Audrey informed her audience on something that most of them consumed every day: soft drinks. She discussed different brands and types of soft drinks and sought to give her audience a better understanding of the beverage industry. From a graph she saw in *USA Today* she constructed a pie graph (Figure 13.4) to show the market share of the leading soft drink companies.[4] In the

Cross-Reference:
Have your students look at the statistics in paragraph 6 of William Fort's speech in Appendix C. What type of visual aid(s) could the speaker have constructed to make those statistics more vivid and memorable?

Cross-Reference:

References to related topics and examples found elsewhere in the text.

VIEW SPEECH MAKING POSITIVELY

Poet Howard Nemerov has said about perception, "What we know is never the object, but only our knowledge."[10] In other words, we do not experience the world directly, but only through the various labels we have attached to things and experiences. More and more we are discovering and investigating the mind's ability to affect behavior. Doctors have discovered, for example, that patients' attitudes about their illnesses significantly affect the speed of their recuperation or their chances for recovery. Athletes have demonstrated improved performance after visualizing themselves competing successfully, and a study of 430 college speech students revealed lowered speech anxiety among those who visualized themselves delivering an effective presentation.[11]

Related Readings:
Ayers, Joe, and Theodore S. Hopf. "Visualization: A Means of Reducing Speech Anxiety." *Communication Education* 34 (1985): 318–323.
Fanning, Patrick. *Visualization for Change.* Oakland, CA: New Harbinger, 1988.
Shone, Ronald. *Creative Visualization: How to Use Imagery and Imagination for Self-Improvement.* Rochester, VT: Destiny, 1988.

Related Reading:

Materials from articles and books to supplement lecture and discussion. Also useful as recommended outside reading for students.

Replace the negative thought . . .
"When I get up to speak, my mind will probably go blank and I'll have nothing to say."

. . . with a positive thought
"I've rehearsed my speech and I have a good set of speaking notes. If I momentarily forget a point, I'll just look at my notecards and then continue."

Replace the negative thought . . .
"My audience will probably be bored with my speech."

. . . with a positive thought
"I found the topic of how 3-D films are made interesting, and my audience probably will too."

Discussion Prompt:
Ask students whether they agree or disagree with this statement, and why: The only people who don't get nervous before speaking in public are those who don't expect much of themselves, or who have decided they don't do anything well.

Discussion Prompt:

Questions, statements, and class exercises designed to stimulate critical thinking and class discussion.

Notice that the appropriate citation above not only tells the listener who Professor Botkin is, but also explains exactly where his words appeared in print. With that information, any listener wanting to read the entire article could go to a library and find it quickly.

To avoid plagiarizing, let these five simple rules guide you.

1. *Establish a clear and consistent method of notetaking when you research.* As you review your notes, you should be able to discern which words, ideas, examples, and organizational structures belong to which authors.

2. *Record complete source citations on each sheet of notes or write this information on each photocopied article.*

Teaching Strategy:
Ask students to examine the source citation in paragraph 13 of Susanne Landowski's speech, "Academic Laboratories: Risking Life and Limb for Credit," in Appendix C. What is missing from that citation? Answer: The source in which Dr. Kaufman's words appeared.

Teaching Strategy:

Out of class assignments, related lecture topics, and additional classroom activities.

For a full list and description of supplements to MASTERING PUBLIC SPEAKING, see the BACK COVER of the AIE.

Mastering Public Speaking

George L. Grice *Radford University*

John F. Skinner *San Antonio College*

 PRENTICE HALL, *Englewood Cliffs, New Jersey* 07632

To
Wrenn, Evelyn, Carol, and Leanne

To
Suzanne, Drew, and Devin;
Gertrude and Beverley;
Rick, Randy, G.W., and JFS;
and
In Loving Memory of
Leon L. Barton

Editorial/production supervision: Mary Kathryn L. Bsales
Acquisitions editor: Stephen Dalphin
Editorial assistant: Caffie Risher
Prepress buyer: Kelly Behr
Manufacturing buyer: Mary Ann Gloriande
Cover design: Bruce Kenselaar
Editor-in-chief: Charlyce Jones Owen
Development editor: Virginia Feury-Gagnon
Marketing manager: Chris Freitag
Copy editor: Eleanor Ode Walter
Art directors: Florence Dara Silverman and Anne T. Bonanno
Designer: Andy Zutis
Photo research director: Lori Morris-Nantz
Photo researcher: Anita Dickhuth
Supplements editor: Sharon Chambliss
Cover art: (left) Robert Daemmrich/Tony Stone Worldwide;
          (right) Charles Gupton/Tony Stone Worldwide

© 1993 by Prentice-Hall, Inc.
A Simon & Schuster Company
Englewood Cliffs, New Jersey 07632

Printed in the United States of America
10 9 8 7 6 5 4 3 2 1

ISBN 0-13-554395-9

Prentice-Hall International (UK) Limited, *London*
Prentice-Hall of Australia Pty. Limited, *Sydney*
Prentice-Hall Canada Inc., *Toronto*
Prentice-Hall Hispanoamericana, S.A., *Mexico*
Prentice-Hall of India Private Limited, *New Delhi*
Prentice-Hall of Japan, Inc., *Tokyo*
Simon & Schuster Asia Pte. Ltd., *Singapore*
Editora Prentice-Hall do Brasil, Ltda., *Rio de Janeiro*

Contents

Preface   xiii

1

An Introduction to Public Speaking   1

Why Study Public Speaking?   2
   Personal Benefits of Studying Public Speaking   2
   Professional Benefits of Studying Public Speaking   3
   Public Benefits of Studying Public Speaking   4
Definitions of Communication   5
Levels of Communication   7
   Intrapersonal Communication   7
   Interpersonal Communication   8
   Group Communication   8
   Public Communication   10
   Mass Communication   10
Components of Communication   12
   Linear Model of Communication   12
   Interactive Model of Communication   13
Overview of the Text   15
Summary   18   **Exercises**   19   **Notes**   19

2

The Ethics of Public Speaking   20

Definition of Ethics   22
Principles of Ethics   23
Ethical Speaking   25
Ethical Listening   30
Plagiarism   32
Summary   36   **Exercises**   36   **Notes**   37

3

Speaking Confidently 38

Pervasiveness of Speaker Nervousness   40
Controlling Speaker Nervousness   42
Coping Strategies   42
   Know How You React to Stress   43
   Know Your Strengths and Weaknesses   44
   Know Speech Principles   44
   Know Your Audience   44
   Know Your Speech   46
   View Your Topic Positively   46
   View Speech Making Positively   47
   Project Control   47
   Test Your Message   48
   Practice   48
   Learn from Experience   49
Summary   50   **Exercises**   50   **Notes**   51

4

Listening 52

The Importance of Listening   54
Listening vs. Hearing   56
The Process of Listening   57
   Receiving   58
   Selecting   58
   Interpreting   59
   Understanding   59
   Evaluating   59
   Resolving   60
Obstacles to Effective Listening   60
   Physical Distractions   60
   Physiological Distractions   60
   Psychological Distractions   60
   Factual Distractions   61
   Semantic Distractions   61
Promoting Better Listening   61
   Desire to Listen   62
   Focus on the Message   62
   Listen for Main Ideas   63
   Understand the Speaker's Point of View   63
   Withhold Judgment   64
   Reinforce the Message   65
   Provide Feedback   66

Listen with the Body   66
Listen Critically   66
Summary   67   **Exercises**   69   **Notes**   69

5

Analyzing Your Audience   70

The Importance of Audience Analysis   73
Audience Analysis *Before* the Speech   75
Analyze Audience Demographics   75
Analyze Audience Needs   81
Analyze Audience Psychology   84
Gather Information about Your Audience   87
Analyze Specific Speaking Situations   87
Audience Analysis *During* the Speech   92
Audience Analysis *After* the Speech   94
Summary   94   **Exercises**   95   **Notes**   96

6

Selecting Your Speech Topic   98

Generating Ideas   101
Self-Generated Topics   102
Audience-Generated Topics   105
Occasion-Generated Topics   106
Research-Generated Topics   108
Selecting Your Topic   111
Focusing Your Topic   112
Determining Your General Purpose   113
Speeches to Inform   113
Speeches to Persuade   113
Speeches to Entertain   114
Formulating Your Specific Purpose   114
Wording Your Thesis Statement   115
Developing Your Speech Title   116
Summary   118   **Exercises**   119   **Notes**   119

7

Researching Your Topic   120

Assess Personal Knowledge   123
Develop a Research Plan   125
Collect Your Information   126

Magazines and Journals 127
Newspapers 129
Government Documents 129
Books 131
Reference Works 133
Interviews 135
Writing and Calling for Information 139
Electronic Media 140
Record Information 140
What to Record 140
How to Record Information 141
Evaluate Information 143
Summary 143   **Exercises** 144   **Notes** 145

8

Supporting Your Speech

Purposes of Supporting Materials 148
Clarity 148
Vividness 149
Credibility 149
Types of Supporting Materials 150
Examples 150
Definition 153
Narration 155
Comparison and Contrast 157
Statistics 159
Testimony 160
Summary 164   **Exercises** 165   **Notes** 165

9

Organizing Your Speech

The Process of Organization 168
Organizing the Body of the Speech 169
Divide the Speech into Key Ideas 169
Develop the Key Ideas 174
Connect the Key Ideas 176
Organizing the Introduction of the Speech 178
Get the Attention of Your Audience 179
State Your Topic 185
Establish the Importance of Your Topic 186
Preview Your Key Ideas 186
Organizing the Conclusion of the Speech 187
Summarize 188

Provide Closure   188
Summary   191   **Exercises**   192   **Notes**   193

10

Outlining Your Speech   194

Functions of Outlining   196
Principles of Outlining   198
Stages of Outlining   200
    The Working Outline   201
    The Formal Outline   206
    The Speaking Outline   208
Summary   210   **Exercises**   211   **Notes**   211

11

Wording Your Speech   212

Functions of Language   215
    Communicating Ideas   215
    Sending Messages about User   216
    Strengthening Social Bonds   216
    Serving as Instrument of Play   217
    Checking Language Use   217
Principles of Effective Language Use   219
    Use Language Correctly   219
    Use Language Clearly   221
    Use Language Vividly   223
    Use Language Appropriately   231
Summary   234   **Exercises**   235   **Notes**   236

12

Delivering Your Speech   238

Principles of Nonverbal Communication   241
Qualities of Effective Delivery   243
Elements of Vocal Delivery   244
    Rate and Pause   244
    Volume   246
    Pitch and Inflection   247
    Voice Quality   248
    Articulation and Pronunciation   249
Elements of Physical Delivery   251
    Appearance   251

Posture 253
Facial Expression 254
Eye Contact 254
Movement 255
Gestures 256
Methods of Delivery 257
Speaking Impromptu 257
Speaking from Memory 257
Speaking from Manuscript 257
Speaking Extemporaneously 258
Summary 259 **Exercises** 260 **Notes** 260

13

Using Visual Aids 262

The Importance of Using Visual Aids 264
Increases Message Clarity 265
Reinforces Message Impact 265
Increases Speaker Dynamism 265
Types of Visual Aids 266
Objects 266
Graphics 267
Projections 272
Handouts 274
Audio Aids 275
Strategies for Using Visual Aids 276
Before the Speech 276
During the Speech 278
Summary 280 **Exercises** 280 **Notes** 281

14

Speaking to Inform 282

Characteristics of a Speech to Inform 285
Types of Informative Speeches 286
Speeches about People 287
Speeches about Objects 289
Speeches about Places 289
Speeches about Events 290
Speeches about Processes 292
Speeches about Concepts 293
Speeches about Conditions 294
Speeches about Issues 294
Guidelines for Speaking to Inform 296
Summary 301 **Exercises** 302 **Notes** 303

15
The Strategy of Persuasion   304

The Importance of Persuasion   306
A Definition of Persuasion   308
Types of Influence   308
The Pyramid of Persuasion   310
Types of Persuasive Speeches   313
   Speeches to Convince   313
   Speeches to Actuate   314
   Speeches to Inspire   314
Principles of Persuasion   315
Persuasive Speaking Strategies   320
   Establishing Speaker Credibility   321
   Enhancing Emotional Appeals   324
Summary   327   **Exercises**   329   **Notes**   329

16
The Structure of Persuasion   330

Structuring Arguments   333
   Steps of an Argument   333
   Types of Argument   334
   Fallacies of Argument   342
Selecting Propositions for Persuasive Speeches   347
   Characteristics of Propositions   348
   Types of Propositions   349
Organizing Persuasive Speeches   351
   Refutational Strategy   352
   Problem-Solution Division   353
   Need-Plan Division   353
   Monroe's Motivated Sequence   354
Summary   355   **Exercises**   358   **Notes**   359

17
Speaking on Special Occasions   360

The Speech of Introduction   362
The Speech of Presentation   365
The Acceptance Speech   367
The Speech of Tribute   369
The Oral Report   372
The Speech to Entertain   374
The Impromptu Speech   377
The Question-Answer Period   379

The Videotaped Speech 381
Summary 385 **Exercises** 386 **Notes** 387

18

Speaking in Small Groups   388

The Importance of Small Groups 390
Small Groups Defined 391
Types of Groups 391
Group Discussion and Decision Making 392
    Principles of Group Decision Making 393
    The Process of Group Decision Making 394
    The Responsibilities of Group Members 397
    The Responsibilities of Group Leaders 399
The Group Presentation 402
    Formats for the Presentation 402
    Preparing a Group Presentation 402
Summary 405 **Exercises** 406 **Notes** 407

Appendixes

A
Critiquing Speeches   408

B
A Speaker's Journal   415

C
Sample Speeches   424

"A Stitch in Time," Emlyn Kathryn Carley 424
Persuasive Speech, William Fort 429
Persuasive Speech, Shelley Schnathorst 432
    Judges' Comments on Shelley Schnathorst's Speech 434
"Academic Laboratories: Risking Life and Limb for Credit," Susanne
    Landowski 436
"The Dilemma of Whistleblowers," Shannon Dyer 440
Remarks at a Memorial Service for the Crew of the Space Shuttle
    Challenger, Ronald Reagan 442
Keynote Address, Mario Cuomo 444
"I Have a Dream," Martin Luther King, Jr. 451

Credits   455

Index   457

Preface

*T*HE word began as the *spoken* word. Long before anyone devised a way to record messages in writing, people told one another stories and taught each other lessons. Societies flourished and fell, battles were waged and won on the basis of the spoken word. Ancient storytellers preserved their culture's literature and history in their memories and transmitted them orally to eager audiences. Crowds could wander away from the unprepared, unskilled speaker, but the most competent, skilled storytellers received widespread attention and praise.

After the development of script and print, people continued to associate marks on the page with the human voice. Even today, linked as we are by radio, television, and computer networks, a speaker standing at the front of a hushed room makes a special claim on our attention and our imagination. As you develop and deliver speeches in this class—and in future years as you deliver reports, sell products, present and accept awards, or campaign for your candidates—you are a part of an oral tradition as ancient as the race. This book is about the contract that always exists between a speaker and an audience, and about the choices you make in your roles as speaker and listener.

We developed this book with two principles in mind. First, public speaking, like ancient storytelling, requires a level of competence that is teachable, skills that can be handed down from patient teacher to interested student. Yet this is more than a skills course. Although a working knowledge of skills is fundamental to your mastery of public speaking, the master speaker is principled as well as skilled. We want to instruct you in *how* to make wise choices as you choose topics, and then research, organize, practice, and deliver your speeches. Just as important, however, we also want to spur you at each point in the speech-making process to think about *why* you make the choices you do.

The second principle guiding us has been most economically stated by British journalist and author Gilbert K. Chesterton: "There are no uninteresting subjects, there are only uninterested people." This book is for those who believe, as we do, that the lessons we have to teach one another can enrich the lives of every listener. The student of art history can learn from the business major, just as the business student learns from the art historian. This course will give you the chance to investigate subjects that appeal to you. We challenge you to develop speech topics creatively and to listen to one another's speeches expecting to learn.

Public speaking is an important part of communication, and communication is not only part of your education, but is also the way you gain and apply your learning. A liberating and lifelong education occurs only through communication, with ourselves and with those around us. We wish each of you the kind of education Steven C. Beering, president of Purdue University, described so eloquently in a speech inaugurating his university's School of Education:

> Education is dreaming, and thinking, and asking questions. It is reading, writing, speaking, and listening. Education is exploring the unknown, discovering new ideas, communicating with the world about us. Education is finding yourself, recognizing human needs, and communicating that recognition to others. Education is learning to solve problems. It is acquiring useful knowledge and skills in order to improve the quality of life. Education is an understanding of the meaning of the past, and an inkling of the potential of the future. Education represents self-discipline, assumption of responsibility, and the maintenance of flexibility, and most of all, an open mind. Education is unfinishable. It is an attitude and a way of life. It makes every day a new beginning.[1]

■ Acknowledgments

Mastering Public Speaking is the product of more than just two co-authors. Though we have tried to speak with one voice for the sake of our readers, the truth is that many voices resonate throughout this text — voices of our teachers, our colleagues, our editors, and our students. What we know, what we value, and thus what we write is shaped in part by their influence and insights. Wherever possible we have tried to acknowledge their contributions. For all their influence on this manuscript, we are thankful.

We would like to thank our former student Pam Lancaster, a district sales manager at Prentice Hall, for first encouraging us to write this book. Mark Hartman, then a Prentice Hall sales rep, was a friendly source of information and assurance. Steve Dalphin, executive editor, and Ray Mullaney, editor in chief of College Book Editorial Development, deserve our gratitude for their faith in the project and for their suggestions. We are grateful to our development editor, Virginia Feury-Gagnon, the worst enemy a slack phrase ever had, for her early and unflagging enthusiasm about this project and for her patience. Our meticulous copy editor, Eleanor Ode Walter, caught our inconsistencies, brought our ideas into focus, and polished our style. We are grateful to Katy Bsales, our production editor, for orchestrating that process so capably and for not laughing at our Type-A questions. We are also grateful to many authors and publishers for their permission to quote material in this book.

We have benefited from the encouragement and advice of some former colleagues and our fellow faculty members at Radford University and San Antonio College: Maresa Brassil, Mary Crow, M. Anway Jones, J. Drew McGukin, David Mrizek, Rick Olsen, Ray Penn, Larry Pollard, Janet Stahl, and Richard Worringham. We are especially grateful to Gwen Brown, Cynthia Cone,

---

[1] Steven C. Beering, "The Liberally Educated Professional," *Vital Speeches of the Day*, 15 April 1990: 400.

Mike Cronin, Suzanne Skinner, and Barbara Strain who gave us their insights, suggestions, and encouragement.

In addition, *Mastering Public Speaking* has been shaped and refined by the close readings and thoughtful suggestions of a number of reviewers: Pamela Cooper, Northwestern University; Elizabeth Bell, University of South Florida; David B. McLennan, Texas Christian University; Kimberly Batty Herbert, Eastern New Mexico University; Beth M. Waggenspack, Virginia Polytechnic Institute and State University; Carl R. Burgchardt, Colorado State University; Edward H. Sewell, Jr., Virginia Polytechnic Institute and State University; Barbara L. Baker, Central Missouri State University; Dayle C. Hardy-Short; Idaho State University; Doris Werkman, Portland State University; and Francis Swinny, Trinity University. Former student Carroll Iverson gave us helpful feedback on several chapters.

Finally, we are indebted to all our public speaking students who have crafted their messages, walked to the front of the classroom, turned to the audience, and informed, persuaded, entertained, and challenged us. Without their ideas and experiences, writing this book would have been impossible, just as without tomorrow's students it would have been unnecessary.

George L. Grice   **John F. Skinner**
Radford, Virginia   *San Antonio, Texas*

An Introduction to Public Speaking

1

Why Study Public Speaking?
Personal Benefits of Studying
  Public Speaking
Professional Benefits of Studying
  Public Speaking
Public Benefits of Studying Public
  Speaking

Definitions of Communication

Levels of Communication
Intrapersonal Communication

Interpersonal Communication
Group Communication
Public Communication
Mass Communication

Components of Communication
Linear Model of Communication
Interactive Model of
  Communication

Overview of the Text

"Speech is civilization itself. The word, even the most contradictory word, preserves contact—it is silence which isolates." THOMAS MANN

"The most important thing I learned in school was how to communicate. . . . You can have brilliant ideas, but if you can't get them across, your brains won't get you anywhere." LEE IACOCCA

"All the great speakers were bad speakers at first."

RALPH WALDO EMERSON

■ Why Study Public Speaking?

You may be taking this class as an elective because you want to improve your public speaking skills. Chances are, however, that you are in this class because it is a requirement for graduation. If that's the case, you may be asking, "Why should I take a course in public speaking?" The answer: Studying and practicing public speaking benefits you personally, professionally, and publicly.

PERSONAL BENEFITS OF STUDYING PUBLIC SPEAKING

Discussion Prompt:
If your class includes international students, ask them to describe the roles speaking plays in their native cultures. Are students encouraged to speak, discuss, and argue in classes? Or are such behaviors discouraged? Are speaking skills considered more important for one gender than the other? What differences do international students notice in the speaking skills of U. S. students compared with those of their own nationalities?

This course can benefit you personally in three ways. First, it can help you acquire skills important to your success in college. According to a recent Carnegie Foundation report, "To succeed in college, undergraduates should be able to write and speak with clarity, and to read and listen with comprehension. Language and thought are inextricably connected, and as undergraduates develop their linguistic skills, they hone the quality of their thinking and become intellectually and socially empowered."[1]

Look at some of the chapter titles in this textbook. They include words such as listening, analyzing, researching, organizing, wording, and delivering. These are skills you will use in constructing and delivering your speeches. They are also *transferable* skills; they can help you throughout your academic studies, as well as in your chosen career.

Second, public speaking can help you become more knowledgeable. There is a saying that we learn:

> 10 percent of what we read,
> 20 percent of what we hear,
> 30 percent of what we see, and
> 70 percent of what we speak.[2]

Consider for a moment two different ways of studying lecture notes for an exam. One method is to read and re-read your notes silently. An alternate technique is more active and makes you a sender of messages. You stand in your room, put your lecture notes on your dresser, and deliver the lecture *out loud*, pretending you are the instructor explaining the material to the class. Which method do you think promotes better understanding and retention of the course material? You will not be surprised to learn that it's the second method.

Speaking is an active process. You discover ideas, shape them into a message, and deliver that message using your voice and body. The act of speaking is a crucial test of your thinking skills. As author E.M. Forster observed, "How do I know what I think until I've seen what I've said?" The process of developing and delivering an idea clarifies it and helps make it uniquely your own. In this course you will learn a lot about the topics on which you choose to speak. By learning how to construct an effective public speech, you will also become a better listener to others' speeches, oral reports, and lectures, and this will further increase your learning.

A third personal benefit of this course is that it can help build your confidence and self-esteem. We devote Chapter 3 to discussing the most common fear of adult Americans: the fear of speaking to a group of people. In this course you will learn how to turn this apprehension into confidence. You will do so by reading this textbook, by listening to your instructor, and, most important, by *doing*. The confidence and poise you gain as you begin to master public speaking will help you when you give that oral report on "Gender Roles in the Plays of Shakespeare" in your British literature class, when you address your school board urging them to expand the district's arts education program, or when you are asked to say a few words upon receiving the Outstanding Community Service award for your involvement in the neighborhood watch program. As the Emerson quotation suggests, great speaking requires practice, but your efforts will bring you these three rewards.

PROFESSIONAL BENEFITS OF STUDYING PUBLIC SPEAKING

Studying communication, and specifically public speaking, is not only important to you personally, but it will also benefit you professionally, as Lee Iacocca's quotation at the beginning of this chapter makes plain. In fact, numerous studies document a strong relationship between communication competence and career success. Effective speaking skills enhance your chances of first securing employment and then advancing in your career. John Hafer and C.C. Hoth surveyed thirty-seven companies, asking them to rate the characteristics they considered most important when hiring an employee. Out of twenty-six total characteristics, oral communication skills ranked first.[3]

More recently three speech and business professors collected 428 responses from personnel managers in business organizations to determine the "factors most important in helping graduating college students obtain employment." Oral communication skills ranked first and listening was second.[4] The researchers concluded:

> From the results of this study, it appears that the skills most valued in the contemporary job-entry market are communication skills. The skills of oral communication (both interpersonal and public), listening, written communication, and the trait of enthusiasm are seen as the most important. It would appear to follow that university officials wishing to be of the greatest help to their graduates in finding employment would make sure that basic competencies in oral and written communication are developed. Courses in listening, interpersonal, and public communication would form the basis of meeting the oral communication competencies.[5]

This course will instruct you in two of those vital skills: public speaking and listening.

Teaching Strategy:
Have students select a business or professional person to interview. From these interviews they should gather information about the importance of oral communication to job performance and career advancement. Instruct students to inquire specifically about the value of public speaking skills. Have the students write a brief report on their findings and discuss in class what they discovered.

Related Reading:
Curtis, Dan B., Jerry L. Winsor, and Ronald D. Stephens. "National Preferences in Business and Communication Education." *Communication Education* 38 (January 1989): 6–14. This article presents compelling evidence of the importance of oral communication skills in the business and professional world.

Once hired, your speaking skills continue to work for you, becoming your ticket to career success and advancement. Researcher Roger Mosvick found that managers and technical professionals spend approximately twice as much time speaking and listening as they do reading and writing.[6] A survey of 500 executives found that speaking skills "rated second only to job knowledge as important factors in a businessperson's success." That same study also showed that effective communication helped improve company productivity and understanding among employees.[7]

Although you will likely spend only a small portion of your career-related communication giving presentations and speeches, your ability to stand in front of a group of people and present your ideas is important to your career success. One survey of sixty-six companies found that 76 percent of executives gave oral reports.[8] Another survey found that while on-the-job public speaking accounted for only 6 percent of managers' and technical professionals' time, it nevertheless ranked as more important to job performance than did time spent reading mail and other documents, dictating letters and writing reports, and talking on the phone.[9] Oral communication and public speaking clearly play a critical role in your professional life.

PUBLIC BENEFITS OF STUDYING PUBLIC SPEAKING

Finally, public speaking can help you play your role as a member of society. As Thomas Mann noted in the opening quotation in this chapter, it is communication that connects us with each other. Public speaking is an important part of creating a society of informed and active citizens.

A democratic society is shaped, in part, by the eloquence of its leaders:

Related Reading:
For an interesting description of the significance of political speeches, read: Noonan, Peggy. *What I Saw at the Revolution.* New York: Random, 1990: 68–69.

a Franklin Delano Roosevelt, who rallied a nation during the Great Depression declaring, "We have nothing to fear but fear itself";

a John F. Kennedy, who urged citizen involvement, exhorting us to "Ask not what your country can do for you; ask what you can do for your country";

a Martin Luther King, Jr., who challenged us to dream of a day when people will be judged not "by the color of their skin but by the content of their character";

a Ronald Reagan, who spoke the words that helped us "mourn the loss of seven brave Americans" aboard the space shuttle *Challenger.*

But a democratic society is also shaped by the quiet eloquence of everyday citizens:

a police officer who informs residents of a crime-plagued area how to set up a neighborhood watch program;

a social worker who addresses the city council and secures funding for a safe house for abused and runaway children;

an elementary school teacher who speaks to civic clubs generating their support for a meals-on-wheels program for elderly citizens confined to their homes;

a priest who consoles a grieving congregation after the fatal crash of a bus bringing their children home from summer camp.

In each of these instances, the speaker used the power of the spoken word to address a need and solicit an appropriate audience response.

While we recognize effective speaking when we meet the person who always says "just the right thing" or who says things in funny and colorful ways, few of us have been trained to speak well. To appreciate the power of communication you must understand just what it is. That requires a look at some definitions of communication and at some of its essential components.

Discussion Prompt:
Have students reflect on their own training in communication, from kindergarten to now. In which of the following have they received the least formal training: reading, writing, or speaking? If they are typical, they will have had the least instruction in learning how to speak.

■ Definitions of Communication ————————

The word **communicate** comes from the Latin verb **communicare,** meaning "to make common to many, share, impart, divide."[10] This concept of sharing is important in understanding communication and is implicit in our definition of the term. Simply stated, when you communicate you share, or make common, your knowledge and ideas with someone else.

You can understand communication best when you view it as both a *process* and a *product*. Some scholars believe communication is basically a process. For example, Thomas Scheidel provides a process perspective when he defines communication as "the transmission and reception of symbolic cues."[11] Other scholars see communication as an outcome or a product and define it simply as **shared meaning.** We believe both of these perspectives offer insights into the concept of communication. **Communication,** *then, is the sharing of meaning by sending and receiving symbolic cues.*

You can understand how meaning is shared by studying Figure 1.1, Charles Ogden and I.A. Richard's **triangle of meaning.**[12] This figure illustrates the three elements necessary when someone communicates; those elements are interpreter, symbol, and referent. The word **interpreter** refers to both the sender and the receiver of a message. The interpreter is simply the person who is communicating, with words or other symbols.

The second element of this model, the **symbol,** is anything to which people attach or assign a meaning. Symbols can be pictures, drawings, or objects. We know, for example, that a sign in an airport showing a fork, a spoon, a glass, and an arrow means that we can find a restaurant or a snack bar in the direction the arrow points. The police officer's uniform and squad car are symbols of the authority of the police. The most familiar symbols, however, are words in a particular language. Many words refer to particular objects, places, and people:

communication: the process of sharing meaning by sending and receiving symbolic cues.

interpreter: any person using symbols to send or receive messages.

symbol: anything to which people attach meaning.

Discussion Prompt:
Begin your discussion of the Triangle of Meaning by showing a videotape, or playing an audiotape, of Bud Abbott and Lou Costello's classic comedy routine "Who's on First?" The sketch is funny because symbols (words) trigger different referents (thoughts) in the minds of the two characters (interpreters).

FIGURE 1.1 The Triangle of Meaning

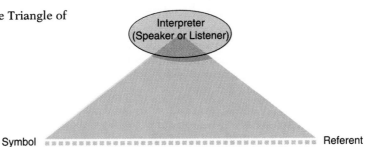

Interpreter
(Speaker or Listener)

Symbol   Referent

referent: the object or idea each interpreter attaches to a symbol.

Discussion Prompt:
Have the class provide examples from situation comedies they watch of humor created when people respond differently to the same symbols. For example, a patient overhears a doctor telling someone that the patient "can go any time now." The patient assumes she is dying, when the doctor actually meant "she is ready to be released from the hospital."

Related Reading:
If you are fortunate to have some foreign students in your class, you will have excellent examples of how different referents shape communication. In analyzing their U.S. peers, foreign students may want to consult books introducing them to cultural, social, and political aspects of this country. One excellent book is: Lanier, Alison R. *Living in the U.S.A.* Yarmouth, ME: Intercultural Press, 1988.

Discussion Prompt:
Have students jot down a few of their most embarrassing experiences. Ask them to review their lists, noting incidents that resulted from a breakdown in communication because they did not share similar referents with someone else. Ask your students to share some of these examples with the class. Continue the discussion with other examples of miscommunication based on individuals' having different referents for the same symbols.

"chair," "Long Beach, California," and "Eudora Welty," for example. Some words refer to concepts, such as "freedom of expression," "existentialism," and "fair play."

The third and final element of the triangle of meaning is the **referent,** the object or idea for which the symbol stands. Both the sender and the receiver of a message have a referent for the symbols used. This referent depends upon each individual's knowledge and experience. People cannot exchange referents in the way they can exchange objects. For example, someone can hand you a paper clip, and that paper clip is the same in your hand as it is in your friend's. Your friends, however, cannot transfer their ideas or information to you. All they can do is to code their ideas into symbols and hope that as you decode them, the ideas you receive will be similar to the ones they intended. In short, as senders we select a symbol based on our referent. That symbol, in turn, triggers the receiver's referent. To check your understanding of how interpreters, symbols, and referents interact, consider this incident one of your authors experienced.

> A father casually asked his son one evening, "How's your homework coming?" The boy, a seventh-grader taking his first computer class, said, "I have to summarize some articles on computers. I've got three, and I need four." The father, planning to go to a book store later that night, said, "OK, I'll buy you a new computer magazine." However, the next morning when his father showed him the magazine with the article on computers, the boy asked, "Where are the others? I told you I need four."

The *interpreters* in this case, the boy and his father, obviously had a communication problem centering around the symbols "I've got three, and I need four." The *son's referent*, the idea he had in mind, was, "I've got three articles, and I need four more." The *father's referent*, however, was, "He's got three of the four articles he needs."

As this example demonstrates, communication is successful only when the interpreters involved attach similar referents to the message being communicated. *The New Yorker* cartoon illustrates the consequences of speaker and listener having different referents. You can, no doubt, think of similar experiences you have had when people misinterpreted what you said because they attached a different referent to your words. The most important thing to remember about the triangle of meaning and the process of communication is this: *Words and other symbols have no inherent meaning. People have meaning; words do not.* The word takes on the meaning that the interpreter attaches to it.

What does the triangle of meaning have to do with public speaking? As you will discover throughout this book, this model applies to public speaking just as it does to all other forms of communication. If speakers and listeners always used specific symbols, interpreted them objectively, and attached similar referents to them, we would experience few if any communication problems arising from the content of the message. As a result, your work in a public speaking class could be limited to improving your organization and polishing your style of delivery. Yet many of our communication problems can be traced directly to difficulties in the relationships between interpreters, the symbols they use, and the referents behind those symbols.

As a public speaker, you must try to ensure that the message your audience hears matches as closely as possible the message you intended. You do that by

Drawing by Shanahan; © 1989 The New Yorker Magazine, Inc.

Discussion Prompt:
Have students provide examples of words that trigger different referents because of differences in the users' ages, genders, religious experiences, educational backgrounds, political affiliations, economic status, and so forth. Discuss how a speaker could enhance shared meaning in each of these examples.

paying particular attention to your content, organization, and delivery, major subjects of this book. To understand the complexity of public speaking, you need to realize how it relates to other levels of communication.

■ Levels of Communication

Communication can occur on five different levels: intrapersonal, interpersonal, group, public, and mass communication. Each of these levels is distinguished by the number of people involved, the formality of the situation, and the opportunities for feedback. One of these levels, public communication, is the subject of this book and the focus of the course you are now taking. Yet public speaking incorporates elements of the other four levels of communication, and a brief look at each of them will help you better understand public speaking.

INTRAPERSONAL COMMUNICATION

Simply stated, **intrapersonal communication** is communication with yourself. The prefix "intra-" means "within." Intrapersonal communication serves many functions, and we all practice it every waking moment. If you woke up late this morning, for example, and panicked because you overslept for a class, you were communicating intrapersonally. If you sit in class worrying about a problem, or reminding yourself to do something later in the day, or

intrapersonal communication: cognition or thought; communicating with oneself.

daydreaming about someone or something, you are communicating intrapersonally. If in the middle of a public speech you tell yourself, "This is really going well," or "I can't believe I just said that," you are also communicating intrapersonally.

As these examples demonstrate, much intrapersonal communication is geared toward a specific, conscious purpose: evaluating how we are doing in a particular situation, solving a problem, relieving stress, or planning for the near or distant future. Though we all have probably uttered something aloud to ourselves at times of stress, joy, puzzlement, or discouragement, intrapersonal communication is typically silent. We sit quietly as we reflect on a speaker explaining the difference between whole life and term life insurance. We are attentive as we hear another speaker explain the necessary preparations for a first sky dive. These examples show the connection between public speaking and intrapersonal communication. Both as public speakers and as audience members for others' speeches, we communicate intrapersonally a great deal. Key features of intrapersonal communication to keep in mind are that it is a continuous process of self-feedback and that it involves only one person.

INTERPERSONAL COMMUNICATION

interpersonal communication: communication between individuals in pairs; also called *dyadic communication.*

As soon as our communication involves ourselves and one other person, it moves to a second level, that of interpersonal communication. **Interpersonal communication** occurs between people, usually two of them. Interpersonal communication is sometimes called dyadic communication; *dyad* is Latin for "pair." Conversations between friends, colleagues, or acquaintances are a common form of interpersonal communication. Yet even strangers communicate interpersonally: A police officer questioning a witness to a crime, a company interviewer meeting a job applicant, and a new student talking to a teacher are all communicating interpersonally.

Teaching Strategy:
Point out to your students that a public speech should echo the tone of good interpersonal communication. A speech should appear to be more a *conversation* with audience members than a *performance* in front of them. Listeners should feel that the speaker is talking *with* them, not talking *at* them.

Whenever two communicators are face to face or speaking over the telephone, the opportunity for verbal interaction always exists. Consider, for example, your last conversation with your best friend, and how easily and naturally you interacted. In fact, if someone had secretly tape-recorded that conversation and typed a transcript of it for you to read, you would probably be surprised by the number of incomplete sentences you and your friend spoke. Ideas that do not appear to make much sense in writing were likely quite clear in conversation. Your best friend is someone who is really on your wavelength, often knows how you are going to finish a sentence, and either finishes it for you or nods agreement and switches to another idea.

In some interpersonal situations, of course, the verbal interaction is less frequent and more self-conscious. We do not interrupt the interviewer sizing us up for a job or the police officer who has just pulled us over for a traffic violation as easily as we do a close friend. Yet the opportunity for verbal interaction exists in even those relatively stressful situations, and is always a characteristic of spoken interpersonal communication.

GROUP COMMUNICATION

group communication: three or more people interacting and influencing one another for a reason and with a sense that they belong together.

As we add to the number of people involved, the next level is **group communication.** Although we discuss group interaction more thoroughly in Chap-

*Face-to-face communication
helps speakers to communicate
more effectively because they
have greater opportunities to
observe and evaluate the feedback of listeners.*

ter 18, we will present some important points about it here. Group communication generally takes place with three or more people interacting and
influencing each other in pursuit of a common goal. Though researchers place
varying limits on the size of a group, everyone recognizes that a sense of cohesion or group identity is essential to any definition of this level of communication.

A dozen members of a neighborhood organization discussing a local traffic
problem are obviously engaged in group communication. A company's sales
staff meeting to review last quarter's sales patterns is similarly involved in a
process of group communication. When you present your speeches in class,
you will not be engaged in group communication. However, if your presentation on a particularly interesting topic generates questions and discussion, your
public speaking class might qualify as an example of group communication.

The important thing to remember about group communication is that the
people involved must have a sense of group identity. A group of fourteen people, for example, is not just seven dyads or pairs of people. They must be aware
that they belong together for some reason, whether they face a common problem, share similar interests, or simply work in the same division of a company.

Group communication may be informal, with all group members free to
discuss issues as they wish, or formal, operating under the rules of parliamen-

tary procedure. As long as members are relatively free to contribute to the discussion, what occurs is clearly group communication. However, once someone stands up and begins to present a report or make a speech, the communication shifts to a different type, public communication.

PUBLIC COMMUNICATION

public communication: one person communicating face to face with an audience.

Public communication, the subject of the course you are taking, occurs when one person speaks face to face with an audience. That audience may be as small as your public speaking class or as large as the masses of people who fill stadiums and other public areas to hear certain speakers. As the size of the audience grows, the flow of communication becomes increasingly one-directional, from speaker to audience. When the audience is large, individual members have less opportunity for verbal interaction with the speaker.

Class Activity: Have students list careers they are considering. Then ask them to write how the different levels of communication may be important to success in each of those careers. Have the students discuss the role that good public speaking skills may play in their career success. Students may want to draw on information gathered in interviews conducted with business or professional persons.

For example, your public speaking class is probably small enough that you feel free to have your instructor answer any questions you have during class. In a lecture class of several hundred students, however, you might feel more pressure to keep silent, even if you had a legitimate question. If you were part of an audience of several thousand people, not only would you feel pressure to keep quiet during a speech, but even if you did voice a question the speaker probably could not hear it.

The key characteristics of public communication, therefore, are a more one-directional flow of information and a more formal feeling than the other types of communication we have discussed so far. Whether the audience is as small as a class of twenty, as large as a convention assembly of 2,000, or a congregation of 200,000 standing outside the Vatican to hear an Easter message from the Pope, public communication always involves one person communicating to an audience that is physically present.

MASS COMMUNICATION

mass communication: one person communicating to a large audience through some print or electronic medium.

But what happens if we sit in front of our television sets and see videotape clips from that Easter service at the Vatican or a telecast of an Academy Awards ceremony? In such a situation we have entered the fifth and final level of communication, **mass communication.** Once the audience becomes so large that it cannot be gathered together in one place, some type of print or electronic medium — newspaper, magazine, radio, or television, among others — must be placed between speaker or writer and the intended audience. As you can imagine, the physical isolation of speaker and audience severely limits the possibilities for spontaneous, instant interaction between them. In fact, an important characteristic of mass communication is that audience feedback is *always* delayed. Assume, for example, that a magazine or newspaper article inspires or angers you enough that you write a letter to the editor. Your response will be slowed by the necessities of composing the letter and mailing it. Then, before your response can be shared with the magazine or newspaper readership, someone must review it, decide to publish it, have it typeset and printed, and distribute it to readers. You have the opportunity to send feedback, but it is delayed.

A second characteristic we should consider about mass communication is that the method of message transmission can become very important. Advertising agencies and the people who use them know very well that the *way* a message is sent can be as important as the *content* of that message, something public speakers should also remember. Advertisements for products and services reach different sizes and types of audiences via radio, television, billboards, magazines, or newspapers.

Politicians and political consultants also understand the impact that different media can have in getting their views to the people. Still the best example of this, more than thirty years after it occurred, is the first of the four 1960 Kennedy-Nixon presidential debates. People who heard that debate on radio but did not see it on television or read transcripts of it believed that Nixon won. People who read the transcripts of the debate but did not see it on television or hear it on radio also believed that Nixon won. People who saw the debate on television, however, said that Kennedy won without much difficulty. Why would television viewers evaluate the debate so differently?

A significant difference in those three situations is the way the message was sent. In the transcripts, people had access only to the words the two men used. Radio listeners could hear the speakers' words and the way they were spoken. However, members of the television audience were able to judge not only the men's words and manner of speaking, but also how Kennedy and Nixon looked and behaved. A sure sign of television's importance to political candidates is the fact that all participants in televised presidential and vice-presidential debates since that fateful Kennedy-Nixon debate in 1960 have had consultants advise them what to wear, where to look, how and when to gesture, and how forcefully to speak, in addition to what to say. We devote a portion of Chapter 17 to the special challenges of speaking before a video camera because future technology will surely expand the importance of mass media in getting messages across to the public.

You will master public speaking skills more quickly and easily if you remain aware of the connections between public communication and the four other levels of communication. In this class, you may use interpersonal and group

Teaching Strategy:
On the 30th anniversary of the Kennedy-Nixon debates, the Arts and Entertainment Network re-broadcast the series of debates and a special about their significance. You may want to play portions of the debates for your students, letting them see how both men adapted to the medium.

Millions of Americans observed democracy at work when Senator John Kennedy and Vice President Richard Nixon faced each other in the first such televised debate during the 1960 presidential election.

communication to determine your speech topics and how you approach them. You may interview an expert on a topic you are considering for a speech. Through informal conversations with your classmates you will form a clearer picture of your audience by discovering their interests, attitudes, and values. You may offer others feedback on their speeches and receive their comments regarding your speech. If you have the opportunity to videotape one or more of your speeches, you will gain experience with one of the important electronic media of mass communication, even if your speech is not broadcast publicly. Certainly, you will consult print or electronic media resources as you research your speech. And all the time you are delivering your public speeches you will be giving yourself intrapersonal feedback about the job you are doing and the positive responses we hope you are receiving.

■ Components of Communication

Teaching Strategy:
Point out the advantages and disadvantages of using models. They aid understanding and retention by translating a theoretical concept into visual form. Their chief weakness is that models always oversimplify what they represent.

Now that you have an understanding of the different levels of communication, we will look at the various components common to any type of communication and, specifically, to public speaking. Remember, the better you understand how communication works in *general*, the better you will be able to make communication work for you in *specific* speaking situations. A brief look at the elements in two communication models will allow us to develop a more accurate view of this complex phenomenon. Just as important, these models will let us see where some common communication problems arise.

LINEAR MODEL OF COMMUNICATION

The earliest models devised by scholars show three basic elements of communication: a *speaker* sending a *message* to a *listener* (see Figure 1.2). The speaker might also be called the sender, the source, or the encoder. **Encoding** is the process of putting ideas into symbols, and we encode so much and so well that we are aware of the process only when we find ourselves "at a loss for words," while either speaking or writing. The ideas of the message originate with the speaker, who determines the form that the message will take. Unless the communication is *intra*personal, the message is sent to a listener or receiver. This person then **decodes** the message, attaching meanings to the words, gestures, and voice inflections that are received.

encoding: the process of selecting symbols to carry a message.

decoding: the process of attaching meanings to symbols received.

Those three elements—speaker, message, listener—*are* important to communication. So what was wrong with the early, linear models of communication? First, they assumed that a person is *either* a sender *or* a receiver of messages. The truth is that we perform both of these roles simultaneously. The early one-directional model of communication shown in Figure 1.2 does not account for this.

The second weakness of this simple model is its suggestion that communi-

Speaker ➤ **M e s s a g e** ➤ Listener

A speaker sends a message to a listener

FIGURE 1.2 Linear Model of Communication

cation involves only one message. Yet remember our earlier discussion of the triangle of meaning. The truth is that there are as many messages as there are communicators involved. The message the speaker intends is never identical to the one received. As long as they are similar, communication will usually be effective.

INTERACTIVE MODEL OF COMMUNICATION

Once communication scholars began to see the limitations of this early linear, three-element model, they began to add other components. Today, the most widely accepted model of communication has seven elements. In addition to the three already mentioned—speaker, message, and listener—we add channel, feedback, environment, and noise. Figure 1.3 illustrates this more complete model of communication.

Channel. The first element we need to add is the **channel** or **medium,** which refers to the way the message is sent. In public speaking the medium is vibrations in the air between speaker and listener, set in motion by the speaker's voice. The message could also be written in any language, put into some code known to both speaker and listener, tape-recorded or videotaped, put into sign language, translated into Braille, or even sent by smoke signal, among other methods. As you realize, voice and words are not our only media for communi-

FIGURE 1.3 Interactive Model of Communication. *A speaker encodes a message, sending it through a channel to a listener, who decodes it. The listener provides feedback, sending it through a channel to the speaker. This interaction takes place in an environment with varying levels of internal and external noise.*

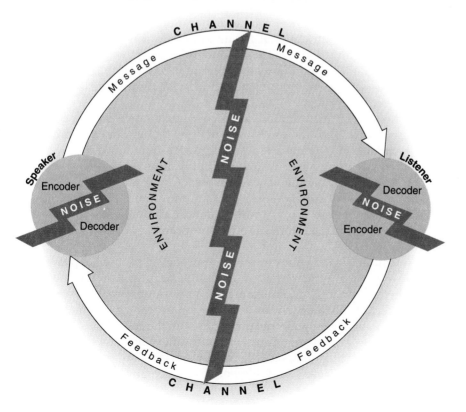

channel or **medium:** the way a message is sent.

Discussion Prompt: We encode so many messages so effortlessly that we rarely stop to think about the process. Ask your students what situations make them aware of the process of encoding a message? Answers may include times when the speaker does not know the name of something, when a speaker says something that sounds wrong, or when a speaker begins to deliver bad news in a way that sounds callous or unsympathetic.

Class Activity: Using these components of communication (and any others students wish to add), have students meet in groups to design their own models of communication. Have each group draw its model on the chalkboard and discuss it.

cation. In fact, communication scholar Albert Mehrabian has estimated that nonverbal cues are more important than verbal cues in communicating your feelings or attitudes to others. He summarized his research in the following equation:

Total feeling = 7% verbal feeling + 38% vocal feeling + 55% facial feeling[13]

Mehrabian's formula means that any time you communicate with someone, the majority of the *feeling* behind your message is carried by visual elements such as facial expression, eye contact, gestures, and movement. More than one-third of your message is carried *paralinguistically*, or by vocal elements such as rate, volume, voice quality, and changes in pitch level. Your actual words carry less than 10 percent of the message about how you feel. As a public speaker, you must learn to manipulate and control all three of these channels: visual, vocal, and verbal. As you can see, public speaking, like every other level of communication, is more complicated than just saying the right words.

Feedback. A second element added to that preliminary model of communication is **feedback**. Feedback includes all messages, verbal and nonverbal, sent by listeners to speakers. If you tell a joke, your listeners will tell you through vocal (laughter), verbal, and visual feedback whether they understood the joke and how they evaluated it. If you are paying attention, you will know who liked it, who didn't, who hasn't understood it, and who was offended by it. "If you are paying attention" is the particularly important clause, for in order to be effective, feedback must be received.

Because public speaking is an audience-centered activity, you as speaker must be sensitive to feedback from your audience. Some feedback is deliberate and conscious; some is unintentional and unconscious. But your audience will always provide you with feedback of some kind. If you are paying attention to it, you will know when they appreciate your humor, understand the point you are making, disagree with the position you advocate, or are momentarily confused by something you have said.

Environment. The third element we need to add to make a more accurate model of communication is the **environment**. Two factors shape a communication environment: (1) the occasion during which communication occurs, and (2) the physical setting or site where communication occurs. The *occasion* refers to the reasons why people have assembled. Circumstances may be serious or festive, planned or spontaneous. Occasions for communication may be as relaxed and informal as a party with friends, as rule-bound as a college debate, or as formal and traditional as a commencement address at a graduation ceremony.

The physical *setting* for your classroom speeches is probably apparent to you. You know the size of the room and the number of people in the audience. You know whether the seating arrangement is fixed or changeable. You know whether a lectern, a chalkboard, or a projection screen are available. You know, or will soon discover, potential problems with the room: The table at the front of the room is wobbly; the air seems stuffy about halfway through each class meeting; one of the fluorescent lights flickers. Each of these distracting elements is a form of noise, a fourth element for which any accurate model of communication must account.

feedback: verbal and nonverbal responses between communicators.

Discussion Prompt:
Ask students to provide examples of the following situations: Someone failed to act on the feedback you gave them. You misinterpreted another's feedback to something you said. You changed your behavior as a result of feedback from another person. What were some of the consequences of these actions?

environment: the physical setting and the occasion for communication.

Related Reading:
For a discussion of the characteristics of the environment, see: Trenholm, Sarah. "The Nature of the Environment." *Persuasion and Social Influence.* Englewood Cliffs, NJ: Prentice, 1989: 163–65.

Noise. **Noise** is anything that interferes with communication, and some form of noise is always present. We will discuss three different forms of it. First, much noise is **physical;** that is, it occurs in the physical environment in which people are communicating. When we think of noise, we usually think of physical noise: the sounds of traffic, the loud whoosh of an air conditioner or a heater, the voices of people talking and laughing as they pass by your classroom. Some physical noise may not involve a sound at all, however. If your classroom is so cold that you shiver or so hot that you fan yourself, then its temperature is a form of noise. If the lighting in the room is poor, then that form of noise will certainly affect the communication occurring there. If your classroom is near a construction site and the heavy, acrid smell of creosote is nauseating you, then that odor is a form of noise. Anything in the immediate environment that interferes with communication is physical noise.

A second type of noise is **physiological:** A bad cold that affects your hearing and speech, a headache, or an empty, growling stomach are examples. Each of these bodily conditions can shift your focus from communicating with others to intrapersonal communication, thinking about how uncomfortable you feel.

A third and final type of noise is **psychological.** This type of noise refers to mental rather than bodily distractions. Anxiety, worry, daydreaming, and even joy over some recent event can distract you from the message at hand. Each of these forms of noise — physical, physiological, and psychological — can occur independently or in combination, and as we have said, some form of noise is always present. Music lovers continually search for better audio equipment — a compact disc player, for example — to reduce the noise involved in playing recorded music. As a speaker you must make similar efforts to minimize the effects of noise in public communication: by varying your rate, volume, and pitch, for example, or through lively physical delivery that combats noise and rivets the audience's attention to your message.

noise: anything that distracts from effective communication.

physical noise: distractions originating in the communication environment.

physiological noise: distractions originating in the bodies of communicators.

psychological noise: distractions originating in the thoughts of communicators.

Class Activity:
Divide your class into small working groups and have them complete Exercise 3 at the end of this chapter.

■ Overview of the Text

We have wrestled with the title of this book for some time. Adopted originally as a working title, *Mastering Public Speaking,* we gradually decided, seems to promise more than it can possibly deliver. Can any student *master* public speaking by studying one textbook and applying its principles in one college course? In our years of combined college teaching, we have yet to see that happen. What *does* happen is that students enter a college public speaking course with varying backgrounds and varying experiences in public speaking. With study and intensive practice, many become far better public speakers at the end of such a course than when they entered; almost all become much more confident about their speaking abilities. But does any communication teacher mold "master" public speakers during the eighteen weeks of a typical college semester or the ten weeks of a college quarter?

In truth, mastering public speaking is a life-long process. This course is neither the beginning nor the end of your development as a public speaker. You bring to this course specific skills and experiences that will help you prepare and publicly present your messages. You have, for example, already developed some degree of skill in communicating interpersonally and in groups. This class is an intensive laboratory that will enable you to learn, experiment with, practice, and refine your skills in public speaking. If you take full advantage of your opportunities to speak, you should leave this course with both a greater understanding of public speaking and greater proficiency in it.

Each time that you speak in public, you are, in effect, entering a contract with your listeners. You are assuming responsibility for being well prepared, for having something interesting or useful to say, and for speaking in the best interests of your listeners. Among the terms of the contract for you as a listener are requirements that you listen expecting to learn, that you listen without prejudging speakers or their ideas, and that you evaluate the messages presented to you. Our view of public speaking stresses the ethics of this speaker-audience contract. Beginning with the next chapter, we discuss a cluster of issues that we feel deserve your attention and understanding before you begin to plan your first graded speech. One of these is ethics, from both the speaker's and listeners' perspectives. An ethical issue that should be of particular concern to any speaker is plagiarism. We will show you how it occurs and suggest some ways you can make certain that you avoid plagiarizing.

We have organized this book in a logical and chronological pattern, taking you step-by-step through the public speaking process. We believe that delivering an effective public speech requires you to do the following:

1. Understand the nature, importance, and ethical responsibilities of public speaking;
2. Understand the role of the audience in the speech-making process;
3. Select a topic you are genuinely interested in, and narrow it;
4. Determine the purpose of your speech;
5. Research and support your speech;
6. Organize your speech;
7. Word your speech;
8. Practice your speech;
9. Deliver your speech; and
10. Evaluate your speaking.

This first chapter has laid a foundation for your impending roles as public speaker and listener. We have demonstrated the importance of public communication and have offered a definition of communication. We have surveyed the levels of communication, from intrapersonal to mass communication, to show you how public speaking utilizes other types of communication with which you have more experience. Finally, we discussed how the various elements of communication interact. Remaining chapters will guide you to control those elements of communication so that your speeches achieve their desired effects.

The greatest asset you can bring to this class as you work through the remaining steps in speech preparation is not previous public speaking experience, or intelligence, or personality, or a disc jockey's voice. The quality that we believe will go further than any other toward ensuring your success as a public speaker is interest — in your audience, in your topic, and in communicating effectively. If you have these interests *and* the energy to follow up on them, you have greatly simplified your task as a public speaker.

If you are interested in developing self-confidence as a speaker, you are certainly in the right place. You are among friends who experience the same types of fears about facing an audience that you do. We realize the prevalence of stage fright. We know that some of you have delayed taking this course because of your apprehension. For that reason, we devote an entire chapter early in the book to this fear, its causes, and ways to cope with it.

If you are interested in issues, events, people, places — in short, the world around you — you should enjoy selecting topics for your speeches and listening to the subjects other speakers have chosen. We will suggest a number of techniques for generating speech topics, both informative and persuasive. We encourage you to be imaginative and creative as you consider possible subjects. If you choose interesting topics, you will enjoy researching them and selecting supporting materials for your speech. We will teach you how to get the most out of your research time and how to select forms of support that are appropriate to your topic and your audience.

If you are interested in *speaking* your ideas as clearly as you can *think* them, we will show you how to structure your speech's main points and how to develop the parts of your speech. You will learn the steps of effective speech introductions and conclusions, and we will teach you a four-step procedure for developing each major idea in your speech. Of all the speaking skills you can possess, clear organization may be the easiest to teach and to learn. We believe that clear organization is critical to an effective speech, and that speaking in an organized manner can also help you think and write more clearly.

If you are interested in people, you should have no trouble analyzing your audience before you speak and interacting with them as you speak. We will show you why audience analysis is so important, and how to study your audience before, during, and after your speech.

If you are interested in polishing your speaking skills, we will teach you how to use your voice and body as you speak to establish natural, lively rapport with your listeners. In addition to offering you guidelines for effective speech practice and delivery, we will help you give specific, useful feedback to your classmates about their speeches. Then, in "A Speaker's Journal," toward the end of the book, you can read both a student's speech and her discussion of how she developed, practiced, and delivered that speech.

If you are interested in wielding influence and achieving results, you should welcome the opportunity to inform, persuade, or entertain your listeners. We will guide you so that you should have no trouble determining your purpose and keeping it clearly in focus as you speak. We devote one chapter to selecting topics and organizing the body of your informative speech. We discuss the complex task of persuasion in two chapters. In the first of these, we will define persuasion, discuss the types of influence you can have on an audience, outline some principles of persuasive speaking, and discuss ethical and emotional appeals. The second chapter on persuasion explains the steps in constructing an argument, the types of arguments, some common fallacies of reasoning, types of persuasive propositions, and organizational patterns that lend themselves particularly well to persuasion.

If you are interested in being able to use language creatively and powerfully, we will instruct you in how to use words to communicate your ideas clearly, forcefully, and memorably. There, as in every other part of this textbook, we use examples from our students and from people in the business and professional world to show you what to strive for and what to avoid.

Each of the speaking skills you develop in this course will serve you well beyond the semester or quarter. For this reason, a separate chapter covers the types of speeches you may be making on special occasions outside of the classroom — speeches of introduction, presentation, acceptance, and tribute; speeches to entertain; impromptu speeches and oral reports; videotaped speeches and question-answer sessions.

Finally, if you skipped the preface to this book, we urge you to take the few minutes necessary to turn back and read it. Written primarily for you, not just for your instructor, the preface condenses our philosophy about this course and about education in general.

Summary

Public speaking offers personal, professional, and public benefits for the individual. On a personal level, public speaking teaches you skills you can use in other courses of study. It is also an active form of learning and can increase your retention of information. Finally, gaining public speaking skills and experience will build your confidence and self-esteem. On a professional level, public speaking is an important form of communication, and excellent communication skills increase your chances of getting the job you want and advancing in it. On a public level, public speaking binds people into groups and propels social movements and social change.

We may view communication as either a process or a product, but the most accurate definition of the term probably includes both perspectives. Effective communication is the sharing of meaning by sending and receiving symbolic cues.

Public communication, the focus of this textbook, is one of five levels of communication. *Intrapersonal communication* refers to the communication we do with ourselves individually. *Interpersonal* or *dyadic communication* is that carried out between pairs of people. *Group communication* involves three or more people communicating for some purpose,

and with a clear sense that they belong together. *Public communication* occurs when one person speaks face to face with an audience, either large or small. *Mass communication* involves one person communicating to a large audience through some print or electronic medium. These five levels of communication are differentiated by the numbers of people involved, the direction of communication flow, and the opportunities for audience feedback.

Terms to be used throughout this book include seven components of communication. The *speaker* or sender is the person originating the *message*, the ideas being communicated. The *channel* or medium of communication is the way the message is sent. Public speaking involves verbal, vocal, and visual channels. The *listener* is the person receiving and interpreting the message. *Feedback* refers to all verbal and nonverbal responses from listener to speaker, either intentional or unintentional. The *environment* includes the speaking occasion and the setting where communication occurs. Finally, *noise* is the name given to anything that interferes with communication. Noise can be physical (environmental), physiological (bodily), or psychological (mental).

Exercises

1. Using the interactive model of communication as a guide (Figure 1.3), analyze a lecture given by an instructor in one of your classes. Focus specifically on the listeners and feedback. Was the instructor attentive to the verbal and nonverbal behaviors of the students? If your answer is no, what could the instructor have done to make the communication event more of a two-way experience? If your answer is yes, give examples to illustrate the instructor's attentiveness to student feedback.
2. Find an article in a magazine or journal discussing speech communication in business and professional environments. Write a one-page summary and attach it to the article. Be prepared to discuss the article in class.
3. Analyze the physical noise present in your classroom. As a listener, how does this affect your reception of your instructor's message? As a speaker, how might you minimize the effect of this noise? If you were redesigning the classroom, what changes would you make to lessen this type of noise?
4. On a sheet of paper make two lists: "My Communication Strengths" and "My Communication Weaknesses." In the first list, indicate those you think will help you in this public speaking course. In the second list, note those you would most like to improve in this course. Keep the lists and refer to them at the conclusion of this course. What changes would you make to the lists at that time?

Notes

1. Ernest L. Boyer, *College: The Undergraduate Experience in America* (New York: Harper, 1987) 73.

2. Cited in Judy Self, "The Picture of Writing to Learn," *Plain Talk: About Learning and Writing Across the Curriculum* ed. Judy Self (Richmond: Virginia Dept. of Education, Spring 1987) 13.

3. John C. Hafer and C.C. Hoth, "Selection Characteristics: Your Priorities and How Students Perceive Them," *Personnel Administrator* March 1983: 26.

4. Dan B. Curtis, Jerry L. Winsor, and Ronald D. Stephens, "National Preferences in Business and Communication Education," *Communication Education* 38 (January 1989): 11.

5. Curtis 13.

6. Roger K. Mosvick and Robert B. Nelson. *We've Got to Start Meeting Like This!* (Glenview, IL: Scott, 1987) 225.

7. Survey was conducted by Communispond, Inc., and is reported in "Executives Say Training Helps Them Speak Better," *Training: The Magazine of Human Resources Development* October 1981: 20–21, 75.

8. James Wyllie, "Oral Communications: Survey and Suggestions," *ABCA [American Business Communication Association] Bulletin* June 1980: 15.

9. Mosvick 224.

10. *The Oxford English Dictionary*. 2nd ed. (Oxford: Clarendon, 1989) 577.

11. Thomas M. Scheidel, *Persuasive Speaking* (Glenview, IL: Scott, 1967) 2.

12. C.K. Ogden and I.A. Richards, *The Meaning of Meaning*, 9th ed. (New York: Harcourt, Brace, 1953) 10–12. Chapter 1, "Thoughts, Words and Things" (pp. 1–23), explains in detail the relationships between symbols, referents, and interpreters.

13. Albert Mehrabian, *Silent Messages* (Belmont, CA: Wadsworth, 1971) 44.

The Ethics of Public Speaking

2

Definition of Ethics

Principles of Ethics

Ethical Speaking

Ethical Listening

Plagiarism

Cross-Reference:
Shannon Dyer's speech, "The Dilemma of Whistle-blowers," in Appendix C, focuses on important ethical issues for speakers and listeners.

Speech making is an artistic process. A good speech is not developed by routine or formula. It needs the spark of creativity to live. The accomplished artist will tell you, however, that although inventiveness is an essential component in the creation process, it alone cannot produce excellence. Excellence results from combining that spark of creativity with a good deal of hard work. How does that process happen?

The successful author begins with a blank sheet of paper. The successful director begins with an empty stage. In order to achieve a finished product — a book or a play — both must go through several complicated steps. For example, in order to stage a play, directors must study the literary form, understand its dynamics, research the script, generate ideas, focus and organize those ideas, and then translate them into performance. In so doing, they give the finished product their individual signatures. Writers follow a similar process to complete a project.

As a public speaker, you are both author *and* director, and you seek to fill two voids: a blank sheet of paper and an empty space before an audience. As an artist you will use your creativity as well as your skills of research and organization to transform your ideas into a living speech. At the end of this process, you will be able to stand in front of an audience and impart information and ideas in a meaningful and memorable way.

Before you can exercise your artistry with language, your persistence as a researcher, or your organizational skills, you must first make the decision to speak and you must have an audience. Your goal in mastering public speaking is not to develop skills as ends in themselves, but to serve the various audiences that you may face throughout your life. *Effective public speakers understand and respect their audiences.* They demonstrate this respect by entering into and honoring an unwritten contract with their listeners. In this chapter we focus on issues concerning that contract between speaker and audience: ethical speaking and listening, and plagiarism. Since each speech you make will reveal aspects of your personality and your values, you should study and consider these issues before even planning your first speech.

■ Definition of Ethics

It is virtually impossible to read a newspaper or listen to a newscast today without encountering the topic of ethics. We hear of politicians "selling out" to special-interest groups, stockbrokers engaged in insider trading, contractors taking "shortcuts" in construction projects, musicians accepting awards for music they did not record, and college officials illegally recruiting student athletes. We read stories of people who agonized over the decision to allow, and in some cases even help, a terminally ill loved one to die. We watch news clips of rallies and demonstrations where constituents accuse their elected officials of abusing the public trust. Society is so concerned with unethical behavior that many professions even include the term "ethics" as a component: We have all heard of medical ethics, business ethics, bioethics, journalistic ethics, environmental ethics, and so forth.

When we talk about **ethics** we are referring to the standards we use to determine right from wrong, or good from bad, in thought and behavior. Our sense of ethics guides the choices we make in all aspects of our professional and private lives. You should not be surprised that your academic studies include a discussion of ethics. You are, after all, educating yourself to function in a world where you will make ethical decisions daily. You may be surprised to learn, however, that colleges throughout the United States offer more than 11,000 courses in ethics.[1] In Chapter 1 we established the importance of speech communication in our lives. We will now examine why it is important for you to ensure that you communicate ethically.

■ Principles of Ethics

In discussing communication ethics, Donald Smith notes that "speaking skill is frequently studied as an ethically neutral instrument. . . ." He compares communication skills to the skill of shooting a rifle. It is not wrong to practice your marksmanship shooting skeet; ethical concerns arise, however, when your target is another human being. "From this point of view," Smith writes, "speaking skill *per se* is neither good nor bad. The skill can be used by good persons or bad persons. It can be put to the service of good purposes [or] bad purposes. . . ."[2] In this course you will learn fundamental communication skills that will empower you as both a speaker and a listener, just as the act of picking up a gun empowers an individual. How you exercise these skills will involve ethical choices and responsibilities.

Two principles frame our discussion of ethics. First, we contend that *all parties in the communication process have ethical responsibilities*. Assume, for example, that one of your instructors had been denied promotion or a requested leave of absence, or had some other reason for holding a grudge against your college administrators. Assume as well that this instructor, without revealing his or her true motives, used class time to provoke and anger you about inadequate parking or poor food quality in the student center at your school, then led you across campus to take the school president hostage, barricade yourselves in the administration building, and tear up the place.

Anyone who knew the facts of this case would agree that the instructor acted unethically; it is wrong to manipulate people, keeping your true motives hidden from them. Yet we contend that any students who let themselves be exploited by participating in such a violent and destructive episode would also share ethical responsibility for what happened. College students, no matter what their age, know that their actions have consequences. As this outlandish example demonstrates, all parties involved in communication share ethical obligations.

In spite of this, public speaking textbooks often discuss ethics only from a speaker's perspective, presenting ethical standards as a list of "do's" and "don'ts" for the sender of the message. Certainly, a speaker has ethical respon-

ethics: standards used to discriminate between right and wrong, good and bad, in thought and action.

Discussion Prompt:
Ask students to discuss examples of business practices they consider unethical. Examples might include junk mail designed to resemble checks or legal notices; diet and fitness centers advertising special low enrollment fees without mentioning high initiation or processing fees; companies urging children to make long distance phone calls.

Discussion Prompt:
Is it unethical for college professors to criticize conditions or policies of the schools employing them? Is such criticism unethical in the classroom? You may want to initiate this discussion by quoting the section on academic freedom from your school's employee handbook or policy manual.

Discussion Prompt:
Everyone agrees that con artists and people running scams are acting unethically. But to what extent do we share responsibility for our own losses to con artists? What mental habits would protect us from con artists while still letting us help people in need?

All parties in the communication process — speakers and listeners — have ethical responsibilities.

sibilities, but a speaker-centered approach to ethics is incomplete. Communication, as we suggest throughout this textbook, is an activity shared by both speaker and listener. As such, both parties have ethical responsibilities. For that reason, we will discuss the ethics of speaking and listening.

Second, we contend that *ethical speakers and listeners possess attitudes and standards that pervade their character and guide their actions before, during, and after their speaking and listening.* In other words, ethical speakers and listeners do more than just abstain from unethical behaviors. Ethics is as much a frame of mind as it is a pattern of behavior. Ethics is not something you apply to one speech; it is a working philosophy you apply to your daily life and bring to all speaking situations. Consider the actions of the speaker in the following incident that one of us witnessed in a classroom.

Lisa presented a persuasive speech on the need for recycling paper, plastic, and aluminum products. To illustrate the many types of recyclables and how overpackaged many grocery products are, she used as an effective visual aid a paper grocery bag filled with empty cans, paper products, and a variety of plastic bottles and containers. After listening to her well-researched, well-delivered speech, with its impassioned final appeal for us to help save the planet by recycling, the class watched in amazement as she put the empty containers back in the bag, walked to the corner of the room, and dropped the bag in the trash can! After a few seconds that seemed like minutes, someone finally asked the question that had to be asked:

"You mean you're not going to take those home to recycle them?" "Nah," said Lisa. "I'm tired of lugging them around. I've done my job."

As Dana Carvey's Church Lady might have said of Lisa's behavior, "How conve-e-enient!" You may or may not believe that people have an ethical responsibility to recycle. But regardless of your views on that issue, you likely question the ethics of someone who insists, in effect, "Do as I say, not as I do." Lisa's actions were simply careless, thoughtless, but they made the entire class question the sincerity with which she spoke. Ethical standards cannot be turned on and off at an individual's convenience.

■ Ethical Speaking

"A speech is a solemn responsibility. The man who makes a bad thirty-minute speech to 200 people wastes only a half hour of his own time. But he wastes 100 hours of the audience's time — more than four days — which should be a hanging offense."
                                                        JENKIN LLOYD JONES

The first and perhaps the most basic obligation of speakers is that they have something meaningful to say to their listeners. Speakers and listeners participate in a transactional relationship; both should benefit from their participation. As the Jones quotation above suggests, listeners give speakers their time; speakers should provide something interesting or useful in return.

You may often speak for personal benefit, and this is not necessarily unethical. You may speak to a group, urging them to support you for president of the student body, or you may listen to a speech on résumé-writing strategies in order to improve your chances of getting a job. There is nothing inherently wrong with pursuing such personal goals, but ethical speakers do not try to fulfill personal needs at the expense of their listeners. As one popular book on business ethics states, "There is no right way to do a wrong thing."[3] Speakers whose objective is to persuade, for example, should do so with the goal of benefiting both the audience and themselves. Even informative speakers have an ethical obligation to benefit their audiences. Here's an example of how this can work in your public speaking class.

Assigned to give an informative speech demonstrating a process or procedure, plant lover Evelyn decided to show how to plant a seed in a pot. Her instructor, who had asked students to write down their topic choices, was privately worried that this topic was too simple, something everyone already knew. Evelyn was, after all, speaking to college students who presumably could read the planting instructions on the back of a seed packet. The instructor did not want to discourage Evelyn, but wanted the class to benefit from her speech.

Without saying, "You cannot speak on this topic," the instructor shared her concerns with Evelyn. She found out that Evelyn had several other plant-related topics in mind. Evelyn agreed that a more unusual topic would be more interesting to the class and more challenging for her to deliver. On the day she was assigned to speak, Evelyn presented an interesting speech demonstrating how to propagate

Discussion Prompt:
State representative Joan Richards is running for a seat in the state senate. She worked hard as a legislator and was voted best representative by the Better Government League (BGL). The BGL voted her opponent, incumbent Mike Letner, as one of the ten worst senators in the state. Many political analysts think Richards would be the superior senator. Letner has taken a "no new taxes" pledge and has challenged Richards to do the same. Richards personally thinks taxes may have to be raised in order to keep the state solvent. Nevertheless, she knows that unless she promises to oppose any new taxes, she will lose the election. What should Richards do?

Effective speakers connect with their audiences and speak about issues that are important to them.

tropical plants by "air layering" them. Evelyn got a chance to demonstrate her green thumb and her classmates learned something most had never even heard of before.

Notice how Evelyn finally paid attention to her audience. At her teacher's suggestion, she rejected the simple, familiar topic that would probably not have taught her audience anything.

Discussion Prompt:
Is it unethical for students to give classroom speeches advocating positions with which they disagree? Or is there value in being able to argue from an opponent's point of view?

Having something meaningful to say leads to the second ethical consideration for speakers: deciding whether or not to speak. Silence is certainly an option, and probably one that is too infrequently exercised. There are times, though, when you need to convey information or when you feel strongly about an issue or an injustice. *Ethical speakers voice their opinions and champion causes.* Our nation's history has been shaped by the voices of Thomas Jefferson, Patrick Henry, Frederick Douglass, Susan B. Anthony, Martin Luther King, Jr., and other advocates. That shaping continues today in the voices of Jeane Kirkpatrick, Cesar Chavez, Ralph Nader, William F. Buckley, Coretta Scott King, Jesse Jackson, and Elie Wiesel, among many others.

You may not have the forum or the impact of those famous speakers, but you do have an opportunity to better the communities of which you are a part. This class provides you with an opportunity to share information your classmates can use to help them get more from their college experience, or to help them function better in their careers and personal lives. You also have a chance to educate others about problems you feel need to be confronted. Students do this effectively a great deal of the time, but we remember one student who showed special sensitivity in addressing a topic she opposed on ethical grounds.

Pam, a sophomore public relations major, had been an animal welfare advocate for a long time, but she knew from class discussions and conversations before class that a number of her classmates hunted for sport or for food. She realized that if she turned her ten-minute persuasive speech into a general sermon against killing animals she would only make a number of her classmates feel defensive. She wanted to speak on some aspect of animal welfare but knew she had to narrow and focus the topic.

As a volunteer worker for several animal protection agencies, Pam had become aware of the problems associated with the use of steel leg hold traps. Inside city limits, they posed a threat to pets, children, and adults who did not know where they had been set. She also opposed their use in the wilderness because, she said, they inflict pain and suffering and kill non-target animals. Pam delivered a well-documented speech to persuade her listeners that the use of these traps should be outlawed. Her carefully worded thesis was not that killing animals is wrong, but that use of this particular trap is cruel and inhumane. In her speech she even discussed two other types of traps as humane alternatives. The class listened intently to Pam, and toward the end of the speech she was gratified to see that many of her classmates, hunters included, were nodding in apparent agreement with her.

Much of your speaking in this class and later in life may not be on significant social or political issues. Yet this class provides you with the training ground to hone your skills as speaker and listener. Use these skills as you move from involvement in class and campus issues to improvement of your community.

Third, ethical speakers pay attention to the values implied in their topic choices. Selecting a topic is one of the first ethical choices you will make as a speaker. Unless you are assigned a topic, you can choose from a wide range of subjects. In a real sense, you give your topic credibility simply by selecting it. As an ethical speaker, your choice should reflect what you think is important for your audience.

In the courses we teach, many student speeches have expanded our knowledge or moved us to act on significant issues. But consider the following list of informative speech topics:

How to get a fake I.D.
How to "walk" (avoid paying) a restaurant check
How to get a faculty parking permit
How to beat police radar
How to get out of a speeding ticket.

We have heard speeches on each of these topics. Even though they were informative rather than persuasive speeches, each of these "how-to" topics implies that its action is acceptable. We do not know why students chose these topics, but we suggest that all of those speakers disregarded their listeners, failed to consider the values they were promoting, and presented unethical speeches.

Fourth, ethical speakers present their listeners with ideas that are logically developed and supported. Listeners have a right to know not only the speaker's ideas but also the material supporting those claims. Ethical speakers are well

Discussion Prompt:
You read an article by a noted medical expert. The author reports a study supporting your claim that the shortage of nurses is a serious problem. She begins her next paragraph, though, with the statement, "However, there are several significant limitations to this study, not the least of which is sample size." Should you present just the researcher's initial claim and make your case seem stronger, or should you acknowledge the study's limitations?

informed, and should thus test their ideas for validity and support. They should not knowingly use false information or faulty reasoning.

We recently witnessed two students presenting incomplete or out-of-date material:

Discussion Prompt:
In researching your speech on discrimination against women in the workplace, you discover two polls with conflicting conclusions. One shows that experts generally agree with your position; the other shows that they disagree. Is it ethical to present your listeners only the poll that supports your position, or should you acknowledge the other? On what basis should you make this decision?

> Janet presented an informative speech on the detection and treatment of breast cancer. Her discussion of the disease's detection was thorough, but when she got to her second point, she said that the only treatments were radical mastectomy, partial mastectomy, radiation therapy, and chemotherapy. She failed to mention lumpectomy, a popular surgical measure often combined with radiation or chemotherapy. Her bibliography revealed that her research stopped with sources published in the early 1980s, explaining the gap in her speech content.
>
> A second speaker, Bill, delivered a persuasive speech on the destruction of the ozone layer and global warming. Toward the end of the speech, he said that a big cause of the problem was polystyrene foam used in packaging fast foods. He singled out one fast-food company, urging classmates to put consumer pressure on this company to abandon such packaging. After the speech, one classmate asked, "Bill, didn't you hear that this company announced a few days ago that they were changing all their food packaging to paper?"

Discussion Prompt:
Many speakers say simply "experts say" or "research shows" when supporting their position. Do speakers have an ethical obligation *always* to identify their sources or the data for their conclusions?

Janet and Bill did not necessarily act unethically; they were simply uninformed and ended up being embarrassed. But what if Janet had known of the lumpectomy procedure and had just not wanted to do further research to find out about it? Then we would question her ethics. If Bill had heard news of the fast-food chain's announcement and ignored it so that he would not have to revise his speech, he would also be acting unethically.

In both of these cases, certain listeners did not notice the factual errors and the lapses in content, while others did. Not getting caught in a factual or logical error does not free the speaker of ethical responsibility to present complete, factual information. If you speak on a current topic, you need to use the most recent information you can find and try to be as well informed as possible.

Fifth, ethical speakers make their intentions clear to the audience. In other words, they do not intentionally manipulate the audience. Allan Cohen and David Bradford define manipulation as "actions to achieve influence that would be rendered less effective if the target knew your actual intentions."[4]

We are familiar with one company whose sales strategy certainly matched that definition of manipulation. This company relied on door-to-door salespersons, especially college students, and instructed new employees to make a list of friends who might be interested in purchasing the product. The employees were told to contact these friends and tell them the good news about their new job. The company also coached employees to say that part of the job involved making presentations to potential customers and to ask if they could practice giving their presentation to the friend in order to get some helpful feedback. In addition, because the company wanted to encourage its workers to succeed, employees offered each volunteer "critic" a gift. However, the company also told each salesperson confidentially that the presentations were actually a test to see if they could sell the product, and that they should take advantage of this sales opportunity.

Discussion Prompt:
News reporters occasionally attribute statements to "a high government official" or "a highly placed source." Should reporters reveal their sources?

We consider this strategy manipulative and unethical. The salespersons make the appointments under false pretenses. The company exploits its employees' friendships; the employees in turn exploit their friends' willingness to be helpful. These helpful critics might not participate if they knew their friends' real intent. A public speaker may try to inform, convince, persuade, direct, or even anger an audience. Ethical speakers, however, do not deceive their listeners. They are up-front about their intentions, and those intentions include benefiting the audience.

Sixth, ethical speakers concern themselves with the consequences of their speaking. Mary Cunningham observed, "Words are sacred things. They are also like hand grenades: Handled casually, they tend to go off."[5] Ethical speakers have a respect for the power of language and the process of communication.

It is difficult to track, let alone predict, the impact of any one message. Statements you make are interpreted by your immediate audience and may be communicated by those listeners to others. Individuals may form opinions and behave differently because of what you say or what you fail to say. Incorrect information and misinterpretations may have unintended, and potentially harmful, consequences. If you provide an audience with inaccurate information, you may contaminate the quality of their subsequent decisions. If you persuade someone to act in a particular way, you are, in part, responsible for the impact of the person's new action. With that principle in mind, consider the following experience a friend of ours had.

> A colleague approaching retirement has had a long and distinguished career teaching communication. She returned to her office visibly upset after a class one day. When questioned, she said she had just had a student announce in the introduction to his speech that his purpose was to teach the class how to make a lethal poison using ingredients people either already had in their homes or could easily buy. "Moreover," she said, "to stress the significance of the topic, he assured us that this substance would kill any living animal, certainly even the heaviest human being."
>
> Upon hearing this, her colleagues' reactions were, "That's scary" or "That's frightening. What did you do?" Her answer told us that our friend really was upset for two reasons. She said, "I sat there thinking of the rash of teenage suicides, even copycat suicides, we've been hearing about lately, and all the other meanness in the world. I wrestled with my conscience for about a minute and a half, and then, for the first time since I started teaching, I interrupted a speaker, told him I didn't think we needed to hear this information, and asked him to be seated."

Placed in that teacher's position, what would you have done? Such an obvious clash between a speaker's freedom of expression and the ethical standards of listeners leads us to consider the standards of ethical listening.

Discussion Prompt:
Some public access cable television stations have caused controversy by airing programs that show how to make explosives or how to jam automatic teller machines. Are such messages, which could harm individuals or lead them to crime, ethical? Is it ethical to suppress this kind of speech?

Discussion Prompt:
Was the teacher's action justified? Did she violate the student's freedom of speech?

KEY POINTS
Responsibilities of an Ethical Speaker

1. Say something meaningful.
2. Speak up about issues you consider important.
3. Choose topics that promote positive ethical values.
4. Use truthful, accurate supporting materials and valid reasoning.
5. Let the audience know your true motives for speaking.
6. Consider the consequences of your words and actions.

■ **Ethical Listening** ─────────────────────────

"A mind that is stretched to a new idea never returns to its original dimension."
OLIVER WENDELL HOLMES

The ethics of listening involves four basic principles. *First, ethical listeners seek out speakers who expand their knowledge, increase their understanding, introduce them to new ideas, and challenge their beliefs.* These listeners reject the philosophy, "My mind's made up, so don't confuse me with the facts." A controversial speaker visiting your campus can expand your knowledge or intensify your feelings about a subject, whether you agree or disagree with the speaker's viewpoint. Even in situations where students are a captive audience for other students' speeches, such as this class, ethical listening should be the standard.

Second, ethical listeners listen openly without prejudging speakers or their ideas. This may be difficult. Listening without bias requires that we temporarily suspend impressions we have formed from the other person's past actions. But the rewards of doing so can be great, as in this example.

Linda's first speech in class completely confused her classmates. She seemed nervous and unsure of herself and what she was going to say, and the point of her speech really eluded everyone. Class discussion after the speech focused primarily on Linda's delivery, and some of the distracting mannerisms she exhibited and needed to control. Weeks later when she went to the front of the room to begin her next speech, no one was really expecting to be impressed. But they were.

Linda's second speech dealt with the problem of homelessness. Her opening sentence told the class that three years ago she had been living on the street for a time. She had their attention from that point on. In addition to citing recent newspaper and magazine articles, Linda had conducted a great deal of original research. She had interviewed the directors of local shelters and a number of the homeless people who took refuge there, and she quoted these individuals in the speech. Her speech was well organized and well delivered. It was both educational and inspiring.

When discussing the speech later, classmates kept referring to her first speech and noting the remarkable improvements Linda had made. One person was blunt, but apparently summed up the feelings of a number of listeners that day: "Linda, I wasn't expecting much from you because your first speech was so unclear to me, but today you had a topic that you obviously care about and you made us understand and care about it, too. I can't get over the difference between those two speeches!"

When listening to your classmates, you should assume that you may learn something important from each speaker, and therefore listen intently. Information and ideas are best shared in such an atmosphere of mutual respect.

Listening eagerly and openly does not imply a permanent suspension of evaluation, however. *A third standard is that ethical listeners evaluate the messages presented to them.* A listener who accepts a premise without evaluating its foundation is like someone who buys a used car without looking under the hood. The warning "let the buyer beware" is good advice not only for consumers of products but also for consumers of messages. As a listener, you should critically evaluate the ideas of the speaker. Is each idea logically constructed? Is each supported with evidence that is relevant, sufficient, and authoritative?

Ethical speakers and listeners read and listen critically. To see how some students listen more critically than others, consider the example of the following persuasive speaker.

> Sharon presented a speech arguing that all of the problems high school students face today—drug use, gang violence, teenage pregnancy, lack of discipline in class, academic failure—resulted from the Supreme Court decision that ended prayer in school. She had two primary supporting materials: quotations from a local religious leader and a comparison of school conditions in the 1950s with conditions in the 1990s.
>
> Sharon argued her case with a great deal of conviction. As she spoke, many listeners indicated agreement with her by nodding their heads and looking concerned. But after her speech, several students asked, "Sharon, aren't there other differences between schools in the '50s and the '90s? There are more students today, and more peer pressure. Drugs that were not even known in the '50s are readily available today. Could it be that teachers in the '50s expected more of students than they do today?" Finally one student said, "I personally agree with you. I think prayer or at least a moment of silence for voluntary prayer might encourage students to be more reverent or thoughtful. But you haven't proved to me that all of these problems you mentioned are a direct result of lack of school prayer. There's a logical flaw in your speech."

Whether offered a product, an idea, or a proposed course of action, ethical listeners evaluate critically.

Fourth, ethical listeners concern themselves with the consequences of their listening. As the following example illustrates, listeners who assimilate only part of a public speaker's message because they fail to listen actively are responsible for the distorted message that results.

> Hank listened to his classmate Jeff deliver a speech about problems with their college's registration procedures. As Jeff spoke, Hank remembered problems he had encountered: long lines, inconvenient registration times, filled classes. At one point Hank heard Jeff talking about experimental phone registration the school was offering next semester to students with last names beginning from A to L. At the next class meeting, Hank said to Jeff, "I called the registrar's office yesterday to register by phone. They asked for my last name. When I said it was Thompson, they told me phone registration this semester was only for students with last names beginning from A to L." "I told you that in my speech," Jeff said. "Weren't you listening?"

Hank may have been embarrassed, but he did not suffer greatly as a result of not listening carefully to Jeff. In other cases, however, the consequences of not listening are more serious. When you fail to listen to someone's directions and are late for an interview, you miss an employment opportunity. In both of these examples, the listener, not the speaker, bears responsibility for the breakdown in communication.

At other times, listener and speaker may share responsibility for unethical behavior. For example, audience members who become victims of "scams" because they did not listen critically share with the speaker responsibility for

Discussion Prompt:
If a political campaign is underway, have students generate a list of candidates' statements and behaviors that they consider unethical. List ways in which members of the public have responded to these statements. Are those responses ethical or unethical?

Related Reading:
For another discussion of the ethical responsibilities of the agent and receiver of persuasive messages, see: Trenholm, Sarah. "The Ethics of Control." *Persuasion and Social Influence.* Englewood Cliffs, NJ: Prentice, 1989: 17-20.

their behavior. Voters who tolerate exaggerated, vague, and inconsistent campaign statements from those who ask to represent them similarly become part of the problem and not of the solution.

KEY POINTS **Responsibilities of an** **Ethical Listener**	1. Seek exposure to well-informed persuasive speakers. 2. Listen openly, without prejudging the speaker or the speaker's ideas. 3. Evaluate the logic and credibility of the speaker's ideas. 4. Beware of the consequences of not listening carefully.

Most of us begin learning ethical principles as children: "It's wrong to lie." "It's wrong to deceive others." "It's wrong to blame others for what we say and do." In the past, views of communication ethics implied a dotted line across the front of a classroom, with ethics being solely the speaker's responsibility. In contrast, we view ethics as a shared responsibility of the speaker and each listener. An absence of ethical motives among speakers and listeners devalues the currency of communication. One aspect of ethics, however, *does* begin as the speaker's responsibility: plagiarism. We feel that the topic of plagiarism deserves special attention, so we discuss it here.

■ Plagiarism

"You must renounce imagination forever if you hope to succeed in plagiarism. Forgery is intention, not invention."　　　　　　　　　　　HORACE WALPOLE

"Your manuscript is both good and original; but the part that is good is not original, and the part that is original is not good."　　　　　SAMUEL JOHNSON

plagiarism: the unattributed use of another's ideas, words, or pattern of organization.

Discussion Prompt: Stimulate and moderate class discussion and debate on the topic: "It is unethical for politicians and businesspersons to deliver speeches they did not write." (See Exercise 6 at the end of this chapter.)

The word **plagiarize** comes from a Latin word meaning "to kidnap," so in a sense, a plagiarist is a kidnapper of the ideas and words of another. A modern definition of plagiarism is "literary — or artistic or musical — theft. It is the false assumption of authorship: the wrongful act of taking the product of another person's mind, and presenting it as one's own."[6]

When you write a paper and submit it to a teacher, you are in effect publishing that work. If in that paper you copy something from another source and pass it off as your own work, you are plagiarizing. This act is such a serious offense that in most colleges and universities it is grounds for failing the course, or even dismissal from the school. Yet recent history has shown us numerous examples of politicians, educators, and other public figures caught plagiarizing materials, either consciously or unconsciously. An offense serious enough to derail a candidate's campaign for office, to force the resignation of a corporate officer, or to end a student's academic career certainly deserves the attention of students in a public speaking class.

Of course, some spoken language is repeated from person to person with no real thought given to the question of copyright or "ownership." Facts or ideas considered common knowledge ("Water freezes at zero degrees Celsius" or "Ronald Reagan served two terms as our fortieth president") do not have to be attributed to a source. Jokes are another example of speech that does not have to be footnoted orally. You may tell your listeners where you heard the joke, but people do not typically concern themselves with copyright law where jokes, tall tales, or popular sayings are concerned. The facts and the wording of a public speech are quite another matter, though. For one thing, most speeches are more formal than joking or conversation. Second, the audience for a public speech assumes that the ideas expressed and the words used are the speaker's, unless they are told otherwise.

Just as you publish the paper you write and submit to your teacher, when you deliver a speech in this class or on any other occasion you are also "publishing" your material. Even without putting your words in print or placing a copyright notice on them, you hold the copyright on your ideas expressed in your own words. The current copyright law is interpreted to say, "Even if a speech has merely been delivered orally and not [formally] published, it is subject to copyright protection and may not be used without written permission."[7] Plagiarism of well-known speeches or speakers is both unethical and foolish, as the following example shows.

> Both of your authors are fans of comedian George Carlin. Some years ago one of us judged a high school speech tournament event called speaking to entertain or after-dinner speaking. Even though the contest rules stipulated that the speech must be the student's original work, one student copied virtually his entire speech word for word from a particular Carlin concert recording. Of course that blatant plagiarism, noted by several judges, led to the student's prompt disqualification from the competition.

As we have said, repeating a joke a friend tells you is one thing; memorizing and reciting a comedy routine by George Carlin, Rita Rudner, Marsha Warfield, or Robin Williams is quite another. Repeating distinctive, well-known material as though it were your own may be the most foolish type of plagiarism. No less serious, however, is plagiarizing from obscure sources. If you deliver a speech someone else has researched, organized, and worded, you are presenting another's work as your own. You are plagiarizing.

Plagiarism applies to more than simply the copying of another's words, however. You may also plagiarize another's ideas and organization of material. For example, if you presented a speech organized around the five stages of dying (denial, anger, bargaining, depression, and acceptance) and did not give credit to Elisabeth Kübler-Ross, you would be guilty of plagiarism. On the other hand, if your speech analyzed the political, economic, and social implications of a pending piece of legislation, you would probably not be guilty of plagiarism. Kübler-Ross developed, explained, and published her framework or model in her book *On Death and Dying*, whereas the second example relies on a commonly accepted pattern of analyzing public policy initiatives. As you can see, the line between legitimate appropriation of material and plagiarism is sometimes unclear. As a speaker you must always be on guard to credit the source of your ideas and their structure.

As another example of potential plagiarism, suppose a speaker, after reading *Game Plans: Sports Strategies for Business*, selected as his or her specific

Teaching Strategy:
Share with your students your college's policy regarding plagiarism. Share your own policy if it differs from the college's.

purpose to explain business management using sports as models. Using three chapter titles from that book, the speaker could word the major ideas of the speech as follows:

I. Filling Out the Lineup Card (Baseball)
II. Preparing the Game Plan (Football)
III. Managing the Flow (Basketball)[8]

Such a speaker would be guilty of plagiarism if he or she did not attribute the ideas to Robert W. Keidel, the author of *Game Plans: Sports Strategies for Business*. Keidel not only supported these ideas, he created them. To avoid plagiarism the speaker could change the wording of the specific purpose: to explain to the audience Robert Keidel's use of sports models for business management. In this way the speaker clearly attributes the ideas in the speech to Keidel.

As we mentioned earlier, plagiarism may be intentional or unintentional. *Intentional plagiarism* occurs when speakers or writers knowingly represent another person's words, ideas, or organization as their own. *Unintentional plagiarism* is "the careless paraphrasing and citing of source material such that improper or misleading credit is given."[9] Intentional plagiarism is considered the more severe offense. Unintentional plagiarism may be done out of ignorance, but the effect is still the same: You are taking credit for the work of another.

Sometimes unintentional plagiarism occurs because of a common misconception that by simply changing a few words of another's writing you have paraphrased the statement and need not cite it. Michael O'Neill refers to this "hybrid of half textual source, half original writing" as a "paraplage."[10] Note the differences and similarities in the original and adapted passages of the following statement by Daniel Botkin.

Practice Speaking:
Have students look at Peter Schjeldahl's description of a ride on the roller coaster The Cyclone, quoted in Chapter 11. Ask them to use the information in the end-notes to introduce those quotations orally.

Statement by Professor Botkin
Forests are not static. They have a biography not unlike a human's. Their infancy is the open field or devastated forest. First, "pioneer species" begin to grow: herbs, grasses, and then shrubs. Afterward there are several stages of trees. These stages are dynamic and diverse. The forest's maturity is known as its "climax"—a more stable and less diverse mix of species that will persist for some time. In old age, a forest, such as the Tabernacle Pines, becomes susceptible to fire or hurricane. These stages of development, or forest succession, are quite interconnected. Take your fallen trees. Certain seeds regenerate best when they fall into the nest of a rotting log.[11]

Speaker's Paraplage of Professor Botkin
Forests are dynamic and have a biography much like a human's. In infancy, a forest is either an open field or a devastated forest. In time, grasses, herbs, and shrubs develop and then give way to several stages of trees. The diversity and dynamism of the forest slow as it reaches its climax in maturity. Much later, in old age, the forest is an easy victim of fires, hurricanes, and other acts of nature.

Speaker's Appropriate Citation of Professor Botkin
Forests have a dynamic and a biography much like a human's, according to Daniel Botkin, professor of biology and environmental studies at the University of Califor-

Practice Speaking:
Use this example to introduce the concept of *oral footnoting*. Give the class copies of statements from published articles. Have them present those statements orally to the class with proper attribution.

nia at Santa Barbara. In his article in the April 1990 *Harper's Magazine,* he discusses

35
*The Ethics of
Public Speaking*

nia at Santa Barbara. In his article in the April 1990 *Harper's Magazine,* he discusses the infancy, growth, maturity, and old age of the forest. From infancy in an open field or a devastated forest, the young forest develops a series of diverse tree species. Botkin notes that at maturity, or "climax," the forest is a "more stable and less diverse mix of species that will persist for some time."

Notice that the appropriate citation above not only tells the listener who Professor Botkin is, but also explains exactly where his words appeared in print. With that information, any listener wanting to read the entire article could go to a library and find it quickly.

To avoid plagiarizing, let these five simple rules guide you.

1. *Establish a clear and consistent method of notetaking when you research.* As you review your notes, you should be able to discern which words, ideas, examples, and organizational structures belong to which authors.

2. *Record complete source citations on each sheet of notes or write this information on each photocopied article.*

3. *Clearly indicate in your speech any words, ideas, examples, or organizational structures that are not your own.* If you cite a source early in your speech and then use another idea from that author later, you must again give that author credit. You need not, however, repeat the complete citation. The statement "Botkin notes" in the appropriate citation above signals the listener that the speaker is again quoting or paraphrasing the words of Daniel Botkin.

4. *When you paraphrase ideas, credit their originator.* Remember that another's statements are characterized by both content and structure. When paraphrasing, you should use not only your words but also your own language style and thought structure.

5. *When in doubt, cite the source.* At times you will be unsure whether you need to acknowledge a source. It is always wise to err on the side of caution.

We have discussed some reasons *not* to hide the true authorship of words and ideas. There are also at least two reasons why speakers *should* mention their sources. The first reason may seem selfish or self-centered, but it is nevertheless true that speakers who cite their sources increase their credibility or believability with the audience. When you quote from a book, an article, or an interview and name the author or speaker of those words, you show the audience that you have researched the topic and that you know what you are talking about. Second, and far more important, acknowledging your sources is the right thing to do. It is honest. Good ideas and memorably worded thoughts are rare enough that the original thinker and writer deserves credit.

Teaching Strategy:
Ask students to examine the source citation in paragraph 13 of Susanne Landowski's speech, "Academic Laboratories: Risking Life and Limb for Credit," in Appendix C. What is missing from that citation? Answer: The source in which Dr. Kaufman's words appeared.

Teaching Strategy:
You may want to advise students who photocopy research materials to copy the table of contents or title page as added insurance against attributing sources incorrectly.

Class Activity:
Ethical behavior is something we should demand in national, state, and local political campaigns. We should also expect it of candidates and the electorate in campus politics. Have students develop a code of ethics that they think should govern speech in student government campaigns on your campus.

1. Take clear and consistent notes while researching.
2. Record complete source citations for notes or photocopied pages.
3. Indicate any quoted material as you deliver the speech.
4. Credit the source of any ideas or structures you paraphrase.
5. Cite the source when in doubt.

**KEY POINTS
Guidelines To Avoid
Plagiarism**

Summary

Ethics and plagiarism are topics of concern to students and teachers of public speaking. *Ethics* refers to fundamental questions of right and wrong in thought and behavior. We offer some positive observations on ethics from the viewpoints of both speaker and listener. Ethics is not a standard for acceptable practice that we turn on before speaking and off after the speech is over; it is a value system pervading our lives. We believe that everyone involved in public communication should be guided by the following ethical considerations.

First, ethical speakers have something meaningful to say. Their messages interest and benefit the audience. Second, ethical speakers are willing to voice their opinions on issues that concern them. They make the decision to speak out, even when remaining silent would be easier. Third, ethical speakers care about the values reflected in their topic choices. Fourth, ethical speakers develop and support the ideas of their speeches accurately and logically. Fifth, ethical speakers make their intentions clear to their audiences and avoid conscious manipulation. Finally, ethical speakers care about the consequences their speaking may have for listeners.

Listening should be guided by four ethical principles. First, ethical listeners welcome challenges to their beliefs just as they embrace learning. Second, ethical listening means listening openly, without prejudging the speaker's ideas. Third, ethical listeners evaluate the speaker's ideas before acting upon them. Finally, ethical listeners care about and accept responsibility for the consequences of their listening.

Both speakers and listeners need to be aware of the issue of *plagiarism*, the unattributed use of another's ideas, words, or organization. Plagiarism may be either *intentional* or *unintentional*. To avoid plagiarizing sources, speakers should (1) establish a clear and consistent method of notetaking, (2) record a complete source citation on each page of notes or on each photocopied article, (3) clearly indicate in the speech any words, ideas, or organizational techniques not their own, (4) orally cite sources for paraphrased, as well as quoted, materials, and (5) when in doubt, acknowledge the source. Careful source citation not only increases a speaker's credibility with the audience, but also is ethically right.

Exercises

1. Select two individuals prominent on the international, national, state, or local scene whom you consider ethical speakers. What characteristics do they possess that make them ethical? Select two people you consider unethical. What ethical standards do you think they abuse?
2. Answer each of the following questions and be prepared to defend your position.
   a. Should a speech instructor have the right to censor topics students select for their speeches?
   b. Should students have the right to use profanity and obscenity in their speeches in this class?
   c. Should the Ku Klux Klan be allowed to hold a rally on your campus?

d. Should public prayers be a part of opening ceremonies at athletic contests at publicly supported schools?

e. Should lawyers defend clients they know are guilty?

3. In the news, find a company that has been accused of some ethical wrongdoing. Follow the story as it is reported for a week, and then discuss the ethics of the company's statements and actions.

4. Read the statement about George Smathers on page 214 of Chapter 11. Discuss the ethics of Smathers and his listeners.

5. Find an article on any subject written by an expert. Summarize the article in one or two paragraphs. Use appropriate source citation, paraphrasing, and quotations to avoid plagiarism.

6. Politicians often do not write the speeches they deliver, instead relying on the words of speechwriters. Lyndon Johnson used a record twenty-four writers for his State of the Union address in 1964.[12] Journalist Ari Posner laments this tradition, observing, "If college or high school students relied on ghosts the way most public figures do, they'd be expelled on charges of plagiarism."[13] Be prepared to defend your answers to the following questions: Is the practice of ghostwriting in politics unethical? What are the advantages and disadvantages of politicians relying on speechwriters? Should students be permitted to use ghostwriters for their classroom speeches?

Notes

1. James A. Jaksa and Michael S. Pritchard, *Communication Ethics* (Belmont, CA: Wadsworth, 1988) xi.

2. Donald K. Smith, *Man Speaking: A Rhetoric of Public Speech* (New York: Dodd, 1969) 228.

3. Kenneth Blanchard and Norman Vincent Peale, *The Power of Ethical Management* (New York: Fawcett-Ballantine, 1988) 9.

4. Allan R. Cohen and David L. Bradford, *Influence Without Authority* (New York: Wiley, 1990) ix.

5. Mary Cunningham, "What Price 'Good Copy'?" *Newsweek* 29 November 1982: 15.

6. Alexander Lindey, *Plagiarism and Originality* (New York: Harper, 1952) 2.

7. *Prentice Hall Author's Guide* (Englewood Cliffs, NJ: Prentice, 1978) 9.

8. Robert W. Keidel, *Game Plans: Sports Strategies for Business* (New York: Berkley, 1987).

9. John L. Waltman, "Plagiarism: Preventing It in Formal Research Reports," *ABCA [American Business Communication Association] Bulletin* June 1980: 37.

10. Michael T. O'Neill "Plagiarism: Writing Responsibly," *ABCA Bulletin* June 1980: 34, 36.

11. Daniel Botkin, in "Only Man's Presence Can Save Nature," *Harper's* April 1990: 38.

12. Jo Ann Tooley, "Database," *U.S. News and World Report* 28 January 1991: 10.

13. Ari Posner, "The Culture of Plagiarism," *New Republic* 18 April 1988: 19.

Speaking Confidently

3

Pervasiveness of Speaker Nervousness

Controlling Speaker Nervousness

Coping Strategies
Know How You React to Stress
Know Your Strengths and
   Weaknesses

Know Speech Principles
Know Your Audience
Know Your Speech
View Your Topic Positively
View Speech Making Positively
Project Control
Test Your Message
Practice
Learn from Experience

■ Pervasiveness of Speaker Nervousness ─────────

"The idea of making a speech does more than make me a nervous wreck; it terrifies me. Acting, though, is different. I'm always doing things with other people. But a speech! I'd rather scrub floors — without knee pads."

CAROL BURNETT[1]

Teaching Strategy:
Play videotaped excerpts of winners accepting an Oscar, Tony, or Grammy award. Ask your students to note any symptoms of nervousness among the award recipients. Stress that nervousness is natural, even among those who are professional performers with extensive experience before audiences.

Carol Burnett is an accomplished comedian and actor, having appeared in her own television series, in movies, and as host of various televised award shows. Nevertheless, she fears public speaking. She is not alone. Meryl Streep, one of America's most versatile actors, said in a 1988 interview, "It's odd: I have this career that spans continents, but the pathetic thing is that I can't get up in front of people and speak. I get really, really nervous." When the interviewer, playwright Wendy Wasserstein, suggested that the reason might be that she was speaking as herself rather than as a character, Streep replied, "Yes. Fiction is something you can lie down and wrap yourself up in. In reality, you're alone on the mountaintop in the wind and the storm and you don't know if you're going to be blown away."[2]

Joanne Woodward's reaction to the prospect of making a speech echoes Burnett and Streep. She says, "Speaking is not something I do well. I guess because I'm a character actress, it's very hard for me to stand up in my own skin." As a result, she practices in the shower for any speech she has to do, "because I sweat so. It's terrifying."[3] Lee Iacocca, former chief executive officer of the Chrysler Corporation, confesses that "to this day I still get a little nervous before giving a speech."[4] And the list of performers and public figures who have disclosed their nervousness about public speaking includes former president Ronald Reagan, NBC weatherperson Willard Scott, singer Barbra Streisand, actor Tom Selleck, and quarterback Joe Montana.

Teaching Strategy:
You may want to administer the Personal Report of Public Speaking Anxiety (PRPSA) survey to your class and use this information to assess the students' levels of public speaking apprehension. Another survey instrument is the Personal Report of Communication Apprehension (PRCA-24). In addition to a total score, the PRCA-24 provides subscores in four communication contexts: public speaking, interpersonal conversations, group discussion, and meetings. These instruments and scoring instructions can be found in: Richmond, Virginia, and James C. McCroskey. *Communication: Apprehension, Avoidance, and Effectiveness*. 2nd ed. Scottsdale, AZ: Gorsuch, 1989, pp. 123–28.

These examples demonstrate that if you are nervous about public speaking and experience what we sometimes call "platform panic," you are in good company. In fact, *The Book of Lists* reports a survey that asked 3,000 Americans, "What are you the most afraid of?" "Speaking before a group" came in first, ahead of the fear of heights, insects and bugs, financial problems, deep water, sickness, and even death![5] Psychiatrists John Greist, James Jefferson, and Isaac Marks contend that public speaking anxiety is "probably the most common social phobia."[6] Today, when so many people are apprehensive about even striking up a conversation with a stranger, is it any wonder that the fear of public speaking is so widespread?

Our experience and research confirm the prevalence of this common fear among college students. When asked to list their communication weaknesses, a clear majority of our students rank speaking before a group of people as their primary fear. James McCroskey has studied the anxieties of public speaking extensively and scientifically. McCroskey's Personal Report of Public Speaking Anxiety assesses the fear college students have about giving public speeches. His data, collected from several thousand students, confirm that public speaking generates greater apprehension than other forms of communication and that this fear spans several levels:

high anxiety	40%
moderately high anxiety	30%
moderate anxiety	20%
moderately low anxiety	5%
low anxiety	5%

Note that nearly three-fourths of college students fall into the moderately high to high anxiety range! This means that even the person who always has the quick response, who can make others in the class laugh, who always looks together, may be just as worried as you are right now about getting up in front of this class to give a speech! Virginia Richmond and McCroskey conclude: "What this suggests, then, is that it is 'normal' to experience a fairly high degree of anxiety about public speaking. Most people do. If you are highly anxious about public speaking, then you are 'normal.' "[7]

What is this platform panic and how does it affect us? Chemically and physiologically, we all experience stage fright in the same way. Adrenalin is suddenly pumped into the bloodstream. Respiration increases dramatically. So do heart rate and "galvanic skin response"—the amount of perspiration on the surface of the skin. All of these things occur so that oxygen-rich blood can be quickly channeled to the large muscle groups. You may have heard stories of a 135-pound person who lifts the front of a car to help rescue someone pinned under it. Such incidents happen because the body is suddenly mobilized to do what must be done.

Yet the body can be similarly mobilized in stressful but non-life-threatening situations: musicians before the opening selection, athletes before the game begins, actors before the curtain goes up, and speakers before they rise to face the audience. In each of these cases, the body is marshalling all its resources either to perform to capacity or to get away from the threatening situation. For that reason this phenomenon is called, appropriately, the "fight or flight" syndrome.

Though our bodies' chemical and physiological responses to stress are identical, the outward signs of this anxiety vary from person to person. As the time approaches for your first speech in this class, you may experience any of several symptoms to varying degrees. Our students tell us that their symptoms include blushing or redness, accelerated heart rate, perspiring, dry mouth, shaking, churning stomach, increased rate of speech, forgetfulness and broken

Teaching Strategy:
To demonstrate the pervasiveness of anxiety among performers, ask students to locate a magazine or journal article describing how people in one of their fields of interest cope with nervousness. For example, *Keyboard* magazine often features articles describing techniques musicians use to deal with stress before a recital or concert.

Discussion Prompt:
Have students list on a sheet of paper several symptoms they experience when speaking to a group of people. Ask them to volunteer to share some of these symptoms with the class, and record them on the chalkboard. Note that many class members share the same symptoms and that some nervousness appears to be common to most of the class.

Reprinted by permission of UFS, Inc.

speech, and nervous mannerisms such as playing with jewelry, tapping fingers, and clutching the lectern.

As we indicated earlier, it is important to realize that these symptoms are typical, not atypical, of a public speaker. If you experience any of these symptoms, you have plenty of company.

■ Controlling Speaker Nervousness

Before discussing what your goal should be regarding speaker nervousness, it is important to note what it should *not* be. Your objective should *not* be to eliminate nervousness. Such a goal is counterproductive for at least two reasons. First, as we have noted, nervousness is natural. Attempting to eliminate it is therefore unrealistic and probably undesirable. Speakers with far more experience in front of the public have failed to do so—remember Burnett, Streep, Woodward, and Iacocca. It is unlikely that you will be able to do so. In fact, the more you concentrate on your nervousness, the more nervous you may become. As someone has said, "You never get rid of the butterflies in your stomach, but you can teach them to fly in formation."

A second reason why you should not try to eliminate nervousness is that some nervousness can actually benefit a speaker. Nervousness is energy. Use that energy to enliven your delivery and to give your ideas impact. Instead of nervously tapping your fingers on the lectern, for example, you can gesture. In place of shifting your body weight from foot to foot, you can incorporate motivated movement in your speech.

Your goal, then, is not to eliminate nervousness but to *control* and *channel* it. The coping strategies we suggest in the next section, and in Chapter 12 on delivery, will enable you to control the symptoms of nervousness and to channel that energy into dynamic, effective vocal and physical delivery.

Related Readings:
Daly, John, and James C. McCroskey, eds. *Avoiding Communication: Shyness, Reticence, and Communication Apprehension.* Beverly Hills: Sage, 1984.
Desberg, Peter, and George D. Marsh. *Controlling Stagefright: Presenting Yourself to Audiences from One to One Thousand.* Oakland, CA: New Harbinger, 1988.
Phillips, Gerald M. *Communication Incompetencies: A Theory of Training Oral Performance Behavior.* Carbondale: Southern Illinois U P, 1991.
Richmond, Virginia, and James C. McCroskey. *Communication: Apprehension, Avoidance, and Effectiveness.* 2nd ed. Scottsdale, AZ: Gorsuch, 1989.

■ Coping Strategies

One popular, non-academic book on public speaking suggests the following "quick-fix" for reducing stage fright:

> Take an orange crate to a busy downtown street where you're not known, get up on the crate and, using all your lung power, proceed to exhort the passersby with the speech you're preparing. I'm serious. This works because you can't continue feeling the really paralyzing fear of stage fright over and over—your nervous system rebels against going through all that turmoil for no reason.[8]

Before you panic further, note that we do not suggest that you try this. In fact, we disagree with the exercise suggested above as well as its rationale. If you are nervous about speaking in front of your classmates, you would no doubt be nervous shouting to strangers on a street corner. You might even risk arrest and still not reduce your nervousness.

We advocate a far less dramatic approach to ease your nervousness. We offer eleven suggestions to help you become a more confident communicator. If you consider each suggestion seriously, you will control your nervousness and learn to channel that nervousness into a dynamic and effective public speaking style.

---

1. Know how you react to stress.
2. Know your strengths and weaknesses.
3. Know speech principles.
4. Know your audience.
5. Know your speech.
6. View your topic positively.
7. View speech making positively.
8. Project control.
9. Test your message.
10. Practice.
11. Learn from experience.

KEY POINTS
Guidelines To
Control Speaker
Nervousness

KNOW HOW YOU REACT TO STRESS

We have already noted that nervousness affects different people in different ways. You may feel that your hands or knees are shaking uncontrollably as you speak in public. The people sitting next to you might not ever experience those symptoms of nervousness, but they might have difficulty breathing comfortably and feel that their voices are shaky or quivery. Whatever your individual responses to stress, don't wait until you are delivering a public speech to discover them.

Knowing your reactions to stressful situations helps you in two ways. First, this knowledge lets you predict and cope with the physical conditions you may experience as you deliver your speech. Your dry mouth or sweaty palms will not surprise you; instead, you will recognize them as signs that your body is performing well under pressure. Second, since you are anticipating these physical conditions, you will be better able to mask them from the audience. How do you do this?

If you know that your hands shake when you are nervous, don't hold a sheet of paper during the speech; the shaking paper will only amplify the movement of your hands and will telegraph this sign of nervousness to your audience. If your voice is likely to be thin and quivery as you begin speaking, take several deep, slow breaths before you begin to speak. If you get tense before speaking, try some muscle relaxation techniques: Tense your hands, arms, and shoulders, and then slowly relax them. If you get flustered before speaking, make sure you arrive on time or even a little early—never late. If looking at an audience intimidates you, talk to audience members before class, and when you speak, look for friendly faces in the audience.

KNOW YOUR STRENGTHS AND WEAKNESSES

Surgeons spend many hours learning how to use the equipment they need to perform operations. Each surgeon knows just what each instrument is capable of doing and can use it to maximum effectiveness. As a public speaker, your instruments are your voice, body, mind, and personality. You will use all these instruments together to create and communicate messages.

To know yourself you must honestly appraise both your strengths and your weaknesses. You should use your strengths to communicate your message with force and impact. If you are a lively and enthusiastic person, use that energy to reinforce your speech physically and enliven your listeners. If you have a talent for creating memorable phrases, use that creativity to help your listeners attend to and remember your ideas. Just as you can tap your strengths in these ways, you can minimize or avoid your weaknesses if you know them. If you are not effective in delivering humor, you probably should not begin your speech with a joke. To do so would risk failure at this critical point in the speech, and that would make you even more nervous.

The more you understand your strengths and weaknesses, the better you will be able to craft your speech to your abilities. The more confident you are that you can accomplish what you set out to do, the less nervous you will be. One note of caution, however: Don't be too critical of yourself and construct a "safe" speech because you have exaggerated your weaknesses. Instead, expand your abilities by incorporating new strategies into your speech making. Only through thoughtful, measured risk taking will you develop as a public speaker.

KNOW SPEECH PRINCIPLES

If you are confident that you have constructed an effective speech, you will be more confident as you step to the lectern. This textbook and your instructor will assist you in learning speech principles. What are the four steps of an effective speech introduction? How should you construct the body of your speech, and how should you develop each key idea? What strategies help you conclude your speech? How can you use your voice and body to communicate your ideas dynamically? What strategies help you word ideas correctly, clearly, and vividly? We address all of these questions, and many others, in this book. As you begin to answer these questions and apply what you learn, you will feel more confident about the content, organization, and delivery of your ideas.

KNOW YOUR AUDIENCE

A confident speaker must believe that the content of a speech will interest or satisfy a need of the audience. If your listeners are bored with your topic, you will sense it, and that will make you more nervous. If the audience is interested in the content of your speech, they will be attentive. They will provide you with nonverbal cues affirming that they are benefiting from, and even enjoying, your speech. The more they focus on *what* you say, the less attention they will pay to *how* you speak, the specifics of your delivery.

We also believe in the adage that it always looks worse from the inside. Because you feel nervous, you focus on your anxiety, exaggerate it, and become more nervous. Remember, though, your audience cannot observe your internal state! Many times our students have lamented their nervousness after concluding a speech, only to learn that classmates envied them for being so calm and free from stage fright. The authors of a study of ninety-five speakers found this experience to be typical. The results of their research, they say, "suggest that untrained audiences are not very good at detecting the self-perceived anxiety of beginning speakers."[9] Even if you feel extremely nervous, then, it probably does not show to the audience. Knowing this should make you more secure and lessen your nervousness.

As an extreme example, one of our students, Susan, wrote the following in her self-evaluation of her first graded classroom speech:

> Too fast, too rushed. I forgot 1/2 of it. Yuck! Yuck! Yuck! I used to think I was a good public speaker. People ask me to speak — I'm not going to do it *ever again*. I was so nervous my insides were on fire. I got up to give my speech, and I felt like I went "mind blank." I looked out at my audience, and I just knew they could feel my fear as I gripped the lectern and my mouth went dry.

The truth is that Susan experienced her speech in a radically different way than her instructor and classmates did. In fact, here are a few of her peers' comments about her speech:

"Wow! You seemed really relaxed! Your speech was organized, informative, and interesting."
"I really saw no weakness in the speech."
"Definitely the best speech given so far."
"She seemed to know what she was talking about."

When the instructor gave Susan her classmates' written comments, he asked her to write how she felt as she read them. Here is some of what Susan wrote:

> Dr. Grice. Excuse me, Dr. Grice. You've given me the wrong feedback sheets. These just can't be mine. This person, they all say, seemed relaxed, well organized, interesting, and informative. These just can't be mine. . . . If only I could get with this person, maybe she could help me with my upcoming speech. . . . Are you sure, Dr. Grice, that these [critiques] are mine?

Susan concluded her reaction paper, "Wow! What you said is definitely true. It does look worse from the inside."

If Susan had not received feedback from her audience, she would probably have retained her high level of fear of public speaking, perhaps even avoiding future opportunities to share her ideas with others. By offering honest evaluation, her classmates let her see her speech from "the other side," helped her relieve some of her anxieties, and motivated her to continue to improve her public speaking skills.

In addition, remember our earlier statement about the pervasiveness of nervousness. Your audience is composed of individuals who, like you, are apprehensive about speaking to a group of people. Like you, too, they respect the person who makes public speaking look effortless. View your listeners as supportive individuals, because good speaker-listener rapport minimizes any speaker's nervousness.

Teaching Strategy:
To provide students with another example of peer testimony, try this early in the semester. After students' speeches, have both speakers and their listeners evaluate the speeches in writing. Collect these critiques. Before distributing them to the speakers, see if there are examples of speakers evaluating themselves more harshly than their audience did. Use these examples in class to make the point that it often looks worse from the inside.

Confident speakers are physically involved in the delivery of their messages. Like this speaker, their facial expression is animated, their eye contact with the audience is direct, and they gesture naturally as they communicate with their audience.

KNOW YOUR SPEECH

Practice Speaking:
Have students deliver ungraded 3-minute maximum impromptu speeches based on family narratives. Ask them to re-tell a funny story that someone usually repeats at family gatherings. Students' vocal delivery will usually be fluent and their physical delivery animated; they will be physically involved in their speeches. Point out how relaxed they appear because they know the speech content (the story) so well. This exercise also demonstrates the usefulness of narratives as supporting materials (see Chapter 8).

Knowing your strengths and weaknesses, speech principles, and your audience gain you little, however, if you do not know your speech. This textbook will acquaint you with strategies enabling you to remember the ideas and supporting material of your speech. If you don't know what you want to say, you won't say it. If you think you will forget, you probably will. The more confident you are, the less nervous you will be.

Keep in mind that we certainly do not believe you need to memorize the entire speech. Yet, if you are well prepared, you should have memorized the outline of major points for your speech and the order in which they are to be presented. If you forget your notes, or drop them on the way to the lectern and cannot get them back into proper order, you should still be able to deliver the speech. (Take a minute to number your note cards, of course, and you have one less worry.)

VIEW YOUR TOPIC POSITIVELY

If you are giving an informative speech, you must believe that what you say will benefit your listeners—that hearing your speech will improve them in some way. If you are giving a persuasive speech, be committed to the belief you attempt to instill or the action you attempt to initiate in your audience. Convincing your audience that they should listen to your speech is easier if you believe that the topic is important. The more you believe in your topic, the more earnestly you will want to inform or convince your listeners. In short, if you doubt the importance of the topic, you will feel and seem tentative.

VIEW SPEECH MAKING POSITIVELY

Poet Howard Nemerov has said about perception, "What we know is never the object, but only our knowledge."[10] In other words, we do not experience the world directly, but only through the various labels we have attached to things and experiences. More and more we are discovering and investigating the mind's ability to affect behavior. Doctors have discovered, for example, that patients' attitudes about their illnesses significantly affect the speed of their recuperation or their chances for recovery. Athletes have demonstrated improved performance after visualizing themselves competing successfully, and a study of 430 college speech students revealed lowered speech anxiety among those who visualized themselves delivering an effective presentation.[11]

If you view public speaking as a tedious chore, your audience will sense that from your vocal and physical delivery, perhaps even from your choice of speech topic. On the other hand, if you look upon public speaking as an opportunity, your positive attitude will help you control your nervousness. The following examples illustrate how you can replace negative thoughts with positive ones.

Replace the negative thought . . .
"When I get up to speak, my mind will probably go blank and I'll have nothing to say."

. . . with a positive thought
"I've rehearsed my speech and I have a good set of speaking notes. If I momentarily forget a point, I'll just look at my notecards and then continue."

Replace the negative thought . . .
"My audience will probably be bored with my speech."

. . . with a positive thought
"I found the topic of how 3-D films are made interesting, and my audience probably will too."

Thinking positively can help turn anxiety into anticipation. Genuine enthusiasm about the chance to speak in public will guide your choice of topic and will reveal itself to the audience through your lively delivery. Seek out opportunities to test and develop your communication skills. Volunteer for oral reports in classes; speak out at organizational meetings; offer to introduce a guest speaker at your club's banquet. This positive attitude, coupled with practice and experience, will help make you less apprehensive and more confident.

PROJECT CONTROL

Most people would probably agree that our attitudes help determine our behavior. Yet ample evidence suggests that our behavior also helps determine

Related Readings:
Ayers, Joe, and Theodore S. Hopf. "Visualization: A Means of Reducing Speech Anxiety." *Communication Education* 34 (1985): 318–323.
Fanning, Patrick. *Visualization for Change.* Oakland, CA: New Harbinger, 1988.
Shone, Ronald. *Creative Visualization: How to Use Imagery and Imagination for Self-Improvement.* Rochester, VT: Destiny, 1988.

Class Activity:
Ask students to write a few negative self-statements regarding their public speaking on the left side of a sheet of paper. Instruct them to replace each negative statement with a positive one, writing it on the right side of the paper.

Discussion Prompt:
Ask students whether they agree or disagree with this statement, and why: The only people who don't get nervous before speaking in public are those who don't expect much of themselves, or who have decided they don't do anything well.

our attitudes. Daryl Bem's theory of self-perception states that if you perceive yourself acting one way, you will assume you feel that way.[12] Thus, if you want to feel confident, act confidently.

You convey your nervousness in a variety of ways: You shift your body weight from foot to foot, you play with your ring, you tap your fingers on the lectern, or you jingle the change in your pocket. Bem would argue, and we agree, that before you can change your *perception* that you are nervous, you must eliminate your nervous *behaviors*. In other words, project control. Stand erect, gesture emphatically, look directly at your audience, and speak force-fully. These are characteristics of the confident speaker. If you assume these behaviors, you should take on a feeling of confidence.

TEST YOUR MESSAGE

Advertisers know the importance of message testing. Before they print an ad or air a commercial, they test the message to gauge public reaction. As a speaker, you can test your message by practicing your speech in front of friends. Can they restate your main points after listening to you? Do they find the supporting materials believable? Is your vocal delivery lively and varied? Does your physical delivery detract from or reinforce your message? Answers to these questions will guide your subsequent practice sessions. The more confi-dent you are that your message will achieve its desired effect, the less nervous you will be.

PRACTICE

Several of the foregoing suggestions imply the importance of practice. Practicing your speech is so important, however, that it deserves inclusion as a separate category. Jack Valenti, former presidential speechwriter and now president of the Motion Picture Association of America, correctly observes, "The most effective antidote to stage fright and other calamities of speech making is total, slavish, monkish preparation."[13]

Your approach to your practice sessions will vary, depending on how your presentation develops. Sometimes you may practice specific sections of your speech that give you difficulty. But you should also practice your speech several times from start to finish without stopping. Too often when students "mess up" in practice, they stop and begin again. This is not a luxury you have when you address an audience, so as you practice, practice recovering from mistakes. Knowing that you can make it through your speech despite blunders in practice should make you more confident.

We also recommend that you occasionally practice your speech in an envi-ronment laden with distractions. Students who practice only in the silence of an empty classroom may not be prepared for distractions that arise when they actually deliver the speech—for example, a student coming into the classroom during the speech, a lawnmower passing by the window, two students talking in the back of the room, or a classmate inadvertently pushing books off a desk. These distractions, especially those stemming from rudeness, should not occur; in reality, though, they do. Practicing with the television on in the back-ground or in your room with noise in the hallway forces you to concentrate on what you are saying and not on what you are hearing. You develop poise as a speaker only through practice.

LEARN FROM EXPERIENCE

You've heard the expression, "Experience is the best teacher." Well, there's some truth in that folk wisdom. After your speech, assess your performance. What did you try that worked? What didn't work? How did you react when you walked to the front of the room, turned, and looked at the audience looking at you? Did you remember what you planned to say? Did you have trouble finding your place in your notes? How nervous did you feel? Did you get more or less nervous as the speech progressed? Your instructor will give you feedback to help you answer some of those questions; others you will need to answer for yourself, since you alone know the true answers. This is difficult for most of us to do. Especially if you think you made mistakes, your reaction may be to put the whole episode out of your mind. Resist this temptation. You can learn a great deal from reviewing your performance.

On the other hand, don't be too critical as you evaluate your performance. You will do some things well, and this should build your confidence. Other aspects of your speech you can improve, and you should work on these. Suppose, however, that you do encounter a serious problem: You completely lose your place, your mind goes blank, and so you bury your head in your notes and race to the end of your speech. Rather than trying to forget this, use it as a learning experience. Ask yourself why you forgot. Did you try to memorize your speech instead of speaking from a set of notes? Were your notes disorganized, or did they contain too little or too much information? Did you focus too much on your instructor and not enough on the entire audience? Once you face the problem and determine its cause, you will be better able to plan so that it does not occur again.

We have devoted this entire chapter to speaker nervousness because we know that it is a real worry for most people. We have suggested some techniques

Teaching Strategy:
Share with your students your own experience(s) with speaker nervousness.

Teaching Strategy:
We know of some teachers, among them winners of teaching excellence awards, who have gone to the wrong classroom and begun a lecture, who have lectured on material they had already covered, or who have done other embarrassing things. Collect stories of such episodes from other faculty members and share them with your students to illustrate that even experienced public speakers make mistakes and briefly embarrass themselves.

Effective public speakers are not born, but learn from experience and develop their own speaking styles.

to help manage and channel your "platform panic" into a lively, enthusiastic speech. If you stop to think about public speaking for a moment, though, you will realize that the worst thing that could happen to you is that you might embarrass yourself. Stop and ask yourself, "Have I ever embarrassed myself before?" Unless you never leave your house, the answer to that question will be "yes." You may have even embarrassed yourself so badly that you thought, "I'll never be able to face them again" or "I'll never live this down." But you do. The sun rises the next day. None of us is perfect, and it is unreasonable to expect perfection of ourselves or the people around us. So the best advice of all may be, "Keep public speaking in perspective." Your audience is made up of colleagues. They support you and are pulling for you. Use this friendly atmosphere as a training ground to become a more effective speaker.

Summary

The topic of this chapter is the widespread and normal phenomenon of speaker nervousness or stage fright. Caused by the body's preparation to perform to capacity, stage fright is a condition the speaker should try not to eliminate, but rather to control. We offer eleven suggestions for controlling nervousness: (1) Know how you react to stress. (2) Know your strengths and weaknesses. (3) Know basic speech principles. (4) Know your audience, so that you realize they are not expecting you to be perfect. (5) Without memorizing it, know what you plan to say in your speech. (6) Have a positive attitude about your topic. (7) Have a positive attitude about speech making. (8) Project control. (9) Test your message prior to delivering it in class. (10) Practice as much as possible in a variety of situations. (11) Learn from your experience and keep public speaking in its proper perspective. Only by reflecting on your performance and on criticisms others give you can you develop as a speaker and deliver your next speech with less anxiety.

Exercises

1. Divide a sheet of paper into two columns. In Column A, list nervous symptoms you experience when speaking to a group of people. In Column B, list ways you can control each symptom. For example:

   Column A
   Play with ring on my finger, turning it while speaking

   Column B
   Remove ring before speaking
   Keep hands apart by gesturing more often

2. Again, divide a sheet of paper in two columns. In Column A, list ten of your strengths. In Column B, state how those strengths can benefit you in your public speaking. For example:

   Column A
   Like to read a lot

   Column B
   Have lots of ideas for possible speech topics
   Can put this skill to good use when I start researching my speech

3. Interview someone who occasionally gives public speeches asking how he or she handles speaker nervousness. Based on your interview, compile a list of suggestions for controlling nervousness. How does that list compare with the one in this chapter?

Notes ──────────────

1. Carol Burnett, in *Family Weekly* 28 January 1979: 2.

2. Wendy Wasserstein, "Streeping Beauty: A Rare Interview with Cinema's First Lady," *Interview* December 1988: 90.

3. *Houston Chronicle* 19 Sept. 1984, Sec. 5, p. 3.

4. Lee Iacocca with William Novak, *Iacocca: An Autobiography* (New York: Bantam, 1984) 16.

5. David Wallechinsky, Irving Wallace, and Amy Wallace, *The Book of Lists* (New York: Morrow, 1977) 469–470.

6. John H. Greist, M.D., James W. Jefferson, M.D., and Isaac M. Marks, M.D., *Anxiety and its Treatment* (New York: Warner, 1986) 33.

7. Virginia P. Richmond and James C. McCroskey, *Communication: Apprehension, Avoidance, and Effectiveness,* 2nd ed. (Scottsdale, AZ: Gorsuch, 1989) 41–42.

8. Ed McMahon, *The Art of Public Speaking* (New York: Ballantine, 1986) 4.

9. Ralph B. Behnke, Chris R. Sawyer, and Paul E. King, "The Communication of Public Speaking Anxiety," *Communication Education* 36 (1987): 140.

10. Howard Nemerov, *Figures of Thought: Speculations on the Meaning of Poetry and Other Essays* (Boston: Godine, 1978) 19.

11. Joe Ayres and Theodore S. Hopf, "Visualization: A Means of Reducing Speech Anxiety," *Communication Education* 34 (1985): 321.

12. Daryl J. Bem, *Beliefs, Attitudes, and Human Affairs* (Belmont, CA: Brooks/Cole, 1970) 57.

13. Jack Valenti, *Speak Up with Confidence* (New York: Morrow, 1982) 19.

Listening

4

The Importance of Listening

Listening vs. Hearing

The Process of Listening
Receiving
Selecting
Interpreting
Understanding
Evaluating
Resolving

Obstacles to Effective Listening
Physical Distractions
Physiological Distractions

Psychological Distractions
Factual Distractions
Semantic Distractions

Promoting Better Listening
Desire to Listen
Focus on the Message
Listen for Main Ideas
Understand the Speaker's Point of
  View
Withhold Judgment
Reinforce the Message
Provide Feedback
Listen with the Body
Listen Critically

■ The Importance of Listening ─────────

Class Activity:
Ask four students to volunteer to leave the room. Give every student remaining in the room a slip of paper with the following paragraph: "Every year James and Joan take $750 to $1,000 dollars out of their Christmas Club savings account and go to the L-Mart Emporium to buy Christmas gifts for themselves. This year their purchases included clothes, fiction books, an exercise machine, and a stereo radio/cassette recorder. They had $125 left over, which they spent on a lavish meal at Le Petit Cafe." Tell them that this exercise is similar to the "telephone game" they may have played as children. Select one student in the room to read the story aloud to the first student you call into the room. That student will then repeat the story to a second student you bring in, and so on. After the last student has heard the story, have him or her repeat it to the class. Discuss what happened as the three sentences were told and retold: What details were changed? Omitted? Added? Use this discussion to illustrate the difficulties of listening.

No wonder Dagwood is confused! Poor listening is the most common cause of message distortion, and when communication is *serial*, or composed of a chain of transactions between people, the cumulative message distortion can be severe. You probably remember playing the game of "telephone" when you were a child. Someone whispered a phrase or sentence to another person, who whispered it to the next one, and so on. The last person to receive the message then said it aloud. Usually, the final message bore little resemblance to what the first person whispered, and the group laughed at the outcome.

Unfortunately, examples of poor listening exist in areas of life where the results are often far from humorous. In fact, researchers estimate that U.S. businesses lose billions of dollars each year simply because of ineffective listening. The following explains why:

> Because of poor listening, letters have to be retyped; appointments have to be rescheduled; shipments have to be reshipped; individuals and organizations are unable to understand and respond to customers' and clients' real needs; employees feel ignored, disgruntled, and ultimately alienated from management; ideas are distorted by as much as 80 percent as they travel through communication channels; unnecessary conflicts disrupt operations and decrease production; and entire organizations are manipulated by propaganda techniques.[1]

Of course, ineffective listening is not confined just to commercial settings. You can probably think of several examples of problems, or at least embarrassing situations, caused by your own ineffective listening. You went to the wrong building to begin registering for classes, or you went to the right place at the wrong time. You asked a question the teacher had just answered. You didn't realize that the biology exam covered your lab notes as well as the lecture material, or that a complete sentence outline of your informative speech on the Japanese tea ceremony was due a week before you were scheduled to speak. You arrived at a party dressed in jeans and a flannel shirt only to find everyone else dressed in suits and cocktail dresses.

Each day you send and receive both oral and written messages. Of the four roles you perform—speaker, listener, writer, and reader—you spend more time listening than doing all the other actions. In his pioneer study, Paul Rankin showed that people spent almost 70 percent of their waking time communicating with others. Of this, approximately 42 percent was spent listening, 32 percent speaking, 15 percent reading, and 11 percent writing.[2]

Today, listening is still our most common communication activity. In fact, because of the prevalence of television and radio, listening seems to consume even more of our time than it did when Rankin completed his investigation. College students, for example, spend approximately 53 percent of their communication time listening.[3] You listen to your parents, teachers, and friends; to television, radio, and movies; and to many other sounds around you. Yet, despite listening's monopoly on your time, you probably know less about this activity than you do about your other forms of communication. While you have taken several courses teaching you to read and write, you have probably never taken a course in listening. In short, you have received the *least* training in what you do the *most*!

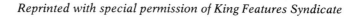

Class Activity:
Recite the following words to your class: *bloom, petal, rose, root, stem, bud, bouquet, pot, seed, blossom, corsage, florist*. After you read the list, have students write the words they remember. Use this exercise to demonstrate principles of listening. How many did they remember? The principle of association (all the words relate to flowers) may have helped them remember. A problem of listening, however, is not just that we fail to remember all that *was* said, but that we may think we heard something that was *not* said. Ask students to raise their hands if they included the word "flower" on their lists. Several, no doubt, will have included this word. Point out that the word "flower" was not on the list.

Reprinted with special permission of King Features Syndicate

It will probably not surprise you, then, to learn that most of us are inefficient listeners. In fact, immediately after listening to your classmates' speeches, chances are high that you will remember, at most, only 50 percent of what you heard, and two days later only 25 percent. This doesn't surprise listening expert Robert Montgomery, who summarizes the sad plight of listening as follows: "Listening is the most neglected and the least understood of the communication arts. It has become the weakest link in today's communications system. Poor listening is a result of bad habits that develop because we haven't been trained to listen." But there is good news, as Montgomery adds: "Fortunately, it is a skill that can be learned."[4] This chapter focuses on the process, problems, and potential of listening in order to give you the tools to improve your listening skills.

■ Listening vs. Hearing

Has the following ever happened to you? You are watching a rerun of *Cheers*, listening to a new Anita Baker tape, or doing accounting homework when one of your parents walks by and tells you to put out the trash. Fifteen minutes later, that person walks back to find you still preoccupied with television, music, or homework, and the trash still setting by the door. Your parent asks, "Didn't you hear me?" Well, of course you did. You heard the direction to put out the trash just as you heard Carla Tortelli insulting Cliff, Anita Baker harmonizing, the dog barking at a passing car, and the air conditioner clicking on in the hall. You *heard* all of these things, but you might not have been *listening* to any of them.

listening: the intermittent, learned, and active attention to aural stimuli.

hearing: the continuous, natural, and passive process of receiving aural stimuli.

What is the difference between **listening** and **hearing?** Listening differs from hearing in at least four important ways.

Listening Is Intermittent. Listening is not a continuous activity, but occurs from time to time when we choose to focus and respond to stimuli around us. Hearing, on the other hand, is a continuous function for a person with normal hearing ability.

Listening Is a Learned Skill. Unless you were born with a hearing loss, hearing is a natural capacity for which you need no training. We hear sounds before we are born; fetuses grow accustomed to certain voices, noises, and music. For this reason, pediatricians advise new parents not to tiptoe or whisper around the infant they have just brought home from the hospital. The child is already used to a lot of noise and must grow accustomed to the rest of it. Throughout our lives, we hear sounds even as we sleep.

Listening Is Active. Hearing means simply receiving an aural stimulus. The act of hearing is passive; it requires no work. Anytime the tiny bones of the inner ear are set in vibration, we are hearing something, and the activity requires no expenditure of energy. The only ways we can limit hearing are by trying to reduce or eliminate the sources of sound stimuli in the environment, or by covering our ears.

Listening, in contrast, is active. It requires you to concentrate, interpret, and respond—in short, to be involved. You can hear the sound of a fire engine as you sit at your desk working on your psychology paper. You *listen* to the sound of the fire engine if you concentrate on its sound, identify it as a fire engine rather than an ambulance, wonder if it is coming in your direction, and then turn back to your work as you hear the sound fade away.

Listening Implies Using the Message Received. Audiences assemble for many reasons. We choose to listen:

1. to gain new information;
2. to learn new uses for existing information;
3. to discover arguments for beliefs or actions;
4. to assess those arguments;
5. to laugh and be entertained;
6. to provide emotional support for a speaker;
7. to celebrate a person, place, object, or idea; and
8. to be inspired.

Suppose a speaker begins a speech this way: "When your ship comes in and you have the time to travel, forget the Bahamas, Hawaii, and the Virgin Islands. Forget Tahiti, because it too is now overrun with tourists. Instead, consider Moorea, a tiny island in French Polynesia, just northwest of Tahiti, with its turquoise bays, undeveloped coastlines, and ivory beaches." Would you listen carefully to what followed? If the subject, Moorea, is unfamiliar to you, your answer is probably yes. We are attracted to novel ideas and information just because we may have some future use for that data.

There are literally thousands of topics you could listen to; for example, converting to electronic currency, using the services of a personal shopper, adapting Japanese management style to American businesses, using ergonomics to enhance worker productivity, preparing lemon grass chicken, ten ways to enliven a party, the history of Arlington National Cemetery, and the life of Rosa Parks. Some of these topics might induce you to listen carefully. Others might not interest you, so you choose not to listen. The perceived usefulness of the topic helps determine how actively you will listen to a speaker. Listening implies a choice; you must choose to participate in the process of listening.

■ The Process of Listening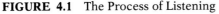

In Chapter 1 we introduced the listener as one component of communication. Indeed, the listener is vital to successful communication; without at least one listener, communication cannot occur beyond the intrapersonal level. Remember that any time two people communicate, two messages are involved:

FIGURE 4.1 The Process of Listening

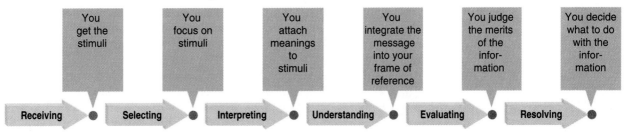

the one the sender intends and the one that the listener actually receives. As we discussed in Chapter 1, these messages will never be identical because people operate from different frames of reference and with different perceptions. You can better understand why the intended and received messages are never identical if you look at the six steps in the process of listening shown in Figure 4.1. We discuss these steps in greater detail here.

RECEIVING

The first step in listening is the act of **receiving** sounds. In face-to-face communication, we receive sound waves set in motion through the air by the speaker; on the telephone, those same sound waves are transmitted electronically. In either case, the first step in listening to the speaker is receiving the sounds, the auditory stimuli. In other words, hearing is the first step in effective listening.

You may have heard people say, "I can't hear without my glasses." What they usually mean is that they can't hear as well if they cannot clearly see the person speaking. Normally, we validate one sense by checking it against others. Thus, even if you recognize the voice of a classmate behind you asking a question, you are likely to turn around and look to make sure. At other times, we may use our senses of taste, smell, or touch to confirm or contradict the auditory message we have received.

Some people unintentionally filter or leave out part of the stimulus. People with a hearing loss, for example, unintentionally filter parts of the messages around them. Whenever we filter, parts of the messages available to us are going to be lost.

SELECTING

"Millions of items of the outward order are present to my senses which never properly enter into my experience. Why? Because they have no interest for me. My experience is what I agree to attend to."[5]

WILLIAM JAMES, PSYCHOLOGIST

Individuals choose differently among stimuli competing for their attention, a phenomenon sometimes called **selective perception.** Think, for example, of the different reports the police gather from witnesses to a traffic accident. Each bystander's report will be shaped by where the person was standing or sitting, what the person was focusing on at the moment of impact, how the person was feeling, and a host of other factors. All these witnesses had selective perceptions of what they saw and heard.

In public speaking situations, the same thing can happen. One person in the audience may focus primarily on what speakers are saying, another on their tones of voice or their gestures, still another on what they are wearing, or even the distracting hum of the heating system. If you are intrigued by the speaker's accent, you have selected to focus on that element of speech delivery, and you will probably hear a slightly different speech than the person sitting next to you. You may even be distracted by internal noise, such as worrying about an upcoming chemistry exam or trying to resolve a conflict with your roommate. As

Teaching Strategy:
Arrange outside of class to have a typically quiet student get into an argument with you at the beginning of the next class meeting. The student might try, for example, to hand in an assignment that was due much earlier. The argument could be over whether you will accept it, or over how many points you will deduct. At the loudest point of the argument, interrupt the student, thank him or her, and ask each class member to write three sentences describing what they just saw and heard. Have students share their versions of the episode with the class. Use this exercise to demonstrate how our preoccupations at any given moment shape our perceptions of events.

William James said over 100 years ago, our view of the world is truly shaped by what we decide to heed.

INTERPRETING

Not only do individuals choose differently among stimuli competing for their attention, they also interpret those stimuli differently. **Interpreting** is the process of decoding the message. When you interpret you attach meanings to the cluster of verbal and nonverbal symbols the speaker provides — words, tone of voice, and facial expression, for example. At this stage the listener is paying careful attention to those verbal and nonverbal symbols and their meanings. When a speaker introduced her speech on "euthanasia," one listener heard "youth in Asia." Only after correcting this misinterpretation was the listener prepared to understand the speaker's message. As we noted in our discussion of the triangle of meaning in Chapter 1, the speaker's frame of reference must be similar to the listener's if communication is to be clear and effective.

UNDERSTANDING

Once you have decoded, or attached meanings to, a speaker's symbols, you begin fitting the message into your framework of existing knowledge and beliefs. **Understanding** a speaker requires you to move beyond message *content* to message *context*. Is the speaker attempting to inform or persuade you? Is the speaker serious or joking? In short, what is the speaker trying to do?

It is easier to judge the context of communication when you listen to friends rather than strangers. You probably know when your friends and acquaintances are joking, upset, or teasing by a particular facial expression or tone of voice, but you do not necessarily know those idiosyncrasies about strangers. Communication from friends provides you more familiar cues to understand context than does communication coming from strangers. As you learn more about speakers, then, you enable yourself to understand their messages more accurately.

EVALUATING

Before acting upon the message you have decoded and understood, you evaluate it. **Evaluating** is the process of judging both the reliability of the speaker and the quality and consistency of the speaker's information. If the speaker is someone you know, you reflect on the history of that person's interactions with you. Has the person ever tried to deceive you? Or does the speaker have a track record of honest, open communication with you? If the speaker is a stranger, you often gauge the person's credibility based on the nonverbal cues of communication. Is the speaker making eye contact with you? Does he or she speak fluently, without unnecessary pauses or filler words? Do the speaker's gestures and other body language seem relaxed and spontaneous? In short, does the person seem well prepared, confident, and sincere? If your answer to any of these questions is no, you may wonder whether the speaker has ulterior motives for speaking to you. As you evaluate the speaker's message, you decide

Practice Speaking: Bring two neckties to class. Ask for two volunteers — one who knows how to tie a tie and one who does not. Have them stand back to back at the front of the room, their profiles to the class. The individual who knows how to tie a tie should begin to do so, giving instructions to the person who does not know how. The latter person should follow the first person's directions exactly. View the finished product. If the second person's tie looks strange (it usually does!), discuss the breakdown in communication. If the tie looks great, discuss how the instruction-giver was able to minimize message distortion.

Practice Speaking: Divide the class into groups of three. Two individuals should sit back-to-back; the third person is the observer. The instructor should give one of the seated individuals a drawing of a geometric design (for example, two triangles, a rectangle, and a circle that overlap). That student should describe it to the second seated person, who will draw it on a sheet of paper. After the exercise is concluded, the observer should comment on when and how directions were misinterpreted, if they were, to produce a design different than the original one. All three persons should discuss how directions might have been changed to minimize message distortion.

whether you believe the data presented, and whether you agree or disagree with the position the speaker advocates.

RESOLVING

The final step in listening, **resolving,** involves deciding what to do with the information we have received. As listeners, we can accept the information we have received, reject it, take action on it, decide to investigate further, or just try to remember the information so that we can resolve it later.

Obviously, we do not consciously go through and dwell upon each of these six steps each time we listen to someone. As the significance of the message increases for us, however, we become more involved in the process of listening —a point each speaker should remember.

■ Obstacles to Effective Listening

physical distractions: listening disturbances that originate in the physical environment and are perceived by the listener's senses.

Speakers and audience members should recognize some of the reasons why effective listening is so difficult. Learning to listen better is easier if you know what you're up against. For this reason, you need to identify the major obstacles to effective listening. We list and discuss five barriers to listening in this section.

PHYSICAL DISTRACTIONS

Have you ever told someone that he or she was being so loud that you couldn't hear yourself think? If so, you were commenting on one obstacle to effective listening: **physical distraction.** Physical distractions are interferences coming to you through any of your senses, and they may take many forms: glare from a sunny window, chill from an air conditioner vent, or the smell of formaldehyde in your anatomy and physiology lab. We've even heard that to reduce physical distractions to its patrons, one New York restaurant has this sign at its entrance: "No cigars or Giorgio perfume in the main dining room." Like a diner whose enjoyment of a meal is spoiled by cigar smoke, you may have trouble focusing on the message of a speech on toxic waste if you concentrate on the speaker's outlandish clothing, on a P.E. class playing a vigorous game of touch football outside, on classmates chatting behind you about a new movie, or on the overpowering smell of Aqua Velva on the person near you.

physiological distractions: listening disturbances that originate in a listener's illness or unusual bodily stress.

PHYSIOLOGICAL DISTRACTIONS

Physiological distractions have to do with the body. Any illness or unusual physiological condition is a potential distraction to effective listening. A bout of flu, a painful earache, or a sleepless night all place obvious and familiar limitations on our willingness and ability to listen.

psychological distractions: listening disturbances that originate in the listener's attitudes, preoccupations, or worries.

PSYCHOLOGICAL DISTRACTIONS

Your attitudes also affect your listening behavior. **Psychological distractions,** such as a negative attitude toward the speaker, the topic, or your reason for attending a speech, can all affect how you listen. If you are antagonistic toward the speaker or the point of view the speaker is advocating, you may resist or debate in your mind the statements you hear. If you are coerced to be in the audience, you may also be more critical and less open-minded about what is being said. In short, if you are concentrating on thoughts other than what the speaker is saying, you will receive less of the intended message.

FACTUAL DISTRACTIONS

College students, who should be among the most adept listeners in our society, find that they are often hampered by **factual distractions,** such as the flood of facts presented to them in lectures. You may be tempted to treat each fact as a potential test question. But this way of listening can pose problems for you. For example, have you ever taken copious notes in your Western civilization class only to find when you re-read them that, although you have lots of facts, you missed the key ideas? Students and other victims of factual distractions sometimes listen for details while missing the general point that the speaker is making.

factual distractions: listening disturbances caused by attempts to re-call minute details while missing the main idea being communicated.

SEMANTIC DISTRACTIONS

Semantic distractions are those caused by confusion over the meanings of words. Listeners may be confused by a word they have never before seen or heard, one they have seen in print but have never heard spoken, or a word the speaker is mispronouncing. If a student gave a speech about her native country, Eritrea, without showing that word on a visual aid, the typical listener would probably begin wondering, "How do I spell that?" "Have I ever seen that word on a map before?" "Is this a new name for an established country?" "Is the speaker pronouncing correctly a word I've always heard mispronounced?" These thoughts divert you from the serious business of listening to a speech filled with new and interesting information. In Chapter 11, Wording Your Speech, we will discuss some ways speakers can minimize misunderstandings about the meanings of words.

semantic distractions: listening disturbances caused by confusion over the meanings of words.

Discussion Prompt:
You are asked to speak to a group of students at a local high school on the topic "What College Offers You." Half the audience plans to attend college; the rest does not. All the students have been required to stay after school on the first sunny day this spring to attend the assembly. What are your listeners' likely psychological distractions with which you must contend? What strategies might you use to minimize them in your speech?

■ Promoting Better Listening ——————————————

Once you understand the obstacles to effective listening, you can develop a plan of action to improve your listening behavior and that of your audience. A major theme of this book, as you no doubt are now aware, is that each party in the communication process has a responsibility to promote effective communication. Promoting better listening should be a goal of both the sender and the receiver of the message. How can you encourage better listening?

As a speaker, you can use many of the suggestions in the chapters that follow to increase the chances that your audience will hear and retain your message. You enhance the audience's retention, for example, when you select your ideas carefully, organize your ideas clearly, support your ideas convincingly, word your ideas vividly, and deliver your ideas forcefully.

Related Reading:
Golen, Steven. "A Factor Analysis of Barriers to Effective Listening." *The Journal of Business Communication.* 27.1 (1990): 25–35. Golen compiled a list of common barriers to effective listening mentioned in research literature on listening. He then asked college students to rate the frequency of these barriers based on their own listening experiences. Golen's resulting list is available in the transparency set.

As a listener, you must also work hard to understand and remember the speaker's message. So far in this chapter we have examined the process of listening and have discussed the obstacles to effective listening. The following nine suggestions will help you become a more effective listener. As you master these suggestions, you will find yourself understanding and remembering more of what you hear.

DESIRE TO LISTEN

Teaching Strategy:
If you are requested to read announcements to your class from various campus departments, clubs, committees, and administrators, alter one of them to include a mention of money. Read the announcement in a matter-of-fact way, not calling special attention to it. If students show unusual interest in it, use the experience to illustrate the phenomenon of selective interest. Be sure to correct the announcement.

Your attitude will determine, in part, your listening effectiveness. In this class you have the opportunity to learn a great deal of information from your classmates' speeches. Some topics will interest you; others, no doubt, will not. Good listeners, however, begin with the assumption that each speech can potentially benefit them. You may not find a speech on how financial institutions determine a person's credit rating of great interest right now. Nevertheless, the first time you apply for a loan you may be happy that you paid attention and prepared for your visit to the bank.

Some speeches you hear in this class will be excellently prepared and delivered; others will not. Again, good listeners can learn something from *any* speech, even if it is poorly prepared and awkwardly delivered. For example, you can determine what the speaker could have done to improve the poorly developed speech. This experience enables you to apply speech principles you have learned and improve your own speaking.

In your class you may also have the opportunity to offer helpful suggestions to your colleagues who present speeches. You will want to listen carefully so that you can help them improve. If you have a genuine desire to listen to a speaker, you will understand and remember more.

Speakers can promote better listening by demonstrating early in their speeches how the information will benefit the audience. Let your audience know quickly just why it is in their interest to listen carefully to your speech. We believe this step is so important that we discuss it in Chapter 9, Organizing Your Speech, as one of the four steps of an effective speech introduction.

FOCUS ON THE MESSAGE

Teaching Strategy:
To simplify listening to speeches early in the semester, you might assign certain groups of students (certain rows, for example) to pay particular attention to one aspect of each speech, such as content, organization, source citations, vocal delivery, or physical delivery.

Your first responsibility as a listener is to listen attentively to the speaker's message. Yet, a speaker's message competes with other stimuli for your attention. These distractions can often be quite powerful. One of your authors once conducted a seminar entitled "First Impressions—Lasting Impressions" in a large room adjacent to a hallway that was being painted. The smell of the paint became a powerful distraction for both speaker and audience. During the presentation one of the audience members opened a door allowing outside air to freshen the room. In addition, the speaker moved from behind the lectern and enlivened his delivery by changing his speaking tone and using more varied gestures. In this situation both the speaker and the audience worked to focus more on the message and less on the distracting smell.

Often speakers themselves create distractions. They may play with change in their pockets, be dressed inappropriately, sway nervously from side to side, use language their listeners find offensive, or say "um" throughout the speech. These quirks can be very distracting. We have had students, for example, who actually counted the number of "ums" in a speech. After a classmate's speech, they would write in their critiques, "You said 'um' thirty-one times in your speech." While this may have provided the speaker with some valuable feedback, we suspect these listeners learned little else from the speaker's message.

Another of our students gave a persuasive speech opposing censorship of song lyrics. She began her speech quoting from a song some in her audience believed to be obscene. While this strategy certainly got the attention of the entire audience, several listeners were offended by the language. Some tuned out the speaker after her introduction rather than listen to the rest of her speech. You may not be able to ignore distractions completely as you listen, but you can try to minimize them.

As we discussed earlier, messages may be both verbal and nonverbal. For this reason, listeners should listen with their eyes as well as their ears. We have all heard someone begin a statement, "I'm not saying this to be critical, but. . . ." That preface often reveals more about the speaker's intent than the words that follow; usually, the person *is* being critical. When we perceive a discrepancy between a person's verbal and nonverbal messages, we tend to believe the nonverbal message, and this response may be justified. People are better at disguising their emotions with their words than with their bodies. You can often read body and voice cues to see what speakers think is important and their degree of commitment to what they are saying.

Speakers, of course, can help listeners focus on the message by eliminating distracting mannerisms and incorporating nonverbal behaviors that reinforce rather than contradict their ideas. For example, appropriate gestures can make a speech easier to remember by describing objects, providing directions, and illustrating dimensions.

LISTEN FOR MAIN IDEAS

You are familiar with the cliché that you can't see the forest for the trees; well, that saying applies to listening. A person who listens for facts often misses the main point of the message. While it is important to attend to the supporting material of a speech, you should be able to relate it to the major point being developed. When listening to a speech, pay close attention to the speaker's use of the organizational techniques we will discuss in Chapter 9. The structure of a speech provides a framework for both speaker and listeners to organize the supporting points and materials of the speech. Speakers who clearly enumerate their key ideas and repeat them at several points in their speeches give their audience a better opportunity to be attentive listeners than do disorganized speakers.

UNDERSTAND THE SPEAKER'S POINT OF VIEW

As we discussed in Chapter 1, each of us has different referents for the words we hear or speak because we have different life experiences. These life experiences affect how we view our world.

Speaking in favor of agricultural programs that would preserve the family farm, our student Cathy tried to involve her audience in her speech by tapping their memories. She asked her classmates to think of the houses they grew up in and the memories created there.

> Think of Thanksgiving and Christmas gatherings. Think of slumber parties and birthday celebrations. Of how you changed your room as you moved from child to teenager to young adult. Think of your feelings as you left home to come to college, and of your feelings when you return to those comfortable confines.

After the speech several students said they were moved by Cathy's eloquence and passion. She had tapped memories important to them. Others in the audience, however, said there were unable to relate to the topic in the way the speaker intended. Several had grown up in more than one house. Some were in military families and had moved often. Still others said they lived in rented townhomes or apartments. And a few commented that their childhood memories were not fond ones. Both speakers and listeners need to remember that different experiences shape and limit our understanding of another's message.

When speakers and listeners come from different cultures, the chances for misunderstanding increase. Differences in language, education, and customs challenge listeners to work especially hard at understanding the speaker's message and intent. These differences are often evident in classes which include both native and non-native students. Some foreign students, for example, come from educational environments that are more structured and formal than the typical American college classroom. They may interpret a speaker's casual dress and use of humor as an indication that the speaker is not serious about the speech. On the other hand, American students may perceive the more formal presentations of some of their foreign counterparts as stiff, indicating a lack of interest in the topic. Understanding each other's frame of reference minimizes this distortion.

Speakers should do two things to clarify the point of view of their speech. First, explain early in the speech if you have some particular reason for selecting your topic, or some special qualifications to speak on the subject. If you speak on radio formats because you work at your campus radio station or because you are a radio-television-film major, tell the audience a little about your background. If you are a registered gemologist and decide to speak on the subject of emeralds, be sure to tell the audience about your qualifications. Second, try to relate your subject to your listeners' frames of reference. Technical jargon and complex explanations impede effective listening. Use examples and language your audience will understand.

WITHHOLD JUDGMENT

You have probably listened to some political debates and heard discussions of them afterwards. You and a friend may even have argued about which candidate presented himself or herself better and who "won." What you thought was important and remembered may have been so different from your friend's perspective that you wondered if you had been watching the same debate.

In a sense, you and your friend *did* watch two different debates. Two people with contrasting perspectives receive two different messages while watching one communication event. You filtered what you heard through your set of beliefs and values. You began judging the candidates and the debate before it ever took place. Many of us have a problem withholding judgment. We hear something and immediately label it as right or wrong, good or bad. The problem is that once we do that, we cease to listen objectively to the rest of the message.

Withholding judgment, of course, is most difficult when you are listening to a speech advocating a position you strongly oppose. The following list includes topics student speakers sometimes discuss: legalization of drugs, capital punishment, mandatory drug testing, abortion, flag burning, euthanasia, gun control, and hiring quotas. We suspect you have some fairly strong opinions on most of those issues. You might even find it difficult to listen to a speech opposing your view without silently debating the speaker. Yet, as you mentally challenge those arguments, you miss much of what the speaker is saying. If you can suspend evaluation until after speakers have presented and supported their arguments, you will be a better listener.

REINFORCE THE MESSAGE

Most Americans speak at rates between 125 and 190 words per minute. Those numbers may seem high to you, but consider the average speaking rates of the following people. Gene Shalit, the *Today* show's cantankerous movie critic, rarely strays from an average rate of 190 words per minute. Former president Jimmy Carter, a Southerner often described as a plodding speaker, averages 160 words per minute. Ronald Reagan, our oldest president when he began his first term, speaks an average of 170 words per minute. If you speak at a rate between 120 and 140 words per minute, your listeners may think you ill or just plain dull.[6] Why? As listeners, we can process 400 to 500 words per minute. This means that, depending on the situation, we may be able to listen at a rate four times faster than a particular person speaks! As a result, we can get bored and move our attention back and forth between what the speaker is saying and some extraneous message, perhaps a personal problem that concerns us. Sometimes, the unrelated thought takes over and psychological noise, which we discussed earlier, drowns out the speaker's message. To be a better listener, you must make better use of this extra time.

You can fill some of this time and better focus on the message by repeating, paraphrasing, and summarizing what the speaker is saying. You use **repetition** when you state exactly what the speaker has said. Consider, for example, a speaker who argues that a tuition increase is necessary to preserve educational excellence at your college or university. The first reason she offers is this: "A tuition increase will enable us to expand our library." If after the speaker makes this claim you repeat her argument in your mind, you are using repetition to help you remember the speaker's message.

Using **paraphrase** is a second way of helping yourself remember the message. By putting the speaker's ideas into your own words, you become actively involved in message transmission. Suppose the same speaker offers this statement to justify one benefit of a tuition increase:

Teaching Strategy: You may be familiar with this exercise to illustrate to your students that they process information much faster than they speak. Write the words that are in parentheses on the board while saying the following: "If I tell you that this word (polk) is pronounced 'poke' and that this word (folk) is pronounced 'foke,' and I then ask you what the white part of an egg is, your answer would be _____." Often the entire class will respond "yolk" immediately. Point out that you asked about the white part of an egg, the albumen. Students answer incorrectly because they are busy thinking of other words with similar spellings and pronunciations, rather than listening to the question.

A tuition increase would generate funds that could be used to enhance our library facilities and resources. In the Chancellor's budget proposal one-third of the tuition increase would go directly to the library. The Chancellor estimates that this would enable us to increase our library holdings of books, periodicals, and audiovisual resources by 10 percent. Also, projected construction would create at least twelve new study rooms.

Obviously, it would be difficult to restate the speaker's explanation word for word. Yet you could paraphrase and summarize her message this way:

A tuition hike would increase our library holdings by 10 percent and increase the number of study rooms by twelve.

Practice Speaking:
Announce to your class that after each student speech you will call on an audience member to summarize the key ideas discussed. This exercise not only encourages students to listen closely to each speech, it also provides the basis for class discussion of the speech's effectiveness.

You use **summary** when you condense what a speaker says. The above paraphrase includes summary as it leaves out some of the specific information the speaker presented. As a speaker concludes his or her message, you should recollect the key points of the speech. Your summary might be, for example, "A tuition increase will help us expand the library, increase the number of faculty, and renovate some of the older dormitories." By getting you actively involved in the communication process, repetition, paraphrase, and summary increase your chances of understanding and remembering the message.

PROVIDE FEEDBACK

A listener can enhance the communication process by providing feedback to the speaker. Although there is greater opportunity for verbal feedback in interpersonal and group environments, it is nevertheless possible in public speaking contexts. The effective speaker will read the nonverbal cues of the audience to assist in the presentation of the speech. If you understand and accept the point of the speaker and nod in agreement, the speaker can move to the next idea. If you appear perplexed, that signal should prompt the speaker to explain the idea more fully before moving to the next point.

Teaching Strategy:
Require students to sit in a different seat and next to a different classmate each class period for the first few weeks. After this time period, ask students if their location in the classroom affected their listening attentiveness. If so, how?

Teaching Strategy:
Get students into the habit of listening critically. Announce that you have included an error in your lecture or discussion material. Tell them to write it down on a sheet of paper when they hear it. After your lecture, ask them to identify the mistake. Be sure to clarify and correct the mistake before the class is over.

LISTEN WITH THE BODY

We listen with more than our ears. In a sense, we listen with our entire bodies. If, as your instructor lectures, you lean back, stretch your legs, cross your arms, and glance at a fellow classmate, you detract from your listening effectiveness. Part of listening is simply being physically ready to listen.

You can ready yourself for listening if you sit erect, lean slightly forward, and place both feet flat on the floor. As you listen, look at the speaker. As important as the message you *hear* is the message you *see*. Remember, you want to detect any nonverbal messages that intensify or contradict the speaker's verbal message.

LISTEN CRITICALLY

Even though listeners should understand a speaker's point of view and withhold judgment, they should nevertheless test the merits of what they hear.

Listeners' nonverbal feedback helps speakers adapt their messages and delivery to specific audiences.

If you accept ideas and information without questioning them, you are in part responsible for the consequences. If the speaker advocating a tuition increase quotes from the Chancellor's budget proposal before it has even been submitted, you have every right to be skeptical. "Will the final budget actually earmark one-third of the tuition increase for library use? Will the Board of Regents accept the Chancellor's proposal? Or is this all speculation?" Decisions based on incorrect or incomplete data are seldom prudent and often disastrous.

Critical listeners examine what they hear by asking several questions: Is the speech factually correct? Are sources clearly identified, and are they unbiased and credible? Does the speaker draw logical conclusions from the data presented? Has the speaker overlooked or omitted important information? Speakers help listeners answer those questions by presenting credible information, identifying their sources, and using valid reasoning.

John Marshall, Chief Justice of the United States from 1801 to 1835, once stated, "To listen well is as powerful a means of communication and influence as to talk well." If you follow these nine suggestions, you will become a better listener.

Cross-Reference:
If your students are about to give a first speech, either graded or for practice, you may want to have them read Appendix A, Critiquing Speeches, in conjunction with this chapter on listening.

Summary

Poor listening costs American businesses billions of dollars yearly. The personal costs of poor listening include lost opportunities, embarrass- ment, financial losses, and, probably most important, lost time. We spend more time listening than we do involved in any other communication activity. Yet, ironically, we receive less instruction in listening than we do in reading, writing, or speaking. Luckily, we *can* teach and learn effective listening.

Listening differs from hearing in four ways. First, we listen only from time to time throughout the day, while hearing is continuous. Second, listening is a learned behavior, while hearing is a natural capacity for most people. Third, listening is active, hearing passive. Finally, listening implies doing something with the message received.

The complex act of listening contains six steps or phases. First, the listener *receives* sound stimuli from various senders or sources. Second, the listener *selects* particular parts of the total stimulus field for attention. Third, the listener *interprets* or decodes the message, attaching meanings to the various symbols received. The fourth step, *understanding*, involves matching the speaker's message with the listener's frame of reference. In the fifth step, the listener *evaluates* the reliability of the speaker and the speaker's message. Finally, after the reflection involved in the previous steps, the listener *resolves*, or decides what to do with, the information received.

One of five obstacles to effective listening is *physical distractions* from any part of the environment. *Physiological distractions*, a second category, arise from conditions in the listener's body. A third obstacle is *psychological distractions*, such as worry or preconceived attitudes toward the speaker or the message. *Factual distractions* are caused by our tendency to listen for small supporting details, even when we miss the main point the speaker is trying to make. Fifth and finally, listeners may be victims of *semantic distractions*, or confusion over the meanings of words.

Both speakers and listeners can contribute to effective listening in nine ways. First, listeners should *develop a genuine desire to listen.* Speakers promote this openness to listening by expressing a sincere desire to communicate. Second, listeners should *focus on the speaker's message* rather than distracting elements of delivery. Speakers assist listening when they minimize or eliminate distracting behaviors and employ forceful delivery to underscore their messages. Third, listeners should *listen for the speaker's main ideas,* and speakers make this task much easier by careful speech organization. Fourth, listeners should try to *understand the speaker's point of view,* and speakers ought to reveal their credentials and explain their reasons for speaking on a particular topic. Fifth, listeners should *withhold judgment about the speaker and the message* until after hearing and considering both. Sixth, listeners should *reinforce the speaker's message* by using repetition, paraphrase, and summary. Seventh, effective listeners should *provide the speaker with feedback,* and speakers should adapt to those responses. Eighth, listeners should be ready to *listen with the whole body.* Finally, though we have urged you to listen objectively to avoid prejudging speakers and their ideas, *effective listening is ultimately critical listening.* Gauging the credibility of the speaker's information is easier if the speaker has presented logically supported ideas and has cited credible sources.

Exercises ──────────────────────────────

1. On a sheet of paper, list your listening strengths and weaknesses. Beside each weakness, indicate specific strategies that could minimize or eliminate the problem.
2. Listen to a speech or lecture, paying particular attention to the five types of distractions discussed in this chapter. Give examples of distractions you encountered. What could you or the speaker have done to minimize these interferences? Discuss these options.

Notes ──────────────────────────────

1. Meada Gibbs, Pernell Hewing, Jack E. Hulbert, David Ramsey, and Arthur Smith, "How to Teach Effective Listening Skills in a Basic Business Communication Class," *The Bulletin of the Association for Business Communication* 47.2 (1985): 30.

2. Paul T. Rankin, "The Importance of Listening Ability," *The English Journal* 17 (1928): 623–30.

3. Larry Barker, Renee Edwards, Connie Gaines, Karen Gladney, and Frances Holley, "An Investigation of Proportional Time Spent in Various Communication Activities by College Students," *Journal of Applied Communications Research* 8 (1980): 101–9.

4. Robert L. Montgomery, *Listening Made Easy* (New York: AMACOM, 1981) n.p.

5. William James, *The Principles of Psychology*, vol. 2 (Cambridge: Harvard University Press, 1981), 380. (This is a reprint of the original 1890 Henry Holt edition.)

6. Lyle V. Mayer, *Fundamentals of Voice and Diction*, 8th ed. (Dubuque, IA: Brown, 1988), 178.

Analyzing Your Audience 5

The Importance of Audience Analysis

Audience Analysis *Before* the Speech
Analyze Audience Demographics
  Age
  Gender
  Ethnicity
  Education
  Religion
  Economic Status
  Group Membership
Analyze Audience Needs
  Maslow's Hierarchy
  The Importance of the Hierarchy
Analyze Audience Psychology
  Values
  Beliefs
  Attitudes
  Behaviors

Gather Information About Your Audience
Analyze Specific Speaking Situations
  Types of Audiences
  Audience Disposition
  Size of the Audience
  Occasion
  Physical Environment
  Time

Audience Analysis *During* the Speech
Analyze Audience Interest
Analyze Audience Understanding
Analyze Audience Evaluation of Your Message

Audience Analysis *After* the Speech

WE have all heard stories so amazing that they seem to take on the qualities of legends. One well-known example is that of Abraham Lincoln and the "Gettysburg Address." As the story goes, Lincoln was such a fine man and such a great thinker that he wrote his now-famous speech on some scraps of paper while on the train to Gettysburg, Pennsylvania.[1] Repeated for many, many years, the story has been made more plausible by the fact that the speech is only 272 words long. Like many other stories that seem too good to be true, however, this one is false. Today, we have a better picture of how Lincoln composed the "Gettysburg Address" and why it is as brief as it is. A more accurate account follows.

President Lincoln was asked to speak at a ceremony dedicating a memorial cemetery for soldiers who had died in the Civil War battle at Gettysburg. He was not to be the main speaker on this occasion, however. Edward Everett, the most famous orator of his day, was the featured speaker at Gettysburg. Everett spoke for an hour and fifty-seven minutes to an audience estimated at between 15,000 and 50,000 people seated and standing outdoors.[2] Afterward, Lincoln rose and, holding two pieces of paper, spoke ten sentences in less than three minutes.[3] Why were Lincoln's remarks so brief?

The answer is that Lincoln had done some excellent analysis of the audience and the speaking occasion. He knew, first, that Everett's speech would be lengthy because of the orator's reputation for making long speeches. Lincoln undoubtedly knew that if he also spoke for two hours, he would lose part of his audience: either their attention or their presence. Remember, the speech was to be given outdoors, with the audience relatively free to leave whenever they chose!

Second, Lincoln knew, as did his audience, that he was not the featured speaker on this occasion and was, therefore, not expected to make a major address. He had been asked only two weeks ahead of time to make "a few appropriate remarks." Everett, on the other hand, was invited six weeks earlier, and the date for the dedication had actually been changed to fit his schedule. Even though he was president, Lincoln was losing popular support by 1863 and knew that a long speech would seem an inappropriate challenge to the importance of Everett's.

The third and final reason for the length of Lincoln's "Gettysburg Address" was that he had been anticipating for some time an occasion for an important speech on the same theme. The words of the speech began to take shape in his mind long before he wrote them on paper. For example, Lincoln began his speech at Gettysburg by saying, "Four score and seven years ago our fathers brought forth on this continent a new nation, conceived in liberty and dedicated to the proposition that all men are created equal." Yet Thomas Scheidel points out that, in informal remarks four months before delivering the "Gettysburg Address," Lincoln had said:

> How long ago is it? — eighty-odd years since, on the Fourth of July, for the first time in the history of the world a nation by its representatives, assembled and declared as a self-evident truth, that "all men are created equal." . . . Gentlemen, this is a

Cross-Reference:
Use speeches in Appendix C to illustrate how speakers adapt their messages to specific audiences. Excellent examples are Susanne Landowksi's speech, "Academic Laboratories: Risking Life and Limb for Credit," Martin Luther King, Jr.'s "I Have A Dream" speech, Ronald Reagan's eulogy for the *Challenger* crew, and Mario Cuomo's address to the 1984 Democratic National Convention. As your students read or listen to these speeches, remind them to identify the audiences each speaker tried to reach.

glorious theme, and the occasion for a speech; but I am not prepared to make one worthy of the occasion.[4]

Making speeches "worthy of the occasion" requires meticulous audience analysis today, just as it did in Lincoln's time. Just as Lincoln's audience analysis caused him to reflect on the circumstances around his remarks at Gettysburg, smart speakers today conduct careful listener analysis. Consider the following situation:

> A hydrologist from an area water district is asked to address a monthly neighborhood association meeting. Instead of speaking the jargon of his field and confusing his audience with a technical discussion of "recharge zones," "reverse osmosis," and "desalination," he explains "xeriscaping," a method of landscaping using native plants with low water requirements. As a result of his speech, every homeowner and renter listening to him gains valuable information about lowering water bills and conserving water while maintaining an attractive lawn during the area's frequent droughts.

What happens when a speaker fails to analyze listeners' needs? Look at the following example:

> A professor of child development who specializes in the design of playgrounds and parks is invited to speak to an elementary school PTA. The parents and teachers attending want to know how they can update their school playground by replacing dangerous, old equipment and also meet the recreational needs of the school's new, booming pre-kindergarten population. The PTA president has explained these concerns to the speaker by phone when she asked the professor to speak. Yet instead of addressing those interests, the speaker narrates a lengthy slide show on the history of playgrounds in the country.

You can imagine how the audience reacts.

Teaching Strategy:
Ask students for the following information on notecards at the beginning of the semester: name, major, academic classification, type of work (if currently employed), previous public speaking experience (if any), and type of work they hope to do after graduation. You may want to provide a profile of the class to all class members, or use this information later as students begin to consider speech topics, organization, motivational appeals, and language.

■ The Importance of Audience Analysis ——————

Every speech in a college public speaking class such as this might be considered a speech of introduction. That is, each speech introduces new facets of your personality and builds on your relationship with the audience. As you and your

Reprinted by permission of UFS, Inc.

classmates select the topics for your speeches, keep in mind that the most effective speeches will be those on subjects in which you are genuinely interested. Each topic that you consider interesting or valuable enough to speak on says something about you as a person. Even if your instructor assigns the topics, your approach to the subject will be unique and will reveal aspects of your personal values and your personality. Yet the phrase "public speaking" always implies the presence of an audience. Public speaking is an **audience-centered**, not speaker-centered, activity. To be a successful speaker you must learn to be an audience-centered speaker. How can you accomplish this?

To be an audience-centered speaker you must develop three important characteristics:

1. You must recognize your place as part of the audience.
2. You must respect your listeners.
3. You must recognize and act on audience feedback.

First, you must recognize your own place as part of the speech audience. This means that the topics you are genuinely interested in hearing about probably reflect the interests of some other people in the classroom. Being aware of your place in the audience also requires you to admit that you are only one part of the total audience, a fact that should make you want to learn as much as possible about those other "parts."

Second, as an audience-centered speaker, you will respect your listeners, as we mentioned in discussing ethics in Chapter 2. Respect and care for the audience means wanting to improve them by providing interesting or useful information. Respect also means recognizing and appreciating their values. In addition, consideration for the audience means trusting the opinions and advice of individual audience members. If you honor the worth of your listeners, you will value their questions and suggestions about your speech. This, in turn, leads to a third and final characteristic of audience-centeredness: recognizing and acting on the feedback from your audience, whether that feedback is verbal or nonverbal.

How can you as a speaker better relate to your audience? You might consider the ways in which you as an individual are part of various audiences. To what magazines do you subscribe, for example? What newspaper do you read? What television shows do you make it a point to watch? What are your favorite clubs and restaurants? What station is your car radio tuned to right now? Your answers to those questions place you in several different audiences.

Television is another interesting place to study various audiences. Notice some time, for example, what your public broadcasting station programs the next time it holds pledge week. Linda Ronstadt's *Canciones de mi Padre?* A superb production of African-American playwright Lorraine Hansberry's *A Raisin in the Sun*, featuring actors such as Esther Rolle and Danny Glover? Concerts by musicians you like? Or by those your parents like and remember? Classic films of Bette Davis, Cary Grant, or Humphrey Bogart? In each case, the PBS affiliate is trying to attract different segments of an audience it believes will benefit from public broadcasting, as well as to draw in people who may seldom watch PBS. In the same way, speakers attuned to their audience members will try to discover and cultivate interests the listeners already have, as well as challenge them with new, useful topics.

Discussion Prompt:
To get students to consider the variety of audiences, lead a discussion comparing the target audiences of several cable television channels, such as MTV, VH1, and Nickelodeon—all products of MTV. Which of these channels attracts the oldest viewer? The youngest? What other assumptions can you make about these audiences?

Discussion Prompt:
To generate some lively class discussion, ask students to compare the clientele at several local nightclubs. What qualities characterize the patrons? What have club owners/managers done to attract that particular group of people?

We believe audience analysis is a process that shapes and molds the preparation, delivery, and evaluation of any well-thought-out public speech. In other words, audience analysis occurs *before, during,* and *after* the act of speaking. Let's consider more closely how this process works.

■ Audience Analysis *Before* the Speech

The amount of time you spend analyzing your audience before you speak will be far greater than your analysis during or after the speech. Your speech may last only five or ten minutes, for example. Yet if you care about doing well, you will spend much more than five or ten minutes considering the audience before you speak.

Your public speaking class is a special type of audience and provides you with unique challenges and opportunities. At the beginning of the semester or quarter, you may know few if any of your classmates. Much as you would do for any general, unfamiliar audience you were preparing to address, you initially analyze your classroom audience by active sleuthing, as well as using your own common sense. You will likely have to make a point of asking around about people's knowledge of or interest in a particular subject area. This is because you will give your first speech before you know your listeners well.

On the other hand, this class provides you the rare opportunity to "live" with your audience for the duration of the course. From the comments they make in and outside of class, from the questions they ask other student speakers or the instructor, and from their nonverbal feedback while listening to classroom speeches, you will gradually assemble an increasingly accurate portrait of this group of people. They will disclose, or you will deduce, information about their beliefs, values, interests, likes, and dislikes. Your audience analysis will be a semester- or quarter-long process, and by the time you deliver your final speech in the class, your audience analysis should be both easier and more accurate than it was at the beginning of the term.

Class Activity:
If your students have selected their topics for an upcoming speech, ask them to list questions about the audience that they would like to have answered to help them develop those speeches. After reading this chapter, have the students return to their lists and try to answer those questions using the techniques discussed. Use those questions that still cannot be answered as the basis for a class discussion on the value and limitations of audience analysis techniques.

ANALYZE AUDIENCE DEMOGRAPHICS

Your first step as a speaker is to discover and evaluate as many specific characteristics of your audience as possible. **Demographics** is the term for those characteristics. Discovering the specifics about your audience will help you answer the question, "Who is my target audience?"

Demographic analysis helps you tailor a message to a specific audience. You will never know everything about your listeners, and so you will make generalizations from the information you do know. One note of caution is in order, however: Be careful not to turn these generalizations into stereotypes about audience members. This will undermine your speech-making efforts. For example, we have observed speakers who assumed that audiences of similar demographic makeup inherently have similar interests. They selected topics they thought would "fit" those groups. Sometimes the speeches were well received; other times they were perceived as patronizing or even insulting.

Some topics may be appropriate to only one type of audience; most sub-

demographics: characteristics of the audience, such as age, gender, ethnicity, education, religion, economic status, and group membership.

Discussion Prompt:
Select several topics that on first glance appear to be of interest primarily to people of one particular age group, gender, economic status, etc. —for example, the Lamaze method of childbirth, sports and male bonding, and expensive wines. Discuss how speakers could justify these topics as important to a broader audience.

audience segmentation: the strategy of targeting a speech primarily toward one portion of the total audience.

Discussion Prompt:
To make certain that students understand audience segmentation, ask them to identify some of the subgroups, or "segments," within the class as a whole. These could include students older than average, campus residents, commuter students, business majors, and so forth.

jects, however, have broader appeal. A speech on the Seneca Falls Declaration of Sentiments is not just a women's topic but could be informative to both men and women. So could a speech on gender bias in language. The solvency of the social security system may be of immediate concern to someone approaching retirement, but with some creative thinking you can make it interesting to anyone who is a taxpayer or who plans to retire some day. The economic plight of the American farmer should interest not only the agriculture major but anyone who eats.

The function of education is to introduce us to new ideas and information. As a speaker, you defeat that goal when you stereotype an audience and choose only topics you think they will find familiar and comfortable. As a listener, you similarly undermine the goal of education when you tune out speeches on topics you do not find immediately interesting.

Sometimes speakers choose to speak to only one segment of a larger audience, a strategy called **audience segmentation** or **audience selection.** If you know that there are people of legal voting age in your class who have not yet registered to vote, you might direct a persuasive speech on the rights and duties of voting to that part of the audience. If there are athletes in your audience, an informative speech on the dangers of heatstroke and heat exhaustion might be appropriate for those listeners. If you know there are cigarette smokers in your class, they are an obvious target for a speech on the hazards of smoking. But we all know that smokers are targets lately, so part of your audience analysis needs to take this issue into consideration.

In each of these cases, your target audience is a subgroup of the audience as a whole; you direct your speech to them, hoping that others will also be interested or find your information useful. Notice, though, that even this strategy requires careful audience analysis. You must be sure that your target audience does exist, and that it is sufficient in size to justify giving them your primary focus. Generally, the more you know about your audience, the more secure you will be and the better speech you will deliver.

Seven of the most common characteristics you will want to know about your potential audience are age, gender, ethnicity, education, religion, economic status, and group membership. Although you will not always be able to learn this much information about your audience, the more you know, the better prepared you will be to present a successful speech.

Age.

"Communicating with college students is always somewhat of a challenge. It is not that I have too much difficulty understanding your changing expressions and attitudes. It is that I forget what you never saw."

TERRY SANFORD, U.S. SENATOR[5]

One of the most obvious concerns you have as you research your audience is their **age.** You may need to find out not only what the *average age* of your audience is, but what the *age range* will be. Your public speaking class may include first-year college students, people returning to college to change careers, and others pursuing interests after retirement. People who are eighteen to twenty years old today relate to the stock market crash of 1929, World War II,

Successful speakers avoid stereotyping their audiences, but view them as collections of individual listeners.

Practice Speaking:
To make students aware of the age range in their class and to provide an opportunity for an ungraded or credit/noncredit speaking assignment, have students use a newspaper index to prepare a 2–4 minute newscast of events that happened on the day they were born. Have them look at local, national, and international news, but urge them also to check the classified ads, grocery and clothing prices, and the movie ads and television log. You may adapt the assignment to your specific objectives: Students may deliver the newscast seated or standing; they may use a script or a set of notes. Students born on a day when a specific paper was not published (for example, a holiday or Sunday) should select the paper of the preceding or following day. You may want to refer students to the section on researching newspapers in Chapter 7.

Discussion Prompt:
Have class members share their first political memories. What does this collective class memory tell you about topics you might select for speeches to this audience? What are some examples of topics that would likely require speakers to provide background information?

Related Reading:
See: Arliss, Laurie P. *Gender Communication*. Englewood Cliffs, NJ: Prentice, 1991.

and the assassination of John F. Kennedy only as important topics of history. While that means that they may be eager to learn more about those topics, it also means they may not understand most casual references to those historical events. If you compare 1973's long gasoline lines to food rationing during World War II, an audience of eighteen-year-olds won't remember either of those events. To make a clear speech on one of the preceding topics, a speaker must use supporting materials that are familiar to the audience, and age is one of the most obvious influences on the audience's frame of reference.

Gender. The next factor you need to consider in your audience analysis is **gender.** It is obviously easier to determine gender than age. Some students run into difficulties with stereotyping when they take gender into consideration for speech making, however. For example, we remember college men who would deliver speeches with purposes such as "to inform you girls about the rules of football so that you don't drive your boyfriends crazy by asking silly questions when you watch a game with them." Most women today would listen to such a speech only under protest.

Yet even today what seems to be consideration for the gender of audience members sometimes turns out to be disguised sexism. We remember a speech informing women how to change a flat tire. While a speaker with genuine safety concerns might be able to deliver such a speech effectively, this particular speaker patronized the women in his audience by repeatedly talking down to them: "Take off your pretty little high heels and put on the pair of running shoes I told you to put in the trunk." "Cover up your fancy little dress with that work shirt I told you to carry in the trunk." Women in the class understandably bristled at the speaker's suggestion that they didn't know enough to change a tire.

Women are sometimes equally guilty of stereotyping. Helen, a student of ours, selected microwave technology as her speech topic. When discussing the advantages of microwave ovens, she said that "the guys" in the audience should seriously consider purchasing a microwave oven because it makes cooking easier. She was surprised at some of the responses her audience made after her speech. Some males were offended that the speaker in effect labeled men cooking klutzes. One man said he was a gourmet cook. Some females objected to Helen's assumption that they liked to cook or that they were good cooks. "Just because I'm female, does that mean I am supposed to enjoy cooking?" Helen could have avoided these reactions had she not stereotyped her audience according to gender. She could have phrased her statement, "Anyone who wants to make cooking easier and faster should seriously consider purchasing a microwave oven."

As these examples show, speakers make a mistake if they stereotype listeners according to their gender. You would be wise to *disregard* the advice found in one college public speaking text published in the mid-1960s:

Discussion Prompt:
Even though this example is extreme, are there topics today that are more appropriate for one gender than the other? If so, what are those topics? How could you try to make them relevant to both sexes?

Generally, women are more interested than men in subjects related to the feminine gender, such as women's clothing, cosmetics, housework, the rearing of children, the local ladies' aid society, home decoration, etc. On the other hand, men show strong masculine interests in rough competitive sports like football. More than women, men tend to enjoy technical and scientific subjects, particularly those related to mechanics, electronics, and engineering. Since more men than women serve as chief breadwinners for their families, they are more apt to be interested in matters pertaining to occupations and professions—but remember the possible exceptions.[6]

Today, those "possible exceptions" are ordinary and routine. As society continues to remove barriers based on gender, gender-specific topics will become fewer. Audience-centered speakers need to remember that.

Ethnicity. **Ethnicity** means the classification of a subgroup of people who have a common cultural heritage with shared customs, characteristics, language, history, and so on. Because members of an ethnic group may share a collective heritage and exhibit strong ethnic pride, it is entirely appropriate for speakers to tap these common experiences and feelings as they construct their speeches for audiences with similar ethnic backgrounds. Speaking to an audience of African-Americans, John Jacob, president of the National Urban League, observed: "Too often, we approach racial issues in a conceptual vacuum. We take a historical view. We forget that while most Americans' forebears came to this nation seeking freedom and opportunity, ours came in chains and were enslaved and oppressed."[7] Jacob's statement was entirely appropriate for his audience, yet he would not have said the words "our forebears" were he speaking, for example, to a white audience, or to listeners of mixed ethnic backgrounds.

As with the issue of gender, speakers should avoid ethnic stereotypes. Never assume that because individuals share the same ethnicity they also share similar experiences and attitudes. If you come from a working-class Irish Catholic ancestry, do not assume that others with Irish surnames are working-class or Catholic. Two people of the same ethnicity may have diverse attitudes, interests, and experiences because of differences in their ages, education, income levels, and religion.

Education. The **educational level** of your audience affects not only what subjects you choose, but also how you approach those particular subjects. You could speak about AIDS to a group of fourth graders, a class of college students, and an audience of biochemists. In each case your speech must be tailored to suit the contrasting educational backgrounds of the audience.

Discussion Prompt:
Ask students to discuss times they remember a speaker talking down to them or talking over their heads. Which situation produced boredom? Which produced anxiety? Why?

Even your audience of college students in this class has a variety of educational backgrounds. Some may have attended private schools, had home schooling, or earned graduate equivalency degrees after interruptions in their high school educations. Others may have lived and studied overseas. Smart speakers will find out as much as they can about the levels and types of education their listeners have.

Remember, also, that education can be informal as well as formal. Just as a high school diploma is unfortunately no guarantee of a solid educational background, listeners who have not completed high school or college are not necessarily uneducated. They may in fact have a wealth of specialized, practical knowledge and training.

If you have the opportunity, find out not only what your audience knows about a potential speech topic, but also whether they have experience relevant to that topic. The speaker in the following example put such knowledge to good use:

> Matt, a movie buff, decided to speak on how to audition for a movie. He went to the library, prepared a research bibliography, and began collecting information. The week before he was to give his speech, he learned that Sarah, a classmate and drama major, had auditioned for a role in a movie that was shot in town last summer. Matt decided to talk with Sarah about the experience. Although she had not gotten the part, Sarah talked excitedly about the experience. This information helped Matt fill in some of the gaps in his research. In addition, mentioning Sarah's experience in his speech connected the topic to the audience and made it seem more immediate.

Religion. Your college public speaking class may contain members of various Protestant denominations, Catholics, Jews, Muslims, Hindus, and Buddhists, as well as agnostics and atheists. Native American classmates may have religious beliefs with which you are not familiar. Students from other countries may also practice **religions** you do not know, or they may practice familiar religions in a different way. Even among people who belong to a particular denomination, religion will be very important to some and relatively unimportant to others. You have formulated your religious beliefs, whatever they are, over a period of time and you may feel defensive about those beliefs when they are challenged.

Stereotyping people on the basis of what you know of their religious views is as difficult and potentially inaccurate as making generalizations based on other demographic characteristics. Do all Catholics oppose birth control and the ordination of women as priests? Do all Jews observe Hanukkah and Yom Kippur, or observe them in the same way? Do all Protestants interpret scripture in the same manner? The obvious negative answer to all these questions should remind you of the limitations of simply finding out the religious sects represented in your audience. If your audience's religious views are truly important to a topic you are considering, you will need to find out more than the labels they prefer.

Economic Status. Economic status, or economic security, is another key factor affecting audience attitudes and behaviors. If a family earns barely enough to subsist, they will probably be more concerned with filling basic life needs than with social or status needs. For that reason, they may relate more readily than their wealthier counterparts to a speaker who advocates expanded health care benefits and automatic cost-of-living adjustments. They may be more receptive to a progressive income tax than to a flat-rate sales tax on products and services. Analyses of survey data and voting behavior suggest that, generally, the higher the income of a family, the more conservative their political attitudes. Even though many students in your class may not yet have significant incomes, their political attitudes are often similar to those of their parents.

Judging the range of incomes of your classmates' families may be difficult. Certainly, it would be impolite to ask. However, you can probably locate or construct several general profiles of the typical students at your college, as the following speaker did.

> For her first informative speech Julie decided to discuss demographics of students at her college. Her primary sources were student profiles based on registration surveys and later released by the administration. This proved to be a subject her classmates enjoyed because it was about them and their friends. Some of the information Julie presented was surprising but seemed reasonable; other items were so funny that they seemed to be mistaken. Julie's research provided her information to analyze her own classroom audience. In addition, it helped others in their audience analysis for future speeches.

If you speak on significant national concerns, consult public opinion surveys on those issues. Such polls categorize responses according to several demographic characteristics, and often one of them is income.

Overall, be realistic, be fair, and be sensitive when choosing topics dealing with economic issues. We remember one student who was offended when a speaker said that students shouldn't go home for spring break but should travel with friends to different parts of the United States to expand their historical and cultural knowledge. The offended student argued that some students simply did not have that option. They needed to work in order to remain in college. Speeches that urge college students to consider investing in the stock market or in real estate usually ignore one important fact: Most college students do not have money to spend for these purposes. On the other hand, we have observed student speakers generate lively audience interest on topics such as how to select an excellent yet inexpensive wine, summer employment opportunities at national parks and historic sites, and how to negotiate the price of a new or used

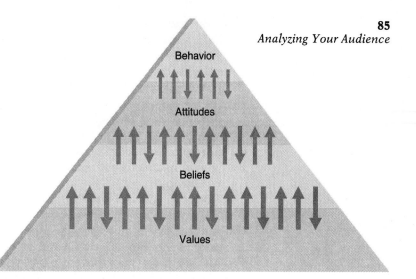

FIGURE 5.2 Levels of Influence

which are based on our beliefs, which are validated by our values. In order to understand better the interaction among these elements we will look at each level of the pyramid, beginning with values and moving upward.

Values. We value something because we deem it to be desirable, or to have some inherent goodness. **A value** expresses a judgment of what is desirable and undesirable, right and wrong, or good and evil. Values are usually stated in the form of a word or phrase. For example, most of us probably share the values of equality, freedom, honesty, fairness, justice, good health, and family. These

values: judgments of what is right or wrong, desirable or undesirable.

How would you describe the person who displayed these bumper stickers? What do you think are some of this person's values, beliefs, attitudes, and behaviors?

values comprise the principles or standards we use to judge and develop our beliefs, attitudes, and behaviors.

If we value honesty, for example, we are probably offended when we learn that a political leader has lied to us. If we value equality and fairness, we will no doubt oppose employment practices that discriminate on the basis of gender, ethnicity, religion, or age. While our actions may not always be consistent with our values, those standards nevertheless guide what we believe and how we act. When we act contrary to our values, we may experience conflict or even guilt. That perceived inconsistency will often motivate us either to change our behavior to match our beliefs and values, or to change our beliefs by rationalizing our behavior.

beliefs: declarative statements expressing truths an individual holds.

Related Reading:
For a discussion of how values and beliefs can affect intercultural communication, see Chapters 7-11 in: Borden, George A. *Cultural Orientation: An Approach to Understanding Intercultural Communication.* Englewood Cliffs, NJ: Prentice, 1991: 95-155.

Beliefs. A **belief** is something you accept as true, and it is usually stated as a declarative sentence. We probably do not think about many of our beliefs because they are seldom challenged: Brushing your teeth regularly reduces your chances of getting cavities; observing speed limits saves lives; sexual abuse is psychologically harmful to children; illiteracy in the United States undermines economic productivity; and so on.

Other beliefs are more controversial, and we often find ourselves defending them. Each of the statements below is debatable.

Colleges place too much emphasis on athletics.

Mandatory sentencing deters crime.

The production of nuclear energy is a threat to humans and their environment.

Air travel is safe.

Courts have failed to protect the rights of the victims of crimes.

IQ tests are culturally biased.

There are, no doubt, statements on this list with which you agree and disagree. Those you accept as true are part of your beliefs.

attitudes: statements expressing an individual's approval or disapproval, likes or dislikes.

Attitudes. **Attitudes** are expressions of approval or disapproval. They are our likes and dislikes. A statement of an attitude makes a judgment about the desirability of an individual, object, idea, or action. Examples of statements of attitude include the following: I endorse Bob Barton for SGA president; I favor a decrease in defense spending; I support capping enrollment at our college; I like broccoli; I prefer classical music to jazz; and I favor a pass-fail grading system for our school.

Usually attitudes evolve from our values and beliefs. Several values and beliefs may interact to complicate our decision making. When two values or two beliefs collide, usually the stronger one will predominate and determine attitudes. You may value both the right to privacy and the right to good health. If a speaker convinces you that a proposed government action will diminish the right to privacy, you may oppose the action. If another speaker demonstrates that the plan is necessary to gather information to contain the spread of a deadly disease, you may support the proposal. A single belief, then, in and of itself is not a reliable predictor of a person's attitude. Again, when values collide, the stronger value usually takes precedence.

behaviors: an individual's observable actions.

Behaviors. A **behavior** is an overt action; in other words, it is how we act. Unlike values, beliefs, and attitudes, which are all psychological principles, behaviors are observable. You may feel that giving blood is important (attitude) because an adequate blood supply is necessary to save lives (belief) and because you respect human life (value). Your behavior as you participate in a blood drive and donate blood is a logical and observable extension of your outlook.

GATHER INFORMATION ABOUT YOUR AUDIENCE

If you understand the foregoing components of psychology, you begin to understand the audience you intend to inform, persuade, or entertain. Your knowledge of those principles will help you as you work to analyze your audience, and will help you develop a psychological, or psychographic, profile. However, you must be careful as you develop a psychological profile of your audience. How do you obtain information about your audience's values, beliefs, attitudes, and behaviors? You have two options, both requiring some work.

The first is to use your powers of observation and deduction. You can make educated guesses about people's values, beliefs, and attitudes by observing their behaviors. For example, what are your classmates talking about before and after class? What subjects have they chosen for classroom speeches? How do they respond to various speeches they hear? What do you guess their age range to be? How do they dress? What books do they carry with them to class? The answers to those and many other questions help you infer a psychological profile of your audience. The longer you are around your classmates, the less this profile will be based on stereotypes and the more accurate it will become.

The second way to gather information about your audience's values, beliefs, attitudes, and behaviors is to conduct interviews or administer questionnaires. Interviews and questionnaires may be informal or, if you have the time and resources, formal. You could interview classmates informally during conversation before or after class. Questionnaires administered during class may be as simple as asking for a show of hands to answer a question ("How many of you have access to a personal computer?") or as formal as asking classmates to answer a written questionnaire you have photocopied and distributed. It's true that audience interviews and questionnaires are somewhat artificial; you don't often have the luxury of using them for your presentations outside of your college classroom. Still, if you are invited or required to address a group of strangers, you would be wise to ask your contact person lots of questions about the audience you will be facing.

ANALYZE SPECIFIC SPEAKING SITUATIONS

Types of Audiences. In terms of their reasons for attending a speech, audiences fall into two categories: voluntary and captive. A **voluntary audience** has assembled of its own free will. Most adults who attend a worship service or a political rally are there voluntarily. Similarly, you may be taking this class as an elective, just because you believe it will benefit you. The **captive audience,** in contrast, feels required to be present. Chances are that you have been part of a captive audience at many school assemblies so far in your education. You may even be taking this class to fulfill a requirement. You may attend a speech by someone visiting your campus because you are required to do so for

voluntary audience: a group of people who have assembled of their own free will to listen to a speaker.

captive audience: a group of people who are compelled or feel compelled to assemble to listen to a speaker.

audience disposition: listeners' feelings of like, dislike, or neutrality toward a speaker, the speaker's topic, or the occasion for a speech.

this or some other course. Your reasons for attending a speech, a presentation, or a class may have a significant effect on your disposition as you listen.

Audience Disposition. Listeners may have any of three general attitudes toward speakers or their ideas: **favorable, unfavorable,** or **neutral.** Each of these categories, however, looks deceptively simple. Listeners can be slightly, moderately, or strongly favorable or unfavorable toward your topic, and you should try to determine this level of intensity. A listener who only slightly opposes your position that home schooling is a desirable method of instruction will probably be easier to persuade than one who strongly opposes it.

If you sense that some of your listeners are neutral toward your topic, you should try to uncover the reasons for their neutrality. Some may be *uninterested* in your topic, and you will want to convince those listeners of its importance. Other listeners may be *uninformed* about your topic, and your strategy here should be to introduce your listeners to the data they need to understand and believe your ideas. Still other listeners may simply be *undecided* about your topic. They may be both interested and informed, aware of the pros and cons of your position. They may not have decided, however, which position they support. Your strategy in this instance should be to bolster your arguments and point out weaknesses in the opposition's case. As you can see, evaluating your audience's disposition is a complex activity. The more you know about your listeners, the easier this process becomes.

Listeners can be favorable, unfavorable, or neutral not only to speakers and their topics, but also to the reason for assembling to hear a speech. We are often tempted to view voluntary audiences as friendly and captive ones as hostile, and those situations certainly do occur. A person may go listen to a public lecture at a museum because of interest in the subject or out of respect for the speaker's reputation. On the other hand, members of captive audiences may be so antagonistic about having to be present that they listen to any speaker through a filter of hostility. The connection between the audience's reasons for attending and their attitudes toward the speaker is not this simple and predictable, however. Figure 5.3 offers some hypothetical examples of public speaking situations to demonstrate the relationship between an audience's attitudes and the reasons for their attendance.

An audience that has assembled freely may well be unfavorable to the speaker or the speaker's organization. As examples, consider the people who attend a political speech to protest or to heckle the speaker. And a captive audience, instead of being hostile because they feel coerced into attending, may

FIGURE 5.3 Types of Audiences

	Voluntary	Captive
Favorable	Students attending campus speech by prize-winning author Russell Baker	TV-film majors required to attend campus speech by director Spike Lee
Unfavorable	Students attending board of regents meeting to hear discussion of proposed increases in tuition and fees	Workers required to attend a seminar to develop skills they believe they already have

actually look forward to a speech. Audience dynamics get even more complicated when a voluntary, favorable audience is forced to listen to other speakers before the person they came to hear. Or a captive audience that is initially unsympathetic to the speaker may find themselves becoming friendly as a result of the speaker's interesting message or engaging style of delivery.

Because attendance is a requirement of most college courses, you face a captive audience when you stand before your classmates. That shouldn't frighten you, though; as we've said, a captive audience is not necessarily unfavorable toward the speaker or the speaking occasion. Keep in mind that in this class your colleagues will be especially friendly because they share some of your concerns and apprehensions. However, the situation does pose an added challenge for you and makes your audience analysis especially important. You have a responsibility to choose novel, interesting topics for informative speeches, to choose significant topics for persuasive speeches, and to be thoroughly prepared for any speech you give. Listeners may develop an unfavorable impression of you if they perceive that you are taking your speech too lightly or exploiting the occasion to preach your own political or religious views. Remember that public speaking is an audience-centered activity; keep your listeners' needs and concerns in mind as you construct your message.

If you use the techniques discussed in this chapter, you will be able to construct an **audience profile.** As you do this, however, be aware of the following points. First, your understanding of your audience will never be complete. It is simply impossible (and probably illegal!) to discover *everything* about your listeners. Sometimes you have to make educated guesses based on incomplete data. Second, much of the information you gather may be of little or no help in preparing your speech. How important is it, for example, to know your listeners' religious affiliations if you are informing them on the benefits of interactive video instruction? On the other hand, if you are discussing the issue of prayer in school, your listeners' religious beliefs may be extremely important.

audience profile: a descriptive sketch of listeners' characteristics, values, beliefs, attitudes, and/or actions.

Finally, keep in mind that your audience is not a uniform mass, but a collection of individual listeners with different experiences, values, beliefs, attitudes, behaviors, and personalities. While opinions may overlap, do not think of your audience as having one opinion toward your topic. Rarely will you be able to say, "This audience opposes converting the intramural athletic field to a multistory parking facility." More likely, your audience analysis statement will have to account for a variety of opinions about your topic. If you need more precise information, you may want to construct a questionnaire, distribute it to your classmates, and then collect, compile, and interpret the results, as Trevor did in the following example.

Trevor favored an amendment to the U.S. Constitution mandating a balanced budget. To help him construct his speech, he prepared and distributed to his class the questionnaire in Figure 5.4.

Class Activity:
Have your students construct an audience questionnaire pertaining to the topic of an upcoming speech. They should distribute it to their classmates and then collect, compile, and interpret the results. Have each student write an audience profile based on the results.

Trevor discovered that a significant majority of his classmates believed that the federal budget deficit was serious and that current budget reduction efforts were ineffective. Nearly three-fourths of the class favored an amendment mandating a balanced budget, although slightly fewer than half thought such an amendment would solve the problem. Approximately half the class thought an amendment would hurt social programs, and a clear majority felt taxes would

Audience Questionnaire

Please take a few minutes to complete the following survey to help me in preparing my persuasive speech. Do not put your name on this survey. Thanks!

Using the scale below please circle the number that best indicates your agreement/disagreement with each of the statements in Questions 1–7.

7 = strongly agree	3 = slightly disagree
6 = moderately agree	2 = moderately disagree
5 = slightly agree	1 = strongly disagree
4 = neutral/neither agree nor disagree	

1. The federal budget deficit is a serious problem.

1	2	3	4	5	6	7
strongly disagree			neutral			strongly agree

2. Current efforts to reduce the federal budget deficit are ineffective.

1	2	3	4	5	6	7
strongly disagree			neutral			strongly agree

3. A constitutional amendment mandating a balanced budget would solve the federal budget deficit.

1	2	3	4	5	6	7
strongly disagree			neutral			strongly agree

4. A constitutional amendment mandating a balanced federal budget would result in increased taxes.

1	2	3	4	5	6	7
strongly disagree			neutral			strongly agree

5. A constitutional amendment mandating a balanced federal budget would end up hurting social programs.

1	2	3	4	5	6	7
strongly disagree			neutral			strongly agree

6. A constitutional amendment mandating a balanced federal budget would end up hurting defense programs.

1	2	3	4	5	6	7
strongly disagree			neutral			strongly agree

7. I favor a constitutional amendment mandating a balanced federal budget.

1	2	3	4	5	6	7
strongly disagree			neutral			strongly agree

Place an "X" by the word that best describes you.

1. I have the following politcal affiliation:	2. Politically, I consider myself to be:
____ Democrat	____ liberal
____ Republican	____ moderate
____ Independent	____ conservative
____ other (please specify) _____	____ other (please specify) _____

Please share any additional comments you would like about the federal budget deficit on the back of this sheet.

FIGURE 5.4 Audience Questionnaire

increase and defense programs would suffer. The class was almost equally divided among Democrats, Republicans, and independents. A majority viewed themselves as moderate, with conservative running a close second, and liberal a distant third. A few students shared additional comments, such as: "boring topic," "probably important, but what can we do?," and "who cares?" Trevor reviewed the results of his survey and wrote the following analysis of his audience:

> The challenge doesn't seem to be getting the audience to support my position that the U.S. Constitution should be amended to require a balanced budget. Most already agree. The difficulty may be, first, getting them interested in the topic and, second, getting them to think that they can have an impact on the solution.

In his speech Trevor tried to increase audience involvement in the topic by showing how the deficit affected the pocketbooks of each of his listeners. He attempted to defuse the arguments that a balanced budget would necessarily result in a cutback of needed social programs and hurt U.S. national security. He supported his arguments with a balance of opinions from Democrats and Republicans, mainly those with moderate views. Trevor's hard work paid off. He delivered a speech that was adapted to his specific audience, and the audience responded favorably.

You may not always have the opportunity to get as much detailed information as Trevor did before you prepare your speech. The more specific and accurate your audience analysis, however, the better you can develop your ideas and accomplish your specific purpose. You need to use the demographic and psychographic information you have gathered about your listeners to develop your audience profile.

Size of the Audience. Remember we said in Chapter 1 that the greater the number of people involved in speech communication, the less chance there is for verbal interaction between the speaker and individual listeners. A little reflection on various public speaking situations proves this principle. In speaking before a small group, a speaker may be frequently interrupted with questions. The situation may be so informal that the speaker sits in a chair or on the edge of a table during the presentation. A speaker in such a situation may use jargon and colloquial language; prepared visual aids, as well as those devised on the spot with transparencies and chalkboards; and a relaxed, conversational style of delivery.

As the audience grows larger, however, the speaker will have to use greater volume and larger gestures. The language of the speech may grow more formal, especially if the speaker knows that the speech will be published or videotaped. As the distance between the speaker and the last row of audience members increases, the speaker's volume must increase, gestures and facial expression must be exaggerated slightly, and visual aids must be projected in order to be seen. Unless the audience is encouraged to ask questions after the speech, they will likely remain silent. As you can see, the **size of your audience** affects both the type of speech you deliver and your manner of presentation.

Occasion. The **occasion,** the reason for the speaking event, is a critical factor in determining what type of audience you will be facing. You need to ask

Discussion Prompt: Show videotapes of two speakers addressing different sized audiences. One might be a student delivering a speech in a classroom; the other might be a politician addressing a national political convention. Both speeches should incorporate effective delivery. Analyze how the size of the audience helped shape the speakers' vocal and physical delivery.

yourself (and maybe even some members of the group), "Why is this audience gathering? What special circumstances bring them together?" A class, an annual convention, a banquet, a party, a competition, a reunion, and a regular meeting of an organization are all examples of occasions. Occasions can be formal or informal, serious or fun, planned or spontaneous, closed to the public or open to all.

In addition to a simple description of the occasion, you as a speaker may need to know about the history of the occasion or about the recent history of the group you will address. If officers of an organization have invited you to speak to them, members of the organization may view you skeptically if there has been recent conflict between the members and the officers. To understand any occasion, you must know both the purpose and the circumstances of the gathering.

Physical Environment. In Chapters 1 and 2 we discussed the forms of noise that speakers and listeners must battle. Every **physical environment** or setting contains unique obstacles to communication. The size of the room itself may impede communication. You may be speaking as some audience members finish a meal. You may be speaking to a large audience through an inadequate or defective public address system. You may compete with a variety of physical noise: the sounds of another meeting next door, a room that is too warm, interruptions from caterers bringing in carts of ice water. Just as it makes good sense to practice a speech in the classroom where you will speak, you should always try to find out something about the physical location where you will be speaking to a group.

Time. If you had your choice, would you rather take a college class at 9:00 a.m. or 1:00 p.m.? If you're typical, you'll choose the 9:00 a.m. class, even though you might not consider yourself a "morning person." Both students and faculty seem to agree that classes at 1:00 p.m. are particularly difficult to attend and to teach because everyone's energy seems low.

The **time** your speech is delivered is an obvious part of your analysis of the speaking occasion. An address given at 4:00 p.m. on Friday will almost surely find an audience more fatigued and restless than will one given Tuesday at 9:30 a.m. If you are scheduled to speak first in a class that meets at 8:00 a.m., you may face an audience still awakening, so you may need to boost your own energy.

Your speech's placement in a program may also affect how your audience receives it. If you follow several other speakers, you may need to work harder at getting and keeping the attention of your listeners. In short, if your listeners are not at their best, plan on working extra hard to enliven your delivery. Think about your class and when you will present your speech. The time factor may not cause you to change your topic, but it may affect how you deliver your speech.

■ Audience Analysis *During* the Speech ⎯⎯⎯⎯⎯⎯⎯⎯

If your audience analysis before the speech has been careful and thorough, you will approach any speaking situation—both in this class and outside of it—

with a fairly complete and accurate picture of your audience. Your study of the audience to this point will have guided your selection of a topic and the specific ways that you have developed that topic and plan to deliver the speech. Yet even the most scrupulous, conscientious audience analysis will not guarantee that your speech will be compelling and effective. Whether you speak from notes, from a manuscript, from memory, or on the spur of the moment, your audience analysis must continue *during* the delivery of your speech if you are to make that vital connection with your listeners. Communication scholars suggest that, as a speaker, you must be aware of three things about your listeners *as you speak*.

First, you must be aware of the audience's **attention** or **interest.** Do their eye contact, posture, and other body language indicate to you that they are concentrating on you and your message? Are there physical distractions in the speech setting that are competing with you for the audience's attention? Do you seem to have the audience's attention throughout some parts of the speech, only to lose it during other parts? If you are concentrating on your message and on your listeners, rather than on how you sound and look, you will know the answers to these questions about the audience's attention.

The route to recovering your listeners' attention may be as simple as changing some aspect of your delivery: speaking more loudly or softly, for example, or moving away from the lectern for part of the speech so that you are closer to the audience. Any change in your established pattern of delivery will likely rekindle audience attention and interest. In addition, changing your usual style of delivery may be essential to overcome the distractions of a stuffy room, a noisy heater, or the coughs and other audience noise that occur whenever people assemble.

A second characteristic of your audience that you must try to assess is their **understanding** or **comprehension** of your message. If you have ever produced a false and hollow sounding laugh when you didn't really understand the joke that was just told, you know how difficult it is to "fake" comprehension. No matter how hard most of us try to cover up a lack of understanding, something about our voices or our bodies signals to others that we didn't really "get it."

Of course, your audience may not try to hide their incomprehension. They may deliberately tell you with puzzled expressions and other nonverbals that they are confused. The worst thing a speaker can do under either circumstance is to continue as if there were no problems. Clarifying something for the audience may be as simple as repeating or rephrasing the problem statement. If a particular word seems to be the source of confusion, defining the word or writing it on the board may solve the problem.

The third and final component of audience analysis during the speech is your listeners' **evaluation** of you and your message. Sensitive speakers attuned to their audiences are able to gauge the reactions of those listeners. Does the audience seem to agree with what you are saying? Do they approve of the suggestions you are making? Answers to these questions are particularly important when you are seeking to persuade your audience.

Sometimes the answer to such questions will be "no." You may be delivering bad news or taking what you know will be an unpopular stand on an issue. Having the audience disagree with the content of your message doesn't necessarily mean that your speech has been a failure. Simply knowing that many listeners agree or disagree with you at the end of a persuasive speech shows that you are an audience-centered speaker, and that's an accomplishment in itself.

■ Audience Analysis *After* the Speech ─────────

Too often speakers assume that the speech-making process concludes as you utter your final statement and walk to your seat. Your influence on audience members can continue for some time, however. We encourage you to add one additional step: **post-speech analysis.** Part of this step should be self-reflection as you analyze your performance. Did you accomplish what you hoped you would? What do you sense were the strongest aspects of your speech? What were the weakest? How would you rate the content, organization, and delivery of the speech? What can you do to improve these aspects of your next speech?

Your answers to these questions provide a very subjective evaluation of your speech efforts. You may be much more critical than your listeners were since only you know how you planned to deliver the speech. For that reason, you should also analyze your audience to determine their assessment of the content, organization, and delivery of your speech.

In this class that information may come from oral or written critiques from your peers, or from comments some of them give you after class. If you have given a good speech on an interesting topic, one of the pleasant rewards in a college classroom may be that audience members have questions to ask you. The tone and content of those questions will tell you a great deal about how the audience received your message. You will also receive helpful suggestions from your instructor. If you expect to improve as a public speaker, you should consider the feedback given you by all your listeners and act upon the comments you think are particularly relevant.

Summary ──────────────────────

The best speeches are those that seem exactly right for the audience to whom they are delivered. They focus on interesting topics, use colorful but familiar language and supporting materials, are delivered with enthusiasm, and are the right length for the topic and the occasion. Such an accomplishment requires careful audience analysis before, during, and after delivery of the speech.

Before the speech a speaker should consider audience demographics, audience needs, and audience psychology. *Demographics* refers to charac-

teristics of the audience, including age, gender, ethnicity, education, religion, economic status, and group membership. Information you gather about these characteristics can help you select a topic and then develop and support it for a particular group of listeners. Realize, however, that simply stereotyping listeners in terms of one or more of these characteristics may not only be incorrect, but may also cause a speaker to offend the audience.

Maslow's hierarchy of needs is a useful tool for analyzing audience motivation. That model ranks five human needs in terms of their predominance. The *physiological needs,* the most basic, include our needs for food, water, and rest. The *safety needs* include everything that contributes to a predictable, orderly existence — secure housing, reliable transportation, freedom from civil unrest or war, for example. Once these needs are largely met, we begin to concentrate on our community of friends and associates and the ways that they fulfill our *love and belongingness needs.* Feeling that we "fit in," that we give and receive affection from a group of people, contributes to our *esteem needs.* This fourth level is important, Maslow says, because we all need a pat on the back from time to time. The highest level of needs, the *self-actualization needs,* refers to our desire to fulfill our potential as human beings.

Four key components of audience psychology are values, beliefs, attitudes, and behaviors. *Values,* such as freedom and honesty, are expressions of worth or rightness. Our values are the basis for the development of beliefs and attitudes. *Beliefs* are statements we accept as true. They may be either provable or open to debate. *Attitudes* express our approval or disapproval of individuals, objects, ideas, or actions. Several values or beliefs may interact to form our attitudes. When these values or beliefs conflict, the stronger one usually predominates. A fourth element is *behavior,* an overt action that reflects our values, beliefs, and attitudes.

Gathering information about your audience's values, beliefs, and attitudes can be formal or informal. You can simply observe their behaviors and infer the thoughts behind them. Or you may have the need and the opportunity to question the audience, orally or in writing, by administering questionnaires and surveys to gauge their feelings.

A final part of audience analysis before the speech focuses on the specific speaking situation. Will you be facing a captive or a voluntary audience? Are they likely to be favorable, unfavorable, or neutral to you and your topic? What is the nature of the speaking occasion? Where will the speech take place? What time is it to be delivered? Considering the answers to these questions is the final step in audience analysis before the speech.

During a speech the speaker should pay attention to the audience's *interest* or *attention,* their *comprehension* or understanding of the message, and their *evaluation* of the speech. Speakers can influence each of these elements. Lively, sincere delivery helps generate audience interest in the topic. A speaker can help ensure the audience's comprehension of the message by defining unusual terms, slowing down the delivery of technical materials, and using repetition.

Finally, after the speech has been delivered, a speaker should continue to analyze the audience for signals about their evaluation of the message. What comments do they make about the speech, orally or in writing? What questions do they ask? What suggestions does the class instructor offer? Any student who is serious about improving as a public speaker must be aware of and act upon audience feedback after the speech is over.

Exercises

1. Select a speech from *Vital Speeches* or some other published source. Read the speech to discern how the speaker adapted, or failed to adapt, the mes-

sage to the specific audience. Mark examples of audience adaptation strategies, writing in the margins of a copy of the speech the specific appeal or strategy used. Indicate where the speaker could better have adapted to the audience.

2. Using the speech you selected in the above exercise, discuss how the speaker would need to adapt the purpose, content, organization, and language if he or she were speaking to your class.

3. Based on your analysis of students in this class, predict their opinions on the following questions.
   a. Should women be excluded from combat roles in the U.S. military?
   b. Generally, is a private college education superior to a public college education?
   c. Should the U.S. Constitution be amended to require a balanced budget?
   d. Should women have the right to have an abortion?
   e. Do social fraternities and sororities do more harm than good?
      After you have made your predictions, poll the class to determine their responses to the above questions. Were your predictions fairly accurate? Were you surprised at some of the answers? What factors caused you to predict as you did?

4. Choose a specific brand-name product advertised in several magazines. Analyze how the product is promoted in each publication. Are there differences in the ads' headlines, body copy, and visuals? If so, what do these distinctions reveal about how the advertisers viewed their audiences? If the ads are identical, suggest ways that the product appeal could be tailored to each audience.

5. Each issue of *Congressional Digest* poses a specific policy question; for example, "Should the National Voter Registration Act be approved?" Several speeches are presented, affirming and negating the question. Select a copy of *Congressional Digest* and read the speeches included. Discuss the differences between the "pro" and the "con" sides in terms of the values supporting each side's arguments.

6. To give you some experience in analyzing off-campus audiences, select one of the following groups, find out what you can about it, and report back to the class.
   a. Knights of Columbus
   b. Optimist Club
   c. B'nai B'rith
   d. Veterans of Foreign Wars
   e. League of Women Voters
   f. NAACP
   g. Rotary Club

Notes

1. Mary Raymond Shipman Andrews, *The Perfect Tribute* (New York: Scribner's, 1906) 1–9.

2. Carl Sandburg, *Abraham Lincoln: The Prairie Years and the War Years* (New York: Harcourt, 1954) 443–44.

3. Newspaper reporters the next day began to reflect widely different public views of the president's surprisingly brief speech. The *Chicago Times* referred to "the silly, flat, and dish-watery utterances" of Lincoln; the *Harrisburg* [Pennsylvania]

Patriot and Union simply reported, "We pass over the silly remarks of the President. . ." (Sandburg 445). Other newspapers, however, made entirely positive evaluations of Lincoln's speech. The *Chicago Tribune* predicted, "The dedicatory remarks of President Lincoln will live among the annals of man" (Sandburg 445). The *Philadelphia Evening Bulletin* noted that thousands who would not wade through Everett's elaborate oration would read Lincoln's brief remarks, "and not many will do it without a moistening of the eye and a swelling of the heart" (Sandburg 446). The *Providence Journal* reminded its readers of the adage that the hardest thing in the world is to make a good five-minute speech, and said, "We know not where to look for a more admirable speech than the brief one which the President made at the close of Mr. Everett's oration" (Sandburg 446).

4. Thomas M. Scheidel, *Persuasive Speaking* (Glenview, IL: Scott, 1967) 97.

5. Terry Sanford, quoted in "Commencement Remarks: Learning to Care and Share," *Representative American Speeches 1988–1989*, ed. Owen Peterson (New York: Wilson, 1989) 154.

6. Win Kelley, *The Art of Public Address* (Dubuque, IA: Brown, 1965) 25.

7. John Jacob, "Racism and Race Relations: To Grow Beyond our Racial Animosities," *Vital Speeches of the Day* 15 January 1990: 214.

8. Abraham H. Maslow, *Motivation and Personality*, 2nd ed. (New York: Random, 1970) 35–47.

9. Maslow 38.

10. Maslow 41.

Selecting Your Speech Topic

6

Generating Ideas
Self-Generated Topics
Audience-Generated Topics
Occasion-Generated Topics
Research-Generated Topics

Selecting Your Topic

Focusing Your Topic

**Determining Your General
  Purpose**
Speeches to Inform
Speeches to Persuade
Speeches to Entertain

**Formulating Your Specific
  Purpose**

Wording Your Thesis Statement

Developing Your Speech Title

*F*IRST, the bad news: "A recent study of today's college students concludes that they 'seem to have no confidence or willingness to extend their knowledge.'" Thomas Kopp of Miami University in Oxford, Ohio, the author of the study, notes that college students are "bored by almost everything," and as a result "they are also boring people. Today's college students, more than any other generation, he says, . . . are dogmatic and uncreative, motivated more by desire for good grades than [by] excitement for learning."[1]

The good news is that we don't accept that portrait as a blanket characterization of college students in the 1990s any more than you do. The best news of all, of course, is that this public speaking class provides you the perfect opportunity to prove such studies wrong. Most of your learning in college courses comes from reading textbooks, listening to your instructors, and participating in class discussions. Occasionally, you have the opportunity to research topics raised in the class and present your conclusions, usually in the form of a research paper. Too rarely do you communicate your ideas orally to the class or listen to the researched, documented opinions of your classmates.

In this class you will read this textbook, listen to your instructor, and participate in class discussions. You will also have the opportunity to investigate issues that concern you and present your ideas to your classmates and your instructor. You are studying some fundamental speech principles, and the best way for you to demonstrate your mastery of them is to prepare and deliver interesting, well-researched speeches on topics of your choice.

Selecting a topic for a speech is more complex than you might think. Students often fail to choose a topic wisely because they adopt strategies that are counterproductive. For example, some students select too quickly. They pick up a magazine, find an interesting article, and decide to use its subject as their topic. Later they discover that the topic is really inappropriate for the audience or the occasion, or they find few corroborative articles. If they keep the hastily chosen topic and approach the assignment half-heartedly, the quality of the speech suffers. If they change topics, they lose valuable speech preparation time. Either option presents a no-win situation.

Eric had three weeks to prepare his informative speech, and he wanted to select a topic that would excite him, his audience, and his instructor. Because he enjoyed watching the street performers near campus, he thought this would make an excellent speech topic. He went to the library, looked at a couple of indexes, but couldn't find anything listed under the topic of street performers. So he changed topics. In the library reading room Eric found and skimmed through several magazines. He came across an article in *Discover* magazine on 3-D music. "Everybody's interested in music," Eric said to himself, so he photocopied the article and stuffed it in a notebook.

A couple of days later, he took out a pencil, a notepad, and the article. As he began reading, however, he encountered words such as psychoacoustics, transponder, binaural imaging, and Convolvotron. Eric concluded that the topic was too technical for his audience (and for him!), and he began thinking of other interests he had that he could turn into a speech topic. Eric enjoyed airbrush artwork, but decided that others might find the topic boring. In his psychology class, he was studying dream interpretation, but Eric reasoned that others may have taken the course and would already know much of his information. Recently there had been an earthquake in an adjacent state, and he thought this might be a timely topic. But since it had been in the news, he was afraid that someone else would choose the same topic. As the day of his speech approached, Eric was still selecting and rejecting speech topics.

Students like Eric spend far too long searching for the perfect topic. They jump from one idea to another because none seems quite right. As you can see, this select-and-reject syndrome wastes valuable time that could be devoted to researching and developing a topic. As the speaking date nears, the student usually panics and selects any topic, developing it hastily in the limited time that remains and never feeling really comfortable with the topic. Unfortunately, this lack of preparation and commitment usually shows up as the speech is presented. At some point in the selection process, you must pick your best topic and commit yourself to developing it. Each of Eric's topics, for example, *could* have been both interesting and informative.

Determining your speech topic, then, is an important part of speech making that should not be slighted. If you select a topic of interest to you and your audience, and on which you can find authoritative supporting material, you greatly enhance your chances of a successful speaking experience. You will also probably find the speech construction process more efficient and enjoyable.

Right about now you may be asking yourself, "How am I ever going to pick the right topic?" Choosing your topic involves several steps. You should (1) generate a list of possible topics, (2) select a topic, (3) focus the topic, (4) determine your general purpose, (5) formulate your specific purpose, and (6) word your thesis statement. Depending on the specific speaking situation, you may also want or be asked to develop a speech title. We will devote the rest of this chapter to a discussion of these six crucial steps.

■ Generating Ideas ————————————————

"You can't have good ideas if you don't have a lot of ideas."
                                                      LINUS PAULING

The first step in the process of selecting a speech topic is **brainstorming.** This is a technique of listing all the ideas that come to mind, without evaluating or censoring any of them. Too often a speaker spends insufficient time generating a list of potential topics. Yet as Dr. Pauling suggests, in order to select a good topic you must generate many topics. Author John Steinbeck compared ideas to rabbits, saying, "You get a couple and learn how to handle them, and pretty soon you have a dozen." As a general rule, the larger your list of possible topics, the better the topic you will finally select. It is important that you not evaluate or criticize your list as you brainstorm. What may seem silly to you at first can turn out to be an unusual speech subject with a lot of potential to interest your audience.

For example, a Chicago Cubs fan, puzzling over the team's failure to win a

brainstorming: noncritical free association to generate as many ideas as possible in a short time.

Discussion Prompt:
Have your students volunteer topics they think are too narrow or too bizarre for a speech. Be prepared to offer some examples of your own. Use these ideas to generate related topics that *would* be appropriate for a classroom speech. Make the point that what initially seemed to be a poor topic for a speech can sometimes yield an excellent one.

National League pennant in nearly half a century, might be interested in the question, "Why can't the Cubs win?" Some sports analysts have noted that, without stadium lights until 1988, the Cubs played all home games during the day and most of their road games at night. This time differential, worsened by traveling across time zones, may have affected team performance. Interesting theory, isn't it? If you began researching this topic, you might come across the term *chronobiology*, "the effect of time on living systems."[2] You could also learn about the consequences of jet lag on the performance of athletes, businesspeople, politicians, and others who travel. What began as a narrow topic (why the Cubs haven't won the National League pennant since 1945) has become a topic with broader appeal. Brainstorming, then, is an important first step, and you should jot down all the topics you think of and postpone evaluating them until later.

You can turn brainstorming into productive work toward your speech by asking and then answering four questions:

1. What topics interest you?
2. What topics interest your listeners?
3. What topics develop from the occasion?
4. What topics develop from your research?

Your answers to these questions will help you devise a list of many topics from which you can then select the most appropriate.

SELF-GENERATED TOPICS

self-generated topics:
speech subjects based on the speaker's interests, experiences, and knowledge.

Discussion Prompt:
Have students complete the exercise described in this paragraph and then share some of the ideas they jotted down. One person's idea may trigger topic ideas for other students. In addition, students will learn more about their classmates, which should help them in their audience analysis.

Self-generated topics come from you—your memory, your notes, your interests, your experiences, and your personal files. Take out a sheet of paper and jot down your hobbies, your favorite courses, books you have read, your pet peeves, names of people who intrigue you, and issues and events that excite you. What are your likes and dislikes? On what topics do you consider yourself knowledgeable? Review your list, writing beside each item possible speech topics. If you enjoy listening to music, perhaps a speech on the history of jazz would be informative. If you are irritated by people who are late, you could inform your audience on why people procrastinate, or on how to set and meet goals. If you are uncomfortable in enclosed places, a speech on claustrophobia might interest you and your audience. If you are nearing graduation and have been reading books on how to land your first job, a speech on how to construct a résumé or the do's and don'ts for the employment interview may be fitting.

Self-generated topics may also include subjects you *need* to know. If, for example, you expect to travel soon and will be making your own arrangements for the first time, you may find yourself riding in taxis, staying in hotels, and dining in some good restaurants. You may be unsure as to tipping etiquette for cab drivers, baggage carriers, and waiters. Researching and delivering a speech on tipping will not only serve your needs but will also interest any of your listeners who might later find themselves in similar situations.

Consider the following topics generated by our students, using just their personal interests and knowledge:

Thinking about your own interests, hobbies, and experiences is one way to brainstorm for speech topics.

Aquariums, salt water
Bicycling
Black history in textbooks
Cancer, heredity as a risk factor
Colleges of the future
Extending the school year
Fashion illustration
Gardening, organic
Hazing
Henri de Toulouse-Lautrec, works of
Impressionism
Indian silver jewelry of the
 Southwest
Interior decorating
Learning disabilities
Leukemia, new treatments for
Parachuting, importance to military
Phobias, how to overcome
Photograph restoration
Physical therapy
Profile of typical student at this
 college
Sailing
Spelunking
T-shirt art
Water conservation.

You have a storehouse of information inside you. Use what you know as a starting point in your topic selection process. It is not important that you know enough about each topic at this stage to construct a speech. Research will help you later in focusing, developing, and supporting your topic. *What is important is that you have a list of possible topics that interest you.* Because these topics come from *your* knowledge, experience, and interests, your commitment to them is usually strong. You also have a head start in understanding the subject. Your interest and knowledge will motivate you in preparing your speech. In addition, your enthusiasm for your topic will enliven and enhance your speech delivery.

Self-generated topics can pose some difficulties for a speaker, however. If you become too involved with a topic, you cannot always develop it objectively. Researching your subject is a process of discovery. If you begin with rigid preconceptions, you may disregard important information that doesn't match your preconceived ideas.

When the time came to develop and deliver a persuasive speech for his public speaking class, Ken decided to try to persuade his classmates, most of them freshmen, that the legal drinking age should be lowered from twenty-one to eighteen. He was committed to this point of view. He had been mentally rehearsing his arguments since the day his state raised the legal drinking age to twenty-one: "If I'm old enough to register with Selective Service and defend my country, I'm old enough to drink if I care to." "If I'm old enough to marry without my parents' consent, I should be able to buy and consume any beverage I want."

Yet two days before his speech was due he asked his speech teacher for an extension. The reason, he explained, was that all of the published sources he had researched *supported* the increased legal drinking age. "Some of the sources even had graphs showing decreases in traffic fatalities among eighteen- to twenty-one-year-olds or reductions in juvenile crimes since the drinking age was raised," he complained. Ken's instructor prodded him, "If all the evidence says that the new law is a benefit in these ways, have you considered changing your view?" Ken's answer was "no." He remained sure that, given more time, he could find the evidence that supported his position.

Ken apparently had expected his research to show that raising the legal drinking age to twenty-one had not reduced traffic fatalities, or that it had actually increased them. If so, he was almost surely involved in a library snipe hunt; such evidence probably does not exist. But Ken's predicament is typical of people who form rigid expectations of what their research will reveal. In effect, Ken wore blinders that blocked out other ways of looking at his chosen topic. If, after doing some research, he still supported lowering the drinking age, Ken probably should have abandoned the traffic safety and juvenile crime issues altogether. Instead, he could have pursued those philosophical arguments he believed strongly. Then his primary argument could have been that society sends mixed messages by treating eighteen-year-olds as mature and responsible in many areas of life and irresponsible in others. Make sure you don't follow Ken's example. Wait until you gather some good supporting data before you commit yourself to a specific focus for your topic.

A second potential pitfall of self-generated topics is the use of jargon. If your topic is technical, you must be especially attentive to the language you choose to convey your meaning. The speaker in the following example forgot that advice.

Caryn, a pre-med student with a double major in biology and chemistry, found an interesting article that explained how some animals survive winter by freezing and then thawing in the spring.[3] She chose this as an informative speech topic and did further research. She reasoned correctly that many of her classmates wouldn't know of this phenomenon or how it occurs.

Yet most of her listeners knew they were in trouble when Caryn said in her introduction: "Today I want to explain how some animals such as the wood frog, the gray tree frog, painted turtles, and gallfly larvae use so-called anti-freeze proteins, ice-nucleating proteins, trehalose, proline, and cryoprotect-ants to maintain the integrity of cells while their extracellular fluid freezes." The audience never recovered. The remainder of her speech contained words and phrases such as colligative cryoprotectants, polyhydroxyl alcohols, cyto-plasm, and recrystallization.

Caryn's problem was not with her topic; indeed, it's a fascinating subject.

With simplified language and clear visual aids, she could have made the topic accessible to her listeners and drawn them into the speech. But the technical vocabulary and jargon she found understandable only confused and alienated most of her classmates. They assumed that the topic was over their heads, and, as presented by Caryn, it was. Remember that your speech on any technical topic will lose its intended impact if you fail to define key terms clearly for listeners less knowledgeable about the subject.

A final potential problem with self-generated topics results from a speaker's excessive devotion to the subject. This problem is closely linked to the first problem we discussed above, becoming too involved with the topic. You may choose as a topic an interest or hobby that has been a passion of yours for years. You probably feel great about this choice. You are enthusiastic about the topic, you already have a wealth of information on it, and doing further research will seem a pleasure rather than a chore. What could possibly go wrong?

"The audience will love this topic," you think. Be careful. Your audience may not share your enthusiasm for aardvarks. Likewise, if your hobby is restoring Studebaker cars and you assume that your listeners are already equally interested in this topic, you have likely analyzed the audience incorrectly. Your interest in a topic is just one criterion in the selection process; it should always be balanced with three other criteria we will discuss later in this chapter. For most topics, the speaker must also work to generate audience interest. We are not suggesting that you avoid self-generated topics of great interest to you. Just do not assume that your audience already has the same level of interest as you. Your audience may not initially share your enthusiasm for aardvarks (or Bob Marley or the history of fireworks or optical illusions), but if you *work* at it, you can *make* them interested. Be prepared to work hard to do so.

In addition, be prepared to listen openly to others' speeches. Remember that ethical listeners do not prejudge either a speaker or that speaker's ideas. We started this chapter with a reference to the Kopp study because we encounter a number of students who seem skeptical of any information that won't help them make the car payment. Granted, some topics seem so narrow or so offbeat that you can imagine thinking, "Who cares about aardvarks?" But can't you also imagine a *terrific* speech on aardvarks by a speaker who was genuinely interested in them and who had lots of vivid supporting material? So much education is important just because it makes you a better (smarter, happier, more well-rounded) person. Some information is intrinsically rewarding and just plain fun to know. Don't dismiss information presented in a speech (or anywhere else) just because it won't make you more money, save you time, or whiten your teeth.

AUDIENCE-GENERATED TOPICS

A second strategy for generating topics is **audience-oriented.** What topics are of interest or importance to your listeners? If you are asked to speak to a group, you are often asked because of your expertise in a particular area. Topic selection, in this case, may be predetermined.

On other occasions, such as in this class, you are not provided with topics or topic areas. How can you find out what interests your classmates? There are

audience-generated topics: speech subjects geared to the interests and needs of a speaker's listeners.

three ways to do this. *First, ask them.* In this class you might ask some of your classmates in casual conversation about topics they would like to hear discussed. If you are allowed the opportunity, you might also use a formal questionnaire to seek topic suggestions from the entire class. If you are speaking outside of class to an organization, ask the person who contacted you about issues of probable interest to the group.

Second, listen and read. What do your classmates discuss before and after class? Articles in your campus or local paper, or letters to the editor, may suggest issues of concern. *Finally, use the audience analysis strategies* detailed in Chapter 5 to generate topics. Consider your listeners' needs. If your class is composed primarily of students just entering college, a speech on the history of your school would be interesting, informative, and appropriate. If your class is composed primarily of seniors, a speech on establishing a good credit history may be timely.

You may even find that most members of your audience seem to feel one way about a controversial topic, while you take the opposite view. You may choose to use this situation to develop and deliver a persuasive speech aimed at winning support for your side of the issue.

The following topics were generated by our students using an audience-centered approach:

Career selection	Notetaking, how to improve
Coca-Cola, history of	Recycling
Country and western dancing	Self-defense for women
Date rape	Small businesses, how to start
Garage sales, how to have successful	Stress management
Goal setting	Study skills, improving
Graphology (handwriting analysis)	Superwoman syndrome
Horror movies, appeal of	Test anxiety, how to control
Interviewing skills	Time management
Interviews, dressing for	Tipping, guidelines for
Isometric exercise	Used cars, how to buy
Leadership skills, how to develop	Vitamins.
Life span, how to increase	

OCCASION-GENERATED TOPICS

A third source of topics is the **occasion.** *When* and *where* a speech is given may guide you in selecting a topic. For example, a speech on setting goals may benefit your classmates more at the beginning of the semester or quarter, whereas a speech on stress management may be particularly relevant preceding midterm or final examinations. A speech advocating the use of airbags may be especially effective if you deliver it just before your classmates head home for semester or spring break. A speech on the dangers of overexposure to the sun will have more impact if it is given in the spring or the summer rather than in the fall.

If you are scheduled to speak near a particular holiday, a speech on the history or importance of that holiday may be appropriate. If you have a speech scheduled on or near Victoria Day, for instance, you can take the opportunity to

*Special occasions, such
as the Annual Taos
Pueblo Powwow, provide
speakers excellent topics
for speeches.*

introduce your classmates to a part of Canadian history. To find examples of other holidays, look at your calendar, or examine different calendars at a book store. Often you can find specialty calendars or almanacs listing unusual but interesting holidays, birthdates of notable and notorious people, or anniversaries of important historical events. If you randomly opened *The World Almanac Fact-A-Day Calendar* to July 7, for example, you would find the following birthdays listed:

Marc Chagall, artist (1887);
George Cukor, film director (1899);
Gustav Mahler, composer (1860);
Satchel Paige, baseball player (1906); and
Ringo Starr, musician (1940).

This page of the calendar would also tell you that Satchel Paige was forty-two years old when his pitching helped the Cleveland Indians win the American League pennant in 1948, and that July 7 is the anniversary of the day in 1981 when President Reagan nominated Sandra Day O'Connor to be the first female Supreme Court justice. And if none of those names or events appealed to you or aroused your curiosity, you would be holding 364 other pages of possible occasion-generated speech topics!

We truly are a people who love to celebrate occasions, whether they are established national holidays or quirky, lesser-known designations. Many of these occasions can suggest possible speech topics. A speech detailing cable television's impact on the viewing habits of the American family would seem appropriately timed during National Cable Month. Banned Book Month might be the ideal occasion for a speech on censorship. Consider some of the possible speech topics suggested by the following: Women's History Month, National

Discussion Prompt:
Increasing numbers of African-American families are celebrating Kwanza, a six-day African celebration that begins on December 26th. Ask students for examples of other national, cultural, or religious holidays with which they may be familiar. For example, some may be familiar with the quinceañera, a party given for Hispanic girls on their fifteenth birthday.

Cigar Lovers Day, American Beer Week, International Left-Handers Day, National Pasta Week, Straw Hat Day, National Relaxation Day, American Chocolate Week, National Singles Week, and Mailbox Improvement Week. There are even months to celebrate ice cream, baked beans, and the hot dog.

Our students generated the following topics as they focused on different occasions for speeches:

Discussion Prompt:
Have your class brainstorm for other examples of seasonal occasions: grunion runs, the running of the bulls, or the return of the swallows to San Juan Capistrano.

Airline safety
All Saints Day
Bat mitzvah (female equivalent of bar mitzvah)
Dia de los Muertos
Eulogies, how to write
February, why it is the shortest month
Festival of the Lanterns
Fireworks, designing displays
Guy Fawkes Day
Halloween masks, how to make
Hanukkah
Hurricanes

Ides of March
Juneteenth
Mardi Gras
Parades, history of
Practical jokes
Punxsutawney Phil (Groundhog Day)
Ramadan
Rodeos, history of
Shrove Tuesday
Spring break activity ideas
Telethons, success of
Test-taking skills.

Note that an occasion-generated topic can often lead you to other interesting topic possibilities. Thinking about a current labor strike might spark your interest in the history of labor unions. From there you might decide to focus your informative speech on child labor. Drought conditions in your area might lead you to consider the subjects of cloud seeding or desalting sea water. The occasion of Memorial Day might get you thinking about The Wall, the Vietnam Veterans Memorial in Washington, D.C. You might then decide to focus on the competition for the design of the monument; on Maya Lin, whose design won that competition; or on the aesthetics of the wall and the stirring effect it has on visitors.

RESEARCH-GENERATED TOPICS

research-generated topics: speech subjects prompted by investigating a variety of print sources.

Discussion Prompt:
Bring in copies of a page from an index, or make a transparency of the page and display it on an overhead projector. Ask students to read the index entries and suggest topics they think would make excellent speeches for this class.

A fourth strategy for generating topics is **research,** and this may take several forms. First, you may consult indexes, such as *Readers' Guide to Periodical Literature* or any of the other indexes we list in Chapter 7. Look at the listing of subjects and jot down those that interest you. A second research strategy is to browse through some magazines or journals in the current periodical section of your library or at a local newsstand. Just remember that this exploration is the first step in selecting a speech topic. Don't leap at the first interesting topic you find, as Eric did in that earlier example. A third strategy for generating topics is to peruse book titles at a good bookstore, noting those that interest you. Bookstores are convenient places to discover speech topics because the books are grouped by general subject area and are arranged to catch your eye. By using these three research tools — indexes, magazines and journals, and books — you may not only discover a speech topic, but you may also locate your first source of information.

Consider the following topics. You might not have thought of these on your own, but they are all potentially excellent topics and came from resources our students found.

Adams, Ansel	Kites
Aerobic exercise videotapes, comparison of	Lying, why children do it
	Magic
Art work, airbrush	Malcolm X
Behavior modification	Marley, Bob
Brainwashing and POWs	Movies, how they are rated
Cholesterol, effects of	Mythology
Colors, how they affect mood	Nightmares
Computer crime	Nuclear medicine, future of
Computer-generated music	Photographs, composing good
Cooking, low-calorie	Pyramids, Aztec
Cosmetic surgery	Radio, history of
Cryonics	Rock music of the '60s
Dali, Salvador	Roller coasters
Disney, Walt	Softball, history of
Divorce, effects on children	Solar energy
Etymology	Spouse abuse
Food preservatives	Stonehenge
Genetic engineering	Subliminal messages
High-definition television	Teenage runaways
Hypochondria	Typography
Illiteracy	Western music, history of
Indian folklore	

Class Activity:
Have students bring a copy of a national, local, or campus newspaper to class. Have them brainstorm by skimming through the paper and recording possible speech topics.

Related Reading:
Grun, Bernard. *The Timetables of History.* New York: Simon-Touchstone, 1979. Students may find this book helpful as they brainstorm for topics, particularly for their informative speeches. Grun organizes approximately 30,000 moments from 5000 B.C. to the present into the following categories: history and politics; literature and theater; religion, philosophy, and learning; visual arts; music; science, technology, and growth; and daily life.

It is important for you to use all four of these strategies to generate possible speech topics. If you end your topic generation process too quickly, you limit your options. A substantive list of self-, audience-, occasion-, and research-generated topics gives you maximum flexibility in selecting a topic.

Once you have selected your topic area, we suggest that you use a technique called **visual brainstorming** to investigate the range of possibilities within that topic. Take out a sheet of paper and write your topic in the center. As you look at the topic, think of how you might divide and narrow it. It may help you to think of some generic categories such as "causes," "types," and "solutions" that are appropriate to numerous topics. As you think of subtopics, draw a line from the center in any direction and write the narrower topic.

visual brainstorming: informal written outlining achieved by free-associating around a key word or idea.

As your thinking suggests additional topics, continue your visual representation. In just a few minutes you will probably be surprised at the web of potential speech topics you have created just from your brainstorming. Figure 6.1 illustrates the end product of a visual brainstorming exercise on the topic of "pollution." Certainly, you can add to this list, but in just a few minutes we were able to provide several options for focusing the subject of pollution. Some of these, such as graffiti, are excellent topics that would probably not have come to mind without this brainstorming exercise.

You may incorporate library research into your discovery and focusing process. If you are considering the topic of phobias, consult indexes and see

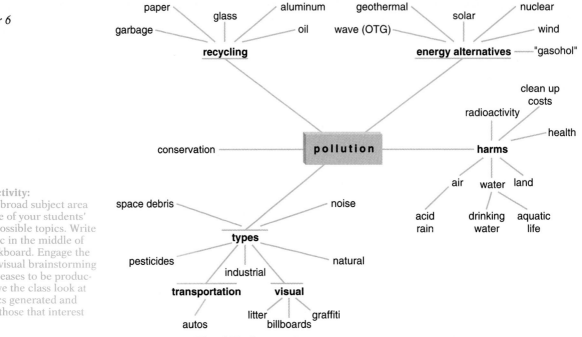

FIGURE 6.1 Visual Brainstorming

how they divide this topic. In just a few minutes, we generated a list of topic areas that included the following:

phobias (sources of fear)
   acrophobia (fear of high places)
   aerophobia (fear of flying)
   agoraphobia (fear of open spaces)
   ailurophobia (fear of cats)
   akousticophobia (fear of sounds)
   aquaphobia (fear of water)
   claustrophobia (fear of closed spaces)
   cynophobia (fear of dogs)
   entomophobia (fear of insects)
   gymnophobia (fear of nudity)
   hypnophobia (fear of sleep)
   logophobia (fear of words)
   mikrophobia (fear of germs)
   misophobia (fear of dirt, contamination)
   nyctophobia (fear of dark)
   ophiophobia (fear of snakes)
   phobophobia (fear of fears)
   phonophobia (fear of speaking aloud)
   pyrophobia (fear of fire)
   thanatophobia (fear of death)
   xenophobia (fear of strangers)

   zoophobia (fear of animals)
phobia predisposition
   biological processes
   learning processes
prevalence
   by age
   by sex
   by culture
treatment
   psychotherapy
   exposure therapy
   drug therapy
   systematic desensitization
diagnosis
panic-prone personality
panic attacks
fear
anxiety
symptoms
   dizziness
   rapid heart rate
   breathing difficulties

Some of these topics may be too narrow, but most would make excellent speech topics.

■ Selecting Your Topic ━━━━━━━━━━━━━━━━━━━━

Once you have generated a list of possible speech topics, you must then select the best one. Determining what is best is an individual choice; neither a classmate, a friend, nor your instructor can make that choice. However, you can apply some criteria to each of your options to help you make a wise selection.

Four questions should guide your choice of topics. First, *"Am I interested or likely to become interested in the topic?"* The more enthusiastic you are about a topic, the greater the time and attention you will give to researching, constructing, and practicing your speech. Speakers motivated by their topics are almost always more productive than those bored with their topics. They always have more fun, and if you enjoy learning, you will learn better.

Second, ask, *"Is the topic of interest or importance to my audience?"* This question helps you avoid choosing a topic you love but one your audience will never care about. Speech making is easier when your listeners are potentially interested in what you have to say. When your audience is more attentive and receptive, you can relax and make your delivery livelier. Sometimes, topics seem to be of little initial interest to audience members but may, nevertheless, be important to their personal or career success. As long as you can demonstrate the importance and relevance of the topic to them, you will motivate your audience to listen.

A third question you should answer in selecting your speech topic is, *"Am I likely to find sufficient authoritative supporting material in the time allotted for researching and developing the speech?"* Rarely do students select topics so narrow that they cannot find sufficient accessible information. You may, however, select a topic so recent that your library has not yet received adequate information. Often, because of your research deadline, you cannot obtain information on your topic through the mail. Occasionally, students contact us just before their speeches are scheduled and tell us that they are unable to complete their speeches because information they ordered has not arrived. That's usually a sign that the student's research started too late or progressed too slowly. In researching your speech, remember the adage that if something can go wrong, it will. Build some flexibility into your schedule so that you can adapt to any crisis that may arise.

Finally, a speaker must also consider the question, *"Do I have an understanding of the topic necessary to undertake and interpret my research?"* A speaker arguing the merits of a tax increase must have an understanding of economics in order to assess research data. A speaker informing the audience about music therapy needs some understanding of psychological treatment techniques and procedures. A speaker may misinterpret the reasons that violent crime in the United States is higher than in Japan if he or she does not understand Japanese culture. You may not need to know much about your topic as you begin your research, but you must know enough to be able to make sense of the data you discover.

1. Does this topic interest me or have the potential to do so?
2. Is this topic interesting or important to my listeners?
3. Am I likely to find sufficient supporting materials on this topic?
4. Do I know enough about this topic to start researching it and to interpret what I discover?

■ Focusing Your Topic

Once you have selected your topic, your next job is to focus it. Even though we have heard students speak on topics that were too narrow, this is rare. More commonly, students fail to narrow their topics sufficiently, leaving too little time to develop the ideas. The result is a speech that is more surface than substance.

When you decide on a topic area, use visual brainstorming to determine some of its divisions, or subtopics. The subject of "loneliness," for example, could focus on any of the following topics: the causes of loneliness, the relationship between loneliness and depression, loneliness and the elderly, loneliness as a cause of teenage suicide, characteristics of the lonely person, the differences between being alone and being lonely, or strategies for coping with loneliness. It is impossible to discuss all of these topics meaningfully in a short speech. Narrowing the scope of your inquiry gives direction to your research and allows you sufficient time to support the ideas you will present to your audience.

Visual brainstorming is an excellent way of focusing your topic. A second way is through research. The more you read about your topic, the more you will likely discover its many dimensions. Some may be too narrow for a complete speech, but others may be suitable for an entire speech or may be combined to form a speech.

For a five-to-seven-minute informative speech assignment, Rob developed three main points in the body of his speech on baseball:

  I. The history of baseball
 II. How the game is played
III. The uniform and equipment used

As you might guess, Rob found himself rushing through the speech, and he still did not finish it within the time limit. You probably noticed that each of his main points is too broad. Rob's problem was that he needed to focus his topic further.

If he was really most interested in the history of baseball, or if his research had revealed a great deal of information on baseball's history, Rob might have focused on a specific era. For example, he could have surprised and enlightened his listeners by discussing baseball during the Civil War. Or he could have focused on the all-black leagues operating from the 1920s until the integration of baseball during the 1950s. He could have spoken about the All-American Girl's Baseball League formed during World War II when many professional baseball players were being drafted. Each of these topics would probably have interested and informed Rob's listeners, regardless of their fondness for baseball. Since each of these narrower topics also places baseball in a sociological context, a speech on the history of baseball becomes a lesson in a particular period of American history and thus has broader appeal for listeners.

■ Determining Your General Purpose _____

Broadly speaking, a speech may have one of three purposes: to inform, to persuade, or to entertain. The general purpose of your speech defines your relationship with the audience. You play the role of mentor when you provide information. You are an advocate when you seek to change beliefs, attitudes, values, or behaviors through a persuasive speech. Your speech to entertain is meant to amuse your audience. As the entertainer, you set a mood to relax your audience through your delivery style, tone, and content.

You may find it difficult at times to distinguish these purposes. Since information may affect both what we believe and how we act, the distinction between informative speaking and persuasive speaking is sometimes particularly blurred. A speech to entertain is frequently persuasive because it may make a serious point through the use of humor. Despite the overlap between these general purposes, you must be secure about your primary purpose any time you speak in public. A closer look at the objectives and intended outcomes of each general purpose will help you distinguish them.

SPEECHES TO INFORM

A **speech to inform** has as its objective to impart knowledge to an audience. You convey this information in an objective and unbiased manner. Your goal is not to alter the listeners' attitudes or behaviors but to facilitate their understanding of your subject and their ability to retain this new information. A speech on any of the following topics could be informative:

The history of photography	Shopping addiction
The teddy bear	The Hispanic film industry
Storytelling	The right and left hemispheres of the
The middle child syndrome	brain.
Surrealism in painting	

speech to inform: a speech designed to convey new and/or useful information in a balanced, objective way.

SPEECHES TO PERSUADE

A **speech to persuade** seeks to influence either beliefs or actions. The former, sometimes called a **speech to convince,** focuses on audience beliefs and attitudes. A speech designed to persuade to belief stops short of advocating specific action. A speaker might argue, for example, that violence on television is harmful to some children without suggesting a specific plan of action. Another example is a speaker who tries to convince listeners of the need for government subsidy of rural health care.

A speech designed to persuade to action, or a **speech to actuate,** attempts to change not only the listeners' beliefs and attitudes, but also their behavior. Persuading others to vote for a ballot proposition, to draft and sign a living will,

speech to persuade: a speech designed to influence listeners' beliefs and/or actions.

speech to convince: a persuasive speech designed to influence audience beliefs and attitudes rather than their behaviors.

speech to actuate: a persuasive speech designed to influence audience behaviors.

to boycott a controversial art exhibit, to contribute money to a charity, or to enroll in a specific course are all examples of speeches to actuate. In each of these cases, the speaker's first goal would be to intensify or alter the audience's beliefs, and then to show how easy and beneficial taking action could be.

SPEECHES TO ENTERTAIN

A third general purpose of speech is to entertain. A speech to entertain differs from speaking to entertain. **Speaking to entertain** is a general phrase covering several types of speaking. It includes humorous monologues, stand-up comedy routines, and storytelling, for example. When you tell your friends jokes or recount a humorous anecdote, you are trying to entertain them. You are probably not trying to develop a key point in an organized, methodical way.

speech to entertain: a speech designed to make a point through the creative, organized use of humorous supporting materials.

A **speech to entertain** is one particular type of speaking to entertain. It is more formal than speaking to entertain because it is more highly organized and its development is more detailed. Speeches to entertain are often delivered on occasions when people are in a festive mood, such as after a banquet or as part of an awards ceremony. For that reason, we discuss the speech to entertain in more detail in Chapter 17, Speaking on Special Occasions (see pages 374–377). Remember that *all speeches*, including those to entertain, should develop a central thought through an organized presentation of supporting material and ideas. Though the ideas in a speech to entertain will be illustrated and high-lighted by humor, a mere collection of jokes does not qualify as a speech. Because of this, we agree with the communication scholars who contend that a speech to entertain is actually either a speech to inform or a speech to persuade, usually the latter.

■ Formulating Your Specific Purpose

general purpose: the broad goal of a speech, such as to inform, to persuade, or to entertain.

When you are asked to state the **general purpose** of your speech, you will respond with two words from among the following: "to inform," "to persuade" (or "to convince" or "to actuate"), or "to entertain." When asked to state your specific purpose, however, you will need to be more descriptive. A *specific purpose* statement has three parts.

**KEY POINTS
To Develop Your
Specific Purpose
Statement**

1. State your general purpose.
2. Name your intended audience.
3. State the goal of your speech.

First, you begin with the general purpose of the speech, stated as an infini-tive; for example, "to convince." Second, you name the individuals to whom the speech is addressed. This is usually phrased simply as "the audience" or "my listeners." Third, you state what you want your speech to accomplish. What should the audience *know*, what should they *believe*, or what should they *do* as a result of your speech? You may want to establish the belief that alcoholism is hereditary. In this example, then, the complete **specific purpose statement** would be: "To convince the audience that alcoholism is hereditary." A speech advocating compulsory national service for all U.S. citizens might have this as its specific purpose: to persuade the audience to write Congress urging the passage of a compulsory national service program. Other examples of specific purpose statements are:

To inform the audience on how to communicate constructive criticism.
To convince the audience that laughter is medically therapeutic.
To convince the audience of the value of a liberal arts education.
To convince the audience that aspartame is harmful.
To convince the audience that hypnotherapy is a credible treatment procedure.
To convince the audience that "men only" social clubs inherently discriminate
    against businesswomen.

specific purpose: a statement of the general purpose of the speech, the speaker's intended audience, and the limited goal or outcome.

Class Activity:
Have students, individually or in groups, work through the three steps of developing a specific purpose statement. They may use topics from any of the lists in this chapter, topics you have prepared, or they may generate topics themselves. Make sure that they write specific purpose statements for both informative and persuasive speech topics.

■ Wording Your Thesis Statement _____

A **thesis statement** is the central idea of the speech. It is a one-sentence synopsis of your speech. Although we discuss it in this chapter, a thesis statement, like the specific purpose, is usually constructed *after* you have finished your initial research and as you decide on your key ideas. The thesis statement of the persuasive speech on compulsory national service, mentioned above, might be this: "Compulsory national service would benefit the nation by promoting the national spirit, promoting the national defense, and promoting the national welfare." This statement is the central idea of the speech, a proposition the speaker will support with evidence and argument.

    Notice that the process of topic selection has, up to this point, enabled you to focus your subject on something specific and manageable. You have a handle on your subject and, as you begin to develop your key ideas, you will be able to determine whether you can support your thesis statement. In organizing the body of the speech, you may realize that your ideas are not balanced or that two of your main points should be collapsed into one. As you research your speech, you may discover additional ideas that are more important than some you had planned to present. That was the experience of our student who spoke on compulsory national service.

    Stuart was developing a persuasive speech advocating a system of compulsory national service (CNS). As he began his research, he planned to focus only on the national security that compulsory military service would provide. He imagined that his thesis statement would be, "Compulsory national service would benefit the nation by ensuring its military readiness." Yet his research quickly revealed many other benefits of CNS.

    Some programs of compulsory national service that have been proposed include a domestic volunteer service that would address issues other than military readiness. For example, Stuart learned that such a program could help conservation and recycling efforts. By training doctors' assistants, CNS could extend quality health care into rural areas. CNS could serve millions of elderly people who need only light assistance in order to be able to live independently in their own homes.

thesis statement: a one-sentence synopsis of a speaker's message.

By the time he had completed his research, Stuart had broadened the focus of his speech and felt he had developed a much stronger case for instituting a CNS program. When he delivered his speech, he presented three main arguments:

  I. CNS would promote the national spirit.
 II. CNS would promote the national defense.
III. CNS would promote the national welfare.

Stuart made certain to revise his thesis statement to reflect his new organization. Remember, you will also need to modify your thesis statement any time you revise the content and structure of your speech.

The following examples illustrate how you can narrow a topic's focus, from a general topic area to a statement of the speech's thesis statement.

Topic area: Hypnosis
Topic: Clinical hypnosis
General purpose: To inform
Specific purpose: To inform the audience of therapeutic uses of clinical hypnosis
Thesis statement: Clinical hypnosis is used to treat post-traumatic stress disorders, sexual dysfunction, and chronic smoking.

Topic area: Surgery
Topic: Elective cosmetic surgery
General purpose: To persuade
Specific purpose: To persuade the audience of the harms of elective cosmetic surgery
Thesis statement: Elective cosmetic surgery leaves physical scars, psychological scars, and financial scars.

■ Developing Your Speech Title

Some speeches do not require titles. Many public speaking instructors, for example, do not insist that their students develop and announce a title before they deliver their speeches in class. In most formal public speaking situations, however, the audience knows the speaker and topic beforehand. The title is often included in a printed program or mentioned by the person introducing the speaker. Therefore, whenever you have the opportunity, you should give a title to all your speeches, including your classroom speeches.

A well-crafted title accomplishes three purposes. First, it generates audience interest in your speech. Similar to a television station's teaser or promotion of an upcoming program, a speech title should arouse interest, secure attention, and make the audience want to listen. By appealing to the needs and interests of your audience, a title can encourage active listening.

Interesting titles may also enhance your image as a communicator and make the audience want to listen to you specifically. If you are speaking to an audience that does not know you, your title may generate the audience's first impression of you. Creative titles engender more interest than general, technical, or overused ones. Which speech would you be more interested in hearing:

one titled "Job Burnout" or one with the title "Making Your Work Relaxing and Rewarding"?

A second purpose of a title is to make your message more memorable. While there is a "up" side to creativity, you should avoid the temptation of selecting a title simply for the sake of creativity. If in the process you sacrifice clarity, you may actually divert audience attention from your central thesis. Remember, when you encapsulate the point of your speech in the title, you prepare the audience to listen for its development or to use it as a reference point when they explain to others what you discussed.

If you study print advertisements you will see that they use this strategy quite successfully. The headline usually contains a selling promise designed to capture the attention of those likely to buy the product or service. Speech titles such as "Converting Anger to Action" or "Making Your Anger Work for You" are clear and direct. A person who frequently experiences anger can expect to learn how that negative emotion can become a positive option. These titles identify the audience (those who experience anger) and include a promise (anger can work for you). A speech describing the healing nature of the grieving process, for example, might be titled simply "Good Grief!" The title is short, attention-getting, and easy to remember, and it highlights the concept that grief can be good.

The following are titles of speeches printed in *Vital Speeches*. You probably have an idea what each speech is about even though you have not heard or read them.

"In Allegiance to the Truth: News, Ethics and Split-Personality Journalism"
"I Touch the Future: I Teach"

"Dirty Business: Money Laundering and the War on Drugs"
"America's Telecommunications: Back to the Future . . . Or Back to the Drawing Board?"

If you accomplish the objectives of securing your listeners' interest and enhancing the memorability of your key ideas *before* you utter your first word, you have gone a long way toward ensuring the success of your speech.

A third and final benefit of a good speech title is primarily for you, the speaker. Giving your speech a title forces you to state the point of your speech clearly and concisely. If you have difficulty constructing a title that encapsulates your key ideas, your speech probably lacks a clear central thought, or else you have strayed from your intended thesis. Discovering this before you speak gives you time to adjust your speech accordingly.

There is no one best way to develop a title for a speech, but consider these three options. First, if your speech contains a key phrase or sentence that is used repeatedly, that statement may be your title. This was the case in Martin Luther King, Jr.'s "I Have a Dream" speech, reprinted in Appendix C. That title captures a key theme of the speech in one phrase. A speech arguing the harm of casual, elective plastic surgery for the sole purpose of making a person feel more beautiful might be titled, "Making Stars, Leaving Scars." The title contrasts the search for physical beauty with the scars it may leave behind. The use of rhyme makes the title easy to remember.

A second option for developing a speech title is to promise your audience something beneficial. A speech on the benefits of exercise might be titled:

Class Activity:
Divide your class into small groups and have them complete all or part of Exercise 5 at the end of this chapter. Have groups report their suggested titles to the entire class. Discuss the strengths and weaknesses of each title.

Class Activity:
Appendix C includes untitled student speeches by William Fort and Shelley Schnathorst. Assign your students to read one of the speeches and develop a title for it.

"Living Longer, Feeling Better." A variation of this approach is the "how to" strategy, commonly used in titles of self-improvement and craft books. It is appropriate when you know the audience is interested in acquiring a skill you can deliver. "How You Can Pass This Course Without Spending Any More Time Studying" may not be the most creative title for a speech, but we bet you and your classmates would listen to it!

Finally, a third strategy is to word your title as a question. A speech investigating laughter therapy might be titled, "Is Laughter Really the Best Medicine?" Posing this question signals to the audience what they will know by the end of the speech. Listeners expect to be able to answer the question. We remember one speech professor who titled a speech convention paper on the effects of humor, "Can Humor Increase Persuasion, or Is It All a Joke?" The title used humor because the paper was about humor, and the fact that we still remember the title attests to its effectiveness.

Summary

By selecting topics for their speeches, students in public speaking classes determine the majority of what they will hear during the course. Six steps can simplify the important process of choosing an appropriate speech topic.

First, brainstorm a list of potential topics focused around your own interests, the needs and interests of your audience, and the occasion for your speech. Your research adds a fourth category of possible topics. Having a large list of subjects gives you the freedom and flexibility to make an appropriate selection.

The second step is to select your topic. Making this decision is easier if you ask yourself four questions while reviewing your topic list: "Am I already interested or likely to become interested in this topic as I develop the speech?" "Is the topic already interesting or important to my audience, or can I interest them in it?" "Am I likely to find adequate, quality supporting materials on this topic in the time I have?" And "Do I know enough about the topic to start researching it and to interpret what I discover?"

The third step is to focus or narrow the subject you've selected. Two ways to accomplish this are visual brainstorming and initial research on the topic. Focusing the topic is important in guiding your research and helping you stay within the time limit for the speech.

The fourth step is to determine your general purpose: to inform, to persuade, or to entertain. The general purpose may be predetermined, as in most classroom speech assignments, or left to the judgment of the speaker. Whether you are determining the purpose or just reminding yourself of it, having that goal clearly in mind will keep you on target as you research and organize the speech.

The fifth step of selecting a topic is to formulate your specific purpose. That statement should specify three things: the general purpose in infinitive form ("to inform," for example), the intended audience, and what you want your listeners to know, believe, or do as a result of your speech.

The sixth step, wording your thesis statement, means distilling the message of the speech into one sentence. This step must come last, since it depends upon your initial research and tentative organization of the speech. With the thesis statement in mind, a speaker is ready to conduct in-depth research and proceed with the development of the speech.

A possible final step, not always required, is to title the speech. Creative, provocative titles achieve three goals. First, they intrigue the audience and make them want to listen to you. Second, they make your message more memorable. Third, they help speakers check to see that the speech has a central focus or thesis.

Exercises

1. On a sheet of paper list eight self-generated, eight audience-generated, eight occasion-generated, and fifteen research-generated topics. Place an "I" by the topics you would develop as informative speeches, and a "P" by those that are persuasive. Place an asterisk (*) by five informative topics and five persuasive topics you think would make the best speeches. Bring your list to class. Meeting in small groups, share your list with your classmates, having them decide the five best topics in each category. Now review your list and decide the topics on which you would like to speak.
2. Choose a topic area and use the technique of visual brainstorming to generate a list of specific topics. Continue diagramming as long as it is productive. Now look at your list and select those that you think are probably the best topics for a speech in this class.
3. Using the topic areas listed below, narrow each subject and write a specific purpose statement for an informative speech and a persuasive speech on each topic.
   a. Fast food   **b.** Funerals   **c.** Illiteracy   **d.** Stress   **e.** UFOs
4. Select and read a speech in Appendix C. Determine its general purpose. Word its specific purpose and thesis statement.
5. Construct at least two titles for a speech on each of the specific purposes listed below. Word the title so that it attracts audience interest or captures the central idea of the speech.
   a. To inform the audience on how to interpret their dreams.
   b. To inform the audience on how the stock market works.
   c. To inform the audience on the history of Valentine's Day.
   d. To inform the audience on the problems of being a single parent.
   e. To persuade the audience of the benefits (or the hazards) of nuclear energy.
   f. To persuade the audience that professional boxing should be outlawed.
   g. To persuade the audience to get involved in campus government.
   h. To persuade the audience that IQ tests are culturally biased.

Notes

1. Hunter S. Thompson, *Generation of Swine: Tales of Shame and Degradation in the '80s* (New York: Vintage, 1989) 209.

2. Patrick Murphy, "Chronobiology: For Athletes It's a Matter of Time," *The Physician and Sportsmedicine* September 1984: 160. Murphy discusses the Cubs and chronobiology in his article on pages 160–62, 164.

3. Kenneth B. Storey and Janet M. Storey, "Frozen and Alive," *Scientific American* December 1990: 92–97.

Researching Your Topic 7

Assess Personal Knowledge

Develop a Research Plan

Collect Your Information
Magazines and Journals
Newspapers
Government Documents
Books
Reference Works
  Dictionaries
  Encyclopedias
  Almanacs
  Yearbooks

  Books of Quotations
Interviews
  Prepare for the Interview
  Conduct the Interview
  Follow Up on the Interview
Writing and Calling for Information
Electronic Media

Record Information
What to Record
How to Record Information

Evaluate Information

"Knowledge is of two kinds. We know a subject ourselves, or we know where we can find information upon it."

SAMUEL JOHNSON

*T*HIS year more than 50,000 books will be published in the United States.[1] Add to this millions of pages of information printed in newspapers, magazines, and other periodicals; volumes of public and private agencies' reports, hearings, and pamphlets; and hours of news and opinions broadcast through television and radio. These print and electronic media have given us access to an explosion of knowledge and opinion. As a result, public speakers can no longer complain about a lack of information. Instead, the challenge confronting public speakers today is to select from this glut of data the information appropriate for their speeches.

In Chapter 6 we discussed how to select a topic. Once you select your topic, you must research it. **Research** is the gathering of evidence and arguments you will need to understand, develop, and explain your subject. It is important to remember that research is not one step of the speech construction process; rather it occurs, or should occur, throughout the process. For example, we have already seen in Chapter 6 how research may initially assist you in selecting your topic. Once you have decided on your topic for certain, additional research will help you focus it and determine your specific purpose. As you move to the next step and begin to construct the body of your speech, you may discover that some

research: the process of gathering evidence and arguments to understand, develop, and explain a speech topic.

"Who is the fairest one of all, and state your sources!"

Drawing by Ed Fisher; © 1984 The New Yorker Magazine, Inc.

of your ideas need further development and support. More directed research is then in order. Your research continues even as you consult dictionaries, thesauruses, and books of quotations to help you word the ideas of your speech before you deliver it in class.

Students often wonder how much research to conduct for a classroom speech. There is no one answer to this question. You should research your topic until you have enough authoritative evidence that you can make an informative or a persuasive statement to your listeners. As the *New Yorker* cartoon suggests, you need to back up your ideas with credible sources. Your instructor may specify a minimum number of sources you are to cite during your speech. Does that mean your research is finished when you have reached that magic number? The answer is, "not necessarily." Sometimes the information you have collected may be insufficient to support your intended central idea, or it may even be contradictory. If additional research does not correct this, you should consider shifting your focus or changing your topic altogether. Research can also lead you to discover new aspects of your subject that you had not considered, but which are more worthwhile to pursue than your original topic. The excellent public speaker, then, does not view research as a phase preceding the construction of the speech, but as an evolving process. We research so that excellent evidence supports excellent ideas that can, in turn, be excellently organized and delivered.

Occasionally, if you are lucky, you may stumble onto one or two sources of great help as you craft your speech. But most of the time you need to be prepared for the hard work of good research to ensure that you collect the information pertinent to your topic. Although your research strategy will depend on your topic and the available research facilities, the following general five-step sequence will assist you in generating excellent ideas and supporting material, regardless of the topic of your speech.

1. Assess your personal knowledge of the topic.
2. Develop your research plan.
3. Collect your information.
4. Record your information.
5. Evaluate your information.

Let us look more closely at each of these steps.

■ Assess Personal Knowledge ─────────────

Samuel Johnson was correct in noting that personal knowledge is the starting point of research. The first question you should ask and answer is, "What do I know that will help me develop my topic?" When you begin your research, do not make the mistake of confining yourself only to library holdings. You are an individual whose memory has been shaped by what you have read, heard, observed, and experienced. Use that knowledge as a starting point for researching your topic.

As we discussed in the preface of this book, our concept of mastering public speaking argues for an ongoing commitment to public communication, and,

Class Activity:
Have students make a list of subjects on which they feel especially qualified to speak. In developing this list, students should ask the following questions: Do I have greater knowledge and expertise in this area than my listeners do? Is this expertise sufficient to support the ideas of my speech? If not, where can I find additional information?

certainly, establishing a personal information base is important for any speaker who wants to be informed and credible. You already have a great deal of personal knowledge. Don't be afraid to tap this resource as you select and develop your speech topic. For example, a student who worked as a plain-clothes security guard for a major department store drew from personal experience in his speech on detecting and apprehending shoplifters. A student who assisted her father in administering polygraph tests chose as her speech topic the use and misuse of lie detectors. A person whose hobby was playing the bagpipes informed his audience on the history of this musical instrument. A vegetarian decided to persuade others to consider her diet. These speakers used their personal knowledge and experiences as starting points for their research. Each developed and delivered an interesting speech.

Throughout your life you will occasionally, perhaps often, be called upon to share your expertise and opinions with others in public speeches. Having a personal filing system will help you retrieve information as you prepare your remarks. We have found three kinds of files helpful in constructing our speeches: a "clipping" file, a quotation file, and a speech file.

clipping file: a collection of newspaper or magazine articles a speaker finds interesting or important.

A **"clipping" file** gives you a head start in selecting a topic and researching your speech. This file includes informative articles cut or copied from newspapers and magazines on topics of interest to you. When you read a provocative passage in a book or an interesting magazine article, photocopy it, record the complete source citation on the photocopy, and file it in a labeled folder. When you are asked to speak to a group, consult your "clipping" file for possible topics appropriate to the occasion and audience.

quotation file: a collection of passages a speaker finds memorable or important, together with the source citation for each passage.

A second useful file is a **quotation file.** Many good books of quotations that are available in the reference section of your library or local bookstore can assist you in wording and explaining your speech. (See a partial list on page 134.) You may also find it helpful to begin generating your own collection of quotations. When you read or hear a memorable statement, copy it and the name of the speaker or writer onto a 3-inch-by-5-inch notecard, putting the card in a filebox. As your collection grows, you can divide the quotations into categories. When preparing your speech, consult your file for statements that illustrate or highlight your ideas.

Quotations can also serve as excellent attention-getting or concluding statements. For example, Jodi began her speech with the statement: "'Memory,' it has been said, 'is the power to gather roses in winter.'" She used that quotation to underpin her thesis that the tragedy of Alzheimer's disease is that by destroying memory, it eliminates one's past. We have also heard several students urge their listeners to action by paraphrasing Edmund Burke: "The only thing necessary for the triumph of evil is for good [people] to do nothing."

speech file: a personal collection of materials about the research, preparation, and delivery of speeches completed or initiated.

A third file, the **speech file,** contains a folder for each speech you have given or have started to prepare. After you present a speech to one audience, a listener may ask you to speak on the same topic to another group. If you have saved your speaking notes, you have also saved yourself valuable research and preparation time. In addition to your speaking notes or manuscript, this file should also include your research notes. You may want to refocus your topic to adapt to the new audience. Such revisions are greatly simplified if you can review your original research notes and articles. It is important to remember, however, that every student speaker should research and develop his or her own speech. One speaker's files should never be used by another speaker to construct a speech.

Winston Churchill was once asked how long he had prepared for one of his speeches. He replied, "For forty years." In discussing this incident, Robert Jeffrey and Owen Peterson observe, "In a sense, a speaker spends his entire life preparing for a speech. Everything that he has learned, the experiences he has had, and the attitudes he has developed all shape and influence the speech."[2] Your knowledge and personal files give you a head start in selecting and developing your topic.

■ Develop a Research Plan

Someone once posed this question: "If you don't know where you're going, how will you know when you get there?" An experienced explorer focuses on a destination. A detailed plan of action and appropriate tools are prerequisites to reaching the target. Similarly, speakers should develop a research plan and marshal the tools necessary to achieve their targets — well-presented speeches. Constructing your research plan begins as you answer several questions:

1. What information do I need?
2. Where am I most likely to find it?
3. How can I obtain this information?
4. How will time constraints affect my research options?

Teaching Strategy:
Once students have tentatively selected a topic for a speech, have them answer each of these four questions.

Your research plan depends, in large part, on your topic and specific purpose. As we mentioned earlier, many speech topics require library research. Topics such as the electronic encyclopedia, mathematical illiteracy, environmental racism, or the history of graffiti would rely heavily on library resources. Other speech topics may rely on personal interviews for most of their information. If, for example, your purpose is to inform your classmates of your school's new registration procedures, your library may be of little assistance. More helpful would be an interview with your college's registrar. A speech explaining new breakthroughs in cancer research may benefit from writing to the American Cancer Society and soliciting information it has compiled. In short, different topics demand different research strategies. A good research plan accounts for these differences.

Not only should you prepare a list of what you need and where you can obtain it, you should also prepare a timetable for constructing your speech. If you are going to speak two weeks from now, you still have time to go to the library and work. You may even have time to set up an interview with an expert, conduct it, and transcribe key quotations. You probably do not have time to write for information and be assured of its arrival in time to integrate it into your speech.

Although you should explore all appropriate options, most of your research will probably take place in your college or community library. One of the most helpful sources of information to assist you in creating your research plan is also one of the least often used: the library staff, particularly those in the reference department. A good reference librarian will assist you in three ways: (1) by acquainting you with the services and holdings of the library, (2) by guiding you to particular sources of information helpful for your research, and (3) by instructing you in the use of library equipment.

Although all libraries have much in common, each is organized to serve its specific constituency. No college library can subscribe to all periodicals and newspapers, for example. It is a waste of your time to copy index citations for periodicals that are not in your library. Your reference librarian is familiar with your library and can guide you to its areas of strength, thus making your research more efficient.

Learning to use a library is similar in some respects to learning to drive a car. A good driver learns driving principles, is familiar with the automobile, and receives qualified instruction before "soloing." The driver's goal is not to remain dependent on the instructor but to become proficient so that he or she can venture out alone. Similarly, the effective researcher learns research principles, is familiar with the library, and solicits guidance toward the goal of becoming proficient in developing a research plan. If pursued aggressively, that research plan will result in a well-researched speech.

■ Collect Your Information ——————————————

Once you have developed a research plan, begin to collect the information you need to understand and develop your topic. Students who complain, "I can't find any information on my topic," usually do not know where to look. For most

The modern college library uses computer terminals to retrieve electronic data bases helpful in researching your speech.

Teaching Strategy:
If your library conducts orientation sessions, schedule one for each of your public speaking classes. After the librarian finishes the presentation, assign each student a research question such as the ones in Exercise 5 at the end of this chapter.

Teaching Strategy:
If available, get a copy of diagrams of your school's library, complete with floor plans and notations of holdings locations. White out key areas such as the reference section, index locations, and government documents. Then photocopy and distribute these diagrams to your class. Have students go to the library and write the names of the appropriate holdings in the blank areas on the diagram. This assignment is designed to familiarize students with the physical layout of their library, thus breaking down one barrier to their research.

topics, your library probably has more information than you can locate and read in the time allotted for your research. If you have developed a good research strategy, you will make efficient use of the following resources in generating the information you need to prepare your speech.

It is impossible to detail in this chapter all, or even most, of the resources available to you. We will confine ourselves to magazines and journals, newspapers, government documents, books, reference works, and alternate research sources. These resources will provide most of the background information you will need. For the serious researcher we also recommend Lois Horowitz's book, *Knowing Where to Look: The Ultimate Guide to Research*, an excellent introduction to where and how to find information.[3]

Practice Speaking:
Prepare a list of specific reference sources (indexes, encyclopedias, dictionaries), including some you know your library does not carry. List at least as many sources as you have students in class. Cut the list into slips of paper and have each student draw one. At the beginning of the next class, each student is to act as a docent, explaining briefly whether the library has the source, exactly where it is located, and what a typical entry looks like. Instruct those whose sources are not in your library to find the name of the closest library that does carry the source.

Class Activity:
To encourage students not only to know magazine titles but also to be able to evaluate their approach to reporting information, assign Exercise 1 at the end of this chapter here.

MAGAZINES AND JOURNALS

Articles in **magazines** and **journals** are probably the most common source of information for student speeches. A resource volume to acquaint you with possibilities for research is *Magazines for Libraries*. This resource provides an annotated listing of 6,500 periodicals, organizing them into 135 subject areas. A sample of these subjects follows:

Aging	Law	Robotics
Agriculture	Medicine and Health	Science
Business	Music	Sports
Civil Liberties	News and Opinion	Transportation
Education	Peace	
Humor	Religion	

Even when you narrow your topic to one of these subjects, you will probably find a list of magazines that is unmanageably long. Take, for example, the topic Medicine and Health. *Magazines for Libraries* lists over 130 periodicals for this entry. How do you keep from being overwhelmed with information? One strategy is to use the list as you narrow your topic choices. For example, two publications are listed under the subheading Arthritis. You could research these two periodicals, narrowing your speech topic further.

A second strategy for filtering useful from extraneous information is to use an index. Several excellent indexes of periodicals exist, and many of the standard paper indexes are now available in compact disk or magnetic tape versions. These indexes can guide you as you focus your search even more. The most commonly used index for researching magazines is the *Readers' Guide to Periodical Literature*, now more than ninety years old. Organized according to author and subject and published every other week, this resource is especially useful because it references more than 200 U.S. publications, including those most frequently found in libraries. You will find the subject index particularly useful, as it specifies articles pertaining to your subject area written during a designated time period. Look at the sample entries and their explanation in Figure 7.1.[4]

Another useful index is the *Public Affairs Information Service (PAIS) Bulletin*, which indexes articles from periodicals as well as selected books, government publications, pamphlets, and reports of public and private agencies.

Another research tool is the *Magazine Index*, a guide to magazine articles

Teaching Strategy:
Even narrower in its focus than the *Reader's Guide to Periodical Literature* is the *Popular Periodicals Index*, which indexes titles not included in the *Readers' Guide*. This resource may be helpful for regional topics because it references magazines not commonly found in other indexes. Magazines represented in this index include, for example, *Texas Monthly, Chicago, Ohio Magazine, Philadelphia Magazine,* and *Southern Magazine.*

Sample subject entry	SPACE RESEARCH Back to the future [meaning of successful Discovery launch] M.D. Lemonick. il *Discover* 10:42- 3+ Ja '89
Explanation	An article on the subject SPACE RESEARCH entitled "Back to the future," by Michael D. Lemonick, will be found, with illustrations, in the periodical *Discover*, volume 10, pages 42-43 (continued on pages of the same issue) in the January 1989 issue. A title enhancement, "meaning of successful Discovery launch," has been added by the indexer to clarify the meaning of the title. Square brackets are used to indicate these editorial interpolations.
Sample name entry	SMITH GARY Dear Mike . . . il pors *Sports Illustrated* 70:58-64+ F 27'89 *about* From the publisher. D. J. Barr. il por *Sports Illustrated* 70:1 F 27 '89
Explanation	An article *by* Gary Smith will be found in *Sports Illustrated*, volume 70, pages 58-64 (continued on later pages of the same issue) in the February 27, 1989 issue. An article *about* Gary Smith by Donald J. Barr will be found in *Sports Illustrated*, volume 70, page 1, in the February 27, 1989 issue.

FIGURE 7.1 *Readers' Guide to Periodical Literature*

from 1977 to the present. On microfiche, this source indexes approximately 400 U.S. magazines, including those in the *Readers' Guide*.

Computer disk systems and on-line searching enable you to conduct a computer search of many databases, and they are becoming increasingly popular in college and local libraries. *InfoTrac*, for example, references popular magazines and periodicals, such as those found in *Readers' Guide* and the *Magazine Index*, as well as selected academic journals. With on-line searching you can customize a bibliography of sources on your topic and print it, thus saving you much time transcribing source citations.

Once you have selected your topic, you may also wish to consult an index to magazines and periodicals in that specific area. Specialized indexes make your research more efficient. A few of the many such indexes include the following:

American Statistics Index
Art Index
Business Periodicals Index
Consumer Health and Nutrition Index
Education Index
Hispanic American Periodicals Index

Humanities Index
Index to Legal Periodicals
Index to Periodicals by and about Blacks
Music Index
Social Sciences Index

Remember that because these indexes are so specialized, the periodicals and journals they lead you to will likely be written for a specialized audience, and may use jargon and technical language familiar only to people in the field. Even if you understand these articles easily, you may have to simplify their language and ideas for the more general audience of your classroom. As you can readily see, however, magazines and journals provide an excellent and abundant source of material that will assist you in preparing your speeches.

NEWSPAPERS

Including articles on topics from aardvarks to zoos, **newspapers** offer abundant information that can be local, national, or international in scope. Use the newspaper indexes to guide you to your specific topic. Newspapers are usually transferred to microfilm or microfiche for easy storage; consequently, most libraries can house many years of newspapers in a few filing drawers. *The New York Times, The Washington Post,* and *The Christian Science Monitor* are all indexed and may be helpful in your research. The citation in Figure 7.2, taken from *The New York Times Index* under the topic "kidnapping," illustrates the type of information typically included in a newspaper index.[5]

FIGURE 7.2 *The New York Times Index*

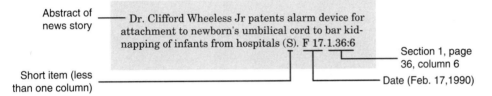

Other indexes will guide you to newspapers targeted at specific ethnic, professional, and geographical audiences. *The Black Newspapers Index,* for example, references newspapers oriented to African-American audiences and often contains stories not found in more mainstream newspapers. *The Wall Street Journal Index* is a source of information on business and economic topics. Your library may also subscribe to the indexes and newspapers of major city papers.

If your city's newspaper is not indexed, it may still be in your library on microfilm. Without an index, however, its usefulness is limited, unless you know the actual or approximate date of the article you want.

Another excellent guide to newspapers is *NewsBank*. Articles on political, economic, social, scientific, legal, health, and international issues are selected, organized, and recorded on microfiche. The *NewsBank Index,* available on computer as well as in hard copy, puts at your fingertips articles from over 450 newspapers it references. Included in the front of the bound volumes of the index is an easy to understand, step-by-step guide to locating articles in *NewsBank*.

GOVERNMENT DOCUMENTS

The most prolific publisher of information in the United States is the **federal government.** Much of our bureaucracy is devoted to collecting, cataloguing, and disseminating information. The U.S. government generates a wealth of information on a wide range of topics from its many congressional, executive, and judicial agencies.

Accessing government documents may initially seem intimidating to you, but learning how to locate this information is well worth your investment of time and effort. Two publications will help you master the process: the *CIS/Index* and the *Monthly Catalog of U.S. Government Publications*. The Congressional Information Service publishes the *CIS/Index* and *CIS Abstracts* to help you select from the 800,000 pages of information produced by Congress each year. The entries in Figure 7.3, taken from the CIS publications, illustrate how to locate a congressional document.[6]

The *CIS/Index* is superior to the *Monthly Catalog* because it is more specific and easier to use. You locate an entry in the *CIS/Index*, and the reference number directs you to a description of the document in the *CIS Abstract*. There, you will find a classification number guiding you to the document's location on the library shelves. The CIS is, however, limited to congressional publications.

FIGURE 7.3 *CIS/Index and CIS Abstract*

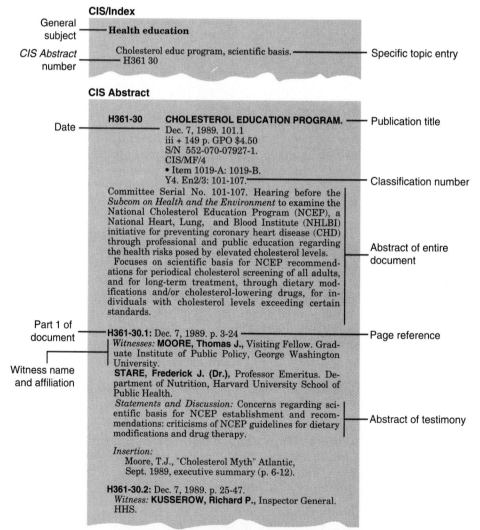

For access to federal statistical publications, you can consult the *American Statistics Index*, also published by the Congressional Information Service.

BOOKS

Books, of course, are excellent sources of information. Longer than magazine and newspaper articles, books allow authors to discuss topics in greater depth, often providing an index to key ideas and a bibliography of sources consulted. Researching, writing, printing, and ordering books usually takes more time than does the same process for periodicals; consequently, information in magazines may be more current and accessible as you prepare your speech than that you find in books. Despite this limitation, books can be an integral part of your research plan.

Your library probably uses one of several cataloguing systems. Three of the most common are the card catalog, the microfilm catalog, and the computer catalog. The trend is toward the computer catalog, although many libraries still use the other two for parts of their collections. The card catalog consists of index cards filed alphabetically according to subject, title, and author, as represented in Figure 7.4.

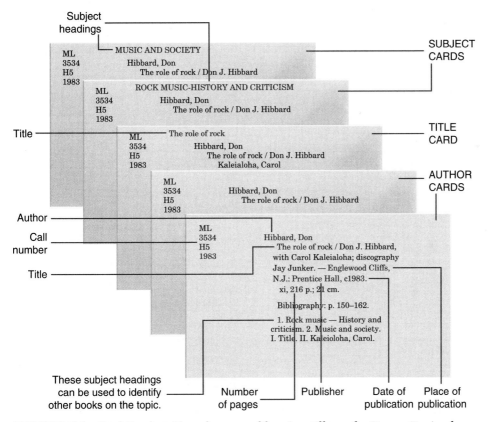

FIGURE 7.4 Card Catalog. Note that some libraries still use the Dewey Decimal System, rather than Library of Congress numbers, for filing books. Others are in the process of converting. If your library is among them, the Dewey Decimal number for Don Hibbard's book would appear as follows: 784.54 H624.

Entries in a microfilm catalog are usually more concise but are still indexed according to subject, title, and author. You could locate information on subliminal persuasion, for example, using any of the following indexes.

Subject Index
Subliminal projection
1989 The age of manipulation: the con in confidence, the sin in
sincere. Key, Wilson Bryan, 1925– . P96 P75 K39 1989

Title Index
The age of manipulation: the con in confidence, the sin in sincere. Key,
Wilson Bryan, 1925– . P96 P75 K39 1989

Author Index
Key, Wilson Bryan, 1925–
The age of manipulation: the con in confidence, the sin in
sincere. 1989. P96 P75 K39

The computer catalog (Figure 7.5) includes the same essential information you find in a card catalog, but permits you to access subject, title, and author listings without having to move from one station to another.[7] The computer catalog usually provides better cross-referencing of related topics than does the card catalog. An additional feature is the "status" column, which indicates whether the book is on the library shelves, checked out, or on order.

FIGURE 7.5 Computer Catalog

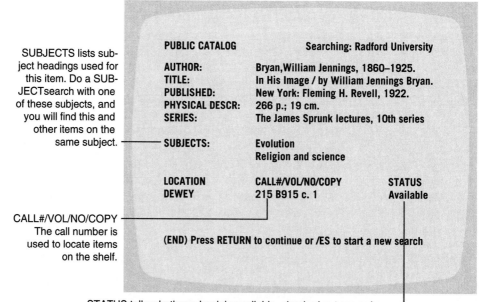

SUBJECTS lists subject headings used for this item. Do a SUBJECTsearch with one of these subjects, and you will find this and other items on the same subject.

CALL#/VOL/NO/COPY The call number is used to locate items on the shelf.

PUBLIC CATALOG   Searching: Radford University

AUTHOR: Bryan,William Jennings, 1860–1925.
TITLE: In His Image / by William Jennings Bryan.
PUBLISHED: New York: Fleming H. Revell, 1922.
PHYSICAL DESCR: 266 p.; 19 cm.
SERIES: The James Sprunk lectures, 10th series

SUBJECTS: Evolution
                 Religion and science

LOCATION   CALL#/VOL/NO/COPY   STATUS
DEWEY   215 B915 c. 1   Available

(END) Press RETURN to continue or /ES to start a new search

STATUS tells whether a book is available, checked out, on order, etc. If a book is checked out, the due date will appear under STATUS.

"There are times when I think that the ideal library is composed solely of reference books. They are like understanding friends—always ready to meet your mood, always ready to change the subject when you have had enough of this or that."

J. DONALD ADAMS

Perhaps the heart of any library is its **reference** section. These resources, usually available for use only in the library, include many types of collections to aid you in your research. A few that you will find helpful are dictionaries, encyclopedias, almanacs, yearbooks, and books of quotations.

Dictionaries. Dictionaries help you clarify the meanings of words and their spellings and pronunciations. There are many good general dictionaries, and you undoubtedly use these regularly. A number of more specialized dictionaries covering a wide range of topic areas are also available. A list of a few of these follows.

The Dictionary of Advertising
A Dictionary of American and British Euphemisms
A Dictionary of Bad Manners
Dictionary of Business and Economics
A Dictionary of Color
A Dictionary of Dates
Dictionary of Literary Themes and Motifs

Dictionary of Modern Political Ideologies
A Dictionary of Slang and Unconventional English
A Dictionary of Statistical Terms
Dictionary of Symbols and Imagery
A Feminist Dictionary
Webster's New World Dictionary of Quotable Definitions

Even a quick glance through that list should tell you that some of these dictionaries would be good places to begin your search for a speech topic.

Encyclopedias. You have, no doubt, used general **encyclopedias,** such as *Encyclopedia Americana, Encyclopædia Britannica,* and *World Book,* to prepare reports and papers in elementary and high school. These multi-volume sets of books organize information on many branches of knowledge. However, did you know there are numerous encyclopedias available focusing on specific bodies of knowledge, such as the following?

Encyclopedia of American Architecture
Encyclopedia of American Humorists
Encyclopedia of American Shipwrecks
Encyclopedia of Black America
Encyclopedia of Jazz

Encyclopedia of Medical History
Encyclopedia of Painting
The Encyclopedia of Sports Talk
Encyclopedia of Terrorism and Political Violence
Encyclopedia of World Mythology and Legend

Discussion Prompt:
Use this list and the list of dictionaries in this chapter to brainstorm for possible speech topics. Wouldn't you be interested in hearing an intriguing speech on famous American shipwrecks, for example?

Class Activity:
Have students select and locate a specialized encyclopedia, skim through it, and report to class on possible speech topics they found.

Examining some of these volumes may both generate topics for future speeches and give you background information on your current topic.

Almanacs. "Almanacs and Bibles were the first books to come to the United States," writes Lois Horowitz. "At a time when there were few newspapers, the settlers used almanacs for a mélange of valuable information and entertainment. Almanacs predicted the weather for the coming year; gave advice on crops and planting; listed home remedies, multiplication tables, interest charts, and even stagecoach schedules. They also included inspirational verse and stories."[8]

Almanacs have changed over the years — certainly, they no longer publish stagecoach schedules — but their character remains the same. Almanacs contain a wide range of specific and statistical information on topics including education, politics, sports, entertainment, and significant events of a particular year. Almanacs are excellent sources when you need specific facts and background information. What is the exact wording of Amendment II of the United States Constitution? Who is the head of state of Zambia? In what year did Mother Teresa win the Nobel Peace Prize? How many hazardous waste sites operate in the state of New Jersey? These questions, and many others, are answered in a good almanac. If you selected the history of manned space flights as your speech topic, an almanac would be a ready reference for the dates, duration, and description of those flights.

General almanacs include *The World Almanac and Book of Facts, Information Please Almanac, The Universal Almanac,* and *The New York Public Library Desk Reference.* Specialized almanacs cover a wide range of subjects, as illustrated by these examples: *Almanac for Computers, Almanac for American Politics, Almanac of Higher Education,* and *Almanac of World Crime.*

Yearbooks. Yearbooks are usually published annually and include information discovered during or pertinent to that year. Encyclopedia publishers, for example, often offer yearbooks as supplements to their main set of books. Yearbooks enable researchers to update information on a particular topic. *Facts on File Yearbook,* for example, digests and catalogs world news originally published in the weekly publication, *Facts on File.* The diversity of topics covered in yearbooks is illustrated by the following titles: *Yearbook of Agriculture, Yearbook of Higher Education, Yearbook of Emergency Medicine, Yearbook of School Law,* and *The World Yearbook of Robotics Research and Development.*

Books of Quotations. Captivating **quotations,** both serious and funny, can enliven the language of your speech. As we noted earlier, they are particularly appropriate in speech introductions and conclusions. Quoting another also adds authority to your comments and, thus, can strengthen the development of your ideas. Fortunately, many excellent books of quotations are available in bookstores and libraries. Some of our favorites follow.

Bartlett's Familiar Quotations
A Book of Irish Quotations
A Dictionary of Economic Quotations
The Dictionary of War Quotations
Famous Last Words
Famous Phrases from History
The Great Thoughts
The International Thesaurus of
   Quotations
The Macmillan Book of Business
   and Economic Quotations
The New International Dictionary of
   Quotations

Oxford Book of Aphorisms
Oxford Dictionary of Quotations
Peter's Quotations
Pocket Book of Quotations
The Quotable Woman: From Eve to
   1799
The Quotable Woman: From 1800 On
The Speaker's Book of Quotations
A Treasury of Jewish Quotations
2,715 One-Line Quotations for
   Speakers, Writers, and Raconteurs

Books of quotations are organized alphabetically by author or subject. You will find a subject organization infinitely easier to use, unless you are searching for a quotation by a specific person.

INTERVIEWS

Although the library will, undoubtedly, be the place where you do most of your research, you can find a wealth of information outside your library, and some of it is not confined to the written word. Depending on your topic, an **interview** may be the best source of firsthand information. The personal interview can aid you in four ways. *First, if published sources are inaccessible, the personal interview may be your only option.* The topic you have chosen may be so recent that sufficient information is not yet in print or, if it is, it has not arrived in your library. Your topic may also be so localized as to receive little or no coverage by area media.

Suppose, for example, your college announces that it will adopt a telephone registration procedure next year. You decide that this will make a timely topic for your informative speech to your classmates. You might make an appointment with the college registrar to learn more about the new procedure. If you learn that other colleges have tried a system similar to the one proposed at your school, you could call officials at those institutions and solicit additional information. Using both telephone and face-to-face interviews, you could generate much of the supporting material you need for your speech, information that would probably not be available at your library.

Related Reading:
Metzler, Ken. *Creative Interviewing*, 2nd ed. Englewood Cliffs, NJ: Prentice, 1989.

A library reference section can unlock a wealth of information in encyclopedias, almanacs, and indexes.

A second advantage of the personal interview is that it permits you to adapt your topic to your specific audience. If your topic is recycling, for example, you would probably present data estimating the amount of resources and landfill space the United States could save annually from such efforts. If you interview the director of your school's physical plant to find out how much trash custodians collect and dispose of each day, you give your speech a personal touch. You could then compute how much your college could contribute to resource conservation. Showing your audience how this topic affects them directly will grab their attention.

Third, personal interviews provide an opportunity for you to secure expert evaluation of your research and suggestions for further research. When interviewing experts, you may find that they challenge some of your assumptions or data. If this happens to you, encourage such feedback and do not get defensive. Knowing all the angles can only help you give a more thoughtful speech. Near the end of your interview, ask your interviewee to suggest additional sources that will help you better research and understand your topic.

Finally, personal interviews can enhance your image as a speaker. In addition to gathering information in the library, you took the time to conduct an interview. Listeners are usually impressed that you went beyond library research in preparing your message for them. Think of the speech topic we just discussed on recycling. Your classmates will probably see your extra effort as confirmation of your commitment to the topic and the speech-making process.

KEY POINTS **Preparing for the** **Interview**	1. Determine whom you want to interview. 2. Decide the format for the interview. 3. Schedule the interview. 4. Research the person to be interviewed. 5. Prepare a list of questions.

Teaching Strategy:
For an upcoming speech, require that students conduct at least one personal interview as part of their research. Have students prepare questions before the interview. Remind them that they should always have more questions prepared than they think they will be able to ask, but that they should note the most important questions to make sure that these are asked.

Prepare for the Interview. Two days before her speech was due, Marie began thinking of a topic. She remembered reading in the campus newspaper that the School of Business was seeking accreditation. Since a majority of students in her public speaking class were business majors, she decided to inform them on the benefits of receiving accreditation and the steps in the accreditation process. She called her accounting professor and arranged for an appointment the next afternoon.

Arriving ten minutes late, she apologized and then explained the reason for the interview. She took out a tape recorder, but Professor Saunders said that he'd rather not be recorded. Since she hadn't prepared a list of questions, Marie began the interview by saying, "Just tell me anything you can about this accreditation thing and how it will benefit the university." Saunders said that he was not involved in the process and didn't think he could be too helpful. He added that he thought accreditation would help the university recruit better students and faculty. After the interview, a disappointed Marie went to the library, found an encyclopedia, photocopied an article on reptiles indigenous to Florida, and went back to the dorm to prepare her speech for the next day's class.

Marie's original topic — accreditation — was a good one; it was timely and relevant to her audience. The personal interview was an appropriate research strategy. Unfortunately, Marie's plan of action was poorly conceived, planned, and executed. Once you decide to conduct a personal interview, you must take several steps in preparation. First, determine whom you want to interview. Your interviewee should be someone who is both knowledgeable on the topic and willing to speak with you. Marie did not bother to find out if her accounting professor was the most knowledgeable person on her topic before she set up the interview.

Second, decide on the format for the interview. Will you conduct it face-to-face, by phone, or by letter? A face-to-face interview will probably give you the most information. People tend to open up more when they interact verbally and nonverbally. As a face-to-face interviewer, you can both listen to what the interviewee says and observe the nonverbal messages. An interview over the phone is another possibility, when you cannot travel or do not have the time or resources to travel to the expert. A third option, conducting an interview through written correspondence, has some disadvantages. It is time-consuming because you must prepare a set of questions, mail or deliver it to the interviewee, and wait for a response. It has an added disadvantage of not allowing for immediate follow-up questions. If something needs clarification, you must submit another question. The written interview, however, often results in more thoughtful and better worded responses than face-to-face or telephone interviews.

The third preparation step is to schedule the interview. When requesting an interview, identify yourself and the topic on which you seek information. Let the person know how you intend to use that information, the amount of time needed for the interview, and any special recording procedures you plan to use. Some people may object to being quoted or to having their comments recorded. If this is the case, it is best to find that out ahead of time rather than at the interview. Marie had not informed her professor beforehand that she wished to tape the interview. You will likely discover that most people you seek to interview are flattered that you selected them as experts and are therefore happy to cooperate.

Fourth, you should research the person to be interviewed before you show up at his or her doorstep. Obviously, your selection of the interviewee suggests that you already know something about him or her. In addition, read any articles the interviewee has published on your topic before the interview. This enables you to conduct the interview efficiently. You will not need to ask questions that the person has already answered in print, and your reading may prompt some specific questions on points you would like clarified. Also, your research will show that you are prepared, and will cause the interviewee to take you and the interview seriously. You will recall that Marie did not do this.

Fifth, prepare a list of questions. Always have more questions than you think you will be able to ask, just in case you are mistaken. Mark those that are most important to your research and make sure you ask them first. You may want to have some closed and some open questions. *Closed questions* are those that

Teaching Strategy:
Have students identify the following questions as *open* or *closed:*

How many charges of student plagiarism have been brought to your attention? (closed)

What is our school's policy regarding plagiarism? (open)

Have students been dismissed from school this semester because of plagiarism? (closed)

How long have you served as director of the university planetarium? (closed)

What special events is the planetarium preparing for? (open)

may be answered with a "yes," a "no," or a short answer. Examples are: "Are elementary school teachers in this state better prepared today to teach subject matter than they were five years ago?" and "What is the average entry-level pay for elementary school teachers in your district?" The first question can be answered by a "yes" or a "no"; the second, with a salary figure. *Open questions* invite longer answers, and can produce a great deal of information. If you ask an educator "What can be done to increase teacher competency in the elementary grades?" sit back and prepare to listen for a while! The less time you have for the interview, the fewer open questions you should ask. Open questions can sometimes result in rambling, unnecessary information. At other times, the interviewee's rambling will trigger ideas you would not have thought of otherwise. When you and the interviewee have plenty of time, and particularly if you are tape recording the interview, you may find that open questions are the best way to get a quantity of information.

Conduct the Interview. The personal interview is an excellent opportunity to practice interpersonal communication skills. Specifically, you should do the following. First, when you arrive introduce yourself, thank the person for giving you his or her time, and restate the purpose of the interview.

Second, conduct the interview in a professional manner. If you are interviewing the president of the local savings and loan, don't show up in cut-off jeans, sandals, and your favorite flannel shirt. Make sure you arrive appropriately dressed and are able to set up and handle any recording equipment with a minimum of distractions. You should try to relax the interviewee, establish a professional atmosphere, pose questions that are clear and direct, listen actively, take notes efficiently, and follow up when necessary. You should be in control of the interview without appearing to be pushy or abrupt.

Third, you should thank the person again for the interview when you have finished.

Follow Up on the Interview. After the interview, review your notes or listen to the tape. Do this as soon as possible after the interview, because the passing of time will dim your memory. If you are unclear about something that was said, do not use that information in your speech. If it will be important to

Related Reading:
For examples of excellent interviews, see: Moyers, Bill. *A World of Ideas.* New York: Doubleday, 1989. Betty Sue Flowers has done an excellent job of editing Moyers' interviews with writers, educators, historians, ethicists, philosophers, and others. These interviews were originally broadcast as part of the PBS series *A World of Ideas.*

Asking questions of experts is another source of information for your speech.

the audience's understanding of the topic, you may wish to contact the person by phone and seek clarification.

As a matter of courtesy you should write to the people you interviewed, thanking them for the time and help they gave you. You may even want to send them a copy of your finished speech if it is in manuscript form.

WRITING AND CALLING FOR INFORMATION

Some years ago, one of us taught a student, Lindahl, who wanted to develop an informative speech on the savant syndrome. This was long before Dustin Hoffman's portrayal of Raymond in the film *Rain Man* made many people aware of the special talents and disabilities of savants. Lindahl had seen a *60 Minutes* segment on the syndrome, but could not find recent written sources in the local libraries she visited. Her best source, she said, was an article from a three-year-old issue of *Time*. Others might have abandoned their research and switched topics, but Lindahl followed a hunch that paid off for her.

The *Time* article quoted several university professors and medical doctors who were engaged in ongoing research on the savant syndrome. Lindahl got their office telephone numbers through directory assistance. She called these experts to see if they could recommend new sources she had been unable to locate. Though she was afraid of imposing on them, Lindahl found that the people she called were all flattered by her attention and complimented her perseverance as a researcher. One psychologist mailed her a photocopy of a book chapter she had written on the savant syndrome; a medical doctor mailed Lindahl a packet of journal articles, including the galleys of an article of his that was about to be published; a psychology professor mailed her a tape of savants with incredible musical talents playing piano concertos they had heard for the first time only moments before. In short, Lindahl received a gold mine of new, expert research as a result of her few long-distance calls.

Lindahl was lucky that she began her research more than a month before her speech was due. To take advantage of pamphlets and brochures available through the mail, you will need to plan ahead as well. But thousands of organizations, such as the American Cancer Society and the United Way, publish their own informational literature. Political parties and lobbying groups prepare position papers on issues that affect them. Corporations distribute annual reports to their stockholders and will share these with people who request them. You can write to any of these organizations. Some have toll-free phone numbers; for others you would have to pay long-distance charges.

Unfortunately, there is no index which conveniently and comprehensively catalogs information available from groups, so you must take the initiative in tracking down what you need. One source that can be helpful is the *Encyclopedia of Associations*. This publication is divided into three volumes: National Organizations of the U.S.; International Organizations; and Regional, State, and Local Organizations. Each volume lists names, addresses, telephone numbers, and descriptions of organizations. The information is also available on computers at some libraries. This research source will not help you if you have five days left before your deadline. But if time permits and research warrants, writing or calling these organizations to request information can add relevant research to your speech.

Related Readings:
Two helpful sources are:

The National Directory of Addresses and Telephone Numbers. Kirdland, WA: General Information, 1987–88.
Levine, Michael. *The Address Book: How to Reach Anyone Who Is Anyone.* New York: Perigee, 1991.

ELECTRONIC MEDIA

News, information, and opinion come to us not only through print media but also through the **electronic media.** In fact, most of us get our news from television. When we think of research, however, we generally focus on magazines, newspapers, books, and other print resources. Information in print is more accessible to the researcher and is usually indexed. Nevertheless, you should not ignore broadcast information as a research option.

You can find some excellent speech topics among the investigative reports presented on television and radio. If you see and hear information you would like to obtain, you should check to see if a transcript of the program is available for purchase. This information is usually given at a program's conclusion. For a nominal cost you can obtain transcripts of many programs such as *60 Minutes, Nightline, 20/20, This Week with David Brinkley, Firing Line, Face the Nation, Meet the Press, Washington Week in Review,* and the *MacNeil/Lehrer NewsHour.*

Your library and video rental stores may have copies of televised broadcasts such as the PBS documentary series *Eyes on the Prize* on the civil rights struggle, or Bill Moyers' *A Walk Through the 20th Century.* Through videotapes you can research topics such as military battles, McCarthyism, and space exploration, to name just a few. Informational tapes can take you on tours of museums such as the Louvre or the British Museum, and distant places such as Australia and Italy. Instructional tapes may teach you how to garden, refinish furniture, and make a sales presentation. As videotape becomes an increasingly valuable and accessible source of information, speakers should consider exploring it. You may even find a trip to your video store or the video section of your library an important part of your brainstorming strategy.

■ Record Information

Once you have located information, you must determine *what* to record and *how* to record it.

WHAT TO RECORD

When in doubt, record more rather than less. Certainly, it is possible to copy too much information. If you find everything potentially important, your topic probably needs better focus. Without some focus, you run the risk of becoming so bogged down in research that you leave little time for organizing and practicing your speech.

On the other hand, if you are too selective, you may be inefficient. As you research your speech, you may shift your topic focus and, hence, the supporting material you previously thought was irrelevant becomes important. Discarding unnecessary information is easier than trying to remember a source, retracing your steps, hoping that the information is still on the library shelves, and then recording that information.

Traditional advice to researchers is to record each piece of information on a separate notecard, along with the source citation, as you find it. This strategy allows you to organize the speech visually and to experiment with different structures. The disadvantage of this method of recording information is that it consumes a great deal of library time that might be better devoted to searching for other sources. In addition, much of what you record on notecards may not be used in your speech at all.

For better or worse, photocopy machines have significantly changed the way that we all conduct library research, and we believe that they should be an important part of your research plan. We all know that sometimes the simplest and most thorough way to record research information is to photocopy pages from books, documents, reference works, or even entire articles. Later, at your leisure and in more comfortable surroundings, you can review, evaluate, and select from the photocopied materials. However, be aware that although they save you time, photocopies may also lull you into a false sense of accomplishment. What you have copied may later turn out to be of little or no use. How can you avoid this problem? You need to keep on top of the material. Do not wait until the night before your speech to read the pile of information you have been collecting on the role of women pilots in World War II.

As long as you have remembered to note your sources on the copied pages, photocopying has two additional advantages over using notecards. First, you may not know what you want to use from an article at the time you first find it. If the focus of your speech changes, a different part of the article may become important. Indeed, sometimes your research forces you to refocus the speech topic. Second, if you are quoting from or paraphrasing one specific part of an article, you may need to check later to make sure that you are not quoting the author out of context. Having a photocopy of the book chapter, the journal article, or the encyclopedia entry lets you check the context and the accuracy of your quotation.

Always record full citations of sources you have consulted in your research in a bibliography at the end of your speech. Most writer's handbooks will recommend a particular bibliographic form. Your **bibliography** is simply a list of works you have consulted in developing your speech. Some of the popular forms include the *Publication Manual of the American Psychological Association*, Kate Turabian's *A Manual for Writer's of Term Papers, Theses, and Dissertations*, and the *Modern Language Association Handbook for Writers of Research Papers*. Be sure to check with your instructor, who may have a preference for one of these or for some other bibliographic form.

bibliography: an orderly list of works consulted or cited during the preparation and delivery of a speech.

Copies of all three style manuals listed above are probably in your library's reference section. If you consult the most recent edition of any of them, you'll be surprised at the range of research materials they cover. In addition to providing examples of bibliographic forms for all sorts of traditional library research materials, each of these books recommends bibliographic forms for interviews, television and radio programs, videotapes, computer software, and pamphlets and brochures. We encourage you to consult a copy of any of these manuals, since examples of them are beyond the scope of this chapter. We can, however, show you sample bibliographic entries for some commonly used sources. Figure 7.6 compares the bibliographic forms of three style manuals. Whether you want to cite a segment of National Public Radio's *All Things*

FIGURE 7.6 Comparison of Popular Bibliography Forms

Book with One Author

Hirsch, E. D., Jr. *Cultural Literacy: What Every American Needs to Know.* New York: Houghton, 1987.

Hirsch, E. D., Jr. *Cultural Literacy: What Every American Needs to Know.* New York: Houghton Mifflin, 1987.

Hirsch, E. D., Jr. (1987). *Cultural Literacy: What Every American Needs to Know.* New York: Houghton Mifflin.

Book with Two or More Authors

Grice, George L., and John F. Skinner. *Mastering Public Speaking.* Englewood Cliffs, NJ: Prentice, 1993.

Grice, George L., and John F. Skinner. *Mastering Public Speaking.* Englewood Cliffs, NJ: Prentice Hall, 1993.

Grice, G. L., & Skinner, J. F. (1993). *Mastering Public Speaking.* Englewood Cliffs, NJ: Prentice Hall.

Article in Weekly Magazine

Samuelson, Robert J. "Why School Reform Fails." *Newsweek* 27 May 1991: 62-66.

Samuelson, Robert J. "Why School Reform Fails." *Newsweek,* 27 May 1991, 62-66.

Samuelson, R. J. (1991, May 27). Why school reform fails. *Newsweek,* pp. 62-66.

Article in Monthly or Bi-monthly Magazine

Waldrop, Judith, and Thomas Exter. "What the 1990 Census Will Show." *American Demographics* January 1990: 20-30.

Waldrop, Judith, and Thomas Exter. "What the 1990 Census Will Show." *American Demographics,* January 1990, 20-30.

Waldrop, J., & Exter, T. (1990, January). What the 1990 census will show. *American Demographics,* pp. 20-30.

Newspaper Article

Wald, Matthew L. "Due Up for License Renewal: The Future of Nuclear Power." *New York Times* 24 June 1991, natl. ed.: A1,8.

Wald, Matthew L. "Due Up for License Renewal: The Future of Nuclear Power." *New York Times,* 24 June 1991, natl. ed., sec A, pp.1, 8.

Wald, M. L. (1991, June 24). Due up for license renewal: the future of nuclear power. *New York Times,* pp. A1,8.

Government Document

United States. Cong. House. Subcommittee on Aviation of the Committee on Public Works and Transportation. *Assuring the Safety of the Aging Airline Fleet.* 101st Cong., 2nd sess. Washington, D.C.: GPO, 1990.

U. S. Congress. House. Subcommittee on Aviation of the Committee on Public Works and Transportation. *Assuring the Safety of the Aging Airline Fleet.* 101st Cong., 2nd sess. Washington, D.C.: GPO, 1990.

United States. Congress. House. (1990). Subcommittee on Aviation of the Committee on Public Works and Transportation. *Assuring the Safety of the Aging Airline Fleet.* Washington, D.C.: Government Printing Office.

MLA Form

Turabian Form

APA Form

Considered, a stop-smoking videotape, or lecture notes you took in an anthropology class last week, the most recent edition of these reference books can likely give you a pattern to follow.

143
Researching Your Topic

■ Evaluate Information ⎯⎯⎯⎯⎯⎯⎯⎯⎯⎯⎯⎯⎯⎯⎯⎯⎯⎯

As you prepare your speech, you must make choices. Your goal is to support your ideas with the most compelling evidence and arguments you can find. The adage "Knowledge is power" certainly applies to speech making; the more you know about your topic, the greater your flexibility in determining its content and, subsequently, its impact. This concept of choice may make your task more complex, but it will also produce a more effective speech.

There is a limit, however, to the time you can spend researching. An important part of effective research is knowing when to stop accumulating materials and when to start using them. In his book *Finding Facts Fast,* Alden Todd provides the following guideline for research projects:

> If the last 10 percent of your planned research time has brought excellent results, you are doubtless on a productive new track and should extend the project. But if the last 25 percent of your scheduled time has brought greatly diminished results, this fact is a signal to wind up your research.[9]

Although Todd's 10/25 formula may not be wholly applicable to your researching a speech for this class, it does highlight an important issue: At some point you must stop concentrating on researching and start concentrating on structuring your speech.

In the next chapter, Supporting Your Speech, we discuss the purposes and types of supporting material. Understanding these topics will help you evaluate your research and select the best information to support the ideas of your speech.

Summary ⎯⎯⎯⎯⎯⎯⎯⎯⎯⎯⎯⎯⎯⎯⎯⎯⎯⎯⎯⎯⎯⎯⎯⎯⎯⎯

Research is the process of gathering information and evidence to understand, develop, and explain your topic. Learning to research is fundamental to mastering public speaking. Even if you are not required to use outside sources for a particular speech, knowing your subject thoroughly greatly reduces your speech anxiety. Of course, knowing your subject probably demands knowing how to use the best library in your area. An agenda for thorough research of a subject involves five steps.

First, assess your knowledge of the subject and begin to organize that knowledge. Chances are good that you chose the topic because you were interested in it or already knew something about it. Keeping a file of articles and quotations on subjects that interest you gives you a head start in your research. As you prepare the speech and after you deliver it, keep your research notes and speaking notes or manuscript in a speech file.

Second, develop a research plan for your topic. What information do you need? Where can you find it? How can you get it in the time you have? Your topic may lead you to interview people or collect printed information from businesses and organizations. Sooner or later, however, you will probably need to learn to use a local library efficiently. Reference librarians can teach you the strengths and limitations of the library you select.

The third step in research is to collect information from a variety of sources. Potential sources include magazines and journals, newspapers, government documents, books, and reference works including dictionaries, encyclopedias, almanacs, yearbooks, and books of quotations. Sources outside the library include interviews and electronic media resources such as radio, television, and videotape. Interviews allow you to collect authoritative, unpublished information on your subject, but they require special planning and preparation. You must select the best interviewee, decide on the format, schedule the interview, research the interviewee you have selected, and prepare a list of questions. After conducting the interview in a competent, professional manner and promptly recording the information you have gathered from it, you should send a note of thanks to the person you interviewed.

The fourth step in research is to record the information you consider important and useful. You may choose to take notes on notecards or to photocopy your information. In either case, be sure to record the source of the information—author, title, and publication information—using a current bibliography form.

The fifth and final step in research is to evaluate the material you are collecting. The quality and quantity of the information you collect will not only help you focus and organize the subject, but should also signal you when you have exhausted your research efforts.

Exercises

1. Locate and look at a recent issue of each of the following magazines: *Mother Jones, National Review, New Republic, Newsweek, The Progressive, Time,* and *U.S. News & World Report.* Based on their content, rank the seven magazines from most liberal to most conservative. Which would you classify as liberal, which as conservative, and which as middle of the road? What information helped you decide your rankings? Were similar topics treated in different ways in these publications?

2. Using any magazine and periodical index listed in this chapter, construct a bibliography of at least seven sources for an upcoming speech. Locate at least three of these articles.

3. Using a newspaper or *NewsBank* index, construct a bibliography of at least five sources for an upcoming speech. Locate at least three of these articles.

4. Using the *CIS/Index* and *CIS Abstract*, locate a congressional document on a topic that would be appropriate for a speech in this class.

5. Using some of the resources listed in this chapter, answer the following questions.
   a. What is the derivation of the word "deadline"?
   b. The Speaker of the U.S. House of Representatives comes from what district and state?
   c. In what year was Henrik Ibsen's play *A Doll's House* published?
   d. What are the chief crops of Cameroon?

    e. On what date did the Alexander Hamilton – Aaron Burr duel occur? Who won?

    f. What is the enrollment of Aquinas College in Grand Rapids, Michigan?

    g. Who was the last U.S. major league baseball player to bat over .400 for the year? What was the year, and what was his batting average?

    h. What is the elevation of Mount Rainier?

    i. What is the preferred pronunciation of the word "data"? In how many other ways can it be correctly pronounced?

    j. Who received the Oscar for Best Actor in 1974? In what movie did he star?

6. Using books of quotations, such as those listed in this chapter, prepare a list of at least two quotations on each of the following topics.

    a. The Art of Conversation

    b. The Importance of Teachers

    c. Overcoming Failure

    d. The Dangers of Apathy

    e. Turning Problems into Opportunities

    Bring your list to class and be prepared to discuss how you might use some of the quotations in a speech. Which would contribute to good introductions or conclusions? Which could be used to illustrate an idea in the body of the speech?

7. Consult the *Encyclopedia of Associations,* and locate at least three organizations you think might have information pertaining to ideas you are considering for upcoming speeches. Write letters requesting relevant information.

8. Select an expert to interview for an upcoming speech. Using suggestions in this chapter, arrange, prepare for, and conduct an interview, and follow up on it.

Notes

1. *The New York Public Library Desk Reference* (New York: Stonesong – Simon, 1989) xi.

2. Robert C. Jeffrey and Owen Peterson, *Speech: A Text with Adapted Readings* (New York: Harper, 1975) 138.

3. Lois Horowitz, *Knowing Where to Look: The Ultimate Guide to Research* (1984; Cincinnati: Writer's Digest, 1988).

4. *Readers' Guide to Periodical Literature* May 1990: n. pag.

5. *New York Times Index* 16 – 28 February 1990: 41.

6. *CIS/Index* April 1990: 51, *CIS Abstract* April 1990: 23.

7. Adapted from *LS/2000 Online Catalog Instruction Tutorial* (Radford, VA: McConnell Library, Radford University, 1990) 4.

8. Horowitz 115.

9. Alden Todd, *Finding Facts Fast,* 2nd ed. (Berkeley: Ten Speed, 1979) 14.

Supporting Your Speech 8

Purposes of Supporting Materials
Clarity
Vividness
Credibility

Types of Supporting Materials
Examples
  Brief
  Extended
  Actual
  Hypothetical

Definition
  By Synonym
  By Etymology
  By Example
  By Operation
Narration
  Personal Narrative
  Third-Person Narrative
Comparison and Contrast
  Literal
  Figurative
Statistics
Testimony

Supporting materials make:
  the general specific. . .
    the abstract concrete. . .
      the mundane memorable. . .
        the impersonal personal. . .
          the remote immediate. . .
            the colorless colorful. . .
              the obscure clear. . .
  the irrelevant relevant. . .
    the unbelievable believable. . .
      the typical atypical. . .
        the routine surprising. . .
          the questionable credible. . .
            the dull vivid. . .
  the complicated understandable. . .
    the usual unusual. . .
      the inaccessible accessible. . .
        the ordinary extraordinary.

*I*N the next chapter of this textbook, Organizing Your Speech, we will present you with a formula for structuring each major idea in your speech. Our students have proved to themselves and to us the usefulness of this pattern, called the 4 S's. This chapter is about the third of the 4 S's: **supporting** your major ideas. In supporting an idea you apply the results of your research and original thinking about your speech topic in the form of examples, comparisons, and statistics, among others. In this chapter you will learn more about the purposes of supporting materials. We will discuss and show you examples of seven types of supporting materials you can use to communicate your ideas clearly, memorably, and authoritatively.

■ Purposes of Supporting Materials ——————

The opening statements above illustrate that supporting materials in a speech serve a variety of purposes. They help give your ideas *clarity, vividness,* and *credibility.*

CLARITY

Early in Operation Desert Storm, Lt. Gen. Thomas Kelly, press liaison for Allied Forces in the Persian Gulf, appeared in a televised press conference. When a reporter asked, "How many aircraft have been lost?" Kelly responded, "The United States has lost nine aircraft. The United Kingdom reports a loss of six aircraft. We have had two losses due to noncombat, mechanical failures."[1] Had the United States lost a total of nine or eleven planes? That depends upon whether the "we" in the third sentence refers to the United States or to other Allied Forces. The statement was unclear, ambiguous. Fortunately, newspaper accounts clarified the general's remarks.

The first goal of any message is to convey the speaker's ideas clearly. **Clarity** refers to the exactness of a message. The clarity of any message you send results partly from your language, as we discuss in Chapter 11, Wording Your Speech. Message clarity is also a function of the material you choose to support your ideas. As you develop your speech, you should frequently ask yourself the question, "Does my supporting material really explain, amplify, or illustrate the point I am trying to make?" If it does not, disregard it and continue your search for relevant material. Clear supporting materials help listeners better understand your ideas.

VIVIDNESS

Which of the following sentences makes a stronger impression on you?

The computer is a helpful teaching tool in the classroom.
The computer is a wise and genial tutor for many subjects, giving immediate, impartial feedback and waiting patiently until the student masters the task at hand.

If you are typical, you chose the second sentence. The first statement seems flat, generic. But that second sentence personalizes the computer, gives it human qualities, and creates an image that may remain with you for a while.

In this chapter we use several excerpts from speeches to illustrate various types of supporting materials. After you finish reading this chapter, you will no doubt remember some of the examples and forget others. Those you remember will be ones you found particularly vivid. **Vivid** supporting materials are striking, graphic, intense, and memorable. A major purpose of supporting materials, then, is to help your audience retain the key points you are developing in your speech. You will accomplish this best by using vivid forms of support chosen with your unique audience in mind.

CREDIBILITY

You gasp as you see the headline: "Scientists Discover Microbial Life on Mars." Would it make a difference whether you saw this on the cover of *Scientific American* or *The National Enquirer?* Of course it would. "Microbial life" is nothing to the folks who write for the tabloids; they've shown photographic evidence of human faces carved into the Martian landscape! A scientific article reviewed and selected for publication by a panel of experts is significantly more believable than an article from any tabloid weekly. **Credibility** refers to the dependability or believability of a speaker or that speaker's sources.

Many ideas in the speeches you prepare will require simple supporting materials: short definitions, brief examples, quick comparisons, for example. In other instances, you may present ideas that are complex or controversial and that require several types of supporting materials. A speech with all of its ideas and support taken from a single source is too limited. Corroborating your ideas

Class Activity:
Write on the blackboard several bland sentences, for example:

The food at the Cozy Cafe is very good.
I have a lot of homework to do.
The students in my speech class are interesting people.
We had a good time.

Have students rewrite these sentences, making them more vivid. Have students share some of their revisions with the class.

Teaching Strategy:
Bring to class a sampling of various magazines, journals, tabloids, and newspapers. Post them around the room and ask your students to rank them in order of their credibility. Discuss the rankings and the criteria students used in evaluating the publications.

credibility: the believability or dependability of speakers and their sources.

and facts among several sources can be a valuable and persuasive tool. Your main points will be more credible if you present evidence that these ideas are shared by several experts.

You establish clarity by explaining your idea so that listeners *understand* it. You establish vividness by presenting your idea so that listeners will *remember* it. And you establish credibility by presenting the idea so that listeners *believe* it. If the supporting materials in your speech get the audience to understand, remember, and believe what you say, you have selected your materials wisely.

You know that you want to present clear, vivid, and believable supporting materials. But you may still be unclear as to just how you can do this. How do you make sure people understand, remember, and believe your message? You have a wide range to choose from as you organize your supporting materials. Below we discuss the most common types of supporting materials and show you how they can work in your speech.

■ Types of Supporting Materials

example: samples or illustrations of a category of people, places, objects, actions, experiences, or conditions.

To help you achieve clarity, vividness, and credibility in your speaking, you should consider seven types of supporting material available to you: examples, definition, narration, comparison, contrast, statistics, and testimony. Keep in mind that there is no one best type of support for your ideas. Select what is most appropriate to your topic, your audience, and yourself. If you accomplish this task, you will have selected the best support for *your* speech.

EXAMPLES

Examples are specific illustrations of a category of people, places, objects, actions, experiences, or conditions. In other words, examples are specimens or representations of some general group. The sound of the word itself gives perhaps the easiest definition to remember, however: an example is a sample of something. Measles, mumps, and chicken pox are examples of common childhood illnesses. New York, Los Angeles, and Miami are examples of the largest

Speakers can explain complex ideas by using supporting materials that are clear and vivid.

cities in the United States. *Broadway Danny Rose, Hannah and Her Sisters,* and *Radio Days* are examples of Woody Allen movies. Soccer, football, and baseball are examples of popular team sports.

The examples you use in your speeches can be either brief, such as those shown in the previous paragraph, or extended. **Brief examples** are short, specific instances of the general category you are discussing. They may be used individually, but are often grouped together. Notice how Jocelyn combined a number of brief examples early in her speech on the attractions of New York City:

> Your walking tour of midtown Manhattan could take you to places as diverse as St. Patrick's Cathedral, Rockefeller Center, the Gotham Book Mart, and the Museum of Modern Art. Try not to gawk as you look at some of the most famous architecture in the world — the Art Deco top of the Chrysler Building, the Empire State Building, and Grand Central Station. Tired of pounding the pavement? Slip into a chair in the Algonquin Hotel's dim lobby, soak up the literary history, ring the bell on your table, and order something to drink. Hungry? You've got the world's table to choose from — everything from four-star restaurants to little holes in the wall serving the best ethnic dishes: Chinese, Vietnamese, Indian, Mexican, Thai.

Extended examples are lengthier and more elaborate than brief examples. They allow you to create more detailed pictures of a person, place, object, experience, or condition. Later in her speech, Jocelyn developed an extended example of one of her favorite New York City attractions:

> Beginning with my second visit to New York, one of my first stops has usually been the Museum of Modern Art. If you're like me you'll need to give yourself at least a

couple of hours here, because for a small admission price you're going to get a chance to see up close art that you've only seen before as photographs in books. Upstairs on my last visit I saw works such as Pablo Picasso's *Guernica* and Roy Lichtenstein's huge pop art paintings of comic strip panels. My favorite Lichtenstein was one called *Oh, Jeff, I Love You Too, But*. . . . On a wall with a number of other paintings was a canvas so small that I almost missed it. I'm glad I didn't. It was Salvador Dali's famous surrealist work, *The Persistence of Memory,* with its melting clock and watch faces. Then over in a corner is a special room that holds only one painting. As you walk in, you see an expanse of gray carpet and several upholstered benches. One wall is glass, two others are white and bare, but the fourth one holds the three panels of Claude Monet's massive painting, *Waterlilies.*

Extended examples such as this have the power to suggest a scene or recreate an experience for your listeners.

Like the spikes mountain climbers use to anchor themselves to the face of a rock, examples give your audience specific points of reference throughout your speech. Whether brief or extended, examples can be of two further types: actual and hypothetical.

actual example: a true instance or illustration.

An **actual example** is real or true. Each of the examples we used above is an actual example. Woody Allen *did* direct the three films listed. Soccer, football, and baseball *are* familiar, established team sports. The Chrysler Building and the Empire State Building *are* famous New York landmarks.

Les McCraw, president of the Fluor Corporation, delivered a speech at Clemson University using a series of actual examples to illustrate the point and title of his speech: "Nothing Much Happens Without a Dream." One example focused on a baseball player named Jim Abbott:

> Jim Abbott had a dream. It takes a special kind of person to make a dream come true against all odds. Jim is the 21-year-old rookie pitcher for the California Angels. He's a left-handed pitcher. He throws left-handed because he was born without a right hand. His parents raised this remarkable man by never treating him too remarkably.
>
> "When I was growing up," he says, "I always pictured myself as a baseball player, but I can't remember how many hands I had in my dreams. I just went out and did things." And he certainly has "done things." He earned the 1987 Sullivan Award as America's best amateur athlete, won the gold medal [in] baseball in the Seoul Olympics, was drafted number 1 by the Angels, and is pitching in the big leagues today.[2]

hypothetical example: an imaginary or fictitious instance or illustration.

Hypothetical examples are imaginary or fictitious. As a speaker, you will often signal hypothetical examples with phrases such as "Suppose that," "Imagine yourself," or "What if." Hypothetical examples clarify and vivify the point you are making, but they do not prove the point.

The following introduction mentions actual products but places them in a hypothetical situation because not all listeners would have all the products listed. The speaker then generalizes from these examples to support the claim that we live in an electronic world.

> We wake up in the morning to soothing music coming from our AM/FM digital clock radio equipped with a gentle wake-up feature. We stumble downstairs, enticed by the aroma of coffee brewed by a pre-set coffee maker with 24-hour digital clock timer and automatic shut-off function. We zap on our 27-inch color TV with

on-screen display of current time and channel and with 139-channel cable-capable tuner. As we sit in our six-way action recliner, we use our 26-function wireless remote to perform the ritual of the morning channel check. Finding nothing that captures our interest, we decide instead to watch the videotape of last week's family reunion, recorded with our 12X power zoom, fully automatic camcorder with self-timer, electronic viewfinder, and "flying erase head for 'rainbow'-free edits." Oh dear! What would our grandparents think? Certainly, we live in an electronic world!

DEFINITION

A **definition** tells us the meaning of a word, a phrase, or a concept. Definitions are essential if your audience is unfamiliar with the vocabulary you use or if there are multiple definitions of a particular term. If you do not clarify terms early in your speech, you risk confusing your listeners and losing their attention. In a speech on computer hacking, for example, you would probably find it necessary to define terms such as *hacker, cracker, virus,* and *worm.* We have found at least three different definitions of "hacker," ranging from favorable to unfavorable. Even if your listeners are familiar with computer terminology, you need to clarify *your* use of the word.

definition: an explanation of the meaning of a word, phrase, or concept.

Definitions may take several forms, four of which are definition by synonym, definition by etymology, definition by example, and definition by operation. Choose the form most appropriate to your audience and to the term you are trying to clarify, and your audience will remember it.

Definition by Synonym. The first type of definition is **definition by synonym.** Synonyms are words that have similar meanings. You have probably used a thesaurus when writing a term paper or a report. A thesaurus is simply a dictionary of synonyms. Consider these pairs of words:

definition by synonym: substituting a word with similar meaning for the word being defined.

mendacity and *dishonesty*   *pariah* and *outcast*
plethora and *excess*   *anathema* and *curse.*
mitigate and *lessen*

Each word is coupled with one of its synonyms. The first word of each pair is probably not a part of your listeners' working vocabulary. As a speaker you would want to use the second word in each pair; those words are more familiar and thus more vivid. The second word of each pair communicates more clearly. If you suffer from "thesaurus-itis," a disease causing you always to choose a fancy word over a simple, more appropriate one, you will be more likely to confuse your listeners. As the joke goes, never use a big word when a diminutive one will do.

A student in one of our introductory public speaking classes used definition by synonym in his speech on the ritual of bullfighting. After introducing each Spanish term, he provided its English translation. Notice how unobtrusively he defines terms in the following excerpt describing the parade to the bullfighting ring: "The *matadores* enter the ring as the band strikes up a *paso doble,* or two-step. Each matador is followed by a *guardia,* or a team of helpers. . . ." By using two languages, the speaker gave his speech a Spanish flavor, yet the English-speaking audience was able to understand his description.

Definition by Etymology. A second type of definition is **definition by etymology.** Etymology is the study of word origins. You may find that describ-

definition by etymology: explaining the origin of the word being defined.

ing how a word has developed clarifies its meaning. For example, the word *decimate* means "to destroy a large portion of," as in: "The hailstorm decimated the soybean crop." You may not know that decimate comes from the Latin word for *ten* or *tenth*. The word *decim* was a common military term used in the days of ancient Rome. If soldiers mutinied against their generals, the entire group was punished. The troops were lined up and every *tenth* soldier was killed, whether guilty or innocent. This arbitrary punishment made others think twice before trying similar action against their leaders. Not only a word's origin but also the history of a word's use can be fascinating.

Most of the time we use definitions to make an unfamiliar term familiar. However, you can also use definition by etymology to highlight the unusual nature of a familiar term. The following etymological definition of the term *debate* is from John Ciardi's *A Browser's Dictionary*. Notice how Ciardi captures both the meaning and the flavor of the word as he traces its historical evolution:

> **debate:** Now signifies a formal presentation of arguments and counterarguments within parliamentary guidelines and time limits. As the formal rules of debate are lost, the discussion descends to wrangling. [Yet wrangling is the root sense. <L. *de-*, down (also functions as an intensive); *battere,* to beat (BATTERY, ABATE). This root sense is nicely expressed by the colorful It. word *battibecco,* hot argument; lit. "a beating of beaks" (as if two birds are fencing).][3]

Related Readings:
A number of good books describe the origins of many of our words and expressions. Four of our favorites were written by Charles Earle Funk: *A Hog on Ice and Other Curious Expressions, Heavens to Betsy! and Other Curious Sayings, Horsefeathers and Other Curious Words,* and *Thereby Hangs a Tale: Stories of Curious Word Origins.*

That image of birds fighting with their beaks certainly enlivens this definition. You will likely find a number of dictionaries of word origins and histories of word usage in the reference section of your library. We enjoy browsing in them, and in Chapter 16, The Structure of Persuasion, we use definition by etymology to explain the red herring and bandwagon fallacies of reasoning (see pages 344, 346).

Definition by Example. As we suggested earlier in this chapter, an example is a specific instance or illustration of a larger group or classification. **Definition by example** uses the specific to make the general more clear. Cactus Pryor, a popular radio personality in Austin, Texas, chose definition by example to explain what he meant when he used the word *Bubba:*

definition by example: providing an instance or illustration of the word being defined.

> Bubba is a good ol' boy. Bubba likes the NRA and Bubba dips snuff and Bubba likes Ollie North and Bubba likes to fish and hunt and eat barbecue and talk about women and frequently is found in Texas politics. Dallas is full of Bubbas, but they dress better. Bubbas are hard to not like because they're friendly. They hate Yankees. Bubba wears cowboy clothes.[4]

Pryor's definition not only clarifies the word *Bubba,* it also makes his use of the concept more vivid.

You need not confine your examples to language, however. Often audible and visual examples can be your quickest and most vivid ways to define a term or concept.

Audible examples are those you let your audience hear. Speeches on types of music, voice patterns, or speech dialects might define key terms by audible examples. For example, if you were using the word "scat" in a speech on jazz, you might offer a dictionary definition of the term: "jazz singing with nonsense syllables."[5] But wouldn't a more interesting and vivid definition be to let your audience hear a taped example of Ella Fitzgerald, Betty Carter, or Al Jarreau singing scat? Other terms appropriate for audible definitions include the following.

bird calls	industrial music
Boston Brahmin dialect	nasality and denasality
conjunto music	sonata form
counterpoint	stuttering and cluttering
fugue	yodeling
glottal fry	

Visual examples define a term by letting the audience see a form of it. Speeches on styles of architecture or painting could benefit from visual definition, as well as any of the following examples.

Abstract Expressionism	concrete poetry	optical illusion
Art Deco	Cubism	photorealism
caricature	Fauvism	
complementary colors	naive painting	

Definition by Operation. Sometimes the quickest and liveliest way to define a term is to explain how it is used. **Definition by operation** clarifies a word or phrase by explaining how it works, what it does, or what it was designed to do. The terms *wok, radar detector, fax machine, food processor,* and *laser scalpel* are but a few of the physical objects best defined by explaining their operation.

You can also define concepts, actions, or processes by operation. To define magnetic resonance imaging, you would have to explain how that technology operates. Notice how the following person defines virtual reality by explaining how musicians and composers of the near future will use it:

> You're ready to enter an alternate reality. You slip on a pair of headphones, a helmet with a tiny video screen for each eye, and a special glove. Three-dimensional, generated images are projected onto your eye screens. Video "hands" match the movements of your own limbs. Sound seems to be coming from all around, not just inside your head, as you'd normally expect with 'phones.
>
> There's a mixing console floating before you. The music is coming from an apparent distance of a couple yards, but when a channel is "soloed," that sound moves to a point inches from your ear, while the rest of the mix stays put. By grabbing the edge of the board and pulling, you get as many input channels as you need, stretching away to infinity.[6]

Definition by operation is often livelier and more complete than most dictionary definitions. And as the example above illustrates, it is especially useful in the case of new technologies whose dictionary definitions have yet to be written.

definition by operation: explaining how the word being defined works, what it does, or what it was designed to do.

NARRATION

Narration is storytelling, the process of describing an action or a series of occurrences. If you come to school on Monday and tell a friend about some-

narration: the process of describing an action or series of occurrences; storytelling.

thing you did during the weekend, you are narrating those events. As a participant in the events, you will probably speak in first person at least part of the time, using the pronouns "I" or "we." Such a story is called a **personal narrative.** We have suggested that you draw upon your own experiences as you select and develop a speech topic, and personal narratives can be rich and interesting supporting materials.

Sultana, a student whose husband is Muslim and who had herself converted to the Muslim religion, used a personal narrative effectively. She told the story of her first experience with the celebration of Ramadan, a period of daylight fasting during the ninth month of the Muslim year:

> My first Ramadan I was a bit nervous. I had just become a Muslim, and I thought, "There is no way I can go from sunup to sunset without food. It's not even logical." I like to eat, as some of you may have noticed. And I thought, "There's no way that I can do this." Also, I was a student at the time, and it was finals. I honestly believe that you can't function if you don't eat. I mean, how can you think and pass a final? But I was determined at least to begin Ramadan; it goes for thirty days. So I set out and the first few days were a bit difficult. You can get hungry; there's no denying that. Your stomach growls out loud in class. But after about three days, the body adjusts. You don't really need as much food as most of us consume. You can live a long time on that stored-up fat we have and survive quite well. But the experience provides a lot of self-confidence, because if you can spend thirty days fasting, you can do just about anything.

Her classmates laughed along with Sultana as she poked fun at students' eating habits during the stress of final exams, as well as her own tendency to be finishing a snack as her speech class started. In addition to creating interest in the topic, Sultana's story reinforced her credibility to speak on the topic of Ramadan. We tend to believe the accounts of people who have experienced events firsthand. That is an important reason for using personal narratives.

Narratives, of course, need not be personal but may relate a series of incidents in the lives of others. When you speak from the point of view of a witness and use the pronouns "he," "she," or "they," you are telling a **third-person narrative.** In the following example, notice how the speaker, a teacher speaking on the subject of education, uses narration to illustrate her point that each child deserves special attention.

> In the pursuit of excellence, it's easy to give more attention to those children who already seem to have a head start toward success and to relegate the more difficult child to the background.
>
> We can't afford such impatience in the name of efficiency. We simply can't predict human success or failure.
>
> I'd like to tell you the story of two children—two educationally handicapped children.
>
> The parents of the first child were not considered successful. His father was unemployed, with no formal schooling. His mother was a teacher—and there was probably tension in the family because of this mismatch.
>
> This child, born in Port Huron, Michigan, was estimated to have an IQ of 81. He was withdrawn from school after months—and was considered backward by school officials.
>
> Physically, the child enrolled two years late due to scarlet fever and respiratory

infections. And he was going deaf. His emotional health was poor—stubborn, aloof, showing very little emotion.

He liked mechanics. He liked to play with fire and burned down his father's barn. He showed some manual dexterity, but used very poor grammar. But he *did* want to be a scientist or a railroad mechanic.

The second child showed not much more promise.

This child was born of an alcoholic father who worked as an itinerant—a mother who stayed at home.

As a child she was sickly, bedridden, and often hospitalized. She was considered erratic and withdrawn. She would bite her nails, and had numerous phobias. She wore a back brace from a spinal defect and would constantly seek attention.

She was a daydreamer with no vocational goals, although she expressed a desire to help the elderly and the poor.

Who were these children?

The boy from Port Huron became one of the world's greatest inventors—Thomas A. Edison.

And the awkward and sickly young girl, became a champion of the oppressed—Eleanor Roosevelt.[7]

COMPARISON AND CONTRAST

Comparison is the process of depicting one item—person, place, object, or concept—in relation to another, more familiar item. **Contrast** functions similarly to comparison except that contrast links items to show their differences. As you can tell, the chief purpose of both comparison and contrast is to clarify that less familiar term or concept. In order for either strategy to serve its purpose and have impact, your listeners must be familiar with one of the items involved in your comparison or contrast.

In a persuasive speech against the practice of late-term abortions, one student, Constance, compared the *Roe v. Wade* decision to the *Dred Scott* decision. She quoted from the *Roe v. Wade* opinion and then said simply, "Sounds a lot like the *Dred Scott* decision, don't you think?" This was not an effective comparison. Constance should have explained what the *Dred Scott* decision was (it validated the ownership of slaves as property). She could then have pointed out the similarities between the two court decisions as she saw them. If she had done this, all of her listeners would have been able to judge the effectiveness of her comparison, rather than the few who remembered quickly what the *Dred Scott* decision said.

Comparison and contrast would logically be the primary types of supporting materials for the following speech topics:

Specific purpose: to persuade the audience that American education could benefit by adopting elements of the Japanese system of secondary education.

Specific purpose: to inform the audience of the differences between lacto-ovo, lacto, and vegan vegetarian diets.

Literal Comparison and Contrast. Just as examples can be actual or hypothetical, comparisons and contrasts can be literal or figurative. A **literal comparison** associates items that share actual similarities. Notice the interesting literal comparison in this quotation from the book *Tribes* by sociologists

comparison: the process of associating two items by pointing out their similarities.

contrast: the process of distinguishing two items by pointing out their differences.

literal comparison and contrast: associations or distinctions between two items that share actual similarities.

Desmond Morris and Peter Marsh. A student, Marcia, used it to support her speech on youth gangs and their dress codes:

> Where a single species of birds inhabits, say, a small island, its members tend to have very dull plumage, lacking in pattern and color. As the number of species or sub-species in any one area increases, so too does the number of species-specific markings in the feathers and beaks. The most extravagant patterns and colors of plumage occur when the variety of avian life in a given area is greatest and the need for identification becomes highly important. Youth groups are, in this sense, very much like species of birds — although, of course, their decoration is of cultural rather than genetic origin.[8]

In a persuasive speech on the dangers of overexposure to the sun, another student, Patricia, also made effective use of a literal contrast:

> Sunblocks are either chemical or physical. Oils, lotions, and creams that claim a certain SPF factor all contain chemical blocks. On the other hand, zinc oxide, the white or colored clay-looking material you see some people wearing, usually on their noses, is a physical sunblock.

Figurative Comparison and Contrast. Unlike their literal counterparts, **figurative comparison and contrast** associate two items that do not necessarily share any similarities. The purpose of figurative comparisons is to surprise us into seeing or considering one person, place, object, or concept in a new way.

Effective figurative comparisons always contain an element of surprise, but the surprise must spark recognition. In a speech of self-introduction where students were to explain some of the events occurring the year they were born, one student, Carolyn, mentioned the low prices advertised for girdles in a 1946 newspaper she had consulted. She then said, "For those of you women who have never had the pleasure of putting on and wearing a girdle, let me tell you that getting into a girdle was the aerobic dancing of 1946." The figurative comparison evokes a vivid and funny image.

One student describing the density of a neutron star quoted from *Sky & Telescope* magazine that "your bathroom sink could hold the Great Lakes if the water were compressed to the density of a neutron star."

Another student introduced his informative speech on karate with the following contrast:

> What images come to your mind when I say the word "karate"? Chuck Norris or Bruce Lee jumping across the movie screen? A flash of fists and feet as dozens of bad guys fall? That's the popular conception of karate. Though it is an excellent form of self-defense, the actual practice of karate is quite different from those images created by the movies.

You can use comparison and contrast together in your speech. If you clarify a term by showing how it is similar to something the audience knows, you can often make the term even clearer by showing how it is different from something the audience also knows.

Discussion Prompt:
Is the comparison William Fort establishes in the opening quotation and first paragraph of his speech on Sick Building Syndrome (Appendix C) *literal* or *figurative*? Why? Answer: Literal. He compares the conditions that caused two epidemics.

figurative comparison and contrast: associations or distinctions between two items that do not share actual similarities.

Discussion Prompt:
Which type of comparison, literal or figurative, does the speaker develop in the example of an impromptu speech in Chapter 17? (Practice speeches are like baseball spring training: figurative)

Statistics are collections of data. Broadly speaking, any number used as supporting material is a statistic. Used appropriately, statistics can also make your ideas clear and vivid, increase your credibility, and prove your point.

We place a great deal of trust in statistics that we feel have been accurately gathered and interpreted. Politicians often trust their pollsters to reveal the probable results of an election even weeks before the actual balloting. We trust statistics to predict certain events in our daily lives, such as price increases or decreases on certain goods and services. Statistics enable speakers to demonstrate trends or compare a situation today with one in the past.

You must be careful about how you use statistics in your speech. Used inappropriately, statistics may baffle or even bore your audience. The following four suggestions should guide you in presenting statistical material.

Do Not Rely Exclusively on Statistics. If statistics are your only form of supporting material, your audience will likely feel bombarded by numbers. Remember, your *listening* audience has only one chance to hear and assimilate your statistics. As a speaker, then, use statistics judiciously and in combination with other forms of support. A barrage of statistics is generally less effective than a few key statistics combined with examples and explanation. Too many statistics will confuse your audience.

Notice in the following speech excerpt how Professor Louis Rader successfully joins statistics with comparison to argue that American industry must commit itself to increasing product quality:

> Many of our CEOs felt that 99 percent good was good enough. If this figure (99 percent good) were converted into our daily non-industrial life, what would it mean?
> More than 30,000 newborn babies would be accidentally dropped by doctors and nurses each year.
> There would be 200,000 wrong drug prescriptions each year.
> Electricity would be off for fifteen minutes each day.
> Ninety-nine percent good means 10,000 bad out of 1 million.[9]

Round Off Statistics. A statistic of 74.6 percent has less impact and is more difficult for your audience to remember than "nearly three-fourths." No one in your audience will remember the statistic of $1,497,568.42; many, however, may be able to remember "a million and a half dollars." Rounding off statistics for your listeners is neither deceptive nor unethical. Instead, it reflects your concern for helping your audience understand and retain key statistical information.

Use Units of Measure that are Familiar to Your Audience. In a speech on the break up of the Soviet Union, telling your audience that the average monthly salary of a Soviet worker in 1990 was 257 rubles would mean little to them. They would also need to know that the official ruble exchange rate at that time was fifty-six cents.[10] Telling your audience that the average monthly salary of a Soviet worker in 1990 was equivalent to $143.92, or nearly $150 in U.S. currency, would be much more vivid. Use familiar units of measure or translate unfamiliar units into familiar ones.

statistics: data collected in the form of numbers.

Discussion Prompt:
Each month *Harper's* magazine publishes the "Harper's Index," a collection of interesting statistics on a wide variety of topics. Their statistics gathered during the 1980s have been collected into the following paperback book: Lapham, Lewis, Michael Pollan, and Eric Ethridge. *The Harper's Index Book.* New York: Holt, 1987. Select a few of these statistics from the magazine or book and ask your students how they could use them to support ideas in a speech.

Teaching Strategy:
Mention to students that they will likely use three types of statistics: (1) measures of incidents or events in the *past;* (2) measures of *current* attitudes, beliefs, or behaviors; or (3) projections of *future* occurrences. Have them bring to class examples of each type.

Use Visual Aids to Represent or Clarify Relationships among Statistics. Suppose you wanted to use the following paragraph in a speech about baseball players:

> Since professional baseball began, in 1876, California has produced 1,282 major leaguers and Pennsylvania has produced 1,260. These states are followed by New York (943), Illinois (859), Ohio (858), and Texas (541).[11]

If you're a baseball fan, you probably find these facts interesting. But remember, even the most avid fans in your audience would probably not remember all these numbers. Your listeners would be more likely to remember the information if you presented the facts both orally and visually. In this case you might construct a chart ranking the states, with the number of players each produced beside the state's name.

TESTIMONY

Examples, definition, narration, comparison, contrast, and statistics are discrete types of supporting materials. Each is a different strategy for validating the ideas of a speech. Speakers sometimes generate these types of support themselves. Other times they glean them from their research, citing their sources but justifying the point in their own words. Still other times speakers find the words and structure of the original source so compelling that they quote directly or paraphrase the source. This strategy is known as **testimony.** Testimony, sometimes called quotation, is another method of presenting types of supporting material. When you quote or paraphrase the words and ideas of others, you use testimony. Look at the two examples below of a speaker making the same basic statement:

testimony: quotations or paraphrases an authoritative source to clarify or prove a point.

> A second characteristic of American families today is that they have two incomes. The days of Ricky and Lucy Ricardo, Ward and June Cleaver, and Archie and Edith Bunker are over. In fact, nearly two-thirds of couples with children are supported by incomes from the husband and wife, many of whom work full-time.

Suppose a speaker, instead, phrased and supported the idea like this:

> A second characteristic of American families today is that they have two incomes. The days of Ricky and Lucy Ricardo, Ward and June Cleaver, and Archie and Edith Bunker are over, at least according to Eugene Fram, a research professor at Rochester Institute of Technology, and Joel Axelrod, president of an international marketing research organization. They write in the October 1990 issue of *American Demographics* that "In 1988, almost two-thirds of married couples with children — 16 million families — had two incomes. In 8 million of these families, both husband and wife worked full-time, year-round."[12]

As you can see, the key idea in each of the examples is the same: The typical American family has two incomes. Both examples rely on statistics to support the key idea. However, by quoting a source in the second example, the speaker has added an additional element of support. The expert testimony increases the credibility of the idea. In this example, testimony or quotation has not changed the *type* of support; it has merely enhanced its *believability*.

Testimony sometimes draws its effectiveness from the content of the quotation, as in the example above. Other times, testimony relies largely on the reputation of the person making the statement. Peter Brown, for example, speaking to a group of fellow lawyers, urged them to renew their professional commitment to enhance justice. He quoted former U.S. Supreme Court Justice William O. Douglas in the conclusion of his speech:

> "As nightfall does not come at once, neither does oppression. In both instances, there is a twilight when everything remains seemingly unchanged. And it is in such twilight that we all must be most aware of *change* in the air, however slight, lest we become unwitting victims of the darkness."
> American lawyers should become strong instruments to advance the ends of justice and to stop the selling of the profession, "lest we become unwitting victims of the darkness."[13]

Notice how in all these examples the speakers used the words and ideas of others to enhance the credibility of their ideas. Expert testimony, however, is not limited to the statements of other people. As a speaker you use *personal testimony* when you support your ideas with your own experiences and observations. Many students select a speech topic because they have some special knowledge or experience with the subject. One of our students, for example, gave a speech comparing retail prices at large supermarkets to those at convenience stores. He was careful to explain his credentials and establish his expertise on the subject. Not only did he wear his store apron and manager's name tag, but he also said early in his introduction, "As a former receiving control manager, I was in charge of purchasing products for the store, so I have some knowledge of how wholesale prices are translated into the retail prices you and I pay." The speaker enhanced his credibility both verbally and nonverbally.

Because a quotation is only as credible as its source, you should ask several questions as you evaluate the testimony you plan to include in your speech. If you intend to use personal testimony, you should ask these questions of yourself.

Teaching Strategy: Ask students to suggest several position statements (e.g., The cost of health care has increased dramatically; doctor assisted suicide should be an option for terminally ill patients; terms of office in the House and Senate should be limited). Write the statements on the blackboard. Have students suggest different types of material that a speaker could use to support each statement. Discuss the advantages and disadvantages of each type.

---

1. Is the source competent?
2. Is the source unbiased?
3. Does the source have special qualifications?
4. Is the source in the "mainstream" of thought?
5. Is the source recent?

KEY POINTS
Tests of Sources

Is the Source Competent? Competence develops from a person's knowledge and experience. We are likely to trust the observation of William O. Douglas on a legal topic if a speaker reminds us that Douglas served many years on the U.S. Supreme Court. The student who discussed the pricing policies of large supermarkets and convenience stores was careful to establish his own credibility both verbally and nonverbally. Speakers who fail to present their qualifications or the qualifications of those they quote give listeners little reason to believe them.

Is the Source Unbiased? Sources perceived to be biased are less credible than those perceived to be objective. You expect representatives of political parties, special-interest groups, business corporations, labor unions, and so forth, to make statements advancing their interests. It will probably not surprise you that the supermarket receiving control manager we quoted earlier concluded that it is more economical to shop at large supermarkets than at convenience stores. When you include testimony and quotations in your speeches, you should try to rely on those who do not have a vested interest in sustaining the position they voice.

Does the Source Have Any Special Qualifications? For a persuasive speech condemning the growth of tabloid news, which source would you find more credible: a cub reporter or a Pulitzer Prize-winning journalist? In an informative speech comparing the philosophies of various environmental action groups, would you be more impressed by testimony from a local member of Greenpeace or a nationally acclaimed environmental expert? If you delivered a speech advocating the licensing of law clerks to draft wills and conduct other routine legal business, would you rather quote a first-year lawyer or a senior law partner of a major legal corporation? Of course it would depend on the specific individuals and what they said, but you would probably place more trust in the latter person in each of the examples just listed.

Certain individuals, because of their position, education, or training, can claim enhanced credibility. The chairperson of a committee that has just studied the effects of a community-based sentencing program may claim to be in a position to know the facts on that issue. A person completing graduate study on the effects of a local Head Start program on literacy has similarly developed an area of expertise. When you have several experts saying essentially the same thing, select those with the most impressive qualifications.

Is the Source in the "Mainstream" of Thought? If you have ever watched television shows such as *Crossfire, Nightline, This Week with David Brinkley,* or the *MacNeil/Lehrer NewsHour,* you have probably observed two experts arguing a point from opposing perspectives. Both advocates may appear to have similar qualifications. Whom should you believe? One way to answer this question is to turn to other experts. Although a majority opinion is not always superior to a minority view, we tend to place greater trust in opinions shared by several experts. If your research uncovers one expert supporting your point and many who discount it, you would be wise to investigate further.

Is the Source Recent? If you were preparing a travel budget for a trip overseas, which would you find more helpful: an airline pricing schedule you had from a year ago or one your roommate picked up at the airport this week? Of course, you would want to rely on your roommate's information. The reason is simple: It is more recent. The timeliness of information is especially important if you are speaking about constantly changing issues, conditions, and events. What you read today may already be dated by the time you give your speech.

Some speech topics, however, are timeless. If you speak about the gods of Mount Olympus, no one would question your use of Thomas Bulfinch's books about mythology, even though they were published in the mid-1800s. Both Edith Hamilton's *Mythology,* published in 1940, and Robert Graves' *Greek Gods and Heroes,* published in 1960, would also add credibility to your speech. As

Cross-Reference:
Assign your students to read William Fort's persuasive speech on the Sick Building Syndrome (Appendix C). Have them analyze the evidence Fort uses to support his contentions. Use the criteria listed in the following annotation to assess the credibility of Fort's ideas.

Teaching Strategy:
In this chapter and in our chapters on research and persuasion, we discuss several guidelines for selecting and using evidence. Remind your students to ask the following questions as they construct their speeches:

1. Is the evidence accurate?
2. Is the evidence quoted in context?
3. Is the source of the evidence an expert?
4. Is the source of the evidence unbiased?
5. Is the evidence relevant to the point being made?
6. Is the evidence specific?
7. Is the evidence sufficient to prove the point?
8. Is the evidence recent? (timely?)

scholars of mythology, Bulfinch, Hamilton, and Graves earned reputations that time is not likely to diminish. Similarly, if you deliver a speech on the ancient Olympic Games, your most authoritative sources might be history textbooks. If, however, your topic concerns current drug-testing procedures in Olympic competition, it would be vital for you to use recent sources of the best quality you can find.

Figure 8.1 summarizes the uses of the types of supporting materials we have discussed.

Type of Support	Use
Example	Provides instances or samples of people, places, objects, actions, conditions, or experiences
Actual Example	Provides clarification and proof
Hypothetical Example	Provides clarification, but does not alone provide proof
Definition	Clarifies an unfamiliar word or phrase
Definition by Synonym	Substitutes a familiar word for the one defined
Definition by Etymology	Explains the origin of the word defined
Definition by Example	Provides an illustration or sample of the word defined
Audible Example	Lets listeners hear sample of the term defined
Visual Example	Lets listeners see sample of the term defined
Definition by Operation	Explains use, function, or purpose of the term defined
Narration	Describes action or event
Personal Narrative	Describes action from participant's point of view; uses "I" and "we"
Third-Person Narrative	Describes action from witness's point of view; uses "he," "she," and "they"
Comparison	Clarifies term by showing its similarity to a more familiar term
Literal Comparison	Associates items with actual similarities
Figurative Comparison	Associates items without actual similarities
Contrast	Clarifies term by showing its difference from a more familiar term
Literal Contrast	Distinguishes items with actual differences
Figurative Contrast	Distinguishes items without actual differences
Statistics	Clarify or prove a point with numbers
Testimony	Clarifies or proves a point using the words of an expert
Personal Testimony	Clarifies a point using the speaker's own words

FIGURE 8.1 Supporting Materials: Types and Uses

Summary

We use supporting materials in a speech to achieve three purposes: clarity, vividness, and credibility. Clarity helps the audience understand your ideas. Vividness assists them to remember your ideas. Credible supporting materials make your ideas believable.

Types of material you can use to support the main ideas of your speech include examples, definition, narration, comparison, contrast, statistics, and testimony. *Examples* are samples or illustrations of a category. Those categories may be people, places, objects, actions, experiences, or conditions. Examples may be brief or extended, and actual or hypothetical. *Actual examples* are real or factual. *Hypothetical examples* are imaginary or fictitious. Both types of examples make a general or abstract term more specific and vivid for the audience.

Definitions are explanations of an unfamiliar term or a word with several possible meanings. We can define terms by synonym, by etymology, by example, or by operation. *Definition by synonym* offers a word or phrase that is the rough equivalent of the word being defined. *Definition by etymology* shows the origin of the word being defined. *Definition by example* gives an illustration or sample of the word in question. *Definition by operation* explains how something works or what it was designed to do. Definitions are crucial if you are using words you suspect your audience will not know, or if you want them to adopt one particular meaning for a term.

Narration is storytelling. Narratives may be personal or third-person. *Personal narratives* originate from the speaker's experience; they use the first-person pronouns "I" or "we." *Third-person narratives* are stories about other people, and they are delivered using either people's names or the third-person pronouns "she," "he," or "they."

Comparisons associate two or more items to show the similarities between or among them. Comparisons can be either literal or figurative. A *literal comparison* links two items that share actual similarities. A *figurative comparison* associates items that do not share any actual similarities.

Contrasts function like comparisons except that their purpose is to distinguish or show differences between two or more items.

Statistics are data collected in the form of numbers. Used properly, statistics can bolster a speaker's credibility and lend vivid support to the ideas of the speech. To ensure your proper use of statistics, you should follow four guidelines. First, don't rely exclusively on statistics, but combine them with other supporting materials. Second, round off statistics to help your listeners remember them. Third, either use units of measure familiar to your audience or else translate your statistics into familiar units. Fourth, use visual aids to clarify the relationships among various statistics.

The final form of support is testimony. You use *testimony* when you cite, quote, or paraphrase authoritative sources. The authorities you cite may employ examples, definitions, narration, comparison, contrast, or statistics. To help ensure that your citations are credible, you should ask five questions of each source you are considering. Is the source competent? Is the source unbiased on this issue? Does the source have any special qualifications? Is the source in the mainstream of thought on this issue? And is the source recent?

think about it, take a break, and come back to your reading when you feel fresher. As a listener, you do not have the freedom to do any of these things. A listener is at the mercy of the speaker. Therefore, the speaker must make the task of listening easier. How does the speaker highlight key ideas and help the audience remember them during and after the speech?

A speaker supplies the missing elements with a clear organizational pattern and effective delivery. Good organization maximizes a speaker's information and arranges ideas so that an audience will remember them. A speaker cannot make use of written cues and so must compensate in other ways. In Chapter 12 we suggest techniques of delivery to help you reinforce the ideas of your speech. This chapter focuses on **structure** — how to organize the supporting materials you have assembled through your research.

A well-organized, well-delivered speech can have as great an impact on your listeners as a well-written essay has on readers. We will teach you how to organize first the body of your speech, and then the introduction and the conclusion. You may find this an unusual order in which to organize the parts of a speech. Be assured that by the end of this chapter you will see the logic of this sequence.

■ Organizing the Body of the Speech ────────────────

Although it is delivered after the introduction, the body of a speech should be constructed first, for in order to "tell us what you are going to tell us," you must first determine what to "tell us." In constructing the body of a speech, your best strategy is to divide the speech into key ideas and then develop each idea.

DIVIDE THE SPEECH INTO KEY IDEAS

In the body of the speech, you develop your key ideas according to a specific organizational pattern. Public speakers employ a wide variety of organizational structures. We will discuss six patterns most commonly used: topical, chronological, spatial, causal, pro-con, and gimmick division. These patterns are appropriate for either informative or persuasive speeches. In Chapter 16 we discuss four additional patterns more suitable for persuasive speeches only: refutational, problem-solution, need-plan, and the motivated sequence.

Keep in mind as you consider these patterns that no one of them is best. In order to achieve the best results, you must select the structure that best achieves the purpose of your speech. In other words, fit the organization to your topic, rather than your topic to the organization. If you study these patterns of organization carefully, you should have no difficulty in finding one that works for any topic you speak on in this class.

Class Activity: Have students brainstorm individually or in groups for topics appropriate for each pattern of organizing a speech. Have them select one topic for each pattern, write a specific purpose statement, and list the ideas to be developed in the speech.

		KEY POINTS
1. Topical division	4. Causal division	**Patterns for Dividing**
2. Chronological division	5. Pro-Con division	**Your Speech into**
3. Spatial division	6. Gimmick division	**Key Ideas**

Topical Division. The **topical division** is the most common organiza-tional pattern for public speeches. This strategy creates subtopics, categories which constitute the larger topic. For example, a speech on the cost of intercol-legiate athletics is divided topically if it focuses on the sports of baseball, bas-ketball, and football. A speech on the great actor Laurence Olivier is arranged topically if the speaker's main points cover Olivier's childhood, his stage roles, and his film career.

Here are more examples of topical division:

Specific Purpose: To inform the audience of the effects of an enhanced self-concept.
Key Ideas: **I.** A good self-concept enhances social interaction.
II. A good self-concept enhances academic achievement.
III. A good self-concept enhances career success.

Specific Purpose: To inform the audience of three views of graffiti.
Key Ideas: **I.** Graffiti as artistic expression
II. Graffiti as political expression
III. Graffiti as vandalism

Specific Purpose: To persuade the audience of the importance of personal dress.
Key Ideas: **I.** Clothing's effects on image
A. The image you have of yourself
B. The image others have of you
II. Clothing's effects on behavior
A. How you behave
B. How others behave when with you

As these examples suggest, topical organization is particularly appropriate as a method of narrowing broad topics, and that may explain its popularity and widespread use. In addition to helping you stay within your time limits, the topical pattern is also attractive because it lets you select subtopics to match your own interests and the interests and needs of your audience.

Chronological Division. The **chronological pattern** follows a time se-quence. Topics that begin with phrases such as "the steps to" or "the history of" are especially appropriate to this organization. Examples of such topics might include the history of your university, the development of computers, the stages of intoxication, the process of silk screening, steps to getting your first job, or how a product is marketed.

The following ideas are developed chronologically:

Specific Purpose: To inform the audience of Elisabeth Kübler-Ross' five stages of dying.
Key Ideas: **I.** Denial
II. Anger
III. Bargaining
IV. Depression
V. Acceptance

Specific Purpose: To inform the audience of the steps to a successful job interview.

Key Ideas: **I.** Prepare thoroughly.
         II. Arrive promptly.
       III. Enter confidently.
       IV. Communicate effectively.
        V. Follow up immediately.

Chronological organization works best if you are explaining procedures or processes. A simple and familiar example of chronological organization is a recipe. Any well-written recipe is organized in a time sequence: First, make sure that you have these ingredients; second, preheat the oven, and so forth.

Although the key ideas of a speech should follow a single method of division, you can use another pattern as you develop one of the key ideas. For example, a speech on ventriloquism could be divided **topically** to include (1) the history of ventriloquism, (2) the types of ventriloquism, and (3) the psychology of ventriloquism. Developing the first idea, however, is best accomplished by a **chronological** format: The speaker might discuss the history of ventriloquism beginning in Ancient Greece and then show its development in the Middle Ages, the Renaissance, and in modern times.

Spatial Division. You divide your topic **spatially** when your main points are organized according to their physical proximity or geography. This pattern is appropriate for a speech discussing the parts of an object or a place. A speech on Scandinavia, for example, might contain three divisions corresponding to the three primary countries of Scandinavia: Denmark, Norway, and Sweden.

Another example of spatial division is:

Specific Purpose: To inform the audience on the design of Shakespeare's Globe Theatre.

Key Ideas: **I.** The stage
       II. The galleries
      III. The "yard"

If you were giving a speech describing current exhibits at a museum of history in your city, you might remember from your last visit that as you enter, the dinosaur exhibit is to your left, a display of antique toys is straight ahead, and the permanent wildlife exhibit is to your right. Letting the spaces in the museum, from left to right, organize your speech, your outline of the main points would be as follows:

Specific Purpose: To inform the audience of the current exhibits at the Museum of History.

Key Ideas: **I.** The dinosaur exhibit
       II. The antique toy collection
      III. The wildlife exhibit

Causal Division. You would choose a **causal organizational pattern** when you want to trace a condition or action from its causes to its effects, or from effects back to causes. Medical topics, in which a speaker discusses the symptoms and causes of a disease, can be easily organized using this method of

Class Activity:
Have students look at the list of audience-generated topics in Chapter 6, selecting several that would lend themselves well to chronological division. What subtopics might each include?

spatial division: organizes a speech according to the geography or physical structure of the subject.

Class Activity:
Have students look at the list of research-generated topics in Chapter 6 and select a topic that would lend itself to spatial division—for example, cosmetic surgery. What are some subtopics a speech on that topic might include?

Class Activity:
Have groups of students generate a list of three medical conditions that a speaker would likely organize causally (e.g. Tourette's syndrome, Alzheimer's disease, Marfan syndrome).

causal division: organizes a speech from cause to effect, or from effect to cause.

division. Informative speeches on topics such as hurricanes, lightning, earthquakes, and other natural phenomena may also use this pattern. The following speech outline illustrates the causal pattern.

> *Specific Purpose:* To inform the audience of the causes and effects of air pollution.
>
> *Key Ideas:* **I.** Causes
>   **A.** Automobiles
>   **B.** Electric-power plants
>   **C.** Industrial processes
>   **II.** Effects
>   **A.** On animal life
>   **B.** On plant life
>   **C.** On buildings and other structures

Because the causal pattern may be used any time a speaker attributes causes for a particular condition, it is suitable for persuasive as well as informative speeches. A speaker might attempt to prove that certain prescription drugs are, in part, responsible for violent behavior among those who use them; that the availability of handguns fosters needless death; that televising executions would lead to a call for an end to capital punishment; or that tobacco use results in disease, debility, and death. For all of these topics the causal pattern would work well as you develop your speech.

Pro-Con Division. The **pro-con division** presents both sides of an issue. You present the arguments *for* a position and the arguments *against*. Because it is balanced in perspective, this pattern is more appropriate for an informative speech than a persuasive one. After discussing each side of an issue, however, you might choose to defend the stronger position. In this case, your division becomes **pro-con-assessment,** and this pattern is more appropriate for a speech to persuade rather than a speech to inform.

An advantage of the pro-con pattern is that it sets an issue in its broader context and provides balance and objectivity. A disadvantage, however, is the time required to do this. You need plenty of time to discuss both sides of an issue in sufficient detail. Therefore, you will probably want to use this strategy only in one of your longer speeches for this class. If you do not devote sufficient time to each idea, a pro-con or pro-con-assessment development may seem simplistic or superficial to your audience.

The following outlines demonstrate pro-con analyses of two controversial issues.

> *Specific Purpose:* To inform the audience of the arguments for and against an increase in the minimum wage.
>
> *Key Ideas:* **I.** Increasing the minimum wage would be beneficial.
>   **A.** The number of poor would decrease.
>   **B.** The number of people on welfare would decrease.
>   **C.** The concept of social justice would be affirmed.
>   **II.** Increasing the minimum wage would be harmful.
>   **A.** Unemployment would increase.
>   **B.** Inflation would increase.
>   **C.** Business bankruptcies would increase.

pro-con division: organizes a speech according to arguments for and against some policy, position, or action.

Class Activity:
Have students brainstorm individually or in groups for topics that can be developed according to a pro-con division. Have them write a specific purpose statement for several of the topics and list the divisions of the body of the speech.

Class Activity:
Students sometimes consider a pro-con division for topics that are really one-sided — such as water conservation or recycling. Ask students to generate several topics that would be *inappropriate* for pro-con division, either because of a lack of opposing arguments or because a speaker favors one side so strongly.

Specific Purpose: To inform the audience of the pros and cons of limiting campaign contributions by political action committees (PACs).

Key Ideas:

   I. Limitations on PAC money are desirable.

      A. PAC money undermines the concept of equal representation.

      B. PAC money undermines the concept of local representation.

      C. PAC money promotes public cynicism.

   II. Limitations on PAC money are undesirable.

      A. Limitations would decrease political participation.

      B. Limitations would strengthen the advantage of the incumbent.

      C. Limitations would violate the right of free expression.

The Gimmick Division. A final organizational strategy you can consider for a speech to inform is the **gimmick,** or what some authors call the formula pattern. The most common use of this strategy develops and words the key ideas in such a way that the first letter of each key idea forms a word. As a student you have been using gimmicks for years to help you retain information you need to know. In elementary school you may have learned to spell "geography" by memorizing the sentence, "*G*eorge *E*liot's *o*ld *g*randmother *r*ode *a* *p*ig *h*ome *y*esterday." In a science class, you might have memorized the order of colors in the visible spectrum by remembering the name "Roy G. Biv": *r*ed-*o*range-*y*ellow-*g*reen-*b*lue-*i*ndigo-*v*iolet.

Gimmicks work so well as memory devices that even advertisers and public service groups occasionally use them. If you can recall what "the four C's" of diamond grading refers to, you probably memorized that information according to a gimmick. The four C's stand for *c*ut, *c*olor, *c*larity, and *c*arat weight. Some health advisers tell us to remember "rice" in the event that we suffer a sprain: *r*est, *i*ce, *c*ompression, *e*levation. We have heard students use both of these gimmicks to organize informative speeches on these topics.

If you were giving a speech explaining how to improve listening, you might want to use the gimmick developed by Robert Montgomery (giving him credit in your speech, of course).[2] Montgomery suggests six guidelines for better listening:

   L — Look at the other person.

   A — Ask questions.

   D — Don't interrupt.

   D — Don't change the subject.

   E — Express emotions with control.

   R — Responsively listen.

No doubt, the word "ladder" would help you remember your major points as you prepared and delivered such a speech. More important, though, the gimmick would help your listeners retain what you had said.

At times the gimmick pattern of organizing a speech may seem corny or trivial to you. If you feel that way about this pattern you probably should avoid it, as your speech delivery may seem self-conscious. When used well and with confidence, however, the gimmick helps your audience remember not only

gimmick division: organizes a speech according to a special memory device, such as alliteration, rhyme, or initial letters that spell a word.

Discussion Prompt: Ask your students what gimmicks they have used recently to help them remember materials in this or another class. Example: Some students may have used "IRS" to help them remember the elements of the triangle of meaning in Chapter 1.

what points you covered, but also the order in which you covered them. That is a major accomplishment! In the next section of this chapter we use another gimmick approach as we introduce you to our "4 S's" of developing the ideas of the speech. See if it helps you remember these important points.

DEVELOP THE KEY IDEAS

Assume that your speech is divided into the key ideas, that you have selected the most appropriate pattern to organize them, and that you have decided their order in the speech. Now you need to develop *each* major point. Obviously, the number of major points you can develop in a speech depends on the time you have been allocated to speak, the complexity of the topic, and the audience's level of education and knowledge of the subject. There is no fixed rule, but most speech instructors recommend that you develop at least two but not more than five main points. Many speakers find that a three-point structure works best.

Regardless of the number of points you select, your responsibility is to explain and support each one sufficiently. The organizational strategy we suggest is one we call the **"4 S's."** Your listeners will better comprehend and remember your speech if you *signpost, state, support,* and *summarize* each idea.

KEY POINTS
The "4 S" Strategy of Developing Key Ideas

1. Signpost the idea.
2. State the idea.
3. Support the idea.
4. Summarize the idea.

Signpost the Idea. Just as a highway signpost tells travelers where they are in their journey, so a signpost in a speech tells the audience where they are in the speaker's message. **Signposts** are words such as "initially," "first," "second," and "finally." They enable your listeners to follow your organizational pattern and, hence, increase the likelihood that they will remember your key ideas.

State the Idea. Each major idea needs to be worded precisely and with impact. Each idea needs to be phrased as a single, declarative sentence stating the point you want the listener to remember.

You can often accomplish the first two S's, signposting and stating your idea, in one sentence. Suppose the specific purpose of your speech is to persuade the audience to oppose mandatory drug testing in the workplace. If you say, "The first reason mandatory drug testing is harmful is that it is cost-prohibitive," you are *signposting*—"first"—and *stating* your idea—"mandatory drug testing is cost-prohibitive." You are now ready to develop that claim with various types of supporting materials.

Support the Idea. This third S is the meat of the "4 S's," similar to the body of the speech as a whole because this step will take you the most time. Once you have signposted and stated the idea, you must **support** it. You have a variety of types of supporting materials at your disposal, limited only by the amount of

Signposting helps listeners organize a speaker's message.

Practice Speaking:
To demonstrate the usefulness of signposting, ask a student to give the class directions for driving to a familiar local landmark (a park, mall, restaurant, or movie theatre, for example). He or she will probably signpost naturally using words such as "then" or "next." Ask students to evaluate the directions given.

research you have done and by time limits on your speech. Some of those types of supporting materials, discussed in detail in Chapter 8, are examples, definitions, comparisons, and statistics.

How would you support your statement that mandatory drug testing is cost-prohibitive? Your strongest form of support will likely be statistics — statistics on the average cost of a single drug screening test, estimates of the number of people currently employed in the United States, and projections of the total cost of testing the entire American workforce for drug use. The figures will be high and will serve as persuasive support for your claim.

Summarize the Idea. A **summary** at the end of each major division helps wrap up the discussion and refocus attention on the key idea. The summary may be as brief as one sentence. To continue with our drug testing example, you might summarize your first subpoint by saying, "Clearly, then, the enormous costs of mandatory drug testing would make it an unreasonable burden on the economy." Such a statement reinforces your point by repeating it — "the cost of drug testing would be too high" — and also provides a note of closure, suggesting that you have said all you plan to about the economics of mandatory drug testing. Now you are ready to introduce your second point, that drug testing results in lost work time — again by signposting, stating, supporting, and summarizing.

Another example of the "4 S" strategy is included in Figure 9.1. Notice how the speaker uses signposting, statement, support, and summary to present her argument that the school year should be extended for American elementary and high school students.

We believe that use of the "4 S's" is fundamental to effective organization within the body of any speech. As you begin to master and apply this four-step strategy, it may seem to be a "cookie-cutter" approach to public speaking. It *is* exactly that. The "4 S's" are to speech organization what the school figures used to be to ice skating and the required movements are to gymnastics. They are all basics that you must learn before you are able to develop your own style or flair. As you master the "4 S's" and gain confidence in public speaking, clear organization will become a habit, almost a reflex reaction performed without conscious effort. As your ability to organize ideas clearly becomes second

Practice Speaking:
After only two or three minutes to collect their thoughts, have students demonstrate their understanding of the 4 S's by speaking without notes for at least a minute and a half on one of these (or similar) topics:

Two Times I've Embarrassed Myself
My Three Favorite Foods
My Two Biggest Accomplishments
My Three Favorite Tapes, CDs, or Records

Stress that you don't want an introduction or conclusion. In addition to clarifying the use of the 4 S's, this activity demonstrates some of the types of support we discussed in Chapter 8. It also shows students that personal narratives, examples, and comparisons can make vivid supporting materials.

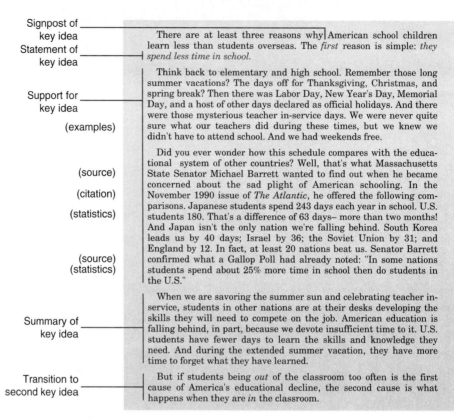

Signpost of key idea

Statement of key idea

> There are at least three reasons why American school children learn less than students overseas. The *first* reason is simple: *they spend less time in school.*

Support for key idea

(examples)

> Think back to elementary and high school. Remember those long summer vacations? The days off for Thanksgiving, Christmas, and spring break? Then there was Labor Day, New Year's Day, Memorial Day, and a host of other days declared as official holidays. And there were those mysterious teacher in-service days. We were never quite sure what our teachers did during these times, but we knew we didn't have to attend school. And we had weekends free.

(source)

(citation)

(statistics)

(source)
(statistics)

> Did you ever wonder how this schedule compares with the educational system of other countries? Well, that's what Massachusetts State Senator Michael Barrett wanted to find out when he became concerned about the sad plight of American schooling. In the November 1990 issue of *The Atlantic*, he offered the following comparisons. Japanese students spend 243 days each year in school. U.S. students 180. That's a difference of 63 days– more than two months! And Japan isn't the only nation we're falling behind. South Korea leads us by 40 days; Israel by 36; the Soviet Union by 31; and England by 12. In fact, at least 20 nations beat us. Senator Barrett confirmed what a Gallop Poll had already noted: "In some nations students spend about 25% more time in school then do students in the U.S."

Summary of key idea

> When we are savoring the summer sun and celebrating teacher in-service, students in other nations are at their desks developing the skills they will need to compete on the job. American education is falling behind, in part, because we devote insufficient time to it. U.S. students have fewer days to learn the skills and knowledge they need. And during the extended summer vacation, they have more time to forget what they have learned.

Transition to second key idea

> But if students being *out* of the classroom too often is the first cause of America's educational decline, the second cause is what happens when they are *in* the classroom.

FIGURE 9.1   The "4 S" Strategy of Developing Key Ideas

nature to you, you will find that the structure of your thinking, writing, and speaking has greatly improved.

CONNECT THE KEY IDEAS

A speech is composed of key ideas, and you have just seen how to develop each one according to the "4 S's." Those key ideas form the building blocks of your speech. In order for your speech to hang together, however, you must connect those ideas, just as a mason joins bricks and stones with mortar. A speaker moves from one idea to the next—puts mortar between the units—with the aid of a transition. A **transition** is a statement connecting one thought to another. Without transitions, the ideas of a speech are introduced abruptly. As a result, the speech lacks a smooth flow of ideas and sounds choppy.

A transition not only connects two ideas, but also indicates the *nature* of the connection between the ideas. Transitions are usually indicated by **markers,** words or phrases near the beginning of a sentence that indicate how that sentence relates to the previous one.[3] Transitions can indicate four basic types of connections: complementary, causal, contrasting, and chronological.

Complementary transitions add one idea to another, thus reinforcing the

transition: a statement that connects parts of the speech and indicates the nature of their connection.

complementary transition: adds one idea to another.

major point of the speech. Typical transitional markers for complementary transitions include the following.

also	and	just as important
next	not only	likewise
in addition		

Each of the following transitions uses the complementary approach to reinforce the speaker's thesis.

> Not only does PAC money undermine the concept of *equal* representation, it also undermines the concept of *local* representation.
> It is clear, then, that clothing affects your image. There is also a second reason why personal dress is important: Clothing affects your behavior.
> Vocal cues, however, are not the only source of information that may help you determine if someone is lying. You may also look for body cues.

Causal transitions emphasize a cause-effect relation between two ideas. Words and phrases that mark a causal relationship include the following.

causal transition: establishes a cause/effect relation between two ideas.

consequently	as a result	because
therefore		

In his speech Victor documented problems resulting from excessive noise. As he shifted his focus from cause to effect, he used the following transition:

> We can see, then, that we live, work, and play in a noisy world. An unfortunate result of this clamor and cacophony is illustrated in my second point: Excessive noise harms interpersonal interaction.

Contrasting transitions show how two ideas differ. These transitions often use words such as the following.

contrasting transition: shows how two ideas differ.

in contrast	on the contrary	in spite of
although	but	on the other hand
nevertheless		

Patricia used a contrasting transition in her speech on theories of alcoholism:

> Although some researchers argue that alcoholism is caused by biological factors, others reject this theory, arguing instead that the cause is cultural.

Chronological transitions show the time relationships between ideas, and use words or phrases such as the following.

chronological transition: shows how one idea precedes or follows another in time.

after	before	while
afterward	as soon as	at last
later	at the same time	

Will informed his classmates on the SQ3R system of studying and remembering written material. He organized his five main points around five key words: survey, question, read, recite, and review. His transitions emphasized the natural sequence of these stages, as in the following:

After surveying, or overviewing, what you are about to read, you are ready for the second stage of the SQ3R system: to question.

Another example of a chronological transition is this:

> If thorough preparation is the first step in a successful job interview, the second step is to arrive on time.

Cross-Reference:
Have students locate and discuss the types of transitions in Shannon Dyer's speech in Appendix C.

A good transition serves as a bridge, reminding listeners of the idea just presented and preparing them for the one to come. It smooths the rough edges of the speech and enhances the cohesiveness of your ideas. Although we have given you a list of key words that signal different types of transitions, you must do more than simply insert a word or phrase between two ideas. If you find yourself using a single word such as "now," "next," or "OK" to introduce your ideas, you need to work on your transitions. You should also avoid using weak and pedestrian phrases as transitions, such as "Moving on to my next point" or "The next thing I would like to discuss." Instead, work on composing smooth, functional transition statements as one of our students did in the following example.

In her persuasive speech Bonnie advocated voluntary school uniforms for students in kindergarten through high school. She previewed her ideas in her introduction by stating that pilot programs demonstrate that "voluntary uniforms would help create a safer school environment, enhance academic achievement, and promote a positive social climate." In the body of her speech Bonnie explained and supported each of these points, connecting them by using smooth transitions. Bonnie used the following excellent transition as she moved from her first to her second idea:

> Every student has a right to learn in a safe environment, and school uniforms help eliminate one cause of school violence. But schools should do more than ensure safety, they should promote learning. A second benefit of school uniforms is that they enhance academic achievement.

As Bonnie moved from her second to her third idea, she said:

Teaching Strategy:
Have students examine the various ways journalists begin stories in one of the following: *Newsweek, Harper's, Atlantic Monthly,* and *Time*. Ask them to report examples to the class. Which of the seven attention-getting devices do the story openings employ? Can others be identified? This exercise can give students experience in introducing and citing sources in their speeches as they report their examples.

> In addition to creating a safer environment and enhancing academic achievement, voluntary school uniforms promote a positive social environment.

■ Organizing the Introduction of the Speech ⎯⎯⎯⎯

After you work on the body of your speech, you are ready to turn your attention to the introduction and the conclusion. An **introduction** should be constructed to achieve four objectives: (1) Get the attention of your audience, (2) state your topic, (3) establish the importance of your topic, and (4) preview the key ideas of your speech. Studying these objectives and the ways to accomplish them will help you get your speech off to a clear and interesting start.

GET THE ATTENTION OF YOUR AUDIENCE

Your first objective as a speaker is to secure the audience's **attention.** If you are fortunate enough to have a reputation as a powerful, captivating speaker, you may already have the attention of your listeners before you utter your first word. Most of us, however, have not yet achieved this reputation. Consequently, it is important to get the audience quickly involved with your speech. The strategy you select will depend on your personality, your purpose, your topic, your audience, and the occasion. We offer you seven possible techniques for getting the audience's attention.

Question Your Audience. A speaker can get an audience involved with the speech through the use of **questions.** Questions can be either rhetorical or direct. A **rhetorical question** stimulates thought, but is not intended to elicit an overt response. For example, consider the following opening questions:

> How did you spend last weekend? Watching television? Going to a movie? Sleeping late?
> If your best friend told you he had AIDS, how would you respond?
> Do you remember when you first learned that there really wasn't a Santa Claus?

A speaker who asks any of the above questions does not expect an overt audience response. In fact, it would probably disrupt the rhythm of the presentation if someone answered orally. A question is rhetorical if it is designed to get the audience thinking about the topic.

A **direct question** seeks a public response. Usually, the response solicited is overt but not necessarily verbal. For example, the following questions can be answered by a show of hands:

rhetorical question: a question designed to stimulate thought without an overt response.

direct question: a question that asks for an overt response from listeners.

How many of you drove to school today? How many wore your seat belts?

Last week the Student Government Association sponsored a blood drive. Who in this class donated blood?

Teaching Strategy:
Have your students identify the following questions as *direct* or *rhetorical.* Then have students reword them to make the direct questions rhetorical and the rhetorical ones direct.

What do you do when a cashier hands you more money in change than you should receive? (Rhetorical) Possible rewording: How many of you would return to a store to give back an extra dollar or two you received in change?

Do you remember how the Ark of the Covenant was depicted in George Lucas's film *Raiders of the Lost Ark?* (Rhetorical) Possible rewording: How many of you remember George Lucas's depiction of the Ark of the Covenant in *Raiders of the Lost Ark?*

What type of food would you be eating if you saw calamari, pesto, and ziti on the menu? (Direct) Possible rewording: Would you know what type of restaurant you were in if you saw calamari, pesto, and ziti on the menu? Point out that if a speaker paused for a response, any of these rhetorical questions could become direct ones.

Like the rhetorical question, a direct question gets the audience thinking about your topic. The direct question has the additional advantage of getting your listeners *physically* involved in your speech and, consequently, making them more alert. This strategy may be especially appropriate if your class meets at 8:00 a.m. and you are the first speaker, or if you have an evening class and are the last speaker, or if you give your speech during mid-term week when your classmates are especially tired.

Sometimes a direct question may invite an oral response. In his speech advocating the use of seat belts, Gene discovered by a show of hands that only a few of his classmates "buckled up" regularly. He then asked the rest of the class why they did not. One classmate complained of wrinkled clothes; another said it was uncomfortable; others said it was too confining. Gene continued, incorporating these excuses into his speech and refuting them.

When you ask a direct question and you want oral responses, you need to pause, look at your audience, and give them sufficient time to respond. If you want your direct question answered by a show of hands, raise your hand as you end the question. In other words, indicate nonverbally how you want the question answered. If you seek and get oral responses, however, make sure that you neither lose control nor turn your public speech into a group discussion. You should probably practice this before your friends first.

A few final cautions about using a question to get the audience's attention. First, avoid asking embarrassing questions of your listeners. "How many of you are on scholastic probation?" "Has anyone in here ever spent a night in jail?" "How many of you come from families earning less than $20,000 a year?" Common sense should tell you that most people would be reluctant to answer direct questions such as these. Second, make sure that you don't answer your opening question nonverbally before asking it. We remember one student who lined up a number of different tennis racquets — wood, aluminum, aluminum and graphite — on the chalk tray under the blackboard. He then turned to the audience and asked, "What would you guess is the fastest-growing sport in the United States?" By asking a silly question in a sincere manner, he got a laugh he did not expect and surely did not want. That student's experience leads us to a final caution: Don't use a question without first considering its usefulness to your speech. Many questions are creative and intriguing. Remember, asking a valid question that listeners answer either openly or to themselves gets them immediately involved and thinking about your speech topic.

Arouse Your Audience's Curiosity. A lively way to engage the minds of your audience is by using the technique of suspense. Get them wondering what is to come. Consider the following passage:

> A 60-year-old plant foreman collapses at his retirement party and dies of a massive heart attack in Oklahoma City; a Boston public relations executive finds he is losing sight in his left eye and eventually becomes totally blind; a 25-year-old waitress in San Francisco has to be hospitalized because of a severe kidney failure; and a 43-year-old garage mechanic in Jackson, Mississippi, has his right foot amputated below the ankle.

What did all these people have in common? They are all victims of diabetes, which if not properly controlled may lead to other physical disorders and even death.[4]

This passage is an excellent attention-getter for a speech introduction. The opening examples create ambiguity or uncertainty and make you want to read further or hear more. The rhetorical question in the second paragraph focuses that uncertainty, and the final sentence solves the puzzle.

You may also arouse curiosity by what you *do* as well as what you say. One student began his speech by placing a small paper sack on the table at the front of the room and saying, "What I have in this sack is imported, costs about five dollars, and is alive." With the audience expecting to see some sort of animal, he then took a bottle of wine from the bag, explaining that its yeast cultures were alive and that his purpose was to inform the audience on how to select good, inexpensive wines.

Another student speaking on sign language began her speech in silence, signing the question, "Can you understand what I am saying?" She paused and then said, "I said, 'Can you understand what I am saying?'," signing as she spoke. She tapped her audience's feelings by arguing that they, undoubtedly, felt the same way a deaf person might feel in a hearing world.

Stimulate Your Audience's Imagination. Another way to engage the minds of your listeners is to stimulate their imaginations. To do this you must know what referents they share, and this requires some good audience analysis on your part. Notice in the following example how the speaker introduces his topic by connecting it to a scene from a popular movie.

> In an amusing scene in a recent popular movie, the intrepid Captain Kirk awakes from the sleep of time travel and, gazing out, sees that his starship is, as hoped, orbiting Earth. "Earth!" he says, "but when?" To which the genetically unflappable Spock, checking his instrument panel, replies, "Judging from the pollution content of the atmosphere, I believe we have arrived at the latter half of the twentieth century." And indeed they had. And so have we. And there is plenty of pollution here to measure.[5]

Even if the audience had not seen *Star Trek IV: The Voyage Home* (1987), most had probably seen the television series or its reruns. As the speaker described the scene, listeners could visualize the characters.

In his speech to the Rotary Club of Philadelphia, Amadeo I.D. Francis, Commissioner of Commerce for the Virgin Islands, used imagery to create interest in his topic:

> When I say the word "Caribbean," I would like you to reflect for just a moment. What images come in mind? I would venture to say that most of you see long stretches of powder-white sand, groves of stately palm trees, emerald-green mountains, vibrant blue water and a sky so clear that it rivals outer space. In short, a vacation paradise.[6]

Francis then attempted to persuade his audience that the Caribbean is more than a tourist resort, that it is a place for business investment. Notice the strong appeals to our sense of sight in this example. In Chapter 11 we discuss the use of language to create other sensory impressions in your audience.

Discussion Prompt:
Have the benefits promised
in thirty-minute television
commercials made us overly
skeptical about such claims?
What are some reasonable
benefits that would get your
attention if a speaker promised them early in a speech?

Promise Your Audience Something Beneficial. We listen more carefully to messages that are in our self-interest. In Chapter 5 we recommended
that you consider your listeners' needs using Maslow's hierarchy: physical
needs, safety needs, love and belongingness needs, self-esteem needs, and self-
actualization needs. If you can promise your audience something that meets
one or more of those needs, you secure their attention very quickly. Beginning
your speech, for example, with the statement, "Every person in this room can
be a millionaire by age thirty!" immediately secures the attention of your
listeners—at least those under the age of thirty! Less dramatic though still
effective examples are ones in which a speaker promises that her information
can save audience members hundreds of dollars in income tax next April, or in
which a speaker says, "The information I will give you in the next ten minutes
will help you buy an excellent used car with complete confidence." Saving
money, the promise of all three of these attention-getters, is directly related to
the interests of every audience member.

Amuse Your Audience. The use of humor can be one of the most effective
attention-getting strategies. Getting the audience to laugh with you makes them
alert and relaxed. Humor can be particularly helpful when used to defuse
hostility. However, any humor you use should be tasteful and relevant to your
topic. As a speaker, you must be able to make a smooth and logical transition
between your humorous opening and the topic of your speech. Telling a joke or
a funny story and then switching abruptly to a serious topic trivializes the topic
and may offend your listeners. Imagine the effect if Lincoln had actually started
the Gettysburg Address with "A guy walks into a bar. . . ."

You can use humor to emphasize key ideas in your speech. The introduc-

THE FAR SIDE   By GARY LARSON

tion below uses humor to highlight the fact that America is experiencing an aging boom.

> During a television interview, an 87-year-old woman was asked: "What were things like in your day?" Smiling, the lady said firmly: "This *is* my day." She was right. This *is* the day of the older American. Our rapidly aging population is already having an impact on government, business, and almost every corner of our society. Looming over the horizon is the huge baby boom generation. When its members reach seniority in just a few years, they will have a profound effect on the workforce, social programs, and the marketplace.[7]

A speaker can also use humor to show a favorable self-image. Journalist Bill Moyers was introduced to the National Press Club with a particularly detailed and glowing account of his life. In the introduction of his speech Moyers used self-effacing humor to relax his audience, engage their attention, and create a more humble image:

> I do appreciate that generous introduction, but let me tell you the other side of it. Three incidents had happened on one trip I took a few years ago when I was still doing commentary on the "CBS Evening News" and working on a summer series weekly with Charles Kuralt. I went out to the airport to go to see my parents down in Texas, and as I was getting out of the cab, the porter reached down and pulled the bag out of the trunk. The bag didn't have my name on it, but it did have the CBS logo, the blue and black logo, on it. And he looked at it, looked at me, looked back at it, looked at me, and he said, "Aren't you in a soap opera?" True story. I started to say, "Yes, 'The CBS Evening News with Dan Rather,'" but I wasn't sure that Dan would appreciate that.
>
> I went on down to the gate and checked in. I was sitting there reading the paper and waiting for them to call my seat number, and I noticed a little bun of gray hair came up over that logo of *The New York Times*. I started to pull it down; it disappeared. I kept reading. In a moment, it came up on this side. I started to pull it down; it disappeared. Finally, I shifted over here, and this time when the gray hair appeared, I jerked the paper down. I was looking right into the eyes of one of our senior citizens, and she said to me, "I know you. Who are you?"
>
> I went on and landed at Shreveport, Louisiana, which is the nearest airport to Marshall, Texas, and I was waiting for that same bag when another elderly lady came up to me, and she said, "Oh, Mr. Kuralt, I love your work. But on television, you look different from the way you look in person." And I said, "Yes, ma'am, on television I'm fatter and balder." She said, "That's all right. I love you both ways." So much for notoriety. Those of us on television do need introductions—maybe not that lengthy, but we do need introductions.[8]

Robert, a student in one of our classes, began his speech with the following attention-getter: "When Mark Twain was asked what he thought of Richard Wagner's music, he said, 'It's not as bad as it sounds.'" The speaker paused, let the audience laugh, and then moved their attention to his topic of America's elderly: "Close examination of the national debate on aging America would indicate that things *are* as bad as they sound."

Another student, Stacey, encouraged her classmates to study a foreign language, introducing her speech this way:

If a polylingual is someone who is fluent in many languages and a bilingual is someone who is fluent in two languages, what would you call a monolingual? The answer is: an American!

This is a joke commonly told among the Japanese. Behind the apparent humor of this joke are some embarrassing truths.

Stacey combined humor and a rhetorical question to get her listeners' attention. She then discussed those "embarrassing truths" and the price we pay for speaking only one language.

Energize Your Audience. Sometimes speakers can command attention simply by their presence. John F. Kennedy, Winston Churchill, and Martin Luther King, Jr., for example, brought to their audiences an expectation that excited listeners. While not everyone can achieve this charisma, most speakers can work to enhance their dynamism. A positive attitude, appropriate dress, a confident walk to the platform, direct eye contact, a friendly smile, erect posture, a strong voice, and forceful gestures give an introduction as much impact as any of the above strategies. Conversely, the absence of these elements can destroy the effect of even the best worded opening statement. The advantages of an "energized" presence, however, extend far beyond a speech introduction. In Chapter 12 we give you specific suggestions for achieving a dynamic delivery throughout your speech.

Acknowledge and Compliment Your Audience. At some point in your life you will probably be called upon to deliver a formal, public speech to an assembled group. Perhaps you will be the keynote speaker for a convention, or maybe you will accept an award from a civic group. The group inviting you to speak may even be paying you, anything from a small honorarium to a substantial fee. Such an occasion usually requires that you begin by acknowledging the audience and key dignitaries.

Notice how Laszlo Csorba III, executive director of Accuracy in Academia, includes his audience in the introduction of his speech given at the William James Forum at Washington College, Maryland. Csorba not only introduces and previews his topic, he thanks the audience for their hospitality and compliments them.

I would like to thank Dr. Peter Tapke and Washington College for inviting me here tonight to express my thoughts on a subject of great importance to college students and professors in America—academic freedom.

I would also like to thank you all for your hospitality, the nice reception, and a fine meal. I always enjoy getting away from Washington, D.C., even if it's only for a few hours. I can tell you, with all the criticism my organization has received and some of the political wars that go on in that town, it's hard to find many friends in Washington, D.C. President Truman once said, "If you want a friend in Washington, buy a dog."

Let me say that I was honored to receive your invitation and noticed that I am among many noted figures who have participated in your forum. As such, I felt compelled to write a speech and offer it to you formally for your pleasure or disgust.

I would like to speak to you tonight about the issue of academic freedom, its function, its proper use, and its definition, and how it occasionally is abused—what we might call academic license.[9]

In this class your classmates make up your audience. You have interacted with them and, by now, probably know them pretty well. To begin your speech formally by acknowledging and complimenting them would seem stiff and insincere. You should not have to compliment fellow classmates; in fact, if you have prepared well, *they* should be thanking *you* for providing excellent information. For your assigned speeches, therefore, you should probably choose one of the other attention-getting strategies.

Class Activity:
Have students examine the attention-getting step of Sandy Gomila's speech in Appendix B. Ask them to rewrite the attention-getter in two ways using two strategies other than the one Gomila uses.

STATE YOUR TOPIC

Once you have the attention of your audience, state the topic or purpose of your speech directly and succinctly. For an informative speech, your statement of purpose should always take the form of a simple declarative sentence. "Today, I will show you how you can improve your study skills" clearly informs the audience of your topic.

This second step in a speech introduction is vitally important, even though the actual statement of purpose will take only a few seconds for you to say. Consider the following beginning section of a speech introduction:

> How many of you have had a cholesterol count taken in the last year? Do you know what your numbers are and what they mean? It seems like we have all recently become much more aware of good cholesterol and bad, high-density lipoproteins and low-density ones, the dangers of high-fat diets and how difficult they can be to avoid in these fast-food, nuke-it-till-it's-hot times. People who never really considered exercising are spending a lot of money to join health clubs and work out. They know that a high cholesterol count can mean you are in danger of developing arteriosclerosis and finding yourself a candidate for surgery. Even if you don't have a heart attack, you may be hospitalized for one of several new procedures to clean out arteries clogged with plaque.

Now answer the following question: This speaker's purpose was to

(a) discuss the interpretation of cholesterol tests;
(b) explain sources of cholesterol in popular foods;
(c) encourage exercise as a key to reducing serum cholesterol;
(d) explain new non-surgical procedures for opening clogged arteries;
(e) I can't tell what the speaker's purpose was.

Unfortunately, in this case, the correct answer is (e). What went wrong? The speaker started off well enough by using two legitimate questions—the first direct, the second rhetorical—as an attention-getter. But then things got out of control; for almost a minute of speaking time, the speaker lapsed into a series of generalizations without ever stating the purpose of the speech. This excerpt represents a minute of wasted time! In a five- to seven-minute speech that minute represents one-fifth to one-seventh of total speaking time. The audience has been confused by the speaker's vague rambling, and their confidence in the speaker may have begun to wane. That is regrettable because any of the purposes (a) through (d) above would be a good one. If you know what your purpose is—and if you're prepared, you *must*—then state that purpose clearly as the second step of your introduction.

ESTABLISH THE IMPORTANCE OF YOUR TOPIC

This third step in organizing the introduction to your speech should convince the listeners that the topic is important to them. You want to motivate them to listen further. A speaker addressing a women's group on rape prevention might include the statement, "One out of three women will at some point in her life be confronted by a rapist. That's one-third of all the women in this room! Because we cannot be sure that we will not be a victim, we must learn how to defend ourselves against rape." If you speak before an audience that includes men, you can easily invite their involvement in the topic. Show them how the potential rape victim may be a girlfriend, wife, sister, daughter, or mother.

PREVIEW YOUR KEY IDEAS

preview: a statement that orients the audience by revealing how the speaker has organized the body of a speech.

The fourth step in organizing your introduction is the **preview step,** where you "tell us what you're going to tell us." Much like a map, the preview step shows a final destination and reveals how the speaker intends to get there. As a result, the audience can travel more easily through the body of the speech. A person discussing the political, economic, and medical implications of national health insurance should inform the audience of these three divisions. A speaker addressing the issue of urban decay might preview her speech by saying, "In order to better understand the scope of this problem, we must look at four measurable conditions: the unemployment rate, housing starts, the poverty level, and the crime rate." That preview lists the four topics to be covered in the body of the speech and prepares the audience to listen more intelligently.

Preview statements are usually from one to three sentences in length. Rarely do they need to be longer. Each of the following examples is appropriately brief and specific in preparing the audience for the key ideas and the organizational pattern of the speech.

> Assuming that you have the necessary materials, the three steps to constructing a piece of stained glass are first, selecting or creating a design; second, cutting the glass; and third, assembling and fixing the individual pieces.

> An enhanced self-concept benefits us in at least three ways. Specifically, it improves our social interaction, our academic achievement, and our chances for career success.

> In selecting a personal computer that's right for you, you need to be guided by three criteria. Utility: Does it meet your needs? Economy: Does it fit your budget? And quality: Will it last?

> A narcoleptic, then, suffers from unexpected attacks of deep sleep. This little-known sleep disorder is better understood if we know its symptoms, its causes, and its treatment.

Notice that the first of these examples uses a chronological, step-by-step organization, while the remaining three employ a topical pattern. Having accomplished this final step of the introduction, these four speakers would be well prepared to begin the bodies of their speeches by signposting, stating, supporting, and summarizing their key points one by one.

How does the introduction sound when you put all four steps together? Our student, Rose, showed us that she certainly knows how to develop a complete and effective introduction:

> According to an old Indian saying, every person dies three times. The first time is the moment your life ends. The second is when your body is lowered into the ground. The third is when there is no one around to remember you. I'm going to talk to you today about death, or rather the celebration of death. This is a special celebration that comes from a Mexican tradition called "Dia de los Muertos," or Day of the Dead. Now it may seem strange and morbid to speak of celebration and death in the same breath, but in the Mexican culture, death is embraced and worshipped just as much as life is. After I give you a little background on Dia de los Muertos, I'll explain the different ways this holiday is celebrated and show you some of the traditional objects used in the celebration.

Kevin, a student with an interest in screenwriting, selected an occasion-generated topic. He delivered the following introduction to his speech on the afternoon before that year's Academy Awards ceremony:

> Oliver Stone rewrote a Vietnam War novel into the successful screenplay *Platoon,* which won an Academy Award, much critical acclaim, and big money. Since Academy Awards are being handed out tonight, I'd like to take this opportunity to teach you some of the basics of writing a screenplay. According to *Successful Scriptwriting* by Kerry Cox and Jurgen Wolff, writing a screenplay is essentially the same as writing a story. Both need three basic elements: a beginning, a middle, and an end, or to use the language of scriptwriters, an introduction, a conflict, and a resolution.

If you have followed the four steps we have outlined, at the end of your introduction the audience should be attentive, know the purpose of your speech, be motivated to listen, and know the major ideas you will discuss. The only remaining part of the speech is the conclusion. Often briefer than the introduction, your conclusion is vitally important to achieving your desired response. As the last section your listeners hear and see, the conclusion must be well planned and carefully organized.

■ Organizing the Conclusion of the Speech _____

The last division of a public speech is the **conclusion.** In concluding a speech, you should **summarize** the key ideas and **provide closure.**

summary: a statement or statements that review the major ideas of a speech.

1. Summarize. **2.** Provide closure.	**KEY POINTS** **Steps of a Speech** **Conclusion**

SUMMARIZE

In the summary you "tell us what you told us." Of all the steps in the process of organization, this should be the easiest to construct. You have already organized the body of the speech and, from it, constructed a preview statement. The summary parallels your preview. If your speech develops three key ideas, you reiterate them. If your speech is on self-concept enhancement, for example, you may simply say, "A good self-concept, therefore, benefits us in three ways. It enhances our social interaction, our academic achievement, and our career success." A speech on dying might be summarized: "Denial. Anger. Bargaining. Depression. Acceptance. These are the five stages of dying as described by Kübler-Ross."

Remember Stacey's introduction to her speech encouraging her classmates to study a foreign language? In the speech she discussed three harms from the nation's failure to promote bilingualism: "First, we lose economically. . . . Second, we lose scholastically. . . . Third, we lose culturally." Notice how Stacey reiterates and reinforces these points in the summary step of her conclusion:

> Clearly, these three points show us that by being monolingual we lose *economically, scholastically,* and *culturally.* Becoming proficient in another language and its culture may help us reduce our deficit and increase our competitiveness in world trade by recognizing possible problems in marketing campaigns. We will gain intellectually by increasing our vocabulary and expanding our minds. We will gain culturally by breaking barriers and possibly eliminating misunderstandings which occur as a result of being unfamiliar with another language, its people, and its culture.

The summary step gives the listener one last chance to hear and organize the main points of your presentation. Thus, the summary step reinforces the ideas of the speech and brings it to a *logical* conclusion.

PROVIDE CLOSURE

While a final summary of your key ideas is important, ending a speech on the summary step is unsatisfying. Such a strategy is what we call, to borrow from Porky Pig, the "b'dee, b'dee, b'dee, that's all folks" conclusion. You should not have to tell your listeners that the speech is finished. That should be clear from your wording, as well as your delivery.

If your summary concludes your speech *logically,* your final statement ends the speech *psychologically.* An effective final statement ties the speech together and provides a strong note of finality or closure. The audience should know that you are about to finish, and they should have the feeling that you have said exactly as much as you need to say. Without resorting to saying, "In conclusion" or "To conclude," you should mark the end of your speech by slowing your rate, maintaining direct eye contact with your listeners, and pausing briefly before and after your final sentence.

An example from literature may clarify what we mean by a psychological conclusion. Remember for a moment Catherine and Heathcliff, the main char-

Discussion Prompt:
How are the introduction and conclusion of a speech similar? What common purposes does each have?

Teaching Strategy:
Present a short lecture on a topic relating to public speaking. Present only the body of the lecture and not an introduction or conclusion. After you have delivered your lecture, ask the class to meet in small groups and write an introduction and conclusion to your lecture using the steps listed in this chapter. This exercise not only reinforces the content of the lecture, it also lets the student apply principles of public speaking to an actual presentation.

acters in Emily Brontë's *Wuthering Heights*. Though they roamed the moors together in their youth, circumstances kept them apart during the rest of their lives. The book ends after both have died. Novelist and short story writer Katherine Anne Porter once wrote: "One of the most perfect and marvelous endings in literature—it raises my hair now—is the little boy at the end of *Wuthering Heights*, crying that he's afraid to go across the moor because there's a man and woman walking there."[10] The final step of your speech conclusion does not have to be dramatic, but it should seem as satisfying as Brontë's final pages.

Sometimes a speaker employs what is called a **circular conclusion,** in which the final statement echoes or refers to the attention-getting step of the introduction. Bonnie used a circular conclusion in her speech advocating voluntary school uniforms. Notice how she refers in her conclusion to the examples she presented in her introduction.

Attention-getting step:

In Los Angeles, a little girl dressing for school puts on her favorite red sweater. Her choice of color results in her being attacked and hit on the head with a rock. The reason: Red is the color worn by one gang, and a member of a rival gang retaliated upon seeing red.

Calvin Wash enjoys football and shows his loyalty to his favorite team by wearing a Cincinnati Bengals jacket. Calvin was shot when he tried to escape from a man who demanded his jacket.

An 18-year-old was shot and killed by someone who wanted his Triple F.A.T. Goose parka and his $70 Nike shoes.

There's an old saying: "Clothes make the person." One thing clothes should not do, however, is make the person a target.

Conclusion:

Currently, Virginia's House of Delegates is considering a bill that would require public schools to implement a voluntary school uniform program. I encourage you to call or write your representative and voice your support of this bill. In addition, if your local school does not already have such a program, contact the school board and urge them to implement one. Remember to tell them that voluntary school programs will help create a safer school environment, enhance academic achievement, and promote a positive social climate.

When a little girl is trying to decide what to wear to school, she shouldn't be faced with a life-or-death decision. When a boy puts on his jacket and shoes, he shouldn't be preparing for combat. A voluntary school uniform is one way of helping schools become what they should be: a place where children can learn and grow.

Your final statement does not have to allude to your attention-getting step. Any of the specific techniques we discussed for gaining audience attention can help bring your speech to a strong, clear, psychologically satisfying conclusion. You may ask a question, even the same one you began with or a variation of it. Or you may answer the question you initially asked. You could arouse the audience's curiosity, though you would need to satisfy it in order to provide closure. You might stimulate their imaginations through vivid imagery, or promise them that the information you have provided can bring them benefits. You could conclude with a joke or humorous story relevant to your topic.

circular conclusion: a conclusion that repeats or refers to material used in the introduction.

Teaching Strategy:
You probably ought to warn students against using tired, overused final statements that begin, "I hope that my speech has . . . ."

Through lively delivery you could energize the audience to act on the information you have provided them. And in a speech other than a classroom assignment, you might end by complimenting and thanking the audience.

Both steps of the conclusion are important. The summary step reinforces the *ideas* of the speech, while the final statement reinforces the *impact* of the speech. Consider the following conclusion of a student's speech opposing capital punishment: "Those in favor of capital punishment should re-examine the issues of dignity, deterrence, and death. We must be motivated by reason rather than retribution if we want our country to be known for 'executing justice, not people.'" The student restated her main divisions and ended with impact through her use of language, voice, and gestures.

Remember Kevin's speech on screenplays (p. 187)? He concluded his speech this way:

> All screenplays carry three basic elements: an introduction, which establishes the storyline and the characters; conflict, which pits the main character against obstacles in the quest of some goal; and a conclusion, which resolves the conflict and reflects on the theme of the work. Let's face it, if *Porky's, Friday the 13th,* and *Attack of the Killer Tomatoes* made it to the big screen, most ideas can make it, if you just have the elements of a good screenplay.

A diagram of the individual elements in a well-organized speech would contain the following:

1. Attention-getting step
2. Statement of topic
3. Emphasis on importance of topic
4. Preview step
5. Body of speech
6. Summary step
7. Closure.

This is the correct order of steps in the *delivered* speech, although you will not *prepare* these steps in the sequence listed above. As we mentioned earlier, you should prepare the body of your speech first. Some instructors recommend that you develop your introduction next and your conclusion last. Others suggest that you prepare your introduction last. Remember, there is no one correct way of constructing a speech. You should select the method that works best for you.

We suggest an alternative strategy (see Figure 9.2), which is divided into

Class Activity:
Bill Wallace, a speech teacher and contest judge, criticizes Shelley Schnathorst's concluding statement in her speech on the safety of medical devices in Appendix C. Do your students believe that criticism is valid? Have students rewrite the concluding statement at the end of that speech using two strategies other than the one Schnathorst uses.

Class Activity:
Ask students to think of (but not reveal) two instructors they've had: one who is an effective lecturer, and one who is not. Have your students identify organizational strategies that contribute to effective lecturing. Discuss how students can incorporate these strategies in their speeches.

FIGURE 9.2 Steps in Organizing a Speech

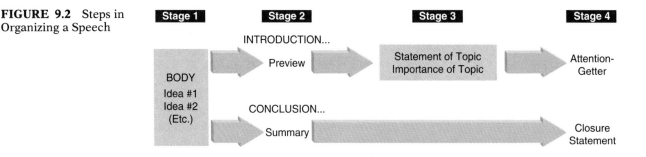

four stages. In Stage 1 you construct the body of your speech, determining the key ideas and developing them using the "4 S's." After completing this stage, you then work outward.

Rather than going just to the introduction or just to the conclusion, you work on both *simultaneously,* focusing on elements that have similar purposes. With your key ideas determined, you are more easily able to word your preview and summary statements. These two steps are similar because they highlight a speech's key ideas. As you complete Stage 2, you have fulfilled the overall organizational strategy we mentioned at the beginning of this chapter: You are ready to "tell us what you're going to tell us," "tell us," and "tell us what you told us."

In Stage 3 you decide how you will state your topic and explain its importance to your audience. This should not be difficult. You have already thought through these steps when you selected your topic. Your choice of words and supporting materials should lead naturally to your preview statement, which you have already worded. In the final stage of your preparation, you devise your attention-getting and closure statements, two crucial steps at the furthest extremes from the body. Developing the attention-getter and the final statement at the same time should increase the total unity of the speech, and this is particularly important if you are using a circular conclusion.

Speakers who begin preparing speeches with the first step as the introduction often end up trying to "fit" the rest of their speech to the introduction. Speakers who write their introduction, body, and conclusion separately often produce three parts rather than a unified whole. The "outward" method of development helps you avoid these pitfalls and enables you to present your ideas clearly, cohesively, and convincingly.

Summary

Teaching Strategy: Have students identify the superstructure of all the speeches in Appendix C by answering the following questions about each: Where does the introduction end and the body begin? Where does the body end and the conclusion begin? Is the organization more obvious in the student speeches than in the professional speeches?

Being sure of your speech organization gives you confidence as a speaker; communicating your information in a well-organized manner makes it much easier for the audience to remember what you have said. The chief goal of speech organization is to assist your listeners in understanding and retaining your information.

The three parts of a speech are the *introduction, body,* and *conclusion.* You should organize the body first because it is the most substantial part of the speech, and because its content determines the content of the introduction and the conclusion. Depending upon your purpose in speaking, you may select any of six organizational patterns for the body of the speech. *Topical division* narrows a broad topic by limiting it to certain subtopics chosen by the speaker. *Chronological division* organizes a historical topic or a speech explaining a process into a time sequence. *Spatial division* lets the geography or physical structure of a place or thing organize the speech for you. *Causal division* allows a speaker to explore a condition or action from its causes to its effects, or from effects back to causes. *Pro-con division* presents the arguments for and against some policy, position, or action, and with the addition of a final assessment step becomes a persuasive speech pattern. The final organizational pattern, the *gimmick division,* uses a memory device such as the first letters of a word to organize key points in the speech and help the audience recall them.

After choosing a general organizational pattern and establishing your main points, you are ready to organize the presentation of each major idea in the speech. To do this we recommend a memory device we call *"the 4 S's"*: *signpost* the idea, *state* the idea, *support* the idea, and *summarize* the idea. Apply these four steps to each major idea in the speech.

Each of the main points you develop needs to be connected to others by *transitions*. Effective transitions indicate the nature of the relation between the ideas: complementary, causal, contrasting, or chronological.

The introduction and conclusion are brief parts of the speech, but they must be well organized and practiced since they are, respectively, your first and last chances to create a favorable impression for yourself or your topic. The introduction should accomplish four steps, in this order: (1) Get the attention of your audience, (2) state your topic or purpose, (3) stress the importance or relevance of your topic, and (4) preview the key ideas you will be developing in the body of the speech. To get your audience's attention you can question your listeners, arouse their curiosity, stimulate their imaginations, promise them something beneficial, amuse them, energize them, or acknowledge and compliment them. An effective conclusion must do two things: (1) summarize, or bring your speech to a logical conclusion, and (2) provide closure, or bring the speech to a satisfying psychological conclusion.

If you follow the suggestions in this chapter, your speech should be well organized. That clear organization will, in turn, make your information easier for the audience to remember, and that's a major goal of public speaking.

Exercises

1. Prepare three introductions for the same body of content. Discuss the advantages and disadvantages of each. Select the one you think is best and explain why.
2. Using the "4 S's," prepare and deliver one major point in the body of a speech. You should document and cite your source(s) in the support step.
3. Prepare three conclusions for the same body of content. Discuss the advantages and disadvantages of each. Select the one you think is best and explain why.
4. Select an organizational pattern you think would be appropriate for speeches with the specific purposes listed below. Could the specific purpose be achieved using other patterns? Are there some patterns that clearly would be inappropriate?
   a. To inform the audience on relaxation techniques.
   b. To inform the audience on the history of Groundhog Day.
   c. To inform the audience on the advantages and disadvantages of raising money for charitable causes by telethons.
   d. To inform the audience on marriage rituals in various cultures.
   e. To persuade the audience that illiteracy is seriously harming national productivity.
   f. To persuade the audience that the health benefits from one exercise program are greater than those from another.

5. Select one topic and show how it could be developed using three different organizational patterns. Which do you think would make the best speech? Why?

Notes

1. Robert Half, "Memomania," *American Way* 1 November 1987: 21.

2. Robert L. Montgomery, *Listening Made Easy* (New York: AMACOM, 1981) 65–78.

3. Glenn Leggett, C. David Mead, Melinda Kramer, and Richard S. Beal, *Prentice Hall Handbook for Writers*, 11th ed. (Englewood Cliffs, NJ: Prentice, 1991) 417–418. We have drawn on examples these authors use in their excellent section on connecting language.

4. Lou Joseph and John J. Lynch, *A Doctor Discusses Diabetes* (Chicago: Budlong, 1977) 1.

5. Gus Speth, "We Are All on This Planet Together," *Representative American Speeches 1988–1989*, ed. Owen Peterson (New York: Wilson, 1989) 88–89.

6. Amadeo I.D. Francis, "America's Stake in the Caribbean: Where Is It Heading?" *Vital Speeches of the Day* 15 April 1981: 394.

7. Robert B. Maxwell, "The 'Graying' of America: Implications for Business," *Representative American Speeches 1987–1988*, ed. Owen Peterson (New York: Wilson, 1988) 158.

8. Bill Moyers, address, National Press Club, Washington, D.C., 27 November 1990.

9. Laszlo Csorba III, "Academic Freedom or Academic License," *Representative American Speeches 1985–1986*, ed. Owen Peterson (New York: Wilson, 1986) 92–93.

10. Qtd. in *The Writer's Chapbook: A Compendium of Fact, Opinion, Wit, and Advice from the 20th Century's Preeminent Writers*, ed. George Plimpton (New York: Viking, 1989) 169.

Outlining Your Speech   *10*

Functions of Outlining

Principles of Outlining

Stages of Outlining
The Working Outline
The Formal Outline
The Speaking Outline

*H*ow long would it take you to memorize and be able to repeat the following twenty-six letters: c-p-s-y-n-i-r-t-y-m-v-i-e-m-r-t-o-i-p-o-e-m-o-m-e-m? If you are typical, you would need a good deal of rehearsal to remember more than the first four to seven letters you just read.[1] Would it help you if the letters were rearranged as follows: y-m-c-o-i-t-p-s-i-p-t-y-m-m-v-e-n-e-o-i-r-r-m-e-o-m? Unless you have an eidetic or photographic memory, such a shuffling of letters is likely no help at all. But what if the letters were scrambled again: m-y-t-o-p-i-c-i-s-p-t-y-m-m-v-e-n-e-o-i-r-r-m-e-o-m? Those first nine letters are now recognizable as the English words "my," "topic," and "is," and you can easily repeat them in correct sequence. Those three words would be even more obvious if we eliminated the dashes and used a familiar pattern of grouping and spacing: "my topic is." If the last seventeen letters were also reorganized as m-e-m-o-r-y-i-m-p-r-o-v-e-m-e-n-t, or "memory improvement," you could master the entire sequence of twenty-six letters in correct order, orally or in writing, without much effort.

Notice that we did not add or delete any letters. We merely reorganized them until they formed a pattern that is easy to recognize and repeat. When you outline, you perform essentially the same task. You organize and reorganize material into a pattern easy to recognize and remember. As you prepare your speech you will find that outlining is an indispensable element of speech organization.

In Chapter 9 we discussed the importance of organization to the delivered speech and suggested some ways of achieving a well-organized presentation. Outlining your speech is the preliminary *written* work necessary to foster clear organization of your *oral* message. In this chapter you will learn why outlines are important to your speech, examine some different types of outlines, and finally, study how to write an excellent outline.

■ Functions of Outlining

A well-prepared outline serves five important functions for a speaker:

1. It tests the scope of the speaker's content.
2. It tests the logical relations among parts of the speech.
3. It tests the relevance of supporting ideas.
4. It checks the balance or proportion of the speech.
5. It serves as notes during the delivery of the speech.

The first purpose of outlining is to *test the scope of the speaker's content.* Have you narrowed the topic sufficiently to cover your key ideas in some depth? Or are you trying to cover too much material, so that you will end up skimming the surface of the subject, merely repeating things your audience already knows? You recall that we said in the previous chapter that a speaker should ordinarily have no more than two to five main points in a speech. Outlining allows you to use paper and pen to organize your main ideas, and then add, delete, regroup, shuffle, condense, or expand them so that the way you approach your topic is manageable. In other words, outlining is a process of setting goals for the speech.

Second, outlining allows speakers to *test the logical relations among the various parts of the speech*. Does one idea in the outline lead to the next in a meaningful way? Do the arguments or subtopics under each of your main points really develop that point? In order to answer these questions, you must understand the concepts of coordination and subordination. **Coordinate** ideas are those of equal value or importance in the overall pattern of the speech. To illustrate the relation between coordinate and subordinate ideas, consider the following hypothetical example.

coordinate ideas: ideas that have equal value in a speech.

Suppose you find in the library Wilson Bryan Key's books *Subliminal Seduction, Media Sexploitation,* and *The Clam Plate Orgy,* works claiming to show evidence of subliminal messages in print advertisements. Intrigued, you do further research on the topic of subliminal messages. You find that audio subliminal messages have increased sales and reduced shoplifting in stores where they have been played under background music. If you decided to deliver an informative speech on subliminal messages, you might arrange your speech topically and focus on those two areas:

Teaching Strategy: Select an outline you have prepared or one you have collected in a previous class. Retype the outline, listing the main and supporting points in random order and with no indentation. Distribute copies to students and have them organize the list of statements into an outline.

    I. Visual subliminals
    II. Audio subliminals

These two topics are coordinate because they are of equal value. You may have more information on one of them than on the other, and consequently spend more time in the speech discussing that topic, but neither is a subtopic of the other. Under that first main topic, you would list subtopics that support it or are **subordinate** to it. Two subordinate points for visual subliminals might be as follows:

subordinate ideas: ideas that support more general or more important points in a speech.

    I. Visual subliminals
       A. Subliminals in print advertising
       B. Subliminals in movies

Notice that A. and B. above are not only subordinate to the main idea, visual subliminals, but are also coordinate with one another since they seem to be equally important. Subordinate ideas for the second main point, audio subliminals, could include:

    II. Audio subliminals
       A. Subliminals to increase sales
       B. Subliminals to reduce theft

With just this much of the outline completed, you as a speaker could begin to ask yourself: "Are my main ideas different enough to qualify as separate points? Do those subordinate points really support the main ideas?" At this stage, the answers to both of those questions seem to be "yes." In this way, the visual form of the outline helps you the speaker test the logical connections between parts of your speech. You continue this process as you further refine and add to the outline.

Third, an outline helps the speaker *test the relevance of supporting ideas*. To understand how this works, assume that you had written the following portion of an outline for a speech on roller coasters:

I. Famous roller coasters
   A. Coney Island's "Cyclone"
   B. Montreal's "Le Monstre"
   C. Six Flags' "Shock Wave"
   D. New design technology

Notice that the fourth subpoint, "design technology," is out of place because it is irrelevant to the main point. How do you solve this problem? Careful study of this portion of the outline should signal you to make "design technology" a separate main point, if you can gather adequate supporting material; if you can't, eliminate it.

A fourth function outlining serves for the speaker is to *check the balance or proportion of the speech*. If you look back to the outline on subliminal messages we used earlier, you will notice that two subpoints support each of the main ideas. As a result, the division of the speech looks balanced, even though a speaker might actually spend more time on one of those main ideas than on the other. The speech would still be balanced if one main point contained three subpoints and the other included two. Yet if the main point of "visual sublimi-nals" contained five subpoints and "audio subliminals" had only two, the out-line may not be balanced. Lack of balance in the outline will be reflected in the speech.

How can you fix an imbalance in your speech? In the speech on subliminal messages, you might decide to focus *only* on visual subliminals rather than having the second topic seem undeveloped or tacked on hastily. As you can see, your outline tests the balance of your speech and can even lead you to alter the specific purpose of the speech.

Fifth, and finally, a special type of abbreviated outline can *serve as notes for the speaker during the actual delivery of the speech*. This outline, called a speak-ing outline and discussed later in this chapter, has only one rule: It must be brief. If you have prepared adequately for your speech, you should need only key words and phrases to remind you of each point you want to discuss. More-over, having your notes in outline form rather than arranged randomly on notecards or sheets of paper should constantly remind you of the importance of clear organization as you are delivering the speech.

■ Principles of Outlining

Correct outlines take one of two possible forms: **complete sentence** and **key word or phrase.** They are exactly what their names imply. Each and every item in a complete sentence outline is a sentence; each item in a key word or phrase outline is a word or group of words. These two forms of outlines should be kept consistent and distinct. Only in the final outline for the speaker's use may complete sentences and phrases be combined. So far in this chapter we have used only phrase outlines. More word or phrase outlines and an example of a complete sentence outline will follow.

1. Each number or letter in the outline should represent only one idea.
2. Coordinate and subordinate points in the outline should be represented by a consistent system of numbers and letters.
3. If any point has subpoints under it, there must be at least two subpoints.
4. Each symbol in a sentence outline should introduce a complete sentence. Each symbol in a word or phrase outline should introduce a word or phrase.
5. Coordinate points throughout the outline should have parallel grammatical construction.

As you begin outlining the ideas of your speech, you will work more efficiently and produce a clearer outline if you follow a few rules, or principles. First, *each number or letter in the outline should represent only one idea*. Remember that a chief goal of outlining is to achieve a clear visual representation of the connections between parts of the speech. This is possible only if you separate the ideas. For example, suppose a speaker preparing a speech on color blindness has worded a key idea as "causes of and tests for color blindness." The phrase contains *two* distinct ideas, each requiring separate discussion and development. Instead, the speaker should divide the statement into two coordinate points: "causes of color blindness" and "tests for color blindness."

Second, *coordinate and subordinate points in the outline should be represented by a consistent system of numbers and letters*. Main ideas are typically represented by Roman numerals: I, II, III, and so forth. Don't worry about brushing up on those higher Roman numerals because you will not have more than five or so main points! Label subpoints under the main points with capital letters: A, B, C, and so forth. Beneath those, identify your supporting points with Arabic numbers: 1, 2, and so on. Finally, identify ideas subordinate to those with lowercase letters: a, b, c. Using this notation system, the labeling and indentation of a typical outline might appear as follows.

I. Main point
  A. Subpoint
    1. Sub-subpoint
    2. Sub-subpoint
    3. Sub-subpoint
  B. Subpoint
    1. Sub-subpoint
    2. Sub-subpoint
      a. Sub-sub-subpoint
      b. Sub-sub-subpoint
II. Main point
  A. Subpoint
  B. Subpoint
    1. Sub-subpoint
    2. Sub-subpoint
  C. Subpoint

A third principle is that *if any point has subpoints under it, there must be at least* two *subpoints*. A basic law of physics is that you cannot divide something into only one part. If you have an A, you must also have a B. (You may, of course, also have subpoints C, D, and E.) If you have a 1, you must also have at least a 2.

Fourth, *each symbol in a sentence outline should introduce a complete sentence. Each symbol in a word or phrase outline should introduce a word or phrase.* In other words, keep the form of the outline consistent. Sentences and phrases should be mixed only in your speaking outline.

Finally, *coordinate points throughout the outline should have parallel grammatical construction.* If you begin the key phrase outline of a speech on how to write a résumé with your first main point labeled "Things to include," your second point should be "Things to omit," rather than "Leaving out unnecessary information." Notice that the first point is worded as a noun phrase and, therefore, you followed it with another noun phrase ("Things to omit") rather than a predicate phrase ("Leaving out unnecessary information"). Of course, you could always change your first point to a predicate phrase by wording it "Including essential information," so that it matches the second point. In this example, all coordinate points have parallel grammatical construction.

Teaching Strategy:
Have students outline the major points in the body of William Fort's speech in Appendix C.

   I. Including essential information
      A. Address
      B. Career objective
      C. Educational background
      D. Employment history
      E. References
  II. Omitting unnecessary information
      A. Marital status
      B. Religious denomination
      C. Political affiliation

As you can see, coordinate main points I and II are verb phrases, while the coordinate subpoints are all nouns or noun phrases.

■ Stages of Outlining

If you have difficulty generating or discovering the main points for a speech topic you have chosen, you are not alone. Many people are intimidated by the prospect of selecting and organizing ideas, particularly for a first speech. We worry if the organization doesn't "come to us" quickly. Or if it *does* come quickly, we worry that it is not the right organizational pattern to use. You can avoid these self-defeating lines of thinking if you keep in mind four guidelines to organizing and outlining.

First, organization is not something that "comes to you," but rather it is something that you must "go after." Structuring a speech requires you to invest time and thought, investments whose dividends may not be apparent until you deliver the speech. Second, there is no one "right" way of organizing all speeches on a particular topic. True, some topics logically lend themselves to certain patterns of organization. As you learned in Chapter 9, speeches about processes often almost organize themselves according to a chronological pattern. Speeches about people may be arranged chronologically or topically. Persuasive speeches on social issues are perhaps most logically organized according to a problem-solution format, discussed in Chapter 16. Yet different speakers may use different structures. You have to determine what works best for you, your topic, and your audience.

Third, during the early stages of organizing and outlining a speech you will have a great deal of uncertainty. Do I have enough main points, too many, or too few? Can I find adequate information to support all of those main points? Am I overlooking other main points the audience would be interested in hearing me discuss? Rather than feeling pressured by such questions, try to enjoy the great freedom and flexibility you have at the early stages of outlining. Remember that the early, informal versions of your working outline are all provisional — temporary and open to change. Fourth, and finally, identifying the main points in a speech is also easier than many people imagine. The remainder of this chapter will guide you through the process of outlining, from those first tentative ideas a speaker puts on paper to the final outline used as speaking notes.

THE WORKING OUTLINE

The first step in preparing an outline is to construct what we like to call a **working outline**, a list of aspects of your chosen topic. Such a list may result from research you have already conducted, or it may simply be a result of some productive brainstorming. Once you have spent significant time researching the subject, you will notice topics that are repeated in different sources on the subject. If, for example, you had selected "Lyme disease" as the topic for an informative speech and had conducted adequate research, your list of possible aspects of the topic would include the following:

Cause   Diagnosis   Prevention
Symptoms   Treatment

Notice that these topics could be applied to any disease, physical illness, or mental condition.

Alternative methods of generating topic areas are brainstorming and visual brainstorming, techniques we discussed in Chapter 6 (see pages 101–110). Not only can brainstorming help you generate topics, it can also help you explore areas of the topic you finally select.[2] Your creative brainstorming might even reveal interesting areas of your topic that have not been adequately treated in the existing research. This discovery provides you an opportunity to conduct original research or experimentation.

As you can see, at this stage the term *outline* is very loose; the list of key ideas you are developing does not have any numbers or letters attached to it. That's fine, since these notes are for your benefit alone. This working outline is not so much a finished product as it is a record of the *process* you go through in thinking about a speech topic.

For a fuller demonstration of this first step in outline preparation, assume that you had read an interesting article on the perfume industry and were

working outline: an informal, initial outline recording a speaker's process of narrowing, focusing, and balancing a topic.

considering "perfumes" as a topic for an informative speech. Using the visual brainstorming technique discussed in Chapter 6, you might generate the related topics shown in Figure 10.1. Your working outline would therefore begin with just the following main points:

History of perfumes	Uses of perfumes
Production of perfumes	Selection of perfumes
Levels of concentration	Care of perfumes

After some preliminary research on perfumes, you might expand your working outline with the following subpoints:

History of perfumes
   In religious worship
   In mythology
   In commerce
   In literature
   In medicine
Production of perfumes
   Research
   Development
   Advertising
   Retailing
Ingredients
   Solvents
   Fixatives
   Essential oils
     Sources
     Methods of extraction
Categories
   Perfumes
   Eau de toilette
   Colognes
   Aftershaves
Uses of perfumes
   In cosmetics
   In household cleaners
   In production of plastics and rubber
   In tanning of leather

FIGURE 10.1 Visual Brainstorming on the Subject "Perfume"

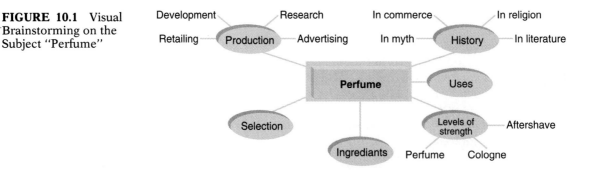

Selection of perfumes
    According to wearer's personality
    According to season
Care of perfumes
    Protection from light
    Protection from heat

Obviously, this is too much material for a typical short classroom speech. How do you decide what to include and what to eliminate? First, consider your interests, those of your audience, and the quantity of research materials you have found on each of these topics.

This is how John focused the topic of perfume from his working outline:

> The history of perfumes is really interesting. When I decided on this topic, I did so partly because it was such an unusual subject and one that's interesting without being too serious. What I found out about the history of perfumes and their uses today in lots of industries showed me that the topic is more important than I thought at first. But I don't think I want to concentrate on either of those aspects of the topic. Maybe I can refer to "history" and "uses" in the introduction to emphasize the significance of the topic, though.
>
>   The care of fragrances is too brief to be the main point of the speech. Most sources mentioned that topic, but they just said "perfumes are volatile chemicals that break down easily. Keep them away from heat and light." I learned a lot in my research about the different categories or levels of strength of perfumes. I now know the difference between a perfume, a cologne, and an aftershave, but that's really a simple point and not enough to base the whole speech on. I think the class would be interested in knowing how the cologne or aftershave you select may reveal aspects of your personality, but most of what I found in two articles was geared toward women, and there are almost as many men as women in our class.
>
>   I've decided to speak on the ingredients of perfumes because three of the sources I've looked at had sections on this subject and it's something the audience won't know. What interested me most in my research were the sources of these different ingredients and how they are collected. While technology is important to the perfume industry today, some of the techniques being used are the same ones that were practiced by alchemists thousands of years ago!

This speaker has narrowed the working outline to one section:

Ingredients
    Solvents
    Fixatives
    Essential oils
        Sources
        Methods of extraction

After some more detailed research in this topic area, John devised another working outline as follows:

  I. Three categories of ingredients
    A. Aromatics or "essential oils"
      1. From flowers
      2. From spices, seeds, woods

> **3.** From synthetic aldehydes
> **4.** Methods of collecting
>> **a.** Distillation
>> **b.** Solvent extraction
>> **c.** Enfleurage
>> **d.** Expression, or "cold pressing"
> **B.** Fixatives or stabilizers
>> **1.** Purpose
>> **2.** Sources
>>> **a.** Natural sources from animals
>>>> (1) Civet from civet cat
>>>> (2) Castoreum from beavers
>>>> (3) Musk from musk deer
>>>> (4) Ambergris from sperm whale
>>> **b.** Synthesis of musk and ambergris
> **C.** Solvents, the "pushers" and "fillers" of perfumes

This version still has problems, but that's OK. Remember the real function of the working outline is to "test the waters" of your topic and reveal the problems in your approach. One obvious problem with this draft of the outline is that it has only one main point, one Roman numeral, and as we discussed earlier, you cannot divide something into only one part. John will have to correct that problem in subsequent versions of the outline. He also felt at this point that the speech ended on a weak note with the relatively simple point of "solvents."

With some shifting, John developed a stronger outline. He had enough interesting information about the four methods of collecting essential oils to qualify them as a main point. Therefore, he decided to begin the first main point on the categories of ingredients with the subpoint solvents, follow with the more interesting points of fixatives and essential oils, and then develop the four methods of collecting as a separate main point. Look at John's revised working outline.

> **I.** Three categories of ingredients
>> **A.** Solvents, the "pushers" and "fillers" of perfumes
>> **B.** Fixatives or stabilizers
>>> **1.** Purpose
>>> **2.** Sources
>>>> **a.** Natural sources from animals
>>>>> (1) Civet from civet cat
>>>>> (2) Castoreum from beavers
>>>>> (3) Musk from musk deer
>>>>> (4) Ambergris from sperm whale
>>>> **b.** Synthesis of musk and ambergris
>> **C.** Aromatics or "essential oils"
>>> **1.** From flowers
>>> **2.** From spices, seeds, woods
>>> **3.** From synthetic aldehydes

II. Methods of collecting essential oils
  A. Distillation
  B. Solvent extraction
  C. Enfleurage
  D. Expression, or "cold pressing"

Notice that this second version of the working outline develops two main points and seems more balanced than the first version. It also begins with a subpoint the speaker thinks will be quick and simple to explain. From there, the outline develops more unusual and complicated ideas.

"The problem now," John noted, "is that I don't think I can cover all of this material in the four- to six-minute time limit for the speech. I'd be racing through it and I doubt that audience members could remember even the main points." Even though he had interesting material on the second point, John decided to develop only the first point in order to meet his time limit. As a result, Roman numeral I became his specific purpose: to inform the audience of the three ingredients in perfumes. Points A, B, and C, became the three main ideas of his speech and, as you will see, John renumbered them I, II, and III.

You might think that as a speaker prepares a speech, the outline would become longer and more complex. To a certain point this is true. As you flesh out your ideas over a period of time, your outline does grow more detailed. What evolves is finally called your formal outline. Once you have decided for certain on the number of main points you can cover in the allowed time, what those points are, and how you will support them, then you select words and phrases from the formal outline to make up your much briefer speaking outline.

Visual aids can clarify your organization for listeners who expect to discuss and act upon the information you provide.

THE FORMAL OUTLINE

formal outline: a complete sentence outline written in sufficient detail that a person other than the speaker could understand it.

Your **formal outline** is a complete sentence outline reflecting the full content and organization of your speech. In its final form it is the finished product of your research and planning for your speech. A stranger, picking up your formal outline, should be able to read how you have organized and supported all your main points. If you keep that goal in mind, you should have no trouble deciding what needs to be included.

The formal outline should probably begin with your speech title. You should also include a statement of your specific purpose and your thesis statement, appropriately labeled. The actual outline should follow the accepted pattern of symbols and indentation, with each item in the outline making up a complete sentence. Your instructor may ask you to label the superstructure of the speech — introduction, body, and conclusion — by inserting these words at the appropriate places in the outline but without Roman numerals or other symbols attached to them. Finally, the formal outline should be followed by a bibliography listing the sources you have used in the development of the speech.

Now let's see how John developed his formal outline for his speech on perfumes. The final version of John's formal outline, with a complete introduction and conclusion, looked like this:

Speech Title: Making Sense of Scents

Specific Purpose: To inform the audience of the three ingredients in perfumes.

Thesis Statement: All fragrances contain solvents, fixatives, and aromatics, obtained from a variety of natural and synthetic sources.

Introduction

Napoleon wouldn't go into battle without them. Egyptian priests used to rub them on statues of gods and goddesses each morning. Doctors used to put them in leather "snouts" over the noses of the sick. Cultured women used to carry them in lockets or in the hollow heads of canes. Today, Americans spend one and a half billion dollars a year on them. "Them," in each of these cases, refers to perfumes. Perfumes have been the prize for which battles were fought, have affected trade routes, and have had a place in every advanced culture on earth. Today, even if you don't buy perfumes, colognes, or aftershaves, you're a perfume consumer every time you buy soap, a household cleaner, a cosmetic, or a piece of leather or plastic. Knowing what actually goes into perfumes is not only interesting information, but also helps explain the variety of perfumes available and their typically high costs. Every ingredient in a perfume, cologne, or aftershave falls into one of three categories: solvents, fixatives, and aromatics or essential oils.

Body of speech

I. Solvents are the "fillers" and "pushers" of perfumes.
    A. Pure, sterile water is the biggest component of perfumes.
    B. Purified ethyl alcohol is the other solvent.

II. Fixatives are the stabilizers in fragrances.
  A. Fixatives stabilize the rates of evaporation of the various aromatics used.
  B. Without fixatives, fragrances would change suddenly and dramatically.
  C. Fixative sources may be natural or synthetic.
    1. Natural fixatives come from animals.
      a. Civet comes from the small East African civet cat.
        (1) Civet is collected from both male and female cats.
        (2) Civet can be removed from captive cats twice a week without harming the animals.
      b. Castoreum is collected from two abdominal sacs of Russian and Canadian beavers.
      c. Musk comes from the tiny musk deer of western China.
        (1) The male deer has a sac to secrete musk as a sexual signal.
        (2) Hunters remove the sacs from slaughtered deer.
      d. Ambergris comes from the sperm whale.
        (1) Whales produce the substance to lubricate their digestive tracts against the bones of the cuttlefish, their primary food.
        (2) Ambergris has an extremely sweet smell and great fixative properties.
    2. Both musk and ambergris are now commonly synthesized.
      a. Perfume manufacturers have voluntarily agreed not to purchase ambergris to protect the sperm whale population.
      b. Synthesized musk and ambergris are much less costly than their natural counterparts.
III. Aromatics or "essential oils" are the primary scents.
  A. Most aromatics come from flowers.
    1. Rose, jasmine, and iris are typical floral scents.
    2. Perfumes may be based on a single flower or a combination.
  B. Some aromatics come from spices, seeds, or woods.
    1. Rosemary, mint, and cloves are typical spices used.
    2. Almond, apricot, and sesame seeds are typical seeds used.
    3. Sandalwood, pine, and cedar are typical woods used.
  C. Some of the brightest aromatics today are the synthetic "aldehydes."
    1. Like formaldehyde, these aromatics are strong.
    2. Though immediately detectable, they don't last long.

Conclusion

The perfume, cologne, or aftershave you're wearing now or saving for a special occasion probably began one morning as workers gathered flowers, spices, or wood bark before dawn. After a costly and time-consuming collection process, the essential oils were shipped to laboratories where chemists began their combination with fixatives and solvents. Knowing these ingredients may help you explain why you pass over some fragrances, but for others you're willing to pay your part of that one and a half billion dollars we Americans spend on fragrance each year.

Bibliography

Boyer, Pamela. "Selecting a Perfect Scent." *Prevention* February 1989: 88+.

Green, Annette. "Perfume." *The Encyclopedia Americana: International Edition.* 1986.

Lamotte, Michael. "Bottled Up." *Esquire* May 1989: 162–65.

Morris, Edwin T. *Fragrance: The Story of Perfume from Cleopatra to Chanel.* New York: Scribner's, 1984.

Oliver, Joan D. "Making Sense of Scent." *Health* November 1989: 57+.

"Perfume." *Encyclopædia Britannica.* 1971.

Weber, Bruce. "Nose Job." *New York Times Magazine* 5 Feb. 1989: 78.

THE SPEAKING OUTLINE

speaking outline: a
brief outline for the
speaker's use alone and
containing source cita-
tions and delivery
prompts.

The **speaking outline,** the one you actually use to deliver your speech, is a pared-down version of your full formal outline. You construct the formal outline for an interested reader with no necessary prior knowledge of your topic. However, you write the speaking outline for *yourself* as a unique speaker. As we mentioned earlier, the only rule for the speaking outline is that it be brief.

Why should the speaking outline be briefer than the formal outline? Chances are that your instructor will want most or all of your speeches delivered from *notes* rather than a written manuscript. By condensing the formal outline to essential words and phrases, you can meet the requirements of the assignment. But more important, if you spoke from a complete sentence outline, you might be tempted to read the speech, sacrificing eye contact and other vital interaction with your audience. Alternately, you might try to memorize the formal outline, another dangerous tactic since you then face the prospect of forgetting part of the speech. If instead you speak using the outline with just key words and phrases to jog your memory, your delivery will seem more natural and conversational, and you will find yourself freer to interact with your audience.

Though the speaking outline leaves out a lot of what the formal outline includes, it also contains some important items not found in the formal outline. For example, you can include directions to yourself about the delivery of the speech. If you know that you have a tendency to drop your volume, you can prompt yourself in the margins of the speaking outline to speak louder by writing "project" or simply "volume!" You may want parts of the speech delivered especially forcefully and write "VOLUME!" or "Louder!" in the margins there. Or you may find that you need notations to mark pauses, or to caution you to slow down, or to remind you to show visual aids in parts of the speech. Some speakers find it particularly helpful to make these delivery notes in a different color ink from the rest of the outline.

Second, most speaking outlines include any supporting material you plan to use. Quotations and definitions should be written out in complete sentences, even though the rest of the outline is in words and phrases. When you quote others, you must be exact. Examples, illustrations, and statistics may be noted in only a few words or numbers. In a speech on America's billionaires, for example, if you plan to describe how Sam Walton made his fortune as founder of Wal-Mart Stores, you might simply write "Sam Walton" in your notes. If your explanation includes specific dates or statistics, you may include those. In addition, you should insert the sources you will cite.

For the speech on perfumes, John condensed the formal outline and then added the following notations for the actual delivery of the speech:

Introduction
  Napoleon
    Egyptian priests
      Doctors
        Cultured women
  $1 1/2 billion (*Encyc. Americana* '86)
Solvents — Fixatives — Aromatics
  I. *Solvents*
    A. Water
    B. Ethyl alcohol
                         PAUSE
          (Solvents . . . canvas / fixatives . . . acrylic)
  II. *Fixatives* — stabilizers
    A. High molecular weight — evaporate slowly
    B. Sources (Edwin Morris, *Fragrance*)
      1. Natural
        a. Civet cat
        b. Castoreum — Russian/Canadian beaver
        c. Musk — deer, western China
        d. Ambergris — sperm whale
      2. Musk & ambergris synthesized
        a. Protects species
        b. Saves money
                    PAUSE
        (Fixatives stabilize aromatics.)
  III. *Aromatics or essential oils* — primary scents
    A. Flowers (*Encyc. Brit.*)
      1. Rose . . .
      2. Single scent / blend
    B. Spices, seeds, woods
      1. Rosemary . . .
      2. Almond . . .
      3. Sandalwood . . .
    C. Synthetic aldehydes (Morris, *Fragrance*)
      1. Strong but pleasant
      2. Don't last long
      3. Usually balanced with other aromatics
        PAUSE BEFORE CONCLUSION
Conclusion
  Solvents, fixatives, aromatics
  $1.5 billion / year

Someone who knows nothing about the topic of perfumes might not be able to make much sense of John's speaking notes. That's OK. As long as your notes make sense to you, you're fine. For example, you are probably puzzled by John's note, "Solvents . . . canvas / fixatives . . . acrylic." For John, though, those four words triggered the following transitional statement: "If solvents are the canvas the perfumer paints on, fixatives are the acrylic or oil holding the paints together." Similarly, "Fixatives stabilize aromatics" prompted John to say, "Fixatives give perfumes stability, but the ingredients they stabilize, the most distinctive elements of a perfume, are the aromatics." If you practice your introduction, conclusion, and transitions as carefully as John did, you should need only a few words to remind you of what you planned to say in those important sections of your speech.

Summary ───────────────────────────────

Outlining serves five main purposes for a speaker preparing a speech. First, it allows the speaker to check the *scope* of the topic. Is the topic too broad? Are you trying to cover too much or too little? Second, the outline permits a speaker to test the *logical relations* between main points and subpoints. Are the points related and yet distinctive enough to qualify as separate ideas? Third, outlining provides a check of the *relevance* of subpoints. Supporting ideas should all be related to the main idea under which they are listed. Fourth, a speaker can use an outline to gauge the *balance* of the speech. Does it look as though you will be spending too much time on one of your points and too little on others? Should you eliminate the points that have little support and reorganize those with a great deal of support? Finally, an outline can function as *speaking notes*, jogging the speaker's memory with key words in correct order.

Outlines can take one of two possible forms: *complete sentence* and *key word or phrase*. In the first of these outlines, each item introduced by a number or letter is a complete sentence. The key word or phrase outline avoids complete sentences. The two forms of outlines should generally not be combined.

Effective outlining is greatly simpli-fied if the speaker keeps in mind these traditional principles or rules. First, each symbol — number or letter — in the outline should represent only one idea. Second, coordination and sub-ordination should be represented by a consistent system of letters and numbers properly indented. Third, any point divided into subpoints must have at least two subpoints. Fourth, complete sentences and key words should be mixed *only* in the speaking outline. Finally, coordinate points throughout the outline should have simple, parallel grammatical construction.

The first phase of outlining is a *working outline*, an informal list of different aspects of the selected speech topic. From there, the speaker should develop a complete sentence outline, or *formal outline*, that is clear and thorough enough to communicate the essence of the speech to any reader. Having checked the scope of the topic, and the logical connections, relevance, and balance of the subpoints, the speaker can then select key words and phrases for a *speaking outline*. That outline may also include transitions, quotations, and source citations, as well as personal directions or "prompts" for the delivery of the speech.

A speaking outline provides a visual test of the organization of a speech.

While effective outlining does not guarantee clear organization in the delivered speech, chances are good that any well-organized speech has been carefully outlined at some stage in its development.

Exercises

1. Select one of the speeches in Appendix C and prepare a key word or phrase outline of the speech. Identify three ways the outline reveals whether the speech was well organized, whether the ideas are balanced, and whether each point directly relates to the specific purpose of the speech.
2. Using the outline you constructed in Exercise 1, reword it as a complete sentence outline. When is it better to develop a key word or phrase outline? When is a complete sentence outline preferred?
3. Listen to a speech in person or on radio, television, or videotape, and outline its main and supporting ideas. Review the outline. Did the speaker try to cover too many points? Are the main points and subpoints relevant, balanced, and logically sequenced? Based on the outline, what suggestions could you give the speaker to improve the speech?
4. Select one of the following topics: superstitions, hiccups, mandatory retirement, or amusement parks. Without doing any research, brainstorm ideas you could include in a speech. Prepare a key word or phrase outline developing coordinate and subordinate ideas.
5. Using the entries below, construct an outline of three major points on the topic of "plastics." The major headings are included in the entries.

clarity	toys	amino plastics
silicon plastics	kitchenware	resistance
piping	types	cellulose plastics
uses	containers	properties
strength	vinyl plastics	auto body parts
polyurethane plastics		

Answer:
The three major headings are types of plastics, properties of plastics, and uses of plastics. The subpoints under each main topic are: TYPES—amino plastics, cellulose plastics, polyurethane plastics, silicon plastics, vinyl plastics. PROPERTIES—clarity, resistance, strength. USES—auto body parts, containers, kitchenware, piping, toys. The order of the main points or the subpoints under each may vary.

Notes

1. E.D. Hirsch, Jr. *Cultural Literacy: What Every American Needs to Know* (New York: Random-Vintage, 1988) 34.

2. Many people who teach creative writing prefer visual brainstorming, or "branching," to the traditional, linear outlines such as the ones we illustrate. For interesting discussions of how outlining by visual brainstorming draws on both sides of the brain, see Henriette Anne Klauser, *Writing on Both Sides of the Brain: Breakthrough Techniques for People Who Write* (San Francisco: Harper San Francisco, 1987) 47–55, and Gabriele Lusser Rico, *Writing the Natural Way: Using Right-Brain Techniques to Release Your Expressive Powers* (Los Angeles: Tarcher, 1983).

Wording Your Speech

11

Functions of Language
Communicating Ideas
Sending Messages About User
Strengthening Social Bonds
Serving as Instrument of Play
Checking Language Use

Principles of Effective Language Use
Use Language Correctly
Use Language Clearly

Use Specific Language
Use Familiar Language
Use Language Vividly
  Use Active Language
  Appeal to Your Listeners' Senses
  Use Figures and Structures of Speech
Use Language Appropriately
  Use Oral Style
  Use Nonsexist Language

Language really is a very, very important part of your delivery. It's one of the main thing separating man from the lower animals and stuff like that. A speaker's language reflects his educational level, his socioeconomic background, and his attitudes about the world around him. So it's really, really important that you think about the words and stuff that you will use to communicate your ideas in a public speech.

We have planned the beginning of each chapter to get you to think about various aspects of public speaking and communication in general. We expect that the opening paragraph of this chapter got your attention with its bland, vague language. The opening lines needlessly repeat the adverbs "really" and "very." They use empty words like "thing" and "stuff." The second sentence contains a grammatical mistake: "thing" should be "things," and then it should be kicked out of the paragraph altogether, replaced by another, more descriptive noun. Beginning with the second sentence, the opening section is also sexist because it implies that all speakers are male. In short, the paragraph is plagued by a poor use of language, especially inappropriate for a chapter on the subject of language. In this chapter we will try to show you how to avoid these and other problems so that you use language powerfully and imaginatively.

A more interesting way to start a discussion of how to use language in a public speech would be to look at a particularly vivid example. One of our favorite actual stories about language use occurred during an unusually heated 1950 U.S. Senate race in Florida. In that campaign, challenger George Smathers used words as weapons against the incumbent Senator Claude Pepper. As *Time* magazine reported it:

> According to the yarn, Smathers had a little speech for cracker voters who were presumed not to know what the words meant except that they must be something bad. The speech went like this:
>
> "Are you aware that Claude Pepper is known all over Washington as a shameless extrovert? Not only that, but this man is reliably reported to practice nepotism with his sister-in-law, and he has a sister who was once a thespian in wicked New York. Worst of all it is an established fact that Mr. Pepper before his marriage habitually practiced celibacy."[1]

Listeners unfamiliar with the words extrovert, nepotism, thespian, and celibacy may have questioned Senator Pepper's integrity.

Unfortunately, this campaign tactic is not an isolated example. Politicians still use language as a primary weapon during a campaign. During the 1990 elections one campaign group, for example, prepared a pamphlet entitled, "Language: A Key Mechanism of Control." The authors presented two lists of words. One list, "Optimistic Positive Governing Words," included terms to describe the candidate's campaign and ideas, words such as crusade, family, freedom, hard work, prosperity, truth, and vision. The other list, "Contrasting Words," specified labels that might be attached to the opponent. This list included anti-child, anti-flag, betray, decay, sick, taxes, and traitors. The authors of the pamphlet encouraged candidates to memorize the words and, "like any tool," use them.[2]

We are all given access to the same number of words. How we use those

Discussion Prompt:
What were the "buzz words" or "trigger words" used by candidates during the 1992 presidential election, or another recent election? What effect did these words have?

214

words helps determine what we accomplish, how we feel about our lives, and how we are remembered. Words are indeed tools speakers can use to advance their causes. Words empower us, and we can employ them to serve both ethical and unethical purposes. As one speaker explains:

> Words, as symbols of ideas and ideals, have the power to make people fall in love or out of love, to be faithful or unfaithful to their vows and pledges. . . . They can produce tears or laughter, success or disaster. They can bring luster or brightness to the face of a child or send him to bed sobbing and sorrowful. . . .
>
> Words can change the face of a city, build churches, schools, playgrounds, boys' clubs, scout groups, civic forums, civic clubs, Little Theatres, Civic Music organizations, garden clubs, and better governments. . . .
>
> The force of words is great, good, glorious, or terrifying.[3]

In this chapter you will learn five functions language serves for us. We will also discuss four principles of language use and offer suggestions for achieving them. This chapter is important because the more you know about language, the greater control you will have as you communicate in public.

> It is hard to stretch a small vocabulary to make it do all the things that intelligent people require of words. It's like trying to plan a series of menus from the limited resources of a poverty-stricken war-torn country compared to planning such a series in a prosperous, stable country. Words are one of our chief means of adjusting to all the situations of life. The better control we have over words, the more successful our adjustment is likely to be.[4]

■ Functions of Language ─────────────

Language fulfills at least five functions for those who use it.[5]

1. Language communicates ideas.
2. Language sends messages about the people using it.
3. Language strengthens social bonds between groups of people.
4. Language can be an instrument of play.
5. Language checks and controls our use of language.

**KEY POINTS
Functions
of Language**

COMMUNICATING IDEAS

Our language can communicate an infinite number of ideas because it has a structure of separate words. For example, unlike the sounds most animals make to signal danger, our language allows us to specify the type of threat, the immediacy of the danger, and any number of other characteristics of the situation.[6] As we mentioned in Chapter 1 in discussing the "triangle of meaning," as

Teaching Strategy:
Ask students to generate examples of words and phrases
that identify a speaker as
being from a particular region of the country. Examples could include the pro-
noun "y'all," the salutation
"yo!," or the use of "pop"
for carbonated soft drinks.
Do these examples also suggest stereotypes about the
educational levels of the
speakers?

Class Activity:
Ask students to list syn-
onyms with stronger emo-
tional impact for each of the
following terms:

accident (collision, catas-
trophe, tragedy);
question [vb] (interrogate,
cross-examine, grill);
party (revelry, fiesta, celebration);
creature (beast, monster,
ogre);
meal (banquet, feast, smor-
gasbord);
fight [n] (battle, brawl, holocaust).

Related Readings:
Pick examples of college
student jargon from Pamela
Munro's book *Slang U.* New
York: Random, 1991. See if
your students are familiar
with that jargon or if they
use other terms to express
similar meanings. See also:
Dickson, Paul. *Slang! The
Topic-by-Topic Dictionary of
Contemporary American Lin-
goes* (New York: Pocket,
1990).

long as a speaker and listener attach similar referents to the words they use, the two can communicate indefinitely. "Like coins, words get their value from the community at large, which must agree on what they represent. The word *dog* may mean a furry creature with four legs and a wagging tail, for instance, but *hippopotamus* or *ziglot* would serve just as well, as long as both speaker and listener agreed on its meaning."[7]

SENDING MESSAGES ABOUT USER

Our vocabulary may reveal aspects of our educational background, our age, and even what area of the country we call home. Consider the two following statements about Natalie: "Regardless of the occasion, Natalie is noticed by all who attend." "Wherever she goes, Natalie stands out like a blackeyed pea in a plate full of grits." You probably formed contrasting images of the two speakers based solely on the words they used.

In addition, language expresses the feelings or emotions of the speaker. The words we select communicate how we feel about both our listeners and the subject under discussion. Which of these terms suggests the strongest emotion, for example?

fire   blaze   inferno

"Inferno" obviously suggests a stronger emotional response from the speaker than either of the other terms. Consider another example:

crisis   dilemma   problem

In this case, "crisis" suggests more feeling than the other terms. Language can carry considerable emotional impact, and the words you select carry some-times obvious, sometimes subtle messages about your background and the nature and strength of your emotions.

STRENGTHENING SOCIAL BONDS

Precisely because it communicates ideas and emotions between people, language serves a social function. For example, we often use language to iden-tify ourselves as part of a particular group. Think of the slang expressions you used around friends when you were younger to signal that you were a member of a certain group and in the know. A ten-year-old child comes home from school one day and suddenly begins calling everything "radical." The next week everything is "radical, dude." The following week he bewilders everyone over the age of ten by calling things "dudical." We have had to guess at that spelling because, of course, dudical is not yet in any dictionary. Is it a contrac-tion of "radical, dude"? We may never know, because after using it for a week or so the child has never repeated the word. The boy's social group apparently dropped the term and moved on to some more interesting expression.

Language other than slang also serves a social function. A group of kinder-garten students reciting the alphabet or counting from one to twenty strengthen their group identity and celebrate the group's accomplishment.

Similar group feelings can occur among adults repeating a pledge, oath, or prayer. Or consider the words we use to greet one another. The exchange "Hi, how are you?" and "Fine, how are you doing?" may be a hollow, automatic social ritual. Nevertheless, such rituals acknowledge the social bond that exists even between strangers.

SERVING AS INSTRUMENT OF PLAY

Our language not only works, it also entertains. For example, entertainment trivia buffs tell the story that once when she was writing a story on the young actor, Hedda Hopper, famed gossip columnist of the fifties, sent Cary Grant the following telegram: "How old Cary Grant?" Grant responded by telegram: "Old Cary Grant fine. How old Hedda Hopper?"

We use language not only for that kind of verbal dueling, but also for the pleasure of its sounds. Many linguists believe we all vocalize as children because it feels and sounds good. Luckily, we do not entirely lose that capacity for play as we mature. The "Ob-la-di, ob-la-da" refrain in the Beatles song of the same name and the "uh-oh" chorus in Hammer's "Here Comes the Hammer" are but two examples of language used for the sheer fun of its sounds.

CHECKING LANGUAGE USE

When in doubt, we as speakers will sometimes check with our listeners to see whether they are decoding a message similar to the one we intended: "Do you understand?" "Get it?" As listeners during interpersonal communication, we may even interrupt a speaker to signal our misunderstanding: "Wait a minute. I don't follow you."

These five functions of language should be obvious to you by this point in your public speaking class. The fact that most of your classmates understood the speeches you have given so far testifies to the power of language to carry a speaker's ideas. Yet your listeners have learned more than the ideas you communicated. From your language during your speeches and while commenting on others' speeches, they have learned about your likes and dislikes. They may have even made accurate guesses about aspects of your background. During the semester or quarter, the language you used in your speeches and in class discussion has also established and strengthened the social bonds between you and your classmates. Anytime anyone used humor or showed any verbal virtuosity, they were inviting you to play with language. And whenever you used an interjection such as "Get this" or "This is important," or whenever you questioned a speaker after a speech, you were using language to check and measure your understanding.

Language has many registers, from chatty and confidential, to simple and direct, complex and technical, lofty and formal. You know that you speak differently to different people, depending upon the environment, the subject under discussion, and the relationship between you and your listeners. Though public speaking is generally more formal than casual conversation, the precise level of language you use will depend on what you want the speech to accomplish.

Cross-Reference:
Take this opportunity to stress the importance of using first and second-person pronouns ("I," "you," "we," "our," "your") in public speeches. Have students look at Mario Cuomo's use of pronouns in his convention speech in Appendix C. Where and how does he separate himself from his listeners? Where and how does he identify with them?

Teaching Strategy:
See if students in your class can recall Lewis Carroll's poem "The Jabberwock" from memory. See if they can remember other examples of nonsense rhymes that are vivid because they are fun to say.

Class Activity:
Have students examine an issue of *Newsweek* noticing how the level of language changes depending upon the subject.

Related Reading:
For another discussion of the differences between oral and written style, see Einhorn, Lois. "Oral and Written Style: An Examination of Differences." *Southern Speech Communication Journal* 43 (Spring 1978): 302–11.

Before we briefly discuss language from a speaker's point of view, consider the ways you respond to language as a reader. Do you read a recipe or a textbook the same way that you do a favorite novel or short story? Do you read a plot summary of *King Lear* the same way that you read Shakespeare's play? The answer to both questions is almost surely, "no." When you read a textbook for a class, you focus on what you get out of it: the main ideas, how they are developed, and how you can use this information. In addition, as a student you are most likely imagining possible test questions you may be asked about this material. To that extent, you value textbook language that is clear, simple, and direct.

In the case of a favorite novel, however, you pay a great deal more attention to its language. As a result, you read imaginative literature more slowly than you do textbooks, newspapers, or instructions for using a new VCR. You may even re-read a passage you particularly like, or read it aloud to someone. As you savor the language of a fictional work, your focus is not so much what you get out of it, but rather what you and the author together create from the language of the text.[8]

We not only read and respond to language in these two ways, we also speak in two different ways. At times we want our language to be **transparent,** almost to disappear. At such times, we focus on getting our meaning across to our listeners as quickly and clearly as possible. If you were reporting a fire, a gas leak, or some other emergency to a group of people and advising them to vacate their building, you would try to communicate that information as directly, simply, and quickly as possible without causing panic. You would not waste time mentally editing and practicing the message to make it more clever or more memorable. Your goal is to get your message across quickly and clearly. In giving instructions or issuing a warning, you would never want to use language your audience did not know. Because your goal in these circumstances is getting your message across to a listener, you would use language with clear denotations. **Denotation** is the dictionary definition of a word.

denotation: the literal meaning or dictionary definition of a word or phrase.

On other occasions, our purpose as speakers is not just to get a message across, but to convey it in an especially vivid way. At such times we pay particular attention to the way we encode the message, choosing words as carefully as we might select a birthday gift for an important friend. When your purpose is to signal your feelings about a subject, to strengthen the social bonds between you and your listeners, or to engage them in verbal play, you will likely use language with strong connotations. **Connotation** is the emotional association that a particular word has for an individual listener. The word "fire" may have strong, pleasant connotations for you if you spent some time around a campfire recently. The same word will have negative connotations for someone whose home was burned down.

connotation: the emotional associations that a word or phrase may evoke in individual listeners.

Your choice of language depends on the purpose of your speech. Usually, you will use a combination of denotative and connotative language registers. Whether the wording of your speech is straightforward or evocative, direct or highly embroidered, however, you must use language carefully. The following section offers guidelines for using language correctly, clearly, vividly, and appropriately.

"Language is the armory of the human mind, and at once contains the trophies of its past and the weapons of its future conquests."

SAMUEL TAYLOR COLERIDGE

Words are sometimes compared to tools and weapons, and in a sense you draw from that arsenal every time you speak. The words you choose help determine your success in informing, persuading, and entertaining your audience. Four principles should guide your use of language and make you a more effective speaker.

1. Use language correctly. **2.** Use language clearly. **3.** Use language vividly. **4.** Use language appropriately.	**KEY POINTS** **Principles of Effective Language Use**

USE LANGUAGE CORRECTLY

"Socrates was a famous Greek teacher who went around giving people advice. They killed him. Socrates died from an overdose of wedlock. After his death, his career suffered a dramatic decline." (from a student paper)[9]

"If the people don't want to come out to the park, nobody's going to stop 'em." (Yogi Berra)

"And you don't need to draw me any diaphragms neither!" (Archie Bunker)[10]

"Sisters Reunited After 18 Years in Checkout Line at Supermarket" (newspaper headline)[11]

Whether it be a Yogiism, an Archieism, or some other kind of "ism," language abuse is all around us. We see our language assaulted in letters, term papers, newspapers, and magazines. We hear it abused on radio, on television, and in conversations with our friends.

As a speaker, your first requirement is to use language correctly, and you achieve this goal in two ways. First, you must select the right word for the thought you wish to convey. Socrates died of an overdose of hemlock, not wedlock. The correct word for Archie's referent is diagram, not diaphragm. After you select the correct words, you must then phrase them correctly. We doubt that the sisters mentioned above had to wait in the supermarket checkout line for eighteen years, even if there were lots of double coupon days!

When you use language incorrectly in your speech you run the risk of sending unintended messages, as well as undermining your credibility and the causes you support. Poorly worded ideas are sometimes evaluated as poor ideas, although this may not be the case. For example, in a speech on how to dress and groom for an interview, a student of ours recently advised, "Men should not wear long hair to a business interview. Long hair has a real *astigmatism* attached to it." The speaker's advice is probably sound, but he has worded it incorrectly; the student meant that long hair has a stigma attached to it. Another student, concerned about the increase of sexually transmitted diseases, encouraged her listeners to commit to "long-term *monotonous* relationships." She should have used the word "monogamous."

Most of the cases of incorrect language you hear in your class will, no doubt, be more subtle than the examples given above. Nevertheless, it is important for speakers to rid their speeches of *all* unnecessary intrusions. Speakers perceived to care about *how* they state their ideas are also perceived to care about *what* they say.

The following examples illustrate some common language errors we have observed in student speeches:

1. The first criteria for selecting a good wine is to experience its bouquet. (The speaker should use the singular noun: criterion.)
2. If our school is to remain financially solvent, we must choose between three options: (1) increasing tuition, (2) laying off faculty and staff employees, or (3) forgoing the planned construction of a new athletic complex. ("Among" is the correct word when more than two options are included.)
3. Because she failed to wear her seat belt, she was hurt bad: a broken leg, fractured ribs, and a mild concussion. (She was hurt badly.)
4. Because they conduct most of their missions at night, a drug trafficker often alludes our understaffed border patrol. ("They" is plural, so the speaker should use "drug traffickers." Also, the correct word is elude, not allude.)
5. He don't realize that his poor credit history as a college student will continue to follow him after graduation. (The verb should be singular: doesn't.)
6. Members of our legislature voted theirselves a pay raise at the same time they voted down an increase in the state's education budget. ("Theirselves" is not a word. The correct word is "themselves.")

Some of these transgressions may seem less severe to you than others. Remember, though, that your language is an important part of the delivery of your speech, and like your physical and vocal delivery, your language should be free of *all* distractions. Errors in subject/verb agreement, misplaced modifiers, and incorrect word choice immediately attract the attention of everyone who recognizes these errors. You won't upset anyone if your language is grammatically correct, but even small errors run the risk of monopolizing some people's attention. In turn, they stop listening carefully to *what* you say because they are paying attention to *how* you speak.

You can speak correctly if you follow a few simple guidelines. *First*, make a note of grammatical mistakes you hear yourself and other people make in casual conversation. Attentive listening is a first step to improving your use of language. *Second*, when you are unsure of a word's meaning, consult a dictionary. *Third*, if you have a question about proper grammar, refer to a handbook for writers. *Fourth*, when practicing your speech, record it and play it back, listening for mistakes you may not have noticed as you were practicing. *Fifth*, practice your speech in front of friends and ask them to point out mistakes. These

Related Reading:
An excellent source for questions of grammar is: Leggett, Glenn, C. David Mead, and Melinda G. Kramer. *Prentice Hall Handbook for Writers.* 11th ed. Englewood Cliffs, NJ: Prentice, 1991. See, especially, their unit on "Basic Sentence Faults," pages 63–133.

strategies will help you detect and correct errors. Not only will your speaking improve, but you may also save yourself some embarrassment. As Mark Twain noted, "The difference between the right word and the almost right word is the difference between lightning and the lightning bug."

USE LANGUAGE CLEARLY

How would you respond if a friend said to you: "Let's work on our project for a while after dinner. Could you bring a quire with you?" You would probably ask several questions because your friend failed to communicate clearly. What specifically is "our project"? How long is "for a while"? What time is "after dinner"? Where will this meeting take place? Your friend would have communicated the first part of the message more clearly if she had said, "Let's meet in my room from 6:00 to 7:00 this evening to work on our group report for Psychology 100." You would also certainly have asked, "What's a quire?" Though it is specific, your friend's request that you bring a *quire* will still be confusing unless you know that it means twenty-four sheets of paper.

Language use must not only be correct, it must also be clear. In order to achieve clarity a speaker should use language that is **specific** and **familiar.** If you sacrifice either criterion, your language may confuse your listeners.

Use Specific Language. In Chapter 1 we mentioned that many of our communication problems spring from the fact that there are always two messages involved whenever two people are communicating. There is, first, the message that the speaker intends. To this, however, we must add the message that the listener infers or interprets. If you tell your instructor that you missed an assignment deadline because you were "having some problems," you leave yourself open to a wide range of possible interpretations. You may be having health problems, or suffering from discord in your family, or undergoing stress from a personal relationship. You could be having trouble juggling a work schedule with your study time, or having trouble getting to class because of car problems. You could be grieving over the loss of a loved one, or struggling with one particularly difficult course. These and other interpretations are possible because "problem" is an abstract term.

To clarify your ideas, use the lowest level of abstraction possible. Words are not *either* abstract or concrete, but take on these qualities in relation to other words. Look at the following lists of terms, for example.

Related Readings: Students whose primary language is not English are often confused by Americans' use of the English language. Two excellent references that may help your students for whom English is a second language are: (1) Makkai, Adam, ed., *Handbook of Commonly Used American Idioms,* 2nd ed. NY: Barron's, 1991. (2) Spears Richard A., *Common American Phrases in Everyday Contexts.* Lincolnwood, IL: National Textbook, 1992.

theatre
Western theatre
twentieth-century Western theatre
documentary theatre
plays of Michael Hastings
The Silence of Lee Harvey Oswald

transportation
automobile
General Motors car
late model Pontiac
1991 Grand Prix
blue 1991 Grand Prix
loaded, blue 1991 Grand Prix with white interior

class
college course
American history
History 1305: America 1945 – Present
History 1305 at Northwestern University
History 1305 with Prof. Yates at Northwestern University

The terms at the top of these lists are more abstract than those at the bottom. As we add those limiting, descriptive words, or **qualifiers,** the referent becomes increasingly specific. The lower the level of abstraction used, the more clearly the listener will understand the speaker.

Suppose you were giving a speech on how citizens can protect their homes from burglaries, and you made the following statement:

> Crime is rampant in our city. Burglary alone has gone way up in the past year or so. So you can see that having the right kind of lock on your door is essential to your safety.

What is wrong with this statement? The language is vague. What does "rampant" mean? How much of an increase is "way up" — 15 percent, 50 percent, 400 percent? Is "the past year or so" one year, two years, or more? What is "the right kind of lock"? As a speaker you should help your audience by making these ideas more concrete. After some research, you might rephrase your argument like this:

> Last week I spoke with Captain James Winton, head of our City Police Department's Records Division. He told me that crime in our city has increased by 54 percent in the last year, and the number of burglaries has doubled. We can help deter crime by making our homes burglar-proof, and one way of doing this is to make sure that all doors have solid locks. I brought one such lock with me: It's a double-keyed dead-bolt lock.

Notice the improvement in the second paragraph. Your message is clearer, and with that clarity you would gain added credibility as a speaker.

Use Familiar Language.

"The chief virtue that language can have is clearness, and nothing detracts from it so much as the use of unfamiliar words."   Hippocrates

Anyone who has purchased a video cassette recorder has suffered through the complicated instructions that accompanied it. According to Karen Schriver, English professor at Carnegie Mellon University, those awkward, unclear instructions are usually written by entry-level engineers who are more concerned with describing the equipment's features than is the poor consumer who will be using it. Mitsubishi Electronics America recently recruited Schriver to help rewrite their VCR user manuals. A sample of her changes follows:

> *Before:* "This VCR employs direct function switching where any playback mode may be directly entered from any other playback mode (normal playback, still frame, speed search, etc.) simply by pressing the appropriate buttons."

After: "When you use a feature (like Play or Rewind), you can go directly to another feature (like Speed Search) without first pressing Stop."[12]

223
Wording Your Speech

Both sentences are specific, but the second communicates the message in a language style more familiar to non-engineers.

Your language may be specific but still not be clear. If listeners are not familiar with your words, communication is impaired. The statement "The Sultan of Swat was famous for his batboy shots" is specific but probably unclear to most listeners. Some may know that the Sultan of Swat is a nickname for baseball great Babe Ruth. Probably only the most avid baseball enthusiast, however, knows that the term *batboy shot* refers to a home run hit so powerfully that the batter knows instantly that it is out of the park and has time to hand the bat to the batboy (no batgirls in Babe Ruth's time) before rounding the bases.

Occasionally we hear speeches in which students try to impress us with their vocabularies. We suspect they drafted their remarks with a pen in one hand and a thesaurus in the other. Phrases such as "a plethora of regulations," "this obviates the need for," "the apotheosis of deceit," and "the anathema of censorship" detract from rather than enhance the speaker's message. "We must ever be mindful to eschew verbosity and deprecate tautology" is good advice and fun to say. But if you are trying to communicate with another person, it's probably better simply to say, "Avoid wordiness."

The use of jargon may also undermine clarity. **Jargon** is the special language of a particular activity, business, or group of people. Computer experts, for example, talk about "RAM" and "ROM," bytes and bits, shells and crashes —abbreviations and words with specialized meanings when applied to computers. Real estate agents will say that a particular house has a good "drive up," meaning that it makes a good first impression. Doctors, nurses, and other medical technicians talk about performing "CAT scans" and administering "D5W." Stockbrokers and their clients discuss "bear markets," "selling short," and "buying on the margin." If you are certain that the people you are addressing know such terms, jargon presents no problem. In fact, it is usually quite specific and can save a lot of time. Jargon can even increase your credibility by indicating that you are familiar with the subject matter. If you have any doubts that your listeners know the jargon, however, either avoid such terms or else define each one the first time you use it.

USE LANGUAGE VIVIDLY

In addition to selecting language that is correct and clear, speakers should choose language that is colorful and picturesque. Vivid language engages the audience and makes the task of listening easier. Read the following critiques of the speeches of our twenty-ninth president, Warren Harding:

1. Warren Harding was not an effective public speaker. His speeches often were confusing and uninspired. He did not make his points well.
2. His speeches left the impression of an army of pompous phrases moving over the landscape in search of an idea; sometimes these meandering words would actually capture a straggling thought and bear it triumphantly a prisoner in their midst, until it died of servitude and overwork. (William G. McAdoo, Democratic party leader)[13]

Related Reading:
Government officials and advertisers are sometimes criticized for using *doublespeak*, language which says one thing on one level but conveys something else on another level. For example, a tax increase is a "revenue enhancement" and a pencil is a "portable, hand-held communications inscriber; and an employee who has been fired is experiencing "negative employee retention." For an entertaining and informative discussion of doublespeak, see Lutz, William. *Doublespeak.* New York: HarperPerennial, 1990.

jargon: the special language used by people in a particular activity, business, or group.

Related Reading:
See Barry, John A. *Technobabble.* Cambridge: MIT P, 1991.

Answers:
"CAT" is the abbreviation for computerized axial tomography; "D5W" stands for a solution of 5% dextrose in sterile water.

Teaching Strategy:
The final page of most recent issues of *The Atlantic* lists new words and expressions, tells where the words have been seen in print, and explains each word's background. In its "Periscope" section at the front of every issue, *Newsweek* now also features a column of "Buzzwords"—jargon and slang currently used by people in various fields. Collect some of these to use in class as examples of colorful, vivid language use.

Practice Speaking:
Quotations 2 and 3 are a lot of fun to say out loud. Have your students try reading them aloud. What attitudes of the writers are communicated when the words are sounded?

3. He writes the worst English that I have ever encountered. It reminds me of a string of wet sponges; it reminds me of tattered washing on the line; it reminds me of stale bean soup, of college yells, of dogs barking idiotically through endless nights. It is so bad that a sort of grandeur creeps into it. It drags itself out of the dark abysm (I was about to write abscess!) of pish and crawls insanely up to the topmost pinnacle of posh. It is rumble and bumble. It is flap and doodle. It is balder and dash." (H.L. Mencken)[14]

Which of these three statements did you most enjoy reading? Which characterization of Harding's speaking did you find the most colorful? Which paragraph contains the most vivid images? Which would you most like to read again? While we don't know your answers to these questions, we're fairly certain that you did *not* select the first statement. Why?

The language of the first critique communicates an idea as simply and economically as possible without calling attention to itself. To use a term we introduced earlier in this chapter, its language is transparent. It is also drab and colorless, and displays little creativity. Its language style is not nearly as lively and its images are not as vivid as the other two paragraphs. The language of the second and third statements is opaque; it calls attention to its sounds, textures, and rhythms. Vivid language helps listeners remember both your message *and* you.

cliché: a once-colorful figure of speech that has lost impact from overuse.

One of the fiercest enemies of vivid language is the **cliché,** a once-colorful expression that has lost most of its impact through overuse. Many clichés involve comparisons. For example, complete the following phrases:

"Cute as a _____."   "Burning the midnight _____."
"Dead as a _____."   "Colder than a _____."
"Between a rock and a _____."

Did you have any trouble completing the expressions above? Probably not. In fact, button, doornail, hard place, oil, and mackerel most likely popped into your mind without much thought. Each of these sayings is a cliché, an overworked expression that doesn't require (or stimulate) much thinking. Clichés are bland, commonplace, hackneyed, and pedestrian. Avoid them!

Perhaps the speech genre most susceptible to clichés is the commencement speech. Robert Leestamper remembers receiving this advice as he prepared his commencement address for Richmond College of London: "Commencement speeches are easy. Just do what any good advertising man does. Take several clichés, quotes, and brief passages that worked in the past, rearrange them and offer them to the public as a wonderful new creation." Borrowing from Churchill, Jefferson, Kennedy, Kipling, Lincoln, Shakespeare, and others, Leestamper created this parody:

Members of the graduating class, lend me your ears: These are the times that try men's souls, but tell me not in mournful words that life is but an empty dream, for when in the course of human events it becomes necessary to strive, to seek, to find, and not to yield, then we must summon up remembrance of things past, recalling that our forefathers brought forth new nations, and asked not what they could do for them, but said instead "we have nothing to fear, but fear itself." In this our time, ask not for whom the bell tolls, for ours is not to reason why, ours is but to hang

For more than twenty years Will Rogers was America's foremost humorous political commentator because of his ability to spin a rope and turn a phrase.

together or we will all hang separately! I want to make one thing perfectly clear: The world will little note nor long remember what I say here, but generations yet unborn will hold this truth to be self-evident: To thine own self be true, for no man is an island. Fear not the slings and arrows of outrageous fortune, but keep your head when all about you are losing theirs and blaming it on you — and then, like a bridge over troubled waters, from sea to shining sea, a brighter day will dawn and bring your finest hour, and never before will so many have owed so much to so few.[15]

How do you suppose an audience would react if he had really delivered this speech?

Now that you have seen some of the effects of dull wording, what techniques can you use to make your language more vivid? The answer to this question may be limited only by your imagination. Three strategies, though, are to (1) use active language, (2) appeal to your listeners' senses, and (3) use figures and structures of speech. Using these suggestions will give you a good start on making your speeches more colorful and, thus, more memorable.

Use Active Language. Which of the following statements is more forceful?

It was decided by the Student Government Association that the election would be delayed for one week.

The Student Government Association decided to delay the election for one week.

The second one, right? The first sentence uses passive voice; the second active. **Active voice** is always more direct because it identifies the agent producing the action and places it first in the sentence. In addition, active voice is more economical than passive voice; the second sentence is shorter than the first by five words.

Active language, however, involves more than active voice. **Active language** is language that works. It has energy, vitality, and drive. It is not bogged down by filler phrases such as "you know," "like," and "stuff like that." Rather than being cliché-ridden, it may convert the commonplace into the unexpected. In the following example, notice how the speaker changes the cliché "between a rock and a hard place" to highlight his point:

Consumers today are stuck between a clock and a hard place . . . and the '90s will be governed by demand for convenience and speed in virtually everything that touches our lives. *Faster food, faster news, faster mail, fax, fax, fax.*[16]

Coining a word or phrase is another way of making your language work for you. When the San Francisco 49ers sought their third consecutive Super Bowl championship, sports columnists labeled it an attempt to "three-peat." The word's novelty makes it memorable. It also conveys more information than the word "repeat." (The 49ers were unable to fulfill this goal, however.) A "well-turned phrase" also actively engages the minds of your listeners as they hear the interplay of words and ideas. Indian nationalist leader Mohandas Gandhi, for example, urged his listeners to "live simply so others might simply live."

Appeal to Your Listeners' Senses. You can achieve impact with language by appealing to your listeners' senses. The obvious and familiar senses are sight, hearing, touch, taste, and smell. To these we can add the sense of motion or movement and the sense of muscular tension. Colorful language can create vivid images that appeal to each of these various senses. Those sharp images in

Reprinted by permission of UFS, Inc.

turn heighten audience involvement in the speech, inviting them to participate with their feelings and thereby increasing their retention of what you have said.

Assume that you are a roller coaster enthusiast and have decided to deliver an informative speech on roller coasters. Such a topic certainly begs for language to create or re-create the various sensations of a coaster ride for your audience. But what if you are not confident about your ability to appeal to your audience's various senses in your speech? You can always do some research on this topic and use the words of others, as long as you accurately attribute your quotations. We easily found four recent magazine articles on roller coasters. Let's look at examples from two particularly vivid articles written to tap all the senses of a reader. Notice how the examples vivify the topic by using the eight sensory images we list below.

Visual images recreate the sight of a person, place, or thing. Speakers can use visual images to set the scene for future action or further explanation. The following passage re-creates the sight of walking up to and boarding the famous roller coaster at Coney Island:

> The Cyclone differs from other roller coasters in being (a) a work of art and (b) old, and not only old but old-looking, decrepit, rusting in its metal parts and peeling in its more numerous wooden parts, filthy throughout and jammed into a wire (Cyclone!) fence abutting cracked sidewalks of the Third World sinkhole that Coney Island is, intoxicatingly.[17]

Visual images can even be used to speculate what an imagined person, place, or thing might look like.

Auditory images suggest the sound of something by appealing to our sense of hearing. You may be familiar with the term *onomatopoeia* for a word that evokes specific sounds, as in "buzz," "crack," or "snarl." Notice the use of that device in this description of the first part of the ride:

> Yes, it may be anguishing initially . . . Terrifying, even, the first time or two the train is hauled upward with groans and creaks and with you in it. At the top then — where there is sudden strange quiet but for the fluttering of two tattered flags. . . .[18]

Tactile images re-create the feel of something. Tactile images spark the audience's memories of textures, shapes, and temperatures, as in this example:

> I should mention that a heavy, cushioned restraining bar locks down snugly into your lap and is very reassuring, although, like everything upholstered in the cars, it may be cracked or slashed and leaking tufts of stuffing from under swatches of gray gaffer's tape. One thing consistently disquieting is how, under stress, a car's wooden sides may *give* a bit.[19]

A special type of tactile image called a **thermal image** creates impressions of heat or cold or any temperature in between those extremes. Notice the vivid thermal image toward the end of this description:

> One time the vibration, with the wheels shrieking and the cars threatening to explode with strain, made me think, "This is *no fun at all!*" It was an awful moment, with a sickening sense of betrayal and icy-fingered doubt: Was my love malign?[20]

visual image: language that causes listeners to remember or imagine the way a thing looks.

auditory image: language that causes listeners to remember or imagine the way a thing sounds.

tactile image: language that causes listeners to remember or imagine the way a thing feels.

thermal image: language that causes listeners to remember or imagine the temperature of a thing.

gustatory image: language that causes listeners to remember or imagine the way something tastes.

kinetic image: language that causes listeners to remember or imagine a sensation of motion.

kinesthetic image: language that causes listeners to remember or imagine states of muscular tension or relaxation.

olfactory image: language that causes listeners to remember or imagine the way something smells.

Gustatory images vividly remind the audience of how something tastes, for example:

Nothing matches the faint metallic taste of fear you experience as the clanking stops and you feel the train set free to begin falling from the top of that first hill.

Kinetic images create feelings of motion or movement, as in this example from the middle of the ride:

This time the drop was a mere 18 degrees, but stretched out over a long, curving length of track, to make the torture of acceleration more exquisite. At nearly 65 mph, the train shot into a tunnel and spun 540 degrees around a banked helix, slowed down only by the screaming of one rider, who felt like a bug being sucked down a bathtub drain.[21]

Kinesthetic images appeal to the audience's sense of muscular tension or relaxation.

A sharp, wincing intake of breath (expletive deleted) and the feeling of innards popping up like a parachute in my rib cage. My hair flew back, and my eyes peeled wide and filled with tears, a product of the 60-mph wind and also of self-pity. My teeth clenched and my knuckles locked bone-white around the lap bar.[22]

Olfactory images appeal to our sense of smell by re-creating pleasant or unpleasant aromas. Fragrances have a strong capacity to evoke our memories of people, places, and objects. Even an unpleasant smell may have pleasant associations, as at the end of a coaster ride:

The payoff is intimacy in the sweet diminuendo, the jiggling and chuckling smart little bumps and dandling dips that bring us to a quick, pillowy deceleration in the shed, smelling of dirty machine oil, where we began and will begin again.[23]

Synesthesia is the combination of sensory appeals in a single image. If you speak of a "stoney silence," that phrase evokes auditory, tactile, and possibly thermal sensations. Notice how the following two sentences combine vivid kinetic, kinesthetic, and even auditory images:

[Riding a coaster is] like driving your car with your head out the window at 70 miles per hour. But to get the full effect, you have to drive it off a cliff.[24]

Discussion Prompt:
What is the main type of sensory appeal Shelley Schnathorst uses in paragraph 6 of her speech in Appendix C? Answer: Kinesthetic.

Discussion Prompt:
What sensory appeal is featured in paragraph 18 of Martin Luther King's "I Have a Dream" speech, in Appendix C? Answer: Thermal.

Notice how many of these examples of sensory impressions are not only evocative but also funny and fun to say. Active language and appeals to the senses are not your only techniques for enlivening your speech language, however. Public speaking gives you an opportunity to devise some of the figures of speech and special language structures you may have studied before in English classes.

Use Figures and Structures of Speech. Important ideas are easier to remember if they are memorably worded, so don't be afraid of sounding "flowery." You can use many figures and structures of speech to enliven your language. Some of the most common are alliteration, parallelism, repetition, antithesis, personification, simile, and metaphor.

Alliteration. **Alliteration** is the repetition of beginning sounds in adjacent or nearby words. A speaker who asks us "to dream, to dare, and to do" uses alliteration. The sounds of words give your speech impact. A student speaking on the topic of child abuse described the victims as "badly bruised and beaten." Not only did these words themselves convey a severe problem, but the repetition of the stern, forceful "b" sound vocally accentuated the violence of the act.

In defending the oil industry C.J. Silas, chairman of Phillips Petroleum Company, used alliteration to characterize the attacks of oil industry critics:

> Perhaps more than at any time in recent memory our industry is perceived as an evil juggernaut: intent on bulldozing the wilderness . . . blackening the waterways . . . and bullying the public. All in the effort to pave a broad path to the shrine of the almighty dollar.[25]

Speaking on the subject of educational reform, Vincent Ryan Ruggiero, professor of humanities at State University of New York at Delhi, complained of "mindstuffing," a current practice in education "which renders students passive and transforms the 3 Rs into Receiving, Recalling, and Regurgitating information."[26]

Parallelism and repetition. Speakers use **parallelism** when they express two or more ideas in similar language structure. When they restate words, phrases, or sentences, they use **repetition.** Parallelism and repetition work in concert to emphasize an idea or a call for action. President Ronald Reagan's moving tribute to the crew of the space shuttle *Challenger* effectively connected ideas by using parallelism. Toward the beginning of the speech, Reagan used repetition to introduce the goal of his speech: "The best we can do is remember our seven astronauts, our *Challenger* seven, remember them as they lived. . . ." Then, for at least half of the rest of the eulogy, included in Appendix C, he issued a final roll call of the ill-fated crew:

> We remember Dick Scobee, the commander who spoke the last words we heard from the space shuttle *Challenger*. He served as a fighter pilot in Vietnam, earning many medals for bravery and later as a test pilot of advanced aircraft before joining the space program. Danger was a familiar companion to Commander Scobee.
> We remember Michael Smith, who earned enough medals as a combat pilot to cover his chest, including the Navy Distinguished Flying Cross, three Air Medals, and the Vietnamese Cross of Gallantry with Silver Star in gratitude from a nation he fought to keep free.
> We remember Judith Resnick, known as J.R. to her friends, always smiling, always eager to make a contribution, finding beauty in the music she played on her piano in her off-hours.

The list continued, "We remember Ellison Onizuka," "We remember Ronald McNair," "We remember Gregory Jarvis," "We remember Christa McAuliffe," each repetition of "we remember" like the forlorn tolling of a bell.[27]

Another excellent example of the use of parallel construction is Martin Luther King, Jr.'s "I Have a Dream" speech (see Appendix C). King repeats the phrase "one hundred years later" to dramatize the "shameful condition" of inequality. He prefaces his hopes for the future with the phrase "I have a dream." And near the end of his speech he uses parallelism and repetition to create a dramatic climax:

alliteration: the repetition of beginning sounds in words that are adjacent or near one another.

parallelism: the expression of ideas using similar grammatical structures.

repetition: restating words, phrases, or sentences for emphasis.

Teaching Strategy:
Ask your students to identify the example of parallelism in paragraph 6 of Shannon Dyer's speech on whistleblowers in Appendix C. Answer: "They are social workers," "they are . . .," "they are. . . ."

Cross-Reference:
The complete text of this speech is in Appendix C. The manuscript is rich with parallelism throughout. In addition to the large patterns such as this one, have your students identify examples of parallelism within individual sentences.

So *let freedom ring* from the prodigious hilltops of New Hampshire. *Let freedom ring* from the mighty mountains of New York. *Let freedom ring* from the heightening Alleghenies of Pennsylvania! *Let freedom ring* from the snowcapped Rockies of Colorado!

But not only that. *Let freedom ring* from Stone Mountain of Georgia! *Let freedom ring* from Lookout Mountain of Tennessee! *Let freedom ring* from every hill and molehill of Mississippi. From every mountainside, *let freedom ring*.

And when this happens . . . we will be able to join hands and sing, in the words of the old Negro spiritual, "*Free at last! Free at last!* Thank God almighty, we are *free at last!*"

antithesis: the use of parallel construction to contrast ideas.

Antithesis. **Antithesis** uses parallel construction to contrast ideas. You can probably quote from memory John Kennedy's statement: "Ask not what your country can do for you, ask what you can do for your country." The fact that it is so memorable attests to its power. Mario Cuomo used antithesis in his keynote address to the 1984 Democratic National Convention (see Appendix C):

We must get the American public to look past the glitter, beyond the showmanship —to reality, to the hard substance of things. And we will do that not so much with speeches that sound good as with speeches that are good and sound. Not so much with speeches that bring people to their feet as with speeches that bring people to their senses.[28]

personification: a figure of speech that attributes human qualities to a concept or inanimate object.

Teaching Strategy: Have your students find an example of personification in paragraph 6 of William Fort's speech in Appendix C.

Personification. **Personification** gives human qualities to objects, ideas, or organizations. One speech teacher used personification as the organizing concept of her speech titled "The Anatomy of an Association." In her address she argued that an association's muscle is its unity, its brains are the knowledge it generates, its lifeblood is its ability to renew its membership, and its heart is its people.[29]

Virginia Postrel, editor of *Reason* magazine, began her speech on the environmental movement using personification this way:

On Earth Day, Henry Allen of *The Washington Post* published a pointed and amusing article. In it he suggested that we've created a new image of Mother Nature:

"A sort of combination of Joan Crawford in *Mildred Pierce* and Mrs. Portnoy in *Portnoy's Complaint,* a disappointed, long-suffering martyr who makes us wish, at least for her sake, that we'd never been born.

"She weeps. She threatens. She nags. . . .

"She's a kvetch who makes us feel guilty for eating Big Macs, dumping paint thinner down the cellar sink, driving to work instead of riding the bus, and riding the bus instead of riding a bicycle. Then she makes us feel even guiltier for not feeling guilty enough.

"'Go ahead, use that deodorant, don't even think about me, God knows I'll be gone soon enough, I won't be here to see you get skin cancer when the ozone hole lets in the ultraviolet rays. . . .'"[30]

simile: a comparison of two things using the words "as" or "like."

Simile and metaphor. Simile and metaphor are comparisons of two seemingly dissimilar things. In **simile** the comparison is explicitly stated, using words such as *like* and *as;* for example: "Trying to pin the Senator down on the issue is like trying to nail a poached egg to a tree."

In **metaphor** the comparison is not explicitly stated but is implied. *Like* and *as* are omitted. Sportscasters who call quarterback Joe Montana's passes "heat-seeking missiles" are using metaphor. Peter Schjeldahl, author of the article on Coney Island's Cyclone, uses metaphor when he compares that roller coaster to a poem:

metaphor: an implied comparison of two things without the use of "as" or "like."

> The coaster is basically an ornate means of falling and a poem about physics in parts or stanzas, with jokes. The special quality of the Cyclone is how different, how *articulated,* all the components of its poem are, the whole of which lasts a minute and thirty-some seconds—exactly the right length, composed of distinct and perfect moments. By my fifth ride, my heart was leaping at the onset of each segment as at the approach of a dear old friend, and melting with instantaneous nostalgia for each at its finish.[31]

Notice that near the end of the description Schjeldahl introduces personification, and the roller coaster begins to take on human characteristics.

Extraordinary circumstances sometimes require extraordinary responses. One such event was triggered by the death of President John F. Kennedy. Kennedy's successor, Lyndon Johnson, chose to respond to the nation's sorrow and uncertainty in a televised address to Congress and the American people. His purposes were four: (1) to honor the memory of the assassinated president, (2) to assure the citizenry that their government continued to function, (3) to unite the American people, and (4) to point the nation to the challenges ahead. Notice in the following excerpt how Johnson used several of the techniques mentioned above to help him accomplish his objectives:

Teaching Strategy: Have your students look at paragraphs 4-6 of King's "I Have a Dream" speech in Appendix C. What extended figure of speech did King develop there? Answer: Metaphor. Coming to Washington in peaceful demonstration is like going to the bank to cash a check.

> We meet in grief, but let us also meet in renewed dedication and renewed vigor. Let us meet in action, in tolerance, and in mutual understanding. John Kennedy's death commands what his life conveyed—that America must move forward. The time has come for Americans of all races and creeds and political beliefs to understand and to respect one another. So let us put an end to the teaching and the preaching of hate and evil and violence. Let us turn away from the fanatics of the far left and the far right, from the apostles of bitterness and bigotry, from the defiant of law, and those who pour venom into our Nation's bloodstream.[32]

Alliteration, parallelism, repetition, antithesis, personification, simile, and metaphor enable speakers to create vivid language and images. One note of caution, however: Always remember that your objective as a speaker is *not* to impress your listeners with your ability to create vivid language. Vivid language is not an end in itself but rather a means of achieving the larger objectives of the speech. As William Safire, a language expert, notes, "A good speech is not a collection of crisp one-liners, workable metaphors, and effective rhetorical devices; a good speech truly reflects the thoughts and emotions of the speaker. . . ."[33]

USE LANGUAGE APPROPRIATELY

As we have discussed throughout this book, appropriateness has several dimensions. Your language should be appropriate to you, your topic, your audience, and the occasion. Sometimes achieving all four of these goals may seem impossible. We have heard speakers criticized for poor grammar or incorrect pronunciation respond, "But that's the way I talk." They apparently believe it's more important for language to reflect their speaking style than for it to be correct. While some listeners may neither detect nor be offended by your incorrect language use, others are. They are the ones who should concern you. The safest rule for you to follow is this: Correct language never offends and incorrect language is never appropriate.

If your language is correct, clear, and vivid, you have a good start on achieving appropriateness. Two other dimensions of propriety, however, are noteworthy: oral style and nonsexist language.

Use Oral Style. Part of speaking appropriately is recognizing that your oral style differs from your written style. Unless your instructor asks that you deliver some speeches from a manuscript, we believe that you will be better off if you think of "developing" speeches rather than "writing" them. We can give you two good reasons for avoiding writing your speeches. First, you will likely try to memorize what you have written, and the fear of forgetting part of the speech will add to your nervousness and make your delivery seem stiff and wooden.

The second and more important reason for not writing out a speech is that the act of writing itself often affects the tone of the communication. **Tone** is the relationship established by language and grammar between a writer or speaker and that person's readers or listeners. Many of us think of writing as something formal and "correct." In fact, many of us are intimidated by writing specifically *because* we think it must be formal and correct. For that reason, we tend not to write the way that we speak.

Our oral style differs from our written style in at least four important ways. First, in speaking we tend to use shorter sentences than we write. Speakers who write out their speeches often find themselves gasping for air when they try to deliver a long sentence in one breath.

Second, when we communicate orally we tend to use more contractions, colloquial expressions, and slang. Our speaking vocabulary is smaller than our writing vocabulary, so we tend to speak a simpler language than we write. Speakers who write out their speeches often draw from their larger written vocabularies. As a result, their presentational style seems formal and often creates a barrier between them and their listeners.

Third, oral style makes greater use of personal pronouns and references than written style does. Speakers *must* acknowledge the presence of their listeners, and one way of doing this is by including them in the speech. Saying "We must rid our speech of sexist language" is more powerful than "People must rid their speech of sexist language." Using the pronouns "I," "we," and "you" makes your speech more immediate and enhances your rapport with your listeners. You may even want to mention specific audience members by name: "Last week John told us how to construct a power résumé. I'm going to tell you what to do once your résumé gets you a job interview. In preparing for an employment interview, there are three steps you should keep in mind." Notice how the name of the student coupled with several personal pronouns brings the speaker and audience together and sets up the possibility for lively interaction.

A fourth difference between oral and written style is the frequency of repe-

tone: the relation established by language and grammar between speakers and their listeners.

tition. Oral style uses more repetition. As we discussed in Chapter 4, Listening, readers can slow down and reread the material in front of them. They control the pace. Listeners do not have that luxury. Speakers must take special care to reinforce their messages, and one way of accomplishing this is by using repetition.

Use Nonsexist Language. Language is sexist if it "promotes and maintains attitudes that stereotype people according to gender. It [**sexist language**] assumes that the male is the norm — the significant gender. **Nonsexist language** treats all people equally and either does not refer to a person's sex at all when it is irrelevant or refers to men and women in symmetrical ways when their gender is relevant."[34]

Notice the gender identification in each of the following two statements:

> One of the most important qualities a company executive must possess is effective communication. In fact, the higher he advances in the company, the more important it is that he be able to speak clearly and convincingly.

> A secretary is no longer only a receptionist and a typist. Today she performs the role of information manager for the office.

Both of these examples are sexist because they imply that executives are male and secretaries female. Nonsexist language allows for the fact that either gender can assume the roles of executive or secretary.

One way of eliminating sexist language in these statements is to replace each "he" and "she" with "he or she." This remedy, however, can be wordy and intrusive at times, especially when a sentence includes several third person singular pronouns. You can solve this problem by using the plural form if it is appropriate. Note how the statements change when they are reworded with this approach:

> One of the most important qualities company executives must possess is effective communication. In fact, the higher they advance in their companies, the more important it is that they be able to speak clearly and convincingly.

> Secretaries are no longer only receptionists and typists. Today they perform the role of information manager for the office.

A more serious form of sexism occurs when language creates special categories for one gender, with no corresponding parallel category for the other gender. Man and wife, for example, are not parallel terms. Man and woman or husband and wife *are* parallel. Other examples of non-parallel language are nurse and male nurse, chairman and chairperson, and Wildcats and Lady Wildcats. We remember hearing about one high school whose mascot was the hen. Its football and boys' basketball teams were the Hens. Yet the school called its girls' basketball team the Lady Hens, a redundancy at best and sexist at worst! One university named its official host student group the "Statesmen and First Ladies," changing the name only after several individuals complained that it assigned men and women to inherently unequal positions. A colleague tells us that when she worked at a television station she was called a "weather girl,"

sexist language: language that excludes one gender, creates special categories for one gender, or assigns roles based solely on gender.

nonsexist language: language that treats both genders fairly and avoids stereotyping either one.

Related Readings: See Chapter 3, "Debates about Language and Sexism," pages 27–41 in: Arliss, Laurie P. *Gender Communication*. Englewood Cliffs, NJ: Prentice, 1991. See also: Sorrels, Bobbye D. *The Nonsexist Communicator*. Englewood Cliffs, NJ: Prentice-Spectrum, 1983.

even though a male employee of the same age was referred to as a "weather man."

Speakers exhibit fairness when they express their ideas and examples in language that treats all members of the audience equally and fairly. If you have difficulty selecting a gender-free term for one that may be considered sexist, consult a dictionary such as *The Nonsexist Word Finder: A Dictionary of Gender-free Usage* by Rosalie Maggio.

Related Reading:
Lederer, Richard. *The Miracle of Language.* New York: Simon-Pocket, 1991.

Like the unique voice and body you use to deliver your speeches, your language is an extremely important part of your delivery. No matter which of the world's roughly 5,000 languages you speak, the words you choose telegraph messages about your background, your involvement with your topic, and your relationship with your listeners.[35] If you are conscientious, you must know when to speak simply and directly, and when to embellish your language with sensory images, figures of speech, and unusual structural devices. In short, you don't have to be a poet to agree with poet Robert Frost, "All the fun's in how you say a thing."[36]

Summary

Language is a distinctly human instrument, no less important than any other tool we have developed for building and creating. Though other animals produce sounds and noises, the human language alone is articulated into words, and alone is capable of expressing an infinite variety of thoughts.

Language serves five functions for those who use it. First, it communicates ideas between speaker and listener. Second, language sends messages, either intentional or unintentional, about the person who uses it. Your choice of language may reveal your age, your background, and your attitudes about the subjects you discuss. Third, language establishes and strengthens social bonds between groups of people. Fourth, language is an instrument of play since it is the arena for joking and the battle of wits. Fifth, we use language to monitor and check our use of language.

As a speaker you use different language on different occasions, depending on the environment, the topic, and your relationship with your listeners. Four principles should guide your use of language: (1) Use language correctly, (2) use language clearly, (3) use language vividly, and (4) use language appropriately.

As a speaker, your first requirement is to *use language correctly*. Select the right word for the thought you wish to convey, and then phrase the thought correctly. Incorrect language may communicate unintended messages as well as undermine a speaker's credibility. Five guidelines will help you detect and correct language errors. First, listen to the language you and others use and focus on how it can be improved. Second, consult a dictionary when you are unsure of the meaning of a word. Third, refer to a writing handbook when you have a question about proper grammar. Fourth, use a tape recorder to help you detect incorrect language use. Fifth, practice your speech in front of friends and ask them to point out your mistakes.

A second principle of language use is to *use language clearly*. To achieve clarity your language should be both specific and familiar. Language has varying levels of abstraction, and the more concrete your language, the more closely your referents will match those of your listeners. In addition to being specific, language must also be familiar. Listeners must know the meanings of the words you use. One type of language that may undermine clarity is jargon, a special language of a particular activity, business, or group of people. If you doubt that your listeners know the jargon either avoid such terms or else define each one the first time you use it.

A third guideline is to *use language vividly*. Colorful language makes the task of listening easier and the message more memorable. Three strategies for making your language more vivid are to use active language, appeal to your listeners' senses, and use figures and structures of speech. Active language avoids clichés and filler phrases, using instead active voice, coined words, and well-turned phrases.

A speaker can use any of eight types of sensory images to appeal to listeners' senses. *Visual images* appeal to the sense of sight. *Auditory images* suggest sounds. *Tactile images* recreate the feel of an object. *Thermal images* suggest temperatures. *Gustatory images* appeal to the sense of taste. *Kinetic images* suggest movement or motion. *Kinesthetic images* recreate states of muscular tension or relaxation. *Olfactory images* appeal to the sense of smell. *Synesthesia* is the combination of two or more sensory appeals in a single image.

A third way to achieve vividness is to use figures and structures of speech. *Alliteration* is the repetition of beginning sounds. *Parallelism* expresses two or more ideas in similar language structure. *Repetition* is the restatement of words, phrases, or sentences. Like parallelism, *antithesis* uses parallel construction, but it does so to contrast ideas. *Personification* attributes human qualities to objects, ideas, or organizations. *Simile* and *metaphor* are comparisons of two dissimilar things. In simile the comparison is explicit, using words such as "like" and "as." These words are omitted in metaphors because the comparison is implied.

A final criterion for effective language is to *use language appropriately*. You should select language that is appropriate to you, your topic, your audience, and the occasion. Two additional dimensions of appropriateness are oral style and nonsexist language. Oral style differs from written style in at least four important ways. First, in speaking we tend to use shorter sentences. Second, when we communicate orally we use more contractions, colloquial expressions, and slang. Third, oral style makes greater use of personal pronouns and references. Fourth, we use more repetition when we speak than when we write.

Nonsexist language treats both genders symmetrically and fairly. It does not create special categories or assign roles based solely on gender. Speakers who have difficulty selecting gender-free language should consult a dictionary of nonsexist terms.

Exercises

1. Select a one- or two-paragraph passage from a book or magazine. Using the guidelines listed in this chapter, rewrite the passage for a speech, incorporating elements of oral style.

2. Decide on nonsexist words that could be substituted for each of the following examples:
   a. policeman
   b. enlisted men
   c. Fatherland
   d. tomboy
   e. Clothes make the man.
   f. man's best friend
   g. All men are created equal.
   h. brotherly love
3. Listen to an album, cassette tape, or compact disc of your favorite vocal recording artist. Try to identify at least one example of each of the following language devices in song lyrics:
   a. alliteration
   b. metaphor
   c. simile
   d. personification
   e. visual image
   f. tactile image
   g. olfactory image
   h. gustatory image
   i. auditory image
   j. kinesthetic image
   k. kinetic image
4. Select a speech from *Vital Speeches of the Day* or another published source. Identify examples of as many types of the language devices listed in Exercise 3 as possible.

Notes

1. *Time* 17 April 1950: 28.

2. *Harper's* November 1990: 17–18.

3. E.C. Nance, "The Power and the Glory of the Word: Civilization Is Where It Is Today by the Force of Words," *Vital Speeches of the Day* 1 April 1957: 382.

4. Bergen Evans, "The Power of Words," in *Language Awareness* 5th ed. eds. Paul Eschholz, Alfred Rosa, and Virginia Clark (New York: St. Martin's, 1990) 34.

5. This discussion of functions of language is based on Roman Jakobson, "Closing Statement: Linguistics and Poetics," in *Style in Language*, ed. Thomas A. Sebeok (Cambridge, MA: MIT P, 1964) 350–74.

6. Charles L. Barber, *The Story of Speech and Language* (New York: Crowell, 1965) 9–10.

7. William F. Allman, "The Mother Tongue," *U.S. News & World Report* 5 November 1990: 62.

8. This discussion of two different ways of responding to language is based on Louise M. Rosenblatt, *The Reader, the Text, the Poem: The Transactional Theory of the Literary Work* (Carbondale: Southern Illinois UP, 1978), particularly Chapter 3, "Efferent and Aesthetic Reading."

9. Richard Lederer, *Anguished English: An Anthology of Accidental Assaults upon Our Language* (Charleston, SC: Wyrick, 1987) 8.

10. Alfred Rosa and Paul Eschholz, "Bunkerisms: Archie's Suppository Remarks in 'All in the Family,'" *Language Awareness*, 10th ed., eds. Paul Eschholz, Alfred Rosa, and Virginia Clark (New York: St. Martin's, 1982) 125.

11. Gloria Cooper, ed., *Red Tape Holds Up New Bridge, and More Flubs from the*

Nation's Press (New York: Perigee, 1987) n. pag.

12. Jeffrey Bair, "'Techno-dolts' Face Obstacle of Electronic Manuals," *San Antonio Light* 14 October 1990: Classified 44.

13. Miriam Ringo, *Nobody Said It Better!* (Chicago: Rand, 1980), 201.

14. Ringo 201.

15. Robert E. Leestamper, "Run Richmond Graduates, Run! Today's Challenges," *Vital Speeches of the Day* 15 December 1989: 156.

16. Richard Kostyra, "Communications in the Future: The Changing Media Environment," *Vital Speeches of the Day* 15 October 1990: 22.

17. Peter Schjeldahl, "Cyclone! Rising to the Fall," *Harper's* June 1988: 70.

18. Schjeldahl 68.

19. Schjeldahl 70.

20. Schjedlahl 70.

21. Richard Conniff, "Coasters Used to Be Scary, Now They're Downright Weird," *Smithsonian* August 1989: 85.

22. Conniff 84.

23. Schjeldahl 70.

24. Conniff 84. Conniff is quoting coaster enthusiast Paul Ruben.

25. C.J. Silas, "Bastille Day in the Oil Patch: When Passion Guides Energy Policy," *Vital Speeches of the Day* 1 January 1990: 187.

26. Vincent Ryan Ruggiero, "The Role of Business in Educational Reform: Pessimism and Popular Culture," *Vital Speeches of the Day* 15 February 1989: 287.

27. Ronald Reagan, "Remarks at the Johnson Space Center in Houston, TX, January 31, 1986," *Weekly Compilation of Presidential Documents* 3 February 1986: 118.

28. Mario Cuomo, Keynote Address, Democratic National Convention, *Vital Speeches of the Day* 15 August 1984: 647.

29. Maridell Fryar, "The Anatomy of an Association," address, First General Sess., Texas Speech Communication Association Convention, Dallas, 30 September 1983.

30. Virginia I. Postrel, "The Environmental Movement: A Skeptical View," *Vital Speeches of the Day* 15 September 1990: 729.

31. Schjeldahl 68.

32. Lyndon B. Johnson, Address Before a Joint Session of the Congress, November 27, 1963, *Public Papers of the President: Lyndon B. Johnson 1963–64*, vol. 1 (Washington: G.P.O., 1965) 10.

33. William Safire, "On Language: Marking Bush's Inaugural," *The New York Times Magazine* 5 February 1989: 12.

34. Rosalie Maggio, *The Nonsexist Word Finder: A Dictionary of Gender-free Usage* (Boston: Beacon, 1988), 165.

35. Allman 60.

36. Quoted in George Plimpton, ed., *The Writer's Chapbook: A Compendium of Fact, Opinion, Wit, and Advice from the 20th Century's Preeminent Writers* (New York: Viking, 1989) 176.

Delivering Your Speech *12*

**Principles of Nonverbal
   Communication**

Qualities of Effective Delivery

Elements of Vocal Delivery
Rate and Pause
Volume
Pitch and Inflection
Voice Quality
Articulation and Pronunciation

Elements of Physical Delivery
Appearance
Posture

Facial Expression
Eye Contact
Movement
Gestures

Methods of Delivery
Speaking Impromptu
Speaking from Memory
Speaking from Manuscript
Speaking Extemporaneously

JOHNNY CARSON once asked comedian Dana Carvey of *Saturday Night Live* how he had developed his deadly accurate impression of President George Bush. Carvey explained that he began with an unlikely combination of two of his other favorite impressions: the late John Wayne and Fred Rogers of *Mr. Rogers' Neighborhood.* To the audience's amazement, Carvey then demonstrated how Bush's physical delivery includes gestures that start out big and swaggering like Wayne's were, but end up limited and constrained like those of Rogers.

Barbara Jordan, former U.S. Representative from Texas, and Jeane Kirkpatrick, former U.S. Representative to the United Nations, are two women whose deep voices and patterns of clear, careful articulation and enunciation make them immediately recognizable to many people. Two African-American ministers, Jesse Jackson and the late Martin Luther King, Jr., are known and remembered for their impassioned voices. In 1984 many Democrats feared that Jackson would lend only lukewarm support to the party's presidential and vice-presidential candidates, Walter Mondale and Geraldine Ferraro. In part of its coverage of Jackson's address to the 1984 Democratic National Convention, *Newsweek* spotlighted Jackson's distinctive speech delivery:

> The moment of highest drama came early, when Jackson met the fears head-on. Suddenly, Jackson's voice grew quiet — and with it, the vast, packed hall. "If in my low moments, in word, deed, or attitude, through some error of temper, taste, or tone, I have caused anyone discomfort, created pain, or revived someone's fears, that was not my truest self," he said. "If there were occasions when my grape turned into a raisin and my joy bell lost its resonance, please forgive me. . . . I am not a perfect servant. I am a public servant doing my best against the odds. As I develop and serve, be patient. God is not finished with me yet." All apprehension evaporated. And by the time Jackson's voice rose again to its perfect preacher's pitch, almost the entire rainbow congregation was on its feet, . . . many weeping with exhilarated pride.[1]

Most of us do not have mannerisms as famous as George Bush's or voices as impassioned as Jesse Jackson's. But each of us has a unique voice, body, and way of wording ideas. The way you present your speech — through your voice, body, and language — makes up your style of delivery. In other words, *what* you say is your speech **content,** and *how* you say it is your **delivery.** If you and a classmate presented a speech with the same words arranged in the same order (something we don't recommend!), your listeners would still receive two different messages. This is because your delivery not only shapes your image as a speaker, but also changes your message in subtle ways. Your presentational style can amplify or undermine your intended message. Your speech delivery is bound to be either an asset or a liability, for as author Hermann Hesse observed, "Everything becomes a little different as soon as it is spoken out loud."

Speech delivery is so important that one of the criticisms of televised presidential debates is that they turn into "beauty contests," emphasizing looks and poise and minimizing the importance of what the candidate says. Very strong

Discussion Prompt:
Ask students to list famous people whom they think are exciting speakers and ones they find boring. Have them focus on vocal and physical delivery, making the point that delivery can add to or detract from the ideas of a speaker.

Teaching Strategy:
Play a portion of a videotape of Jesse Jackson's address to the 1984 Democratic National Convention to illustrate his speaking style and the audience's response.

delivery: the way a speaker presents a speech, through voice qualities, bodily actions, and language.

delivery can no doubt mask weak content for some listeners. More important, though, effective delivery can bolster important, well-organized ideas, and poor delivery can diminish the impact of those same ideas.

Paul Lorain has compared a printed speech to "a dried flower: The substance, indeed, is there, but the color is faded and the perfume gone." As Lorain suggests, your delivery gives color and fragrance to your words. To help you understand how that invigoration occurs, we will discuss the qualities and various elements of effective delivery in this chapter. Before we examine the individual physical and vocal elements that constitute delivery, let's consider some rules that apply to all nonverbal communication.

■ Principles of Nonverbal Communication _____

Your nonverbal behavior communicates a great deal of information about how you feel about what you say. Recall Albert Mehrabian's formula from Chapter 1 (see page 14). In particular, four principles of nonverbal communication help account for the importance of speech delivery. These principles are important because they provide a framework we will use later to evaluate the specific elements of vocal and physical delivery.

1. Part of Our Nonverbal Communication is Conscious and Deliberate, While Another Part is Unconscious and Unintentional. You do certain things deliberately to make other people feel comfortable around you or attracted to you. You dress in bright natural fabrics that flatter you or make you feel comfortable. You cut your hair in a style that is fashionable, traditional, or uniquely flattering. When speaking or listening to others, you look them directly in the eyes. You smile when they tell you good news and show concern when they share a problem.

On the other hand, you may have habits you are not aware of until someone points them out. You fold your arms, assuming a closed and defensive body position, or jingle your keys when nervous. You tap your fingers on the lectern when anxious or look down at the floor when embarrassed. Because we can control only those things of which we are aware, the first step toward improving your speech delivery is to identify and isolate any distracting nonverbal behaviors you exhibit.

In this chapter we discuss the following nonverbal elements of speech delivery: rate, pause, volume, pitch, inflection, voice quality, articulation, pronunciation, appearance, posture, facial expression, eye contact, movement, and gestures. Of these elements, only one — vocal quality — is very difficult to change or control. The others are much easier to modify. But how can you learn whether you have annoying and distracting habits? Feedback from your instructor and your classmates can show you areas in which you need to improve. If you have access to a cassette recorder, you can listen to your voice as you practice your speech, and a video camera will enable you to observe and assess your physical delivery. Keep in mind that discovering and improving your delivery weaknesses is not a quick, one-shot event, but continues with each successive speech you deliver in class.

Discussion Prompt:
If there are students in your class who have lived in other nations, ask them to give examples of how the meanings of nonverbal signals can differ from one culture to another.

Discussion Prompt:
How can/should a speaker adapt his or her delivery if there are international students in the audience who have some trouble understanding the English language?

Related Reading:
Ekman, Paul. *Telling Lies: Clues to Deceit in the Marketplace, Politics, and Marriage.* New York: Norton, 1985.

2. Few if Any Nonverbal Signals Have Universal Meaning. Standing at a bakery in Paris, France, you can't resist the aroma of long, golden loaves of bread hot from the oven. Unable to speak French, you get the clerk's attention, point to the loaves, and hold up two fingers, as in a V for victory. The clerk nods, hands you three loaves, and charges you for all three. Why? The French count from the thumb, whether it is extended or not. The same thing would happen if you used an identical gesture to order another two drinks in a German tavern. The French and German people simply apply different rules to their counting gestures than we do.

Just as the meanings of gestures and movements can change from one culture to the next, nonverbal delivery that is appropriate and effective in one speaking situation may be inappropriate and ineffective in another. Smiling and lively gesturing are appropriate if you are informing your audience on the history of clowning. On the other hand, your body should show more tension and your face more concern if you were persuading others of the devastating effects of unnecessary surgery. Though this chapter focuses on improving delivery of your classroom speeches, you can adapt many of our suggestions to your delivery in other speaking situations.

3. When a Speaker's Verbal and Nonverbal Channels Send Conflicting Messages, We Tend to Trust the Nonverbal Message. A used car sales representative rushes you into signing a purchase agreement while saying, "Man, this is the best deal on the lot. You are so lucky!" A supervisor at work tells you privately that she is impressed with your work, but then doesn't allow you to speak at staff meetings. A person keeps saying, "I love you," but never does anything to show consideration for you. Would you doubt the sincerity of these people? If you are typical, you certainly would.

We have each been interpreting and responding to other people's nonverbal communication for so long that we lose sight of its significance. Few things remind us of its importance quicker than having someone break a nonverbal rule. One of those rules is that a person's words and actions should match. Nonverbal messages should complement and reinforce verbal ones. When they do not, "actions speak louder than words." In those cases, we tend to trust the nonverbal message to help us answer the question, "What's really going on here?" As a result of this, one final principle of nonverbal communication becomes extremely important.

4. Ultimately, Your Intentions Do Not Matter Nearly as Much as the Meanings that Other People Attach to Your Nonverbal Communication. You stare out the window while delivering your speech because you feel too nervous to make eye contact with your listeners. The audience, however, probably assumes that you are bored and not really interested in speaking to them. Because we cannot read one another's minds, your audience's perception that you are disinterested is the only important one in this case, even though it may be far from the truth. You must eliminate any distracting behaviors that mask your good intentions if you care about presenting the best speech you can.

In this chapter we will discuss several guidelines to help you improve your vocal and physical delivery. We will also discuss four methods of delivery and how you can give a successful speech, whether it is delivered impromptu, from memory, from manuscript, or extemporaneously. But first let us make sure we understand the qualities of effective delivery.

■ Qualities of Effective Delivery ————————————

As you begin to think about the way you deliver a speech, keep in mind three characteristics of effective delivery. First, effective delivery helps the listeners as well as the speaker. If you are well prepared for a particular speech, you have probably spent a good deal of time formulating and rehearsing it. You know what you want to say, but your audience does not. Your audience has only one chance to receive your message. Just as clear organization makes your ideas easier to remember, effective delivery can underscore your key points, sell your ideas, or communicate your concern for the topic.

Second, keep in mind that the best delivery looks and feels natural, comfortable, and spontaneous. Former tennis great Helen Wills Moody once said, "If you see a tennis player who looks as if he is working very hard, then that means he isn't very good."[2] The same thing could be said of a speaker's delivery. No one should notice how hard you are working to deliver your speech effectively. Some occasions and audiences require you to be more formal than others, of course. Speaking to a large audience through a stationary microphone, for example, will naturally restrict your movement. For a presentation in this class, on the other hand, you may find yourself moving, gesturing, and using visual aids extensively. You want to orchestrate all these elements so that your presentation looks and feels relaxed and natural, not strained or awkward. You achieve spontaneous delivery such as this only through practice.

Third, and finally, though it may sound contradictory, delivery is best when the audience is not aware of it at all. Your goal should be delivery that is free of distractions and that reinforces your ideas. When the audience begins to notice how you twist your ring, count the number of times you say "um," or categorize the types of grammatical mistakes you make, your delivery is momentarily distracting them from what you are saying. Your delivery has now become a liability rather than an asset. To avoid this you need to concentrate first on eliminating distractions, and second on using elements of delivery to reinforce your purpose in speaking.

---

1. Effective delivery helps everyone—the listener as well as the speaker.
2. The best delivery looks and feels natural, comfortable, and spontaneous.
3. Delivery is best when the audience is not aware of it.

**KEY POINTS
Characteristics of
Effective Delivery**

You go a long way toward ensuring effective delivery when you are concentrating on your ideas and how the audience is receiving them, rather than on how you look or sound. If you are really interacting with your listeners, you will be paying attention to their interest in your speech, their understanding of your message, and their acceptance or rejection of what you are saying. If you notice listeners checking their watches, reading a paper, whispering to a friend, or snoozing, they are probably bored. Enlivening your delivery with movement and changes in volume may be sufficient to revive their interest. If your listeners' facial expressions convey confusion, they may not understand the point you are making. Slowing down your rate of delivery and using descriptive gestures to reinforce your ideas may enhance their understanding. If you observe frowns or heads shaking from side to side, you've encountered a hostile audience! Looking directly at such listeners, establishing a conversational tone, incorporating friendly facial expressions, and using body tension to demonstrate your involvement with your topic may help break down their resistance to you and your ideas. Once you have mastered the basics of speech delivery, you will be flexible and able to adapt to any of these situations. Your delivery will complement your message, not detract from it.

Any prescription for effective delivery will include three basic elements: the **voice,** or vocal delivery; the **body,** or physical delivery; and **language.** In Chapter 11, we discussed how your language contributes to your delivery style. In this chapter we focus on vocal and physical delivery. Vocal delivery includes rate, volume, pitch, voice quality, articulation, and pronunciation. The elements of physical delivery are appearance, posture, facial expression, eye contact, movement, and gestures. Let us take a closer look at how vocal delivery can enhance your speech.

■ Elements of Vocal Delivery ────────────

KEY POINTS
Elements of Vocal Delivery

1. Rate and pause
2. Volume
3. Pitch and inflection
4. Voice quality
5. Articulation and pronunciation

RATE AND PAUSE

You have probably heard the warning, "Look out for him; he's a fast talker," or words to that effect. Such a statement implies that someone who talks fast may be trying to put something over on us. At the other end of the spectrum, we often grow impatient with people who talk much slower than we do, even labeling them "uncertain," "dull," or "dense." Though these stereotypes may be inaccurate, we have already noted that the impressions people form based on our nonverbal communication are more important than anything we intend to communicate.

Your **rate** or speed of speaking can communicate something, intentionally or unintentionally, about your motives in speaking, your disposition, or your involvement with the topic. Your goal in a speech, therefore, should be to avoid extremely fast or slow delivery, but instead to use a variety of rates. Your various rates should, in turn, reinforce your purpose in speaking and make you seem conversational.

rate: the speed at which a speech is delivered.

In Chapter 4, Listening, we told you that the typical American speaker talks at a rate between 125 and 190 words per minute. To test your own rate of speaking, read the following paragraphs once silently. Then read aloud from them at a rate that seems natural and conversational, using pauses to mark transitions from one idea to the next. Imagine yourself presenting this information to someone who has not read it. Ignore the slash marks and make a note of the word you have reached after one minute:

Grassroots democracy depends on small groups of people meeting to talk about topics they consider important. Voluntary membership in such groups isn't easy today. People seem to connect with others mainly through television, radio, magazines, and newspapers. In reaction to the isolation many people feel, salons — groups of people meeting for directed discussion — are springing up at a rate not seen in recent history.

Salon comes from the French word for "drawing room," and a meeting place is necessary for almost all salons. Gossip is an important ingredient in the recipe for a successful salon, but it's only secondary. The/ salon must be focused on an exchange of ideas. A salon must also meet on a regular basis, on established days and at established times, whether it's once a week, every two weeks, or only once a month. The salon may have a core group that attends each meeting, but// it's also important to have new guests from time to time.

The development of the electronic salon is a recent phenomenon. People with access to computers hooked up to modems can become a part of a lively network known as the WELL (Whole Earth 'Lectronic Link), for example. Electronic salons/// lack the spark of face-to-face interaction, though in the world of ideas, this may even be an advantage. Jon Carroll, one WELL fanatic, notes that the medium "favors people who are articulate in print" and that "it provides an absolutely level playing field in terms of physical appearance."[3]

How fast did you read? The first slash mark (/) indicates 100 words, and you probably passed that mark easily. The double slash (//) indicates 150 words, the triple slash 200, and the final word of the third paragraph is number 250. You probably did not finish the final paragraph if you were using pauses and reading conversationally. Chances are that your final word falls somewhere between the single and triple slash marks, between 100 and 200 words per minute.

This exercise cannot accurately measure your normal speaking rate, and is not intended to do so. You may, after all, speak faster or slower than you read aloud. But the experiment should give you some idea of how easy it is to speak more than 100 words a minute. To get an idea of how slow a rate of 100 words per minute actually is, try taking exactly one minute to read up to the first slash mark. You probably feel that you are plodding along sluggishly.

Although we can process information at rates faster than people speak, our comprehension depends on the type of material we are hearing. You should slow down, for example, when presenting detailed, highly complex informa-

Cross-Reference:
You may want to review the discussion of speaking and listening rates in Chapter 4.

tion, particularly to a group that knows little about your subject. Our student René did just that in his informative speech detailing the history of political and religious conflict in the Middle East. Not only did he speak slower than he had in other speeches, but he also used a clearly labeled map of the area and a timeline showing the splintering of groups into smaller factions. His reduced rate of delivery and his repetition of information in visual form showed his concern for his audience's comprehension. In other situations, however, speaking slightly faster than the rate of normal conversation may actually increase your persuasiveness by carrying the message that you know exactly what you want to say.

pause: an intentional or unintentional silence in a speaker's vocal delivery.

Pauses or silences are an important element in your rate of delivery. You may pause to allow the audience time to reflect upon something you have just said or to heighten suspense about something you are about to say. Pauses mark important transitions in your speech, helping you and your audience shift gears. World-renowned violinist Isaac Stern was once asked why some violinists were considered gifted and others merely proficient or competent when they all played the correct notes in the proper order. "The important thing is not the notes. It's the intervals between the notes," he responded.

Let's take a sentence from Jesse Jackson's speech quoted earlier in this chapter. Try reading it without any internal punctuation or pauses.

> If in my low moments in word deed or attitude through some error of temper taste or tone I have caused anyone discomfort created pain or revived someone's fears that was not my truest self.

The sentence makes sense only if you insert pauses. And the statement becomes powerful when you make those pauses meaningful! Speakers reading from a written text sometimes mark their manuscripts to help them pause appropriately. Now try reading Jackson's sentence, pausing a beat when you see one slash (/) and pausing a bit longer when you encounter two (//).

Practice Speaking:
Have students practice marking pauses and reading aloud the final two paragraphs of Adlai Stevenson's eulogy of Eleanor Roosevelt in Chapter 17. You may also want to select portions of Ronald Reagan's *Challenger* speech in Appendix C.

> If in my low moments, / in word, / deed, / or attitude, // through some error of temper, / taste, / or tone, // I have caused anyone discomfort, / created pain, / or revived someone's fears, // that was not my truest self.

Did you notice how much more impact the statement had when you included pauses? You may even disagree with our interpretation of the placement and length of pauses. You might say the sentence differently, and that's fine. Public speaking is, after all, a creative and individual process. Remember, though, that to be effective in a speech, pauses must be used *intentionally* and *selectively*. If your speech is filled with too many awkwardly placed pauses, or too many vocalized pauses, such as "um" and "uh," you will seem hesitant or unprepared and your credibility will erode quickly.

VOLUME

volume: the relative loudness or softness of a speaker's voice.

Your audience must be able to *hear* you before they can *listen* to your ideas. **Volume** is simply how loudly or softly you speak. Though it's rare that a person speaks too loudly in a classroom speech, we may consider such a speaker boisterous or obnoxious. In contrast, we often label the inaudible speaker unsure, timid, "wimpy." The truth could be that you speak too loudly because you have suffered a hearing loss and are not aware that your volume is uncomfortable to your listeners. The frustratingly quiet speaker may have grown up in a household with six other children and parents who were constantly yelling, "Quiet!" But your audience will not know about your history. What they *will* know is that you are shouting or whispering your speech and they will judge you by that behavior. Remember that hearing is the first step in listening. If you frustrate your audience or divert their attention with inappropriate volume, your chances of getting them to listen carefully to your message are slim.

Make sure you adapt your volume to the size of the room where you speak. In your classroom you can probably use a volume just slightly louder than your usual conversational level. When you speak before a large group, a microphone may be helpful or even essential. If possible, practice beforehand so that you will not be startled by the sound of your amplified voice. You may even be called upon to speak before a large audience without a microphone. This is not as difficult as it sounds. In fact, your voice will carry well if you support your breath from your diaphragm. To test your breathing, place your hand on your abdomen while repeating the sentence "Those old boats don't float" louder and louder. If you are breathing from the diaphragm, you should feel your abdominal muscles tightening. Without that support, you are probably trying to increase your volume from your throat, a mistake that could strain your voice.

At times, you may have to conquer not only a large space but also external noise, such as the chattering of people in a hallway, the roar of nearby traffic, or the whoosh of the air conditioning system. That may require hard work. If you are fortunate enough to have the use of a microphone in such a situation, speak at normal volume and let the public address system do the work for you. If a microphone is available but is really unnecessary, don't use it; in a small room, a microphone distances you from the audience. We discuss the use of two different types of microphones in more detail in Chapter 17 (see pages 383–384).

PITCH AND INFLECTION

Pitch is a musical term, and when we talk about vocal pitch we are referring to the highness or lowness of vocal tones, similar to the notes on a musical staff. Every speaker has an optimal pitch range, or "key." This is the range in which you are most comfortable speaking, and chances are good that in this range your voice is also pleasant to hear. People who speak in unusually high or low voices are rare, and in these cases work with speech therapists helps them to achieve a flexible, useful pitch range.

Speakers who are unusually nervous sometimes raise their pitch. Other speakers think that if they lower their pitch, they will seem more authoritative. (If you have seen reruns of the *Mary Tyler Moore Show*, you will recognize this as the Ted Baxter factor.) In truth, speakers who do not use their normal pitch usually sound artificial.

The following practice technique may help you retain or recapture a natural, conversational tone in your delivery. Begin some of your practice sessions seated. Imagine a good friend sitting across from you, and pretend that she asks

Class Activity:
If you are in a large classroom or a room with ambient noise, have each student speak several sentences from the front of the room. Have students seated throughout the room assess the speaker's volume. Is it too loud, too soft, or just right?

Practice Speaking:
Distribute a double-spaced copy of a paragraph from a speech. Read the paragraph to the class trying not to use vocal emphasis or varying the length of your pauses. Have students underline words they think should be emphasized and put a slash (/) at points where they think a pause is appropriate. Call on students to read the passage to the class to show that vocal delivery can enhance the liveliness and meaning of a presentation, and that different speakers may use different vocal delivery.

pitch: the highness or lowness of a speaker's voice.

you what your speech is about. Answer her question by summarizing and paraphrasing your speech: "Mary, I'm going to talk about the advantages of mandatory school uniforms in elementary and middle schools. I've divided my speech into three main arguments. School uniforms will enhance student self-esteem; they will reduce discipline problems; and they will save parents money." Listen closely to the tone of your voice as you are speaking. You are having a conversation with a friend. You're not tense; you feel comfortable.

Keeping this naturalness in mind, stand, walk to the lectern, and begin your speech. Your words will change, but the tone of your speech should be comfortable and conversational, as it was before. In a sense, you are merely having a conversation with a larger audience. We have found this technique helpful for students whose vocal delivery sounds artificial or mechanical. Not only do they find their natural pitch range, but they also incorporate more meaningful pauses.

inflection: patterns of change in a person's pitch level while speaking.

A problem more typical than an unusually high- or low-pitched voice is vocal delivery that lacks adequate **inflection,** or changes in pitch. Someone who speaks without changing pitch delivers sentences in a flat, uniform pitch pattern that becomes monotonous. Indeed, the word "monotone" means "one tone," and you may have had instructors whose monotonous droning invited you to doze. People whose voices sound monotonous are usually actually using three tones: one in the middle, one slightly higher, and one lower. That's still too little vocal variety, however. Your inflection is an essential tool for conveying meaning accurately. A simple four-word sentence such as "She is my friend" can be given four distinct meanings by raising the pitch and volume of one word at a time:

"**She** is my friend." (Not the young woman standing with her.)
"She **is** my friend." (Don't try to tell me she isn't!)
"She is **my** friend." (Not yours.)
"She is my **friend**." (There's nothing more to our relationship than that.)

If you have ever made a comment jokingly only to have people take you seriously, chances are that you did not adequately signal with your inflection that it was a joke. In public speaking, women can generally make wider use of their pitch ranges than men can without sounding affected or unnatural. For this reason, men often find that they need to vary other vocal and physical elements of delivery—volume, rate, and gestures, for example—to compensate for a limited pitch range.

VOICE QUALITY

voice quality or **timbre:** the unique characteristcs that distinguish one person's voice from others.

Voice quality or **timbre,** the least flexible of the vocal elements discussed here, is the characteristic that distinguishes your voice from other voices. You may have called a friend on the phone and had difficulty telling him from his father, or her from her mother or sisters. Most of the time, however, even through the telephone, an instrument causing a lot of distortion, you recognize the voices of friends easily. In general, our individual voices are easily recognized as distinct. In fact, you may have heard that police investigators often use voice prints to identify and distinguish individual voices on tape recordings.

Sometimes the clarity and resonance of your voice can be temporarily affected by colds, by allergies, or by strain after hours spent screaming support for a favorite team. That temporary change should not cause alarm. However, if many people describe your voice as strident, harsh, nasal, breathy, or hoarse over a long period of time, you may want to consult a speech therapist.

ARTICULATION AND PRONUNCIATION

The final elements of vocal delivery we will discuss are articulation and pronunciation. **Articulation** is the mechanical process of forming the sounds necessary to communicate in a particular language. Most articulation errors are made from habit. You tell your parents that you're going to the "libary," for example. Even though you know how to spell the word and would say it correctly if pressed to do so, you have fallen into a habit of misarticulating it. Sometimes our articulation errors are reinforced by people around us who make the same mistakes. Sometimes illness or fatigue affect our articulation temporarily.

Articulation errors take four principal forms: deletion, addition, substitution, and transposition. One of these, represented by the example of "libary," is the **deletion** or leaving out of sounds. Saying "goverment" for "government" is another example of a deletion error. If you have heard someone say "athalete" for "athlete," you've heard an example of an articulation error caused by the **addition** of a sound. Examples of errors caused by the **substitution** of one sound for another are "kin" for "can" and "git" for "get." The final type of articulation error is one of **transposition,** or the reversal of two sounds that are close together. This error is the vocal equivalent of transposing two letters in a typed word. Saying "brethern" for "brethren" or "hunderd" for "hundred" are examples of transposition errors.

If you make articulation errors as a result of habit, the pattern may be so ingrained that you can no longer identify your mistakes. Your speech instructor, your friends, and your classmates can help you significantly by pointing out articulation problems. You may need to listen to tape recordings of your speeches to locate problems and then practice the problem words or sounds to correct your articulation.

Pronunciation, in contrast to articulation, is simply a matter of knowing how the letters of a word sound and where the stress falls when that word is spoken. We all have two vocabularies: a speaking vocabulary and a reading vocabulary. Your speaking vocabulary — the group of words you use in day-to-day conversation — is much smaller than your reading vocabulary. To test this, think of the times you have been reading something and encountered a word you have never spoken or even heard spoken: "Her *vitriolic* parting words stung him," for example. You may have seen the word before in print. Even though you may have never looked up its pronunciation or meaning in a dictionary, you probably feel that you know more or less what it means in the context of the sentence. Such a word is part of your reading vocabulary.

Most of us make errors in pronunciation primarily when we try to move a word from our reading vocabulary over to our speaking vocabulary without consulting the dictionary. In a public speech, the resulting pronunciation error can range from a minor distraction to a major disaster, depending upon how far off your mispronunciation is and how many times you speak the word during

articulation: the mechanical process of forming the sounds necessary to communicate in a particular language.

pronunciation: knowing how the sounds of a word are to be said and which parts are to be stressed.

Teaching Strategy:
Put some commonly mis-
pronounced words on the
blackboard and discuss their
preferred pronunciations.
The following words are on
many linguists' lists of most
frequently mispronounced
words:

amicable	longevity
athlete	medieval
berserk	mischievous
bestial	niche
charisma	nuclear
chasm	often
dais	omnipotent
drowned	picture
environment	preferable
escape	recognize
February	respite
formidable	statistics
genuine	surprise
gesture	theater
height	twenty
hundred	ubiquitous
incomparable	unscathed
irreparable	vehement
larynx	virile

your speech. For example, one of our students delivered a persuasive speech against "apartheid" in South Africa, mispronouncing that important word more than fifty times during the presentation! (Both "a PART hite" and "a PART hayt" are acceptable pronunciations; "A par theed" is not.) The real misfortune is that this mispronunciation was what almost all listeners remembered most vividly about the speech. Although the speaker presented a well-researched speech on a topic that was of obvious concern to him, the audience was left thinking, "If he is so concerned about it, why didn't he learn to pronounce the word correctly?" If you have *any* doubt about the pronunciation of a word you plan to use in a speech, look it up in a current dictionary and then practice the correct pronunciation out loud before the speech. Apply this rule to every word you select, including those in quotations. If you follow this simple rule, you will avoid embarrassing errors of pronunciation.

Pronunciation of proper nouns — the names of specific people, places, and things — can also pose difficulties. Suppose that for your speech on mountain climbing you want to quote from a fine book entitled *Beyond Boredom and Anxiety: The Experience of Play in Work and Games.*[4] You copy an excellent passage about the psychology of the sport onto a notecard. Then you turn to the title page to find the author's name: Mihaly Csikszentmihalyi! Don't tear up the notecard.

Obviously proper nouns should be pronounced the way that the people who have the name (or who live in the place, or who named the thing) pronounce them. The large city on the Texas Gulf Coast is pronounced "HEW stun"; the street in New York City spelled the same way is pronounced "HOW stun." The surname "Koch" can be pronounced "Kotch" (as in former New York mayor Ed Koch) or "Koke" (as in poet Kenneth Koch). But many people with the last name "Koch" pronounce it "Cook." When you see the name "Schroeder," you may think of the *Peanuts* character and mentally pronounce the word with a long "o" sound. Yet the late William Schroeder, world's first artificial heart recipient, pronounced his family's name as though the "oe" were a long "a."

If you refer to people who are well known and are or were mentioned frequently on radio and television, as in the Ed Koch and William Schroeder examples, make sure that your pronunciation corresponds to common usage. If you quote or refer to a person who is unfamiliar to your audience — as Csikszentmihalyi will almost certainly be — your listeners will not know that you have mispronounced the name unless you appear to stumble uncertainly over it. The only way to confirm your pronunciation of a name like "Csikszent-mihalyi" would be to locate the person, place a long-distance call, and ask. No one expects you to do that. Instead, decide on a reasonable pronunciation, practice it, and deliver it with confidence in your speech. For names of places, consult the Pronouncing Gazetteer or list of Geographical Names found at the back of many dictionaries.

Once you have mastered the elements of vocal delivery we have discussed, your speaking voice will be free of articulation errors and mispronounced words. Your unique voice quality will be pleasant to hear. Your voice will be well modulated, with enough inflection to communicate your ideas clearly. You will speak loudly enough that all your listeners can hear you easily. You will adapt your rate to the content of your message, and you will pause to punctuate key ideas and major transitions. In short, your sound will be coming through loud and clear. Now let's consider the picture your listeners will see by examining the aspects of physical delivery.

■ Elements of Physical Delivery ————————————

1. Appearance
2. Posture
3. Facial expression
4. Eye contact
5. Movement
6. Gestures

APPEARANCE

As we have mentioned earlier in this text, we all form quick impressions of people we meet based on subtle nonverbal signals. **Appearance,** in particular our grooming and the way we dress, is an important nonverbal signal that helps people judge us. Why is appearance so important? You may ask, "What about the inner me? Does it really come down to 'it's not who you are but what you wear?'" Of course, that is not the case. But you would be foolish to underestimate the power of first impressions and the initial reactions people have to your appearance.

appearance: a speaker's physical features, including dress and grooming.

Studies demonstrate that people whom we consider attractive can persuade us much more easily than those we find unattractive. In addition, high-status clothing carries more authority than does low-status clothing. For example, studies show we are more likely to jaywalk behind a person dressed in a dark blue suit, a crisp white shirt, and a dark tie, and carrying an expensive black-leather briefcase, than we would behind a person dressed in rags or even in jeans. We will also take orders more easily from that well-dressed person than we would from someone poorly dressed. These studies reinforce the adage that "clothes make the person," a saying any public speaker would do well to remember.

Since John T. Molloy's first book, *Dress for Success,* came out in 1975, we have all been getting plenty of advice about the best colors, fabrics, and styles of clothing for the business office. Dressing for success has become big business. Today, "image consultants" across the country teach men and women how to dress for increased productivity and influence. Some of this may seem unrealistic or inappropriate for you as a public speaker. If you use a little common sense in preparing for your speech, however, you will have no problems.

Related Reading:
Bixler, Susan. *Professional Presence.* New York: Putnam, 1991. See, especially, Chapter 10, "The Impact of a Business Wardrobe," pages 141–70.

The safest advice we can offer the public speaker on appearance is to avoid extremes in dress and grooming. Use clothes to reinforce your purpose in speaking, not to draw too much attention to themselves. Every moment that the audience spends admiring your European-cut navy blue suit, or wondering why you wore the torn Metallica T-shirt when you're not talking about rock music, is a moment they are distracted from your message.

Here are some "dress for address" guidelines for you to follow. In selecting your attire, take into consideration the occasion, audience, topic, and speaker.

1. Consider the Occasion. The formality or informality of your clothing is dictated in part by the speaking occasion. A student delivering a valedictory would dress differently than one delivering an impromptu campaign speech in the school cafeteria. A speech in your classroom permits you more informality than would a business presentation to a board of directors, a sermon to a congregation, or an acceptance speech at an awards ceremony.

2. Consider Your Audience. Some of your listeners dress more casually than others. In any audience there is a range of attire. As a rule, we suggest that you dress at the top of that range. For speeches outside the classroom, traditional, tasteful, and subdued clothing is your wisest choice. Your aim is to appear as nicely dressed as the best dressed in your audience. In other words,

Discussion Prompt:
Ask students to answer the questions posed in the caption to these photographs.

Clothing can send powerful messages about a speaker's attitude toward the topic, the occasion, and the audience. What topics do you think would be appropriate and inappropriate for this student dressed these three ways?

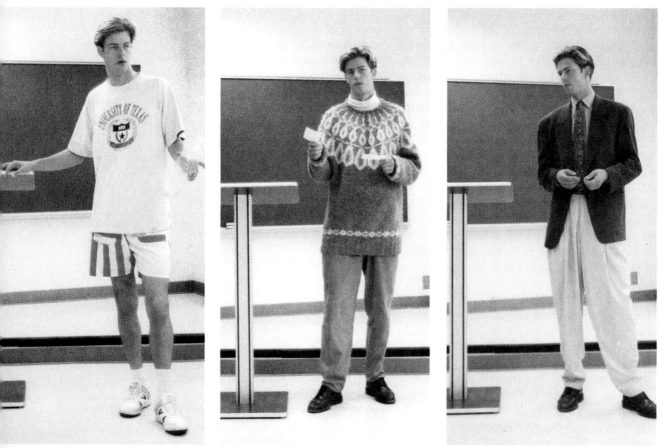

when in doubt, dress "up" a little. An audience is more easily insulted if you appear to treat the speaking occasion too casually than if you treat it too formally. Remember, your listeners will make judgments based on your appearance before you even open your mouth.

3. Consider Your Topic. Your topic may also affect your choice of clothes. While the public speech is not a costumed performance, clothing can underscore or undermine the impact you want your speech to have. A hot pink dress or lime green shirt would be appropriate for a speech on the festival of Mardi Gras, but not for one on the high cost of funerals. On the other hand, you would look foolish presenting a speech on health and physical fitness if you demonstrated exercises dressed in a business suit.

4. Consider Your Image. Finally, the image you want to create as a speaker should shape your selection of clothing. Darker colors, for example, convey authority. Lighter colors establish a friendlier image. A student perceived as the class clown might dress more formally on the day of his or her speech to help dispel this image.

Clothing not only influences our perceptions of others, it also shapes our self-perception. Just think of your own experiences. You probably have certain clothes that give you a sense of confidence or make you feel especially assertive or powerful. You feel differently about yourself when you wear them. Dressing "up" will not only convey to your listeners that you take them and the speaking occasion seriously, it also establishes this same positive attitude in your own mind.

As a practical matter, we suggest that you decide what you will wear before the day of your speech and that you practice, at least once, in those clothes. You will discover that this benefits you in three ways. First, you reduce by one the number of decisions you must make on the day of your speech. Second, you will be more comfortable as you deliver your speech. If you wear a suit coat and are not used to doing so, you will have practiced gesturing with it on. You will have decided if it is best buttoned or unbuttoned. Third, practicing in what you actually plan to wear alerts you to problems and enables you to correct them. Make sure that what you plan to wear is clean and pressed. You may also discover, for example, that a favorite bracelet creates a distracting sound as it taps on the lectern when you move your arm. One of our students complained that she was distracted during her presentation because every time she moved her arms to gesture her coat made a "rustling" sound. She could have eliminated this distraction had she practiced in that suit coat before the day of her speech. Whatever the problems, it's best to encounter and fix them before the speech. You can then concentrate fully on the speech itself.

POSTURE

A public speaker should look comfortable, confident, and prepared to speak. You have the appropriate attire. Your next concern is your **posture,** the position or bearing of your body. In posture the two extremes to avoid are rigidity and sloppiness. Don't hang on to or drape yourself across the lectern, if you are using one. Keep your weight balanced on both legs and avoid shifting your weight back and forth in a nervous swaying pattern. Equally distracting is

posture: the position or bearing of a speaker's body while delivering a speech.

standing on one leg and shuffling or tapping the other foot. You may not realize that you do those things. Other people will have to point them out to you. Remember that before your delivery can reinforce your message, it must be free of annoying mannerisms.

FACIAL EXPRESSION

facial expression: the tension and movement of various parts of a speaker's face.

Researchers estimate that the human face is capable of 250,000 — a quarter of a million — different facial expressions.[5] That's a vast amount of communication potential! Yet, ironically, many people giving a speech for the first time put on a blank mask, reducing their **facial expression** to one neutral look. We have often seen our students do this, and we know why it occurs. Inexperienced speakers are understandably nervous and may be more concerned with the way they look and sound than they are with the ideas they are trying to communicate.

To articulate clearly you must open your mouth freely; as you speak, your face must move. Not just any facial expression will serve your purposes, however. Your facial expression must *match* what you are saying. The speaker who smiles and blushes self-consciously through a speech on date rape will simply not be taken seriously by the audience, and may offend many listeners. If you detail the plight of earthquake victims, your face should reflect your concern. If you tell a joke and your listeners can't stop chuckling, you certainly should break into a smile rather than a frown. In other words, your face should register the thoughts and feelings behind your words.

The way to use facial expression appropriately to bolster your message is really simple: Concentrate as much as possible on the ideas you are presenting and the way your audience is receiving and responding to them. Try not to be overly conscious of how you look and sound. This takes practice, but your classroom speeches provide a good forum for such rehearsal. You will learn to interact with the audience, maintain eye contact, and respond with them to your own message. Chances are that if you do those things your facial expression will be varied and appropriate and will reinforce your spoken words.

EYE CONTACT

eye contact: gaze behavior in which a speaker looks at listeners' eyes.

We've all heard the challenge, "look me in the eye and say that." We use direct eye contact as one gauge of a person's truthfulness. **Eye contact** can also carry many other messages: confidence, concern, sincerity, interest, and enthusiasm. Lack of eye contact, on the other hand, may signal deceit, disinterest, or insecurity.

Try this simple experiment. The next time you are talking to a good friend, look at a spot on that person's hair rather than looking him or her in the eyes. What will happen? Chances are good that your friend will either ask you, "What's the deal?" or else use one of those nervous, self-directed, preening gestures we all have to make sure that there's nothing wrong with our hair. Your friend may even do both, because the speaker who avoids eye contact with us, or who looks beyond us, will frustrate or anger us or at least make us very self-conscious.

Your face is the most important source of nonverbal cues as you deliver your speech, and your eyes carry more information than does any other facial feature. As you speak, you will probably look occasionally at your notes or manuscript. You may even glance away from the audience briefly as you try to put your thoughts into words. Yet you must keep coming back to the eyes of your listeners to check their understanding, interest, and evaluation of your message.

As a public speaker, your goal is to make eye contact with as much of the audience as much of the time as possible. The way to do that is to make sure that you take in your entire audience, from front to back and from left to right. Include all those boundaries in the scope of your eye contact, and make contact especially with those individuals who seem to be listening carefully and responding positively to your message. Whether you actually make eye contact with each member of the audience is immaterial. You must, however, create that impression. Again, this takes practice before you feel comfortable.

MOVEMENT

Effective **movement** benefits you as a speaker, your audience, and your speech. First, physical involvement such as place-to-place movement can actually help you relax. Your comfort is not, by itself, a compelling reason to include movement in a speech, but moving to a visual aid, for example, can help you energize and loosen up physically. From the audience's perspective, movement adds visual variety to your speech, and appropriate movement can arouse or rekindle the listeners' interest. Most important, though, physical movement serves your speech by guiding the audience's attention. Through movement you can underscore key ideas, mark major transitions, or intensify an appeal for belief or action.

movement: a speaker's motion from place to place during speech delivery.

Related Reading: For a discussion of how movement and gesture affect communicator style, see: Richmond, Virginia, James McCroskey, and Steven Payne. *Nonverbal Behavior in Interpersonal Relations,* 2nd ed. (Englewood Cliffs, NJ: Prentice, 1991), pp. 66–72.

Remember that your speech starts the moment you enter the presence of your audience. Your behavior, including your movement, sends signals about your attitudes toward the audience and your speech topic. When your time to speak arrives, approach your speaking position confidently, knowing that you have something important to say. Addressing a large audience through a microphone mounted on the lectern will naturally restrict your movement. If the lectern is there as a matter of convenience, and particularly if you are speaking to a relatively small audience, don't automatically box yourself into one position behind the lectern. Remember that even the smallest lectern puts a physical barrier between you and your audience. Moving to the side or the front of it reduces both the physical and the psychological distance between you and your listeners, and may be especially helpful whenever you conclude your speech with a persuasive appeal.

Make certain that your movement is selective and that it serves a purpose. Avoid random pacing. Movement to mark a transition should occur at the beginning or the end of a sentence, not in the middle. Finally, bring the speech to a satisfying psychological conclusion and pause for a second or two before gathering your materials and moving toward your seat in the audience.

gestures: movements of a speaker's hands and arms while delivering a speech.

GESTURES

Gestures are important adjuncts to our verbal messages; at times, they can even replace words altogether. As a public speaker you can use gestures to draw a picture of an object, to indicate the size of objects or the relationships between them, to re-create some bodily motion, to emphasize or underscore key ideas, to point to things such as visual aids, or to trace the flow of your ideas. If you don't normally gesture in conversation, force yourself to include some gestures as you practice your speech. You may feel self-conscious about gesturing when you first begin to practice it. With adequate rehearsal, your gestures will become more spontaneous and look more natural. They are well worth whatever time you spend practicing them. Not only do they reinforce your ideas and make you seem more confident and dynamic, but gestures, like movement, can help you relax.

To be effective, then, gestures must be coordinated with your words, and must appear natural and spontaneous. In addition, any gesture should be large enough for the audience to see it clearly. The speaker who gestures below the waist, or whose gestures are barely visible over the top of a lectern, may appear timid, unsure, or nervous. Speakers who gesture too much — who talk with their hands — may also be perceived as nervous, flighty, or excitable. The two extremes to avoid, therefore, are the *absence* of gestures (hands clenched in a death-grip on the sides of the lectern) and *excessive* gestures (gestures emphasizing everything, with the result that nothing stands out). Remember, if your audience is waiting for you to gesture or counting your many gestures, they are distracted from your message.

The following two generalizations from research on gestures are particularly helpful for the public speaker. First, people who are confident, relaxed, and have high status tend to expand into the space around them and use gestures that are wider than those of other people. Speakers who wish to emphasize their authority, or to seem more authoritative, can therefore help do so by increasing the width of their gestures. Second, a wide, palm-up gesture with both hands creates an openness that is entirely appropriate when a speaker is appealing for a certain belief or urging the audience to some action. A palm-down gesture with one or both hands carries more force and authority, and can be used to command an audience into action or to exhort them to a certain belief. Stand up and deliver the following statement, gesturing with both hands palms-up: "We need to communicate our message to the university administration: It's time to get serious about adequate funding of our library. Give us the resources we deserve!" Now repeat those sentences gesturing with both hands palms-down. Did you feel a subtle difference in tone and intensity?

As a speaker you should adapt the size of your gestures to the size of your audience. On stage before a crowd of several thousand, you will need to gesture much more expansively than you do while standing at the front of a small classroom. In a cavernous auditorium, you must adjust your gestures, as well as your facial expression and eye contact, so that they will be clear to those in the back rows.

These, then, are the tools of vocal and physical speech delivery, from rate of speaking to hand gestures. Your goal throughout this class and in your future public speaking experience will be to eliminate any distracting elements and then work toward delivery that is conversational, forceful, and as formal or informal as your audience and subject require. Once you have marshaled these aspects of vocal and physical delivery to work for you, you can then use them in any of four ways of delivering a speech.

■ Methods of Delivery ───────────────────

The four basic ways you can deliver your public speech are (1) impromptu, or without advanced preparation, (2) from memory, (3) from a manuscript, or (4) extemporaneously, or from notes. The impromptu and the memorized methods have very limited applications, particularly for an important speech, but they deserve at least brief attention.

SPEAKING IMPROMPTU

We speak **impromptu** whenever a teacher, a colleague, or a boss calls on us to express an opinion on some issue, or whenever someone unexpectedly asks us to "say a few words" to a group. We deal with those special occasions and offer specific guidelines for impromptu speaking in Chapter 17 (see pages 377 – 379). In those informal situations, other people do not necessarily expect us to be forceful or well organized, and we are probably more or less comfortable speaking without any preparation. Yet the more important the speech is, the more inappropriate the impromptu method of delivery. In short, impromptu speaking is excellent practice for anyone, but no conscientious person will risk a grade, an important proposal, or professional advancement on an unprepared speech.

impromptu speaking: speaking without advanced preparation.

SPEAKING FROM MEMORY

Speaking from **memory** is similarly appropriate only on rare occasions. We speak from memory when we prepare a written text and then memorize it word for word. At its best, the memorized speech allows a smooth, almost effortless-looking delivery, since the speaker has neither notes nor a manuscript and can concentrate on interacting with the audience. For most of us, however, memorizing takes a long time. Our concentration on the memory work we've done and our fear of forgetting part of the speech can also make us sound mechanical or "programmed" when reciting. For these reasons, the memorized method of delivery is usually appropriate only for brief speeches: introducing another speaker, or presenting or accepting an award, for example.

speaking from memory: delivering a speech that is recalled word-for-word from a written text.

SPEAKING FROM MANUSCRIPT

The **manuscript** speech, delivered from a complete text prepared in advance, not only ensures that the speaker will not be at a loss for words, but is also essential in some situations. An address that will be quoted or later published in

speaking from manuscript: delivering a speech from a text written word-for-word and practiced in advance.

its entirety is typically delivered from a manuscript. Major foreign policy speeches or State of the Union addresses by U.S. presidents are always delivered from manuscript, because the premium is not just on being understood, but on not being misunderstood. Speeches of tribute and commencement addresses are often also scripted. Any speaking situation calling for precise, well-worded communication is appropriate for manuscript delivery.

Having every word of your speech scripted should boost your confidence, but it does not ensure your effective delivery. When you write the manuscript, you must take care to write in an oral style. In other words, the manuscript must sound like something you would say in conversation. The text of your speech thus requires a good deal of time to prepare, edit, revise, and type for final delivery. In addition, if you do not also take time to practice delivering the manuscript in a fluent, conversational manner and with appropriate emphasis, well-placed pauses, and adequate eye contact, you are preparing to fail as an effective speaker.

SPEAKING EXTEMPORANEOUSLY

**speaking extemporane-
ously:** delivering a
speech from notes or
from a memorized out-
line.

The final method of delivery, and by far the most popular, is speaking **extemporaneously,** or from notes. Assuming that you have researched and organized your materials carefully, and that you have adequately practiced the speech, speaking from notes offers several advantages over other methods of delivery. You don't have to worry about one particular way of wording ideas, since you have not scripted the speech. Neither do you have to worry that you will forget something you have memorized. With your notes before you, you are free to interact with the audience in a natural, conversational manner. If something you say confuses the audience, you can repeat it, explain it using other words, or think of a better example to clarify it. Your language may not be as forceful or colorful as with a carefully prepared manuscript or a memorized speech, but speaking from notes helps ensure that you will be natural and spontaneous.

When speaking either from a manuscript or from notes, you need to keep several practical points in mind:

1. Practice with the notes or manuscript you will actually use in delivering the speech. You need to know where things are on the page so that you have to glance down only briefly.
2. Number the pages of your manuscript or your notecards so that you can check their order just before you speak.
3. Determine when you should and when you should not look at your notes. Looking at your notes when you quote an authority or present statistics is acceptable. In fact, it may even convey to your audience your concern for exactness in supporting your ideas. However, do not look down while previewing, stating, or summarizing your key ideas. If you cannot remember your key points, what hope is there for the audience? Also, avoid looking down when you use personal pronouns such as "I," "we," and "you," or when you address members of the audience by name. A break in your eye

contact at those points suddenly distances you from the audience, and creates the impression that the speech is coming from a script rather than from you.

4. Slide the pages of your manuscript or notes rather than turning them. As a rule, if you use a lectern, do not let the audience see your notes after you place them in front of you. The less the audience is aware of your notes, the more direct and personal your communication with them will be.

5. Devote extra practice time to your conclusion. The last thing you say can make a deep impression, but not if you rush through it or deliver it while gathering up your notes and walking back to your seat. Your goal at this critical point in the speech is the same as your goal for all of your delivery: to eliminate distractions and to reinforce your message through your body, voice, and language.

The most satisfactory way of delivering your classroom speeches combines all four of the methods we have discussed. We have advised you not to look at your notes during the preview of your introduction or the summary step of your conclusion. We stressed the importance of the introduction and conclusion in Chapter 9. To demonstrate that you are well prepared and to ensure contact with your audience, you may want to have your introduction and conclusion memorized. That won't be difficult, since they are brief sections. You may decide or be assigned to deliver the body of your speech extemporaneously, looking at your notes occasionally. Just don't look at your notes while you are stating or summarizing each main point. If you quote sources at different points in your speech, you are, in effect, briefly using a manuscript. Finally, as an audience-centered speaker you should be flexible enough to improvise a bit. You speak impromptu whenever you repeat an idea or think of a better example to increase your clarity or your persuasiveness. If you are well prepared, this combination of delivery methods should look natural to your audience and feel comfortable to you.

One standard in the American work ethic has been the traditional saying, "If it's worth doing, it's worth doing well." That's wise counsel for the public speaker. Your gestures, rate of delivery, and grammar may seem trivial until they begin to interfere with your communication, undermine your credibility, and dilute your persuasiveness. Delivery is a vital part of your public speech, and effective delivery is an asset worth cultivating.

Summary

The nonverbal elements of delivery include everything about your speech that could not be captured and recorded in a manuscript of the speech. Vocal delivery is comprised of your *rate*, use of *pauses*, *volume*, *pitch* and *inflection*, *voice quality*, *articulation*, and *pronunciation*. Your *appearance, posture, facial expression, eye contact, movement,* and *gestures* make up the physical elements of your delivery. With each of these elements, your goal as a speaker should be to eliminate distractions and to work for variety so that you look and sound natural. Once you are aware of unconscious mannerisms you *may* have and of the characteristics of effective delivery that you *should* have, you can make significant improvements in the way you deliver a speech. You exercise a good deal of control over most of these physical and vocal elements of delivery. With the confidence that comes from practice, you should be able to adapt your delivery to different speaking situations and audience sizes. Though this chapter examined several different elements of delivery, speech delivery is best when *none* of those elements makes an impression on the audience. Instead, delivery should reinforce the clear, forceful communication of your ideas.

With a repertoire of effective vocal and physical skills at your command, you can then select one of four methods of delivery: *impromptu,* or speaking without advanced preparation; speaking from *memory;* speaking from a *manuscript;* and speaking *extemporaneously,* or from notes. While each of those types of delivery is appropriate under certain public speaking circumstances, impromptu speaking and speaking from memory should almost certainly be avoided for prepared, graded classroom speeches. Speeches from a manuscript and, particularly, from notes, have far fewer limitations and more applications than the other two methods of delivery. Those who can speak clearly and emphatically from a few notes after the necessary period of practice have gone a long way toward ensuring success, not only in the public speaking classroom but also in future public speaking situations.

Exercises

1. Select a short passage from a novel, short story, speech, or other prose selection and photocopy it. Study the meaning and emotion of the excerpt. After marking the copied text, read the passage aloud, emphasizing key words and phrases and using pauses to enhance the message's impact.
2. Record your speech on audiotape and listen to it. Analyze your use of rate, pauses, volume, pitch, inflection, articulation, and pronunciation. What can you do to ensure that your delivery is lively and reinforces the message of the speech?
3. Record your speech on videotape. Watch and listen to it. Analyze your physical delivery, focusing on those aspects discussed in this chapter. What are your strengths? What are your weaknesses? What can you do to improve the physical delivery of your message?
4. Attend a speech and analyze the speaker's vocal and physical delivery. Was the message delivered effectively? What nonverbal elements enhanced and what detracted from the speech? What suggestions could you give the speaker to improve the delivery of the speech?

Notes

1. Sylvester Monroe, "Let the Joy Bells Ring," *Newsweek* 30 July 1984: 22.

2. Laurence J. Peter, *Peter's Quotations: Ideas for Our Time* (New York: Bantam, 1979) 476.

3. Information in these paragraphs is

based on two articles: Stephanie Mills, "Salons and Beyond: Changing the World One Evening at a Time," *Utne Reader* March/April 1991: 68–77, and John Berendt, "The Salon," *Esquire* November 1990: 48. Jon Carroll is quoted on page 75 of the Mills article.

4. Mihaly Csikszentmihalyi, *Beyond Boredom and Anxiety: The Experience of Play in Work and Games* (San Francisco: Jossey-Bass, 1975).

5. Ray L. Birdwhistell, *Kinesics and Context: Essays on Body Motion Communication* (Philadelphia: U of Philadelphia P, 1970) 8.

Using Visual Aids

13

The Importance of Using Visual Aids
Increases Message Clarity
Reinforces Message Impact
Increases Speaker Dynamism

Types of Visual Aids
Objects
Graphics

Projections
Handouts
Audio Aids

Strategies for Using Visual Aids
Before the Speech
During the Speech

A three-year-old boy with bangs and short pants saluting at his father's funeral . . .

An anguished woman kneeling over the body of a student shot by the National Guard . . .

An American president lifting his pet beagle by its ears . . .

Two helmeted figures saluting an American flag staked into a desolate, gray landscape . . .

A space shuttle exploding in a cloudless azure sky . . .

A tiny, battered girl being lifted from a well . . .

A young man standing motionless in a street in front of four tanks . . .

People dancing and spraying champagne all night from atop a wall . . .

The strange fireworks of anti-aircraft tracers in a night sky . . .

Discussion Prompt:
We selected these images knowing that older students will relate to more of them than younger students will. What other images evoke strong memories among your students?

If you form a vivid mental image at the description of any of these events, you prove the haunting power of pictures.[1] We have all grown up in a visually oriented society. Even our language reflects the power of the visual message. Consider these familiar sayings:

"A picture is worth a thousand words."

"Don't believe anything you hear and only half of what you see."

"Missouri — the Show Me State."

"I wouldn't have believed it if I hadn't seen it with my own eyes."

Today television and film are our primary entertainment media. We colorize classic movies for people who will not tolerate black-and-white films. Most Americans today get the majority of their news from television. Even our newspapers are filled with pictures, many in color. When the news is bad, we expect to see pictures or videotape of the airplane wreckage, the flooding, or the aftermath of the earthquake. When the news is good, we expect to see pictures of the winning team, the successful space mission, or the heroic rescue. We are, indeed, people for whom "seeing is believing."

Because pictures are such an important part of life, delivering a public speech without considering using visual aids is a little like playing tennis with your racquet hand tied behind your back. As a speaker, you need not rely only on words to communicate your ideas precisely and powerfully. You can add force and impact to your message by incorporating a *visual* dimension as well.

■ The Importance of Using Visual Aids

A well-designed, appropriate **visual aid** can add significantly to the effectiveness of the speech and the speaker. Effective visual aids serve three important functions. First, they add clarity to a speaker's message. Second, they reinforce the impact of the message. Third, they increase the dynamism of a speaker's delivery. Considering these three functions should help you determine whether to incorporate visual aids in a particular speech.

how the lines on the cans clearly spelled out the word "sex" when two cans were stacked and aligned in a certain way.

Also included under the category of objects are any people you use to help demonstrate a procedure, such as cardiopulmonary resuscitation or the Heimlich maneuver. Objects used effectively give your speech immediacy and carry a great deal of impact.

GRAPHICS

The term **graphics** includes a variety of two-dimensional visual aids used to clarify or illustrate a point being made orally. Five types of graphics to consider are pictures, diagrams, graphs, charts, and maps.

Pictures can make a speaker's oral presentation more concrete and vivid. It is difficult to imagine how a speech on the artistic styles of Georgia O'Keeffe or Edward Hopper could be effective without pictures or prints of some of their paintings. A speaker trying to persuade the audience that subliminal messages are common in advertising would be both vague and unconvincing unless he or she presented actual examples.

Pictures can also be used to dramatize a point, as with photographs showing the extent of tornado damage in a particular area. A speaker who advocates legislation mandating seat belt use might display two pictures of badly mangled automobiles. The impact of the message would be clear and forceful as the speaker observes, "The driver of the car in the first picture was not wearing his seat belt and died. The driver in the second picture was wearing hers and walked away."

When you use pictures, make sure that you select them with size and clarity in mind. A small snapshot of the Palace of Versailles or a picture of it in an encyclopedia held up for audience view detracts from, rather than reinforces, the speaker's purpose. Pictures used as visual aids often must be enlarged. Luckily, color laser copiers found at many copy shops today make enlarged copies of pictures quickly and inexpensively. Or you can check the library for books with large pictures. The picture you want to show may even be available as an inexpensive poster from a local museum gift shop or a bookstore. For very large audiences, you may need to project pictures for easy viewing. Here again, you may be able to borrow slides from your school's art department library or to purchase them from a museum gift shop.

Diagrams are graphics, typically drawn on posterboard, showing the parts of an object or organization, or the steps in a process. Posterboard is ideal for diagrams used in classroom speeches because its large size makes it easy for audience members to see. It is also thick and rigid enough to make handling it easy. You might use a diagram to show the features of a new aircraft design, the organizational structure of the U.S. judicial system, or the steps in the lost wax method of casting jewelry, for example. The best diagrams achieve their impact by simplifying and exaggerating key points. For example, no diagram of manageable size could illustrate all the parts of a six-cylinder engine clearly enough for the audience to see easily. A carefully constructed diagram could isolate and label key parts of that engine design, however.

Steven's speech on Poplar Forest, Thomas Jefferson's getaway home, sought both to capture the uniqueness of Jefferson's architectural style and to

graphics: two-dimensional visual aids, including pictures, diagrams, graphs, charts, and maps, used during the delivery of a speech.

pictures: photographs used to make a point more vivid or convincing.

Teaching Strategy: Invite a faculty member or staff member with expertise in graphic design to speak to your class. Ask the person to talk about the basics of preparing graphics for effective visual aids in speeches.

Discussion Prompt: Refer students to the picture at the beginning of this chapter. Discuss when this style of delivery (speaker holding a picture) would and would not be appropriate. For example, when speaking to a small audience and referring to the visual aid for a short period of time, such delivery might be effective. However, if speaking to a large audience and referring to the visual aid throughout the presentation, the speaker would need to enlarge the visual aid and position it on an easel, or project the visual aid.

diagrams: graphics, usually drawn on posterboard, showing the parts of an object or organization, or the steps in a process.

Teaching Strategy:
If students have no objection, save some of their visual aids for use in future classes. Use these visual aids to illustrate effective and ineffective visual aids.

FIGURE 13.1 Picture: Poplar Forest, Home of Thomas Jefferson

re-create life in those post-presidential years. Steven used two visual aids: a picture (Figure 13.1) and a diagram (Figure 13.2). He based his diagram on one he found in a brochure he had picked up when he toured Poplar Forest. Steven knew he did not have time to discuss each of the ten areas identified. In his speech he cited the brochure as a source, mentioned each area in passing but focused on four key areas: (1) the west bedroom, (2) the dining room, (3) the east bedroom, and (4) the parlor. In preparing his visual aid, he labeled each area and then covered the words with slips of white paper. He used the diagram to guide the audience through the house, removing the slips of paper so that the audience could identify each location as he discussed it. When he had concluded his speech, the audience had a better understanding of the house's layout.

FIGURE 13.2 Diagram: Floor Plan of Jefferson's Poplar Forest Home

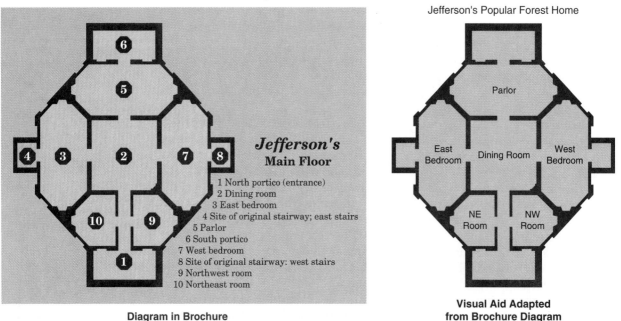

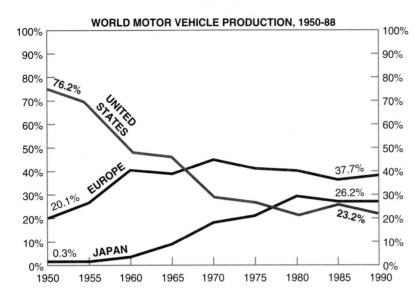

WORLD MOTOR VEHICLE PRODUCTION, 1950-88

76.2%

UNITED STATES

EUROPE

20.1%

0.3%   JAPAN

37.7%

26.2%

23.2%

1950   1955   1960   1965   1970   1975   1980   1985   1990

Class Activity:
Distribute to the class copies of a statistical table or chart from an almanac, a government report, *The Gallup Poll Monthly,* or some other source. Have students work in groups to decide how they could convert the information to a line, bar, or pie graph. Have them construct the graph on a sheet of posterpaper. Display the class work and discuss the choices the groups made.

FIGURE 13.3   Line Graph

Graphs are visual aids that illustrate some condition or action, and graphs take several familiar forms. A **line graph** is useful in depicting changes over time. A speaker might convincingly illustrate the rising cost of a college education during the past twenty years. Some line graphs trace two or more variables at once in contrasting colors: income and expenditures, for example.

Doug used a line graph (Figure 13.3) in his speech advocating legislation to make the U.S. automotive industry more competitive in the world market. Notice how his graph dramatizes the decline of the U.S. share as compared with increases for Europe and Japan. Doug found the graph in an almanac, and it highlighted the U.S. decline in blue.[3] When he constructed his visual aid, Doug substituted red for blue to contrast more vividly with the black lines. He also thought it would reinforce the image of being "in the red."

A **bar graph** is useful in showing quantitative comparisons.One measure of the economic health of an institution, a company, or a nation, for example, is whether it is "in the red" or "in the black." A bar graph contrasting deficits and profits, showing their relative size, provides us a clear, visual indication of economic health, particularly when income is represented in black and deficits in red.

A third type of graph, the **pie graph,** is helpful when you want to show relative proportions of the various parts of a whole. If you are analyzing the federal budget, for example, a pie graph could illustrate the percentage of the budget allocated for defense. Pie graphs could illustrate proportions of how people spend their time in a typical day, the causes of cancer deaths, how the average grocery dollar is spent, and the composition of your university according to the majors chosen by the student population. The speaker should probably emphasize the pertinent "slice" of the pie graph with a contrasting color.

Audrey informed her audience on something that most of them consumed every day: soft drinks. She discussed different brands and types of soft drinks and sought to give her audience a better understanding of the beverage industry. From a graph she saw in *USA Today* she constructed a pie graph (Figure 13.4) to show the market share of the leading soft drink companies.[4] In the

line graph: a diagram used to depict changes among variables over time.

bar graph: a diagram used to show quantitative comparisons among variables.

pie graph: a diagram used to show the relative proportions of a whole.

Cross-Reference:
Have your students look at the statistics in paragraph 6 of William Fort's speech in Appendix C. What type of visual aid(s) could the speaker have constructed to make those statistics more vivid and memorable?

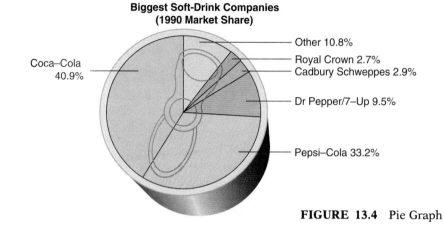

**Biggest Soft-Drink Companies
(1990 Market Share)**

Coca–Cola 40.9%

Other 10.8%

Royal Crown 2.7%

Cadbury Schweppes 2.9%

Dr Pepper/7–Up 9.5%

Pepsi–Cola 33.2%

FIGURE 13.4 Pie Graph

charts: graphics, usually drawn on posterboard, used to condense a large amount of information, to list the steps in a process, or to introduce new terms.

magazine *Beverage World* she found a chart listing the top ten soft drink brands.[5] Using this information and citing her sources in her speech, she was able to compare the growth of sugared, diet, and decaffeinated drinks. She converted the chart into a bar graph to dramatize the different rates of growth (Figure 13.5).

Similar to diagrams and graphs, **charts** are used to condense a large amount of information into a small space. For visibility and ease of handling,

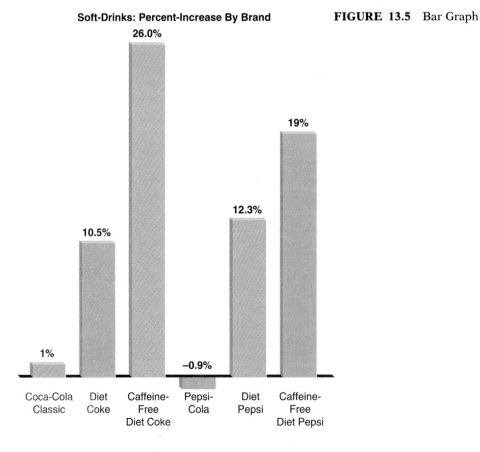

Soft-Drinks: Percent-Increase By Brand

FIGURE 13.5 Bar Graph

26.0%

19%

10.5%

12.3%

1%

−0.9%

| Coca-Cola Classic | Diet Coke | Caffeine-Free Diet Coke | Pepsi-Cola | Diet Pepsi | Caffeine-Free Diet Pepsi |

charts are also usually drawn on posterboard when used as visual aids for a small audience. Speakers introducing an audience to new terms will sometimes list those words on a chart, a strategy particularly effective if the words can be uncovered one at a time in the order they are discussed. Using charts, you could list the top ten states in per capita lottery ticket sales, or rank professional sports according to players' average salaries. Charts are particularly appropriate for medical and other technical topics. A speaker detailing the solution phase of a problem-solution speech might list steps advocated on a chart and introduce them in the order they are discussed.

As a speaker, you can either prepare charts in advance or draw them during the speech. For example, charts might show how regular investment in an Individual Retirement Account can lead to financial security in later life, and those calculations could be done ahead of time or during the course of the presentation. If you plan to draw one or more charts during your speech, rehearse the drawing. Make sure that you can draw as you continue to speak, so that your speech is not marred by long gaps of silence. If a chart is so complex that you cannot draw it as you speak, prepare it in advance. You can use a flip-chart, a large sketch pad bound at the top, to accommodate a series of charts. Available at most art supply stores, flip-charts have a sturdy backing that will stand up straight on an easel. They allow you to flip each visual aid back after using it. If you need to show one chart briefly, speak for a while, and then show another chart, simply leave a blank page between charts that need to be separated.

As part of her presentation to incoming students, Marcia used a chart to reveal student enrollment in the various colleges of the university (Figure 13.6). Had she wanted to emphasize one college, she could have used a pie chart with the appropriate slice highlighted in another color.

Maps, the final type of graphic visual aid, lend themselves especially well to speeches discussing or referring to unfamiliar geographic areas. Speakers informing an audience on the islands of Hawaii, the Battle of Gettysburg, or threats to the Alaskan wildlife refuge would do well to include maps to illustrate their ideas. Though commercial maps are professionally prepared and look good, they may be either too small or too detailed for a speaker's purpose. If you cannot isolate and project a section of the map for a larger audience, you will probably want to prepare a simplified, large-scale map of the territory in question.

> **Class Activity:** Distribute to the class copies of complicated or detailed tables or charts. You might select these from technical or business periodicals, or any of the sources listed in the previous annotation. Have students work in groups to design a visual aid that simplifies and highlights the data.

> **maps:** graphics representing real or imaginary geographic areas.

FIGURE 13.6 Chart

Total Student Body Enrollment by College	
College	Percent
Arts & Sciences	34%
Business	29%
Education	22%
Communication	9%
Nursing	6%

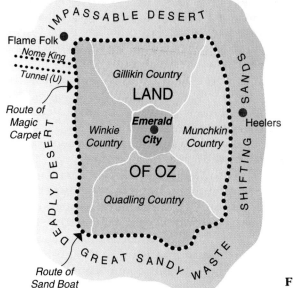

FIGURE 13.7 Map: The Land of Oz

Will generated his speech topic by brainstorming about his favorite childhood movie, *The Wizard of Oz*. In his research he discovered that L. Frank Baum wrote fourteen Oz books, and Will decided to inform his audience on the Land of Oz. He found a map of Oz and surrounding countries in *The Dictionary of Imaginary Places*.[6] Will photocopied the map, edited out the surrounding countries, added color, and enlarged the map of Oz so that his audience could see it as he described this mythical nation (see Figure 13.7). Will's audience will probably find *The Wizard of Oz* more enjoyable the next time they watch it.

PROJECTIONS

projections: a manner of presenting visual aids by casting their images onto a screen or other background.

Projections refer not so much to a type of visual aid as to a *manner of presentation*. Any of the graphics mentioned above—pictures, diagrams, graphs, charts, or maps—can be projected. This is especially appropriate when your audience is too large to see the visual aid easily and clearly. In such a case, you might want to use projections, such as slides, transparencies, or opaque projections. For convenience, we can group projections into two categories: *still projections* (slides, filmstrips, opaque projections, and transparencies) and *moving projections* (films and videotapes).

Still and moving projections can be critical to business and other public presentations. They may not, however, always serve the purpose of the public speaker and, particularly, the student of this class. Two notes of caution are in order. First, filmstrips, films, and videotapes are lengthy, and the organization of their content is predetermined. It is important that you, not a visual aid, organize and present the ideas of your speech. Second, as a beginning public speaker, you need to control and be the primary focus of the public speaking event. Standing at the back of the room, with lights dimmed, and narrating a slide show gives you little experience in speaking before an audience. For this reason, your instructor may not allow you to give a slide show, although you may be allowed to present a few relevant slides. Visual aids must always support, not become, your speech.

Still Projections. Slides are small mounted transparencies projected one at a time, and most of us associate slides with photographs or pictures. Yet any of the graphics we discussed earlier can be photographed and developed into slides. Whereas maps, charts, graphs, and diagrams may be cumbersome and subject to wear, *slides* of those visual aids are easily transported and easily reproduced. If you are considering using slides as visual aids, be aware of two disadvantages. One is that slides require projection equipment that is frequently noisy and intrusive. The second disadvantage is that slides must be projected in darkness to be easily visible, and this, of course, takes the focus away from you, the speaker.

slides: small mounted transparencies projected one at a time.

Filmstrips are familiar to most of us from as far back as our elementary schooling, but that does not mean that filmstrips are necessarily simplistic. Filmstrips can be used to instruct a group in parliamentary procedure or on how to conduct a business meeting, for example. Not only are a wide variety of filmstrips commercially available, but certain companies will design and manufacture filmstrips to meet the needs of speakers in specific businesses or professions. You will probably find filmstrips a more useful visual aid in your career than in your classroom speeches.

filmstrips: a series of pictures, diagrams, or any other graphic projected one at a time from a roll of plastic.

The **opaque projection** is an image projected directly from a sheet of paper. Any of the graphic visual aids discussed earlier can be projected in this manner. Opaque projections offer the advantage of enlarging and projecting visual aids without the work or expense of preparing transparencies. Two disadvantages of this type of visual aid are that the opaque projector is not as widely available as the slide projector, and it is certainly noisier to operate. In fact, its noise may rule out its use for extended periods of time in a small classroom.

opaque projections: images cast directly from a sheet of paper by use of an opaque projector.

Transparencies are clear or tinted sheets of plastic with words or images drawn or printed on them. Shown with an overhead projector, the transparency may be either prepared in advance or drawn with a felt-tip marker during the presentation. Many computer graphics programs can generate professional-looking transparencies. Overhead transparencies allow you to work through a problem, for example, without turning your back to the audience, thus helping you maintain audience involvement and interaction. If you plan to use transparencies in your very first speech, you will want to prepare them beforehand. You will be nervous enough without having to worry about drawing your visual aid as you speak.

transparencies: sheets of clear or tinted plastic with images drawn or printed on them and projected using an overhead projector.

Each of these types of still projections can visually enhance a presentation. They help ensure that the images are big enough for even the largest audiences to see clearly. All require special projection equipment, however. You may need to reserve that equipment through the audio-visual department of your school library. Or your instructor may have some basic equipment in the department. You will need to check all of this in advance and practice with the equipment so that you know how to operate it and how to minimize any noise it makes. On the day of your speech you will need to be extremely well organized and punctual since projection equipment requires time for setup and focusing and is subject to mechanical failure. Your diligence can pay off handsomely, however. If you are sure that the visual aid is important enough to project, its contribution to your speech will probably outweigh these potential disadvantages and reward your extra effort.

film and **videotape:** moving projections used to enhance a speaker's point.

Moving Projections. Moving projections include **films** and **videotapes,** and they are appropriate whenever action will enhance a visual presentation. Moreover, with the widespread popularity of video cassette recording equipment, this particular type of visual aid is becoming easier and cheaper to use. The choice between films and videotapes is dictated both by the projection equipment available to you and by the size of the audience. Images are clearer and can be projected larger from film than from videotape, making film a wise choice for presentations to large groups. Videotapes are entirely appropriate for presentations to small audiences or before larger groups that have multiple viewing monitors. Again, it is important that you use only short clips from videotapes to illustrate the ideas of your speech. Do not let the visual aid monopolize your presentation.

Videotapes have one obvious advantage over films: They do not require you to darken the room for projection. Though both the film and the videotape carry with them possible distractions, their potential impact is undeniable. We will remember for many years a persuasive presentation one of our students, George, gave on the problem of teenage inhalant abuse, or "paint sniffing." After establishing the problem with statistics and testimony from experts, George pressed the play button on the remote control. Suddenly his audience was seeing videotaped excerpts from news features on the problem: young people on downtown streets and under bridges, unable to answer quickly when the reporter asked, "What's your name?" Such flesh-and-blood examples of the effects of the problem are difficult to dismiss. Many speeches on social problems are significantly more compelling if the audience not only hears about but also sees graphic evidence of the problem.

HANDOUTS

handout: any graphic visual aid distributed to individual audience members.

A final method of visually presenting material is the **handout.** Copies of any graphic visual aid — pictures, diagrams, graphs, charts, or maps — may be handed out to individual audience members.

Handouts are appropriately used under two conditions: (1) when the information cannot be effectively displayed or projected, or (2) when the audience needs to study or refer to the information after the speech. Gwen, a student presenting a speech on "The Power Résumé," used a handout to great benefit. She handed out a sample power résumé and referred to it at key intervals in her speech: "If you turn to line fifteen, you will see. . . ." She made sure to number the lines of the résumé in the margin so that the audience could find the reference without fumbling. Not only could the audience refer to the résumé as Gwen discussed its key features, but many also probably saved it to use later as they prepared to enter the career world upon graduation. Gwen's speech and her visual aid made a convincing argument for the importance of the power résumé. In a similar way, if you try to persuade your audience to contribute time and money to local charities, you will more likely achieve your goal if you distribute a handout with the name, address, telephone number, and brief description of each charity.

AUDIO AIDS

Audio aids include records, tapes, and compact discs, and certainly there is an audio dimension of films and videotapes. Certain speech topics lend themselves to audio reinforcement of the message. A speech on Janis Joplin, for example, would be more vivid and informative if the audience could see and hear a videotaped clip of one of her performances. Lindahl, a student whose research we mentioned in Chapter 7, began her speech on the savant syndrome by playing half a minute of a taped piano performance of Chopin's *Polonaise #6 in A-Flat Major*. Her first words were, "The person who was playing that music is considered handicapped, but he heard this piece of music for the first time only minutes before sitting down to play it." The audiotape was a compelling example of one form of the savant syndrome. A speech comparing the jazz styles of Ellis, Wynton, and Branford Marsalis could hardly be effective without letting listeners hear examples from each of those artists. A speech comparing and contrasting the protest music of World War I with that of the Vietnam War would certainly be more powerful with audio examples.

Audio aids need not be confined to music topics, however. A speech on Winston Churchill might benefit from listening to his quiet eloquence as he addressed Great Britain's House of Commons and declared, "I have nothing to offer but blood, toil, tears, and sweat." A speaker analyzing the persuasive appeals of radio and television advertisements could play pertinent examples. Dan, a criminal justice major and intern with the police department, began his speech by playing an audiotape recorded in a police squad car. The officers were deciding whether they should stop a motorist suspected of driving while intoxicated. The audience heard the law enforcement officials describe what they saw that alerted them to a possible DWI and heard them discuss criteria for stopping the motorist. As the siren sounded, Dan stopped the tape. He used the audio aid to introduce his topic on the criteria for making a DWI arrest.

We have discussed the importance and major types of visual aids. What follows are some practical guidelines, showing you how to prepare and use visual aids in your public speech. Remember, even the most brilliant visual aid cannot salvage a poorly planned, poorly delivered speech. Visuals can aid, but they cannot resuscitate a weak speech. On the other hand, even the most carefully designed and professionally executed visual aid can be spoiled by clumsy handling during a presentation. The effect of public speaking is cumulative, with each element contributing toward one final effect. If you use visual aids in a presentation, you cannot afford to use them poorly.

audio aids: cassette tapes, compact discs, or records used to clarify or prove a point by letting listeners hear an example.

KEY POINTS
Strategies for Using
Visual Aids

Before the Speech
1. Determine the information to be presented visually.
2. Select the type of visual aid best suited to your resources and speech.
3. Ensure easy viewing by all audience members.
4. Make sure that the visual aid communicates the information clearly.
5. Construct a visual aid that is professional in appearance.
6. Practice using your visual aid.
7. Arrange for safe transportation of your visual aids.
8. Carry back-up supplies with you.
9. Properly position the visual aid.

During the Speech
1. Reveal the visual aid only when you are ready for it.
2. Talk to your audience—not to the visual aid.
3. Refer to the visual aid.
4. Keep your visual aid in view until the audience understands your point.
5. Conceal the visual aid after you have made your point.
6. Use handouts with caution.

BEFORE THE SPEECH

Determine the Information to be Presented Visually. Sections of a presentation that are complex or detailed may be particularly appropriate for visualization. Be careful, however, not to use too many visual aids. The premium in a speech is on the *spoken* word. Multimedia presentations can be exciting; they may also be extremely difficult to coordinate. Handling too many charts and posters quickly becomes cumbersome and distracting.

Select the Type of Visual Aid Best Suited to Your Resources and Speech. The visual aid you select will be influenced by the information you need to present, the amount of preparation time you have, your technical expertise at producing the visual aid, and the cost involved. In the business and professional world, professionally produced visual aids can be costly, but they are worth the investment. As a student, your budget, time, and expertise are important criteria. If preparing videotape clips to illustrate your speech is beyond your budget, or you lack either the time or the skill to prepare them, you are probably better off without them. A visual aid that calls attention to its poor production is a handicap, no matter how important the information it contains.

Ensure Easy Viewing by All Audience Members. A speaker addressing an audience of 300 would not want to use a videotaped presentation displayed on a single television monitor. A bar graph on posterboard should be visible to more than just the first four rows of the audience. If possible, practice with your visual aids in the room where you will speak. Position the visual aid and then sit in the seat of your farthest possible audience member. (In an auditorium, make it the back row; people will not move forward unless forced to.) If you can read your visual aid from that distance, it is sufficient in size. If you cannot, you must either enlarge the visual aid or eliminate it.

Make Sure that the Visual Aid Communicates the Information Clearly. Simplicity should be your guiding principle in constructing your visual aid. Too much information may clutter or confuse. For example, speakers sometimes construct posters in technicolor to make them lively and interesting. Remember that the purpose of visual aids is to inform, not impress, the audience. You may use red to indicate a budget deficit, but, as a general rule, black or dark blue on white is the most visually distinct color combination for graphics.

Construct a Visual Aid that is Professional in Appearance. In the business and professional world, a hand-lettered poster, no matter how neatly done, is inappropriate. Professionals understand the importance of a good impression. You may not have the resources to secure a professionally produced visual aid, and your instructor may not require it. How can you make a professional-looking graphic without spending a fortune? A simple solution is to use inexpensive, commercially prepared "press-on" letters. A print shop near you may have word processors and printers with many different sized fonts for your use for about $5 an hour. You can then enlarge your graphics on a copy machine. Hiring an art student to draw and letter a visual aid you have designed is another alternative. If you throw together a chart or graph the night before your speech, that is exactly what it will look like. Your hastily prepared work will undermine an image of careful and thorough preparation.

Practice Using Your Visual Aid. If you are conscientious, you will spend hours preparing your speech; visual aids are a part of that presentation. Just as you rehearse the words of your speech, you should rehearse referring to your visual aid, uncovering and covering charts, advancing slides, and writing on overhead transparencies. In short, if you plan to use visual aids, learn how *before* your speech; no audience will be impressed by how much you learn during the course of your presentation.

Arrange for Safe Transportation of Your Visual Aids. Visual aids worth using are worth transporting safely. Posterboards should be protected from moisture and bending. Cover your visual aid with plastic to protect it from a freak rainstorm or that flying Frisbee you encounter just before speech class. Do not roll up paper or posterboard charts, carrying them to different classes or leaving them in a car trunk throughout the day, and then expect them to lay flat when you speak. You will have a cylinder, not an effective visual aid.

Carry Back-up Supplies with You. An exciting and informative presentation can be ruined when a projector bulb blows as you are preparing to speak. Make an inventory of equipment you may need, such as extension cords, bulbs, and batteries, and then take them with you.

Properly Position the Visual Aid. Arrive at the place where you will give your speech *before* the audience arrives. Position your visual aid in the most desirable location. Make sure that the maximum number of people will see it and that there are no obstructions between it and the audience. If you are not the first speaker, have your visual aid and equipment conveniently located so that you can set up quickly and with little disruption.

DURING THE SPEECH

Reveal the Visual Aid Only When You are Ready for It. A visual aid is designed to attract attention and convey information. If it is visible at the beginning of the speech, the audience may focus on it rather than on what you are saying. It is important that the visual aid be seen *only* when you are ready to discuss the point it illustrates.

If your aid is on posterboard, cover it with a blank posterboard or turn the blank side to the audience. At the appropriate time, expose the visual aid. If you are using projections, have someone cued to turn the lights off and the projector on at the appropriate time.

Occasionally, a speaker will stop speaking, uncover a visual aid, and then continue. This is where rehearsal can really help you. You want to avoid creating unnecessary breaks in the flow of your speech. With practice you will be able to keep talking as you uncover your visual aid.

Talk to Your Audience — Not to the Visual Aid. Remember, eye contact is a speaker's most important nonverbal tool. Sustained visual interaction with your audience keeps their attention on you and allows you to monitor their feedback regarding your speech. Turning your back to your listeners undermines your impact. For this reason, use prepared graphics rather than a blackboard.

Refer to the Visual Aid. Speakers sometimes stand at the lectern using their notes or reading their manuscript, relatively far from their visual aid. This creates two lines of vision and may be confusing for the audience. It may also give the impression that you must rely on your notes since you do not fully understand what the visual aid conveys.

Other speakers carry their notes with them as they move to the visual aid, referring to them as they point out key concepts. Not only is this cumbersome, but it also reinforces that same image that the speaker is unsure of what he or she wants to say.

A well-constructed visual aid should be used as a set of notes. You should not need to refer to anything else as you discuss the point your visual aid illustrates. The key ideas represented on the aid should trigger the explanation you will provide. When you practice your speech, use your visual aid as your notes.

If you use a pointer to refer to the visual aid, have it easily accessible, use it *only* when pointing to the visual aid, and set it down immediately after you are finished with it. Too many speakers pick up a pen to use when referring to their visual aid and end up playing with the pen during the rest of the speech.

Finally, you should point to your visual aid with the hand closer to it. This keeps your body open and makes communication physically more direct with your audience.

General Norman Schwarzkopf uses a map during a press conference to explain the military strategies that had just brought Operation Desert Storm to a quick finish.

Keep Your Visual Aid in View until the Audience Understands the Point. Remember that you are more familiar with your speech than is your audience. Too often, a speaker hurries through an explanation and covers the visual aid before the audience fully comprehends its significance or the point being made. Just as you should not reveal your visual aid too soon, do not cover it up too quickly. You will have invested time and effort in preparing the visual aid. Give your audience the time necessary to digest the information it conveys. If you are interacting with and responding to your audience, many will likely signal their understanding of the visual aid by nodding their heads or changing their posture.

Conceal the Visual Aid after You have Made Your Point. Once you proceed to the next section of your speech, you do not want the audience to continue thinking about the visual aid. If the aid is an object or posterboard, cover it. If you are using projections, turn off the projector and turn on the room lights.

Use Handouts with Caution. Of all the forms of visual aids, the handout may be the most troublesome. If you distribute handouts before your remarks, the audience is already ahead of you. Passing out information during a presentation can be distracting, especially if you stop talking as you do so. Disseminating material after the presentation eliminates distractions but does not allow the listener to refer to the printed information as you are explaining it. In general, then, use handouts in a public speech only if that is the best way to clarify and give impact to your ideas.

You will encounter some speaking situations, such as the business presentation, that not only benefit from but may also demand handout material. The audience is often a decision-making group. During an especially technical presentation, they may need to take notes. Afterward, they may need to study the information presented. Handouts provide a record of the presenter's remarks and supplementary information the speaker did not have time to explain.

Visual aids can make your speech more effective. By seeing as well as hearing your message, the audience becomes more involved with your speech and more responsive to your appeals.

Summary

We live in a visually oriented world, expecting not only to hear about events around the globe, but also to see color pictures and videotapes of those events. Various studies show that visual aids complement the spoken word by increasing audience involvement with a speech and aiding their retention of the information presented. Visual aids can contribute to the clarity and impact of a speaker's message and, when handled well, can make a speaker's delivery seem more dynamic.

The four categories of visual aids discussed in this chapter are objects, graphics, projections, and handouts. *Objects* are three-dimensional and may be either actual items or models of large or small items. *Graphics* refers to a large group of two-dimensional visual aids, including pictures, diagrams, graphs (line, bar, or pie graphs), charts, and maps. *Projections* may be either still or moving. Still projections include slides, filmstrips, opaque projections, and transparencies. Any type of graphic may be shown by a still projection. Moving projections include films and videotapes. *Handouts* of any type of graphic may be given to audience members when no other method of presentation is possible. In addition to these strictly visual supports, a speaker may choose audio aids such as records, tapes, and compact discs of music, spoken words, and other sounds.

To use visual aids for maximum impact, a speaker needs to prepare them carefully using the following steps as guidelines: (1) Determine the amount of information to be presented visually; (2) select the type of visual aid best suited to the speaker's resources and speech topic; (3) ensure easy viewing by all audience members; (4) ensure that the visual aid communicates its information clearly; (5) construct a visual aid that appears carefully or professionally done; (6) practice using the visual aid; (7) arrange for safe transportation of the visual aid; (8) carry back-up supplies in case of equipment failure; and (9) properly position the visual aid before beginning the speech.

During the actual delivery of the speech, the speaker using visual aids needs to remember the following: (1) Reveal the visual aid only when ready to use it; (2) talk to the audience, not to the visual aid; (3) refer to the visual aid; (4) keep the visual aid in view until the audience understands the point it makes; (5) conceal the visual aid after making your point with it; and (6) use handouts with caution.

Visual aids can greatly enhance many speeches, and some speeches would be difficult to deliver without appropriate audio or visual aids. Effective use of those visual aids, however, requires careful planning and practice to integrate them into your speech delivery without distraction.

Exercises

1. Select a graph, diagram, or chart that you find in a magazine article. Describe how you would adapt it as a visual aid for a speech.

2. Sketch a visual aid you could construct for one of the speeches in Appendix C. Describe how the aid would make the message of the speech clearer and more memorable.
3. Describe at least two types of visual aids you could use for speeches with the following specific purposes:
   a. to inform the audience on techniques of handwriting analysis.
   b. to inform the audience on origami, the Japanese art of paper folding.
   c. to inform the audience on the process of photograph restoration.
   d. to persuade the audience that more money should be spent on AIDS research.
   e. to persuade the audience that the government should invest more money in the U.S. space program.
   f. to persuade the audience that [name of building on campus] should be razed and replaced with another facility.
4. Go to the library and consult a book on graphic design or read a chapter on the topic in an advertising textbook. What suggestions concerning layout and illustration are appropriate for a speaker's visual aids? What suggestions seem unsuited to the medium?

Notes

1. We adapted this chapter opening from four images in an effective Nikon advertisement we saw for the first time in *American Photo* March/April 1991: 19.

2. Michael Antonoff, "Meetings Take Off with Graphics," *Personal Computing* July 1990: 62.

3. *The Universal Almanac 1991*, ed. John W. Wright (Kansas City, MO: Andrews and McMeel, 1990) 277.

4. "Biggest Soft-Drink Companies," *USA Today* 4 Feb. 1991, B1.

5. "Beverage World Top 10 Soft Drink Brands of 1989," *Beverage World* March 1990: 24.

6. Alberto Manguel and Gianni Guadalupi, *The Dictionary of Imaginary Places*, expanded ed. (San Diego: Harvest–Harcourt, 1987) 287.

Speaking to Inform

14

Characteristics of a Speech to Inform

Types of Informative Speeches
Speeches about People
Speeches about Objects
Speeches about Places

Speeches about Events
Speeches about Processes
Speeches about Concepts
Speeches about Conditions
Speeches about Issues

Guidelines for Speaking to Inform

"We are drowning in information and starving for knowledge."

JOHN NAISBITT[1]

*I*F YOU consider this statement for a moment, you will, no doubt, agree wholeheartedly. In fact, we respond to information today in an almost schizophrenic way. On one hand, study after study reveals that young people seem to know less and less about the world around them. A few years ago, a test of nearly 8,000 high school juniors representing all sections of the country and all subgroups revealed that on average, students got only half the history and literature questions correct.[2] As two authors studying those test results point out, if we think of this as a national report card in history and literature, eleventh graders in the United States fail both these crucial subjects. What is more troubling is that students at this age do not seem particularly worried about this failure.

By the time those people begin their various careers, however, they will have changed and become convinced of the value of knowing as much as possible. The problem is that just as we learn to appreciate information, we are bombarded with too much of it. Some people begin to suffer stress from trying to keep up with the avalanche of available information. The average adult American now reads 100 newspapers, thirty-six magazines, and 3,000 forms and notices in one year. This same person listens to 730 hours of radio, watches 2,463 hours of television, and talks on the phone for almost sixty-one hours.[3] Did you know that more information has been published during the past thirty years than during the previous 5,000?[4] According to William Banach, executive director of the Institute for Future Studies, "Information is doubling every $2\frac{1}{2}$ years — every 900 days! By the time today's kindergartner moves through the grades to graduation, the body of knowledge will quadruple!"[5]

As a college student, you suffer greater information overload than most other people. Not only are you bombarded by the same media aimed at every other citizen, but you also spend much of your time receiving, interpreting, evaluating, and committing to memory information presented in books, articles, handouts, lectures, and discussion. With this extensive experience as receivers of information, why are most students intimidated by the prospect of sending information in informative speeches?

The answer is that informative speaking poses three challenges to you as a speaker. First, you must be able to select an appropriate informative topic. You don't want to repeat information that your audience already knows. Yet you may hesitate to speak on a topic you find personally interesting for fear that it will be irrelevant to your listeners. Second, once you select a topic, you must then sift through what may be a huge amount of available information to determine what supporting material is most suitable for your audience and relevant to your purpose. Finally, once you narrow the topic and select your supporting materials, you must organize your information in the most fitting manner. Those three tasks form the essence of informative speaking, the subject of this chapter.

Related Reading:
Wurman, Saul. *Information Anxiety: What To Do When Information Doesn't Tell You What You Need To Know.* New York: Doubleday-Bantam, 1990. This book is an excellent source of statistics, surprising facts, and quotations about the stresses of trying to keep up with information or trying to make sense of vague information.

Class Activity:
Have students use the information in the first two paragraphs to write an introduction for a speech with this specific purpose: to inform the audience of the technology of the information explosion. Remind students to use the four-step strategy discussed in Chapter 9, "Organizing Your Speech."

Dr. Jones, your geology professor, entered the classroom, took out a folder of notes, put up the first of a series of slides, and began to lecture on the differences between active and inactive volcanoes. During the news blackout surrounding the war in the Persian Gulf, Lieutenant General Thomas Kelly appeared at the Pentagon for occasional press briefings on the most recent war news. Scott, a classmate in your business communication class, spent half the period summarizing his outside reading on factors that shape a company's culture. The lecture, briefing, and oral report these people delivered are three of the forms informative speeches can take. We discuss the oral report in Chapter 17, Speaking on Special Occasions; in this chapter we focus on the **speech to inform.**

At the most fundamental level we seek knowledge for three reasons: We want to *know, understand,* and *use* information. The goals of any informative speaker, in turn, are to impart knowledge, enhance understanding, or permit application. Suppose you decided to prepare an informative speech on the general subject of advertising. You could select as your specific purpose to inform the audience on advertising in ancient times. Your listeners probably know little about this topic and you can readily assume that your speech would add to their **knowledge.** Alternately, you could have this as your specific purpose: to inform my audience on how effective advertising succeeds. Using examples your audience already knows, you could deepen their **understanding** of advertising strategies and principles. A third specific purpose might be to inform your listeners on how they can prepare effective, low-cost advertisements when they want to promote a charity fund-raising project or a garage sale. In this instance you would help the audience **apply** basic advertising principles.

Speakers inform us, then, when they provide us with new information, when they help us understand better some information we already possess, or when they enable us to apply information. You must make sure, when you prepare an informative speech, that you do not slip into giving a persuasive speech. How can you avoid this problem? After all, a persuasive speech also conveys information. In fact, the best persuasive speeches usually include supporting material that is both expository and compelling.

You must be able to distinguish between informative and persuasive speeches. Some topics, of course, are easy to classify. A speaker urging audience members to sign and carry an organ donor card is clearly trying to persuade; the speaker is attempting to intensify beliefs and either change or reinforce behavior. On the other hand, a speech charting the recent increases in organ transplant procedures is a speech to inform. A speech on the history of computers is informative, while a speech advocating an IBM clone as the best computer buy for the college student is persuasive. A speech describing different forms of alcohol addiction is informative, whereas a speech advocating the Alcoholics Anonymous program to overcome addiction would be persuasive.

Many speakers, both beginning and experienced, at times have trouble distinguishing between informing and persuading. The reason is that speakers sometimes begin preparing a speech with the intention to inform, only to discover that somewhere during the speech construction process their objec-

speech to inform: a speech to impart knowledge, enhance understanding, or facilitate application of information.

Class Activity:
Ask students to write and bring to class five specific purpose statements for speeches on any topics they choose. Two or three statements should be for informative speech topics; the remainder for persuasive topics. Students should *not* identify the type of speech. At the beginning of class, have students exchange their papers with another person (or have groups exchange their papers with another group). Each person or group should write "informative" or "persuasive" by the appropriate specific purpose statements. Use this exercise as a starting point for discussing the differences between informative and persuasive speeches. Note topics you think would be especially good for informative and persuasive speeches.

tive has become persuasion. In other instances, speakers deliver what they intended to be an informative speech only to find that their listeners received it as a persuasive message. How can this happen? Let us look at the experience of one speaker, Sarah.

Sarah designed a speech with the specific purpose of informing the audience of the arguments for and against allowing women to serve in military combat. In her speech she took care to represent each side's arguments accurately and objectively. After her speech, however, Sarah discovered that some listeners previously undecided on the issue found her pro arguments particularly persuasive and now support permitting women to serve in combat roles. But Sarah also learned that others in her audience became more convinced that women should be excluded from such roles. Did Sarah's speech persuade? Apparently for some audience members the answer is yes; they changed their attitudes because of this speech. Yet Sarah's objective was to inform, not to persuade.

In determining the general purpose of your speech, remember that both speakers and listeners are active participants in the communication process. As we discussed earlier in this text, listeners will interpret what they hear and integrate it into their frames of reference. Your objectivity as a speaker will not stop the listener from hearing with subjectivity. As a speaker, though, you determine the motive for and manner of your presentation. Your goal in your informative speech is not to advocate specific beliefs, attitudes, and behaviors on controversial issues. Your objective is to assist your hearers as they come to know, understand, or apply an idea or issue. As you word the specific purpose of your speech, you should be able to determine whether your general purpose is to persuade or to inform.

Teaching Strategy:
Select several issues and ask students to prepare at least two informative and two persuasive specific purpose statements for each of the topic areas. Use the students' statements to test their understanding of the differences between the two types of speeches. Point out that even controversial issues have elements that are appropriate for informative speeches.

■ Types of Informative Speeches ━━━━━━━━

Teaching Strategy:
To help students generate creative ideas for informative speeches, suggest that they combine the eight topic categories discussed in this chapter with the sources of speech topics discussed in Chapter 6 (self-generated, audience-generated, occasion-generated, and research-generated). The transparency pack provides such a grid.

We can identify several ways of classifying informative speeches. We have chosen one pattern which we think will work well for you. This pattern is based on the type of topics you may choose for your speech. But first let us give you a couple of guidelines to help you use these informative categories. First, approach each category of topics with the broadest possible perspective. Second, recognize that the categories overlap, that the boundaries between them are not distinct. Whether you consider the Great Pyramid of Cheops an object or a place, for example, is much less important than the fact that it is a fascinating informative speech topic. The purpose of the categories is to stimulate, not to limit, your topic selection and development. If you can concentrate on these matters, you will avoid the dangers of persuading your audience rather than informing them. As you begin brainstorming, consider information you could provide your listeners regarding people, objects, places, events, processes, concepts, conditions, and issues. In the following sections we discuss those eight major topic areas for informative speeches and the patterns of organization appropriate for each.

1. Speeches about *people*
2. Speeches about *objects*
3. Speeches about *places*
4. Speeches about *events*
5. Speeches about *processes*
6. Speeches about *concepts*
7. Speeches about *conditions*
8. Speeches about *issues*

KEY POINTS
Subject Categories
for Informative
Speeches

SPEECHES ABOUT PEOPLE

Activities and accomplishments of other people fascinate us. We gravitate toward books, magazine articles, television programs, films, and even supermarket tabloids that reveal the lives of celebrities. We are interested in the lives of the rich and the famous. We are also interested in the lives of the poor and the not-so-famous. There is even a popular periodical entitled simply *People*.

People, then, are an abundant resource of topics for your informative speech. Choosing to inform about a person lets you be as historical or as contemporary as you wish. A speech about a person allows you the opportunity to expand your knowledge in a field that interests you while sharing those interests with your listeners. If you are majoring in computer and information sciences, you might speak on Steve Jobs or Steve Wozniak, founders of Apple Computer, as contemporary leaders or Thomas J. Watson, founder of IBM, as a historical figure. If you are studying art, speeches on Claude Monet or Edward Hopper are just two of hundreds of options available to you. If you are an avid photographer, an informative speech assignment gives you the opportunity to discover and communicate something about the life and accomplishments of Ansel Adams, Diane Arbus, Alfred Stieglitz, or Annie Leibovitz, for instance.

Of course, you don't need to confine your topic to individuals associated with your major or areas of interest. You could interest and inform audiences by discussing the lives and contributions of people such as the following:

Gary Larson	Alfred Kinsey
Eleanor Roosevelt	Andy Warhol
Demosthenes	Margaret Mead
Frank Lloyd Wright	Eudora Welty
Reinhold Niebuhr	e.e. cummings
Sally Hemings	D.W. Griffith
Jimi Hendrix	Walt Disney
Jackie Robinson	Clarence Darrow.

Perhaps your class meets in a building bearing the name of a person with whom you are not familiar. A speech telling your class about this person could be enlightening and memorable. Our student Margaret began her first informative speech of the semester as follows:

If you're like me, the first semester you registered here on campus and got a printout of your course schedule, you had to ask someone what LH stands for. Or you looked it up on a campus map: Laughton Hall. We've been meeting here in LH203 for three weeks, and some of us have had other classes in this building before. But did you ever wonder who this Laughton person is — or was? Well, John H. Laughton not only bequeathed the money to build this classroom building when he died, but was also a graduate of the school, the founder of Laughton Electronics, and a former mayor of the city.

You may choose to discuss not one person but a group of people, such as the Marx Brothers, FDR's brain trust, the "Four Horsemen of Notre Dame," or the rock group Aerosmith. You might even compare and contrast two or more individuals to highlight their philosophies and contributions. The following pairs of noted figures might generate lively exposition:

Malcolm X and Martin Luther
  King, Jr.
Sam Ervin and Richard Nixon
Rachel Carson and Ralph Nader
J. Edgar Hoover and Elliott Ness
The Dalai Lama and Pope John Paul II

Mao Tse-tung and Joseph Stalin
Rosalynn Carter and Barbara Bush
Edward R. Murrow and Joseph
  McCarthy.

Class Activity:
Distribute to students a copy of a short article about a person from an encyclopedia (or similar source). Ask students to read the article and then, in small groups, outline the body of a speech about that person, noting information they would use as supporting material. Discuss the groups' products. Do the speeches focus on a few key points, or are they detailed biographical listings? What information that is appropriate for the written article would be inappropriate for a speech? What other sources could students consult?

In considering a speech to inform about a person, you must decide not only what is important but also what the audience will remember. Too often speakers organize speeches reminiscent of a biographical listing in an encyclopedia, presenting a seemingly limitless compendium of dates. This is a mistake. Even the most attentive listener will remember few of the details in such a speech.

If you selected the life of Thomas Jefferson as your speech topic, for example, you would need to narrow and focus that subject. Listeners would probably not remember that Jefferson was born on April 13, 1743, according to the modern calendar and April 2 according to the old calendar; that he entered the College of William and Mary in 1760; that he was admitted to the Virginia bar in 1767; and that he married Martha Wayles Skelton on January 1, 1772. On the other hand, an audience might remember that Jefferson died on the fiftieth anniversary of the Declaration of Independence, July 4, 1826.

Speeches about people are often organized either chronologically or topically. One chronological pattern for a speech about Jefferson could be:

I. Jefferson's Early Life
II. Jefferson's Middle Years
III. Jefferson's Last Years.

You could organize your speech topically based on the epitaph Jefferson wrote for his tombstone:

I. Author of the Declaration of Independence
II. Author of the Statute of Virginia for Religious Freedom
III. Father of the University of Virginia.

If you wanted to focus on the three major roles Jefferson assumed in different stages of his life, you could develop your speech topically *and* chronologically, as in the following example:

I. Jefferson as Revolutionary
II. Jefferson as President
III. Jefferson as Elder Statesman.

SPEECHES ABOUT OBJECTS

A second resource of informative topics is **objects.** Speeches about objects focus on what is concrete rather than what is abstract. Again, consider objects from the broadest perspective possible so that you can generate a maximum number of topic ideas. Topics for this type of speech could include the following:

electric cars
volcanoes
endangered species
the Great Wall of China
coffee
smart roads

crocodiles
the Great Pyramid of Cheops
Fabergé eggs
the Parthenon
the Acropolis.

Class Activity:
Bring to class several objects (or pictures of objects). Divide the class into small groups and give each group an object. Have the groups brainstorm about how they could develop an informative speech about the object. Have the groups put on the blackboard an outline of the key ideas of their speeches. Lead a class discussion on the types and appropriateness of the organizational patterns selected.

Speeches about objects may use any of several organizational patterns. A speech on the Cathedral of Notre Dame or the Statue of Liberty might be organized spatially. A speech tracing the development of cyclones and anticyclones evolves chronologically. A speech on condors discussing (1) the Andean condor and (2) the California condor is organized topically. A speaker discussing the origins, types, and uses of pasta also uses a topical division. If the speech focused only on the history of pasta, however, it might be best structured chronologically.

SPEECHES ABOUT PLACES

One of the favorite pastimes for many of us is the summer vacation. Families pack their suitcases and, maps in hand, take to the road in search of historical, cultural, and recreational sites. Returning with souvenirs, pictures, postcards, and informational literature, we are able to "relive" our vacation.

Places are an easily tapped resource for informative speech topics. These speeches introduce listeners to new locales or expand their knowledge of familiar places. Topics may include real places, such as historic sites, emerging nations, national parks, famous prisons, and planets. Topics may also include fictitious places, such as the islands of Scylla and Charybdis, the Island of the Lord of the Flies, and the Sea of Frozen Words. Speeches about places challenge speakers to select words that create vivid images.

To organize your speech about places you would typically use one of three organizational patterns: spatial, chronological, or topical. A speech about the Nile, the world's longest river, is organized spatially if it discusses the upper, middle, and lower Nile. A presentation about your college might trace its development chronologically. A speech on Poplar Forest, Thomas Jefferson's getaway home, might use a topical pattern discussing Jefferson's architectural style.

Suppose you selected as your informative speech topic Ellis Island, the site

Class Activity:
Have students bring to class a travel brochure, travel magazine, or article from an encyclopedia which features a significant place or landmark. Let students brainstorm in groups how they might develop some of these examples as informative speeches. Require that they use several organizational patterns in their examples.

of the chief U.S. immigration center from 1892 to 1954. You could choose any of the following patterns of development.

> *Pattern:* spatial
> *Specific Purpose:* to inform the audience about Ellis Island's Main Building.
> *Key Ideas:*   **I.** The Registry Room
> **II.** The Baggage Room
> **III.** The Oral History Studio

> *Pattern:* chronological
> *Specific Purpose:* to inform the audience of the history of Ellis Island.
> *Key Ideas:*   **I.** Years of Immigration, 1892–1954
> **II.** Years of Dormancy, 1954–84
> **III.** Years of Remembrance, 1984–present

> *Pattern:* topical
> *Specific Purpose:* to inform the audience of the history of Ellis Island.
> *Key Ideas:*   **I.** The Process of Immigration
> **II.** The Place of Immigration
> **III.** The People Who Immigrated

Notice that each of these outlines is organized according to a distinct pattern. The key ideas in the first outline are organized spatially. Although the specific purposes of the second and third speeches are identical, the former is organized chronologically and the latter topically.

If you choose to speak about a place, be aware of a couple of common pitfalls. First, avoid making your speech sound like a travelogue. The speaking occasion is not an opportunity to show a captive audience slides you took during your last vacation ("And here are my cousins Lois and Louie. If you look closely, you can see part of Berkeley Plantation, the site of the first Thanksgiving and the birthplace of William Henry Harrison and Benjamin Harrison."). Your speech should identify and develop ideas contributing to the general education of your listeners.

A second pitfall to avoid is inappropriate visuals. While visual aids often enhance the presentation of speeches about places, we have too often seen speakers illustrate their ideas visually by holding up postcards or books and magazines containing pictures of places. This strategy is a mistake. These pictures are too small to be seen. As we advised in the previous chapter, use visual aids that are large enough to be viewed by *all* audience members. On other occasions, students speaking about places have distributed photographs or postcards to be passed among audience members during the speech. Although listeners could see the visual aids clearly as they held them, they often became preoccupied with the pictures and missed much of what the speaker was saying at the time. Remember, your visual aids should not distract your audience from the main attraction: you, speaking to inform.

SPEECHES ABOUT EVENTS

When we have been on the go from morning to night, we sometimes comment that we have had an "eventful day." When we look forward to an impor-

Broadcast journalists speak to inform when they report news to the public.

tant happening, we say we anticipate a "big event." **Events** are important or interesting occurrences in our lives. When we speak of the events of history, we include those happenings that shaped our nation, society, or world. Speeches about events focus on these important occurrences, personal or historical, and seek to convey knowledge so that an audience can better understand those events.

Examples of topics for this type of speech might include the following:

the sinking of the *Titanic*
the *War of the Worlds* broadcast
the Woodstock festival
D-Day

the Scottsboro case
the explosion of the zeppelin Hindenburg
the Chautauqua movement.

For a speech assignment that does not require you to conduct research, you might speak about an event in your life you consider important, funny, or instructive. Examples of such topics could include "the day I registered for the first time in college," "the day my first child was born," or "my most embarrassing moment."

Speeches about events typically use a chronological or topical pattern. For example, if your topic is the daring Great Train Robbery that took place in Britain in 1963, you could organize your speech chronologically, describing what happened before, during, and after those famous fifteen minutes. If your specific purpose is to inform the audience about aerial sports, you might use a topical pattern and discuss (1) gliding, (2) ballooning, and (3) skydiving.

A speaker wanting to inform the audience about the Scopes "Monkey" Trial could use any of the following developmental patterns.

Pattern: topical
Specific Purpose: to inform the audience of the theological dispute of the trial.
Key Ideas: **I.** The literal interpretation of the Scriptures
              II. The figurative interpretation of the Scriptures

Pattern: topical
Specific Purpose: to inform the audience of the key players of the drama.
Key Ideas: **I.** John T. Scopes, the defendant
              II. Clarence Darrow, the defense attorney
             III. William Jennings Bryan, the prosecutor

Pattern: chronological
Specific Purpose: to inform the audience of the background and outcome of the controversy.
Key Ideas: **I.** The law
              II. The challenge
             III. The verdict

The first two speeches are organized topically; the third is structured chronologically. Notice how each organizational strategy neatly matches the specific purpose of the speech.

SPEECHES ABOUT PROCESSES

Class Activity:
Divide the class into groups and assign each a speech topic focusing on a process. Students should be able to develop key ideas from their discussion and should not have to rely on outside research. For example, appropriate topics could include ways to study for an exam, how to decide on a major, and planning the perfect weekend. Have students use a chronological pattern to organize the key ideas in a speech. After listing the key ideas, the students should write a transitional statement connecting one key point to the next.

A process is a series of steps producing an outcome. Your informative speech about a **process** could explain how something works, functions, or is accomplished. We have had students give informative speeches on such "how-to" topics as how to read a food packaging label, detect plagiarism, write an effective term paper, administer first aid for burns, suit up and enter a "clean room," and tie-dye T-shirts. Informative topics, such as how batik materials are made, how radar works, and how to make children "waterproof" (a speech on the process of teaching water safety), are all process speeches. Speeches on critical path analysis, the Nielsen ratings, nuclear medicine, and cryptography (encoding and decoding messages in a code known only to those who understand) are also potentially good informative topics about processes.

Because a process is by definition a time-ordered sequence, speeches about processes commonly use chronological organization. They are not, however, confined to this pattern. As we have argued earlier, the best organization is the one that achieves the purpose of the speech. A student presenting a speech on colorization of black-and-white movies might choose a chronological pattern if the specific purpose is to explain how the process works. A pro-con division detailing the arguments for and against colorization would also be informative if the speaker discussed both sides in an unbiased manner.

Suppose you select cartooning as a topic area for a speech to inform. You would choose the organizational pattern best suited to your specific purpose. Let us look at some examples illustrating how you can narrow your topic on cartooning and what organizational patterns fit each topic.

Pattern: topical
Specific Purpose: to inform my audience on cartooning.
Key Ideas: **I.** Definition of cartoons
              II. Purposes of cartoons
             III. Types of cartoons

Pattern: chronological
Specific Purpose: to inform my audience on the process of creating a comic strip.
Key Ideas: **I.** Designing a comic strip
              II. Drawing a comic strip
             III. Producing a comic strip

Pattern: spatial
Specific Purpose: to inform my audience on how to draw a cartoon character.
Key Ideas: **I.** Drawing the head
              II. Drawing the upper body
             III. Drawing the lower body

Notice that each of the speeches outlined above is progressively narrowed and that each uses the type of organizational pattern best suited to it. The first is organized topically, the second chronologically, and the third spatially.

SPEECHES ABOUT CONCEPTS

Speeches about **concepts,** or ideas, focus on what is abstract rather than what is concrete. Whereas a speech about an object such as the Statue of Liberty might focus on the history or physical attributes of the statue itself, a speech about an idea might focus on the concept of liberty. Other topics suitable for informative speeches about concepts include eco-tourism, concrete poetry, nihilism, traumatic obsessions, the Doppler effect, nirvana, and religious dualism.

Speeches about concepts challenge you to make specific something that is abstract. These speeches typically rely on definitions and examples to support their explanations. Appropriate organizational patterns vary. A speech on Norse mythology might use a topical division of materials and focus on key figures.

Drew, a student of ours, entertained and involved all his listeners with a speech on onomastics, or the study of names. You can see from the preview at the end of his introduction that he also used a topical organization for this speech about a concept:

These are some actual names reported by John Train in his books *Remarkable Names of Real People* and *Even More Remarkable Names.* Let me repeat: These are *actual* names found in bureaus of vital statistics, public health services, newspaper articles, and hospital, church, and school records: E. Pluribus Eubanks, Loch Ness Hontas, Golden Pancake, Halloween Buggage, Odious Champagne, and Memory Leake.

Train says in *Even More Remarkable Names* that "what one might call the free-form nutty name—Oldmouse Waltz, Cashmere Tango Obedience, Eucalyptus Yoho—is the one indigenous American art form."

We're lucky. No one in here has a name as colorful as any of those. But we all have at least two names—a personal and a family name. Today, I'll tell you, first, why personal names developed, and second, the legal status of names. Finally, I have something to tell each of you about the origin of your names.

Speeches about theories, particularly if they are controversial, sometimes use a pro-con division. A discussion of the merits and shortcomings of Felice Schwartz's "Mommy Track" theory of career advancement reflects a pro-con development.

SPEECHES ABOUT CONDITIONS

Each spring, professional baseball players report to training camps. Some players arrive out of shape. Those who weigh too much or too little or who suffer from a physical injury are placed on a conditioning program. Their goal is to be in good condition by the time the season starts. Therefore, one way of viewing a **condition** is as a state of fitness or health. Conditions are also particular situations: living conditions in a third-world country; or the social and political climate that gives rise to movements like witchcraft hysteria in Salem, Civil War in the United States, McCarthyism, the women's movement, labor movements, the civil rights movement, and national independence movements.

Speeches about conditions can focus on a person's health and, indeed, medical topics are a popular source of student speeches. A speaker may choose the specific purpose: to inform the audience on the symptoms, causes, and treatment of myasthenia gravis. This topical organization is a pattern appropriate for many speeches about specific diseases or other health conditions. Another excellent topic for a speech to inform is "affluenza," a word coined to denote chronic psychological disorders afflicting the wealthy.

Conditions are not limited to the state of a person's physical or psychological health. Recession, "stagflation," and full employment are all terms economists use to describe the health of the economy. Social and cultural conditions also provide opportunities for informative speech topics. Depression, for example, is a condition that can apply to a person, a community, or the economy.

SPEECHES ABOUT ISSUES

Speeches about **issues** deal with controversial ideas and policies. If your informative speech is on an issue, you might talk about the use of polygraphs as a condition for employment; uniform sentencing of criminals; freedom of expression vs. freedom from pornography; regulation of big trucks on roads; and systematic instruction vs. child-oriented activities in preschools. Any issue being debated in your school, community, state, or nation can be a fruitful topic for your informative speech.

Class Activity:
Select a few emotionally charged issues (sexual harrassment, hiring quotas, and legalization of drugs, for example). Ask your students to brainstorm aspects of these issues that would be appropriate for *informative* speeches. Have them state the specific purpose of each speech and briefly describe what the speaker might discuss. In discussing these topics, point out what makes the speech informative rather than persuasive, and point out instances where topics have strayed into the realm of persuasion.

You might be thinking that controversial issues are better topics for persuasive speeches, but they can also be appropriate for speeches to inform. If you choose a controversial topic, research and develop it so that you present the issue objectively, and you are informing your audience.

Two common organizational patterns for speeches about issues are the topical and pro-con divisions. If you use a topical pattern of organization for your speech about issues, it will be easier for you to maintain your objectivity. If you choose the pro-con pattern, you may run the risk of moving toward a persuasive speech. As you recall, a pro-con strategy presents two sides of an issue, letting the listener decide which is stronger. If your informative speech on an issue is organized pro-con, guard against two pitfalls: **lack of objectivity** and **lack of perspective.**

Speakers predisposed toward one side of an issue sometimes have difficulty presenting both sides objectively. One such student, Carl, presented a speech on the increasingly popular practice of adopting uniforms for public schools. He presented four good reasons *for* the practice: (1) Uniforms are more economical for parents, (2) uniforms reduce student bickering and fighting over designer clothes, (3) uniforms increase student attentiveness in the classroom, and (4) uniforms identify various schools and promote school spirit. Carl's only argument *against* public school uniforms was that they limit students' freedom of expression. His speech was obviously out of balance. Though the assignment was an informative speech, Carl's pro-con approach was ultimately persuasive. If, like Carl, you choose a topic and feel committed to one side of the issue, save that topic for a persuasive speech.

A second pitfall that sometimes surfaces in the pro-con approach is characterizing an issue as two-sided when, in reality, it is many-sided. For example, one of our students spoke on the issue of child care. He mentioned the state family leave laws that permit mothers of newborn infants to take paid leaves of absence from work, and fathers to take unpaid leaves, while their jobs are protected. The speaker characterized advocates of such bills as pro-family and opponents as pro-business. He failed to consider that some people oppose such laws because they feel the laws don't go far enough; many state laws exempt small companies with fewer than fifty employees. If you fail to recognize and acknowledge the many facets of an issue in this way, you polarize your topic and lose the benefit of alternative perspectives.

In the preceding sections we have discussed eight types of informative speeches. As you begin working on your own informative speech, remember to select a topic that will benefit your listeners and communicate your information clearly and memorably. Use these eight subject categories to narrow and focus your topic. As you go through each category, use the self-, audience-, occasion-, and research-generated strategies we discussed in Chapter 6 on pages 102 – 9. These strategies will help you come up with a list of many topics to consider for your informative speech.

As you review this list you will, no doubt, find several persuasive topics. Before excluding them, see if there are related topics suitable for an informative speech. For example, you may have some strong feelings about intercollegiate athletic programs and their role in colleges and universities. To argue their merits or to suggest that they be scaled back would make your speech persuasive rather than informative. However, you could change your focus to a more informative topic related to the issue of intercollegiate athletics. You could inform the audience of the history and intent of Proposition 48, the National Collegiate Athletic Association's statement of academic entrance requirements for college athletes. You might trace the history of the athletic conference to which your school belongs.

As you go about selecting your topic, keep in mind this question: "How will the audience benefit from my topic?" Remember, your informative speech must bring new information or enhance the understanding of your audience. A speech detailing what employers look for in an employment résumé, for example, is clearly relevant to a class of students ready to enter the job market. But what about topics such as the golden age of vaudeville, the origins of superstitions, the history of aviation, the effect of music on livestock production, or the psychological aspects of aging?

Maybe you think that these topics are not relevant to your audience. But keep in mind that part of the process of becoming an educated individual is learning more about the world around you. We are committed to this perspective and believe it is one you should encourage in your listeners. For example, in his speech on kites and competitive kite flying, our student Ken recently informed us about the use of kites in ancient religious worship. After a bountiful harvest, early tribes would tie a handful of the first wheat harvested to the tail of a kite and literally offer it up to the gods in thanks. After this historical background, Ken traced the evolution of kite designs. He showed examples of the large, colorful, aerodynamic kites he takes to the coast to fly on weekends. Speeches on such subjects that are interesting and fun to know can always contribute to anyone's general education.

Once you have selected a topic that meets criteria discussed in Chapter 6, ask yourself the following three questions: (1) What does the audience already know about my topic? (2) What does the audience need to know to understand the topic? (3) Can I present this information in the time allotted in a way that the audience can understand and remember it? If you are satisfied with your answers to these questions, you can then begin developing the most effective strategy for conveying that information. Table 14.1 should help you as you select an appropriate organizational pattern.

Discussion Prompt:
To help students develop audience- and occasion-centered approaches to public speaking, select an informative speech topic, perhaps relating to an important campus or local issue. Lead a class discussion of the topic, answering the three questions included in this paragraph.

■ Guidelines for Speaking to Inform _____

As you prepare your speech to inform, keep in mind several guidelines. We discuss some of these more fully elsewhere in the text, but they are worth mentioning here.

Stress Your Informative Purpose. In presenting an informative speech, you must make clear from the outset that your objective is to **inform.** This is particularly important if your topic is controversial or related to other topics that are controversial. For example, if you are discussing the different methods

Speeches about . . .	Use . . .	If your purpose is to . . .
People	Topical organization	Explain various aspects of the person's life
People	Chronological organization	Survey events in the person's life
Objects	Topical organization	Explain various uses for the object
Objects	Chronological organization	Explain how the object was created or made
Objects	Spatial organization	Describe various parts of the object
Places	Topical organization	Emphasize various aspects of the place
Places	Chronological organization	Chart the history of or developments in the place
Places	Spatial organization	Describe the elements or parts of the place
Events	Topical organization	Explain the significance of the events
Events	Chronological organization	Explain a sequence of actions or events
Events	Causal organization	Explain how one event produced or resulted in another
Processes	Chronological organization	Explain how to do something or how it is done
Processes	Pro-Con organization	Explore the arguments for or against the procedure
Processes	Causal organization	Discuss the causes and effects of the process
Concepts	Topical organization	Discuss aspects, definitions, or applications of the concept
Conditions	Topical organization	Explain aspects of the condition
Conditions	Chronological organization	Trace the stages or phases of the condition
Conditions	Causal organization	Show the causes and effects of the condition
Issues	Topical organization	Discuss aspects of the issue's significance
Issues	Chronological organization	Show how the issue evolved over time
Issues	Pro-Con organization	Present opposing viewpoints on the issue

TABLE 14.1 Organizing Informative Speeches

of therapeutic abortions, you must take into account that many in your audience will have already adopted a pro-life or pro-choice perspective. Those who oppose abortion may perceive you to be advocating abortion. They will resist the information you are presenting, and your speech will not be successful.

Be Specific. At times we have had students tell us they will deliver a brief informative speech on "sports." This topic is far too broad and reflects little or no planning. Many of us know *a little about a lot* of subjects. An informative speech gives you the perfect opportunity to fill in the gaps by telling your audience *a lot about a little*. Narrow the topic. To help you do that, we have suggested in this chapter that you focus on **specific** people, objects, places, events, processes, concepts, conditions, and issues. Your "sports" topic can be narrowed to sports commentators; the history of astroturf; Forest Hills, former home of the U.S. Open tennis championships; competitive team sports and male bonding; and so on. If you are specific about your topic, your purpose, and the materials you use to support your speech, you will save yourself time during your research and make your speech easier for the audience to remember.

Be Clear. If you choose your topic carefully and explain it thoroughly, your message should be **clear.** Do not choose a topic that is too complex. If your speech topic is on particle accelerators or Boolean polynomials, you run the risk of being too technical for most audiences. You would never be able to give your audience the background knowledge necessary to understand your presentation in the limited time you have. You should also be careful about using jargon. Impressing the audience with your vocabulary is counterproductive if they cannot understand your message. The purpose of informative speaking is not to impress the audience with complex data, but to communicate information clearly.

Be Accurate. Information that is inaccurate does not inform; it misinforms and has two negative consequences. First, inaccuracies can hurt a speaker's credibility. If listeners recognize misstatements, they may begin to question the speaker's credibility: "If the speaker's wrong about that, could there be other inaccuracies in the speech?" **Accurate** statements help develop a positive image or protect one you have established earlier.

Second, inaccurate information can do potential harm to listeners. Such harm can be mental or physical. For example, you give an informative speech on the life-threatening reactions some people have to sulfites, a common ingredient in some food preservatives. Your audience leaves the class worried about their health and the damage they may have suffered. You neglected to mention that these reactions are rare. Your misinformation has harmed your audience. Another example is giving a speech on how to apply and check a tourniquet, but using outdated methods. If people in your audience later try your method, they could do serious physical damage. As you can see, if audience members are unaware of factual errors, they may form beliefs that are not valid or make decisions that are not prudent.

Not only should your information be accurate, but you must accurately cite any sources you have used to develop your speech. Some speakers assume that because they do not take a controversial stand in an informative speech, they need not cite sources. An informative topic may require fewer sources than you would use to establish your side of a debatable point. Demonstrating the truth of your ideas and information is nevertheless important. Also, as we mentioned in Chapter 2, you must cite the sources for any quotations you use.

Limit Your Ideas and Supporting Materials. Perhaps the most common mistake speakers make in developing the content of their speeches is including too much information. Do not make the mistake of thinking that the more information you put into a speech, the more informative it is. As we have mentioned previously, listeners cannot process all, or even most, of what you present. If you overload your audience with information, they will stop listening. Remember the adage that **"less is more."** To spend more time explaining and developing a few ideas will probably result in greater retention of these ideas by your listeners than the "speed and spread" approach.

Be Relevant. As you research your topic, you will no doubt discover information that is interesting but not central to your thesis. Because it is so interesting, you may be tempted to include it. Don't. If it is not **relevant,** leave it out.

One student, Larry, delivered an intriguing informative speech on the Jains, a tribe of monks in India whose daily life is shaped by reverence for all living things. As you would guess, the Jains are vegetarians. Yet they don't eat vegetables that develop underground because harvesting them might kill insects in the soil! Larry had done a good deal of research on this topic, including his own travels in India. His firsthand knowledge was both a blessing and a curse. Listening to someone who had visited the Jains' monasteries certainly made the topic immediate and compelling. But because he knew so much about the country, Larry included a lot of information about India that was interesting but irrelevant to his main point. His speech became much too long. To avoid this

Teaching Strategy:
Select an informative speech topic on which your students have lots of ideas— for example, how to study for an exam. Have the class brainstorm for ideas. Assign a student to record these suggestions on the chalkboard. After the class has generated many suggestions, discuss how a speaker might focus these ideas into a well-organized speech suitable for a five-to-seven minute presentation. Ask the class questions such as: (1) Which of these ideas are most important and should be included in the speech? (2) Which ideas are least important and need not be included in the speech? (3) Are there ideas that overlap and could be combined?

Much of our learning comes from the informative messages of our parents, teachers, and peers.

problem and keep yourself on track, write out your central thesis and refer to it periodically. When you digress from your topic you waste valuable preparation time, distort the focus of your speech, and confuse your audience.

Be Objective. One of the most important criteria for an informative speech is **objectivity.** If you take a stand, you become a persuader. Informative speakers are committed to presenting a balanced view. People representing political parties, charitable organizations, business associations, and special-interest groups are understandably committed to the objectives and policies of those groups. Your research should take into account all perspectives. If as you develop and practice your speech you find yourself becoming a proponent of a particular viewpoint, you may need to step back and assess whether your orientation has shifted from information to persuasion. If you do not think you can make your speech objective, save the topic for a persuasive speech.

In Chapter 11, Wording Your Speech, we discussed the use of language. Nothing betrays the image of objectivity that is essential in an informative speech as quickly as the inappropriate use of language. For example, in an informative speech on the pros and cons of juvenile curfew laws, one of our students used language that telegraphed his personal opinion on the issue. Even when explaining the arguments *for* such laws, he described them as "silly," "costly," and "unenforceable." If your speech is to remain informative rather than persuasive, your language should be descriptive rather than evaluative or judgmental.

Use Appropriate Organization. As we stated earlier, there is no one best organizational pattern for informative speeches. You choose the pattern that is most appropriate to your topic and specific purpose. However, some patterns are inappropriate for an informative speech. While a pro-con approach is appropriate, a pro-con-assessment strategy moves the speech into persuasion. Problem-solution, need-plan, and motivated sequence patterns, to be discussed in Chapter 16, are also traditionally used for persuasive, not informative, speeches. Again, Table 14.1 offers suggestions for selecting an **appropriate organizational pattern.** If you have any doubt that your organization is informative rather than persuasive, check with your instructor.

Use Appropriate Forms of Support. As with persuasive speeches, speeches to inform require **appropriate supporting materials** such as those we discussed in Chapter 8. These materials should come from sources that are authoritative and free from bias. If you discuss a controversial issue, you must represent each side fairly. For example, if your specific purpose is to inform your audience on the effects of bilingual education, you must research and present information from both its proponents and its critics.

Use Effective Delivery. Some speakers have a misconception that **delivery** is more important for a persuasive speech than for an informative speech. Regardless of the type of speech, you should become involved physically and vocally in delivering your speech. The suggestions we offered in Chapter 12, Delivering Your Speech, are appropriate for the speaker who informs as well as one who persuades. Your voice and body should reinforce your interest in and enthusiasm for your topic. Your delivery should also reinforce your objectivity. If you find your gestures, body tension, or voice conveying an emotional urgency, you have likely slipped into persuasion.

1. Stress your informative purpose.
2. Be specific.
3. Be clear.
4. Be accurate.
5. Limit your ideas and supporting materials.
6. Be relevant.
7. Be objective.
8. Use appropriate organization.
9. Use appropriate forms of support.
10. Use effective delivery.

We hope that after reading this chapter you *know* the principles and characteristics of informative speaking, that you *understand* how they contribute to effective speaking, and that you will be able to *apply* them as you prepare your speeches. If you have that information and can use it, the chapter has been informative and you have been a careful reader.

Summary

Never in human history have we had so much information so readily available. Deluged with this overflow of information, many of us respond by giving up and refusing to process this information. Those who understand the value of information to their personal and professional growth must figure out ways to contain the flow. As part of your work in this class, you will present informative speeches. An informative speech assignment provides you with the opportunity to be the sender rather than the receiver of information; it requires you to research a subject of your choice, synthesize data from various sources, and pass it on to your listeners. Your goals as an informative speaker are to expand listeners' knowledge, assist their understanding, or help them apply the information you communicate.

Classifying informative speeches by subject gives you an idea of the range of possible topics and the patterns of organization each subject typically uses. Speeches about *people* are often arranged chronologically, but may explore subtopics, such as aspects of the subject's life. Speeches about *objects* use spatial organization if your purpose is to describe various parts of the object, chronological organization if your purpose is to explain how the object was created, and topical organization if your purpose is to explain how the object is used. Speeches about *places* use chronological organization if your purpose is to explain the history or stages of development of the place, topical organization if you want to emphasize various aspects of the place, and spatial organization if your purpose is to describe the parts of the place. Speeches about *events* also use any of the following three methods of organization: Use chronological organization to explain a sequence of events; use topical organization if your purpose is to explain the significance of the event; use causal organization if you want to show how one event produced or led to another.

Speeches about *processes* can also use any of the following three organizational patterns. A chronological pattern helps you tell listeners how to do something or how something is done. A pro-con pattern is appropriate if you want to explore the arguments for and against the process. A causal pattern lets you discuss what caused or causes some process and the effects that result. You might instead begin with the effects and trace back to the causes. Speeches about *concepts* typically use topical organization as the speaker discusses various aspects, definitions, or applications of the concept.

Speeches about *conditions* may use topical organization to discuss various aspects of the condition, chronological organization to trace the stages or phases of a condition, or causal organization to show the causes of the condition and the effects that the condition has. Finally, speeches about controversial *issues* may use a pro-con organization if your purpose is to explore opposing viewpoints on the issue, topical organization if your purpose is to discuss the significance of the issue, or chronological organization if your purpose is to discuss how the issue has evolved.

As you begin to prepare an informative speech on a subject from one of these categories, ask yourself three questions: (1) *How much does the audience already know about this topic?* (2) *What does the audience need to know in order to understand this topic?* (3) *Can I present this information in the allotted time so that the audience will understand and remember it?* When you answer these questions, you can be sure that your topic is narrowed sufficiently and is appropriate to your listeners.

Finally, we offer ten guidelines to help you develop and deliver an effective informative speech. (1) Begin with an overall picture; let your audience know that your purpose is to inform. (2) Be specific; narrow the topic you have chosen. (3) Be clear; remember that your audience probably knows much less about this topic than you do. (4) Be accurate; misinformation can harm your listeners. (5) Limit the ideas and supporting material that you try to include. Covering a few ideas in depth is usually more informative than giving a shallow treatment of many ideas. (6) Be relevant; do not be sidetracked by interesting but irrelevant information. (7) Be objective in your approach to the topic and the language you use. (8) Use the pattern of organization best suited to achieving your specific purpose. (9) Use appropriate forms of support. (10) Use lively, effective speech delivery.

Exercises

1. Using techniques of brainstorming and research, generate a list of two informative speech topics for each of the following categories: people, objects, places, events, processes, concepts, conditions, and issues. Place an asterisk (*) by the five topics you think are most appropriate for a speech in this class.
2. Using the list you generated in Exercise 1, select one topic from four categories and write a specific purpose statement for each. Think about how you could develop each specific purpose and then discuss what organizational pattern you think would be most appropriate.
3. Select an informative speech from *Vital Speeches of the Day* or some other published source. Analyze the speech to see if it adheres to the guidelines

discussed in this chapter. If it does, show specifically how it fulfills the goals of each of these guidelines. If it does not, list the guidelines violated and give examples of where this occurs in the speech. Suggest how the speaker could revise the speech to meet the guidelines.

4. Using the speech you selected in Exercise 3, identify and write down the specific purpose of the speech. Does it meet the characteristics of a speech to inform? Why or why not? What is the method of organization used in the speech? Do you think this is the best pattern to achieve the speech's specific purpose? Why or why not?

5. Analyze a lecture by one of your instructors to see if it adheres to the guidelines listed in this chapter. Which guidelines for informative speeches do you think also apply to class lectures? Which do not apply? If the instructor violated any guidelines you think apply to lecturing, how might the instructor remedy this?

Notes

1. John Naisbitt, qtd. in *Knowing Where to Look: The Ultimate Guide to Research*, Lois Horowitz, ed. (Cincinnati: Writer's Digest, 1984) 339.

2. Diane Ravitch and Chester E. Finn, Jr. *What Do Our 17-Year-Olds Know? A Report on the First National Assessment of History and Literature.* (New York: Harper, 1987).

3. Richard Saul Wurman, *Information Anxiety* (New York: Doubleday, 1989), cited in Stacey Okun, "Info Overload" *Self* October 1989: 164.

4. Bob Richmond, "Time Not on Side of Information Age" *San Antonio Light* 7 July 1990: B1.

5. William J. Banach, "Are You Too Busy to Think?" *Vital Speeches of the Day* 15 March 1991: 351.

strongly	**Oppose** moderately	slightly	**Neutral**	slightly	**Favor** moderately	strongly
− − −	− −	−	0	+	+ +	+ + +

Remember, when you speak to persuade you are speaking to listeners who may oppose, be indifferent to, or support your position. What strategy will you adopt to reach them? The information you gather and the assumptions you make about your audience before your speech determine the strategy you use as you develop your speech.

When preparing their persuasive speeches, many students make the mistake of thinking that they must change their audiences' opinions from "oppose" to "favor," or vice versa. Take the example of Chris, who argued in his persuasive speech that the National Collegiate Athletic Association should adopt a playoff system to determine the college football champion. After his speech, only one classmate who had opposed a playoff system said that Chris had persuaded him to support the proposal. Chris thought he had failed to persuade. Further class discussion, however, proved him wrong. A few listeners said they had changed their position from strong opposition to mild opposition. In addition, several who already supported the playoff system said that Chris' arguments had strengthened their opinion. And several listeners who were neutral before the speech found that Chris persuaded them to agree with him. As you can see, even though Chris persuaded only one audience member to move from "oppose" to "favor," his speech was quite successful. *Persuasion occurs any time you move a listener's opinion in the direction you advocate, even if that movement is slight.*

The most dramatic response you can request of your listeners is that they **change** a value, belief, attitude, or behavior. For example, if you know the audience supports asbestos removal programs and you urge them to oppose such programs, you are asking them to change an attitude. If they oppose putting rating labels on music albums, tapes, and CDs, you may argue for such a policy. If individuals eat foods laden with cholesterol, you may want to encourage them to alter their diets. Depending on your topic and your approach, you will try to move the audience from a negative to a positive position, or from a positive to a negative one.

You may, secondly, attempt to **instill** a value, an attitude, a belief, or a behavior. You instill when you address a particular problem of which your listeners are unaware or undecided. If you persuade them that a problem exists, you have instilled a belief. If you persuade hearers neutral on the subject to recycle aluminum cans, for example, you have instilled a behavior. One of our students was active in the animal welfare movement. Ginger chose as the specific purpose of her speech to persuade the audience to boycott products made from animal fur. In her speech she presented data and pictures that she claimed documented cruelty to animals because of the sale of fur products. Although some students found the argument unconvincing, a few listeners said they had not been aware of a problem and were more concerned about it after the speech. Ginger was successful in moving those individuals from a neutral to a supportive position. In short, she had instilled an attitude.

Finally, you may try to **intensify** values, beliefs, attitudes, or behaviors. In

Class Activity:
Write on the chalkboard a statement that a persuader might make in a speech— for example, "Social fraternities and sororities contribute significantly to a well-rounded college experience." Have students state their opinions regarding this statement using the continuum on this page. Record class opinions on the board. Use these results in discussing the three types of influence a persuader might seek. Discuss the types of appeals that might be most effective to the different segments of the audience. Given the numerical breakdown of this class, how would this group develop a speech supporting the above statement?

this case you must know that audience members already agree with your position or act as you wish. Your goal is to strengthen your listeners' positions and actions. For example, your audience may already believe that recycling is desirable and they may even do it occasionally. If your persuasive speech causes your listeners to recycle more frequently, you have intensified their behavior. You may even encourage them to persuade others to adopt an environmental ethic. Among those who heard Ginger's speech opposing the fur industry were those who already agreed with her position. A couple of those students said that the speech increased their concern. After class they asked Ginger how they could become involved in the animal welfare organization to which she belonged. When you change believers into advocates and advocates into activists, you have intensified their attitudes and behavior.

■ The Pyramid of Persuasion

You cannot know *how* to change your audience until you know *what* you want to change. As our definition of persuasion implies, you may target one of several changes in your listeners in your persuasive speech. You may seek to influence their values, beliefs, attitudes, behaviors, or a combination of these. Recall that we discussed these four concepts in Chapter 5 and illustrated them as a pyramid (see Figure 5.2, page 85). In that discussion we suggested that our behavior is typically shaped by our attitudes, which are based on our beliefs, which are validated by our values. Figure 15.1, the Pyramid of Persuasion, reproduces that model. We do this to emphasize that persuasive speaking is an audience-centered activity. To be a successful persuader, you must *connect* with your audience. Organizing values, beliefs, attitudes, and behaviors into a pyramid will help you visualize your speaker-listener connection as you work on your persuasive speech.

FIGURE 15.1   The Pyramid of Persuasion.

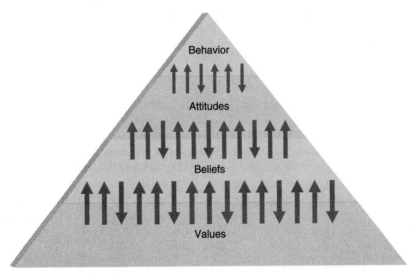

Class Activity:
A criticism of the pyramid model is that it is too linear and segmented. We recognize that the four elements co-mingle and interact with each other. Divide the class into groups and ask them to develop a more dynamic, interactive model. You might encourage them to consider a three-dimensional model or one with overlapping circles, for example.

This pyramid can help you formulate the specific purpose of your speech by identifying what you seek to change in your audience. Do you want to influence what they believe, how they feel, or how they act? More specifically, do you want to influence their values, beliefs, attitudes, or behaviors? You may wish to affect more than one of those, perhaps all of them. As you work on this with a specific topic in mind, you will see that it is difficult to change one without changing another. For example, if you convince an audience that a new convention center would help revive the economy of your city (belief), they may consequently favor its construction (attitude) and vote for the necessary bond issue to pay for it (behavior).

As the Pyramid of Persuasion suggests, our values and beliefs interact to affect our attitudes; attitudes, in turn, affect our behavior. The upward arrows in the model reflect this traditional view of how we produce change. A speaker trying to persuade you not to smoke might express the argument in the following way: You shouldn't smoke because it is a bad habit. It is a bad habit because it increases your chances of getting cancer. Getting cancer is bad because it imperils your health, and you should value your health. Notice that the speaker uses values the listener is presumed to possess in order to justify the behavior sought. The pyramid helps you visualize the process of persuasion and develop your arguments accordingly. As you prepare your persuasive speech, use this pyramid to help you develop your strategy.

When you develop your persuasive strategy, begin by clarifying why you feel strongly about an issue. "Providing reasons" for your feelings moves you to consider the first and second levels of the pyramid—in other words, your values and beliefs. The example of Tony, whose persuasive speech called for a boycott of a department store, will give you an idea of how you can use the pyramid for your persuasive speech.

Tony was bothered when his friend Mike told him about the hiring and promotion policies at the department store where Mike worked. Men and single women were given priority over married women whose husbands were employed. When a newspaper investigated and reported the charge, Tony decided to make this issue the topic of his persuasive speech. Using the pyramid structure, Tony sorted out his feelings and planned his persuasive strategy. He first asked himself, "Why do I think this topic is important to discuss?" His answer was that the store's policies were unfair. Knowing this, he worked through the various levels of the pyramid as follows:

Statement of values: I value equality and fairness.
Statement of belief: The local department store has discriminated against married women in its hiring and promotion decisions and policies.
Statement of attitude: No one should be denied employment on account of gender or marital status. I disapprove of the store's employment practices.
Statement of behavior sought: Therefore, I will not shop at this store, and I will urge others to join in the boycott.

Once he identified the values and beliefs underlying his and his listeners' attitudes and behaviors, Tony was able to generate the materials he needed to construct his persuasive appeal. Tony reminded his audience of their respect for the values of equality and fairness. He then quoted from a newspaper article

Class Activity:
Have students write a statement of a behavior they might advocate in a speech. Select several and, in class discussion or in small groups, have students work "down" the pyramid writing a statement of attitude supporting the behavior, then a statement of belief supporting the attitude, and finally a statement of value underpinning the belief.

to document that the local department store had discriminated against two married women. Arguing that an injustice had been committed, Tony declared that everyone should be incensed by the store's employment practices and he urged a boycott.

The examples we have shown so far suggest that our beliefs affect our attitudes and our attitudes affect our behavior. Looking at the Pyramid in Figure 15.1, you can see this upward movement. But persuasion and influence do not move in only one direction — up. If you turn back to page 48 in Chapter 3, you will remember the discussion of self-perception. Just as beliefs and attitudes influence behavior, so too can behavior influence beliefs and attitudes. As the arrows in the pyramid suggest, influence moves up and down. Our behavior may "filter down" and affect our attitudes. This principle is practiced in a variety of contexts, as illustrated in the following examples.

Business executives assume that dressing the part of a "company person" will help create a company attitude. Parents assume that children who are taught to share with others will develop a respect for others. Behavior modification clinics sometimes have clients speak publicly about their addiction in the belief that this public behavior will bolster the speaker's attitudes and beliefs. In each of these instances, the persuader targets a change in behavior and assumes that a change or reinforcement in beliefs and attitudes will follow. The philosophy behind this assumption is simple: People are often uncomfortable when what they *believe* and what they *do* are inconsistent. One way to resolve that discrepancy is to modify their beliefs.

Right about now you may be wondering how those examples relate to you as a public speaker. Certainly, you do not want to force your audience into a public declaration and demonstration of support at the conclusion of each persuasive speech. You can, however, use the basic principle to your advantage. Take a close look at the following example.

Class Activity:
Give the class copies of an editorial from your campus newspaper, a local paper, *The New York Times,* or one found in *Editorials on File.* Have the students identify beliefs, attitudes, and values implicit in the editorial, as well as any behaviors being advocated.

> Beverly worked as a volunteer for a community literacy project and decided to use this experience as the basis for her persuasive speech. She realized that many people consider illiterate adults to be either stupid or lazy. Beverly decided that the best way to get them to change their belief would be to concentrate on convincing them to volunteer a few hours to work at the adult literacy center or in a tutorial program. From her own experience Beverly knew that the volunteers would see how hard these adults worked to improve themselves. She believed that through this volunteer work her classmates might also begin to understand the social, economic, and language barriers that keep some of these adults from becoming literate in English. By securing a behavior (getting listeners to work with an adult literacy program), she would give her classmates a firsthand experience that, she hoped, would change their beliefs and attitudes in a more permanent way than any speech alone could accomplish.

You can also use behavior to effect change by pointing out an existing behavior that is inconsistent with an existing belief or attitude. Note how Mike used this strategy in his persuasive speech.

> Two weeks before his persuasive speech, Mike distributed to his classmates a short questionnaire regarding their beliefs and attitudes about a state lottery. Mike supported a state lottery, but found that almost half of his audience opposed it, believ-

ing that gambling is morally wrong. In his speech he pointed out that if any of his classmates had ever played bingo or had participated in an office "pool," their behavior was technically gambling and, like a state lottery, it was done on a voluntary basis. Some audience members' commitment to the behavior (gambling) was stronger than their commitment to their attitude (gambling is wrong). They adjusted their attitude to accommodate their behavior, and ended up thinking, "Some gambling is worse than others." While they might still oppose a state lottery on other grounds, Mike successfully weakened one argument against it. Other audience members had beliefs that were apparently stronger than their behavior. At the end of Mike's speech they still opposed the lottery and said they would quit the forms of betting he had pointed out.

As you see from these examples, your persuasive speech will target your audience's thoughts and actions. It's true that we sometimes act without fully considering the consequences of our actions; we also sometimes think about certain actions without ever actually acting. For this reason, your persuasive speech may aim to change your listeners' thoughts, actions, or both. Your goal determines the type of persuasive speech you will be giving, so let's consider your options in more detail.

■ Types of Persuasive Speeches —————————

Persuasive speeches are generally classified according to their objectives. An effective persuasive speech may change what people *believe*, what people *do*, or how people *feel*. Persuasive speeches, then, may be divided into speeches to *convince*, to *actuate*, and to *inspire*, and our discussion in this chapter centers on these three divisions. These divisions can help you determine your primary objective as you work on your speech, but keep in mind that persuasive speeches often include two or more objectives. For example, do you remember the example a few pages back of Ginger and her speech on animal rights? In order for Ginger to get her audience to boycott animal fur products (see page 309), she must convince them of the rightness of her cause. We usually act or become inspired after we are convinced.

SPEECHES TO CONVINCE

In a **speech to convince,** your objective is to affect your listeners' beliefs or attitudes. Each of the following specific purpose statements expresses a belief the speaker wants the audience to accept:

speech to convince: a persuasive speech designed to influence listeners' beliefs or attitudes.

To convince the audience that exit polls harm the balloting process.
To convince the audience that air travel is safer than ground travel.
To convince the audience that there is a constitutional right to privacy.
To convince the audience that Franklin Roosevelt was a better president than his cousin, Theodore Roosevelt.
To convince the audience that Robert E. Lee was a better general than Ulysses S. Grant.

In each of these speeches your purpose is to establish belief. While a speech to convince does not require listeners to act, action may be a natural outgrowth of their belief. So be aware that you might need an action step in your speech. For example, if you convince your audience that exit polling harms democracy but you suggest no remedy for the problem, you may leave your audience frustrated. In this case you can suggest a simple action step, such as urging your listeners to express their views to their elected representatives. When a speech includes this step, it becomes a speech to actuate.

SPEECHES TO ACTUATE

speech to actuate: a persuasive speech designed to influence listener behaviors.

A **speech to actuate** may include establishing beliefs, but it always calls for the audience to act. The specific purpose statements listed here illustrate calls for action:

To move, or actuate, the audience to donate nonperishable food to a local food bank.
To move the audience to investigate charities before making cash donations.
To move the audience to spay or neuter pet cats and dogs.
To move the audience to begin a low-impact aerobic workout program.
To move the audience to vote for a limitation on the term of service of city council members.

SPEECHES TO INSPIRE

speech to inspire: a persuasive speech designed to influence listener feelings.

A third type of persuasive speech is the **speech to inspire.** The speech to inspire attempts to change how listeners feel. Examples include commencement addresses, commemorative speeches, eulogies, and pep talks. Some specific purposes of speeches to inspire follow:

To inspire the audience to respect those who volunteer their time to help others.

A commencement address is an example of a speech to inspire.

To inspire the audience to honor the journalistic integrity of Edward R. Murrow.

To inspire the audience to appreciate those who made their education possible.

To inspire the audience to give their best efforts to all college courses they take.

The purposes of inspiration are usually noble and uplifting. These speeches typically have neither the detailed supporting material nor the complex arguments characteristic of speeches to convince and actuate. Adlai Stevenson's eulogy of Eleanor Roosevelt in Chapter 17 (see pages 370–72) is an example of a speech to inspire. In this class you will most likely be giving persuasive speeches to convince or to actuate.

Thus far we have seen the importance of audience involvement in the important process of persuasion. We have provided a definition of persuasion and discussed the various goals that persuasive speakers can have. In the following section we will discuss nine important principles that apply to all persuasive speeches.

■ Principles of Persuasion

Throughout this text we have emphasized that a speech is shaped by the speaker, topic, audience, and occasion. Each element affects the finished product. Because each element is variable, no person can give you a simple formula to make your persuasive speech effective. After all, no two people will give the same speech on the same topic to the same audience. Your strategy for each speech must be based on your unique situation and your own creativity. Nevertheless, we can give you a few principles, or guidelines, to study as you prepare your persuasive speech.

1. Persuasion is more likely if goals are limited rather than global.
2. Persuasion is more permanent if achieved incrementally.
3. Persuasion is more likely if the audience lacks information on the topic.
4. Persuasion is related to how important the audience considers the topic.
5. Persuasion is more likely if the audience is self-motivated in the direction of the message.
6. Persuasion is more likely if the speaker's message is consistent with listeners' values, beliefs, attitudes, and behaviors.
7. Persuasion is more likely if arguments are placed appropriately.
8. Persuasion is more likely if the source is credible.
9. Persuasion is more likely if the speaker establishes common ground with the audience.

**KEY POINTS
Principles
of Persuasion**

Persuasion is More Likely if Goals are Limited Rather than Global. A common mistake many beginning speakers make is to seek *dramatic* change in the values, beliefs, attitudes, and behaviors of their listeners. In our experience it is the rare speaker who can accomplish this, particularly if you seek change on highly emotional and controversial issues such as abortion, gun control, capital punishment, religion, or politics. Keep in mind that the more firmly your audience is anchored to a position, the less likely you are to change their attitudes. It is unrealistic for you to expect dramatic change in a person's beliefs and values in a one-shot, five- to ten-minute speech. Instant conversions occur, but they are rare. Rather than try to convince your audience to support (or oppose) the death penalty, try convincing them of a smaller aspect of the topic: that capital punishment deters crime (or does not), for example. Once a listener accepts that belief, you or another speaker can build on it and focus on a successive objective: support for (or opposition to) the death penalty.

Which specific purpose statement in the following pairs is the more limited and reasonable goal?

Specific purpose: To persuade the audience to oppose the use of all animals in laboratory tests, *or*
Specific purpose: To persuade the audience to oppose the use of animals in laboratory tests of cosmetics and cleansers.
Specific purpose: To persuade the audience that violence on television promotes aggression in viewers, *or*
Specific purpose: To persuade the audience that violence in television programs aimed at children promotes aggression in children.
Specific purpose: To persuade the audience that U.S. weapons systems are worth the investment, *or*
Specific purpose: To persuade the audience that U.S. land-based missile systems are worth the investment.

In each case, the second statement is more limited. To be successful as a persuasive speaker, you must view persuasion as a process of moving a listener incrementally through a range of positions; your speech may be only one part of this process. Select a realistic goal and channel your efforts toward achieving it.

Persuasion is More Permanent if Achieved Incrementally. This principle builds on the previous one. To be effective and long-lasting, persuasion should occur incrementally, or one step at a time. This principle becomes more important if your audience is likely to hear counterarguments to your argument. In any speech, you speak for a fixed amount of time. The greater the number of points you must prove, the less time you have to support and explain each. Because you must move through several steps, your limited time may force you to abbreviate your support of some of these steps. When your listeners hear another speaker attack one of those steps later, they may lack sufficient evidence to counter those attacks; hence, what you accomplished may be only temporary. Your goal should be to "immunize" your listeners to possible counterarguments. The stronger your arguments, the greater the likelihood that you will bring about enduring change in the opinions of your audience. If you know your audience has been exposed to counterarguments, you may need to address those arguments before introducing your own.

Persuasion is More Likely if the Audience Lacks Information on the Topic. In the absence of information, a single fact can be compelling. The more information your listeners possess about an issue, the less likely you are to alter their perception. Sandra used this principle in a speech designed to persuade her audience that many medical tests give false or inaccurate results. She cited statistics from the American College of Obstetricians and Gynecologists that the Pap smear fails to detect cervical cancer as much as 40 percent of the time. She went on to say that "according to a report of the National Cholesterol Education Program, almost 50 percent of cholesterol screenings are wrong by 5 percent or more from their correct values."[3] Sandra gave her audience information that was new and surprising, and it had great persuasive impact. This principle, of course, has significant ethical implications. Ethical speakers will not exploit their listeners' lack of knowledge to advance positions they know are not logically supported.

Persuasion is Related to How Important the Audience Considers the Topic. Ken, Andrea, and Brad gave their persuasive speeches on the same day. Ken's purpose was to persuade the audience to support the school's newly formed lacrosse team. He urged his listeners to show their support by attending the next home game. Andrea's topic concerned the increasing number of homeless adults and children in the city. She told the class about Project Hope, sponsored by the Student Government Association, and asked everyone to donate either a can of food or a dollar at designated collection centers in campus dining halls or in the Student Center. Finally, Brad advocated legalization of marijuana, citing the drug's medical and economic potential. Which speaker do you think had the most difficult challenge? In answering this question you must consider the audience. A significant factor is how important the audience considers the topic.

The importance of a topic can *increase* the likelihood of persuasion. Audience members in the above example probably agreed with both Ken and Andrea, and both may have been successful persuaders. Listeners who viewed combatting hunger as a more important goal than supporting the lacrosse team were probably more persuaded by Andrea and may have contributed to Project Hope.

Just as the importance of a topic can work for you as a persuasive speaker, it can also work against you and *decrease* the likelihood of persuasion. It is surely easier, for example, for someone to persuade you to change brands of toothpaste than to change your religion. The reason is simple: Your religion is more important to you. Brad probably had a tougher time persuading his listeners than did either Ken or Andrea. Legalizing marijuana probably ran counter to some deeply held audience opinions, and the intensity of those beliefs and values may have made them more resistant to Brad's persuasive appeals. The importance of an issue will vary according to each audience member, and you need to take this into account as you prepare your persuasive appeal.

Persuasion is More Likely if the Audience is Self-Motivated in the Direction of the Message. People change their values, beliefs, attitudes, and behaviors because they are motivated to do so. To be an effective persuader, you must discover what motivates your listeners. This requires an understanding of their needs and desires. How can you do this? You can enhance your persuasive appeal by following three steps. First, identify as many of the needs and desires

Cross-Reference:
Refer students back to the discussion of Maslow's theory of motivation in Chapter 5.

Teaching Strategy:
To help your students prepare for their persuasive speeches, ask them to brainstorm a list of needs and desires students in your class probably possess. Write these on the chalkboard as the class names them. Have the class decide on those that are strongly felt needs and desires. Have students write this list down and suggest that they refer to it as they develop their persuasive speeches.

Related Reading:
For a discussion of consistency theories, see: Trenholm, Sarah. "Creating Contradiction: Cognitive Consistency." *Persuasion and Social Influence.* Englewood Cliffs, NJ: Prentice, 1989: 93-114.

of your listeners as possible. Second, review your list and select those that your speech satisfies. Third, as you prepare your speech explain how the action you advocate fulfills audience needs. If you discover that your speech does not fulfill the needs or desires of your listeners, then you probably have failed to connect with these listeners. They may receive your speech with interest, but your audience probably will not exercise the sustained concern necessary to retain and act on your message. What you intended as a persuasive speech may in fact be received as informative.

Persuasion is More Likely if the Speaker's Message is Consistent with Listeners' Values, Beliefs, Attitudes, and Behaviors. We have discussed the importance of consistency elsewhere in this text, but we think it important enough to mention here. People want to establish consistency in their lives. We expect coherence between our beliefs and actions, for example. In fact, we will call someone a hypocrite who professes one set of values but acts according to another. Your ability to persuade is thus enhanced if you request an action that is consistent with your audience's values.

Use this principle of consistency in constructing your persuasive appeal. For example, we have had students who persuaded their classroom audience to oppose the use of animals in non-medical product testing. They first identified the beliefs that would cause a person to challenge such tests—for example, product testing harms animals and is unnecessary. Next they showed their audience that they share these beliefs. Once they accomplished that, the speakers then asked their listeners to act in accordance with their beliefs and boycott companies that continue to test cosmetics on animals, since continuing to buy such products would be inconsistent with their beliefs.

Persuasion is More Likely if Arguments are Placed Appropriately. Once you have determined the key arguments in your speech, you must decide their order. To do that, you must know which of your arguments is the strongest. Assume for a moment that your persuasive speech argues against mandatory drug testing in the workplace. Assume too that you are using problem-solution organization. Your arguments supporting the first point in your speech body might be as follows:

    I. Mandatory drug testing in the workplace poses problems.
        A. Mandatory drug testing violates the worker's right to privacy.
        B. Mandatory drug testing would be prohibitively expensive.
        C. Drug tests are not always accurate.

One of these three arguments will likely be stronger than the other two. You may have more evidence on one; you may have more recent evidence on it; or you may feel that one argument will be more compelling than the other two for your particular audience. Assume that you decide point B is your strongest. Where should you place it?

Two theories of argument placement are the primacy and recency theories. **Primacy** theorists recommend that you put your strongest argument first in the body of your speech to establish a strong first impression. Because you are most likely to win over your listeners with your strongest argument, this theory suggests that you should win your listeners to your side as early as possible. Primacy theorists would tell you to make your strongest argument point A.

Recency theorists, on the other hand, believe that you should present your strongest argument last, thus leaving your listeners with your best argument. They would have you make your strongest argument point C. How do you as a persuasive speaker resolve this conflict?

Though the primacy and recency theorists argue whether the first or last position is stronger, they generally agree that the middle position is weaker than either. Therefore, do not place your strongest argument in the middle position. When you sandwich a strong argument between weaker ones, you reduce its impact.

Persuasion is More Likely if the Source is Credible. We are persuaded by those whom we respect and trust. We often defer to their opinions because we have neither the time nor the expertise to investigate and evaluate the issue under discussion. We cannot, for example, directly observe the relationship between capital punishment and the deterrence of crime, so we trust the opinions of those who have researched that relationship. We choose to see a movie because critics we respect praise the film. Trusted experts in a field are credible sources for us.

How do you use this principle as you prepare your persuasive speech? As you research your topic you will, no doubt, find a variety of sources making similar statements. How do you decide which sources to include in your speech? Your decision should be based, of course, on the qualifications of the source, but consider also how your audience will view the source. For example, whom would your audience probably view as the most credible source discussing the rights of defendants: a college law professor, a court judge, a defense attorney, a police officer, or a public opinion poll? The answer may vary according to the specific audience. For example, a college law professor might have the highest credibility with college students. You will want to select a source appropriate to your audience.

Persuasion is More Likely if the Speaker Establishes Common Ground with the Audience. Which source advising you to "Take Smith for public speaking; she's a great teacher" would you find more persuasive: a friend who is also a college student or a counselor at your school? If you are typical, your answer is "my friend," particularly if that friend has already taken a public speaking class with Professor Smith. The counselor might have taken Smith's public speaking class, might know Smith personally, or might have heard many complimentary remarks about Smith from her former students. But the counselor might also just be trying to fill a class that other students are avoiding.

As this example shows, you are probably more easily persuaded by people similar to you than by those who are different. Your friends, for example, are credible sources, not because they possess special expertise, but because they share your values and interests. We all reason that individuals with backgrounds like ours will view situations and problems as we would. Furthermore, we believe that people who share our beliefs will investigate an issue and arrive at a judgment in the same manner we would if we had the time and the opportunity.

One way to increase your persuasion, then, is to identify with your listeners. Sonja, a weekend news anchor for a local television station, was asked to speak to a college television production class on employment opportunities in television. Notice how Sonja used the strategy of identification in her introduction as she focused on experiences she shared with her listeners.

> Seven years ago a timid freshman girl sat in a college classroom much like this. Just like you, she was taking a TV production class. And like some of you, I suspect, she dreamed of being in front of a camera someday, sitting at an anchor desk, reporting the news to thousands of families who would let her come into their homes through the magic of television.
>
> There was little reason to predict that this girl would achieve her dreams. In many ways she was rather ordinary. She didn't come from a wealthy family. She didn't have any connections that would get her a job in broadcasting. She was a B student who worked part-time in the university food service to help pay for her education. But she had a goal and was determined to attain it. And then one day, it happened. An instructor announced that a local TV station had an opening for a student intern. The instructor said the internship would involve long hours, menial work, and no pay. Hardly the opportunity of a lifetime! Nevertheless, after class she approached the instructor, uncertain of what she was getting into. With her instructor's help she applied for and received the internship. It is because of that decision that I am now the weekend anchor of the city's largest television station.

The rest of Sonja's speech focused on the importance of student internships in learning about the reality of the broadcast media and making contacts for future references and employment. Her opening comments made Sonja a more believable speaker by bridging the gap between her and her listeners. Sonja's suggestions had more impact on her audience because she had established common ground with them.

As this final principle demonstrates, who you are may be as persuasive as what you say. Even before you complete your research or organize and practice your speech, you may have one powerful, persuasive instrument already working for you: your reputation with your listeners. In the final section of this chapter, we discuss the persuasive potential of speaker credibility and the speaker's emotional appeals.

■ Persuasive Speaking Strategies ─────────────

We can find evidence as far back as the era of Ancient Greece of people giving advice on how to be an effective persuasive speaker. Aristotle, for example, devoted much space in his classic work *The Rhetoric* to the subject. Aristotle discussed three modes of persuasion speakers have at their disposal: *ethos, logos,* and *pathos.*[4] These three modes remain an important foundation today for our understanding of persuasive speaking. What do these terms mean and how can they help you as you prepare a persuasive speech?

ethos: speaker credibility.

logos: logical appeal.

pathos: emotional appeal.

Ethos, or speaker credibility, derives from the character and reputation of the speaker. *Logos,* or logical appeal, relies on the form and substance of an argument. *Pathos,* or emotional appeal, taps the values and feelings of the audience. In Chapter 16, we will discuss *logos* in greater detail. We will introduce you to the elements of an argument, describe five types of arguments you can use in your speaking, and define several categories of faulty reasoning you should avoid. Below we discuss the two other modes of persuasion—*ethos* and *pathos*—and offer several suggestions to assist you in building them into your persuasive speech.

ESTABLISHING SPEAKER CREDIBILITY

As a speaker, your first available source of persuasion is your own credibility, or *ethos*. **Credibility** is simply your reputation, and it helps determine how your listeners evaluate what you say. The higher your perceived credibility, the more likely the audience is to believe you.

Speaker credibility is fluid, varying according to your listeners. You possess only the credibility your listeners grant you. If you pepper your speaking with humor, for example, some listeners may see you as lively and interesting while others may think you frivolous. You probably have as many different images as you have audience members.

Credibility also varies according to time. Your credibility can be divided chronologically into the time before, during, and after your speech. These chronological divisions are sometimes referred to as initial, derived, and terminal credibility.[5] Your image or reputation prior to speaking comprises your **initial credibility,** sometimes called **antecedent *ethos.*** The more the audience knows about you, the more rigid your image.

But what if your listeners do not know you personally? Even in this case, you still bring varying images to the speaking occasion. For example, if you are a spokesperson for an organization, you may assume the image of that organization in the minds of your audience. Think about how you would describe the kind of person who belongs to the Democratic Party, the Republican Party, the Sierra Club, or the National Rifle Association. An image probably comes to your mind quite easily. If a representative from one of those associations were to speak to you, you would make certain assumptions about the individual based on what you know about that organization. Just as you do with strangers, you form impressions of your classmates based on what they say in class, how they dress, whether they arrive at class on time, their age and appearance, and any organization to which they belong. They have also formed impressions of you, of course. Such images constitute your initial credibility.

Derived credibility is the image the audience develops of you as you speak. The moment you enter the presence of your listeners, you provide stimuli from which the audience can evaluate you. As you begin your speech, the number of stimuli multiplies quickly. If you begin your speech with an offensive joke, listeners' images of you will become more negative. However, when you appeal to your listeners' values and present reasoned arguments to advance your position, you enhance your image. The credibility you derive during your presentation is a function of many factors. Your information, of course, helps your audience judge your credibility. Your audience will also judge your nonverbal behaviors (see Chapter 12), such as gestures, posture, eye contact, and appearance, to name a few. If you convey confidence, authority, and a genuine concern for your listeners, you will enhance your credibility.

Terminal credibility is the image the audience has of you after your speech. Even this credibility is subject to change. The listener may be caught up in the excitement and emotion of your speech and end up with an elevated

credibility: the degree to which listeners believe a speaker.

Teaching Strategy: Have students brainstorm names of well-known individuals whose credibility they would say has changed over time, either positively or negatively.

initial credibility or **antecedent ethos:** a speaker's image or reputation before speaking to a particular audience.

Teaching Strategy: Write the name of some groups on the board. Ask the class to name some words and phrases that in their opinion describe those groups. List those words under the appropriate group's name. Now have the class look at their descriptions of these groups. What information does that provide a speaker? What do these lists reveal about the audiences? What do the lists reveal about students in this class?

derived credibility: the image listeners develop of a speaker as he or she speaks.

terminal credibility: the image listeners develop of a speaker by the end of a speech and for a period of time after it.

opinion of you. As time passes, that evaluation may moderate. As you can see, the process of generating and maintaining credibility is ongoing. In this class, for example, your credibility at the conclusion of one speech will naturally shape your initial credibility for your next speech.

Numerous studies demonstrate that a speaker with high credibility is more successful in persuading others than a speaker with low credibility. Clearly, you need to pay careful attention to your credibility at each stage in order to deliver a successful persuasive speech. How do you go about enhancing your image? Communication theorists agree that speakers who come across as competent, trustworthy, and dynamic are viewed as credible speakers.[6] If your audience believes you possess competence, trustworthiness, and dynamism, you will probably be effective in persuading them.

competence: listeners' views of a speaker's qualifications to speak on a particular topic.

Competence. If people believe you are knowledgeable on your topic, they will be more likely to believe what you say. In this class you are among peers, and so your audience probably considers you as a fellow student rather than an expert on your chosen topic. Your task, then, is to establish an image of **competence** on your subject. Several strategies will help you. We discuss four below.

KEY POINTS
Guidelines for Enhancing Your Image of Competence

1. Know your subject.
2. Document your ideas.
3. Cite your sources.
4. Acknowledge personal involvement.

First, the obvious: **Know your subject.** From which of these people would you be more likely to buy a new video disc player: a salesperson who can answer all your questions about the product, or someone who doesn't know the answers and doesn't care to find out? The answer is obvious, isn't it? In a persuasive speaking situation, you as speaker are a salesperson and your audience members are consumers. To speak ethically, you must be well informed about your subject. You will discover that the more you read and listen, the easier it is to construct a message that is both credible and compelling.

Not only should you know your specific topic, you should also understand how it interacts with related topics. Just as the salesperson must know the video disc player and how it will operate with other equipment you own, you should comprehend both the *content* and the *context* of your persuasive message. Persuading your classmates to begin recycling low-density plastics does you little good if your area has no processing plant for LDPs and thus recyclers will not accept them. In addition, you will feel foolish if an audience member asks after your speech, "Did you know that no recycling center will accept those plastics?" This is where your research helps you by enhancing your expertise on your subject. A well-researched speech increases persuasion by contributing to your image as a well-informed individual. In a public speaking course such as this, the image building you do is cumulative. Thorough, quality research not only enhances your credibility on the immediate topic, but also generates positive initial credibility for your next appearance before the same group.

Second, you can bolster your image of competence if you **document your ideas.** Unsupported ideas are mere assertions. Though your listeners don't expect you to be an expert on your topic, they need assurance that what you say is corroborated by facts or by experts. Providing documentation supports your statements and increases your believability.

A third strategy for enhancing your credibility is to **cite your sources.** Simply presenting the data upon which your conclusions are based is insufficient. Remember, your audience is not going to have the opportunity to read your bibliography. You need to tell your listeners the sources of your information. Citing sources enhances the credibility of your ideas by demonstrating that experts support your position. Of course, it also requires that your sources be of good quality. We remember one student who cited *Hustler* magazine as the source for his contention that soft-core pornography does not exploit women, and thereby destroyed his credibility.

Fourth, **acknowledge any personal involvement** or experience with your subject. Listeners will probably assume that you have an edge in understanding color blindness if you let them know you are color-blind. They will probably make the same positive assumption if you are diabetic and speaking on diabetes, or if you are a child of an alcoholic and are speaking on codependency. If you have worked with terminally ill patients and are speaking on a related topic, mentioning your experience will add authority to your ideas.

Trustworthiness. A second criterion of speaker credibility is **trustworthiness,** and it should tell us two things about you. First, we should trust you as an individual: You are *honest* in what you say. Second, we should trust you with your topic: You are *unbiased* in what you say. A speaker can demonstrate trustworthiness in two simple, practical ways.

1. Establish common ground with your audience. If listeners know that you understand their values, experiences, and aspirations, they will be more receptive to your arguments. When you let them know you identify with those values, experiences, and aspirations, you increase your persuasiveness.

2. Demonstrate your objectivity in approaching the topic. The information and sources you include in your speech should demonstrate thorough, unbiased research. One student gave his speech on cigarette smoking, arguing that its harmful effects were greatly exaggerated. In presenting his arguments, he relied on studies conducted by the tobacco industry. Few in the audience were persuaded by the speaker. The speaker undermined his image of trustworthiness because he limited his research to sources the audience considered biased on the topic, sources that had a financial interest in supporting one side of the issue.

Dynamism. A third element of credibility is **dynamism.** Competence and trustworthiness are obviously legitimate criteria used to determine speaker credibility, but you may wonder why we include personal dynamism on this list. Dynamism is more closely associated with delivery than with content. We enjoy listening to speakers who are energetic, vigorous, exciting, inspiring, spirited, and stimulating. But should speakers whose delivery is static, timid, and unexciting be considered less credible than their more exuberant counterparts? Perhaps not, and the ethical listener will focus more on the content than on the form of the message. Yet you should know that studies continue to document

Discussion Prompt: What special experience, involvement, or knowledge do your students have that would give them heightened credibility if they revealed it in a persuasive speech?

trustworthiness: listeners' views of a speaker's honesty.

dynamism: a speaker's confidence, energy, and enthusiasm for communicating.

dynamism as an element of speaker credibility, and it would be prudent for you to develop this attribute.

Dynamism contributes to persuasion because it conveys both confidence and concern. You show **confidence** largely through your speech delivery. If you appear tentative or unsure of yourself, the audience is not assured. To the extent that you can strengthen your verbal, vocal, and physical delivery, you can enhance your image of confidence and, hence, your credibility. No one expects you to give a professional-level performance. Remember that mastering public speaking is a process that involves study and practice. If you take yourself and your speech seriously, you will do fine.

Dynamism also demonstrates a **concern** for the audience and a desire to communicate with them. If your delivery seems flippant, distracted, or detached from the audience, your listeners will assume that you are not concerned about the topic or about them. On the other hand, conveying enthusiasm for your topic and your listeners communicates a strong positive message.

As a speaker, then, you should present a well-researched and documented message and communicate it in an honest and unbiased manner. Your verbal, vocal, and physical delivery should show you to be a fluent, forceful, and friendly individual who takes seriously the issues you address. If you are perceived to be competent, trustworthy, and dynamic, you will have high source credibility and, hence, be an effective persuader.

ENHANCING EMOTIONAL APPEALS

As we have indicated earlier, *pathos* is the appeal to emotions. Among the emotions speakers may arouse are your anger, envy, fear, hate, jealousy, joy, love, or pride. When they then use these feelings to try to get you to believe something or act in a particular way, they are using emotional appeals.

Many of the feelings listed above seem negative—anger, fear, hate, and jealousy, for example. Consequently, you may consider emotional appeals as unacceptable or inferior types of proof. Perhaps you have even heard someone say, "Don't be so emotional; use your head!" It is certainly possible to be emotional and illogical, but keep in mind that it is also possible to be both emotional and logical. Is it wrong, for example, to be angered by child abuse, to hate racism, or to fear chemical warfare? We don't think so. The strongest arguments combine reason with passion. *Logos* and *pathos* should not conflict but complement each other.

Class Activity:
Have students identify and evaluate some of the emotional appeals in Appendix C speeches by William Fort, Shannon Dyer, and Mario Cuomo.

In his persuasive speech Chris examined problems caused by inadequate vaccination. He presented data gathered by the Centers for Disease Control showing that measles, rubella, tetanus, mumps, influenza, and pneumonia cause much unnecessary suffering. After discussing each disease, Chris concluded:

> All told, every year diseases that we can prevent kill an estimated 70,000 people, take over 20 billion dollars worth of lost productivity and so-called free medical benefits from our pockets as taxpayers, and cause pain and suffering to hundreds of thousands of others.[7]

In this speech Chris' specific purpose was to advocate a nationwide vaccination campaign to save lives, reduce suffering, and conserve tax dollars. Did Chris

Highly visible public figures bring to speaking situations strong initial credibility, which may be favorable, neutral, or unfavorable.

construct a logical argument? Yes. He used statistics from a reliable source and explained how they supported his position. Did Chris construct an emotional argument? Again, yes. He appealed to his listeners' fear of death and their compassion toward others. *Logos* and *pathos* coalesced to form a compelling argument.

As you can see, when properly constructed, emotional appeals make your listeners active participants in the development of your message. By tapping their *feelings*, you involve them psychologically and physiologically. The following four guidelines will help you develop and enhance the *pathos* of your persuasive speech.

1. Tap audience values.
2. Use vivid examples.
3. Use emotive language.
4. Use effective delivery.

KEY POINTS
Guidelines
for Enhancing
Emotional Appeals

Teaching Strategy:
Have students brainstorm
(individually, in groups, or
as a class) a list of values
they think the majority of
the class holds. You might
use the PERSIA framework
(*political, economic, religious, social, intellectual,*
and *artistic*) to get your students thinking about a broad
range of values. Refer to this
list as you discuss how to develop an audience-centered
persuasive speech.

Practice Speaking:
Have students bring to class
a picture from a magazine,
newspaper, or some other
printed source. Have them
construct and present an argument that uses the picture
to tap their listener's emotions.

The first, and probably most important, guideline for developing emotional appeals is to **tap audience values.** As we have mentioned repeatedly in this chapter and elsewhere in this text, you must conduct careful audience analysis before you can deliver an effective speech. Demonstrate in your speech how your audience's values support your position. You can use some of the strategies we discussed in Chapter 5, Analyzing Your Audience, when we presented Maslow's hierarchy and explained how you can relate your topic to audience needs (see pages 81–84). The more attached listeners are to the values a speaker promotes, the more emotional is that speaker's appeal. Part of your responsibility as a speaker is to make that connection evident to your listeners.

A second strategy for enhancing emotional appeals is to **use vivid, emotionally toned examples.** The example may not be sufficient to prove your point, but it should illustrate the concept and generate a strong audience feeling. Kellie used this strategy in her speech against marital rape exemptions in state laws. She told of a woman she had counseled:

. . . Bill began to take his frustrations out on Jane, by beating her violently and demanding sex on call. One time, Jane refused his demands; Bill threw her to the bed with a gun to her head and tied her up. When she began to scream and fight, he wrapped the phone cord around and around her neck to keep her quiet; she almost couldn't breathe. While she lay there, helpless, with the gun on the nightstand, he repeatedly raped and sodomized her. When he was finished he just left her there. Sometime later, she got herself loose. She had bruises on her wrists, ankles, throat, inner thighs, breasts, and vaginal areas.[8]

Who can respond to Jane's situation without feeling compassion or anger?

Visual and audio aids can also enhance a speaker's *pathos.* Duncan selected as the specific purpose of his speech to persuade the audience to become members of Amnesty International. He had joined the organization because he felt that as an individual, he could do little to help end torture and executions of prisoners of conscience throughout the world. As part of a concerted world-wide effort, however, he saw the opportunity to further social and political justice. His speech included ample testimony of persecution coupled with statistical estimates of the extent of the problem. Duncan wanted to infuse his speech with convincing emotional appeals to support the data. After presenting the facts, he paused and spoke these words to his listeners: "In the last four minutes you've heard about the anguish, the pain, the suffering, and the persecution experienced by thousands of people, simply because they want to be free and follow their consciences. I want you not only to *hear* of their plight, but also to *see* it." Duncan pushed the remote control button of a slide projector and proceeded to show five slides of people brutalized by their own governments. He did not speak, but simply showed each slide for ten seconds. After the last slide, he spoke again: "They say a picture is worth a thousand words. Well, these pictures speak volumes of man's inhumanity to man. But these pictures should also speak to *our consciences.* Can we stand back, detached, and do nothing, knowing what fate befalls these individuals?" Duncan then told the audience how they could become involved in Amnesty International and begin to make a difference. Duncan's speech had a powerful effect because he touched his audience's emotions with vivid examples.

Duncan also employed *pathos* by using a third technique: he **used emotive language,** such as "the anguish, the pain, the suffering, and the persecution. . . ." In Chapter 11, Wording Your Speech, we discussed the power of words. Nowhere can words be more powerful than when they work to generate emotional appeals. Take the example of Theresa, who argued for derecognition of fraternities and sororities, citing as one reason the harms of hazing. Notice in the following passage how Theresa first presents statistics to document the problem, and then uses emotive language to intensify her argument.

> According to the November 1988 issue of the *Washington Monthly,* in the past ten years alone, hazing incidents have killed about fifty college students and injured innumerable others. They've been beaten, branded, burned, buried, stabbed, shot, drowned, frozen, and poisoned. In fact, electric cattle prods, two-handled paddles, Jew baiting, gay bashing, alcohol poisoning, group grope encounters, and black-face slave auctions, have all made national headlines as a result of what are politely called "fraternity mishaps."[9]

Beaten, branded, burned, buried, stabbed, shot, drowned, frozen, and poisoned are all strong, emotion-producing words. Whether you agree with her argument or not, you were probably moved by her language.

As a final method, you can **use effective delivery** to enhance emotional appeals. As we discussed in Chapter 12, Delivering Your Speech, when a speaker's verbal and nonverbal messages conflict, we tend to trust the nonverbal message. For that reason, speakers who show little physical and vocal involvement with their speeches usually come across as uninterested or even insincere. By displaying emotion yourself you can sometimes generate audience emotion.

Before leaving the subject of *pathos*, a few parting comments are in order. Emotional appeals are powerful persuasive tools. They can stir passions, intensify beliefs, and impel actions. Speakers have an ethical responsibility to use emotional appeals wisely. Emotional appeals are never in order if the speaker disregards the logical basis of the speech. Emotion and logic are best used in concert with each other.

It is important to remember that these three modes of persuasion — *ethos, logos,* and *pathos* — all work to enhance your persuasive appeal. The best persuasive speeches combine all three. Effective persuaders are credible, present logically constructed and supported arguments, and tap the values of their listeners.

Summary ———————————————————————————————

Persuasion is a dynamic activity requiring the participation of a speaker, a message, and at least one listener. Politicians, educators, business people, and religious leaders flood us with persuasive appeals daily. In order to benefit from sound persuasion, and avoid the pitfalls of flawed or unethical persuasion, speakers and listeners must understand what persuasion involves.

Persuasion is the process of influencing another person's values, beliefs, attitudes, or behaviors. Influencing can mean changing attitudes or actions, instilling new beliefs, or simply intensifying people's feelings about their existing beliefs or behaviors. The Pyramid of Persuasion helps you determine the specific purpose of your speech and generate arguments you can use to achieve that purpose. A persuasive speech aimed at changing beliefs and attitudes, but not requesting any overt behavior of listeners, is called a *speech to convince*. A *speech to actuate* seeks to change behaviors. A *speech to inspire* encourages positive changes in the way listeners feel about their beliefs or actions.

Whether you target values, beliefs, attitudes, behaviors, or a combination, your job as an effective persuader will be easier if you keep in mind nine principles of persuasion. First, you are likelier to persuade if you seek modest and limited, rather than dramatic, changes in audience attitudes and behaviors. Second, persuasion is more lasting if achieved step by step, or incrementally. Third, the audience is more easily persuaded on topics they do not know well. Fourth, persuasion depends upon how important the audience considers the topic. Fifth, persuasion is obviously easier when the audience is already self-motivated in the direction of the message. Sixth, an audience is more easily persuaded if they sense some inconsistency in their values, beliefs, attitudes, and behaviors. Seventh, persuasion is more likely if the speaker's arguments are appropriately placed within the speech. Eighth, persuasion is more likely if the audience considers the speaker's sources credible. Ninth, and finally, persuasion is more likely if the speaker establishes common ground with the audience.

Three modes of persuasion, discussed at least as early as the time of Aristotle, are *ethos*, *logos*, and *pathos*. *Ethos*, the first source of persuasion available to speakers, is their credibil-ity or believability. *Logos* is a logical appeal based on the form and substance of the message. It appeals to the listener's intellect and reasoning. *Pathos*, an emotional appeal, relies on the audience's feelings for its persuasive impact.

Some speakers have *initial* or *antecedent credibility* with a particular audience, based on the listeners' prior knowledge of the speaker. An unknown speaker may take on the credibility of the organization he or she represents. All speakers have *derived credibility*, developed from the ideas they present in their speech and their speech delivery, and *terminal credibility*, based on the audience's evaluation of speaker and message after the speech.

Competence, trustworthiness, and dynamism are three components of a speaker's credibility. To build images of competence, speakers should know their speech subjects, document their ideas, cite their sources, and mention any special experience they have with their topics. To demonstrate trustworthiness, speakers should establish common ground with their audiences and show evidence of thorough, unbiased research. Since listeners associate dynamism with the energy, vigor, and friendliness of a speaker's delivery, developing a dynamic image requires showing confidence about speaking and concern for the well-being of the audience.

Pathos, or emotional appeal, is the final persuasive strategy discussed in this chapter. To develop powerful emotional appeals a speaker should tap audience values; use vivid, emotionally toned examples; use emotive language; and display emotion in the physical and vocal delivery of the speech. *Pathos* should complement rather than replace the logical structure of a speech.

1. Select three print or broadcast advertisements for the same kind of product (soft drinks, insurance, automobiles, and so on). Discuss the persuasive appeals of each ad. Which one do you think is the most effective? Why? Could any of these strategies of persuasion be incorporated in a speech? Provide some examples.
2. Select a topic and write a specific purpose statement that seeks dramatic change in the behavior or attitude of your audience. Divide the change you seek into several incremental steps. Discuss what you would need to prove to achieve each step. Could any of these steps be the basis for a speech by itself?
3. Listen to a speaker on C-SPAN, *The MacNeil/Lehrer News Hour, Nightline,* a news interview show, or some other broadcast. Keep a chronology of the speaker's initial, derived, and terminal credibility. What changes occurred in your impression of the speaker? What accounted for those changes? What might the speaker have done to improve his or her credibility?

Notes

1. "The 30-Second President," narr. Bill Moyers, *A Walk Through the 20th Century*, exec. ed. Bill Moyers, PBS, 1984.

2. Charles U. Larson, *Persuasion: Reception and Responsibility*, 5th ed. (Belmont, CA: Wadsworth, 1989) 10.

3. Linda J. Heller, "How Accurate Are Medical Tests?" *Parade* 3 Feb. 1991: 4.

4. *The Rhetoric of Aristotle*, trans. Lane Cooper (New York: Appleton, 1960) 8.

5. James C. McCroskey, *An Introduction to Rhetorical Communication*, 2nd ed. (Englewood Cliffs, NJ: Prentice, 1972) 63–64.

6. In his book *An Introduction to Rhetorical Communication*, p. 65, McCroskey credits D.K. Berlo and J.B. Lemert with labeling those three dimensions of credibility in "A Factor Analytic Study of the Dimensions of Source Credibility," a paper presented at the 1961 convention of the Speech Association of America, New York.

7. Chris Thomas, "Better Safe Than Sorry," *Winning Orations, 1989* (Mankato, MN: Interstate Oratorical Association, 1989) 61.

8. Kellie Rider, "Happily Ever After?" *Winning Orations, 1990* (Mankato, MN: Interstate Oratorical Association, 1990) 95.

9. Theresa McGuinness, "Greeks in Crisis," *Winning Orations, 1990* (Mankato, MN: Interstate Oratorical Association, 1990) 73–74.

The Structure of Persuasion

16

Structuring Arguments
Steps of an Argument
Types of Arguments
Argument by Example
Argument by Analogy
Argument by Cause
Argument by Deduction
Argument by Authority
Fallacies of Argument
Hasty Generalization
Post Hoc Ergo Propter Hoc
Slippery Slope
Red Herring
Appeal to Tradition
False Dilemma
Bandwagon
Ad Hominem

**Selecting Propositions for
  Persuasive Speeches**
Characteristics of Propositions
Types of Propositions
Propositions of Fact
Propositions of Value
Propositions of Policy

Organizing Persuasive Speeches
Refutational Strategy
Problem-Solution Division
Need-Plan Division
Monroe's Motivated Sequence

"There are about 650,000 lawyers in the United States—one for each 365 people—and their number is increasing at a rate seven times faster than our population. If that rate continues until the year 2074, everyone in the United States will be a lawyer."[1]

In the space of one hundred and seventy-six years the Lower Mississippi has shortened itself two hundred and forty-two miles. That is an average of a trifle over one mile and a third per year. Therefore, any calm person, who is not blind or idiotic, can see that . . . just a million years ago next November, the Lower Mississippi River was upwards of one million three hundred thousand miles long . . . and forty-two years from now the Lower Mississippi will be only a mile and three-quarters long. . . . " MARK TWAIN, *LIFE ON THE MISSISSIPPI*[2]

"More than at any time in history, mankind faces a crossroads. One path leads to despair and utter hopelessness, the other to total extinction. Let us pray we have the wisdom to choose correctly." WOODY ALLEN[3]

DO THOSE arguments seem unconvincing to you? Do they seem more humorous than persuasive? If so, you probably have detected some flaws in them and would not be persuaded by the speakers. In order to be an effective and ethical speaker, you must be able to construct sound arguments and organize them in a convincing fashion. Speakers who knowingly use faulty reasoning are acting unethically. Understanding how to reason also benefits you as a listener. In order to make rational decisions, you must be able to analyze and assess what you hear.

The ability to structure sound arguments and detect flawed reasoning is an important skill for the public speaker. Thomas Gilovich, associate professor of psychology at Cornell University, explains:

> Thinking straight about the world is a precious and difficult process that must be carefully nurtured. By attempting to turn our critical intelligence off and on at will, we risk losing it altogether, and thus jeopardize our ability to see the world clearly. Furthermore, by failing to fully develop our critical faculties, we become susceptible to the arguments and exhortations of those with other than benign intentions. In the words of Stephen Jay Gould, "When people learn no tools of judgment and merely follow their hopes, the seeds of political manipulation are sown." As individuals and as society, we should be less accepting of superstition and sloppy thinking, and should strive to develop those "habits of mind" that promote a more accurate view of the world.[4]

In the previous chapter we discussed the **strategy** of persuasion. You learned not only what persuasion is but also some principles and strategies you can use to develop a convincing message. In this chapter we discuss the **structure** of persuasion. We will show you how to construct an argument and how to detect faulty arguments. In addition, you will study characteristics and types of persuasive propositions and special organizational patterns you can use in your persuasive speeches.

332

"A speech has two parts. Necessarily, you state your case, and you prove it."[5]

ARISTOTLE

Aristotle's description of the effective persuasive speech sounds simple, doesn't it? Before you can prove your case, however, you must understand the structure of arguments and how those arguments are organized in your speech. In the previous chapter we referred to this type of persuasive appeal as *logos*. Let's see how all this works.

STEPS OF AN ARGUMENT

Suppose you make the following statement: "I am more confident about public speaking now than I was at the beginning of this course." If someone asked you to justify your statement, you might respond in this way:

> Well, I experience fewer symptoms of nervousness. I seem to worry less about facing an audience. The night before my speech, I sleep better than I used to. I establish eye contact with my audience now rather than avoiding looking directly at them, as I did in my first speech. I no longer nervously shift my body weight from foot to foot, and I've stopped playing with my high school class ring and have started gesturing.

Your statement and response together constitute an argument. You have made a claim ("I am more confident about public speaking now") and then supported it with evidence, in this case, examples from personal observation. Aristotle would be pleased!

At its simplest level an argument includes three steps:

1. You make a claim.
2. You offer evidence.
3. You show how the evidence proves the claim.[6]

The **claim** is the conclusion of your argument. It is a statement you want your listeners to accept. Some examples of claims are:

Crime in our nation is rampant.
Textbook prices are too high.
Alcoholism is a disease.
The most important thing you can learn in college is how to learn.
Pornography is not a constitutionally protected form of free expression.

Visual aids make ideas easier to remember.
Cleanliness is next to godliness.
The certainty of punishment is a greater deterrent to crime than the severity of punishment.
Pizza is the ultimate health food.

The validity of any claim depends on the evidence supporting it. **Evidence** is the supporting materials you use to prove a point. As an advocate, you have an obligation to support your position with valid arguments. In other words, you must offer your listeners *reasons* to accept your conclusion. In her speech entitled "Campus Safety: The Forgotten Priority," Jenelle used the following supporting materials to make her point:

Related Reading:
For a discussion of the Toulmin model of argument, see: Rybacki, Karyn C., and Donald J. Rybacki. *Advocacy and Opposition* 2nd ed. Englewood Cliffs, NJ: Prentice, 1991: 46-57.

Teaching Strategy:
Review the types of supporting materials in Chapter 8. Have the class identify types of supporting materials they could use to prove these claims.

evidence: supporting materials a speaker uses to prove a point.

Teaching Strategy:
Encourage your students to
think critically about messages they hear and read.
Have them evaluate how
Jenelle used evidence to
support her points. She did
some things well: for example, she used a variety of
sources, supported some
points with statistical proof,
and identified the qualifica-
tion of her source, Michael
Smith. However, sometimes
she was vague. Point out her
use of the phrases "experts
say," "many campus offi-
cials," and "many campus
crimes."

Violent crimes on our college campuses are becoming a major concern all across
the nation. In that *USA Today* survey published just last October, they revealed that
in 1987 alone there were over 1,800 armed robberies, 13,000 physical assaults, and
over 600 *reported* rapes on our college campuses. Michael Smith, criminal justice
professor at the University of Southern Mississippi, states, "Campuses are supposed
to be an idealistic sanctuary where crime doesn't occur; unfortunately that is not a
valid assumption today."

But the problem is even worse than the statistics reveal. *Why?* Simply because in
many instances, campus crimes go unreported. All too many times, students fail to
confide in their campus officials. Experts say nine out of ten rapes on our college
campuses have gone unreported. In other instances, many campus officials fail to
share any inside information with anyone outside the academic community. One
Georgia Tech study found that many campus crimes went unreported simply because it would not look good for the university. But this lack of reporting is not
isolated to just this one southern school. In fact, a 1986 edition of *Education Digest*
suggests that "the most common problem in schools with chronic violence or
disruption is *failure* of school officials to report and effectively deal with these
violent or criminal incidents."[7]

In her speech Jenelle followed the three steps in constructing and presenting an argument. First, she stated her claim (violent campus crime is a major
concern). Second, she offered evidence to support the point, referring to a *USA
Today* survey. Finally, she explained how the evidence proved the claim, using
her own words, the words of a criminal justice professor, and additional evidence suggesting an even greater magnitude to the problem.

TYPES OF ARGUMENT

*"He who will not reason is a bigot; he who cannot is a fool; and he who dares
not is a slave."*   WILLIAM DRUMMOND

Speakers can justify their claims by using any of five types of argument. You
may offer proof by arguing from example, analogy, cause, deduction, or authority. The type of argument you select will depend on your topic, the available
evidence, and your listeners. You may combine several types of argument in a
single persuasive speech. In fact, the best speeches usually combine types of
argument. Let's look in more detail at these five basic types of argument available to you as a persuasive speaker.

argument by example or
inductive argument:
says that what is true of a
few instances is true generally.

Argument by Example. **Argument by example** is an inductive form of
proof. **Inductive argument** uses a few instances to assert a broader claim. For
example, if you have struggled through calculus and analytic geometry, you
may conclude that math is a difficult subject for you. You arrive at this conclusion by generalizing from the few specific math classes you studied.

We form many of our opinions through proofs provided from argument by
example. We read of several murders in Chicago and assume that the city is
plagued with violence. We hear a few friends complain of electrical problems
with a particular General Motors car and decide not to buy that model. A
speaker relates several examples of corruption in city hall, and we conclude
that political corruption is widespread. Those are all examples of inductive
reasoning.

Notice how James used a few instances to establish a broader claim in his speech on cosmetic plastic surgery:

> The number of Americans undergoing aesthetic plastic surgery has increased dramatically. According to the American Society of Plastic and Reconstructive Surgery, in just seven years there have been increases of 215 percent in the number of "tummy tucks," 40 percent in eyelid surgeries, and 34 percent in nose jobs.[8]

While there are many other types of elective plastic surgery, James based his conclusion that elective aesthetic plastic surgery is increasing on the three procedures he mentions.

Perhaps as you read the preceding arguments you questioned the validity of some of them. How can you test whether the examples used to support an argument are sound? The validity of argument by example hinges on the quality of the examples a speaker chooses. Ask yourself the following four questions to test the validity of argument by example. Keep in mind that argument by example is valid *only* if you can answer "yes" to *each* of these four tests of argument:

---

1. Are the examples true?
2. Are the examples relevant?
3. Are the examples sufficient?
4. Are the examples representative?

KEY POINTS
Tests of Argument by Example

---

1. Are the examples **true?** The first test of argument by example is to determine if the examples are true. In Chapter 8 we noted that hypothetical or imaginary examples can clarify a point, but they do not prove it. Only when true examples are presented should you proceed to the next question.
2. Are the examples **relevant?** Suppose a speaker presented evidence that three murders were committed during the past weekend in a major city and concluded, "So you can see that it is not safe to walk the streets of this city." Do these examples relate to the claim? If these three homicides resulted from *domestic* violence, they would not relate to *street* crime and, thus, would not prove a threat to the city's visitors. The examples, in this case, are not relevant.
3. Are the examples **sufficient?** Three murders in one weekend is statistically significant for a small town like London Mills, Illinois, but, even though tragic, that number is actually below the average number for several of our larger cities. In general, the greater the population for which you generalize, the more examples you need.
4. Are the examples **representative?** The examples you use as evidence should be typical, not exceptions. Was this weekend typical, or was the number of murders abnormally high?

Argument by Analogy. An analogy is a comparison. **Argument by analogy** links two objects or concepts and asserts that what is true of one will be true of the other. Arguing that computerized phone registration would work at your college because it works at State U is an example of reasoning by analogy.

Teaching Strategy: Have students read paragraphs 5-9 of Susanne Landowski's speech (Appendix C). Identify the argument she makes in paragraph 6 and the examples she uses in paragraphs 7-9 to support that argument. Ask students to evaluate these examples using the four tests of argument. Are there some questions that cannot be answered without more information provided? How does the information in paragraphs 10-13 reinforce Susanne's use of examples?

argument by analogy: says that what is true in one case is or will be true in another.

Argument by analogy is particularly appropriate when the program you advocate or oppose has been tried elsewhere. Some states have lotteries, no-fault insurance, and the line-item veto; others do not. Some school systems allow corporal punishment, offer magnet programs, and require a passing grade for participation in extracurricular activities; others do not. A speech defending or disputing one of these programs could demonstrate success or failure elsewhere to establish its position.

William Schaefer, governor of Maryland, used argument by analogy to urge an expanded federal role in providing child-care services:

> Today's parents do all they can to keep their children safe. They scrutinize the toys they play with, the food they eat and clothes they wear. Because our world is so complicated, however, with thousands of children's products available to families, parents can't monitor everything. As a result, we the people, through the federal government, act to ensure the health and safety of children. Children's toys, food, and clothing are all tested. The federal government requires special caps on prescription drug bottles to prevent children from taking potentially harmful medication.
>
> These practices are accepted by our society as necessary for the protection of children, because we recognize that our kids are often too young or inexperienced to know what is harmful to them. If it is good policy to regulate what children play with, eat, and wear, is it not also prudent that we ensure safety in the places where they learn and grow while their parents are at work?[9]

The preceding example illustrates the persuasive appeal of argument by analogy. You introduce a situation that is familiar to the audience and explain why we respond to it as we do. You then assert that your idea or proposal is analogous and, therefore, deserves a similar response. The key to this pattern of argument is the similarity between the two entities. In testing the validity of your argument by analogy, you need to answer this question: "Are the two entities sufficiently similar to justify my conclusion that what is true of one will be true of the other?" If not, your reasoning is faulty. This question can best be answered by dividing it into two questions.

KEY POINTS
Tests of Argument by Analogy

1. Are the similarities between the two cases relevant?
2. Are any of the differences between the two cases relevant?

---

1. Are the **similarities** between the two cases relevant? If you decide to argue by analogy for a computerized phone registration system, you may find many similarities between your college and State U. However, the fact that both schools have similar library facilities and the same mascot is irrelevant to registration. Equivalent student enrollments, advising procedures, and periods for registration *are* highly relevant and can be forceful elements as you build your case.

2. Are any of the **differences** between the two cases relevant? If so, how do those differences affect your claim? If you discover that, unlike State, your college has neither an integrated computer network nor the technical staff

The force of persuasion can topple or sustain governments.

PROBLEM-SOLUTION DIVISION

The **problem-solution division** is a simple, rigid, organizational approach for a persuasive speech. In this approach the major divisions of your speech and their order are predetermined: You first establish a compelling problem and then present a convincing solution. Because you advocate a plan of action, this method is by nature persuasive.

A speaker discussing rape prevention might divide the **problem** area into physical and psychological effects of rape. The **solution** phase might include a six-step plan to prevent rape. Speeches that call for a law or some action often use a problem-solution format. Speeches may also **oppose** an action that is demonstrated as harmful, as in the next example.

> *Specific Purpose:* To persuade the audience to oppose mandatory drug testing in the workplace.
> *Key Ideas:* I. Mandatory drug testing is harmful.
>   **A.** It is cost-prohibitive.
>   **B.** It results in lost work time.
>   **C.** It undermines employee morale.
>   **D.** It is an unreasonable intrusion of privacy.
>   II. The harms of mandatory drug testing can be avoided.
>   **A.** Employers can better supervise employees.
>   **B.** Legislators should oppose drug-testing legislation.

problem-solution division: a rigid persuasive organizational pattern that establishes a compelling problem and offers one or more convincing solutions.

Teaching Strategy:
Remind students that the amount of time a speaker should spend developing the problem and solution divisions of the speech depends on the topic and the audience. A speaker discussing the topic of child abuse would probably not have to spend much time convincing the audience that child abuse is a problem. Most of that speaker's time should probably be devoted to persuading listeners to work for a particular solution.

NEED-PLAN DIVISION

The **need-plan division** is a variation of the problem-solution division. This fourfold approach (1) establishes a need or deficiency in the present system, (2) presents a proposal to meet the need, (3) demonstrates how the proposal satisfies the need, and (4) suggests a plan for implementing the proposal.

need-plan division: a variation of problem-solution organization that (1) establishes a need or deficiency, (2) offers a proposal to meet the need, (3) shows how the plan satisfies the need, and (4) suggests a plan for implementing the proposal.

Business executives and managers often intuitively employ the need-plan organizational strategy. For example, a company president informs the board of directors of the problem of being located in a town without an airport. Documenting a loss of sales due to unnecessary driving time, the president proposes relocating company headquarters to a city with a major airport. This would permit the company to cover more territory without expanding the sales force. Finally, the president distributes to the board a detailed plan of action for selecting the appropriate city for relocation.

Salespeople also use the need-plan strategy. They demonstrate or create a need, supply the product or service to meet that need, demonstrate or describe how well it will work, and will often even arrange an easy payment plan to guarantee your purchase. This fundamental sales approach is prevalent for one simple reason: It works! You can use this strategy when you want to prompt an audience to action.

Suppose the specific purpose of your speech is to persuade your audience that employers should provide health promotion programs for their employees. Using the need-plan pattern, you could make four arguments. First, employee illness results in absenteeism, lost productivity, and increased health care costs. Second, employers should establish on-site health and fitness centers for their employees. Third, when health promotion programs have been tried, they have reduced absenteeism, increased productivity, and capped health care costs. As your final step you could suggest an implementation strategy to include exercise and conditioning programs, alcohol- and drug-awareness education, stress-management workshops, anti-smoking clinics, and health status testing and evaluation.

MONROE'S MOTIVATED SEQUENCE

In the 1930s, Alan Monroe developed one of the most popular patterns for organizing persuasive speeches and called it "the motivated sequence."[20] This pattern is particularly appropriate when discussing a well-known or easily established problem. Drawing from educator and philosopher John Dewey's work with reflective thinking, Monroe believed that persuasion is best accomplished if a speaker moves a listener sequentially through a series of steps.[21] **Monroe's motivated sequence**, then, includes the following five steps, or stages: attention, need, satisfaction, visualization, and action.

Monroe's motivated sequence: a persuasive pattern composed of (1) getting the audience's attention, (2) establishing a need, (3) offering a proposal to satisfy the need, (4) inviting listeners to visualize the results, and (5) requesting action.

Monroe argued that speakers must first command the **attention** of their listeners. Suppose your geographic area is experiencing a summer drought. You might begin your speech with a description of the landscape as you approached your campus a year ago, describing in detail the green grass, the verdant foliage, and the colorful, fragrant flowers. You then contrast the landscape of a year ago with its look now: bland, brown, and blossomless. With these contrasting visual images you try to capture the attention and interest of your audience.

A speaker's second objective is to establish a **need.** This step is similar to the problem and need steps in the problem-solution and need-plan patterns of organizing a speech. For example, your speech on the drought situation could illustrate how an inadequate water supply hurts not only the beauty of the landscape but also agricultural production, certain industrial processes, and, ultimately, the economy of the entire region.

As you dramatize a problem, you create an urgency to redress it. In the **satisfaction** step of the motivated sequence, you propose a way to solve, or at least minimize, the problem. You might propose voluntary or mandatory conservation as a short-term solution to the water shortage crisis in your area. As a longer-range solution you could suggest planting grasses, shrubs, and other plants requiring less water. You might advocate that the city adopt and enforce stricter regulations of water use by businesses, or that it develop alternate water sources.

However, Monroe argued that simply proposing a solution is seldom sufficient to effect change. Through **visualization,** his fourth step, a speaker seeks to intensify an audience's desire to adopt and implement the proposed solution. You could direct the audience to look out the window at their campus and then ask if that is the scenery they want. More often, though, you create word pictures for the audience to visualize. Without adequate water, you could argue, crops will die, family farms will be foreclosed upon, industries will not relocate to the area, and the quality of life for everyone in the area will be depressed. In contrast, you could refer to the landscape of a year ago, the image you depicted as you began your speech. The future can be colored in green, red, yellow, and blue, and it can represent growth and vitality.

The final step of the motivated sequence is the **action** you request of your listeners. It is not enough to know that something must be done; the audience must know what you want them to do, and your request must be within their power to act. Do you want them to join you in voluntary conservation by watering their lawns in the evening when less water will evaporate, or by washing their cars less frequently? Are you asking them to sign petitions pressuring the city council to adopt mandatory conservation measures when the water table sinks to a designated level? You should conclude your speech with a strong appeal for specific, reasonable action.

The speech in Figure 16.1 was delivered by Mike Espy to his colleagues in the U.S. House of Representatives. His remarks came in debate on a proposal to adopt a National Voter Registration Act designed to make voter registration more convenient. His speech illustrates the natural, logical order that Monroe's organizational pattern advocates.[22]

Summary

Persuasion is the art of affecting other people's values, beliefs, attitudes, or behaviors. The logical impact of a persuasive speech springs from a speaker's evidence and reasoning. To be an effective persuader, you must know how to structure a valid argument, how to detect flaws in reasoning, how to word propositions, and how to select the best general organizational pattern for your persuasive message. The three steps of structuring an argument are (1) to make a claim you want the audience to accept, (2) to supply evidence supporting that claim, and (3) to explain how the evidence proves the claim. The validity of any claim ultimately depends on the quality of the evidence supporting it.

Attention: Appeals to
common values

Need: Introduces problem of
poor voter participation and
voter disenfranchisement

Satisfaction: Introduces
proposed solution

Visualization: Continues
visualization of problem but
points to improvement with
enactment of proposed
legistration

Action: Argues against
impediments to action. Uses
examples from common history
to urge action today.

Hon. Mike Espy
United States Representative, Mississippi

From the House floor debate of February 6, 1990 on H.R. 2190, the National Voter Registration Act.

During the recess I had the privilage of visiting Eastern Europe. I had the privilage of witnessing first hand the people's historic movement for democracy, for the right to elect governments of their own choosing. I was proud to know that our country is the world's democratic model, that people everywhere are looking to the United States to point the way forward toward truly representative government.

And yet, as I watched democracy struggling to be born in Eastern Europe, I was reminded that too many citizens in our country still do not take part in our own electoral process. I was reminded that our country has the worst voter participation rate of the world's major democracies. I was reminded that our own democratic process can and should be improved. That is why I urge my colleagues to support H.R. 2190.

The right to vote is the hallmark of our democracy. However, as we all know, in the beginning of our country's history that precious right to vote was preserved only for those white men who owned enough property to qualify. Blacks were themselves property. Since then, after years of struggle, the right to vote and participate in our democracy has been extended to everyone. But that struggle is not yet over.

Today, many voter registration procedures around the country still effectively disenfranchise those who do not have the means to travel to a registrar. The National Voter Registration Act would effectively eliminate this problem by allowing voter registration by mail in every State where it is currently not allowed.

I represent a very poor, very rural district. I know that many citizens, particularly those who are elderly and without their own transportation, have a difficult time getting a ride to a registrar's office, which could be 10 or 20 minutes away. I have participated in many voter registration drives where the main expenditure is on gas money to take people to register. But many people are still being left behind.

This problem is so great in Mississippi that the Senate Elections Committee of the State legislature just last week approved a bill to allow mail-in voter registration. I am proud that Mississippi is moving in this direction.

I am also excited about provisions in this bill which would allow citizens to register when they apply for driver's licenses, and when they conduct business at government agencies, and public places such as schools and libraries. H.R. 2190 also ends the practice of purging voters because they choose not to vote in certain elections.

I realize that some colleagues are concerned about the proper role of the Federal Government in the registration process. However, I believe that procedures for registering and voting in all Federal elections should be the same, whether a citizen in Maine, Michigan, or Mississippi. On many issues States have the right to go their separate ways. But voting rights should not be one of them.

Lastly, several arguments have been advanced about the probable costs of implementing this legislation. It is true that we must be mindful of the costs to taxpayers of every piece of legislation we enact. However, I believe it is a mistake to oppose this legislation because of its cost in dollars. I don't believe the dollar amounts are prohibitive.

The right to register and vote has been paid for by countless Americans with their lives so that the blessings of liberty would be shared by all Americans.

They died so that America could point the way to genuine democracy for the peoples of the world. We must continue to point the way today.

FIGURE 16.1 Example
of Motivated Sequence

To give listeners a reason to accept a persuasive claim, speakers may use any of five types of arguments. First, *argument by example* uses specific instances to support a general claim. In order for an argument by example to be valid, the speaker must use examples that are true, relevant to the claim, sufficient in number, and representative. Second, *argument by analogy* links two concepts, conditions, or experiences and claims that what is true of one will be true of the other. The validity of argument by analogy depends upon the quality of the comparison a speaker develops. To test that analogy, ask two questions: (1) Are the similarities between the cases relevant? and (2) Are any differences between the two cases relevant?

Argument by cause, the third type of argument, links two concepts, conditions, or experiences and claims that one causes the other. A speaker arguing by cause can move listeners' attention forward from cause to effect, or can trace effects back to their causes.

To test the validity of the cause-effect relationship, speakers and listeners should consider three questions: (1) Does a causal relationship exist? (2) Could the presumed cause produce the effect? and (3) Could the effect result from other causes?

A fourth type of argument, *argument by deduction*, consists of three parts. The *major premise* is a claim about a general group of people, events, or conditions. The *minor premise* places a person, event, or condition into that general class. And the *conclusion* argues that what is true of the general class is also true of the specific instance. The major premise, minor premise, and conclusion together form a type of deductive argument called a *syllogism*. In order for an argument by deduction to be valid, both major and minor premises must be true and they must be related.

Finally, *argument by authority* uses testimony from an expert source to prove a speaker's claim. The validity of this type of argument depends upon the credibility the authority has with the audience. To be credible, the source should be competent and unbiased, should have special qualifications to speak on the topic under discussion, should be in the mainstream of thought, and should be recent.

Both speakers and listeners must watch out for logical flaws or *fallacies* in persuasive arguments. Fallacious arguments are particularly dangerous because they may resemble sound reasoning as we read or listen to them. Unfortunately, eight fallacies of argument are common. The fallacy of *hasty generalization* involves making claims on the basis of insufficient or unrepresentative examples. *Post hoc ergo propter hoc* falsely argues that because event A preceded event B, A caused B. It confuses chronology with causation. The *slippery slope* fallacy asserts that one event inevitably unleashes a series of events. The *red herring* fallacy introduces irrelevant issues to deflect attention from the true question under discussion. The fallacy called *appeal to tradition* asserts that old ways of doing things are correct or best, simply because they are traditional. *False dilemma* argues that we must choose between two alternatives, when in reality we may have a range of options. The *bandwagon* fallacy argues that we should behave or think a particular way because most people do. Finally, the *ad hominem* fallacy urges listeners to reject an idea because of the politics, religion, or lifestyle of the person voicing the idea.

All persuasive speeches advocate propositions, position statements the speaker wants listeners to accept. Persuasive propositions must be stated as a declarative sentence expressing a judgment, must be debatable, and require proof in order to be accepted. The three types of persuasive propositions are propositions of fact, propositions of value, and propositions of policy. *Propositions of fact* ask the audience to accept the truth or falsity of a statement. *Propositions of value* ask the audience to determine the relative worth of an idea or action. *Propositions of policy* ask the audience to support a course of action.

Speakers sometimes select a particular persuasive topic because they hear or read an argument they wish to oppose. The act of countering one argument with another is called *refutation*. To refute an argument, follow this four-step *refutational strategy*. First, state the position you are refuting. Second, state your own position. Third, support your position with evidence. And fourth, show how your position undermines the argument you oppose.

Three other popular methods of organizing persuasive speeches are problem-solution, need-plan, and the motivated sequence patterns. A simple, rigid, organizational plan, *problem-solution* establishes a compelling problem and presents one or more workable solutions to meet that problem. The *need-plan* pattern is a four-step variation of problem solution organization. Using need-plan organization, a speaker (1) establishes a need, (2) suggests a proposal to meet that need, (3) shows how the plan meets the need, and (4) offers a plan for implementing the proposal. A final persuasive speech pattern, *Monroe's motivated sequence*, is a formal, five-step pattern for moving listeners to belief or action. It consists of (1) getting the attention of your listeners, (2) clarifying the need, (3) showing how to satisfy that need, (4) visualizing the solution, and (5) requesting action.

Exercises

1. Select a persuasive speech in Appendix C and determine the speaker's key ideas. Analyze the structure of each major argument: (a) Identify the claim, (b) identify the supporting material, and (c) identify the speaker's explanation of how the support proves the claim. Are any of those steps missing? If so, what is the impact on the argument? Could any of the three steps be strengthened? If so, how?

2. You have been asked to visit your former high school to speak with a group of college-bound students. The school's counselor has asked you to speak on the topic "College Years Are the Best Years of Your Life!" Construct three arguments that support this position. Give an example of how you might use in your speech each of the types of argument: example, analogy, cause, deduction, and authority.

3. Using argument by analogy, construct a short speech on one or more of the following topics. What similarities between the two entities make your analysis credible? What differences undermine the believability of the statement?
   a. Being in college is like being in a demolition derby.
   b. Life is like an athletic contest.
   c. Studying for an exam is like tying your shoe.
   d. Marriage is like gardening.
   e. A job interview is like an audition for a role in a film.

4. Determine whether each of the following statements is a proposition of fact, value, or policy.
   a. The university should build a new library.
   b. A new library would cost the university seven million dollars.
   c. It is more important to build a new library than to expand our athletic facilities.
   d. Sex education encourages sexual activity among schoolchildren.
   e. The FDA should reduce required testing for experimental drugs to fight life-threatening illnesses.
   f. Workers in high-stress jobs should be subject to random periodic drug testing.
   g. *Citizen Kane* is the best American film ever made.
   h. It is more important for a country to *do* good than to *feel* good.
   i. If the proposed tuition increase is adopted, the university may lose up to five hundred students.
   j. U.S. schools should adopt a 12-month schedule.

5. Identify the major premise, minor premise, and conclusion in each of the following groups of statements:

Inquiring Minds should air on the Trashy Cable Network.
Inquiring Minds is a fluffy news show.
All fluffy news shows should be aired on the Trashy Cable Network.

A high grade point average is important to Charlotte.
Today's college students value high grade point averages.
Charlotte is a college student.

A lot of the dance music of the 1990s sounds like disco music of the 1970s.
A lot of the dance music of the 1990s is awful.
The disco music of the 1970s was awful.

6. Locate examples of each of the fallacies discussed in this chapter. Examine advertisements in newspapers, in magazines, on radio, and on television. Read editorials, letters to the editor, and transcripts of speeches.

Answers:
Conclusion *Inquiring Minds* should air . . .
Minor Premise *Inquiring Minds* is a fluffy news show.
Major Premise All fluffy news shows should be aired . . .

Conclusion A high grade point average . . .
Major Premise Today's college students . . .
Minor Premise Charlotte is a college student.

Minor Premise A lot of the dance music . . . sounds like disco music of the 1970s.
Conclusion A lot of the dance music of the 1990s is awful.
Major Premise The disco music of the 1970s was awful.

Notes

1. V.H. Krulak, *Orange County Register*, qtd. in "On the Record," *National Review* 24 November 1989: 8.
2. Mark Twain, *Life on the Mississippi* (New York: Harper, 1917) 156.
3. Qtd. in Mark L. Schannon, "One Businessperson's View of the Ecological Crisis: The Restoration of Trust," *Vital Speeches of the Day* 1 January 1991: 178.
4. Thomas Gilovich, *How We Know What Isn't So* (New York: Free, 1991) 6.
5. *The Rhetoric of Aristotle*, trans. Lane Cooper (New York: Appleton, 1932) 220.
6. For a more elaborate discussion of the structure of an argument, see Stephen Toulmin, *The Uses of Argument* (New York: Cambridge U P, 1974).
7. Jenelle C. Martin, "Campus Safety: The Forgotten Priority," *Winning Orations, 1989* (Mankato, MN: Interstate Oratorical Association, 1989) 14.
8. Statistics are taken from Jonathan Carey, "Scar Wars," *The Spectator* 26 May 1990: 7.
9. William Schaefer, *The Congressional Digest* February 1990: 48, 50.
10. Al Swift, *The Congressional Digest* April 1990: 108.
11. D. Stanley Eitzen, "Problem Students: The Socio-Cultural Roots," *Vital Speeches of the Day* 15 May 1990: 479.
12. Gary Bauer, *The Congressional Digest* February 1990: 59.

13. John M. Ericson and James J. Murphy with Raymond Bud Zeuschner, *The Debater's Guide*, rev. ed. (Carbondale: Southern Illinois U P, 1987) 139.
14. *The New York Public Library Desk Reference* (New York: Stonesong–Simon, 1989) 230.
15. "Bulls, Bears and Bowls," *Forbes* 6 February 1989: 172.
16. Bruce N. Waller, *Critical Thinking: Consider the Verdict* (Englewood Cliffs, NJ: Prentice, 1988) 30.
17. Thomas H. Kean, "Keynote Address," *Vital Speeches of the Day* 15 October 1988: 7.
18. W. Ward Fearnside and William B. Holther. *Fallacy — The Counterfeit of Argument* (Englewood Cliffs, NJ: Prentice, 1959) 92.
19. Ann Richards, "Keynote Address," *Vital Speeches of the Day* 15 August 1988: 648.
20. Bruce E. Gronbeck, Douglas Ehninger, and Alan H. Monroe, *Principles of Speech Communication*, 10th brief ed. (Glenview, IL: Scott, 1988) 271–84. See also Alan H. Monroe, *Principles and Types of Speech* (Chicago: Scott, 1935).
21. See our discussion of Dewey's Steps to Reflective Thinking in Chapter 18, pages 395–97.
22. Mike Espy, in *Congressional Digest* April 1990: 124, 126.

Speaking on Special Occasions

17

The Speech of Introduction

The Speech of Presentation

The Acceptance Speech

The Speech of Tribute

The Oral Report

The Speech to Entertain

The Impromptu Speech

The Question-Answer Period

The Videotaped Speech

*I*N September 1989, President George Bush delivered his first televised speech from the White House to the American people. Speaking from his desk in the Oval Office, the president outlined his new strategies in the war on drugs.

At Ryan White's funeral in 1990, singer Elton John spoke briefly but movingly about Ryan's struggle against AIDS before playing and singing a special version of "Candle in the Wind."

In March 1991, Sophia Loren received a Lifetime Achievement Award and a special Oscar from the Academy of Motion Picture Arts and Sciences. Introduced by Gregory Peck, she accepted the award with brief remarks to an audience that remained standing all the time she was on stage.

At the end of the war in the Persian Gulf, General Norman Schwarzkopf appeared before television cameras to explain the strategies that won the war and to answer questions from the press.

Though none of us has the celebrity or visibility of the individuals mentioned in these examples, you can count on being called upon to deliver a speech on some special occasion: an oral report in a world history class, a speech introducing a guest speaker at a club meeting, a speech accepting an award from a civic group, or a eulogy at the funeral of a relative or friend. In addition to those "ordinary" special occasions, consider that somewhere on a college campus right now is the student who will one day appear on national television to accept the Heisman Trophy, the Tony Award for Best Actress, or the Academy Award for Best Director. Somewhere on a college campus right now is the person who will present breakthrough medical research findings to a national convention of doctors and medical technicians. Somewhere on a college campus right now is the future Andy Rooney or Erma Bombeck, who will be well paid to speak at banquets, roasts, and professional meetings.

To speak your best on any of these special occasions, you must consider the customs and audience expectations in each case. In this chapter we will discuss nine special occasions or special circumstances for public speeches: the speech of introduction, the speech of presentation, the acceptance speech, the speech of tribute, the oral report, the speech to entertain, the impromptu speech, the question-answer period, and the videotaped speech. You will learn guidelines for each of those types of speeches and read examples of many of them. This information can serve you well beyond the classroom and prepare you for any occasion when you are requested, invited, or expected to speak.

■ The Speech of Introduction

speech of introduction: a speech introducing a featured speaker to an audience.

One of the most common types of special-occasion speeches is the **speech of introduction.** Some people use that phrase to indicate speeches by people introducing themselves to an audience. As we use the phrase in this chapter, however, we mean a speech introducing a featured speaker. The following guidelines will help you prepare such a speech of introduction.

---

1. Focus on the featured speaker.
2. Be brief.
3. Establish the speaker's credibility.
4. Create realistic expectations.
5. Set the tone for the speech.

KEY POINTS
Guidelines
for the Speech
of Introduction

The first guideline to remember is to *keep the focus on the person being introduced*. The audience has not gathered to hear you, so don't upstage the featured speaker. Keep your remarks short, simple, and sincere.

In order to achieve the first guideline, you will want to follow the second: *Be brief*. If you can, request and get a copy of the speaker's résumé. This will give you a body of information to select from when preparing your introductory remarks. The key word in that last sentence is *select*. Too often we have heard speeches of introduction begin with a sentence such as "Our speaker tonight was born in Sioux City, Iowa, ..." Your listeners will tune out quickly if your introduction is a lengthy chronology of events in a person's life. A speech of introduction is not a dramatic reading of a résumé. *Highlight* information the audience does not know.

A third guideline is to *establish the speaker's credibility on the topic*. You do this by presenting the speaker's credentials. As you prepare your speech of introduction, ask and answer questions such as these: What makes the speaker qualified to speak on the subject? What education and experiences make the speaker's insights worthy of our belief?

Fourth, remember to *create realistic expectations*. Prepare the audience to listen intelligently to the remarks that will follow. When Lashelle introduced the director of financial aid to her sorority, she included the statement, "I asked Mr. Palmerton to speak with us this afternoon because he's the person in charge of all scholarships. He will tell us how we all can receive financial assistance for next year." Lashelle's overstatement compelled Mr. Palmerton to begin his remarks by noting that the deadlines for most of next year's scholarships had already passed, and that not all in the audience would qualify for the limited number of scholarships still available. His comments embarrassed Lashelle, disappointed several in the audience, and made the speaker feel that he could not live up to audience expectations.

Genuine praise is commendable, just be careful not to oversell the speaker. Can you imagine walking to the microphone after the following introduction: "Our speaker tonight is one of the great speakers in this country. I heard her last year, and she had us laughing until our sides hurt. She will keep you spellbound from her first word to her last. Get ready for the best speech you've heard in your entire life!"

Finally, you should phrase your remarks to *establish a tone consistent with the speaker's presentation*. Would you give a humorous introduction for a

Practice Speaking:
Have students interview one another in pairs for five minutes, making notes as they talk, and then introduce the partner in a 2–3 minute speech.

speaker whose topic is "The Grieving Process: What to Do When a Loved One Dies"? Of course not. On the other hand, if the evening is designed for amusement and merriment, your introduction should help set that mood.

Communication professors should certainly know how to introduce a featured speaker. In the example below, Professor Don Ochs of the University of Iowa did an exemplary job of introducing his longtime colleague, Professor Samuel L. Becker. Becker was the keynote speaker at the Central States Communication Association convention in Chicago on April 12, 1991. You'll see that Ochs uses some communication jargon because he was speaking to a group of communication professionals. Notice, though, how Ochs' brief, cordial remarks focus on Becker, establishing his credibility and setting the tone for Becker's informative and inspirational speech:

> Thirty years ago I walked out of an Iowa City store onto the main street and noticed Sam Becker walking about twenty feet ahead of me. His youngest daughter was alongside Sam but she was terribly upset about something; crying, and obviously hurt about something. Sam put his arm around his daughter and, in the space of two blocks, said something that comforted and fixed the problem. She was smiling when they parted company.
>
> I share this snapshot of Sam with you because, for me, it captures Sam's approach to life, higher education, scholarship, and our profession.
>
> Sam Becker has *figuratively* put his arm around difficulties and problems for his entire career. He's made all of us as teachers and scholars better persons and better professionals with his intellect, his vision, his energy, and his instinctive willingness to help.
>
> As a rhetorician I would much prefer to introduce Sam with figures and tropes, with synechdoche, litotes, and hyperbole. But Sam is a social scientist, so I will be quantitative instead.
>
> How much has Sam helped us? Sam has taught at four universities; written six books; been active in eight professional associations; authored ten monographs; served on twelve editorial boards; worked on evaluation teams for thirty-two colleges and universities; served on thirty-six university committees; lectured at fifty colleges and universities; directed fifty-five PhDs; and authored 105 articles.
>
> Without doubt, he has helped and assisted and supported all of us. Our speaker today, Sam Becker.[1]

The following example is a sharp contrast to Ochs' serious speech of introduction above. The occasion was a debate between British and American debaters, moderated by one of your authors. Billed as the battle of the sexes, the debate was intended to be a lighthearted look at gender roles in business and government. The evening blended entertainment and education. The debaters and moderator had honed their skills of good-natured name calling. Notice how college student Faye introduced the moderator and helped set the tone for the spirited debate that was to follow.

> Dr. Grice has asked me to introduce him as the moderator of tonight's debate. He told me not to make a big fuss over him, just to speak of him as I would any other great man. I realize I need to be careful when I talk about Dr. Grice, because I am talking about the man he loves. Dr. Grice came to Auburn University at Montgomery in 1987 and is currently head of the Department of Communication. AUM

wanted to pay Dr. Grice what he's worth, but found out he wouldn't work that cheaply.

Dr. Grice doesn't have many faults, but he sure makes the most of the ones he has. Dr. Grice is very responsible. No matter what goes wrong in the department, Dr. Grice is always responsible. As an executive, Dr. Grice delegates all the authority, shifts all the blame, and takes all the credit. He deserves some credit too. Dr. Grice is the only professor I know who is always undertaking vast projects with half-vast ideas.

After all this praise, I feel I should balance this introduction with a note of caution. Dr. Grice recently appeared on Channel 8 to analyze the presidential and vice-presidential debates. I'm sure that both of you who saw him noticed his shifty eyes. Those of us who know Dr. Grice well want you to know that his shifty eyes are no indication of his honesty and integrity. In fact, since we have known him, we have seen no indication of his honesty and integrity.

Without further delay, I introduce tonight's moderator, the humble and rightfully so — Dr. George L. Grice.

Faye's use of humor and friendly invective was appropriate to the occasion and prepared the audience for the debate that followed. If the occasion had not placed a premium on humor, however, Faye would have needed to develop a different speech of introduction.

■ The Speech of Presentation ───────────

The **speech of presentation** confers an award, a prize, or some other form of special recognition on an individual or a group. Such speeches are typically made on special occasions: after banquets or parties; as part of business meetings or sessions of a convention; or at awards ceremonies such as the Tony Awards, the Academy Awards, or the Grammy Awards, where many people will be recognized.

We will restrict our discussion of the speech of presentation to prepared statements commenting on and presenting an award to an individual or group. Thus, remarks made by a presenter about an actor or actress honored with the American Film Institute's Lifetime Achievement Award would qualify as a speech of presentation; opening the envelope and reading the winner of the Grammy Award for "Song of the Year" is really an announcement rather than a prepared speech. When you give a speech of presentation, let the nature and importance of the award being presented, as well as the occasion on which it is being presented, shape your remarks. The following guidelines will help you plan this special-occasion speech.

speech of presentation: a speech conferring an award, prize, or some other recognition on an individual or group.

1. State the purpose of award or recognition.
2. State the recipient's qualifications.
3. Adapt organization to audience knowledge.
4. Compliment finalists for the award.

**KEY POINTS
Guidelines
for the Speech
of Presentation**

First, as a presenter you should *state the purpose of the award or recognition.* If the audience is unfamiliar with the award—if it is a new or special award—or if they know nothing about the organization making the award, you will probably want to begin by briefly explaining the nature of the award or the rationale for presenting it. This is especially important if you as the speaker represent the organization making the award. In contrast, an award with a long history probably needs little if any explanation.

A second guideline is to *focus your speech on the achievements for which the award is being made; don't* attempt a detailed biography of the recipient. Since you are merely highlighting the honoree's accomplishments, the speech of presentation will be brief, rarely more than five minutes long and frequently much shorter.

Third, *the way you organize a speech of presentation is determined primarily by whether the audience knows the name of the recipient in advance.* If they do *not* know the name of the individual you are honoring, capitalize on their curiosity. If you begin by announcing the name of the recipient and then explaining why that person was selected, the bulk of your speech will seem anticlimactic. Instead, let ambiguity about who will receive the honor propel the speech and maintain the audience's attention. Begin by making general comments that could refer to several or many people; as the speech progresses, let your comments get more specific. If the person receiving your award is from a group containing both men and women, use gender-neutral pronouns ("this person" or "our honoree") rather than using "he" or "she." In this way, you keep your audience guessing and allow them the pleasure of solving a puzzle. If the audience knows in advance the name of the person being recognized, you will want to change your strategy. Instead of beginning with general statements and gradually becoming more specific, begin the speech honoring someone known in advance with specifics and end with more general statements that summarize the reasons for the presentation.

Finally, if a group of individuals has been nominated and you are announcing the winner with your speech of presentation, briefly *compliment the entire group of people who have been nominated for the award.*

The following speech was delivered at an annual convention of the Texas Speech Communication Association (TSCA) to honor a person giving lengthy and outstanding service to that organization. Notice how the speaker focuses on the reasons for the award and the honoree's qualifications. In addition, the speaker's organization carefully creates suspense for this surprise award.

The key word in "TSCA Outstanding Service Award" is "service." We who have been privileged to serve this association as officers soon learn that what we accomplish is not primarily a function of our own talents and hard work, but a function of the expertise and efforts of many individuals like you—individuals who understand what is important in making the Texas Speech Communication Association a vibrant and vital organization. . . .

Important to TSCA is networking. Through letters, phone calls, and testifying, this year's recipient helped make our voice heard in her local community and in Austin. . . .

Important to TSCA is service on the Executive Committee. As editor of the *TSCA*

Newsletter, this year's recipient gave life to this instrument of communication, establishing the professional format it continues today.

Important to TSCA are the many programs which comprise our convention. Many of you have attended and learned from programs and workshops this year's recipient has conducted.

A Piper Professor and a Danforth Scholar, she was honored by her institution this year as the first recipient of the Dr. and Mrs. Z.T. Scott Fellowship for Excellence in Teaching. This award recognizes excellence in teaching, advising, and support for student organizations.

I have long believed that an important criterion for professional service is that an individual is not offended by doing the menial. This year's recipient is not offended by doing the menial and is capable of accomplishing the significant. She is professional, gracious, amiable, and hard-working.

I suspect that there is only one person in this room who will be surprised at this year's choice for the Outstanding Service Award — and that person is the recipient herself, for she will feel that she was just fulfilling her professional obligations. We know better. She represents the best of our association, the best of our discipline, and the best of our profession.

At the beginning of my remarks I said that this introduction is a personal privilege, for the individual we honor today is perhaps the most significant colleague in my professional life. It is with pleasure that I present to you this year's recipient of the TSCA Outstanding Service Award: Frances Swinny.[2]

Point out to your students how the repetition of the statement "Important to TSCA is" unifies the speech and explains why the award is being given.

■ The Acceptance Speech

At some point in your life, you may be commended publicly for service you have given to a cause or an organization. You may be presented a farewell or retirement gift from your friends or co-workers. You may receive an award for winning a sporting event, an essay contest, or a speech contest. Although these are different occasions, they have at least one thing in common — each requires a response. To accept a gift or an award without expressing appreciation is socially unacceptable. An **acceptance speech,** then, is a response to a speech of presentation. When a recipient acknowledges the award or tribute, he or she provides closure to the process. A gracious acceptance speech usually includes four steps.

acceptance speech: a speech responding to a speech of presentation by acknowledging an award, tribute, or recognition.

---

1. Thank those who bestowed the award.
2. Compliment the competition.
3. Thank those who helped you attain the award.
4. Accept the award graciously.

**KEY POINTS
Guidelines for the
Acceptance Speech**

First, *thank the person or organization bestowing the award.* You may wish to name not only the group sponsoring the award but also the person who made the speech of presentation. In addition, you may want to commend what the award represents. Your respect for the award and its donor authenticates your statement of appreciation.

Second, if you are accepting a competitively selected award, and especially if your competitors are in the audience, acknowledge their qualifications and compliment them. This step need not be lengthy; you can *compliment your peers* as a group rather than individually.

Third, *thank those who helped you achieve the honor.* Seldom do we achieve things by ourselves. Whether you are an accomplished pianist, vocalist, artist, athlete, or writer, you have usually had someone—parents, teachers, or coaches—who invested time, money, and expertise to help you achieve your best.

Finally, you should *accept your award graciously.* An acceptance speech is no time to be cocky or clever. Of well-known acceptance speeches, one of the most gracious and inspirational was delivered by Steven Spielberg on March 30, 1987. He was receiving the Irving G. Thalberg Memorial Award at the fifty-ninth Academy Awards ceremony for his screenwriting accomplishments during 1986. Notice how Spielberg accomplishes each of the steps we have elaborated. He thanks the members of the Academy of Motion Picture Arts and Sciences and the audience. He shows his respect for the recognition by commenting on its history and by naming and complimenting some previous recipients of the Thalberg Award. He thanks those who helped him attain the award by mentioning people who influenced him, and he accepts the award in a particularly gracious and humble manner. His opening remark refers to Sally Field's impromptu remarks when she was named Best Actress for *Places in the Heart.* Field had gushed, "You like me! You really like me!" Spielberg's acceptance speech was as follows:

Discussion Prompt:
What features of this speech's content and organization make Spielberg seem particularly gracious?

Point out how quickly Spielberg offers his thanks.

Spielberg demonstrates his knowledge of the award's history by mentioning former recipients in the first paragraph and the movies nominated for Best Picture in the first year of the Thalberg Award in this second paragraph.

He demonstrates some knowledge of Irving Thalberg by quoting him.

I'm resisting like crazy to use Sally Field's line from two years ago. Thank you very much. Following in the footsteps of some of my heroes, Cecil B. DeMille, and George Stevens, Alfred Hitchcock, William Wyler, Ingmar Bergman, and Robert Wise, this award is truly a great honor for me.

The Thalberg Award was first given fifty years ago in 1937, which was the year of *In Old Chicago, Captains Courageous, Dead End, The Life of Émile Zola, Lost Horizon, Stage Door,* and *A Star is Born*—all having been nominated for Best Picture that year. I'm told Irving Thalberg worshiped writers. And that's where it all begins. That we are first and foremost storytellers. And without, as he called it, "the photoplay," everybody is simply improvising. He also knew that a script is more than just a blueprint. That the whole idea of movie magic is that interweave of powerful image, and dialogue, and performance, and music that can never be separated. And when it's working right, can never be duplicated or even forgotten.

I've grown up—most of my life has been spent in the dark watching movies. Movies have been the literature of my life. The literature of Irving Thalberg's generation was books and plays. They read the great words of great minds. And I think in our romance with technology, and our excitement at exploring all the possibilities of film and video, I think we've partially lost something that we now have to reclaim. I think it's time to renew our romance with the word. I'm as culpable as anyone in having exulted the image . . . at the expense of the word. But only a generation of readers will spawn a generation of writers.

The five films nominated for Best Picture this year *[Children of a Lesser God, Hannah and Her Sisters, The Mission, Platoon,* and *A Room With a View]* are as much the writer's film as the director's. And it's good news that each of these films has found its audience. Because this audience, who we all work for, deserves everything that we have to give them. They deserve that fifth draft, that tenth take, that one extra cut, and those several dollars over budget. And Irving Thalberg knew that. He would have been proud to have been associated with any of these films, as I am proud to have my name on this award in his honor. Because it reminds me of really how much growth as an artist I have ahead of me, in order to be worthy of standing in the company of those who have received this before me. So my deepest thanks to the board of governors of the Academy, and the audience out there in the dark. Thank you very much.

Spielberg compliments the writing of movies currently nominated for Best Picture, and he compliments the audience in the last paragraph.

By thanking the audience at the end of the speech, Spielberg makes all viewers feel responsible for conferring the award on him.

■ The Speech of Tribute

Mr. Crenshaw is retiring after thirty years as a seventh-grade science teacher. At his retirement banquet, three former students tell the audience the important role he played in their lives.

Bonnie Taylor has been promoted to vice-president of sales and will move to the corporate headquarters in Atlanta. On her last day at work her employees throw her a farewell party. Rosa speaks for the employees, commenting on Bonnie's many contributions to the company and her co-workers.

A noted civil rights leader stands on the spot where thirty years earlier a group of 137 disenfranchised African-Americans began a forty-mile march to the state capitol to demand full voting rights. He tells the crowd of the faith and forbearance of those who made those first steps toward justice.

These are all examples of **speeches of tribute.** This type of ceremonial speech honors a person, a group, or an event, and it can be one of the most moving forms of public address. Vivid and memorable examples include Ronald Reagan's tribute to the crew of the *Challenger* after the shuttle's explosion in 1986 (see pages 442–44), Ted Kennedy's eulogy of his brother Robert Kennedy after his assassination in 1968, and Abraham Lincoln's Gettysburg Address.

A special form of the speech of tribute is the **eulogy,** a speech of praise usually given for those who have recently died. Peggy Noonan, speechwriter for presidents Ronald Reagan and George Bush, captures the power of eulogies:

speech of tribute: a speech honoring a person, group, or event.

eulogy: a speech of tribute praising a person who has recently died.

They are the most moving kind of speech because they attempt to pluck meaning from the fog, and on short order, when the emotions are still ragged and raw and susceptible to leaps. It is a challenge to look at a life and organize our thoughts about it and try to explain to ourselves what it meant, and the most moving part is the element of implicit celebration. Most people aren't appreciated enough, and the bravest things we do in our lives are usually known only to ourselves. No one throws ticker tape on the man who chose to be faithful to his wife, on the lawyer who didn't take the drug money, or the daughter who held her tongue again and again. All this anonymous heroism. A eulogy gives us a chance to celebrate it.[3]

Five guidelines will help you write a eulogy or any other speech of tribute.

KEY POINTS **Guidelines for the** **Speech of Tribute**	**1.** Establish noble themes. **2.** Provide vivid examples. **3.** Express audience feelings. **4.** Create a memorable image. **5.** Be genuine.

First, *establish noble themes*. As you begin developing the eulogy ask, "Why is this person worthy of my respect and praise?" Answer this question by developing themes you want the audience to remember. Remember to focus on the positive. A speech of tribute celebrates what is good about a person; it is not an occasion for a "warts and all" biography. You must be careful, however, not to exaggerate a person's accomplishments. To do so may undermine your speech by making it seem insincere or unbelievable.

Second, *develop the themes of your speech with vivid examples*. Anecdotes, stories, and personal testimony are excellent ways of making your speech more vivid, humane, and memorable.

Third, *express the feelings of the audience assembled* or those whom you represent. The audience needs to be a part of the occasion for any speech of tribute. If you are honoring a former teacher, you may speak for yourself, but you can also speak for your class or even all students who studied under Mr. Crenshaw. If the honoree is present, he or she should feel that the tribute expresses more than one person's view.

Your use of noble themes, vivid examples, and audience feelings should combine to *create a memorable image of the person being honored*. Your speech not only honors someone, it also helps audience members focus on that person's importance to them.

Finally, *be genuine*. If you are asked to deliver a speech of tribute about someone you do not know, you may want to decline respectfully. The personal bond and interaction you develop in getting to know someone well is essential for a speech of tribute. Also, the person being honored may find the tribute more meaningful if it comes from a person he or she knows well.

One of the most eloquent and moving speeches of tribute in modern American history was Adlai Stevenson's eulogy of former first lady Eleanor Roosevelt. Mrs. Roosevelt died on November 7, 1962, and was buried three days later. Ten days after her death, an estimated 10,000 people gathered for a memorial service at New York City's Cathedral of St. John the Divine. The occasion called for a formal and substantial eulogy. Notice how Stevenson applied the guidelines we have discussed previously in the following excerpts from that speech.

Discussion Prompt:
How, specifically, does this eulogy illustrate the guidelines for a speech of tribute?

By using "we" early and often, the speaker claims to express the feelings of the audience.

One week ago this afternoon, in the Rose Garden at Hyde Park, Eleanor Roosevelt came home for the last time. Her journeys are over. The remembrance now begins.

In gathering here to honor her, we engage in a self-serving act. It is we who are trying, by this ceremony of tribute, to deny the fact that we have lost her, and, at least, to prolong the farewell, and—possibly—to say some of the things we dared

Adlai Stevenson celebrated the life of the former first lady and comforted the nation in his eulogy of Eleanor Roosevelt.

not say in her presence, because she would have turned aside such testimonial with impatience and gently asked us to get on with some of the more serious business of the meeting.

A grief perhaps not equaled since the death of her husband seventeen years ago is the world's best tribute to one of the great figures of our age — a woman whose lucid and luminous faith testified always for sanity in an insane time and for hope in

Stevenson establishes the noble themes of service and selflessness early.

371

Point out the parallel structure in this section: "lives she salvaged," "battles . . . she fought," "afflicted she comforted," and so on.

This quotation that Mrs. Roosevelt "loved so well" provides an example of her philosophy.

This section reinforces an image of Roosevelt as a modest and selfless person. Can anyone reading or listening to these lines doubt the sincerity of Stevenson's feelings? Point out how these lines bring the eulogy to a satisfying psychological conclusion.

a time of obscure hope—a woman who spoke for the good toward which man aspires in a world which has seen too much of the evil of which man is capable. . . .

We dare not try to tabulate the lives she salvaged, the battles—known and unrecorded—she fought, the afflicted she comforted, the hovels she brightened, the faces and places, near and far, that were given some new radiance, some sound of music, by her endeavors. What other single human being has touched and transformed the existence of so many others? What better measure is there of the impact of anyone's life?

Many of the admonitions she bequeathed us are neither new thoughts nor novel concepts. Her ideas were, in many respects, old-fashioned—as old as the Sermon on the Mount, as the reminder that it is more blessed to give than to receive. In the words of St. Francis that she loved so well: "For it is in the giving that we receive." . . .

And now one can almost hear Mrs. Roosevelt saying that the speaker has already talked too long. So we must say farewell. We are always saying farewell in this world—always standing at the edge of loss attempting to retrieve some memory, some human meaning, from the silence—something which was precious and is gone. . . .

We pray that she has found peace, and a glimpse of sunset. But today we weep for ourselves. We are lonelier; someone has gone from one's life—who was like the certainty of refuge; and someone has gone from the world—who was like a certainty of honor.[4]

■ The Oral Report

You will encounter oral reports throughout your academic life. They will probably play an integral part in your professional life as well. You may be asked to synthesize the critical reactions to the plays of Tennessee Williams for an English class; to provide your history class with an account of the firebombing of Dresden, Germany, during World War II; or to present to your boss and co-workers the results of your two-month study of new software options for the office. Your material and your manner of presentation may affect what others learn and what actions they take, as well as your academic and career success.

oral report: a substantial speech on an assigned or selected topic delivered to an academic or business audience.

Teaching Strategy:
Some students in class will have undoubtedly been required to deliver oral reports in other classes. Ask them to evaluate their own reports or those they heard. What were the general strengths and weaknesses of those reports? What information from this or earlier chapters could have improved the quality of those oral reports?

The **oral report** differs from the other types of public speeches you have done in this class in four important ways. First, your topic for an oral report is usually assigned by a teacher in a class or by a supervisor in a business or professional setting. You may not have even been involved in the process of generating topics for the reports. Second, oral reports are typically longer than speeches, often lasting up to half an hour or more. In the academic environment, however, class size and limited class time may force reports to be shorter. Under these conditions, the problem of covering a lot of information in a short period of time is even more significant. Third, reports are usually informational, compressing a lot of ideas and data. Often this information is important for classroom or business discussions that will follow. Finally, unlike the public speaker's typical audience, the audience for an oral report may be taking notes during the presentation. As a result, they may feel free to interrupt a speaker, asking questions or commenting on items they find interesting.

Individuals assigning reports often have a particular format in mind, and you will want to use your audience analysis skills and adapt your presentation accordingly. Nevertheless, the following five suggestions should help make your oral report more effective.

---

1. Organize your ideas clearly.
2. Synthesize your supporting materials.
3. Document your information.
4. Use visual support when possible.
5. Be creative.

**KEY POINTS
Guidelines for the
Oral Report**

First, *organize your ideas clearly*. Clear organization, important for any speech, is critical for the oral report. You will be presenting a great deal of information, and you want to make certain your listeners don't get lost among the specifics. Remember the "4 S's" (see pages 174–76) and use them!

Second, *synthesize your ideas*. A key objective of an oral report is to help the audience make sense of all available ideas and information. To do this you must integrate and unify the data you have collected, editing and organizing it so that your main ideas are clear and impressive. Synthesis does not mean that you inject your point of view throughout the presentation. If your point of view is requested, give it at the end. In class assignments, for example, an instructor might ask you to offer your evaluation near the end of your report. In business and professional settings, a question-answer period often follows the oral presentation, and you may be asked for your perspective then.

A third guideline to follow as you prepare your oral report is to *document your ideas and cite your sources*. Because others may use your information, they need to know the quality of the information you present. Cite your sources carefully. You may even distribute a handout so that your audience can refer to it later; include your sources of information in that material.

Fourth, *support your ideas with visual aids* when appropriate. As we mentioned above, you will present much information, and these aids can highlight significant points and trends. You may want to refer to handout materials, or to charts, graphs, and diagrams displayed on posterboard or overhead projections. Other students may be responsible for remembering material you cover in your class report and may use your handout as a study guide. In a business or professional setting your company may consider adopting a new policy or implementing a plan of action you recommend. Decision makers may base their decision, in part, on information you present, and they may want to refer to it later.

Finally, though an oral report places heavy emphasis on research, organization, analysis, and synthesis, *don't forget your own creativity*. Certainly, an oral report does not need the same level of creativity as, for example, a speech to entertain. Nevertheless, do not disregard it in this type of presentation. You have already learned that *what* you say is only part of a speech. *How* you say it is also important. Like any other good speech, an oral report should get the audience's attention immediately, highlight key ideas memorably, and conclude vividly. All this requires your ingenuity and inspiration. That spark of creativity may help your audience better understand and remember your message. It may set your report apart from others and give you a more attentive and receptive audience.

■ The Speech to Entertain

As we discussed early in this text, the three main purposes of speaking are to inform, to persuade, and to entertain. Though many informative and persuasive speeches contain elements of humor, the speech designed specifically to entertain is a special case because it is often difficult to do well.

speech to entertain: a speech to make a point through the creative, organized use of the speaker's humor.

The **speech to entertain** seeks to make a point through the creative, organized use of the speaker's humor. The distinguishing characteristic of a speech to entertain is the entertainment value of its supporting materials. It is usually delivered on an occasion where people are in a light mood: after a banquet, as part of an awards ceremony, and on other festive occasions.

A *speech to entertain* is different from *speaking to entertain*. In their opening monologues, Jay Leno, David Letterman, and Arsenio Hall are all speaking to entertain. Their purpose is to relax the audience, establish some interaction with them, and set the mood for the rest of the show. Their remarks are not organized around a central theme, something essential to a speech to entertain. If you combine the following five guidelines with what you already know about developing a public speech, you will discover that a speech to entertain is not only challenging but also fun to present.

KEY POINTS
Guidelines for the
Speech to Entertain

1. Make a point.
2. Be creative.
3. Be organized.
4. Use appropriate humor.
5. Use spirited delivery.

Teaching Strategy:
Have foreign students discuss topics that would not be appropriate for speeches to entertain in their native countries.

The first requirement for a speech to entertain is that it *makes a point*, or communicates a thesis, no less than the most carefully crafted informative or persuasive speech. Frequently the person delivering a speech to entertain is trying to make the audience aware of conditions, experiences, or habits that they take for granted. Here are examples of topics on which we have heard students present successful speeches to entertain:

A speech emphasizing the imprecision and incorrectness of language, especially that used in some advertisements.

A speech criticizing many doctors' failure to speak language that their patients can understand *and* many patients' failure to ask their doctors the right questions.

A speech poking fun at our interest in or curiosity about tabloid news stories.

A speech on "momilies," familiar homilies or sayings that mommies (and daddies) tell their children.

A speech criticizing the routine, expensive date and introducing some creative, less expensive dating options.

In some of these speeches, the speaker had stated the main point fairly bluntly by the end of the speech: take a careful look at the language used to sell you things; you owe it to your health to ask questions of your doctor; you do not have to spend a fortune to have an interesting time on a date. In other speeches, speakers simply implied their thesis: Think about what you say to correct or otherwise manipulate your children. Each of these speeches *does* make a point, however.

Second, *a speech to entertain is creative.* To be creative you must make sure that your speech to entertain is *your* product, and not simply a replay of an Arsenio Hall, David Letterman, or Joan Rivers monologue. A replay like this is not creative, no matter how great a job you think you do delivering the other person's lines. Moreover, if you copy Arsenio's, David's, or Joan's words and don't credit them, you are plagiarizing. Your speech to entertain should be original and creative. It should give your audience a glimpse of *your* unique view of the world.

Third, *a speech to entertain is organized.* It must have an introduction, body, and conclusion just as informative and persuasive speeches do. In other words, the speech to entertain must convey a sense of moving toward some logical point and achieving closure after adequately developing that point. Failure to organize your materials will cause you to ramble, embarrassing both you and your audience. You will feel, quite literally, like the novice comic caught without a finish, a sure-fire joke that makes a good exit line. The audience will sense that you are struggling and will have trouble relaxing and enjoying your humor.

To illustrate how you can organize materials that seem random, consider the experience of Steve, who selected as the topic of his speech to entertain "What This Graduating Senior Will Remember About His College Days." Steve began by thinking of some humorous incidents he had experienced during his four years in college: mistaking a graduate teaching assistant for another student the first day of class and telling him all the bad things he had heard about the course; saying to an instructor "I missed class last Tuesday. Did you say anything important?"; and having roommates soak his mattress with lime Jell-O, then let it congeal. He continued brainstorming, thinking of other examples. Gradually he recognized a possible pattern of organization. Rather than randomly recounting these various embarrassing incidents as a stand-up comic might, Steve organized them around three key ideas: (1) classroom catastrophes, (2) dormitory disasters, and (3) social setbacks. This organiza-

Teaching Strategy:
Steve's experience shows how important it is to brainstorm a number of vivid examples at the same time that you are looking for an organizing pattern. Point out how the alliteration ("classroom catastrophes," "dormitory disasters") reinforces the light tone of the speech.

tional pattern focused Steve's speech, and he concluded by making the following point:

> College is a special time in our lives, a sort of interlude between being a child living at home and being an adult living in the Real World. College is a place where we *learn, live,* and *laugh* with others. Three of us in this class will walk across a stage next month and leave college behind. We will take with us memories of happy days. Most of you, however, still have time to create your own memories. Make the most of these precious days. But remember, keep an eye on your roommates— especially if they've just returned from Kroger's with a bagful of lime Jell-O!

Steve's humor was relevant to his college audience, and *using appropriate humor* is the fourth guideline for a speech to entertain. The speech to entertain is difficult to do well for a simple reason: Most people associate entertainment with lots of laughter and feel that if the audience is not laughing a good deal, they are not responding favorably to the speech. But stop to consider for a moment the range of things that entertain you, from the outrageous antics of the comedian Gallagher to the muttered ramblings of Steven Wright. Your humor should be adapted to your topic, your audience, the occasion, and your own personal style. Four suggestions should guide your use of humor.

Be Relevant. Good humor is memorable and relevant to your general purpose. If humor does not relate to the point you are making, your audience will be diverted from, rather than directed to, your key idea. In his speech on the effect of smiling and laughter on health, Brent used the following personal example. Notice how it relates to and introduces a key point he then makes.

> [O]ur depression affects those around us. My roommate is the king of gloom. To him everything is always awful. He makes [Edgar Allan] Poe look like Ronald McDonald. A game show host could not maintain a smile after ten minutes with my roommate. And let me tell you, his depression rubs off. Because he is being so negative, I begin to think things are bad, which is not only depressing but unhealthy. In December 1988, *Psychology Today* published an article entitled "How We Make Ourselves Sick" that placed a direct link between depression and chronic illness. For the benefit of our own health and those around us, we need to smile and laugh more often.[5]

Be Tasteful. Important to any speech, audience analysis is vital for a speech to entertain. Taste is subjective. What delights some listeners may offend others. Do the best job you can in analyzing your audience, but when in doubt, err on the side of caution. Remember, humor that is off-color is off-limits.

Be Tactful. Avoid humor that generates laughter at the expense of others. There may be times when good natured ribbing is appropriate, as in Faye's introduction of Dr. Grice quoted earlier in this chapter (page 364). But humor intended to belittle or demean a person or group is unethical and unacceptable.

Be Positive. The tone for most occasions featuring speeches to entertain should be festive. People have come together to relax and enjoy each other's company. Dark, negative humor is usually inappropriate as it casts a somber tone on the situation.

Finally, a speech to entertain benefits from spirited delivery. We have often heard good speeches to entertain and looked forward to reading transcripts of them later. We were usually disappointed. The personality, timing, and interaction with the audience that made the speech lively and unforgettable could not be captured on paper. We have also read manuscripts of speeches to entertain that promised to be dynamic when presented, only to see them diminished by a monotonous, colorless, and lifeless delivery.

■ The Impromptu Speech

You are sitting at a staff meeting listening to your co-workers argue about office assignments in the company's new building. Your boss suddenly turns to ask how you would solve the problem. Or you are standing in the back of a crowded orientation session when, to your surprise, your supervisor introduces you and says, "Come up here and say a few words to these folks." Or you receive an award you didn't know you were being considered for. As people begin to applaud and whistle, you start walking to the front of the room to accept an attractive plaque. These are but three situations in which you would deliver an impromptu speech.

The **impromptu speech,** one with limited or no advanced preparation, can be intimidating. You have not had time to think about the ideas you want to communicate. You begin speaking without knowing the exact words you will use. You have not practiced delivering your speech. Don't panic! All is not lost. By now you have a pretty good understanding of how to organize, support, and deliver a speech. You have practiced these skills in prepared classroom speeches. All this practice will help you in your impromptu speech. With experience comes confidence. You already know what it feels like to stand before an audience. "But this is different," you might be saying right about now. "In those cases I had time to prepare." Well, if you follow these four guidelines, you should be ready for almost any impromptu speech that comes along.

impromptu speech: a speech delivered with little or no advanced preparation.

---

1. Speak on a topic you know well.
2. Make the most of the preparation time you have.
3. Focus on a single or a few key points.
4. Be brief.

**KEY POINTS
Guidelines for the Impromptu Speech**

First, if you have a choice, *speak on a topic you know well*. The more you know about your topic, the better you will be able to select relevant ideas, organize them, and explain them as you speak. You will also be more comfortable talking about a subject you know, and your confidence will show in your delivery.

Even though your preparation time is limited or nonexistent, *make the most of what time you've got.* Don't waste "walking time" from your seat to the front of the room worrying. Instead, ask yourself, "What do I want the audience to remember when I sit down? What two or three points will help them remember this?"

Third, *focus on a single or a few key points.* This may be easier if you think a bit like the character Charlie Fox in David Mamet's play *Speed – the – Plow.* As a movie producer, Charlie's test of a screenplay is whether he can condense it to one sentence, so that *TV Guide* can print a blurb about it. As silly as it might seem, this strategy could help you focus on the few ideas you want to get across to your listeners. If you have been asked to explain why you support building a new library instead of renovating the existing facility, think of the two or three most important reasons underlying your position. And remember to use the "4 S's" as you present those reasons to your audience.

Finally, *be brief.* One public speaking axiom is "Stand up! Speak up! Shut up!" Although this can be carried to an extreme, it is probably good advice for the impromptu speaker. An impromptu speech is not the occasion for a long, rambling discourse. Say what you need to say, and then be seated.

One author of this textbook gave an impromptu speech to his public speaking students the second day of class. He had assigned an ungraded speech of self-introduction for that day, and he wanted students to think of the assignment as an important practice opportunity. As he walked to class, he considered how he could set a proper tone and relax his students. He remembered hearing that baseball spring training was just thirty days away. A baseball fan, he decided to illustrate his point with an analogy between baseball and the class. Three aspects of baseball spring training were similar to what he expected in his class. By the time he walked into the class, he was ready to deliver the following impromptu speech:

> In less than a month, major league baseball players will pack their bags and head to Florida and Arizona for spring training. As part of their training, they do three things. They receive instruction from their coaches. They work on fundamental skills. And they play exhibition games in which they practice putting it all together. Spring training is important because it helps baseball players prepare for the regular season, when games really count.
>
> I want you to think of the first weeks of this class as your spring training in public speaking. You will learn from your coach — that's me — public speaking strategies and techniques. You will work on fundamental skills such as supporting, organizing, and delivering your speech. And you will give ungraded, practice speeches to your classmates. If you take this spring training seriously, you'll be ready when it's your turn to walk to the front of the room, look at your audience, and begin giving your first graded speech.

Later he reflected on the speech. He included the non-specific word "things" at the end of his second sentence where a more specific word would serve better. The last sentence seemed OK, but maybe something with a baseball image would be more catchy. What about coming to the plate and hitting a home run? Despite these weaknesses, he was satisfied with his impromptu

Practice Speaking:
Place the following topics (or others we suggest in the Instructor's Resource Manual) on separate slips of paper. Have students draw three, select one, and place the two they didn't pick back into the pot. After a minute's preparation, the student is to deliver an impromptu speech on one of these topics:

If I were the President of the United States, I would . . .
My most important material possessions are . . .
I was really embarrassed when . . .
The biggest problems facing (name of your state) are . . .
My favorite childhood memory is . . .
My idea of a perfect date is . . .
The best thing about my major is . . .
The best way to destroy a friendship is . . .
The biggest difference between men and women is . . .
The best (or worst) things about (your college) are . . .

remarks. Judging from the reactions of the class and their comments, he had succeeded in relaxing them before they gave their first speech to the class. If the instructor uses the strategy in subsequent semesters, he will no doubt reflect on his first attempt, polish his language, and improve his speech.

Notice how the instructor used the guidelines listed above. He selected two topics he knew well: public speaking and baseball. He was comfortable talking about both topics. Had he chosen to compare public speaking preparation with thermonuclear physics, a topic on which he had little knowledge, he would have been in trouble — and so would his audience! He collected his thoughts and outlined the body of the speech in his mind as he walked to class. He focused on a single idea: The ungraded speaking assignments in this class give you an opportunity to prepare for future speeches. He established this position by developing three simple points. The speech was brief and to the point, just eleven sentences. And after the speech was over, he evaluated it in order to do a better job next time.

Impromptu speaking is spontaneous; it requires you to think on your feet. The more you study and practice public speaking principles and skills, the more confident you will be when someone taps you on the shoulder and says, "You're on!"

■ The Question-Answer Period ———————————

TV reporter, asking question of Washington Redskins quarterback before Super Bowl XXII, 1988: *"Doug, how long have you been a black quarterback?"* Doug Williams: *"I've been a quarterback since I was a kid. I've been black my whole life."*[6]

Preparing for a public speech involves a lot of uncertainty. Even the most thorough audience analysis can never tell you everything you'd like to know about your listeners. You have to make a lot of educated guesses and take it from there. Sometimes you are unsure whether you have accurately assessed what your listeners want to hear.

Having the opportunity to field questions from the audience following your speech or oral report reduces this uncertainty. Rather than dreading the **question-answer period,** you should welcome it. First, it offers you an excellent opportunity to adapt to your audience. You know what your listeners want to hear because they ask the questions. Second, it gives you an opportunity to interact directly with your audience. This usually results in a more natural, lively delivery and makes for better speaker-listener rapport.

A third reason to welcome questions is that almost any question asked can help you. If questions are friendly, that is high compliment: The audience is genuinely interested in you and your topic. If questions stem from audience confusion about your presentation, you have an opportunity to clarify. If someone asks you a combative and contentious question, you've just been given a second chance to win this person over to your point of view. Without the Q-A period you would not have had this opportunity. If time permits, then, seize the opportunity to answer your listeners' questions.

Before tackling the Q-A period, study the guidelines in the box. You will find them helpful when you stand in front of an audience and ask, "Are there any questions?"

KEY POINTS
Guidelines
to Answering
Questions

1. Restate or clarify the question.
2. Compliment the question.
3. Answer the question.
4. Check the response with the questioner.

Teaching Strategy:
Have students listen to (or read a transcript of) a question-answer period following a speech or at a press conference. Ask them to analyze the speaker's strategies and effectiveness in responding to audience questions. Sources might include network broadcasts of presidential press conferences; C-SPAN broadcasts of interviews, National Press Club addresses, conference proceedings, news briefings, and call-in shows; and transcripts of presidential press conferences published in *Weekly Compilation of Presidential Documents* and *Public Papers of the Presidents of the United States.*

The first step, *repeating or clarifying the question,* is important for three reasons. First, repetition makes sure that the entire audience has heard the question. At times, your audience will be small enough that you can be reasonably sure everyone heard the question asked. Or if your audience is very large, the person asking the question may have stepped to a microphone located in the audience. As a rule, though, if you have any doubt that everyone in the audience heard the question, repeat it. Second, repeating the question allows the questioner the opportunity to correct you if you misstate it, saving you the embarrassment of beginning to answer a different question. Third, if the question seems confusing to you or somehow misses the point, you should rephrase the question to make it clearer, more focused, and more relevant. Never answer a question you don't understand.

A second step in answering a question is to *compliment the question,* if deserved. We have all heard speakers say, "I'm glad you asked that." Of course, you cannot repeat that same remark after each question. But without seeming insincere you might say, "That's a good (or perceptive or interesting) question," or "I was hoping someone would ask that." If you know the questioner, you might even joke, "Can't put anything past you, Bernie."

You may face hostile questions, and they certainly pose special challenges for a speaker. Remember, though, that a hostile question is not necessarily a bad question. Hostile questions can be quite legitimate. Sincerely complimenting a hostile question or questioner can defuse a tense situation and focus attention on issues rather than on personal antagonism.

You are now ready for the third step: *answering the question.* Of course, the content and the form of your answer depend on the specific questions; nevertheless, the following suggestions may be helpful.

Know Your Topic Thoroughly. Your success during the Q-A period will depend, in large part, on your research and preparation for your speech. You should always know more than you included in your speech. Most of the time, poor answers reflect poor preparation.

Be as Brief as Possible. Obviously, some questions require longer, more thoughtful answers than others. The question "How much did you say it will cost to complete Phase II of the new library?" can be answered simply, "$2.5 million." The question "What will that $2.5 million provide?" will require a much longer answer. There are two reasons for making your answers as succinct as possible. First, short answers are easier to remember than lengthy ones. Second, the shorter each answer, the greater number of questions you can field.

Be Methodical When Giving Lengthy Answers. When you need to give a detailed answer, use the "frame it, state it, and explain it" approach. Suppose you were asked the question "How will the $2.5 million budgeted for Phase II of the new library be spent?" You might answer as follows:

> In order to answer that question, we need to look at three categories of costs: construction, furniture and equipment, and instructional materials.
>
> Mike Phillips, the director of buildings and grounds, estimates cost breakdowns as follows: $1.7 million for construction, $300,000 for furniture and equipment, and $500,000 for instructional materials.
>
> Unlike many institutions, we're fortunate that we can provide a sizable amount of money—half a million dollars—*in addition to* our regular annual budget of $200,000 for instructional resources. This is a one-time infusion of money. You should also know, however, what these figures do not include. *Not included* are personnel costs, energy costs, and costs for purchases of materials and equipment beyond the first year.

If You Don't Know an Answer, Admit It. Making up an answer is potentially damaging. Fabricated answers can not only undermine your credibility, but the audience may also act on incorrect information you have provided. Besides, it's unethical. There is nothing wrong with saying, "I don't know" or "I don't know, but I'll check on it and let you know." If you give the second response, make sure you follow up promptly.

Be Careful About What You Say Publicly. Remember that in a public gathering, there is no such thing as an "off the record" statement. Don't say, "It's not official and I would not want it reported yet, but we expect that the vice-president will be our commencement speaker." You will probably read the following headline in the next issue of your school paper: "Vice-President Possible Commencement Speaker." If the press is present, what you say may indeed be reported. As a general rule, never say anything that would embarrass you or slander others if it appeared in the next morning's paper.

The final step in answering a question is to *check the response with the questioner.* Did you answer the question to his or her satisfaction? Is there a follow-up question? Remember two drawbacks to this approach, however. If each person is allowed a question and a follow-up, you will be able to answer fewer people's questions. Second, if questioners are argumentative, asking them if you answered the question to their satisfaction gives them an opportunity to keep the floor and turn the Q-A period into a debate.

■ The Videotaped Speech

In Chapter 1 we introduced you to the components of the communication process: speaker, message, listener, channel, feedback, environment, and noise. Channel, you remember, refers to the way the message is sent. Messages

A college televison studio gives students valuable experience working with this mass medium and adapting to the camera.

may be written or spoken. If spoken, they may be delivered in person or transmitted electronically. Videotape is one popular electronic medium. Even though you still see and hear the speaker, videotape introduces a new dynamic to the public speech, and that dynamic affects how audience members receive the message.

videotaped speech: a speech taped during practice for the speaker's review or during actual delivery for viewing by another audience.

The **videotaped speech** is increasingly common, for both practice and presentation. If you have access to a camcorder, you may want to use it as you practice your speeches for this class. If you are nervous about your speech and self-conscious practicing in front of another person, just set up a camera, turn it on, walk to the front of the room, and deliver your speech. This rehearsal strategy gives you the advantage of a live critic, one who knows you well and wants to help you become a better speaker. That critic is *you!* You can watch yourself on the videotape and note things you do well and those still needing work. After viewing yourself, you may even ask some friends to look at the tape with you and offer their comments and suggestions. If you use the videotape strategy, keep a copy of your final practice tape for each of your speeches in this class. After you have a few examples, review them. You will probably be surprised to see how much you have improved since your first effort.

Videotaping actual presentations is also increasingly common. Speeches given to community groups or before governmental bodies are often taped for possible broadcast on local news. Corporations use videotaped presentations in their employee training programs. Your instructor may have played tapes of great speeches for you, or speeches other students gave when they took this public speaking class. These examples may have been particularly helpful, because videotape re-creates the event better than a lifeless manuscript does. In this section we discuss videotaping an entire speech for playback, and we offer three guidelines to help you meet this challenge.

---

1. Adapt your delivery to your audience(s).
2. Adapt your delivery to your microphone.
3. Adapt your delivery to your camera shots.

**KEY POINTS
Guidelines for the
Videotaped Speech**

Your first consideration in preparing for a videotaped or filmed speech is your *audience*. Are you speaking primarily to the immediate group assembled or to those who will view the videotape later? Which is your primary audience and which your secondary? Or are both equally important? Unlike traditional speaking situations requiring analysis of one audience, the videotaped speech often requires you to analyze several audiences. If these audiences differ in significant ways, the task of constructing your speech is more difficult.

The audience you expect to view your videotape should also guide the way you respond to the camera. If you are videotaping your speech for your own analysis, you want the camera to see what any audience member in the camera's location might see. In that case, don't look directly into the camera during your entire speech. Make eye contact with all parts of your audience as you practice, treating the camera as just another audience member. If you are speaking only to an external audience, as the president does when speaking to the public from a desk in the Oval Office, you will want to make eye contact only with the camera, treating it as your only listener. As a rule, if the audience viewing a videotape sees another audience in the speaker's presence, they will expect the speaker to be interacting with those people. If audience members watching a videotape believe themselves to be the speaker's only audience, they will expect to receive the full measure of the speaker's eye contact.

A second concern is the *microphone* you will use. A **lapel microphone** is a small one that clips to your shirt, tie, dress, or jacket. It moves with you. A **fixed**, or stationary, **microphone** is often fastened to the lectern or held in place by a microphone stand. You may or may not be given a choice of microphones. What are the advantages and drawbacks of each?

A lapel microphone allows you freedom of movement. You may walk and keep the same voice level. Some media experts believe that because it is attached near the chest cavity, it adds resonance to your voice, making your vocal

Practice Speaking:
To give students a chance to see and hear themselves on videotape, tape their delivery of just the introductions of an upcoming speech. Have students deliver their introductions to a classroom empty except for the person videotaping. Ask them to remember where classmates sit and to visualize and make eye contact with them. This assignment gives you a chance to (1) emphasize the importance of impressions formed during the first seconds of a speech, (2) check the structure and content of the introductions, (3) show students examples of positive and negative elements of their delivery, and (4) help ensure advanced preparation for the speech.

delivery richer. This mike is also unobtrusive, not easily seen by you or your audience. Speakers who experience "mike fright" usually prefer the lapel to the fixed microphone because it is out of their sight. However, if you use a lapel mike, you will need to watch your movement, being careful not to become entangled in the cord. You will also want to select your clothing carefully. If your jacket and shirt or blouse rustle as you move, the mike will pick up distracting noise.

Even a fixed microphone attached to the lectern sometimes picks up distracting noises, such as nervous tapping of fingers on the lectern or shuffling of paper as you move your speaking notes. In order to do your best job as a speaker, you need to be aware of all that the audience hears. A disadvantage of the fixed microphone is that it restricts movement. As you walk away from the mike, your volume may fade. Most fixed microphones today, however, are multi-directional and are able to pick up sound from many directions. You do not need to stand rigidly twelve inches away from the fixed mike, speaking without turning your head from side to side. You may (and should) move your head as you make eye contact with various sections of your audience. Avoid looking at the mike and becoming preoccupied with its presence.

A third factor you should consider when planning and practicing your speech is the *camera*. Where is it positioned? What is its angle of vision? Will it record close-up or long shots? What the camera sees should help determine your delivery. If the camera takes only head shots, your facial expressions become more important and gesturing less so. Glancing down at your notes will be more noticeable. In a full body shot, you will be free to gesture and move about more freely. If the camera sees you from chest up, you will want to ensure that your gestures are high enough to convey your dynamism visibly. Someone videotaping your speech rehearsal or actual presentation may use the camera's zoom lens to get a variety of shots. If possible, find out this person's plans before you speak.

Here are some other tips to make your videotaped presentation more effective:

1. Avoid wearing predominantly white or black clothing. Pastel clothing is usually preferred.
2. Avoid wearing finely striped clothing, or other busy patterns.
3. Avoid wearing large or excessive jewelry.
4. Keep make-up simple and natural. Shiny facial and head areas should be treated with powdered make-up. Men who have "5 o'clock shadows" should shave or use corrective make-up before they speak.
5. Don't blow into or tap on a microphone.
6. Don't make exaggerated movements in front of the camera.
7. Exercise caution in using overhead projectors, slides, or other types of visual aids that require lights to be turned off. The camera may not be able to videotape those projections efficiently.

In summary, try to determine what the viewing audience will see. If possible, find out how your speech will be taped beforehand so that you can practice accordingly. If this is not possible, be prepared to adapt during the event. Arrive early and talk to the camera operator; you may even want to suggest how you would like the speech recorded. Let the camera operator know if you will use a visual aid, and when, so that he or she can zoom in on the chart or graph at the appropriate time. If your primary audience is the tape viewing audience and if you are given a choice, request many close-up shots. Remember, your eyes and face are the most expressive parts of your body. Emphasizing those aspects of your physical delivery can make the speaker-viewer relationship more personal.

As with any speech, practice is the key to effective delivery. Videotaping adds another dynamic to that delivery. You must be concerned not only with how your body and voice carry your message, but also with how the medium of transmission affects the message your listeners receive.

Summary

The *speech of introduction* presents a featured speaker to an audience. If you are called on to introduce another speaker, your speech should not compete with the one you are introducing. You should be brief, focus your remarks on the featured speaker, establish that person's credibility, create positive but realistic audience expectations, and match the tone of the featured speech.

The *speech of presentation* confers an award, prize, or special recognition on an individual or group. Such a speech should state the purpose of the award or recognition, particularly if it is new or unfamiliar to the audience. The speaker should state the recipient's qualifications to reveal why the person deserves the award. If the audience does not know the name of the recipient in advance, the speech of presentation should create suspense, revealing the recipient's name only late in the speech. If the person being honored has been selected from nominees known to the audience, the speech of presentation should compliment these other individuals.

The *acceptance speech* is an honoree's response to a speech of presentation. Social custom dictates that you thank at least briefly any group presenting you an award, prize, or other recognition. When accepting an award you should thank the people bestowing the award, compliment your competitors if you know them, and thank those who helped you attain the award. Your acceptance speech gives you a chance to say thanks humbly and sincerely.

The *speech of tribute* honors an individual, a group, or a significant event. A eulogy, spoken to honor a person who has recently died, is one of the most familiar speeches of tribute. In delivering a speech of tribute you should establish noble or lofty themes built upon vivid examples from the subject's life. As a speaker you should attempt to express the collective feelings of the audience. You should create a memorable image of the subject, and you should be genuine.

The *oral report* is a special type of public speech because the speaker is as likely to be assigned the topic as to have chosen it. Oral reports are usually longer than public speeches and they are usually informative. Because they cover a lot of material, oral reports should be well organized, should synthesize relevant supporting material before evaluating it, should be well documented, should use visual supports when appropriate, and should be creative.

The *speech to entertain* seeks to make a point through the creative, organized use of the speaker's humor. Usually delivered on a light, festive occasion, your speech to entertain should make a point, be creative, be well organized, use appropriate humor, and be delivered in a spirited manner. The humor you use in a speech to entertain should be relevant to your point, tasteful, tactful, and light.

An *impromptu speech* is one delivered with little or no advance preparation. You speak impromptu whenever someone asks you a question or calls on you to speak with only a moment's notice. Under these circumstances, speak on a subject you know well, if possible, and use your limited preparation time in a positive way. Ask, "What do I want the audience to remember from what I say?" Then focus your remarks to achieve that goal. The impromptu speech should focus on only a few key points and it should be brief. To improve your impromptu speaking, reflect on each speech to see how you might have improved its content, organization, and delivery.

The *question-answer period* after your speech gives you the opportunity to adapt your material to the specific needs or wishes of the audience, because listeners will ask you what they want to know. Answering questions from audience members will be easier if you follow four steps. First, restate or clarify the question. Second, compliment the question or the questioner. Third, answer the question. Finally, check your response with the person who asked the question.

The *videotaped speech* is becoming increasingly common, both for practice and for actual presentation of the speech. Videotaping requires speakers to adapt their delivery to their various audiences, to the microphone, and to the camera. The presence of a video camera will influence your eye contact, movement, gestures, and other elements of your vocal and physical delivery.

Exercises

1. Pair up with another member of the class. Discuss each other's speech topic and relevant personal background. Following the guidelines discussed in this chapter, prepare a speech introducing your partner on the day of his or her speech. Your partner will introduce you when you speak.
2. Prepare and deliver a speech of tribute for someone you admire and who is known to the class. This person may be a campus, local, national, or international figure.
3. Pair up with someone and discuss what each of you do well. Create an award that one of you will receive. One of you will give a speech of presentation and the other a speech of acceptance.
4. View a speech that was constructed for both public and mass communication. Examples include speeches at political conventions, inaugural addresses, State of the Union addresses, and State of the State addresses by governors. Analyze the speech in light of the different audiences. Did one audience seem more important to the speaker than the other? If so, what led you to this conclusion? Do you think the speaker adapted well to each audience? If so, what strategies and techniques did the speaker use well? If not, what could the speaker have done better?
5. Listen to a formal speech of introduction. The speech may be one you see on television, as in a C-SPAN broadcast of a National Press Club address. Or you

may attend a campus or community meeting where a speaker is introduced. Using the guidelines in this chapter, critique the speech of introduction. What did the introducer do well? What could he or she have done better? Did the introducer prepare the audience to listen intelligently to the speech that followed?

Notes ———————————————————————————

1. Don Ochs, Introduction of Samuel L. Becker, Central States Communication Association Convention, April 12, 1991, rpt. *The CSCA News* (Spring 1991): 2.

2. George L. Grice, Remarks at the First General Session, Texas Speech Communication Association Convention, October 4, 1986, rpt. *TSCA Newsletter* (January 1987): 12.

3. Peggy Noonan, *What I Saw at the Revolution* (New York: Random, 1990) 253.

4. Adlai Stevenson, "Eulogy on Eleanor Roosevelt," *Representative American Speeches: 1962–1963*, ed. Lester Thonssen (New York: Wilson, 1963) 179–83.

5. Brent Wainscott, Untitled Speech, *Winning Orations 1990* (Mankato, MN: Interstate Oratorical Association, 1990) 71.

6. Barry Wilner, "Thanks for the Memories," *Inside Sports* February 1991: 66.

Speaking in Small Groups

18

The Importance of Small Groups

Small Groups Defined

Types of Groups

Group Discussion and Decision Making
Principles of Group Decision Making
The Process of Group Decision Making

The Responsibilities of Group Members
The Responsibilities of Group Leaders

The Group Presentation
Formats for the Presentation
 The Public Discussion
 The Symposium
Preparing a Group Presentation

"Never doubt that a small group of thoughtful, committed citizens can change the world. Indeed, it's the only thing that ever has." MARGARET MEAD

■ The Importance of Small Groups ————————————

Take out a sheet of paper and start listing all the small groups to which you belong. Think of committees, subcommittees, boards, and councils on which you serve. Include your network of close friends. Add your family to the list. What about athletic teams, honor societies, fraternities or sororities, the chess club, the debating society, the arts council, study groups, and other groups? After a few minutes of this brainstorming, you will probably be surprised at the length of your list. In fact, groups are so prevalent in our society that it is estimated there are more groups in America than there are people.[1]

Not only are groups plentiful, they are also influential. They shape our society and our behavior. Government, businesses, educational institutions, and other organizations depend on groups to gather information, assess data, and propose courses of action. Our families and our close friends give us counsel and support in times of need. We do so much planning, problem solving, and recreating in small groups that we can all relate to the humorist's remark that "there are no great people, only great committees."

Cross-Reference:
If you rarely have time to teach group work but would like your students to make group presentations, the list of ten steps in preparing a group presentation toward the end of this chapter should be particularly helpful.

Because groups significantly influence our lives, it is essential that groups communicate effectively. Unfortunately, small group communication seems not to be a skill most of us master easily. For example, two college professors and communication consultants note that "poor meeting preparation, ad hoc scheduling, and lack of participant training in meeting management are causing many companies to lose the *equivalent of thirty man-days and 240 man-hours a year for every person who participates in business conferences.*"[2] Groups are numerous and influential, and poor group communication can be costly. But why study group work as an adjunct to public speaking? The answer is twofold: (1) Groups of people often make public presentations, and (2) the quality of those presentations depends on how well group members have functioned together.

For most of your work in your public speaking class you have operated alone. *You* selected your speech topics. *You* researched as much as you wanted and at your own convenience. *You* organized your speeches as you thought best and practiced them as much as you thought necessary. As we suggested in Chapter 2, you were the author, artist, and director of your own success or failure.

As part of a group solving a problem and preparing a presentation, your work is more complex. The group's final presentation will allow you to apply everything you have learned about researching, organizing, and delivering a speech. Just as important, however, group processes will test your ability to work productively and congenially with other people. You will do that much more easily if you understand the subjects covered in this chapter: what constitutes a group, the types of groups, principles of group decision making, the responsibilities of group leaders and members, and the most frequently used formats for group presentations.

■ Small Groups Defined

A **small group** is a collection of three or more individuals who interact and influence each other in pursuit of a common goal. This definition includes four important concepts: *individuals, interaction, influence,* and *goal.*

The number of **individuals** in a group may vary. At a minimum, there must be three. Two people are not a group but rather an interpersonal unit, sometimes called a dyad. The addition of a third person adds a new dynamic, a new perspective. Paul Nelson describes the new relationship in the following way:

> Something happens to communication when it involves more than two people: It becomes much more complex. For example, imagine two people, A and B, having a conversation. There is only *one* possible conversation, A-B. Add one more person, C, however: Now there are *four* possible interactions, A-B, A-C, B-C, and A-B-C. Add another person, D, and there are eleven possible interactions. And so on.[3]

small group: a collection of three or more people influencing and interacting with one another in pursuit of a common goal.

Teaching Strategy: Ask students to complete the brainstorming exercise suggested in the opening paragraph of this chapter. Have students select one of the groups they listed. Ask them to describe the group according to the four characteristics discussed here: individuals, interaction, influence, and goal.

Discussion Prompt: Your students, no doubt, have been assigned to working groups in several of their classes. Ask them what group size they liked best. Let them provide examples of problems they encountered with groups that were either too small or too large.

Although we can all agree that three is the minimum number for a small group, we do not always agree on the maximum number. Even communication experts disagree, with some using seven as a workable maximum and others stretching the range to twenty. What characterizes a small group is not a specific number of participants but the *type* of communication they undertake. If a group is too large, meaningful interaction among members may be impossible and the large group may have to be divided into smaller working groups.

A group's size, then, affects a second characteristic of a small group: **interaction.** A small group offers each participant an opportunity to interact with *all* other members of the group. A group cannot function if its participants fail to interact, and it functions ineffectively when a few members dominate. Generally, the larger the group, the fewer opportunities for any one member to participate and the greater the likelihood that a few members will dominate the flow of communication, making certain that meaningful interaction does not take place.

A third characteristic of small groups is **influence.** Members of a group interact in order to influence others. As journalist Walter Lippman observed, "When all think alike, no one thinks very much." Groups function best when members express differences of opinions openly and try to persuade others with data and arguments.

Finally, a group has a purpose. As we noted in Chapter 1, a group is more than simply a collection of individuals who interact; it exists for a reason. Members interact and influence each other in order to achieve a **goal.** The group process fails when members are unsure of their goal or when they fail to resolve conflicting perceptions of that goal.

■ Types of Groups

People form groups for two reasons: because they enjoy interacting with each other or because they need to accomplish a task. Therefore, we can classify groups into two general types: social-oriented and task-oriented. A **social-**

social-oriented group: a small group that exists primarily because its members enjoy interacting with one another.

task-oriented group: a small group that exists primarily to accomplish some goal.

study group: a task-oriented group devoted to researching and learning about a topic.

problem-solving group: a task-oriented group devoted to deciding on courses of action to correct a problem.

action group: a task-oriented group devoted to implementing proposals for action.

oriented group is one whose main goal is social. The group may not have a major task in mind but rather be concerned mainly with relationships, enjoying time spent with other members of the group. **Task-oriented groups** are more formal. Members interact with a specific goal in mind. For example, you and a few classmates may form a study group to review for examinations and to be an audience for each other as you practice your speeches.

The objectives of social-oriented and task-oriented groups often intermingle. Say you and your friends decide to go to a movie. Clearly, this is a social occasion, but you still must accomplish certain tasks: What movie does the group want to see? When is the best time for everyone to see it? Will you carpool or will everyone meet at the theatre? Do you want to get a bite to eat before or after the movie? You have probably, at times, been frustrated when your social group was unable to make some of these "easy" task decisions.

While social-oriented groups may have task objectives, the converse is also true. You form a study group to accomplish certain tasks, but as you get to know the others you discover that you enjoy their company. As social objectives emerge, the group meets more frequently and functions more effectively. If social purposes predominate, however, you may find that your group sacrifices studying for socializing. Even though most groups have both social and task objectives, one purpose usually takes precedence according to the situation. That purpose determines the structure of your group and the nature of the communication among its members.

In this chapter we will focus on *task-oriented groups*, sometimes called working groups, and they include study groups, problem-solving groups, and action groups. The objective of a **study group** is to learn about a topic. It gathers, processes, and evaluates information. When you and your classmates work together to study for an exam, you are a study group. A **problem-solving group** decides on courses of action. This type of group explores a problem, suggesting solutions to remedy it. The objective of an **action group** is, as its name implies, to act. It has the power to implement proposals. Those categories may overlap. In fact, you may be a member of a group that studies a situation, devises a solution, *and* implements it.

As you go through this chapter, you will find that participating in task groups and delivering public speeches are similar in several ways. Both usually involve research, analysis of information and ideas, and the presentation of that information to others. In small groups your presentation may be to other group members, although sometimes a group will present its findings to an external body. Yet despite these similarities, there are notable differences between public speaking and group communication. The effective communicator will seek to master both sets of skills.

■ Group Discussion and Decision Making _____

One of the most important reasons we form groups is to make decisions. We may seek a friend's guidance because we believe that "two heads are better than one." The philosophy behind this statement is the foundation of group decision making. You might have heard the expression that in communication "the whole is greater than the sum of its parts." This is particularly true in group communication. What this means is that, if a group of five functions effectively, its product will be qualitatively or quantitatively superior to the total product of five people working individually. But a group is able to work most effectively when members follow certain principles of group decision making. We discuss these five principles next.

1. Group decision making is a shared responsibility.
2. Group decision making requires a clear understanding of goals.
3. Group decision making benefits from a clear but flexible agenda.
4. Group decision making is enhanced by open communication.
5. Group decision making requires adequate information.

**KEY POINTS
Principles of Group
Decision Making**

PRINCIPLES OF GROUP DECISION MAKING

Group Decision Making is a Shared Responsibility. It is true that the group leader plays a special role in the group. As a matter of fact , we include a separate section in this chapter on the responsibilities of the group leader as well as members. The presence of a group leader does not necessarily establish a leader-follower, or even an active-passive, association. In fact, this relationship is usually better represented as a partnership. Group decision making requires the active participation of *all* members performing mutually reinforcing responsibilities.

Group Decision Making Requires a Clear Understanding of Goals. As we have stated earlier, every group has a goal. Sometimes that goal is predetermined. Your instructor may, for example, divide your class into small groups, assigning each group to generate a list of twenty-five topics suitable for a speech to inform. In your career you may be part of a small group with the task of studying specific job-related problems and proposing workable solutions. In both of these instances the group has a clear statement of its objective. In other situations the goal of your group may be less clear. If that is the case you will have to clarify, specify, or even determine your goals.

Group Decision Making Benefits From a Clear but Flexible Agenda. Every group needs a plan of action. Because a group's process affects its product, it is vital that members spend sufficient time generating an action plan. The leader can facilitate this process by suggesting procedures that the group may adopt, modify, or reject. The best plan, or agenda, however, is one not dictated by the leader but rather developed by both the leader and the members of the group. Remember, the leader and the group members are a partnership.

A group's agenda should be both specific and flexible. Group participants must know what is expected of them and how they will go about accomplishing the task at hand. Raising $1,000 for charity might be accomplished by dividing the membership into five teams, each with the responsibility for generating $200. These teams would need to communicate and coordinate to avoid un-

Teaching Strategy: Have groups discuss the following goal: to present to the class an informed, organized, and well-delivered discussion on [their topic] on the day assigned. Have students determine interim goals; refer them to the section, "Steps in Preparing a Group Presentation," as a guide. You may want to collect this assignment and return it to them later. At that time, ask them to evaluate their interim goals and to note which goals they achieved and which they did not. Remind your students that not meeting interim goals does not necessarily mean the group has failed. An effective group reviews and revises goals and procedures throughout the discussion process.

Teaching Strategy: Remind students that setting goals for groups is an important task, and they should follow three guidelines: (1) goals should be specific; (2) goals may be short-term and/or long-term; and (3) goals should be realistic.

necessary overlap as they decided on their fund-raising projects. Groups also need to be flexible as they pursue their goals. Unexpected obstacles may require revising the agenda. The group needs a backup plan, for example, if their car wash is canceled because of rain.

Group Decision Making is Enhanced by Open Communication. If all members of a group think alike, there is no need for the group. One person can simply make the decision. Diversity is what gives a group breadth of perspective. Both the group leader and individual members should protect and encourage the expression of minority views.

groupthink: excessive agreement among group members who value conformity more than critical evaluation.

What a group wants to avoid is the problem of groupthink, a term coined by Irving Janis. **Groupthink** occurs when group members come to care more about conforming and "not making waves" than they do about exercising the critical evaluation necessary to weed out bad ideas.[4] Groupthink reduces open communication and adversely affects the quality of decision making. In order to be effective, a group must encourage each member to exercise his or her independent judgment.

Group Decision Making Requires Adequate Information. Access to information that is sufficient and relevant is extremely important. A group suffers if its information is based on the research of only one or two of its members. To avoid this problem a group should follow a few simple steps. First, the leader should provide essential information to the group as a starting point. Second, each member of the group should contribute critical knowledge to the group. Third, the group should divide the gathering of information in a way that is efficient and yet provides some overlap. Later in this chapter we provide some suggestions for gathering information. Now that we understand the principles of group decision making, we need to understand *how* the group makes decisions.

Class Activity:
If you followed the teaching strategy two annotations ago, have groups convert the interim goal statements they developed into an action plan. For example, if a short-term goal is to gather the group's initial research by the next group meeting, the action plan will describe how the group will accomplish this goal. Each person may be responsible for bringing to the next group meeting four articles relating to the group's topic. See "Steps in Preparing a Group Presentation," later in this chapter.

Related Reading:
For a brief discussion of groupthink, its symptoms and prevention, see: Ross, Raymond S. *Small Groups in Organizational Settings.* Englewood Cliffs, NJ: Prentice, 1989: 48–50.

THE PROCESS OF GROUP DECISION MAKING

In his celebrated book *How We Think*, published in 1910, John Dewey argued that decision making should be a logical, orderly process.[5] His "Steps to Reflective Thinking" have provided one of the most useful, and we think one of the best, approaches to problem solving. Authors and theorists differ in their adaptations of the reflective thinking model, organizing it around five, six, or seven steps. We prefer a seven-step approach.

If you are a member of a problem-solving discussion group or a task-oriented group and you have not been assigned a topic, the group will need to select a topic and word it. A good discussion topic is current, is controversial, and has a body of data and opinion from which to construct and refute positions. Once you select a topic meeting these criteria, you must word the topic according to the following guidelines.

First, it should be worded as a question the group will seek to answer. "The campus parking problem" fails to meet this criterion and, consequently, does not direct participants in the discussion toward a goal. A better wording is evident in the examples presented in the second criterion.

Second, the question should be open rather than closed. Open wording might include "What can be done to alleviate the parking problem on campus?" or "How should this college solve the campus parking problem?" These questions are open because they do not direct the group to one particular solution. They invite a variety of solutions and can generate lively and productive discussion. The question "Should the campus build a multi-story parking facility to solve the campus parking problem?" is an example of a closed question, because it focuses attention on one solution. This "yes-or-no" question limits discussion of alternative proposals. Because it forces individuals to choose sides, a closed question is probably more appropriate for a debate than for a discussion format.

After members have agreed upon a topic question, the group should begin answering it in a logical, methodical manner. The following seven-step process based on Dewey's model will aid your group. It is important that you go through these steps chronologically and not jump ahead in your discussion. Solutions are best discussed and evaluated only after a problem is thoroughly defined and analyzed.

---

1. Define the problem.
2. Analyze the problem.
3. Determine the criteria for the optimal solution.
4. Propose solutions.
5. Evaluate proposed solutions.
6. Select a solution.
7. Suggest strategies for implementing the solution.

**KEY POINTS
The Steps to Problem Solving**

Define the Problem. Before you can solve a problem, you must first define it. By defining the key terms of the question, group members decide how they will focus the topic, thus enabling them to keep on track and to avoid extraneous discussion. Suppose your college asks you to be part of a student advisory committee to address the issue "What can be done to alleviate the parking problem on campus?" In order to answer the question, members must agree on what constitutes "the parking problem." Are there too few parking spaces? If there are sufficient spaces, are they not geographically located to serve the campus best? Is there congestion only during certain times of the day or week? Is the problem how the spaces are designated—for example, is there adequate parking for faculty but not for students? Is the problem not the number of spaces but the condition of the parking lots? How your group defines the problem determines, to a large extent, how you will solve it. If there is not a problem with the condition of the lots or the number of spaces for faculty, you can safely delete these considerations from your discussion agenda.

Analyze the Problem. In analyzing the problem a group looks at both the symptoms and causes of the problem. We gauge the severity of a problem by examining its **symptoms.** For example, the group needs to know not only the approximate number of students unable to find parking spaces, but also why that is detrimental. Students may be late for class or may avoid going to the library because of parking congestion; accidents may occur as cars crowd into small spaces; the college may spark resentment from students who pay to attend but have no place to park; students may transfer to another school with more convenient access; students walking to dimly lit and distant parking spaces after an evening class may worry about physical attacks. These symptoms point to the magnitude of the problem. Certainly, some symptoms are more serious than others, and it is important that group members identify those needing immediate action.

But the group is still not ready to propose remedies. The group must now consider the **causes** of the problem. By examining how a difficulty developed, a group may find its solution. The parking problem might stem from a variety of causes, including increased enrollment, parking spaces converted to other uses, lack of funds to build new parking lots, too many classes scheduled at certain times, inadequate use of distant parking lots, and some student parking spaces earmarked for faculty and administrators.

Determine the Criteria for the Optimal Solution. Decision making **criteria** are the standards we use to judge the merits of proposed solutions. It is wise to state these criteria *before* discussing solutions. Why select an action plan only to discover later that sufficient funding is unavailable? The group studying campus parking worked to avoid this pitfall. Some of the criteria they considered were as follows:

Criteria	*Explanation*
Economics	The proposal should be cost-effective.
Aesthetics	The proposal should not spoil the beauty of the campus.
Legality	The proposal cannot force residents and businesses adjacent to campus to sell their land to the college.
Growth	The proposal should account for future increases in enrollment.
Security	Students should be safe as they go to and from parking lots.

The group could also have considered ranking parking privileges according to student seniority or giving students parking status equal to faculty.

Propose Solutions. Only after completing the first three steps is the group ready to propose solutions. This is essentially a brainstorming step with emphasis on the *quantity*, not quality, of suggestions. At this stage, the group should not worry about evaluating any suggested solutions, no matter how farfetched they may seem. This group's brainstorming list included the following:

Building a multi-story parking lot in the center of campus
Constructing parking lots near the edge of campus
Reclaiming some faculty spaces for student use
Lighting and patrolling lots in the evening
Initiating bus service between apartment complexes and the campus
Encouraging students to carpool or ride bicycles to campus.

Evaluate Proposed Solutions. Now the group is ready to evaluate each of the proposed solutions. Each possibility is judged using the criteria listed in the third step. Next, the group considers the advantages of the proposed solution. Finally, they assess its disadvantages. The centrally located, high-rise parking garage may not be cost-efficient, and may intrude on the beauty of the campus, but may use valuable land efficiently and limit the extent of late-night walking.

Select a Solution. After evaluating each proposed solution, you and your fellow group members should have a pretty good idea of those to exclude from consideration and those to retain. You will then weigh the merits and deficiencies of each. Your final solution may be a combination of several of the proposed remedies. For example, the group working on the campus parking problem might issue a final report with a three-phase solution: short-range, middle-range, and long-range goals. A short-term approach may involve converting a little-used athletic practice field to a parking facility, creating more bicycle parking areas, and encouraging carpooling. A middle-range solution could involve creating a bus system between student apartment houses and the campus, or trying to get the city transit system to incorporate new routes. The proposal for the long-term might involve building a well-lit multi-story parking facility, not in the middle of campus, but near the athletic complex, to be used during the week for general student parking and on weekends for athletic and entertainment events.

Suggest Strategies for Implementing the Solution. Once the small group has worked out a solution, members would normally submit their recommendations to another body for approval, action, and implementation. Sometimes, however, decision makers should not only select feasible and effective solutions but also show how they can be implemented. How would the small group incorporate suggestions for implementing their solution? They would probably recommend coordinating their plan with the long-range master plan for the college. Other administrators would have to be included. The group would probably also suggest a timetable detailing short-term and long-term projects, and might also identify possible funding sources.

In summary, the reflective thinking model enables a group to define a problem, analyze it, determine the criteria for a good solution, propose solutions, evaluate solutions, select a solution, and suggest ways to implement it. Decisions made by following this process are generally better, and group members are more satisfied with their work. This model can not only benefit groups in business, government, education, and other organizations, but can also improve your individual decision making.

THE RESPONSIBILITIES OF GROUP MEMBERS

As we argued earlier, the leader-member relationship is not an active-passive partnership. In order to enhance the quality of the group's product, all members must participate actively. At this stage you may be asking yourself, "What do group participants do?" If you reflect on our example of the group tackling the campus parking problem, you can see how those group members handled their responsibilities. Productive group members undertake six key responsibilities.

1. Inform the group.
2. Evaluate ideas and proposals.
3. Question other participants.
4. Challenge unfounded conclusions.
5. Advocate personal beliefs.
6. Support other group members.

Members Inform the Group.

"Just the facts, ma'am."   SGT. JOE FRIDAY, *DRAGNET*

Group members should enlarge the information base on which decisions are made and action taken. As we have said elsewhere, a decision is only as good as the information on which it is based. If the group does not know all the causes of a problem, for example, their proposed solution may not solve it. The greater the number of possible solutions a group considers, the greater its chance of selecting the best one.

You enlarge the group's information base in two ways. First, you contribute what you already know about the issue being discussed. Even information that is only hearsay may be worth mentioning, as long as you acknowledge that it is something you have heard but cannot prove. Another member may be able to confirm or refute it, or it can be put on the agenda for further research. Dispelling popular misconceptions so that they do not contaminate the decision-making process is important.

Secondly, group members contribute to a group's understanding of a topic by gathering additional relevant information. Ideas surfacing during a group meeting may help shape the agenda for the next meeting. You may hear ideas that you want to explore further. You may need to check out facts before the group can clarify the dimensions of a problem or adopt a particular plan of action. The research and thought you give to a topic before a meeting will make the meeting itself more efficient and productive.

Members Evaluate. To be effective, a discussion should cover a range of positions on the issue being considered. Each idea should be discussed thoroughly and analyzed critically. A decision based on incorrect information or faulty reasoning may be ineffective or even counterproductive. Thus all group members are obligated to evaluate the contributions of others and to submit their own positions for evaluation. This is sometimes difficult for us to do. Yet participants should not be defensive about their ideas, but open to constructive criticism.

Members Question. Effective discussants not only give but also seek information and opinions. Knowing how and when to ask an appropriate question are important skills for group members. The ability to ask effective questions requires active listening, sensitivity to the feelings of others, and a desire to learn. Group members should seek clarification of ideas they do not understand and encourage others to explain, defend, and extend their ideas.

Members Challenge.

"Freedom rings where opinions clash."   ADLAI STEVENSON

Too often we accept what we hear at face value, or we may remain silent even though we disagree with what we hear. Discussion benefits when facts, opinions, and proposals are challenged. A significant part of this process is separating good ideas from bad. Ideas that have merit withstand rigorous testing, so group members should challenge the assumptions underlying others' opinions.

Members Advocate. Group members should not only provide information to help make decisions but should also use that data to develop positions on the issues being discussed. Discussants should be willing to state and defend their opinions. Although evaluating, questioning, and challenging are important skills, beware of the member who seems to tear down the contributions of others without offering alternative points of view. This person rarely helps the group.

Members Support Other Group Members. A group is a collection of individuals with different personalities. Some may be less assertive than others and may have fragile egos. They may be reluctant to express their ideas because they fear criticism. If this occurs, the group may lose important information and be rushed into a decision. It may even foster the groupthink we discussed earlier. The climate of the group should encourage openness and acceptance. It is the job of both the leader and the group members to create and reinforce a climate of openness and acceptance.

THE RESPONSIBILITIES OF GROUP LEADERS

When individuals complain about the lack of cohesiveness and productivity of their group, much of their criticism is often directed toward the group's leader. Just as effective leadership depends on effective membership, so does effective membership depend on effective leadership. Leaders have certain responsibilities that, if fulfilled, will help the group meet its goal.

Teaching Strategy:
Have students who served as group leaders write a summary and evaluation of their leadership experience, using these ten criteria.

Teaching Strategy:
Have group members write a critique of their group leader using these ten criteria for effective leadership.

1. Plan the agenda.
2. Orient the group.
3. Establish an information base.
4. Involve all members in the discussion.
5. Encourage openness and critical evaluation.
6. Secure clarification of ideas and positions.
7. Keep the group on target.
8. Introduce new ideas and topics.
9. Summarize the discussion.
10. Manage conflict.

**KEY POINTS
Responsibilities
of Group Leaders**

Leaders Plan the Agenda. A group leader has the primary responsibility for planning an agenda. This does not mean dictating the agenda; rather, the leader offers suggestions and solicits group input into the process.

Leaders Orient the Group. How a meeting begins is extremely important in setting expectations that affect group climate and productivity. A leader may want to begin a meeting with some brief opening remarks to orient the group to its mission and the process it will follow. In analyzing business meetings, Roger Mosvick and Robert Nelson conclude, "The chairperson's orientation speech is the single most important act of the business meeting." They describe this speech as follows:

> It is a systematically prepared, fully rehearsed, sit-down speech of not less than three minutes nor more than five minutes (most problems require at least three minutes of orientation; anything over five minutes sets up a pattern of dominance and control by the chairperson).[6]

For some groups that you lead it will not always be appropriate or even desirable to begin a meeting with a structured speech. Still, leaders should try to accomplish several objectives early in the group's important first meeting. They should (1) stress the importance of the task, (2) secure agreement on the process the group will follow, (3) encourage interaction among members, and (4) set an expectation of high productivity.

Leaders Establish an Information Base. Leaders may wish to introduce background information to the group in an opening statement, or distribute some relevant articles with background information to members before the first meeting. This sometimes makes the initial meeting more productive by establishing a starting point for discussion. Leaders should encourage input from all members, however, as the primary means of ensuring sufficient information for making decisions.

Leaders Involve all Members in the Discussion. A leader must make certain that participation among group members is balanced. A person who speaks too much is as much a problem as one who speaks too little. In either case, the potential base of information and opinion is narrowed. Remember our position that all members share the responsibility of group leadership. If someone is not contributing to the discussion, any member of the group can ask the silent person for his or her opinion.

Leaders Encourage Openness and Critical Evaluation. After the group has shared information and ideas, the leader must guide the group in evaluating them. The leader may do this by directing probing questions to specific individuals or to the group as a whole. To achieve and maintain a climate of free and honest communication, the group leader must be sensitive to the nonverbal communication of participants, encouraging them to verbalize both their reluctance and their excitement about the ideas other members are expressing. At the same time, the sensitive leader will keep criticism focused on *ideas* rather than on personalities.

Leaders Secure Clarification of Ideas and Positions. Effective leaders are good at getting members of the discussion to make their positions and ideas clearer and more specific. They do this in two ways. First, the leader may encourage a member to continue talking by asking a series of probing follow-up *questions* ("So what would happen if . . . ?"). Even the use of *prods* ("Uh-huh." "Okay?") can force discussants to think through and verbalize their ideas and positions. Second, the leader may close a particular line of discussion by *paraphrasing* the ideas of a speaker ("So what you're saying is that . . ."). This strategy confirms the leader's understanding, repeats the idea for the benefit of other group members, and invites their reaction.

Leaders Keep the Group on Target. Effective leaders keep their sights on the group's task while realizing the importance of group social roles. There is nothing wrong with group members becoming friendly and socializing. This added dimension can strengthen your group. However, when social functions begin to impede work on the task, the group leader must "round up the strays" and redirect the entire group to its next goal.

Leaders Introduce New Ideas and Topics. We've already mentioned that it is important for leaders to prepare for the first group meeting, either by researching and preparing an orientation speech or by circulating background materials to group members. In addition, the leader should be the most willing researcher among the group. If discussion stalls because the group lacks focus or motivation, the leader must be willing and able to initiate new topics for research and talk. If a lapse in the group's progress signals that research and discussion have been exhausted, the leader must recognize this situation and be willing to move on to the next phase of group work.

Leaders Summarize the Discussion. A leader should provide the group periodic reviews of what has been decided and what remains to be decided. These summaries keep members focused on the group's task. Leaders may begin a group meeting with an **initial summary,** a brief synopsis of what the group decided previously. They may offer **internal summaries** during the discussion to keep the group on target. At the conclusion of the group task, leaders should provide a **final summary,** reviewing what the group accomplished.

Leaders Manage Conflict. Conflict is not only inevitable in group discussion, it is essential. When ideas collide, participants must rethink and defend their positions. This process engenders further exploration of facts and opinions and enhances the likelihood of a quality outcome. It is important, then, that a group not discourage conflict but manage it.

While conflict of ideas contributes to group effectiveness, interpersonal antagonism may undermine it. When conflict becomes personal, it ceases to be productive. Such conflict disrupts the group. Some members may stop expressing their opinions for fear of attack. If the climate becomes too uncomfortable, members may withdraw from the group. Thus, it is essential that when conflict surfaces the group respond appropriately. At some point it may become evident that conflict cannot be solved by the group or in the presence of group members. In this event, the leader may have to meet with the disruptive member one-on-one and discuss the problem.

When a group, following the seven steps of problem solving, is composed of members and a leader fulfilling the various roles just outlined, it should produce results quickly. At times, the problem solving will have been for the benefit of the group alone and no external report is needed. Often, however, the group will be requested or will want to present its findings to a larger group:

company workers, company stockholders, or just an interested public audience, for example. In the following sections of this chapter, we discuss two popular formats for group presentations and provide a systematic checklist to help you develop a first-rate presentation.

■ The Group Presentation

FORMATS FOR THE PRESENTATION

There are several different formats for a group presentation, two of which are the public discussion and the symposium.

public discussion: a small group exchanging ideas and opinions on a single topic in the presence of an audience.

The Public Discussion. In a **public discussion** a group sits, usually in a semi-circle, in front of the audience. Members are aware of an audience but usually address others in the group. The audience, in effect, eavesdrops on the conversation. If your public speaking class includes group presentations, your small group may be asked to use this format to present your ideas to the class.

The problem-solving classroom discussion usually requires extensive preparation. The group has researched the topic, planned the discussion, and possibly practiced the presentation. Members have a general idea of the content and organization of their own and other participants' remarks, although the presentation is not memorized or scripted. The presentation is intended to inform and persuade the audience on the issue being discussed. Sometimes a question-answer period follows.

symposium: a series of public speeches on a single topic, possibly followed by group discussion or a question-answer period.

The Symposium. A **symposium** is a series of speeches on a single topic presented to an audience. It differs from a public discussion in at least two ways. First, there is no interaction among the speakers during the presentation, unless a discussion period follows. Each speaker has a designated amount of time to present his or her remarks. Second, speakers address members of the audience directly. Sometimes speakers are seated at a table; often they use a lectern. In most public symposiums the speakers have not met beforehand to discuss what they will say. If you are assigned to a group for a presentation in this class, you will likely want to meet several times, following some of the guidelines we discuss in the following section.

PREPARING A GROUP PRESENTATION

A group presentation offers you a variety of learning experiences. You will have the opportunity to enhance your research skills, organization skills, oral communication skills, and group interaction skills. This assignment, therefore, is potentially one of the most significant learning opportunities of this class. In addition, your group presentation may be a meaningful learning experience for your classmates.

Although there is no one correct way to prepare for a group presentation, our remaining suggestions should certainly help you make the process more efficient and the product more effective. An asterisk (*) denotes those steps requiring group interaction; the other steps may be done individually.

In a public discussion a group of experts discusses a specified topic in front of an audience of interested listeners.

*Brainstorm About the Topic. If you've read the previous chapters, our first suggestion for preparing a group presentation should not surprise you. Through brainstorming you will discover knowledge that group members already possess, and you will uncover numerous ideas for further research. In addition to providing content, brainstorming also serves a relationship function. By giving all members an opportunity to participate, brainstorming affords you a glimpse of your peers' personalities and their approaches to group interaction. You get to know them, and they get to know you. If there is an atmosphere of openness and respect during this first meeting, the group is off to a good start. Once you have generated a list of areas concerning your group's topic, you are ready for the second step.

* **1.** Brainstorm about the topic.	**KEY POINTS** **Steps in Preparing a** **Group Presentation**
2. Do some exploratory research.	
* **3.** Discuss and divide the topic into areas of responsibility.	
4. Research your specific topic area.	
5. Draft an outline of your content area.	
* **6.** Discuss how all the information interrelates.	
* **7.** Finalize the group presentation format.	
* **8.** Plan the introduction and conclusion of the presentation.	
9. Prepare and practice your speech.	
***10.** Rehearse and revise the presentation.	

Do Some Exploratory Research. Through brainstorming you discover areas that need further investigation. The second phase of your group process is individual research. While there may be some merit in each person's selecting a different topic to research, research roles should not be too rigid. Rather than limit yourself by topic, you may wish to divide your research by resource. One member may look at popular news magazines, another at government documents; a third may interview a professor who is knowledgeable on the topic; and so forth. It is important that you not restrict your discovery to the list of topics you have generated. Exploratory research is also a form of brainstorming. As you look in indexes and read articles you find, you will uncover more topics. Each member of the group should try to find a few good sources that are diverse in scope.

*Discuss and Divide the Topic Into Areas of Responsibility. After exploratory research your group should re-convene to discuss what each member found. Which expectations were confirmed by your research? Which were not? What topics did you find that you had not anticipated? Your objective at this stage of the group process is to decide on the key areas you wish to investigate. You will probably decide that each person in the group should have primary responsibility for researching a particular area. That person becomes the content expert in that area. While this approach makes research more efficient, it has a drawback. If one person serves as a specialist, the group gambles that he or she will research thoroughly and be objective in reporting what is found. If either assumption is not fulfilled, the quantity of information may be insufficient and the quality contaminated. An alternative approach is to have more than one person assigned to a specific area and, as we suggest later, each person should note any good articles that help the group but are outside his or her specific area of responsibility.

Research Your Specific Topic Area. Using strategies we have discussed in Chapter 7, you should research your topic area. Your focus should not be on the quantity but on the quality of the sources you discover. While your primary goal should be to gather information on your topic, you should also note information related to the topics of your colleagues. As you consult indexes, jot down on a card sources that might be helpful to another member in the group. A group that supports each other in this way makes the process more efficient and, hence, more enjoyable. This usually results in a better product.

Draft an Outline of Your Content Area. After you have concluded your initial research but before you meet again with your group, you should construct an outline of the ideas and information you've found. This step is important for two reasons. It forces you to make sense of all the information you have collected, and it will expedite the next step when you will share your information with the rest of the members of your group.

*Discuss How All the Information Interrelates. You are now ready to meet again with the other members of your group. Members should briefly summarize what they have discovered through their research. After all have shared their ideas, the group should decide which ideas are most important and how those ideas relate to each other. There should be a natural development of the topic that can be divided among the members of the group.

*Finalize the Group Presentation Format. The speaking order should already be determined. There are, nevertheless, certain procedural details that the group must decide. Will the first speaker introduce all presenters, or will each person introduce the next speaker? Where will the participants sit when they are not speaking, facing the audience or on the front row? The more details you decide beforehand, the fewer distractions you will have on the day you speak.

*Plan the Introduction and Conclusion of the Presentation.** A presentation should appear to be that of a group and not that of four or five individuals. Consequently, you must work on introducing and concluding the group's comments, and you must incorporate smooth transitions from one speaker's topic to the next. An introduction should state the topic, define important terms, and establish the importance of the subject. A conclusion should summarize what has been presented and end with a strong final statement.

Prepare and Practice Your Speech. By this time in the course you know the requirements of an excellent speech and have had the opportunity to deliver a few. Most of our earlier suggestions also apply to your speech in your group's presentation. Some differences are worth noting, however. For example, as part of a group presentation you will need to refer to members' speeches and perhaps even use some of their supporting materials. The group presentation may also impose physical requirements you haven't encountered as a classroom speaker, such as using a microphone, speaking to those seated around you in addition to making direct contact with the audience, or speaking from a seated position.

*Rehearse and Revise the Presentation.** While individually practicing your speech is important to a good presentation, it is only one part of rehearsal. The group should practice its entire presentation. Group rehearsal will not only make participants more confident of their individual presentations, but will also give the group a feeling of cohesion.

Teaching Strategy:
You may want students to keep a log of their group participation using these ten steps as an organizational structure. Have them discuss accomplishments and obstacles encountered at each step.

Summary

Whether they are part of our business, social, or personal lives, numerous formal and informal groups are important to us because they solve problems, get things done, and provide us with emotional support. A *small group* is a collection of three or more people influencing and interacting with one another in pursuit of a common goal.

Groups usually fulfill both *social* and *task* needs for their participants, though one of these groups of needs will predominate depending upon the situation. Three types of task-oriented groups include the *study group*, which learns about a topic; the *problem-solving group*, which decides on courses of action; and the *action group*, which implements proposals. This chapter focused on the ways

groups function and the tasks they accomplish: gathering, analyzing, and spreading information; formulating, advocating, and implementing courses of action.

Group decisions are usually superior to decisions individuals make by themselves. To ensure valid decisions, groups must abide by five principles. First, group decision making is a shared responsibility and requires active participation of all members. Second, group members must share a goal that is specific and realistic. Third, groups make decisions best under a clear but flexible schedule or agenda. Fourth, groups make the best decisions when members are free to express opinions openly. Fifth, group decision making requires and benefits from the research and information shared by all participants.

Problem-solving groups can speed their progress and simplify their task by following a seven-step modification of John Dewey's steps to reflective thinking. First, define the problem. Second, analyze the severity and the causes of the problem. Third, determine the criteria that an optimal solution to the problem must satisfy. Fourth, propose various solutions to the problem. Fifth, evaluate each possible solution against the established criteria. Sixth, decide on the best solution, and seventh, suggest ways of putting the solution into action. Following these steps in this order will streamline group problem-solving work.

Group participation involves six functions: sharing information, evaluating data and opinions, questioning other participants, challenging unfounded conclusions and opinions, advocating personal beliefs, and supporting other participants in the group. Responsibilities of group leaders include planning the group's agenda; orienting the group to the task at hand; providing background information on the problem to be discussed; involving all members in the group's discussion; encouraging a climate of open, honest critical evaluation; seeking clarification of members' ideas and positions; keeping the group focused on its task; introducing new ideas and topics for discussion; summarizing the discussion at various points; and managing interpersonal conflict. If group participants perform those functions during the seven-step problem-solving process, they should reach a satisfactory conclusion, and may then be asked to present their findings in a public presentation.

The presentation may take the form of a *public discussion* before an audience. In this situation, participants speak to one another about aspects of the problem after researching, organizing, and practicing the presentation. Another popular form of group presentation is the *symposium*, a series of formal individual speeches on different aspects of a problem.

When given the opportunity to meet and plan a group presentation before delivering it, members should always do so. Both those experienced and inexperienced in preparing group presentations can benefit from a logical ten-step approach to developing them. First, brainstorm the topic with colleagues in the group. Second, do some individual exploratory research to gauge the scope of the topic. Third, discuss the topic with group members and divide areas of research responsibility by topic or source. Fourth, individually research your assigned area, noting sources in other group members' areas. Fifth, organize the data your research has yielded. Sixth, discuss with other group members how all of the generated information interrelates. Seventh, determine the presentation format. Eighth, plan the introduction of group members and the material under discussion. Ninth, prepare and practice speeches individually. And tenth, rehearse and revise the entire group presentation.

Exercises

1. Select someone in a leadership position to interview. The person may be a business executive, an officer in an organization, a school principal, a college president, or any other leader. Construct and ask a series of questions

designed to discover his or her views on characteristics of effective and ineffective leaders. Record the answers and be prepared to discuss them in class.

2. Using the topic areas listed below, select a specific problem area and word it in the form of a problem-solving discussion question.
   a. crime
   b. education
   c. international relations
   d. political campaigning
   e. public health

3. Choose four campus problems you think need to be addressed — for example, class registration. Word the topics as problem-solving questions. Analyze each topic asking the following questions:
   a. How important is the problem?
   b. What information do you need to analyze and solve the problem?
   c. Where would you find this information?
   d. What barriers keep the problem from being solved now?
   e. Which steps in the problem-solving process do you think will generate the most conflict? Why?

   Based on your answers to those questions, select the best topic for a problem-solving discussion. Justify your choice.

4. Think of a problem you are experiencing that you need to solve. Work through the seven steps of the reflective thinking model to arrive at a solution to the problem. Did the model help you arrive at a decision? If so, which steps were most helpful? If not, what are some limitations of the model?

5. Observe a meeting of a student, faculty, city, or some other decision-making group. What examples did you observe of good and bad group communication skills? Could the meeting have been conducted better? If so, how?

6. Discuss when it would be better for a group presentation to take the form of a public discussion. When would the symposium format be preferable?

Notes

1. Bobby R. Patton and Kim Giffin, *Decision-Making Group Interaction*, 2nd ed. (New York: Harper, 1978) 1.

2. Roger K. Mosvick and Robert B. Nelson, *We've Got to Start Meeting Like This!* (Glenview, IL: Scott, 1987) 4.

3. Paul E. Nelson, "Small-Group Communication," in *Applied Business Communication* by Lilian O. Feinberg. (Sherman Oaks, CA: Alfred, 1982) 27.

4. Irving L. Janis, *Groupthink: Psychological Studies of Policy Decisions and Fiascoes*, 2nd ed. (Boston: Houghton, 1982) 9.

5. John Dewey, *How We Think* (Boston: Heath, 1910).

6. Mosvick 114.

APPENDIX *A*

Critiquing Speeches

Almost as important as the speeches you make in your public speaking course are the kinds of comments you make about the speeches others give. In this text we have shown you how to prepare and deliver an effective speech. You should use this knowledge as you comment on the speeches you hear others deliver. Appropriate feedback is crucial to your development as a public speaker. Before you can polish your skills, you must learn from your instructor and classmates what distractions of your language, voice, or body you need to eliminate. You, in turn, want to be an incisive and sensitive critic when it is your turn to write or speak about others' speeches. This brief section aims to help you make better critical comments.

For the purposes of this section, our definition of **criticism** includes *all* remarks made about a public speech, whether they evaluate or merely describe, and whether they are written or spoken. If you say, "Your speech was seven minutes and twelve seconds long," you are functioning as a speech critic as you describe an aspect of the speech. If you write an evaluative statement such as "I liked your speech a lot," you are also providing speech criticism. Notice, however, that while this last comment might make speakers feel happy, it doesn't really teach them anything. In fact, finding out how long they spoke is probably more instructive for speakers than hearing, "I liked it." There is nothing wrong with saying to your classmates, "I enjoyed your speech," or "I didn't care for this speech as much as your last one." Just don't stop there. Explain *why*.

All criticism contains three parts: judgments, reasons, and norms.[1] The most familiar and superficial level of critical comments consists of **judgments.** We make them frequently about many different subjects: "I like Christie's restaurant"; "I didn't care for Ron Howard's 1991 movie *Backdraft*"; "Dr. Hudson is a great teacher"; or "I always enjoy your speeches."

Underlying those judgments, whether we voice them or not, are **reasons** of some sort: "I like Christie's restaurant because the food is good and the service is attentive"; "In spite of *Backdraft*'s terrific visual effects, I didn't care about the characters as much as I had in earlier movies Howard directed"; "Dr. Hudson is a great teacher because her lectures make a course I dreaded lively and interesting"; "I always enjoy your speeches because you choose such unusual topics." Statements such as those specify reasons for the critics' judgments.

The statements in the preceding paragraph are instructive and useful because from them a listener can infer your **norms,** the values you believe make something "good" or "effective" or "desirable." Such statements tell us that the individual critics value good food and careful service in a restaurant, compelling characters in movies, liveliness in class lectures, and unusual topics in public speeches. We may, of course, argue with the critics about whether those norms are actually valid. That is healthy and productive. The lesson for us as speech critics is to provide reasons for our judgments; only by doing so do we tell the speaker the basis of our reactions.

Here are some examples of helpful comments made by students about their classmates' speeches:

> I liked Adele's speech about the constellations. The introduction was very interesting and piqued my curiosity. Her organization was clear and she had excellent transitions from one area to the next. She used a good speaking style in easy to understand language and she defined unfamiliar terms. She also seemed *really* interested in what she was talking about and that made me interested, even though I thought she spoke rather fast in places.

> Adele used a lot of description in her introduction, and that caused me to visualize what she was talking about. The body of the speech contained information that was new and interesting to me. Her conclusion was also very creative.

> John's speech on how to improve study habits was the best I heard. It was appropriate and beneficial to everyone in the class. The language was simple and coherent. He explained just what we needed to know in the time he had.

> I liked Ernest's speech on how to construct a sundial and find your direction if lost because he seemed to have involved almost everyone in the classroom. I also thought he spoke with a great deal of confidence.

> One problem I saw was the use of visual aids. Once you have finished with the visual aid, you should put it away rather than leave it where the audience can see it. That way, the audience will focus their attention on you rather than on the object.

One value of receiving written or oral comments from classmates about your speeches is that repetition of a criticism will reinforce it. If your instructor or some classmate tells you that you need to speak louder, you might discount the advice as one person's opinion. If twelve people in the class write or say that they had trouble hearing you, however, the criticism gains impact and you will likely give it more attention.

A second value of receiving criticism from many people is that different people value different aspects of a speech. Some people put a premium on delivery, others on speech content, and still others on organization. Individual classmates may notice different things about your speech simply because of where they sit in the classroom. With such a variety of perspectives and values, it would be a shame if all their criticism were reduced to "Good job!" or "I liked it." To provide the best criticism you can, just remember to specify the reasons for your judgments; ask yourself *why* a speech has the effect it does on you, and then try to communicate those reasons to the speaker.

We should also make a final note about the spirit in which you give and receive speech criticism in this class. Your instructor may invite you to make oral or written comments about the speeches you hear others give. If your comments are written, they may be signed or unsigned. But whether your comments are written or oral, and whether your written critiques identify you or retain your anonymity, you should never make criticisms that are designed to belittle or hurt the speaker. Target the *speech*, not the speaker. Focus on specific *behaviors* rather than the person exhibiting those behaviors. You will probably never hear a speech so fine that the speaker could not make some improvement; and you will never hear a speech so inept or ill-prepared that it does not have some redeeming value. *Listen evaluatively* and then *respond empathically*, putting yourself in the speaker's place, and you should make truly helpful comments about your classmates' speeches.

Keep this advice in mind as you react to the criticisms your classmates speak or write about your work. Some of us are just generally "thin-skinned," easily hurt by anything that seems to be a negative criticism, and at times *all* of us can become defensive. But don't be too quick to dismiss the feedback others give you about your speeches. *Remember that your goal as you move from one speech to the next in a public speaking classroom is not consistency but improvement*. So rather than defending what you said or did in your speech, listen carefully and *act* upon those suggestions for improvement that you receive most frequently. You will make your most accelerated improvement if you graciously accept the compliments of your peers and then work quickly to eliminate problems that they bring to your attention. If you have doubts about the validity of suggestions your classmates are making, discuss the matter with your instructor.

To help you become a better critic for your classmates, we offer nine suggestions you can use as you evaluate their speeches. One of our students, Martina, delivered an informative speech on photography techniques that any person could learn and use to take better pictures. We asked some students to critique her speech, and we have used their comments to illustrate our suggestions.

KEY POINTS
Guidelines for
Critiquing Speeches

1. Begin with a positive statement.
2. Be specific.
3. Be honest but tactful.
4. Personalize your comments.
5. Reinforce the positive.
6. Problem solve the negative.
7. Organize your comments.
8. Provide the speaker with a plan of action.
9. End positively.

Begin With a Positive Statement. Do you remember being told, "If you can't say something nice, don't say anything at all"? Well, that's good advice to follow when you critique your classmates' speeches. Public speaking is a personal experience. You stand in front of an audience expressing *your* thoughts in *your* words with *your* voice and *your* body. When you affirm the positive, you establish a healthy climate for constructive criticism. Demonstrate to speakers that what they said or how they said it was worthy. Fortunately, you can always find something helpful to say if you think about it. Be positive — and be sincere!

Two of our students began their critiques of Martina's speech with the opening statements below. Notice that in addition to complimenting the speaker, the students demonstrate their involvement in the speaking situation.

> As an amateur photographer, I find the topic of your speech extremely fascinating and of enormous help. After the initial question, I think all people in the audience probably realized that this topic may be of interest not only to those who take pictures but also to those who are being photographed.

> The content of your speech was very helpful to me since I like to take pictures. You explained some techniques of picture taking in an easy to understand manner.

Be Specific. Suppose instead of this list of nine suggestions for offering criticism, we simply said, "When you critique your classmates' speeches, be as helpful as possible so that they can improve their speaking." Though that is good advice, it's not very helpful, is it? By being more specific and detailing nine guidelines, we hope to provide you a handle on how you can improve your critiquing skills. Similarly, you will help your classmates if you provide them specific suggestions for improvement.

In order for speakers to become more proficient, they need to know *what* to improve and *how* to improve. One of our students told Martina, "Parts of your speech were hard to follow." That may be the listener's honest opinion, but it doesn't give Martina much direction. What parts of the speech? Why were they hard to follow? What could she have done to minimize the problem? Remember, provide reasons for your judgments. In the two statements below, the listeners' comments are specific.

> Your explanation of lighting and diffusion was simple and direct. The example of how to have the light coming from the side of the subject illustrated clearly the line definition produced by shadows. I thought it was wise to caution your listeners about not using the same technique for portraits, since the shadows would accentuate undesirable facial lines.

> I was glad to hear that you took the photographs for your visuals. I think that you might want to tell that you took the pictures sooner to heighten the effect of your credibility.

Be Honest But Tactful.

"Do not remove a fly from your friend's forehead with a hatchet."
CHINESE PROVERB

Providing suggestions for improvement tests your interpersonal skills. At times you may be reluctant to offer criticism because you think it may offend the speaker. If you are not honest, however, the speaker may not know that the topic was dull, the content superficial, and the delivery uninspiring. However, you must respect your classmates' feelings. The statement "Your speech was dull, superficial, and uninspiring" may be honest, but it is hardly tactful. It may provoke resistance to your suggestions or damage the speaker's self-esteem.

One of our students thought Martina's speech content and organization were excellent, but her delivery to be mechanical and lifeless. The student could have said, "Your delivery lacked excitement." Instead, she wrote: "Obviously, you love photography. Try to display how much you enjoy it by speaking a bit more energetically about it."

Personalize Your Comments. The more interest and involvement your critique conveys, the more likely the speaker is to believe in and act on your advice. You can personalize your comments in several ways. First, use the speaker's name occasionally, as in: "Martina, I think that your use of visual aids was fantastic. The size of your photographs, the way you presented them, and the way you kept them concealed really worked well."

A second way of reducing a speaker's defensiveness and establishing speaker-critic rapport is by using "I-statements" in place of "you-statements." Tell how the speech affected you. Instead of saying "Your organization was weak," say "I had trouble following your key ideas," and then give some examples of places where you got lost. Following is an example of what one of our students *could* have said and what he *did* say in his critique of Martina:

> *He could have said:* "You lost my attention for your entire speech because you spoke so softly that I couldn't hear you."

> *Instead, he said:* "Martina, because I was sitting in the back of the room, I had a difficult time hearing you because you spoke so softly. If you increase your volume, the entire audience will be able to follow your speech better."

A third way of personalizing your comments is by stating how you have benefited from hearing the speech. The opening statements of the two student critiques we included under our first suggestion let Martina know that her speech was interesting and helpful to them.

Reinforce the Positive. Sometimes we want so much to help someone improve that we focus on what the speaker did wrong and forget to mention what the speaker did well. As you enumerate how speakers can improve, don't forget the things they did well and should continue doing. One student was impressed with Martina's use of visual aids and made the following comment:

> Martina, I would like to emphasize how appropriately you matched your pictures with each division of your speech. The overlay used to demonstrate the "rule of thirds" was especially helpful and provided immediate comprehension of that composition concept.

Problem Solve the Negative. If you are serious about wanting to improve your speaking, you will want to know the weaknesses of your speech. Only then can you improve. As a critic, you have a responsibility to help your classmates become better speakers. Don't be afraid to let them know what went wrong with a speech.

As a general rule, though, you should not criticize behaviors that the speaker cannot correct. Martina's delivery, for example, included a slight German accent. She spoke slowly and distinctly so that her accent did not impede her audience's comprehension. Even if her accent did detract from her message, it would have been inappropriate for a student to comment, "I had trouble understanding what you said because of your accent. You need to get rid of it for your next speech." That, of course, would be impossible. On the other hand, it would be useful to suggest that Martina slow her speaking rate so that her ideas are more easily understood.

You will help speakers improve their speaking if you follow two steps in your criticism. First, point out a specific problem, and, second, suggest ways to correct it. Remember, the title of this section is not "List the negatives" but "Problem solve the negative." You want to state ways to overcome problems.

One student was impressed with Martina's visual aids, but observed that she directed them to the center of the audience. This critic offered Martina the following advice:

> I think it would help the audience more if you moved the pictures to show all of the people in the audience. I would vary the direction that the visuals are shown in order to involve the entire audience.

Notice how another student offered solutions to some problems with Martina's delivery.

> The delivery of your speech included a couple of strengths: (1) You involved the audience with a question at the beginning and the end; (2) you maintained eye contact in a natural, poised manner. Yet I felt that through your speech the quality of *dynamism* was lacking. [Your delivery] came across as mechanical. Inject some vocal variety—volume, inflection, and animation. Deliver that same speech with energy, enthusiasm, and vocal variety, and you will transform a good speech into an excellent speech.

Another critic commented on Martina's soft voice and offered a possible solution:

> I had trouble hearing you in places. I have found that if I take deep breaths from the diaphragm before beginning, I have better control of the sound that I am projecting.

Organize Your Comments. A critique, just like a speech, is easier to follow if it is well organized. You can select from several options to frame your comments, and you should select the one that is most appropriate to you, the speaker, and the speech.

For example, you can organize your comments topically into the categories of speech *content, organization,* and *delivery.* A second option is chronological; you can discuss the speech's *introduction, body,* and *conclusion.* A third option is to divide your comments into speaking *strengths* and *weaknesses* (remember, give positive comments first). You might even combine these three options. You could discuss the speaker's content, organization, and delivery, and within each of those categories discuss first the strengths and then the weaknesses.

Provide the Speaker With a Plan of Action. When you give your comments, include a plan of action for the speaker. What should the speaker concentrate on when presenting the next speech? One student focused Martina's attention on her next speaking experience by suggesting the following action plan:

> Martina, overall your speech was very good. However, there are three goals you might work on for your next speech. First, use signposts to strengthen your organization. Signposting will identify your key points more clearly. This will help your audience remember them. Second, move around more. Your primary objective is to include the entire audience. Instead of standing in one place, which tends to include only part of your audience, you could move from left to right. Third, work on projecting your voice to include people in the back of the room, as well as the front. This way your entire audience will hear you. If you use these suggestions for your next speech, your speech will improve and be even more effective.

End Positively. Conclude your critique on a positive note. Speakers should be reminded that both you and they benefited from this experience. One of the highest compliments you can give a speaker is that you learned something from the speech. Two of our students concluded their critiques of Martina's speech as follows:

> In my opinion, Martina, your idea for the topic was interesting and the organization was very good. There are only a few minor things to improve. I am sure many of us will now think about your advice while taking photographs. It was a valuable lesson.

> I really felt as if I could take a better picture with your tips.

Author Isaac Bashevis Singer once said, "The wastepaper basket is the writer's best friend." Yet self-criticism is difficult for both writers and speakers. You master public speaking faster and easier if you can rely on helpful criticism from your classmates, as well as your instructor. To be helpful, criticism must be balanced between positive and negative aspects of the speech. In addition it should be specific, organized, personalized, honest, and tactful. Our years of teaching experience have convinced us that following these guidelines will pay big dividends as you give and receive constructive, beneficial speech criticism.

Note ──────────────────────

1. This model of criticism is adapted from Beverly Whitaker Long, "Evaluating Performed Literature," *Studies in Interpretation*, ed. Esther M. Doyle and Virginia Hastings Floyd, vol. 2 (Amsterdam: Rodopi, 1977) 267–81. See also her earlier article: Beverly Whitaker, "Critical Reasons and Literature in Performance," *The Speech Teacher* 18 (November 1969): 191–93. Long attributes this three-part model of criticism to Arnold Isenberg, "Critical Communication," *The Philosophical Review* (July 1949): 330–44.

A Speaker's Journal

"It's what you learn after you know it all that counts."

QUOTED BY JOHN WOODEN

One way to improve your own public speaking is to observe and analyze the speaking of others. What techniques of support, organization, and delivery do they use? What seems to work for them? What doesn't? How can you learn from their successes and mistakes? All these questions can help you improve as a speaker.

But there are other questions you might find instructive, if only you had the chance to ask: What are some of the decisions behind the speech? How did *this* speaker go about selecting *this* topic and develop it in *this* way? Published speeches rarely provide these insights. In addition, they are often edited from a manuscript, so that speakers appear never to have stumbled, lost their place, forgotten a transition, or been distracted by a loud noise or an audience member wandering into the room late.

The following Speaker's Journal is a record of what one student learned as she applied all she knew about developing and delivering a speech. Her journal is designed to let you see beyond the transcript of her delivered speech; you will "hear" her talk about some of the decisions she made before she walked into a classroom, looked at her audience, and began speaking.

Sandra Gomila, then an undergraduate student, delivered her persuasive speech "Volunteerism: Just Do It!" to a class at Radford University in Virginia during the summer of 1991. Her speech was delivered extemporaneously, and the following manuscript is an unedited transcript taken from her videotaped speech.

Following the speech, we asked Sandy to discuss how she selected her topic, developed her ideas, and rehearsed her speech.

"VOLUNTEERISM: JUST DO IT!"

SANDRA GOMILA, *Radford University*

A man was going down from Jerusalem to Jericho when he fell into the hands of robbers. They beat him, stripped him, and left him for dead. Two men passed right by, but a Samaritan came to where the man was and had compassion for him. He bandaged his wounds, took him to an inn, and took care of him.

The Biblical parable of the Good Samaritan provides one of the earliest examples and one of the best illustrations of the act of volunteerism. A volunteer is simply someone who sees a need and fills it. Volunteerism is something that many of us admire, yet few of us imitate. With this in mind, involvement in volunteerism deserves a closer look.

After all, how many of us would think it would be a waste of our time to go and buy groceries for an elderly woman who is confined to her home? Or how many of us would agree that it's worthless to help someone learn how to read? Probably not many of us would agree with those statements. The obstacle in volunteering lies not in our agreement, but in the movement from agreement to action.

Today, I'll be discussing volunteerism by addressing three questions you may have about volunteering. One, does society still need volunteers? Two, why should I get involved now? And three, how do I get involved?

Well, does society still need volunteers? Many people equate volunteerism with the social activism of the 1960s — seeing each as an idea and an era whose time has passed. But according to Kathy Hillard, who is a University of Illinois student and active volunteer, "Back then it was all talk. But this is action. College students are taken out of their homes to really do something."

We can see that volunteers are used in our society today, but does this mean that they are still necessary? Are they still needed? Well, national estimates for the homeless in the United States range from 250,000 all the way up to 735,000, with approximately one-half of all homeless adults never having finished high school. In the state of Virginia, almost 12 percent of the population lives below the poverty line. And according to the *Statistical Abstract of the United States, 1990,* 14 percent of all persons living right here in the city of Radford live below the poverty line. In addition to statistics regarding lack of education and housing, in 1987 approximately 7,000 alcohol and drug abuse treatment clinics were surveyed, and at that time the number of clients in treatment was nearly 600,000. In addition to all these statistics, we see a plethora of organizations in the United States devoted solely and singularly to volunteer work. These range from APO, the service fraternity right here on campus, to the Woman's Resource Center in the city of Radford, all the way up to national organizations such as COOL (the Campus Outreach Opportunity League), and organizations such as the United Way.

But rather than seeing all of these statistics and all of these organizations as overwhelming, we should see them as opportunities for us to discover our own interests and become personally involved, creating a niche for ourselves in volunteerism based on our own interests. Mr. [Wayne] Meisel, who is the coordinator of COOL, a national organization that attempts to match students with their interests, has this to say: "It's the joy of service! Self-interest is a win-win deal. This whole movement is about complementary needs."

I can personally attest to the benefits of volunteering in an area you feel strongly about. For the past six years the cause I have been involved in is teenage drug abuse and drug addiction and its prevention. Had I not chosen to volunteer in an area I felt strongly about, I'm sure I would not have continued my volunteer work, nor would I have seen it as beneficial to myself. And I'm sure that the people I was working with would have really suffered because it wouldn't have been an issue that I cared about. So when we ask ourselves the question "Does society still need volunteers?" I think we can see that the answer is clearly *"Yes!"*

Which brings us to our second question: "Why should I volunteer now?" Many of us plan on volunteering our time but later on in life—once we've gotten "settled down." But we have just settled down into this community for the next four years. And if you ever change your major, you have possibly settled down for the next five or even six years! So the time to volunteer is *now*. And thus the question becomes: "Is volunteering worth my time?" That's a perfectly legitimate question. College is certainly a busy time. There's homework, socializing, part-time jobs to think about—all these things are making demands of our time. The bottom line is: What's in it for me? Well, let's look at some of the benefits of volunteering.

One benefit is an enhanced résumé. One of the main reasons that we come to college is to enhance our employability, so that when we get out into the workforce we are attractive to prospective employers. Well, volunteer work enhances your employability. Says Carol Carter, author of the book *Majoring in the Rest of Your Life*, "If you've been active in volunteer work, your future employer will realize that you care about people and the community. Employers want to hire people who will be role models for others. Good citizenship is good business." Employers are clearly looking for well-rounded individuals. A résumé containing volunteer work is the résumé of an individual that is headed for success.

A second benefit of volunteerism is the acquisition of life skills. We have not come to college just to learn about what's in our textbooks and fill ourselves with head knowledge. We've come to learn about how to deal with everyday life and the problems it presents. Life skills enhanced by volunteer work include communication skills, relationship skills, and problem-solving skills. By choosing to volunteer in an area that is related to your major, you learn about your field of study both in and out of the classroom. For example, if you are an accounting major, perhaps you want to volunteer your time by filling out tax forms for the elderly. At Tulane University in Louisiana, pre-law students help to prepare clemency arguments for the release of elderly prison inmates. So you can see that it's quite easy to just look at yourself; see what is your major, what are your interests; and match them up with an organization. Says Jeff Segall, a college student involved with volunteer work, "Instead of just going out for beer to take your mind off your studies, it's important to contribute something to your community." We can clearly see that when we do volunteer work, we not only benefit others, but we benefit ourselves.

A third way that volunteerism is personally beneficial is in our own development, our own personal growth. Plato said that the unexamined life is not worth living. Volunteer work is a way of examining our lives. By helping others, we increase our understanding of ourselves. We all carry with us fears and prejudices that are unfounded, that have never been tested by daily experience. Volunteer work is a way of confronting them. Do you believe that all poor people are lazy? Perhaps you're afraid of homeless people. Well, by volunteering in these environments, this helps us to test our beliefs and strengthen our viewpoints with the benefit of firsthand experience.

Other benefits in the area of personal growth include broadening our horizons. When we do volunteer work, we interact with sections of society that we may otherwise know nothing about. In doing this, we learn more about others and we increase our own self-awareness. An added benefit of this in the area of personal growth is enhanced self-esteem, because we can take pride in the work that we do. An example of this would be George Montague, a Wharton student, who uses his skills and his time to help a Sioux Indian reservation that at this time has an 80 percent unemployment rate. Montague's using his skills in farming and agriculture to help bring this reservation closer to self-sufficiency. Says Montague of his experience: "I'll be fulfilled when the fields yield enough crops for them to make a profit."

In answer to question two, "Why should I become involved now?", we've seen that involvement in volunteer work is personally beneficial to us in a variety of ways, ranging from future employability to the development of our life skills and our own personal growth. We can see that society clearly has a desperate need for volunteers, and I believe that this alone should justify our time. And the benefits we've just discussed further justify our involvement.

Which brings us to the third and final question: "How do I get involved?" By matching particular issues with our own interests, we bring a focus and clarity to volunteer work. For example, if you are an education major, don't wait until you are student teaching. Start now! Volunteer with adults or children who need to learn how to read. Maybe you'd like to be outdoors or you're a physical education major. Well, then you can volunteer your time, quite enjoyably, by working with the Special Olympics, or working as a Big Brother, Big Sister, volunteering at a day camp. I would challenge each one of you to discover your own interests and match them to an agency. To aid in this, at the end of my speech I will give you a handout with the names, numbers, and contact people of agencies in our area that are in need of volunteers, as well as a brief description of the work involved. As you can see, the process of becoming involved is a relatively simple one — almost as easy as a phone call. And with that, I would ask each and every one of you to call three numbers on this list and to commit yourself to one organization for a period of just two weeks.

We have seen today that society definitely still has needs, and is in need of volunteers that are willing to give their time and their enthusiasm to the great needs in our society. We have explored some of the ways that volunteerism is personally beneficial, ranging from enhanced employability to the acquisition of life skills to our own development and personal growth. And we can now take the steps necessary to become involved in our community.

In trying to think of a way to wrap up the speech and help you to remember the key points discussed here today, I was reminded of a well-known athletics company whose slogan seems quite appropriate here: "Just Do It!" If we look at the letters of NIKE, we can easily remember the points discussed here today. Question one: Does society still need volunteers? [Visual aid: *N*eeds are everywhere] Today we've seen that needs are everywhere. Question two: Why should I become involved now? [Visual aid: *I*nvolvement benefits me] One reason might be because involvement benefits me in three ways: the development of our résumé and enhanced employability, development of our life skills, and our own personal growth.

In response to the third question, "How do I become involved?", this is where the K comes in — with knowledge of issues and interests. [Visual aid:

Knowledge of interests & issues] Know yourself, know your own interests, and have a working knowledge of the agencies and issues in your area.

Well, this covers the three points discussed here today, and so you may be wondering, "What's she going to use that *E* for?" Well, at the beginning of the speech I discussed the idea that very few people have a problem with volunteerism. Most of us agree that it is a good thing. The problem lies in moving from that agreement into action. And that's where the *E* comes in. The *E* is eliminate excuses. [Visual aid: *E*liminate *E*xcuses] Be a modern-day Good Samaritan. If you're afraid to do it yourself or you don't think you'll stay involved, go out in pairs and become involved in community service. Just eliminate the excuses, become a modern-day Good Samaritan, see what needs to be done, and JUST DO IT!

WORKS CITED

Carter, Carol. *Majoring in the Rest of Your Life.* New York: Noonday, 1990.

"Homeless, Report #14364," *American Statistics Index, 1989.* Washington, D. C.: Congressional Information Service, 1989, Supp. 5: 14.

Lee, Felicia R. "Students Reach Out to Help the Poor." *New York Times* 11 March 1989: 31.

Rice, Faye. "Volunteer Work: Better than Beer." *Fortune* 16 July 1990: 78-81.

Theus, Kathryn T. "Campus-Based Community Service." *Change* September/October 1988: 27-38.

United States. Dept. of Commerce. "Alcoholism and Drug Abuse Treatment Facilities and Clients," *Statistical Abstract of the United States: National Data Book.* Washington, D. C.: GPO, 1990.

—. —. Dept. of Commerce. "Persons Below Poverty Level," *Statistical Abstract of the United States: National Data Book.* Washington, D. C.: GPO, 1990.

Virginia Statistical Abstract. Charlottesville: UVA Center for Public Service, 1989.

■ Interview with Sandra Gomila ————————————

1. HOW DID YOU GO ABOUT SELECTING YOUR TOPIC?

When I first got the assignment, I was trying to decide between two topics: (1) the problems with the 911 emergency phone system and (2) innumeracy, or math illiteracy. I had heard a television report about some problems with 911, and that interested and concerned me. A friend mentioned math illiteracy as a possible topic choice and gave me a copy of a book he had on the subject. I went to the library and looked first for books on these subjects, but found few recent and relevant sources. So I moved to periodicals. With the help of *InfoTrac* and other computer indexes, I soon found some references for newspaper and magazine articles. I located about five or six articles on each subject, brought them home, and read them.

In trying to decide on my topic, I asked other people for their opinions: "Do you think this would make a good persuasive speech?" "Do you see an argument here?" Then one day somebody suggested that I speak on volunteerism —persuading people to volunteer their time. I thought, "Well, that sounds like an interesting topic." I went back to the library and got some more stuff, this time on volunteerism, and I really liked what I saw.

At that point, I still could have chosen any of the three topics: 911, innumeracy, or volunteerism. I continued to work with each of these ideas, weighing the pros and cons of each. When you have a deadline to meet — you know, you have a time and a date to give your speech — it's very important that at some point you pick a topic and run with it. So after I looked at the pros and cons of each topic, I decided to go with volunteerism. The main reason was that it interested me the most, personally. As I said in my speech, I am a volunteer and I've found this experience very rewarding. To develop a speech about something you're interested in makes a huge difference.

2. HOW DID YOU DETERMINE THE KEY IDEAS YOU WOULD COVER IN YOUR SPEECH?

Once I decided to do volunteerism, I had to figure out where to go from there. I bantered around, asking a couple of friends: "If you heard a speech about why we should volunteer, what would you *expect* to see in it? What would you *like* to see in it?" I thought about the topic and bounced some ideas off my roommates. I got this general idea that my main objective would be to talk about why we should volunteer based on the *needs,* the *benefits,* and the *process.*

3. WHAT OBSTACLES DID YOU SEE FOR THE TOPIC OF VOLUNTEERISM?

Well, it's not a tremendously controversial topic. Few people would say, "Volunteering is not worth my time," or "I don't agree with volunteering." So that was one of the obstacles I had to confront: to develop a speech in light of the fact that it did not appear to be a controversial topic. Persuasive speeches usually should have an element of controversy. I had to try to zero in on what the controversy would be.

As I thought about the topic, I decided that the challenge was to get people to volunteer. People say they believe in volunteerism, yet many fail to participate. I really wanted to get the audience to take the next step: *to volunteer.* So as I was reading the articles and talking with some friends, I decided to make my speech different by not focusing so much on the *needs* of volunteering. That's what I'd expect to hear in a typical volunteerism speech (there are this many homeless, this many drug addicts; we have all these needs; get out there and help!). I decided instead to focus on the personal benefits of volunteering. I wanted to get the audience to see volunteerism as a way to enlarge or apply their own interests. You know, "If I know I'm going to live in the city, maybe I ought to get out and volunteer in issues I'll be confronted with in the city." Or, "If I'm an accounting major, I want to volunteer my time to help someone who's not skilled in accounting and that helps me practice my major at the same time." So I was very interested in pursuing this angle of the benefits of volunteerism.

As you can see from the text of the speech, that was my main focus: a brief description of why society still needs volunteers, then a *huge* section on why we should get involved now during college, and then, finally, ending with the process. In my speech I asked three questions: (1) Does society still need volunteers? (2) Why should I volunteer now? and (3) How do I get involved?

4. WHAT STRATEGIES DID YOU USE IN YOUR SPEECH TO HELP THE AUDIENCE REMEMBER AND REINFORCE YOUR MESSAGE?

I decided to include a handout in my speech because, like I said before, the main obstacle is moving listeners from agreement to action. I was trying to focus on how easy it is to become involved. I wanted to make it easy for my audience, so that once they walked away from the speech they would have something tangible to refer to. I also used the N-I-K-E gimmick as my conclusion. Maybe when those who heard my speech see a Nike ad on television, they will think of my speech.

5. DID THE FACT THAT THE SPEECH WAS VIDEOTAPED AFFECT SOME OF YOUR DECISIONS?

When I learned that the speech was going to be videotaped, that brought in some other problems and concerns to deal with. I decided to have a visual aid and do my summary as a gimmick using the letters of Nike. I really wanted the audience to be stimulated in hearing and seeing it. And so once I found out I was going to be videotaped, I chose to have a yellow posterboard with black letters. Otherwise, I probably would have chosen black letters on white posterboard. But since I knew it was being videotaped, and you want to stay away from black on white, I chose yellow posterboard.

If I were doing this speech without being videotaped, I probably would have chosen a much darker dress since I tend to wear darker colors anyway. But because I was being videotaped, I knew that pastels would be a good choice. So that's why I chose what I wore. But I think it's important when we speak to be dressed on a level that's consistent with the seriousness of our topic. I don't think it would be appropriate, at least for me, to come in and give a speech sloppily dressed. Your appearance does make a statement.

One thing that added a lot to my nervousness once I got there was being miked. If I had had the chance to practice with the microphone, with all the wires tripping me up, I would have been much more at ease when I gave the speech.

6. HOW DID YOU PREPARE YOUR VISUAL AID?

I really took time with my visual aid. I chose the colors very carefully. I went out and bought stencil letters that I could rub onto the posterboard. And I chose very carefully the height of the beginning letters and each letter after that. I sat down with a ruler and penciled out how the letters would look best and how they would come across most clearly to the audience. It took a long time, but if you want a visual aid that will really reinforce what you're saying, then it's worth doing well. A visual aid should look professional.

7. HOW DID YOU PRACTICE YOUR SPEECH?

One thing that was especially beneficial before giving this speech was practicing in the room beforehand. I went to the classroom the evening before the speech, set up my visual aid, went through the speech, went through how I was going to move in the room, which was especially important because the speech was being videotaped. The next day when I had a microphone on me and a cord running down to the floor, I realized how important that practice was in getting used to just moving around the room.

So I went into the classroom the night before, got comfortable with where the audience was going to be sitting, and I think most important, I got comfortable with my visual aid. I bought two posterboards so that I could cover up the first with the second. I cut the top posterboard into four strips and paperclipped them over my visual aid. That way, I could uncover one letter at a time: *N*, then *I*, then *K*, then *E*. And so I practiced that, because otherwise I would have been really nervous.

It was also important for me to see how my visual aid was going to fit on the easel. Would it need to be taped? Would the ends curl around the back? How am I going to deal with that? It helped my level of nervousness tremendously to get those things out of the way the *day before* the speech instead of the *morning of* the speech.

8. WHAT ARE SOME OF THE TECHNIQUES YOU USED TO RELATE YOUR SPEECH TO THIS PARTICULAR AUDIENCE?

I thought it was really important to localize the topic, and that's one reason I wanted to use a handout. There are statistics in the speech from the state of Virginia, and even from the city of Radford itself. I used them to localize my speech. Instead of just saying "There are X million homeless people in America," I could say, "X percent of people living right here in our city live below the poverty line," and bring it home. And I thought that was important.

9. HOW DID YOU FEEL ABOUT THE DELIVERY OF YOUR SPEECH?

I guess this was the first time I've given a speech just with notecards. It was difficult for me to get out from behind that lectern with my notes in one hand and still try to use my body and my other hand in my speech. I think I could have used fewer notecards, if I had condensed my notes to include just my key ideas and the quotations and statistics I needed. Using 4-by-6-inch instead of the 3-by-5 cards would probably also have helped.

I was very concerned about my delivery looking artificial instead of natural. It's important to practice, but I don't think we should practice ourselves to death. We should be confident that we know our topic. And if we do know our topic and how it's organized, I think we'll do all right — even if we get lost or trip over something. I know it was a big help for me to sit down and say:

Okay, I start off with the story of the Good Samaritan and I talk about how that's a great example [of volunteerism]. I talk about how people admire volunteerism, but not many people do it. I move into my statement of topic, my rhetorical questions, and my preview step. And that's my introduction.

In just doing that, I've reasoned out how I've organized my speech, so that when I get up and give it, it's clear in my head.

In the actual delivery of the speech, there were a couple of times when I lost my place or stumbled over some words. But I just kept right on going. That's really important — to realize that it's very difficult to give a speech without any mistakes in it. In a public speaking class, I don't think professors are looking for perfection. I think they're looking for a well-rounded speech — good in content, good in organization, good in delivery, but not perfect. It's OK to make mistakes. After I got through the speech, I still felt good about it, even though there had been a couple of blunders here and there.

There was one point in the speech where I say that according to the *Statistical Abstract of the United States,* 14 percent of people living here in Radford live below the poverty line. When I was putting my sources together to turn in after the speech, I discovered that the 14 percent figure actually came from the *Virginia Statistical Abstract.* Even though that didn't change the point I was making, I felt bad that I hadn't quoted the correct source. I could have avoided this mistake if I had taken a little more time when I was researching. After photocopying my articles, I should have divided them, stapled each article, and written the source on the top page of each article.

10. WHAT TECHNIQUES DID YOU USE TO HELP YOU COPE WITH YOUR NERVOUSNESS?

I don't think that when we speak we should expect *not* to be nervous. It's only natural to be nervous. In fact, I get more frightened if I'm *not* nervous a little bit before I speak. If you're serious about your topic and really want to communicate it to your audience, you're probably going to be a little nervous. That's natural.

Practice, of course, is one way of reducing nervousness. As I said earlier, rehearsing in the room where I was going to speak and practicing using my visual aid helped make me more confident.

Another thing that helps me in giving a speech is seeing how the audience is reacting to me: their body language, their eye contact. And I can't analyze those things unless I'm looking at them. So for me, in doing any kind of audience analysis [during the speech], eye contact is critical. From their body language, eye contact, and facial expression, I found that most people seemed to be responding to the speech. There's one point in the speech where I tell a joke, and to see people smile and chuckle, you say, "OK, they must be with me."

Sample Speeches

"A STITCH IN TIME"

EMLYN KATHRYN CARLEY, *San Antonio College, San Antonio*

Lyn Carley delivered the following speech in a public speaking class at San Antonio College during the fall of 1990. Members of her class seemed particularly impressed with Lyn's visual aids, and we are grateful to Judy Martin for her permission to reprint them here. In the marginal annotations, we have indicated the major strengths of Lyn's speech, as well as some improvements she might make.

Lyn begins with a rhetorical question. Her topic is apparent by the time she finished her second sentence. The surprising prices she mentions here certainly give the audience a reason to listen.

This section of the introduction builds the importance of Lyn's subject further.

Her third paragraph clearly previews the ideas she will develop in the body of her speech.

Here Lyn begins to apply the 4 S's to her first point. She signposts ("One") and states her idea (quilts are historical records). She quickly introduces a source to support the idea.

How would you like to go to bed tonight with a dear old friend and find you've woken up with a millionaire? Well, the quilt your great-grandmother made, the one you toss over your bed on those cold winter nights, the quilt you carelessly throw into the washing machine, probably won't be worth a million dollars, but it could be worth a small fortune. Some antique quilts have been valued between $35,000 and $50,000—and some have sold for more than $150,000!

Quilts were treasured in their own day for their beauty, utility, and craftmanship. Today they are perhaps even more highly regarded as documents of our American heritage. They tell us a lot about ourselves, and many of them are just beautiful to look at. But if you're absolutely unsentimental and don't have trouble eventually parting with them, quilts can also be solid investments.

So first, I would like to tell you how quilts are viewed as historical records. Second, I will describe quilting as an art form. Third, I will discuss a quilt's investment value. And finally I will describe and show you a personal history quilt I've put together for a member of this class.

One of the most interesting ways of looking at antique quilts is as historical records. "Quilts are among the few tangible objects that reflect the role women played in the building of America," says Patricia Wilens, editor of the Better Homes and Gardens book, *America's Heritage Quilts*. She notes that "Pilgrim women brought to the New World [the] skills and styles of their European homeland." They also brought memories of those homelands. They created quilt patterns that they called "Windmill Blades" and "Dresden Plate," for example. Wilens says that as quiltmakers designed individual blocks for their patchwork quilts they frequently chose names to commemorate important people or events. Early pioneer women traveling across America named their quilt blocks "Kansas Troubles," "Road to California," "Oklahoma Wonder," or "Rocky Mountain Chain." As their families settled down, the women made quilts out of blocks with names like "Barn Raising" and "Straight Furrow." Blocks with names like "Hands-all-Around" and "Swing-in-the-Center" remind us how important the country dance was to them. With fabric scarce during the Civil War, the "Log Cabin" block, made of thin strips of material, became popular. As you can see, the names early Americans gave their quilt patterns tell us something about their lives.

In addition to telling us about individual lives, certain styles of quilting also identify particular historical periods. Today, if you find a "crazy quilt" made of odd shaped scraps of velvet, satin, silk, and ribbons, it may have been made in the Victorian era, from 1870 to 1900. If it's in good shape, that's probably because it was made to be thrown over a sofa or chair. It was decorative rather than useful. If you find a quilt made of bright, solid colors on a dark background, it could have been made by Amish women whose families settled in Pennsylvania or Kansas. Because their austere religious beliefs prohibited them from using printed fabrics, the Amish put together strong, solid colors that look very contemporary to us.

In the 1920s, quilts reflected the new "modern woman," and Wilens says that the widespread publication of quilt patterns for the first time greatly popularized quiltmaking. The Depression marked another change; quilters again were quilting out of necessity, like their colonial predecessors. Two sentences in a little booklet entitled *Quilts: Heirlooms of Tomorrow*, summarize quilts as historical records: "Today we treasure as part of our American culture the innumerable variety of patchwork patterns that have recorded gallant lives, the growth of our nation, and the symbols of a new society. Thousands of people take pride in preserving and further enriching this heritage by making quilts of beauty that generations to come will prize."

Quilting took a back seat during World War II and through the '50s and '60s. In fact, according to Beth Sherman, in an article in the February 1989 *Harper's Bazaar*, it wasn't until New York's Whitney Museum of American Art exhibited sixty pieced quilts in 1971 that people began to look at quilting as something more than a useful craft. And that second way of appreciating quilts is as a fine art.

Aunt Martha's Favorite Quilts Magazine notes, "For a 'Prize Winning' quilt, design is most important. The selection and combination of materials and colors, the skill of the needle worker, and artistic quilting all go to make the quilt a thing of beauty."

The most important step in achieving a beautiful quilt is the fabric selection. Cotton is the most popular fabric and the most durable of textiles. Cotton's color retention is exceptional as well. I have worked with denim and silk in the past and always return to cotton. Any fabric store will have a large selection of colors and prints to choose from. It takes practice to get the right combinations, but once you get the hang of it, you are on your way. I mentioned Amish quilts earlier, and Amish quilters were experts at combining colors. What they lost in the detail of printed fabric that was forbidden to them, they made up for in color. The neon colors of Amish quilts remind many people of the pop art of the 1960s.

You may be curious as to the actual construction of a quilt. Maggie Malone,

These brief, vivid, examples show that the names of quilt blocks tell a history and evoke images of pioneer life. "As you can see" begins a very brief summary of the point Lyn has made so far.

"In addition" begins a complementary transition. Lyn defines "crazy quilt" and reminds her listeners of the dates of the Victorian era. She uses "if you find" to introduce two brief hypothetical examples.

This quotation serves as an effective summary of Lyn's first point.

The information from *Harper's* serves as Lyn's transition to her next point. In the final sentence, Lyn signposts and states her second point.

Lyn gives no author for this source, nor did she for the "booklet" she quoted earlier.

Lyn mentions her own experience as a quilter. If her topic had been controversial, she would have needed to build her credibility earlier in the speech.

Lyn's use of "I," "you," and "we" throughout the speech helps her involve her listeners and establish a warm, friendly interaction with them. At this point, Lyn used several quilt blocks as visual aids. One was partially quilted so that the audience could see the layers she mentions. Lynn's second point lacks a summary.

Lyn begins her transition to her third point here.

She signposts and states her next idea with "a third way of looking at quilts is as investments."

This is Lyn's best job of explaining a source's qualifications. Again she quickly uses a source to support the idea she has just introduced.

These three actual examples from three different sources seem well organized because the dollar amounts ($6,500, $50,000, $176,000) increase with each one.

Mentioning a local quilt guild localizes the topic and tells listeners where they might go to learn more about the subject.

Here Lyn introduces the idea of the personal history quilt and then signposts it as her "final" point.

author of *500 Full-size Patchwork Patterns,* says, "Quilt patterns consist largely of geometric pieces; it is the different sizes of those pieces and their arrangements that give patchwork its tremendous variety." A quilt top is either pieced together from blocks or is a solid fabric with other materials sewn, or appliquéd, to it. Shirley Thompson, who has a special interest in throws and crib quilts, writes in her book, *Think Small,* "Quilts consist of three layers: top, batting, and backing. Quilting stitches hold the three layers together while adding ornamental surface interest to the quilt." The stitch count on a finely crafted quilt should be eight to twelve stitches per inch, and no area larger than the palm of your hand should be left unquilted. You will often see an obvious mistake somewhere in the pattern of an old quilt. Members of strict religious orders often made these mistakes on purpose as a sign of humility, a recognition that only God is perfect.

If you have absolutely no appreciation of craftsmanship and no eye for color and design, you may still be interested in quilts because of those dollar figures I mentioned at the beginning of my speech. Yes, a third way of looking at quilts is as investments. In their book *Quilts, Coverlets, Rugs, & Samplers,* Dr. Robert Bishop, director of New York's Museum of American Folk Art, and his co-authors tell the story of one quilt. They relate, "In the fall of 1980, an important collection of American textiles was sold at auction in New Hampshire." One particular quilt, signed by its maker and dated 1837, fetched only $85.00 at that time. However, the buyer then sold it to a museum curator in New York City for $650. "Today," they note, "it is one of the most prized examples of Americana in the museum's permanent collection and is valued at $6,500. This is not an isolated incident."

An article in *Business Week,* March 6, 1989, tells of the investment potential of unique quilts. For example, a "1930 quilt depicting interracial scenes, such as a black doctor caring for a white patient, sold for a few dollars in the 1960s. Despite the quilt's ordinary workmanship, a collector purchased it last year for more than $50,000."

Sherman says in her *Harper's Bazaar* article that today, "Quilts generally cost between $500 and $2,000, but in urban areas they may sell for $25,000 or more. The record for a quilt sold at auction was set [in 1987] at Sotheby's when a dealer paid $176,000 for a Baltimore album quilt," made around 1840. As you can see by these examples, these bed covers can be anything but ordinary. But even seemingly ordinary early twentieth-century quilts seem to be appreciating at about 10 percent a year, according to the *Business Week* article. A trip to an antique dealer, a quilt shop, or to an organization such as the Greater San Antonio Quilt Guild might give your great-grandmother's quilt a new value, and even a new lease on life. If it's an heirloom, its value will increase steadily throughout the years.

But you don't have to be made out of money to get yourself a quilt today. With some skill and patience you can make a special type of quilt, the personal history quilt. That's the final topic I'll briefly discuss today.

Quilters seem to take special joy in selecting blocks not only for their aesthetic qualities, but also for the blocks' names. Your quilt can tell a story. It can be a personal history or family sampler quilt. A quilter simply selects blocks with names that have special meaning for the person who is to receive the quilt.

I interviewed classmate Norma Falkner and asked her a few questions

Mother's Day

Emerald Isle

Baby's Breath

about herself. We came up with blocks representative of the special people, places, things, and times that are important to her. These are the blocks I selected for Norma's quilt and why they are significant in her life:

Night Owl — Norma rarely gets to bed before midnight.
Emerald Isle — The emerald is her birthstone.
Sister's Choice — Norma has two sisters.
Collector's Block — Antique collecting is a hobby of hers.
Texas Two-Step — She is a native Texan.
Mother's Day — This must be better than Christmas! Not only was Norma born and married on this day, but she's also the mother of a little boy.
Puppy Dog Tails — She is a pet lover.
Chocolate Lover — Need I say more?
Vagabond — Norma enjoys traveling and plans to see a lot of the world.
Baby Boomer — Without giving away her age, I'll just say that Norma qualifies.
Baby's Breath — For her two-year-old son.
Mexican Star — This final block proudly reflects Norma's heritage.

The fact that Lyn had developed a quilt based on the life of one of her listeners gives an immediacy to this final point.

At this point, Lyn introduced a large visual aid composed of enlarged color copies of quilt blocks. As she mentioned the 12 blocks in Norma's quilt, Lyn pointed to each.

Mexican Star

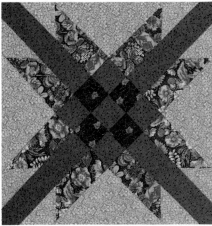

Sister's Choice

Chocolate Lover

Night Owl

Texas Two-Step

Puppy Dog Tails

Collector's Block

Vagabond

Baby Boomer

Lyn shows excellent audience adaptation by mentioning other members of her classroom audience and their interests. Each of these people had spoken on the subject Lyn indicates.

Here Lyn acknowledges the source of the quilt blocks she used in her visual aid.

A quilt made up of those blocks and using fabrics I chose would be as unique as Norma herself. I could also make a personal history quilt for a group of people — a family or a group of friends. From speeches I've heard given in class this semester, I could create a class quilt. Let's start with the block "Classmates." How about "Carnival Ride" for Dianne Bloom's love of the roller coaster? Housebuilder Darin Turner would be well represented with a block entitled "Carpenter's Wheel." "Acrobats" might be the best block to describe our exercise guru John Caballero. To represent Sonja Heldt's expertise in photography, I'd choose a block named "Photo Album." My own block would be "Quilter's Dream." And to date our quilt, how about "Yellow Ribbons," signifying the safe return of our Desert Shield participants? Judy Martin, who was for eight years senior editor of *Quilter's Newsletter Magazine*, lists numerous quilt block patterns in her *Ultimate Book of Quilt Block Patterns*, my source for the blocks I've used in Norma's quilt. You can see the endless possibilities available to quilters today. You need only a subject and a little imagination to create a historical record, treasured for years to come.

Today, I've shown you a personal history quilt fashioned after classmate Norma Falkner's life. I've demonstrated how a quilt can be a valuable investment. I've described quilting as an art form and told you a little about the historical significance of quilts. Personal history quilts are an excellent way to preserve family histories, as they would be handed down from generation to generation. As Dr. Bishop points out, "A quilt is often made as a document of love. It's a record of being in a certain place at a certain time. It's craftsmanship. It's emotional. It's art."

Lyn summarizes her points in reverse order.

Delivered from memory and with appropriate pauses, Lyn's final quotation brings her speech to a solid psychological conclusion.

PERSUASIVE SPEECH[1]

WILLIAM FORT, *California State University, Chico*

William Fort won first place in persuasive speaking at the 1989 American Forensic Association's National Individual Events Tournament. Examining a phenomenon known as Sick Building Syndrome, he discussed its causes, symptoms, and solutions. See if you agree with one judge's comment that "the speech was a textbook example of fine persuasion."

> "What is so terrible as war? I will tell you what is ten and ten thousand times more terrible than war—outraged nature. I see that three persons out of every four are utterly unaware of the general causes of their own ill-health, and that is to stupid neglect, or what is just bad, stupid ignorance."

1   In 1859, Reverend Charles Kingsley used these powerful words to address the cholera epidemic which created a 40 percent infant mortality rate in England, simply because of a lack of sanitation. Today we face a similar situation. There is a problem that most are unaware of, which is causing influenza, smallpox, pneumonia, tuberculosis, meningitis, airborne lead poisoning, and most fatally, Legionnaire's disease. This problem? Sick Building Syndrome. Sick Building Syndrome [SBS] describes any building with actual or potential health hazards due to contaminated air. The incidence of SBS is rising, partially because buildings have been planned with maximum energy savings in mind since the energy crisis of the 1970s. Dr. Tony Pickering, who is currently studying SBS, states in the May, 1987, issue of *World Press Review* that "SBS affects 90 percent of supersealed buildings, and in some cases sickens up to 70 percent of the building occupants." Supersealed buildings describe any building which uses mechanical ventilation. In basic terms, a building whose windows cannot open or close.

2   SBS is a serious problem that we need to become aware of, because if we don't do something to cure the disease today, then like England in the 1860s, thousands of Americans will die in the 1990s. So today we will investigate SBS by first examining the general causes of the problem, then looking at the symptoms of SBS, and finally, we will find ways to end the outraged nature of SBS.

3   There are three major causes of SBS. The first is that buildings are using ineffective heating, ventilation, and air conditioning systems, also known as HVAC systems. Architect William Heineman describes these systems in the December, 1985, issue of *National Safety and Health News*. "Once we enter these air-tight buildings, we are completely dependent upon its support systems

for survival. The quality and quantity of air we breathe are totally contained within the system."

4   Not only do these systems pick up fungus and bacteria and recirculate it throughout a system, but also airborne viruses, germs from co-workers, and cigarette smoke. "Microbiological health hazards are the most widespread of the many hazards in mechanically ventilated buildings," declares environmentalist Sandy Moretz in the February, 1988, issue of *Occupational Hazards* magazine. Moretz goes on to state, "The vast majority of this microbial growth is caused by stagnant water and dirt build-up in air filters, and condensation drainage trays that are not regularly cleaned." Or, in Kingsley's words, "stupid neglect and stupid ignorance."

5   The third major cause of SBS is the lack of governmental support. The Environmental Protection Agency's Eileen Claussen states in the June 6, 1988, issue of *Time* magazine that "Some Americans spend an estimated 90 percent of their time indoors. However no specific federal regulations have been adopted for control of air in offices, even though the air in some buildings is 100 times as polluted as the air outside the buildings."

6   Ineffective HVAC systems, lack of maintenance on existing systems, and no governmental support all perpetuate the problems associated with Sick Building Syndrome. And those problems are significant. The symptoms of SBS don't start out with our building throwing up or your elevator doors getting a fever, rather as minor annoyances such as a dry throat, headaches, or drowsiness. In fact, the May, 1987, issue of *Occupational Health and Safety* printed a survey of over 1,000 office workers, half of whom worked in naturally ventilated buildings, and half in mechanically ventilated buildings. The results showed that while only 15.7 percent of those in naturally ventilated buildings had frequent headaches, 37.4 percent of those in mechanically ventilated buildings did. When it comes to drowsiness, 13.8 percent in naturally ventilated buildings, and 51.4 percent — four times as many — in mechanically ventilated buildings, were frequently drowsy on the job.

7   These lopsided figures translate into a monetary loss by building owners. James Repace, an indoor air specialist with the EPA, states in the January, 1989, issue of *Discover* magazine, "The millions of workdays lost each year [due to SBS] translate into billions of dollars in medical expense, diminished productivity, and compensation claims." In May, 1988, 70 workers boycotted their office building, claiming that the air inside the building was so contaminated it caused frequent headaches, dizziness, eye irritation, chest pains, and breathing difficulties. The Washington, D. C., building is the National Headquarters of the Environmental Protection Agency.

8   Although usually the symptoms of SBS are the ones I've previously mentioned, sometimes just one visit into any supersealed building can be fatal. In May, 1985, 37 men, women, and children who stayed on the fourth floor of Stafford General Hospital mysteriously died. Later the cause was found to be Legionnaire's disease, a harmful bacterium which originated in an air conditioning system which blew the deadly disease through the air ducts right into the unsuspecting patients' rooms. The HVAC system hadn't been cleaned in over a year. This incident, outlined in the *Air Conditioning, Heating and Refrigeration News*, is not an isolated one. In fact, the September 2, 1985, issue of *U. S.*

News and World Report says "Legionnaire's disease strikes 25 to 50,000 Americans a year, and about 15 percent of the victims die." Translating these figures, we can see that the outraged nature of SBS causes around 5,000 deaths annually.

9   Hospitals, hotels, the Environmental Protection Agency, and school buildings are places where we should be able to go and feel safe and secure. However until we, as individuals and as a nation, do something to stop the enraged nature of Sick Building Syndrome, then each and every trip into a supersealed building will be potentially life threatening.

10 On an individual level, the one sure fire way to prevent becoming a victim of SBS is to wear a gas mask at all times. But since gas masks are uncomfortable, hard to find, and — let's face it — unattractive, I'll recommend other means of survival. First, we need to become aware of general causes of our own ill health in these buildings. Realize that if you have frequent headaches, dry throat, drowsiness, eye irritation, chest pains, or breathing difficulties inside a building, that it probably is a sick building.

11 Once this awareness is achieved, please act. Pick up the phone and call your local building inspector and ask him or her to examine your sick building, and let you and the building owner know what actual or potential health hazards are there due to contaminated air. Another practical step we can all take is to tell others about the problem so they can also help find these sick buildings and pressure building owners to start a preventive program against SBS.

12 On a larger level, we can see the need to attack the number one cause of SBS, which is microbial growth in HVAC systems. David Custer, the vice-president of Environmental Management Systems, says in the February, 1987, issue of *Buildings*, "Microbiological health hazards are the most preventable of the many hazards in supersealed buildings. They can be virtually eliminated through simple maintenance." The types of simple maintenance which Mr. Custer speaks of include replacing all dirty air filters, emptying all condensation drainage trays, and treating the entire system with an inexpensive antimicrobial solution. By spending a few dollars today, they can save millions tomorrow, and end their stupid neglect. This is a simple and logical solution which will be easy and inexpensive to implement.

13 Finally, federal legislation which (a) requires building owners to use certain types of tested, effective HVAC systems, and (b) requires them to clean and maintain their existing systems, would be a great help in calming the outraged nature of SBS.

14 In 1859, one of England's major problems was a cholera epidemic which created a 40 percent infant mortality rate. This could have been solved by taking simple preventive measures and being more sanitary. Unfortunately, most ignored Reverend Kingsley, and because of it, hundreds of thousands needlessly died. Research scientist Michael McCawley said in the June 6, 1988, issue of *Time* that "unless we realize the severity of the problem today, Sick Building Syndrome will be one of the major problems in the 1990s." If we follow the simple steps which I've outlined, we can learn from the English mistakes of the 1860s, and end the stupid neglect, stupid ignorance, and outraged nature associated with SBS. And in the process we can all play doctor and save the thousands of lives lost each year to SBS.

PERSUASIVE SPEECH[2]

SHELLEY SCHNATHORST, *University of Northern Iowa*

Shelley Schnathorst was the persuasive speaking champion at the 1988 American Forensic Association's National Individual Events Tournament. In her speech she advocated stricter regulation of medical devices. Following the text of her speech are the comments of her judges.

1   In Roman times the Latin phrase "caveat emptor" or "let the buyer beware" was an appropriate warning to the citizens of that time. In the United States today we pride ourselves on a system which protects consumers from dangerous products. And while we understand that we still have responsibilities in our own protection, we have come to trust the safety of the products we must use. But for thousands of people each year that trust is misplaced. They are the ones who use medical devices ranging from X-rays to incubators and pacemakers to prostheses.

2   There are over 1,600 different types of medical devices in use today by virtually every patient who enters a doctor's office for tests or a hospital for operations. Although the range of medical devices may seem broad, they are all subject to the medical regulatory system.

3   The Food and Drug Administration, or the FDA, has been given responsibility to approve medical devices. Yet Representative Henry Waxman of California stated on May 4th of 1987 that "only a handful have actually been so approved." Because most devices have not gone through rigorous approval processes, they present enormous hazards to us. In testifying before the House of Representatives on May 5th of last year, Stephen Ferguson, president of one of the world's largest manufacturers of medical devices, stated, "Everyone in this room will someday want one of the devices we have under development, as the best available choice for yourselves or someone you know." So that we can improve the safety of those choices, we need to look at the importance of regulating medical devices, flaws in current regulations, and finally workable solutions to ensure that we are adequately protected.

4   Adequate regulation is essential for two reasons. First and foremost, medical devices are often critical to the health and survival of individuals. By definition, a medical device is any instrument or apparatus intended to prevent, diagnose, or treat a human illness or disorder. And of course, when we seek the help of a doctor or a hospital, we hope that the devices they use will make us better, and we trust that they will not make us worse. Yet sometimes devices that are considered life-supporting become life-threatening.

5   John Villforth, an FDA administrator, reported in a May 1986 *FDA Consumer* that a heart resuscitation unit failed when the machine, like many of its type, had no warning device to indicate that the battery's powering units were defective. In addition, a July 2, 1987, segment of *20/20* reported that investigators discovered a flaw in the Therac 25, a radiation machine used in the treatment of cancer. Each of the three patients interviewed complained of being burned by the machine. After the loss of two lives, investigations led to the discovery of a computer program error which had given some patients forty-five times the amount of radiation requested. As amateurs in health care, we

cannot be expected to have a clear understanding of every medical device and its hazards. Yet our lives are at stake.

6   A second reason for adequate regulation was described by Representative Waxman, who is chairman of the House Subcommittee on Medical Devices. He stated that unlike a consumer product such as a child's toy, or even a Toyota, which can be recalled, it is more difficult to deal with medical devices for oftentimes they have been implanted into a human body. Consider the case of Constance Walters, who testified in a videotape before House hearings. To correct a curvature in her spine, she had an operation in which a medical device called a Weiss spring was implanted into her back in February of last year. By April she was experiencing tremendous pain. The Weiss spring, which had never been submitted for testing, snapped inside her. As Walters said, "It is worse now, I can't be anybody. Do something so that someone else's life is not totally ruined like this."

7   According to Waxman, the best solution is to have a system that provides reasonable assurance that devices are both safe and effective. Well, there is a law intended to provide such an assurance. However, that law, the Medical Device Amendment of 1976, is flawed itself.

8   In his May 4, 1987, testimony, Dr. Sidney Wolf, director of the Public Citizen Health Research Group, outlined three specific flaws in current regulation. First, legislation requires that most devices meet FDA performance standards. The catch is the FDA has never devised any standards, and thus cannot regulate the devices.

9   In the absence of standards, the FDA relies upon Article 510K of the Medical Device Amendment. 510K allows a manufacturer to introduce a new device on the market simply by claiming it is substantially equivalent to devices on the market in 1976. There is no need to claim that the devices are any better than the devices in 1976, and the claims that are made go untested. Dr. Wolf stated that this second flaw is perhaps the biggest loophole in the law.

10   In fact, Representative Waxman noted that well over 98 percent of the new medical devices that enter the market each year do so by claiming substantial equivalence rather than going through pre-market safety tests and reviews. What this means is that Americans continue to serve as guinea pigs for new medical devices. Constance Walters was a guinea pig, for the Weiss spring had never been submitted for testing.

11   Now the question that some of you may be asking is how common is such a problem. The third flaw in this system ensures that we will never know the answer, for complete, systematic reporting of defects is not required. Now the law requires that manufacturers report defects directly to the FDA. But hospitals, doctors, distributors, those who actually work with the devices, are not mandated to report the defects to anyone. And for the information that is reported, a General Accounting Office study published in December of 1986 found that there is a funnelling effect. They examined what happened to nearly 1,200 reports of medical device problems and found that because of the informality of the process and lack of required reporting, less than 1 percent of those problems ever reached FDA files.

12   Failure to develop standards, reliance on an equivalent standard instead, and finally incomplete reporting all combine to create inadequate protection. It is protection which Tama and James Jackson wish they had had when their

firstborn baby, a baby boy, developed jaundice. The baby was placed in an illuminated hospital incubator which rid the child's body of the yellow coloration. The next day the incubator was empty. Their baby was found in intensive care with a fever of 106 degrees. The next morning, the Jacksons' firstborn died. The cause of death, the incubator. With a broken thermostat and alarm and a defective on-off switch, the incubator literally became an oven. To prevent such horrors, immediate action needs to be taken. As is evident, current regulation must be modified.

13 First, the FDA should be required to develop the standards called for twelve years ago, so that the design of the device will be safe to begin with. For none of the examples that I have provided is an isolated malfunction, but rather a flaw in the design itself.

14 Second, establishing design standards will close the 510K loophole, and products won't be approved only because they are equivalent to devices in 1976. For as you well know, since 1976, improvements in medical technologies have occurred. Therefore, we should demand that such technologies be incorporated into new medical devices.

15 Third, reporting of defects should be mandated. Not just by manufacturers, but of course by doctors, hospitals, and distributors. There again should be a standardized format of reporting. Now this proposal will work, for when reports of problems do reach the FDA, they have been proven to be quite effective in protecting our interests. For example, when the FDA received reports of faulty sleep apnea monitors, which help children prone to sudden infant death syndrome, they were able to respond quite quickly. The FDA received reports that faulty monitors had electrocuted one child and burned several others. With this information, the FDA was able to issue safety alerts to health care professionals, home users, sleep apnea support groups, and of course the manufacturers who could improve the device.

16 Currently, there is a bill before the House Subcommittee on Health, Environment, and Energy. Although not yet in its final form, this bill will ensure that necessary alterations be made in FDA regulations. It is this bill, HR2595, which you should encourage your legislators to support.

17 Again, although we cannot be expected to know everything about every medical device, there are times that we or someone we know will be using one. Therefore we need to trust the proverb, "let the buyer beware," and become more informed about such devices.

18 The 1976 bill was well-intentioned. However, after a decade of talk and no action, it is time that Congress with our assistance take serious steps in regulating this multi-billion-dollar medical device industry. With timely action we can discover and correct what otherwise might be a fatal flaw. But we must act. For as Helen Keller once wrote, "Science may have found a cure for most evils, but it has found no remedy for the worst of them all, the apathy of human beings."

JUDGES' COMMENTS ON SHELLEY SCHNATHORST'S SPEECH

STEVEN BRYDON, *California State University, Chico*

First, let me extend my congratulations to all of the finalists. This was a very competitive round. . . . The topic of this speech, the lack of standards for medical devices, is clearly a significant one. However, one weakness of the speech, and the principal reason I ranked it second rather than first, was that quantification of the problems with unregulated medical devices could not be provided, beyond several specific examples. While this may be an inherent problem with this topic, I am troubled by the reliance on a few examples for proof of actual harm. If the number of unapproved devices is as widespread as the speech contends, then quantification of harm ought to be more available.

A second weakness with the speech was the attempt to provide a "personal" solution. The suggestion that we become more informed really is not workable, given the reporting difficulties outlined in the speech. How can a patient find out if a particular device has been approved or merely falls under one of the loopholes?

Despite the problems outlined above, on the whole this was a very strong speech. It was well documented, organized, and contained a number of very moving examples combined with testimony by authorities. I also felt that the speaker's delivery was exceptionally strong. Her presentation was both polished and conversational. On the whole, this was a fine example of persuasive speaking and I am pleased that it emerged as the ultimate winner in the collective judgment of the critics.

SARA HOLZBERLEIN, *Arizona State University*

When analyzing speeches there are several aspects to consider. But in these six speeches I had to narrow my critical analysis down to two areas: performance and compelling persuasiveness.

Ms. Schnathorst's performance level was very polished. There were, however, three areas which I believe she could have improved. First, including all of her audience in her speech would have helped in gaining more audience attention. Most of her performance was directed to her right, leaving the other half of the audience at an odd angle. Second, in vocal quality, although very articulate, she needed to pull back and allow the facts to speak for themselves. Instead, there seemed to be too much emphasis on shoving the facts. Her voice became tense. Third, her overall performance needed to be relaxed. Talking "to" an audience rather than "at" them can capture more attention on top of providing great facts and figures.

Compelling persuasiveness is an important area in persuasive speaking. It is the area that pushes a critic to vote. Although Ms. Schnathorst provided her audience with a clean performance, I still had a hard time becoming "moved" to vote. At one point in her speech I thought that she would grasp me when she addressed the point about human apathy, but this point was made at the end.

Weaving this theme throughout may have created "sappiness," but an occasional hinting at the importance apathy has in dealing with medical device approval would have clinched the vote. Because I felt this area was lacking, I had a hard time trying to reason with the "how" and "why" I should react. Hearing an ending line that contained "humaneness" will not always get my vote. I prefer to see consistency throughout.

BILL WALLACE, *Concordia College*

Obviously there are many good things to say about any speech that wins the AFA nationals and this one is no exception. One of the things I liked about Shelley's speech was that she convinced me the topic was both significant and appropriate to her audience. She accomplished this by (1) observing that all of us will have need of medical devices at some point in our lives and (2) using *explicit* and *specific* examples to build her case. These strategies were critical to her success because my reaction to her topic, as with most other topics in the round, was initially rather negative. (It is becoming increasingly difficult for me to leave a persuasion round without experiencing temporary bouts of hypochondria.)

Another strength of the speech was its use of compelling material. Her description of the pain caused by the faulty Weiss spring was particularly effective—not simply because of her initial description but because she returned to the example a few minutes later to refer to the victim of the faulty device as simply a guinea pig. In addition, the legal loopholes are presented in such a fashion as to make them appear enormous and I found myself asking how the FDA could be so incredibly careless in performing its duties.

As with any speech, of course, there were a couple of things I believe Shelley could have done better. First, I have never considered *20/20* to be television journalism at its best. At this level of competition the quality of documentation is critical. She could have improved the credibility of her citation here by seeking an alternative source for the Therac 25 example. Second, I felt that her closing statement was something less than imaginative. While I have immense respect for Helen Keller, I am not convinced that (1) apathy is incurable, or (2) that it is the worst of all human evils. This quotation gave the appearance of being selected simply to fulfill the requirement to have a closing statement.

"ACADEMIC LABORATORIES: RISKING LIFE AND LIMB FOR CREDIT"[3]

SUSANNE LANDOWSKI, *St. Cloud State University, Minnesota*

Susanne Landowski presented this persuasive speech at the 1988 Interstate Oratorical Association Contest where she was a semi-finalist. Her topic, unsafe student laboratories, was well chosen for a student audience.

1   For Ramsey Bittar, a typical day involves private nursing, physical therapy sessions, and communicating simple messages such as "hello" or "mom" on his computer keyboard. Ironically, however, three years ago Bittar was a gifted chemistry student. What happened? An accident that could and should have been prevented. Three years ago Bittar was performing a dangerous chemistry experiment when his flask exploded and an artery in his neck was severed. Before paramedics were summoned, he had lost enough blood to cause serious brain damage.

2   Ramsey Bittar is just one example of shocking lack of safety in student chemical labs. Academic laboratories. We're all familiar with them, from tak-

ing a lab class ourselves or knowing someone who did. Academic labs in high schools or universities are where curious students fearlessly learn about acids and bases or watch photos develop. The thrill of mixing a few milliliters of this with a few milliliters of that, however, easily becomes pain when a lab accident occurs.

3   Today, I will show you just how unsafe student labs are and convince you that steps must be taken to improve their safety. I'll begin by examining the extent and seriousness of unsafe student labs nationwide. Next I'll examine the causes behind this lack of safety. Finally, I'll discuss a three-part solution that must be implemented to protect anyone who has to work in a student laboratory.

4   Most universities and colleges have education requirements that require students to take at least one course involving some laboratory work. The *Journal of Chemical Education*, October 1986, released the results of a survey conducted to determine the number of people involved in student labs over a recent four-year period. Two hundred and fifty schools reported approximately 800,000 undergraduates involved. When you add the number of faculty, graduate students, and support personnel, and the number of schools that did not respond, the number of people involved in student labs, in one way or another, is significant.

5   Many chemical accidents involving these students go unreported for many reasons, thus the exact number is not known. The survey released by the *Journal of Chemical Education* estimates that approximately 60 percent of the students received some type of injury during that four-year period.

6   Now we can assume that some of them were nothing more severe than cuts from a broken test tube, treatable with a Band-Aid. Some of them, however, were severe enough to cause permanent disability or death.

7   For example, in late September of 1987, five high school students and a teacher were rushed to the emergency room with lacerations and burns when a test tube of alcohol exploded during a routine lab procedure.

8   In 1982, an undergraduate student in a freshman lab received third-degree burns when a Bunsen burner accidentally ignited his hair.

9   In 1979, a Southern Massachusetts University graduate student died in an explosion after an attempt to distill a dangerous chemical.

10   Now you may think that any dangerous activity must tolerate some accidents. I agree. However, academic labs have tolerated too much. According to the Occupational Safety and Health Administration, or OSHA, the rate of injury in a student lab is as much as 50 times higher than in the chemical industry. That means that for every one accident in industry, 50 occur in academic labs, a difference we can no longer ignore.

11   Lab accidents are also not limited to chemistry departments. Many non-science departments, such as art, anthropology, and photography, have poor student safety records. Students in art classes routinely mix paints containing chemicals known to cause nasal, lung, and skin cancer. Photography students work with chemicals that can cause kidney damage and nervous system disorders. Harry Teitelbaum, a biochemist at the EPA, states, "Teachers in these areas aren't trained to handle hazardous chemicals safely." In one instance, the National Institute for Occupational Safety and Health, or NIOSH, found that poor ventilation at Columbia College was the cause of skin, eye, and respiratory

inflammations among students in a photography class in 1981. The instructor didn't realize how toxic the fumes would be in an enclosed area.

12   People who have no connection to student labs must also be concerned about their safety, because just being in the same building that houses a laboratory is dangerous. In 1987, at my own university, the physics, geology, and, interestingly, the speech departments had to evacuate their building when the bomb squad was called to remove dangerous chemicals from the chemistry department.

13   Given the number of persons involved in student chemical labs, one would assume that safety measures would be at their finest. However, just the opposite seems to be true. Dr. James Kaufman, a former research chemist for Dow Chemical and current director of the Laboratory Safety Workshop at Curry College, has investigated over 1,000 chemical accidents in educational institutions. He states, "Schools and colleges are notoriously poor in terms of safety performance. There's a tremendous difference in terms of what's considered good sense and practice at a major chemical company versus a school."

14   Unsafe student labs result from two interrelated causes: unsafe students and poor safety instruction. NIOSH states that even in the best of labs, they routinely turn up poor housekeeping, unsafe chemicals, and insufficient safety measures. Chemicals are improperly labeled and do not have disposal information on them. Without this information it becomes very easy for a chemical to be disposed of incorrectly, stored improperly, or accidentally combined with another chemical, causing a dangerous accident. In 1981 a student at the University of Pennsylvania lost an eye, suffered a punctured eardrum, and received lacerations when a chemical exploded during an experiment. The label on the chemical didn't explain that it explodes when exposed to air.

15   In addition to the unsafe lab situations, there is also a serious lack of safety instruction. John Leach, head of the Safety Management Program at the National Institute of Health, states, "The lack of safety consciousness among many teachers is practically criminal. Because of their poor awareness of lab hazards, safety plays a very minor part in the instructional process." This is devastating, because instructors represent the primary method of teaching students safety. Think back to a chemistry, photography, or art class you may have taken. Was your safety instruction as thorough as it could have been? If you can answer yes, consider yourself one of the fortunate few. When I took a chemistry class several years ago, the instructor did not show the class the proper method for smelling a chemical — waving the fumes to your nose instead of directly inhaling them — and I almost cost myself my sense of smell.

16   In another instance, a student in California spilled a flask of phenol. Not knowing the proper emergency procedure, she mopped up the spill with paper towels. Unfortunately, phenol is toxic when ingested, inhaled, or absorbed by the skin, and the student became seriously ill.

17   Student labs are an experiment in poor safety. Having heard about the lack of safety, you might be wondering, Isn't there a law that mandates student safety? The simple answer is no. Even though legislation exists that protects employees who work with hazardous chemicals, there is no regulation that applies to academic institutions. Students are left at the hands of their instructors, who are supposed to teach them safety. The accidents I've discussed suggest that such instruction is not enough. Further, because no national stan-

dard exists for regulating lab safety, insurance companies can only regulate schools on the basis of their own standards, which may or may not be accurate.

18 One part of a solution to this problem is an extension of existing OSHA legislation to educational institutions. Extending such legislation could do a great deal to improve student safety. Ramsey Bittar's accident, which I referred to earlier, could have been prevented. Dr. Kaufman states that had he been performing the same experiment at Dow Chemical, federal guidelines would have required that it be performed under a shield. Also, the lab lacked a phone, posted emergency telephone numbers, and required first-aid training. Such measures would be required if federal regulations were extended to include students.

19 The funding for such legislation would not have to be extensive. I talked to the chairperson of the chemistry department at my university and he asserted that the schools, insurance companies, and accrediting agencies, such as the American Chemical Society, could do a great deal to monitor student labs. All that is needed is a national standard, a standard that is already found in existing legislation.

20 A second part of the solution to unsafe labs would be for schools to develop a comprehensive safety program. Basically, a safety program ensures that relevant information reaches the people who need it. A good safety program addresses the hazards associated with all departmental activities and materials in use, the process for training students to work in labs, the monitoring of labs, and the procedures to be followed in the event of an emergency. The best part of a safety program is that it can be tailored to the needs of each school. The University of California at Irvine implemented just such a safety program in every department that used chemicals in 1986. According to Ron Kolb, the director of news and communication for Irvine, in the two years since, the accident rate has fallen by 25 percent.

21 A final solution involves our own actions. There is a safe way to perform most lab work. We have to make sure we know that method. The book *Safety in Academic Laboratories*, produced by the American Chemical Society, recommends the following as rules for all students in any lab:

- If your instructor does not discuss each experiment and possible hazards, ask before you begin so you know what could happen.
- Never work alone.
- Wear eye protection at all times.
- Wash face and hands before leaving the lab to make sure all traces of chemicals are gone.

22 It's also important just to know that this problem exists. Some of us may never have had a lab class and may never have one. In the past few moments I've told you about the problem of unsafe student labs. As listeners, you can now take the information I've given you and give it to your friends and people you know who are taking lab classes, so they can take every precaution available to them. After all, I can't give my speech to everyone, but you can help.

23 Student laboratories across the country are needlessly unsafe, exposing students, faculty, and bystanders to unnecessary dangers. Both minor and serious accidents occur because of a lack of safety in labs and insufficient safety instruction. A solution to this problem is threefold: Existing legislation must be

extended to include students, schools must develop comprehensive safety programs, and we ourselves must take every available precaution. Student labs have been unsafe long enough. They must be improved before more people risk life and limb for credit.

"THE DILEMMA OF WHISTLEBLOWERS"⁴

SHANNON DYER, *Southwest Baptist University, Missouri*

Referring to them as "our endangered species" and "the conscience of our nation," Shannon Dyer addressed the need to protect whistleblowers in this persuasive speech. Her speech raises some significant ethical questions.

1   Millions of Americans, including most of us in this room, watched with anticipation the 1986 historic flight of the space shuttle *Challenger*. Suddenly, a ball of smoke and flames filled the screen. Dazed, we began to realize that seven people had died as we watched.

2   In Bhopal, India, a toxic gas leak was discovered at the Union Carbide plant, but not before it left a grotesque and prolific path of destruction of over 2,000 dead.

3   Facing two of the greatest tragedies of our time, we are amazed to find that these failures were not due to technology or safety. In fact, safety engineers had fully warned company officials, yet in neither case was any attempt made to correct the problem. Instead the engineers were labeled troublemakers.

4   Today there are countless numbers of these time-bomb tragedies waiting to ignite. It is only the conscience of ethical workers that can defuse — or blow the whistle on — these potential disasters. Unfortunately, most employees who do try to warn us never survive the traumatic experience.

5   Thus, let's examine the dilemma of whistleblowers. First, who are whistleblowers? Then, what is the high personal price of their warnings? And finally, how can we protect these citizens — the watchdogs of our nation's safety?

6   Who are they? Whistleblowers are simply employees who object to a situation they feel is dangerous or illegal. They are social workers, such as Irvin Levin of the Brooklyn Office of Special Services for Children, who reported that serious cases of child abuse and even death were not being properly investigated. They are medical personnel, such as Dr. Grace Pierce of a New Jersey pharmaceutical company, who protested the production of a new drug for infants which she believed would have dangerous — even fatal — side effects. They are security officers such as John Berter of the Veterans Administration Hospital in Cincinnati, who following his conscience exposed two of his superiors for repeatedly beating patients. But whistleblowers are also you and me when we see something illegal or dangerous going on in our professions and we just can't look the other way.

7   Inevitably, these reports aren't always welcome to employers. Thus, whistleblowers become "troublemakers" and "traitors." *Psychology Today*, in August of 1986, tells us that "objectors are driven by feelings of professional ethics, religious values, or allegiance to the community." In fact, *Nation's Business* explains that "we often become whistleblowers out of a concern for our com-

pany." Understanding who whistleblowers are allows us to expose the heart of the problem—the high personal cost to the employee.

8   Judith Penley paid the price of a clean conscience with her life. Immediately after taking part in an outside investigation of her employer, the Watts Bar Nuclear Power Plant, several attempts were made on her life. Scared and confused, Judith told investigators she knew of no one who would even want to hurt her. The next day, Judith was brutally gunned down as she waited for a friend. "With echoes of Karen Silkwood," *Newsweek* reports that investigators drew an obvious connection.

9   Not all whistleblowers pay such a high price. Most just lose their jobs, some lose vacation time, and yet others are demoted to menial or demeaning tasks. No matter what form it takes, "nearly all whistleblowers can count on some form of retaliation." David Ewing, author of *Do It My Way Or You're Fired!*, estimates that at least 500,000 employees are fired unfairly each year. "Since the burden of proof usually falls on the whistleblower, legal bills may mount rapidly. [T]hey may be heavily in debt and face the loss of home, spouse, children, [and] friends."

10   In spite of documented injustice, it has only been in the last two years that Congress has even considered legislation to help reinstate and give redress to these victims. But these efforts have been the equivalent of applying a Band-Aid where a tourniquet is needed. Of the two government agencies designed to protect these citizens, the *Economist* reports only 1 percent of the cases filed "make it through the Office of Special Council's fine sieve," and GAP, the Government Accountability Project, can only "handle 100 cases a year," turning down 95 percent of its requests. So how can we protect these citizens who are only trying to protect us? For our final question, there is a threefold answer. First, stop the retaliation; second, these vital warnings must be heard; and finally, as potential objectors, we must be prepared.

11   To stop the retaliation, Russell Mokhiber of the Center for the Study of Responsive Law explains that the problem is legal deterrence. Corporations have adopted limited liability; thus, no single individual in management can be held accountable for destroying the employee's life. "[But] if you personalize the crime," he explains, "people will start holding management to the kind of moral standards the larger society has." Therefore, we must call for stiff prosecution of individuals responsible for the retaliation.

12   Second, these vital warnings must be heard and separated from everyday complaints. Corporations such as IBM and AT&T have found that the most effective early warning system is a formal "ombudsman" system. "A senior executive operates outside the normal chain of command. He is permanently available at the end of a hotline to deal with employee grievances and alarms on a confidential basis."

13   And finally—and perhaps most important—we should be prepared. We must realize that objecting to our employers will bring retaliation. Is the situation serious enough—dangerous or illegal? Does it warrant the risk? If so, we seek the advice of several veteran whistleblowers. In a recent interview in *Technology Review:* Seek immediate legal council, and if possible, find an anonymous route to make your warnings heard.

14   Realizing what it means to become a whistleblower and the high personal price it exacts, we should demand protection for these workers who literally

hold the safety of our nation in their hands. Unfortunately, it's too late for the 2,000 people in Bhopal, and for the crew of the *Challenger,* but not for Roger Roijoly. Roger was senior engineer of the shuttle who desperately tried to warn his superiors to postpone that fatal flight. As you and I sat bewildered at the explosion, Roger went to his office and wept—he knew exactly what had happened. Amid sleepless nights, Roger testified before the presidential commission investigating the disaster. And yes, he was fired. But now Roger takes his warning on ethical decision making to the college lecture circuit, for the ethical training of engineers. "From where I sit," he states, "the agency is following the same principles that got it into trouble on the shuttle. When I see someone approaching the edge of a cliff, should I whisper—or should I scream?"

15   How many lives will it take for us to learn this lesson? Two thousand more like Bhopal? Or just yours in a needless auto accident? Or mine in an airplane that was improperly tested? Or someone we love who was given a "lifesaving" drug that kills due to medical negligence in testing? If we do not attempt to protect our objectors now, then our endangered species of whistleblowers will become extinct, as will the conscience and safety of our nation.

REMARKS AT A MEMORIAL SERVICE FOR THE CREW OF THE SPACE SHUTTLE *CHALLENGER*[5]

RONALD REAGAN

Following the explosion of the space shuttle Challenger, *President Ronald Reagan delivered this eulogy for the seven shuttle astronauts at the Johnson Space Center in Houston, Texas, on January 31, 1986. Peggy Noonan, one of Reagan's speechwriters, suggests that eulogies "are the most moving kind of speech because they attempt to pluck meaning from the fog, and on short order, when the emotions are still ragged and raw and susceptible to leaps."*

1   We come together today to mourn the loss of seven brave Americans, to share the grief that we all feel, and perhaps in that sharing, to find the strength to bear our sorrow and the courage to look for the seeds of hope.

2   Our nation's loss is first a profound personal loss to the family and the friends and the loved ones of our shuttle astronauts. To those they left behind —the mothers, the fathers, the husbands and wives, brothers and sisters, yes, and especially the children—all of America stands beside you in your time of sorrow.

3   What we say today is only an inadequate expression of what we carry in our hearts. Words pale in the shadow of grief; they seem insufficient even to measure the brave sacrifice of those you loved and we so admired. Their truest testimony will not be in the words we speak, but in the way they led their lives and in the way they lost their lives—with dedication, honor, and an unquenchable desire to explore this mysterious and beautiful universe.

4   The best we can do is remember our seven astronauts, our *Challenger* Seven, remember them as they lived, bringing life and love and joy to those who knew them and pride to a nation.

5   They came from all parts of this great country — from South Carolina to Washington State; Ohio to Mohawk, New York; Hawaii to North Carolina to Concord, New Hampshire. They were so different; yet in their mission, their quest, they held so much in common.

6   We remember Dick Scobee, the commander who spoke the last words we heard from the space shuttle *Challenger*. He served as a fighter pilot in Vietnam, earning many medals for bravery and later as a test pilot of advanced aircraft before joining the space program. Danger was a familiar companion to Commander Scobee.

7   We remember Michael Smith, who earned enough medals as a combat pilot to cover his chest, including the Navy Distinguished Flying Cross, three Air Medals, and the Vietnamese Cross of Gallantry with Silver Star in gratitude from a nation he fought to keep free.

8   We remember Judith Resnick, known as J.R. to her friends, always smiling, always eager to make a contribution, finding beauty in the music she played on her piano in her off-hours.

9   We remember Ellison Onizuka, who as a child running barefoot through the coffee fields and macadamia groves of Hawaii dreamed of someday traveling to the moon. Being an Eagle Scout, he said, had helped him soar to the impressive achievements of his career.

10   We remember Ronald McNair, who said he learned perseverance in the cotton fields of South Carolina. His dream was to live aboard the space station, performing experiments and playing his saxophone in the weightlessness of space. Well, Ron, we will miss your saxophone and we *will* build your space station.

11   We remember Gregory Jarvis. On the ill-fated flight he was carrying with him a flag of his university in Buffalo, New York — a small token, he said, to the people who unlocked his future.

12   We remember Christa McAuliffe, who captured the imagination of the entire nation; inspiring us with her pluck, her restless spirit of discovery; a teacher, not just to her students, but to an entire people, instilling us all with the excitement of this journey we ride into the future.

13   We will always remember them, these skilled professionals, scientists, and adventurers, these artists and teachers and family men and women; and we will cherish each of their stories, stories of triumph and bravery, stories of true American heroes.

14   On the day of the disaster, our nation held a vigil by our television sets. In one cruel moment our exhilaration turned to horror; we waited and watched and tried to make sense of what we had seen. That night I listened to a call-in program on the radio; people of every age spoke of their sadness and the pride they felt in our astronauts. Across America we are reaching out, holding hands, and finding comfort in one another.

15   The sacrifice of your loved ones has stirred the soul of our nation and through the pain our hearts have been opened to a profound truth: The future is not free; the story of all human progress is one of a struggle against all odds. We learned again that this America, which Abraham Lincoln called the last, best hope of man on Earth, was built on heroism and noble sacrifice. It was built by men and women like our seven star voyagers, who answered a call beyond duty,

who gave more than was expected or required, and who gave little thought to worldly reward.

16 We think back to the pioneers of an earlier century, the sturdy souls who took their families and their belongings and set out into the frontier of the American West. Often they met with terrible hardship. Along the Oregon Trail, you could still see the grave markers of those who fell on the way. But grief only steeled them to the journey ahead.

17 Today the frontier is space and the boundaries of human knowledge. Sometimes when we reach for the stars, we fall short. But we must pick ourselves up again and press on despite the pain. Our nation is indeed fortunate that we can still draw on immense reservoirs of courage, character, and fortitude; that we're still blessed with heroes like those of the space shuttle *Challenger*.

18 Dick Scobee knew that every launching of a space shuttle is a technological miracle. And he said, "If something ever does go wrong, I hope that doesn't mean the end to the space shuttle program." Every family member I talked to asked specifically that we continue the program, that that is what their departed loved one would want above all else. We will not disappoint them.

19 Today we promise Dick Scobee and his crew that their dream lives on, that the future they worked so hard to build will become reality. The dedicated men and women of NASA have lost seven members of their family. Still, they, too, must forge ahead with a space program that is effective, safe, and efficient, but bold and committed.

20 Man will continue his conquest of space. To reach out for new goals and ever greater achievements — that is the way we shall commemorate our seven *Challenger* heroes.

21 Dick, Mike, Judy, El, Ron, Greg, and Christa — your families and your country mourn your passing. We bid you goodbye; we will never forget you. For those who knew you well and loved you, the pain will be deep and enduring. A nation, too, will long feel the loss of her seven sons and daughters, her seven good friends. We can find consolation only in faith, for we know in our hearts that you who flew so high and so proud now make your home beyond the stars, safe in God's promise of eternal life.

22 May God bless you all and give you comfort in this difficult time.

KEYNOTE ADDRESS[6]

MARIO CUOMO, *Governor of New York*

The keynote address at a political convention challenges the speaker to unify the party, excite the electorate, and spotlight important issues of the campaign. On July 17, 1984, Mario Cuomo addressed the Democratic National Convention in San Francisco. As you read this speech, try to discern how Cuomo attempted to fulfill these objectives.

1   On behalf of the Empire State and the family of New York, I thank you for the great privilege of being allowed to address this convention.

2   Please allow me to skip the stories and the poetry and the temptation to deal in nice but vague rhetoric.

3   Let me instead use this valuable opportunity to deal with the questions that should determine this election and that are vital to the American people.

4   Ten days ago, President Reagan admitted that although some people in this country seemed to be doing well nowadays, others were unhappy, and even worried, about themselves, their families and their futures.

5   The President said he didn't understand that fear. He said, "Why, this country is a shining city on a hill."

6   The President is right. In many ways we are "a shining city on a hill."

7   But the hard truth is that not everyone is sharing in this city's splendor and glory.

8   A shining city is perhaps all the President sees from the portico of the White House and the veranda of his ranch, where everyone seems to be doing well.

9   But there's another part of the city, the part where some people can't pay their mortgages and most young people can't afford one, where students can't afford the education they need and middle-class parents watch the dreams they hold for their children evaporate.

10   In this part of the city there are more poor than ever, more families in trouble. More and more people who need help but can't find it.

11   Even worse: There are elderly people who tremble in the basements of the houses there.

12   There are people who sleep in the city's streets, in the gutter, where the glitter doesn't show.

13   There are ghettos where thousands of young people, without an education or a job, give their lives away to drug dealers every day.

14   There is despair, Mr. President, in faces you never see, in the places you never visit in your shining city.

15   In fact, Mr. President, this nation is more a "Tale of Two Cities" than it is a "shining city on a hill."

16   Maybe if you visited more places, Mr. President, you'd understand.

17   Maybe if you went to Appalachia where some people still live in sheds and to Lackawanna where thousands of unemployed steel workers wonder why we subsidized foreign steel while we surrender their dignity to unemployment and to welfare checks; maybe if you stepped into a shelter in Chicago and talked with some of the homeless there; maybe, Mr. President, if you asked a woman who'd been denied the help she needs to feed her children because you say we need the money to give a tax break to a millionaire or to build a missile we can't even afford to use — maybe then you'd understand.

18   Maybe, Mr. President.

19   But I'm afraid not.

20   Because, the truth is, this is how we were warned it would be.

21   President Reagan told us from the beginning that he believed in a kind of social Darwinism. Survival of the fittest. "Government can't do everything," we were told. "So it should settle for taking care of the strong and hope that economic ambition and charity will do the rest. Make the rich richer and what falls from their table will be enough for the middle class and those trying to make it into the middle class."

22   The Republicans called it trickle-down when Hoover tried it. Now they call it supply side. It is the same shining city for those relative few who are lucky enough to live in its good neighborhoods.

23 But for the people who are excluded—locked out—all they can do is to stare from a distance at that city's glimmering towers.

24 It's an old story. As old as our history.

25 The difference between Democrats and Republicans has always been measured in courage and confidence. The Republicans believe the wagon train will not make it to the frontier unless some of our old, some of our young, and some of our weak are left behind by the side of the trail.

26 The strong will inherit the land!

27 We Democrats believe that we can make it all the way with the whole family intact.

28 We have. More than once.

29 Ever since Franklin Roosevelt lifted himself from his wheelchair to lift this nation from its knees. Wagon train after wagon train. To new frontiers of education, housing, peace. The whole family aboard. Constantly reaching out to extend and enlarge that family. Lifting them up into the wagon on the way. Blacks and Hispanics, people of every ethnic group, and Native Americans—all those struggling to build their families' claim to some small share of America.

30 For nearly fifty years we carried them to new levels of comfort, security, dignity, even affluence.

31 Some of us are in this room today only because this nation had that confidence.

32 It would be wrong to forget that.

33 So, here we are at this convention to remind ourselves where we come from and to claim the future for ourselves and for our children.

34 Today, our great Democratic Party, which has saved this nation from depression, from fascism, from racism, from corruption, is called upon to do it again—this time to save the nation from confusion and division, most of all from a fear of a nuclear holocaust.

35 In order to succeed, we must answer our opponent's polished and appealing rhetoric with a more telling reasonableness and rationality.

36 We must win this case on the merits.

37 We must get the American public to look past the glitter, beyond the showmanship—to reality, to the hard substance of things. And we will do that not so much with speeches that sound good as with speeches that are good and sound.

38 Not so much with speeches that bring people to their feet as with speeches that bring people to their senses.

39 We must make the American people hear our "tale of two cities."

40 We must convince them that we don't have to settle for two cities, that we can have one city, indivisible, shining for all its people.

41 We will have no chance to do that if what comes out of this convention, what is heard throughout the campaign, is a babel of arguing voices.

42 To succeed we will have to surrender small parts of our individual interests, to build a platform we can all stand on, at once, comfortably, proudly singing out the truth for the nation to hear, in chorus, its logic so clear and commanding that no slick commercial, no amount of geniality, no martial music will be able to muffle it.

43   We Democrats must unite so that the entire nation can. Surely the Republicans won't bring the country together. Their policies divide the nation: into the lucky and the left out, the royalty and the rabble.

44   The Republicans are willing to treat that division as victory. They would cut this nation in half, into those temporarily better off and those worse off than before, and call it recovery.

45   We should not be embarrassed or dismayed if the process of unifying is difficult, even at times wrenching.

46   Unlike any other party, we embrace men and women of every color, every creed, every orientation, every economic class. In our family are gathered everyone from the abject poor of Essex County in New York to the enlightened affluent of the gold coasts of both ends of our nation. And in between is the heart of our constituency. The middle class, the people not rich enough to be worry-free but not poor enough to be on welfare, those who work for a living because they have to. White-collar and blue-collar. Young professionals. Men and women in small business desperate for the capital and contracts they need to prove their worth.

47   We speak for the minorities who have not yet entered the mainstream.

48   For ethnics who want to add their culture to the mosaic that is America.

49   For women indignant that we refuse to etch into our governmental commandments the simple rule, "thou shalt not sin against equality," a commandment so obvious it can be spelled in three letters: E.R.A.!

50   For young people demanding an education and a future.

51   For senior citizens terrorized by the idea that their only security, their Social Security, is being threatened.

52   For millions of reasoning people fighting to preserve our environment from greed and stupidity. And fighting to preserve our very existence from a macho intransigence that refuses to make intelligent attempts to discuss the possibility of nuclear holocaust with our enemy. Refusing because they believe we can pile missiles so high that they will pierce the clouds and the sight of them will frighten our enemies into submission.

53   We're proud of this diversity. Grateful we don't have to manufacture its appearance the way the Republicans will next month in Dallas, by propping up mannequin delegates on the convention floor.

54   But we pay a price for it.

55   The different people we represent have many points of view. Sometimes they compete and then we have debates, even arguments. That's what our primaries were.

56   But now the primaries are over, and it is time to lock arms and move into this campaign together.

57   If we need any inspiration to make the effort to put aside our small differences, all we need to do is to reflect on the Republican policy of divide and cajole and how it has injured our land since 1980.

58   The President has asked us to judge him on whether or not he's fulfilled the promises he made four years ago. I accept that. Just consider what he said and what he's done.

59   Inflation is down since 1980. But not because of the supply-side miracle promised by the President. Inflation was reduced the old-fashioned way, with a

recession, the worst since 1932. More than 55,000 bankruptcies. Two years of massive unemployment. Two hundred thousand farmers and ranchers forced off the land. More homeless than at any time since the Great Depression. More hungry, more poor — mostly women — and a nearly $200 billion deficit threatening our future.

60   The President's deficit is a direct and dramatic repudiation of his promise to balance our budget by 1983.

61   That deficit is the largest in the history of this universe; more than three times larger than the deficit in President Carter's last year.

62   It is a deficit that, according to the President's own fiscal adviser, could grow as high as $300 billion a year, stretching "as far as the eye can see."

63   It is a debt so large that as much as one-half of our revenue from the income tax goes to pay the interest on it each year.

64   It is a mortgage on our children's futures that can only be paid in pain and that could eventually bring this nation to its knees.

65   Don't take my word for it — I'm a Democrat.

66   Ask the Republican investment bankers on Wall Street what they think the chances are this recovery will be permanent. If they're not too embarrassed to tell you the truth, they'll say they are appalled and frightened by the President's deficit. Ask them what they think of our economy, now that it has been driven by the distorted value of the dollar back to its colonial condition, exporting agricultural products and importing manufactured ones.

67   Ask those Republican investment bankers what they expect the interest rate to be a year from now. And ask them what they predict for the inflation rate then.

68   How important is this question of the deficit?

69   Think about it: What chance would the Republican candidate have had in 1980 if he had told the American people that he intended to pay for his so-called economic recovery with bankruptcies, unemployment and the largest government debt known to humankind? Would American voters have signed the loan certificate for him on Election Day? Of course not! It was an election won with smoke and mirrors, with illusions. It is a recovery made of the same stuff.

70   And what about foreign policy?

71   They said they would make us and the whole world safer. They say they have.

72   By creating the largest defense budget in history, one even they now admit is excessive. By failing to discuss peace with our enemies. By the loss of 279 young Americans in Lebanon in pursuit of a plan and a policy no one can find or describe.

73   We give monies to Latin American governments that murder nuns, and then lie about it.

74   We have been less than zealous in our support of the only real friend we have in the Middle East, the one democracy there, our flesh-and-blood ally, the state of Israel.

75   Our policy drifts with no real direction, other than an hysterical commitment to an arms race that leads nowhere, if we're lucky. If we're not — could lead us to bankruptcy or war.

76   Of course we must have a strong defense!

77   Of course Democrats believe that there are times when we must stand and fight. And we have. Thousands of us have paid for freedom with our lives. But always, when we've been at our best, our purposes were clear.

78   Now they're not. Now our allies are as confused as our enemies.

79   Now we have no real commitment to our friends or our ideals, to human rights, to the refuseniks, to Sakharov, to Bishop Tutu and the others struggling for freedom in South Africa.

80   We have spent more than we can afford. We have pounded our chest and made bold speeches. But we lost 279 young Americans in Lebanon and we are forced to live behind sandbags in Washington.

81   How can anyone believe that we are stronger, safer, or better?

82   That's the Republican record.

83   That its disastrous quality is not more fully understood by the American people is attributable, I think, to the President's amiability and the failure by some to separate the salesman from the product.

84   It's now up to us to make the case to America.

85   And to remind Americans that if they are not happy with all the President has done so far, they should consider how much worse it will be if he is left to his radical proclivities for another four years, unrestrained by the need once again to come before the American people.

86   If July brings back Anne Gorsuch Burford, what can we expect of December?

87   Where would another four years take us?

88   How much larger will the deficit be?

89   How much deeper the cuts in programs for the struggling middle class and the poor to limit that deficit? How high the interest rates? How much more acid rain killing our forests and fouling our lakes?

90   What kind of Supreme Court? What kind of court and country will be fashioned by the man who believes in having government mandate people's religion and morality?

91   The man who believes that trees pollute the environment, that the laws against discrimination go too far. The man who threatens Social Security and Medicaid and help for the disabled.

92   How high will we pile the missiles?

93   How much deeper will be the gulf between us and our enemies?

94   Will we make meaner the spirit of our people?

95   This election will measure the record of the past four years. But more than that, it will answer the question of what kind of people we want to be.

96   We Democrats still have a dream. We still believe in this nation's future.

97   And this is our answer—our credo:

98   We believe in only the government we need, but we insist on all the government we need.

99   We believe in a government characterized by fairness and reasonableness, a reasonableness that goes beyond labels, that doesn't distort or promise to do what it knows it can't do.

100 A government strong enough to use the words "love" and "compassion" and smart enough to convert our noblest aspirations.

101 We believe in encouraging the talented, but we believe that while survival

of the fittest may be a good working description of the process of evolution, a government of humans should elevate itself to a higher order, one which fills the gaps left by chance or a wisdom we don't understand.

102 We would rather have laws written by the patron of this great city, the man called the "world's most sincere Democrat," St. Francis of Assisi, than laws written by Darwin.

103 We believe, as Democrats, that a society as blessed as ours, the most affluent democracy in the world's history, that can spend trillions on instruments of destruction, ought to be able to help the middle class in its struggle, ought to be able to find work for all who can do it, room at the table, shelter for the homeless, care for the elderly and infirm, hope for the destitute.

104 We proclaim as loudly as we can the utter insanity of nuclear proliferation and the need for a nuclear freeze, if only to affirm the simple truth that peace is better than war because life is better than death.

105 We believe in firm but fair law and order, in the union movement, in privacy for people, openness by government, civil rights, and human rights.

106 We believe in a single fundamental idea that describes better than most textbooks and any speech what a proper government should be. The idea of family. Mutuality. The sharing of benefits and burdens for the good of all. Feeling one another's pain. Sharing one another's blessings. Reasonably, honestly, fairly, without respect to race, or sex, or geography or political affiliation.

107 We believe we must be the family of America, recognizing that at the heart of the matter we are bound one to another, that the problems of a retired schoolteacher in Duluth are our problems. That the future of the child in Buffalo is our future. The struggle of a disabled man in Boston to survive, to live decently is our struggle. The hunger of a woman in Little Rock, our hunger. The failure anywhere to provide what reasonably we might, to avoid pain, is our failure.

108 For fifty years we Democrats created a better future for our children, using traditional democratic principles as a fixed beacon, giving us direction and purpose, but constantly innovating, adapting to new realities: Roosevelt's alphabet programs; Truman's NATO and the GI Bill of Rights; Kennedy's intelligent tax incentives and the Alliance for Progress; Johnson's civil rights; Carter's human rights and the nearly miraculous Camp David peace accord.

109 Democrats did it—and Democrats can do it again.

110 We can build a future that deals with our deficit.

111 Remember, fifty years of progress never cost us what the last four years of stagnation have. We can deal with that deficit intelligently, by shared sacrifice, with all parts of the nation's family contributing, building partnerships with the private sector, providing a sound defense without depriving ourselves of what we need to feed our children and care for our people.

112 We can have a future that provides for all the young of the present by marrying common sense and compassion.

113 We know we can, because we did it for nearly fifty years before 1980.

114 We can do it again. If we do not forget. Forget that this entire nation has profited by these progressive principles. That they helped lift up generations to the middle class and higher: gave us a chance to work, to go to college, to raise a

family, to own a house, to be secure in our old age and, before that, to reach heights that our own parents would not have dared dream of.

115 That struggle to live with dignity is the real story of the shining city. It's a story I didn't read in a book, or learn in a classroom. I saw it, and lived it. Like many of you.

116 I watched a small man with thick calluses on both hands work fifteen and sixteen hours a day. I saw him once literally bleed from the bottoms of his feet, a man who came here uneducated, alone, unable to speak the language, who taught me all I needed to know about faith and hard work by the simple eloquence of his example. I learned about our kind of democracy from my father. I learned about our obligation to each other from him and from my mother. They asked only for a chance to work and to make the world better for their children and to be protected in those moments when they would not be able to protect themselves. This nation and its government did that for them.

117 And that they were able to build a family and live in dignity and see one of their children go from behind their little grocery store on the other side of the tracks in South Jamaica where he was born, to occupy the highest seat in the greatest state of the greatest nation in the only world we know, is an ineffably beautiful tribute to the democratic process.

118 And on January 20, 1985, it will happen again. Only on a much grander scale. We will have a new President of the United States, a Democrat born not to the blood of kings but to the blood of immigrants and pioneers.

119 We will have America's first woman Vice-President, the child of immigrants, a New Yorker, opening with one magnificent stroke a whole new frontier for the United States.

120 It will happen, if we make it happen.

121 I ask you, ladies and gentlemen, brothers and sisters — for the good of all of us, for the love of this great nation, for the family of America, for the love of God. Please make this nation remember how futures are built.

"I HAVE A DREAM" [7]

MARTIN LUTHER KING, JR.

Speaking from the steps of the Lincoln Memorial in Washington, D.C., on August 28, 1963, Martin Luther King, Jr. delivered his "I Have a Dream" speech to an audience estimated at 200,000. As you read this speech, study the power of its language and see if you agree with many scholars that this is the greatest American speech of the twentieth century.

1   I am happy to join with you today in what will go down in history as the greatest demonstration for freedom in the history of our nation.

2   Five score years ago, a great American, in whose symbolic shadow we stand today, signed the Emancipation Proclamation. This momentous decree came as a great beacon light of hope to millions of Negro slaves, who had been seared in the flames of withering injustice. It came as a joyous daybreak to end the long night of their captivity.

3   But one hundred years later, the Negro still is not free. One hundred years later, the life of the Negro is still sadly crippled by the manacles of segregation and the chains of discrimination. One hundred years later, the Negro lives on a lonely island of poverty in the midst of a vast ocean of material prosperity. One hundred years later, the Negro is still languished in the corners of American society and finds himself an exile in his own land.

4   And so we've come here today to dramatize a shameful condition. In a sense we've come to our nation's Capitol to cash a check. When the architects of our republic wrote the magnificent words of the Constitution and the Declaration of Independence, they were signing a promissory note to which every American was to fall heir. This note was a promise that all men — yes, black men as well as white men — would be guaranteed the unalienable rights of life, liberty, and the pursuit of happiness.

5   It is obvious today that America has defaulted on this promissory note insofar as her citizens of color are concerned. Instead of honoring this sacred obligation, America has given the Negro people a bad check — a check which has come back marked "insufficient funds."

6   But we refuse to believe that the bank of justice is bankrupt. We refuse to believe that there are insufficient funds in the great vaults of opportunity of this nation. And so we've come to cash this check — a check that will give us upon demand the riches of freedom and the security of justice.

7   We have also come to this hallowed spot to remind America of the fierce urgency of now. This is no time to engage in the luxury of cooling off or to take the tranquillizing drug of gradualism. Now is the time to make real the promises of democracy. Now is the time to rise from the dark and desolate valley of segregation to the sunlit path of racial justice. Now is the time to lift our nation from the quicksands of racial injustice to the solid rock of brotherhood. Now is the time to make justice a reality for all of God's children.

8   It would be fatal for the nation to overlook the urgency of the moment. This sweltering summer of the Negro's legitimate discontent will not pass until there is an invigorating autumn of freedom and equality. Nineteen sixty-three is not an end, but a beginning. Those who hope that the Negro needed to blow off steam and will now be content will have a rude awakening if the nation returns to business as usual. There will be neither rest nor tranquility in America until the Negro is granted his citizenship rights. The whirlwinds of revolt will continue to shake the foundations of our nation until the bright day of justice emerges.

9   But there is something that I must say to my people, who stand on the warm threshold which leads into the palace of justice. In the process of gaining our rightful place, we must not be guilty of wrongful deeds. Let us not seek to justify our thirst for freedom by drinking from the cup of bitterness and hatred.

10   We must forever conduct our struggle on the high plane of dignity and discipline. We must not allow our creative protest to degenerate into physical violence. Again and again we must rise to the majestic heights of meeting physical force with soul force.

11   The marvelous new militancy which has engulfed the Negro community must not lead us to a distrust of all white people. For many of our white brothers, as evidenced by their presence here today, have come to realize that

their destiny is tied up with our destiny. They have come to realize that their freedom is inextricably bound to our freedom. We cannot walk alone.

12 As we walk, we must make the pledge that we shall always march ahead. We cannot turn back. There are those who are asking the devotees of civil rights, "When will you be satisfied?" We can never be satisfied as long as the Negro is the victim of the unspeakable horrors of police brutality. We can never be satisfied as long as our bodies, heavy with the fatigue of travel, cannot gain lodging in the motels of the highways and the hotels of the cities. We cannot be satisfied as long as a Negro in Mississippi cannot vote and a Negro in New York believes he has nothing for which to vote. No, no, we are not satisfied, and we will not be satisfied until justice rolls down like waters, and righteousness like a mighty stream.

13 I am not unmindful that some of you have come here out of great trials and tribulations. Some of you have come fresh from narrow jail cells. Some of you have come from areas where your quest for freedom left you battered by the storms of persecution and staggered by the winds of police brutality. You have been the veterans of creative suffering. Continue to work with the faith that unearned suffering is redemptive.

14 Go back to Mississippi, go back to Alabama, go back to South Carolina, go back to Georgia, go back to Louisiana, go back to the slums and ghettos of our Northern cities, knowing that somehow this situation can and will be changed. Let us not wallow in the valley of despair.

15 I say to you today, my friends, so even though we face the difficulties of today and tomorrow, I still have a dream. It is a dream deeply rooted in the American dream.

16 I have a dream that one day this nation will rise up and live out the true meaning of its creed, "We hold these truths to be self-evident, that all men are created equal."

17 I have a dream that one day on the red hills of Georgia the sons of former slaves and the sons of former slaveowners will be able to sit down together at the table of brotherhood.

18 I have a dream that one day even the state of Mississippi, a state sweltering with the heat of injustice, sweltering with the heat of oppression, will be transformed into an oasis of freedom and justice.

19 I have a dream that my four little children will one day live in a nation where they will not be judged by the color of their skin but by the content of their character. I have a dream today.

20 I have a dream that one day, down in Alabama, with its vicious racists, with its governor having his lips dripping with the words of interposition and nullification, one day right there in Alabama little black boys and black girls will be able to join hands with the little white boys and white girls as sisters and brothers. I have a dream today.

21 I have a dream that one day every valley shall be exalted, every hill and mountain shall be made low, the rough places will be made plain and the crooked places will be made straight, and the glory of the Lord shall be revealed, and all flesh shall see it together.

22 This is our hope. This is the faith that I go back to the South with. With this faith we will be able to hew out of the mountain of despair a stone of hope. With

this faith we will be able to transform the jangling discords of our nation into a beautiful symphony of brotherhood. With this faith we will be able to work together, to pray together, to struggle together, to go to jail together, to stand up for freedom together, knowing that we will be free one day.

23   This will be the day — this will be the day when all of God's children will be able to sing with new meaning, "My country 'tis of thee, sweet land of liberty, of thee I sing. Land where my fathers died, land of the pilgrim's pride, from every mountainside, let freedom ring." And if America is to be a great nation, this must become true.

24   So let freedom ring from the prodigious hilltops of New Hampshire. Let freedom ring from the mighty mountains of New York. Let freedom ring from the heightening Alleghenies of Pennsylvania!

25   Let freedom ring from the snowcapped Rockies of Colorado! Let freedom ring from the curvaceous slopes of California!

26   But not only that. Let freedom ring from Stone Mountain of Georgia!

27   Let freedom ring from Lookout Mountain of Tennessee!

28   Let freedom ring from every hill and molehill of Mississippi. From every mountainside, let freedom ring.

29   And when this happens, when we allow freedom to ring — when we let it ring from every village and every hamlet, from every state and every city — we will be able to speed up that day when all of God's children, black men and white men, Jews and Gentiles, Protestants and Catholics, will be able to join hands and sing in the words of the old Negro spiritual, "Free at last! Free at last! Thank God Almighty, we are free at last!"

Notes

1. William Fort, Persuasive Speech, *1989 Championship Debates and Speeches* (Annandale, VA: Speech Communication Association, 1991) 123–26.

2. Shelley Schnathorst, Persuasive Speech, *1988 Championship Debates and Speeches* (Annandale, VA: Speech Communication Association, 1988) 112–16.

3. Susanne Landowski, "Academic Laboratories: Risking Life and Limb for Credit," *Winning Orations, 1988* (Mankato, MN: Interstate Oratorical Association, 1988) 64–67. Coached by Kenneth Haught.

4. Shannon Dyer, "The Dilemma of Whistleblowers," *Winning Orations, 1989* (Mankato, MN: Interstate Oratorical Association, 1989) 63–65. Coached by Robert Derryberry.

5. Ronald Reagan, Remarks at the Johnson Space Center in Houston, TX, January 31, 1986, *Weekly Compilation of Presidential Documents,* February 3, 1986 (Washington: GPO, 1986) 117–19.

6. Mario Cuomo, Keynote Address, *Vital Speeches of the Day* 15 August 1984: 646–49.

7. Martin Luther King, Jr., "I Have a Dream." Reprinted by permission of Joan Daves. Copyright by Martin Luther King, Jr.

Credits

Chapter 1

1   Bob Daemmrich/The Image Works
9   Hill/The Image Works
11   Wide World

Chapter 2

20   Daniel Marcko
24   AP/Wide World
26   Peter Marlow/Magnum

Chapter 3

38   J. Sulley/The Image Works
46   Bob Clay
49   Costa Manos/Magnum

Chapter 4

52   Jim Stratford/Black Star
67   Tim Brown/Tony Stone Worldwide

Chapter 5

70   Lester Sloan/Woodfin Camp
77   Bill Anderson/Monkmeyer Press
85   Paul Conkin/Monkmeyer Press

Chapter 6

98   Daniel Marcko
103   Michael Newman/PhotoEdit
107   Lisa Law/The Image Works

Chapter 7

120   Stan Ries/The Picture Cube
126   Frank Pedrick/The Image Works
135   John Spiner/Uniphoto
138   Grant Leduc/Monkmeyer Press

Chapter 8

146   Michael Newman/PhotoEdit
151   Bob Daemmrich/Tony Stone Worldwide

Chapter 9

166   Gabe Palmer/Mug Shots/The Stock Market
175   Rick Friedman/Black Star

Chapter 10

194   Tim Brown/Tony Stone Worldwide
205   Charles Gupton/Tony Stone Worldwide

Chapter 11

212   Marc Grimberg/The Image Bank
225   UPI/Bettmann Newsphotos

Chapter 12 ───────────────

238   UPI/Bettmann
252   Drew Skinner

Chapter 13 ───────────────

262   Daniel Marcko
266   John Waterman/Tony Stone Worldwide
268   Courtesy of Jefferson's Poplar Forest
272   Courtesy of Lucinda Vardey Agency
279   Gilles Bassignac/Gamma Liaison

Chapter 14 ───────────────

282   Chip Henderson/Tony Stone Worldwide
291   Chris Cross/Uniphoto
299   Brian Smith/Stock-Boston

Chapter 15 ───────────────

304   AP/Wide World
307   Photograph reproduced with the kind permission of American Express
        TRS Co., Inc.
314   Courtesy Duke University, photo by Les Todd
325   AP/Wideworld

Chapter 16 ───────────────

330   David Butow/Black Star
351   Bob Daemmrich/Stock-Boston
353   East News/Sipa Press

Chapter 17 ───────────────

360   UPI/Bettmann
371   UPI/Bettmann
382   Howard Dratch/The Image Works

Chapter 18 ⸺

388   Larry Laufer/The Picture Cube
403   Clark/The Stock Market

Appendix C ⸺

Index

* Boldface page numbers indicate marginal glossary.

A

Abstraction, levels of, 221–22
Acceptance speech, **367**–69
Accuracy of informative speeches, 298–99
Acknowledgement of one's audience, 184–85
Action
    in motivated sequence, 355, 356
    speech to persuade to, 113–14
Action group, **392**
Active language, 226
Active listening, 56–57
Active voice, 226
Actual example, 152
Actuating speeches, **113**–14, **314**
Adams, J. Donald, 133
Addition, 249
Ad hominem, 346–**47**
Advocates, group members as, 399
Agenda
    group decision making and, 393–94
    group leader's responsibility to plan, 400
Age of audience, 76–77
Allen, Woody, 332, 345
Alliteration, **229**
Almanacs, 133–34
American Statistics Index, 131
Analogy, argument by, **335**–37
Antecedent *ethos*, **321**
Antithesis, **230**

Anxieties of public speaking, 40–42
    coping with, 42–50
Appeal(s)
    emotional, enhancing, 324–27
    to tradition, **345**
Appearance, **251**–53
Application of information, 285
Appropriateness of language, 231–34
Argument(s), 333–47
    fallacies of, **342**–47
    steps of, 333–34
    types of, 334–42
        by analogy, **335**–37
        by authority, **341**–42
        by cause, **337**–38
        deductive, 338–40, **339**
        by example (inductive), **334**–35
    See also Persuasion
Argumentum ad populum, 346
Aristotle, 320, 333
Articulation, **249**–51
Attention, audience, 93
    getting, 179–85
    in Monroe's motivated sequence, 354, 356
Attitude(s), **86**
    desire to listen, 62
    influencing, 309
    intensification of, 309–10
    positive, 46–47
    in pyramid of persuasion, 310–13
    speech to convince and, 313–14
Audible examples, 154–55

Audience
    clothing choice and consideration
        of, 252–53
    establishing common ground with,
        319–20, 323
    expressing feelings of, in tribute,
        370
    getting attention of, 179–85
    knowing one's, 44–45
    size of, 91
        adapting size of gestures to, 256
    types of, 87–89
    in videotaped speech, 383
Audience analysis, 71–96
    to generate ideas, 106
    importance of, 73–75
    after speech, 94
    before speech, **75**–92
        audience demographics, **75**–81
        audience needs, 81–84, 182,
            326, 354–55, 356
        audience psychology, 84–87
        gathering information, 87
        specific speaking situations, 87–
            92
    during speech, **92**–94
    tapping audience values through,
        326
Audience–centered speaker, 74
Audience disposition, **88**–91
Audience–generated topics, **105**–6
Audience profile, **89**–91
Audience segmentation, **76**
Audience selection, 76
Audio aids, **275**, 326
Auditory images, **227**
Authority, argument by, **341**–42
Awards ceremonies, speeches at,
    365–69

B

Back–up supplies for visual aids, 277
Balance of speech, checking, 198
Banach, William, 284
Bandwagon fallacy, **346**
Bar graph, **269**
Bauer, Gary, 341

Becker, Samuel L., 364
Behavior(s), **86**–87
    influencing, 309
    intensification of, 309–10
    projecting control, 47–48
    in pyramid of persuasion, 310–13
    See also Nervousness
Beliefs, **86**
    instilling, 309
    intensification of, 309–10
    proposition of fact focusing on, 349
    in pyramid of persuasion, 310–13
    speech to convince and, 313–14
    speech to persuade to, 113–14
Belongingness and love needs, 82–
    83, 84
Bem, Daryl, 48
Benefits of studying public speaking,
    2–5
Bias
    listening without, 30
    of sources, testing, 162
Bibliography, **141**
Black Newspapers Index, The, 129
Blackstone, William, 350
Body, listening with the, 66
Body of speech, organizing, 169–78
    connecting key ideas, 176–78
    development of key ideas, 174–76
    division into key ideas, 169–74
Bonds, language and social, 216–17
Book of Lists, The, 40
Books, research using, 131–32
Bradford, David, 28
Brainstorming, **101**–2, 201
    for group presentation, 403
    proposing solutions to problems,
        396–97
    for speech to entertain, 375
    visual, **109**, 110, 112, 201, 202
Brando, Marlon, 83
Brevity
    of answers in question-answer pe-
        riod, 380–81
    of impromptu speech, 378
    of speech of introduction, 363
Brief examples, 151
Broadcast information, 140
Brontë, Emily, 189

Brown, Peter, 161
Browser's Dictionary, A (Ciardi), 154
Brydon, Steven, 434
Burnett, Carol, 40
Bush, George, 240, 347, 362
Business, importance of listening in, 54

C

Camera, videotape, 384
Captive audience, **87**–89
Card catalog, 131
Carley, Emlyn Kathryn, 424
Carnegie Foundation, 2
Carson, Johnny, 240
Carter, Jimmy, 65
Carvey, Dana, 25, 240
Cataloguing systems, library, 131–32
Causal division, **171**–72
Causal transitions, **177**
Cause, argument by, **337**–38
Cause to effect argument, 337
Ceremonial speech, 369–72
Challenger, tribute to crew of, 229, 369, 442–44
Change, influence causing, 309
Channel (medium), **13**–14
Charts, **270**–71
Chronobiology, 102
Chronological division (organization), **170**–71, 288–93
Chronological transitions, **177**–78
Churchill, Winston, 125
Ciardi, John, 154
Circular conclusion, **189**
CIS Abstract, 130–31
CIS/Index, 130
Citations, source, 35, 323, 373
Claim, 333
Clarification
  group leader's responsibility to secure, 400–401
  of question in question–answer period, 380
Clarity
  of informative speeches, 298

of language, 221–23
  supporting materials for, 148–49, 150, 265
Cliché, **224**
Climate, small group, 399, 401
"Clipping" file, **124**
Closed questions, 137–38
Closure, providing, 188–91
Clothing, 251–53
Cohen, Allan, 28
Coleridge, Samuel Taylor, 219
Common ground with audience, establishing, 319–20, 323
Communication, **5**
  components of, 12–15
  definitions of, 5–7
  interactive model of, 13–15
  levels of, 7–12
  linear model of, 12–13
  nonverbal, 241–43
  open, 394, 400
  See also Delivery; Listening
Comparison and contrast, **157**–58, 163
Competence, **322**–23
  of source, testing, 161
Complementary transitions, **176**–77
Complete sentence outline, **198**
Complimenting one's audience, 184–85
Comprehension, audience, 93
  rate of speaking and, 245–46
Computer catalog, 132
Concepts, informative speech about, 293–94, 297
Concern, dynamism showing, 324
Conclusion
  of critique, 414
  of group presentation, 405
  organizing, 187–91
Conclusion (deductive argument), **339**, 340
Conditions, informative speech about, 294, 297
Confidence, speaking with, 3, 39–51
  coping strategies for, 42–50, 423
  dynamism and, 324
  nervousness of speaker and, 40–42
  controlling, 42

Confidence, speaking with *(cont.)*
  pervasiveness of, 40–42
Conflict management by group lead-
  ers, 401–2
Connotation, **218**
Consequences, concern for
  ethical listening and, 31–32
  ethical speaking and, 29
Consistency in constructing persua-
  sive appeal, principle of, 318
Content
  speech, 240
    scope of, testing, 196–97
  of subject, knowing, 322
Context
  message, 59
  of subject, knowing, 322
Contrast, 157–58, 163
Contrasting transitions, **177**
Control, projecting, 47–48
Controversial ideas and policies,
  speeches on, 294–95
Convincing speeches, **113**, **313**–14
Coordinate ideas, **197**
Coping strategies, 42–50, 423
Copyright law, 32, 33
Correctness of language, 219–21
Creativity
  in oral report, 373–74
  of speech to entertain, 375
Credibility, **321**–24
  admission of not knowing answer
    and, 381
  establishing speaker, 307, 321–24
    in speech of introduction, 363
  ethos, **320**, 321–24, 327
  persuasion and, 319
  of source, testing, 162
  supporting materials for, **149**–50
Criteria, decision making, 396
Critical evaluation
  group leader's responsibility to en-
    courage, 400
Critical listening, 30–31, 66–67
Criticism, 408–14
  defined, 408
  guidelines for critiquing speeches,
    410–14

three parts of, 408–9
value of receiving many people's,
  409
Csorba, Laszlo, III, 184
Cues
  nonverbal, 14, 66, 93, 255
  verbal, 14
Culture
  frame of reference and, 64
  meanings of gestures and move-
    ments and, 242
Cunningham, Mary, 29
Cuomo, Mario, 230, 444
Curiosity, arousing one's audience's,
  180–81

D

Data. *See* Information; Research
Debatable, propositions as, 349
Decision making, group, 392–402
  principles of, 393–94
  process of, 394–97
  responsibilities of leaders, 399–402
  responsibilities of members, 397–
    99
Decoding, **12**, 59, 217
Deduction, gathering audience information using, 87
Deductive argument, 338–40, **339**
Definition, **153**–55, 163
  by etymology, **153**–54
  by example, **154**–55
  by operation, **155**
  by synonym, **153**
Deletion, 249
Delivery, 239–61, **240**, 422–23
  dynamism and, 323–24
  effective, to enhance emotional
    appeals, 327
  importance of, 240–41
  of informative speech, 300
  methods of, 257–59
  nonverbal communication princi-
    ples and, 241–43
  physical, elements of, 244, 251–57

qualities of effective, 243–44
of speech to entertain, 377
time of, 92
vocal, elements of, 244–51
 articulation and pronunciation,
  249–51
 pitch and inflection, **247**–**48**
 rate and pause, 65, 244–46, **245**,
  246
 voice quality or timbre, **248**–49
 volume, **246**–47
Democratic National Convention
 (1984), 240
Democratic society, benefits of
 studying public speaking to, 4–5
Demographics, audience, **75**–81
Denotation, **218**
Derived credibility, **321**
Devotion to topic, excessive, 105
Dewey, John, 394
Diagrams, **267**–68
Dictionaries, 133
Differences in argument by analogy,
 relevance of, 336–37
Direct questions, **179**–80
Discussion
 group. *See* Group discussion and
  decision making
 public, **402**, 403
Disposition, audience, **88**–91
Distortion, message, 54, 55
Distractions
 factual, **61**
 focusing on message despite, 62–63
 physical, 60
 physiological, 60
 practice to overcome, 48–49
 psychological, **60**–61
 semantic, **61**
Documentation
 of ideas, 323
 for oral report, 373
Douglas, William O., 161
Dred Scott decision, 157
Dress for Success (Molloy), 251
Drummond, William, 334
Dyad, 391
Dyadic communication, 8

Dyer, Shannon, 440
Dynamism, 184, **323**–24
 visual aids for, 265–66

E

Economic status of audience, 80–81
Educational level of audience, 79
Effect to cause argument, 337
Either–or fallacy, 345–46
Eitzen, D. Stanley, 337
Electronic media, research using, 140
Emerson, Ralph Waldo, 2
Emotional appeals, enhancing, 324–
 27
Emotive language, 216, 327
Encoding, **12**
Encyclopedia of Associations, 139
Encyclopedias, 133
Energizing the audience, 184
Entertain, speech to, **114**, **374**–77
Environment, **14**
 physical, 92
Espy, Mike, 355
Esteem needs, 83, 84
Ethics, 21–37
 definition of, 22–**23**
 ethical listening, 30–32
 ethical speaking, 25–29
 plagiarism and, **32**–35
 principles of, 23–25
Ethnicity of audience, 78–79
Ethos, **320**, 327
 establishing speaker, 321–24
Etymology, definition by, **153**–54
Eulogy, 229, 315, **369**–72, 442–44
Evaluation, 59–60
 critical listening, 66–67
 ethical listening and obligation of,
  30–31
 group leader's responsibility to encourage critical, 400
 group members' responsibility in,
  398
 of information gathered in research, 143
 of message by audience, 93–94

Evaluation *(cont.)*
  of proposed solutions to problems,
    397
Events, informative speech about,
  290–92, 297
Everett, Edward, 72
"Everybody's doing it" fallacy, 346
Evidence, **333**–34
Example(s), **150**–53, 163
  argument by, **334**–35
  definition by, **154**–55
  in speech of tribute, 370
  types of, 151–53
  vivid, emotionally toned, 326
Expectations, introducing speaker
    and creating realistic, 363
Experience
  credibility and acknowledging
    one's, 323
  learning from, 49–50
Extemporaneous speech, **258**–59
Extended examples, 151–52
Eye contact, **254**–55, 258–59, 278,
  383

F

Facial expression, **254**
Fact, propositions of, **349**
Facts on File Yearbook, 134
Factual distractions, **61**
Factual information, presentation of,
  27–28
Fallacies of argument, **342**–47
False dilemma, **345**–46
Familiar language, clarity and use of,
  222–23
Favorable audience, 88–89
Fear of public speaking, 40–42. *See
  also* Nervousness
Federal government, publications
  by, 129–31
Feedback, **14**
  in intrapersonal communication , 8
  from listener, 66
  in mass communication, 10
  about nonverbal behavior, 241

  in public communication, 10
  See also Criticism
Ferraro, Geraldine, 240
"Fight or flight" syndrome, 41
Figurative comparison and contrast,
  158
Figures of speech, using, 228–31
Files, personal, 124–25
Films, **274**
Filmstrips, **273**
Final statement, 188–91
Final summary, 401
Finding Facts Fast (Todd), 143
First impressions, 251
Fixed microphone, 383, 384
Focus
  in impromptu speech, 378
  of speech of introduction, 363
  of speech of presentation, 366
Forbes magazine, 343
Formal outline, **206**–8
Formats for group presentation, 402,
  404–5
Forster, E.M., 3
Fort, William, 429
"4 S" strategy of developing key
    ideas, 174–76
Frame of reference, understanding,
  63–64
Francis, Amadeo I.D., 181
Frost, Robert, 234

G

Gallup Poll Monthly, The, 81
Galvanic skin response, 41
Gender of audience, 77–78
Generalization, hasty, **342**–43
General purpose, 113–**14**
Genuineness of speech of tribute, 370
Gestures, **256**–57
  variation in meanings of, 242
  visual aids and, 265
Gettysburg Address, 72–73, 369
Gilovich, Thomas, 332
Gimmick division, **173**–74, 421

Goals
  of persuasion, limiting, 316
  of small groups, 391, 393
Gomila, Sandra, 415
Gould, Stephen Jay, 332
Government documents, research
    using, 129–31
Grant, Cary, 217
Graphics, 266, **267**–72
Graphs, 266, 269–70
Greist, John, 40
Group(s)
  social-oriented, **391**–92
  task-oriented, **392**
  See also Small groups
Group communication, **8**–10
Group discussion and decision mak-
    ing, 392–402
  principles of, 393–94
  process of, 394–97
  responsibilities of leaders, 399–402
  responsibilities of members, 397–
    99
Group membership of audience, 81
Group presentation, 402–5
Groupthink, **394**, 399
Gustatory images, **228**

H

Habits, 241
Hafer, John, 3
Hall, Arsenio, 374
Handouts, **274**–75, 279
Harding, Warren, 223–24
Hasty generalization, fallacy of, **342**–
    43
Hearing, listening vs., **56**–57
Hesse, Hermann, 240
Hierarchy of needs, 81–84
Hippocrates, 222
Holmes, Oliver Wendell, 30
Holzberlein, Sara, 435
Honesty in critique, using, 411–12
Hopper, Hedda, 217
Horowitz, Lois, 127, 133
Hoth, C.C., 3

How We Think (Dewey), 394
Hubbard, Elbert, 346
Humor, use of
  appropriate, 376
  to get audience's attention, 182–84
Hypothetical examples, 152–53

I

Iacocca, Lee, 2, 3, 40
Ideas
  coordinate, **197**
  documentation of, 323
  group leader's introduction of
    new, 401
  in informative speech, limiting, 299
  language and communication of,
    215–16
  listening for main, 63
  preconceived, 103–4
  relevance of supporting, testing,
    197–98
  subordinate, **197**
  for topic, generating, 101–11
    audience–generated topics,
      105–6
    occasion-generated topics, **106**–
      8
    research-generated topics, **108**–
      11
    self-generated topics, **102**–5
  See also Key ideas
Image
  clothing choice and, 253
  of person honored in speech,
    creating, 370
Images, sensory, 227–28
Imagination, stimulating audience's,
    181
Impromptu speech, **257**, **377**–79
Incremental persuasion, perma-
    nence of, 316
Indexes
  to newspapers, 129
  of periodicals, 127–29
  research-generated topics and,
    108–10

Inductive argument, **334**–35
Inflection, **248**
Influence, 308
  in pyramid of persuasion, 312
  in small groups, 391
  types of, 308–10
  See also Persuasion
Information
  on audience, gathering, 87
  group decision making and adequate, 394
  persuasion and audience's lack of, 317
  See also Research
Informational literature from organizations, 139
Information base
  group leader's establishment of, 400
  group members' responsibility to contribute to, 398
Information overload, 284
Informative speech (speech to inform), **113**, 283–303, **285**
  characteristics of, 285–86
  guidelines for, 296–301
  organization of, 288–95, 297, 300
  types of, 286–96
    about concepts, 293–94, 297
    about conditions, 294, 297
    about events, 290–92, 297
    about issues, 294–95, 297
    about objects, 289, 297
    about people, 287–89, 297
    about places, 289–90, 297
    about processes, 292–93, 297
InfoTrac, 128
Initial credibility, **321**
Initial summary, 401
Inspiration, speech for, **314**–15
Instilling value, attitude, belief or behavior, influence and, 309
Intensification of values, beliefs, attitudes or behaviors, 309–10
Intentional plagiarism, 34
Intentions, ethical speaking and clarity of, 28–29
Interaction, small group, 391

Interactive model of communication, 13–15
Interest of audience, 93
  speech title and, 116–17
Internal summary, 401
Interpersonal communication, 7, **8**
Interpreter, **5**, 6
Interpreting, 59
Interview
  gathering audience information using, 87
  research based on, 135–39
    conducting, 138
    following up on, 138–39
    preparing for, 136–38
Intrapersonal communication, **7**–8
Introduction
  of group presentation, 405
  organizing, 178–87
    establishing importance of topic, 186
    getting audience's attention, 179–85
    previewing key ideas, **186**–87
    stating topic, 185
  speech of, **362**–65
Investigative reports, 140
Issues, informative speech about, 294–95, 297

J

Jackson, Jesse, 240, 246
Jacob, John, 78
James, William, 58
Janis, Irving, 394
Jargon, 104–5, 128, **223**
Jefferson, James, 40
Jeffrey, Robert, 125
John, Elton, 362
Johnson, Lyndon, 231
Johnson, Samuel, 32, 122, 123
Jones, Jenkin Lloyd, 25
Jordan, Barbara, 240
Journal, speaker's, 415–23

Journals, research using, 127–29
Judgment(s), 408
    proposition expressing, 347, 348
    withholding, 64–65

K

Kean, Thomas, 344
Kelly, Thomas, 148
Kennedy, John F., 11, 230, 231
Kennedy, Robert, 369
Kennedy-Nixon presidential debates
    (1960), 11
Key ideas
    connecting, 176–78
    determining, 420
    development of, 174–76
    dividing body of speech into, 169–
        74
    previewing, **186–87**
Keynote address at political conven-
    tion, sample of, 444–51
Key word or phrase outline, **198**
Kinesthetic images, **228**
Kinetic images, **228**
King, Martin Luther, Jr., 240
    "I Have a Dream" speech, 117,
        229–30, 451–54
Kirkpatrick, Jeane, 240
*Knowing Where to Look: the Ultimate
    Guide to Research* (Horowitz),
    127
Knowledge
    personal, assessing, 123–25
    reasons for seeking, 285
Kopp, Thomas, 100

L

Landowski, Susanne, 436
Language, 213–37
    active, 226
    common errors of, 220

emotive, 216, 327
    functions of, 215–18
    jargon, 104–5, 128, **223**
    objectivity and, 300
    principles of effective use of, 219–
        34
        appropriateness, 231–34
        clarity, 221–23
        correctness, 219–21
        vividness, 223–31
    transparent, 218, 224
    as weapon, 214
Language abuse, 219–20
Lapel microphone, 383–84
Larson, Charles, 306
Leaders, group, 399–402
Learned skill, listening as, 56
Leestamper, Robert, 224
Leno, Jay, 374
Letterman, David, 374
Library cataloguing systems, 131–32
Library research, 125–26, 127–35
Lincoln, Abraham, 72–73, 369
Linear model of communication,
    12–13
Line graph, **269**
Lippman, Walter, 391
Listener analysis. *See* Audience anal-
    ysis
Listening, 53–69, **56**
    active, 56–57
    critical, 30–31, 66–67
    ethical, 30–32
    hearing vs., **56–57**
    importance of, 54–56
    learning correct language usage
        by, 220
    obstacles to effective, 60–61
    participation of listener in persua-
        sive process, 307–8
    process of, 57–60
    promoting better, 61–67
Literal comparison, **157–58**
Literal contrast, **157**, 158
Logos, **320**, 324, 325, 327
Lorain, Paul, 241
Loren, Sophia, 362
Loudness, 246–47

M

McAdoo, William G., 223
McCraw, Les, 152
McCroskey, James, 40–41
Magazine Index, 127
Magazines, research using, 127–29
Magazines for Libraries, 127
Maggio, Rosalie, 234
Main ideas, listening for, 63. *See also* Key ideas
Majority opinion, source as part of, 162
Major premise, **339**, 340
Manipulation, 28
Mann, Thomas, 2, 4
Manual for Writer's of Term Papers, Theses, and Dissertations, A (Turabian), 141, 142
Manuals, style, 141–43
Manuscript speech, **257**–58
Maps, **271**–72
Markers, 176, 177
Marks, Isaac, 40
Marsh, Peter, 158
Marshall, John, 67
Maslow, Abraham, 81–84, 326
Maslow's hierarchy, **81**–84
Mass communication, **10**–12
Mead, Margaret, 390
Meaning
    shared, 5
    triangle of, 5–6
Medium, media
    electronic, research using, 140
    for mass communication, 11
    videotaped speech, 381–85, **382**, 421
Medium (channel), **13**–14
Mehrabian, Albert, 14, 241
Memory
    gimmicks as memory devices, 173
    speaking from, **257**
Mencken, H.L., 224
Message(s)
    clarity, visual aids for, 265
    distortion of, 54, 55. *See also* Listening

evaluation of, by audience, 93–94
facial expression appropriate to, 254
focusing on, 62–63
impact, reinforcing, 265
listening and using, 57
nonverbal, 63
reinforcing, 65–66
about user, language to send, 216
Message context, 59
Message testing, 48
Metaphor, **231**
Microfilm catalog, 132
Microphone, using, 383–84
Minor premise, **339**, 340
Mispronunciation, 249–50
Mitsubishi Electronics America, 222
Modern Language Association Handbook for Writers of Research Papers, 141, 142
Molloy, John T., 251
Mondale, Walter, 240
Monroe, Alan, 354
Monroe's motivated sequence, **354**–55, 356
Montana, Joe, 40
Montgomery, Robert, 56, 173
Monthly Catalog of U.S. Government Publications, 130
Moody, Helen Wills, 243
Morris, Desmond, 157–58
Mosvick, Roger, 4, 400
Motivated sequence, Monroe's, **354**–55, 356
Motivation of audience, persuasion and, 317–18
Movement, **255**
Moving projections, 272, 274
Moyers, Bill, 140, 183
Murrow, Edward R., 345

N

Naisbitt, John, 284
Narration, **155**–57, 163
Need-plan division, **353**–54
Needs, audience, 81–84, 326

getting audience's attention by meeting, 182
in Maslow's hierarchy, **81**–84
in Monroe's motivated sequence, 354–55, 356
Nelson, Paul, 391
Nelson, Robert, 400
Nemerov, Howard, 47
Nervousness, 40–42
controlling, 42
coping with, 42–50, 423
pervasiveness of, 40–42
Neutral audience, 88
NewsBank, 129
NewsBank Index, 129
Newspapers, research using, 129
Newsweek, 240
New York Public Library Desk Reference, The, 342
New York Times Index, The, 129
Nixon, Richard M., 11
Noble themes in speech of tribute, 370
Noise, **15**
Non-parallel language, 233
Nonsexist language, **233**–34
Nonsexist Word Finder: A Dictionary of Gender–Free Usage, The (Maggio), 234
Nonverbal communication, 241–43
Nonverbal cues, 14, 66, 93, 255
Nonverbal messages, 63
Noonan, Peggy, 369, 442
Norms, 409
Notation system for outlining, 199
Notecards, recording information on, 141
Notes, speaking extemporaneously from, 258–59

O

Objectivity
in informative speech, 300
problem of lack of, 295
trustworthiness and, 323
Objects, **266**–67
informative speech about, 289, 297

Observation, audience information using, 87
Obstacles to effective listening, 60–61
Occasion, 14
audience analysis and, 91–92
clothing for, 252
See also Special occasions, speaking on
Occasion–generated topics, **106**–8
Ochs, Don, 364
Ogden, Charles, 5
Olfactory images, **228**
O'Neill, Michael, 34
On-line data searching, 128
On the Waterfront (movie), 83
Opaque projection, **273**
Open communication, 394, 400
Open questions, 138
Operation, definition by, **155**
Oral communication skill in profession, 3–4
Oral report, **372**–74
Oral style, 232–33
Organization, 167–93
alternative strategy for, 190–91
of body of speech, 169–78
connecting key ideas, 176–78
development of key ideas, 174–76
division into key ideas, 169–74
chronological, **170**–71, 288–93
of conclusion, 187–91
of critique, 413
of informative speeches, 288–95, 297, 300
of introduction, 178–87
establishing importance of topic, 186
getting audience's attention, 179–85
previewing key ideas, **186**–87
stating topic, 185
Monroe's motivated sequence, **354**–55, 356
need-plan divison, **353**–54
of oral report, 373
for persuasion, 351–55
problem-solution division, **353**
process of, 168–69

Organization *(cont.)*
  pro-con division, **172**–73, 292, 294, 295
  refutational strategy, **352**
  spatial, **171**, 289, 290, 293
  of speech to entertain, 375
  topical, **170**, 171, 288–89, 290, 293, 294, 295
  See also Outlining
Organizations, informational literature from, 139
Orientation, group leader's responsibility for, 400
Outlining, 195–211
  complete sentence, **198**
  functions of, 196–98
  key word or phrase, **198**
  in preparation of group presentation, 404
  principles of, 198–200
  stages of, 200–210
    formal outline, **206**–8
    speaking outline, 198, **208**–10
    working outline, **201**–5
  See also Organization

P

Paralinguistic communication, 14
Parallelism, **229**, 230
Paraphrasing, 34, 35, 401
  to reinforce message, 65–66
Paraplage, 34
Participation, group leader's responsibility to encourage, 400
Partipulation, 306, 307
Pascal, Blaise, 168
Pathos, **320**
  enhancing, 324–27
Pauling, Linus, 101
Pauses, **246**
Peck, Gregory, 362
People, informative speech about, 287–89, 297
Pepper, Claude, 214
Perception
  selective, 58–59

theory of self-perception, 48
Periodicals, indexes of, 127–29
Personal benefits of studying public speaking, 2–3
Personal interviews, research using, 135–39
Personal involvement, credibility and acknowledging one's, 323
Personalization of one's critique, 412
Personal knowledge, assessing, 123–25
Personal narrative, **156**
Personal Report of Public Speaking Anxiety, 40–41
Personal testimony, 161
Personification, **230**
Perspective, problem of lack of, 295
Persuasion, 305–59
  definition of, **308**
  enhancing emotional appeals, 324–27
  establishing speaker credibility, 307, 321–24
  importance of, 306–8
  informative vs. persuasive speeches, 285–86
  organization for, 351–55
  principles of, 315–20
  propositions for, **347**–51
    characteristics of, 348–49
    types of, 349–51
  pyramid of, 310–13
  speeches to persuade, **113**–14
    samples of, 429–34
    strategies in, 320–27
    types of, 313–15
  structuring arguments, 333–47
    fallacies of, **342**–47
    steps of argument, 333–34
    types of argument, 334–42
  types of influence in, 308–10
Peterson, Owen, 125
Phobia, public speaking anxiety as, 40
Photocopies of information, 141
Photographs, 267
Physical delivery, elements of, 244, 251–57
  appearance, **251**–53
  eye contact, **254**–55

facial expression, **254**
gestures, **256**–257
movement, **255**
posture, **253**–54
Physical distractions, 60
Physical environment, 92
Physical movement, 255
Physical noise, **15**
Physical setting, 14
Physiological distractions, 60
Physiological noise, **15**
Physiological or physical needs, 82, 83
Pictures, **267**
Pie graph, **269**–70
Pitch, **247**–48
Places, informative speech about,
    289–90, 297
Plagiarism, **32**–35
Plan, research, 125–26
Plan of action, critique providing
    speaker with, 413–14
Platform panic, 40–42
    coping with, 42–50, 423
Play, language as instrument of, 217
Point of view, understanding
    speaker's, 63–64
Policy propositions, **350**–51
Political affiliations of audience, 81
Political convention, sample keynote
    address at, 444–51
Politicians, use of language by, 214
Porter, Katherine Anne, 189
Position, proposition expressing
    one's, 348
Positive attitude, 46–47
Posterboard, 267
Post hoc ergo propter hoc, **343**
Postrel, Virginia, 230
Post–speech analysis, 94
Posture, **253**–54
Practice, 48–49, 421–22
    for group presentation, 405
    with visual aids, 277
Preconceived ideas, 103–4
Premises, major and minor, **339**, 340
Presentation
    group, 402–5
    speech of, **365**–67
Preview, **186**–87

Primacy theory, 318
Problem
    analyzing, 395–96
    defining, 395
Problem–solution division, **353**
Problem solving
    in negative critique, 412–13
    steps to, 395–97
Problem–solving group, **392**
Processes, informative speech about,
    292–93, 297
Pro-con–assessment, 172
Pro-con division, **172**–73, 292, 294,
    295
Professional benefits of studying
    public speaking, 3–4
Profile, audience, **89**–91
Projections, **272**–74
Pronunciation, **249**–50
Proof, propositions and requirement
    of, 349
Proper nouns, pronunciation of, 250
Proportion of speech, checking, 198
Propositions, **347**–51
    characteristics of, 348–49
    types of, 349–51
        of fact, **349**
        of policy, **350**–51
        of value, **350**
Pryor, Cactus, 154
Psychological conclusion, 188–89
Psychological distractions, **60**–61
Psychological noise, **15**
Psychology, audience, 84–87
*Public Affairs Information Service
    (PAIS) Bulletin*, 127
*Publication Manual of the American
    Psychological Association*, 141,
    142
Public benefits of studying public
    speaking, 4–5
Public communication, **10**
Public discussion, **402**, 403
Public speaking
    fear of, 40–42
        coping with, 42–50, 423
    positive attitude toward, 47
    reasons for studying, 2–5
        personal benefits, 2–3

Public speaking *(cont.)*
  professional benefits, 3–4
  public benefits, 4–5
Public statements, taking care in
  making, 381
Purpose of speech, 113–15
  determining general, 113–**14**
  formulating specific, 114–**15**
  stressing, in informative speech,
    296–98
Pyramid of persuasion, 310–13

Q

Qualifications of source, 162
Qualifiers, 222
Question-answer period, **379**–81
Questionnaires
  for audience profile, 89–91
  gathering audience information
    using, 87
Questions
  closed, 137–38
  direct, **179**–80
  to get audience's attention, 179–80
  group members' responsibility to
    ask, 398
  for interview, 137–38
  open, 138
  rhetorical, **179**
Quotation file, **124**
Quotations
  books of, 134–35
  See also Testimony

R

Rader, Louis, 159
Radio, information from, 140
Rankin, Paul, 54
Rapport
  speaker-critic, 412
  speaker-listener, 45
Rate of speaking, 65, 244–46, **245**

*Readers' Guide to Periodical Litera-
  ture*, 108, 127
Reagan, Ronald, 40, 65, 442
  tribute to *Challenger* crew, 229,
    369, 442–44
Reasoning, flawed patterns of, 342–
  47
Reasons, 408
Receiving sounds, 58
Recency theory, 319
Recording information, 140–43
Red herring, **344**–45
Reference librarian, assistance from,
  126
Reference works, research using,
  132–35
Referent, **6**
Refutational strategy, **352**
Refute, **352**
Rehearsal of group presentation, 405
Reinforcement
  of message, 65–66
  of positive in critique, 412
Relevance
  of argument by analogy, testing,
    336–37
  of inductive argument, testing, 335
  of information in speech to in-
    form, 299–300
  of speech to entertain, 376
  of supporting ideas, testing, 197–98
Religion(s) of audience, 79–80
Repetition, 65, **229**, 230, 232–33
  of question in question–answer
    period, 380
Report
  investigative, 140
  oral, **372**–74
Representation, testing inductive argument for, 335
Research, 121–45
  assessing personal knowledge and,
    123–25
  collecting information, 126–40
    from books, 131–32
    from electronic media, 140
    from government documents,
      129–31

from interviews, 135–39
from magazines and journals, 127–29
from newspapers, 129
from reference works, 132–35
writing and calling for information, 139
defined, **122**
developing plan for, 125–26
evaluating information, 143
for group presentation, 404
library, 125–26, 127–35
recording information, 140–43
Research-generated topics, **108**–11
Resolving, 60
Resources, choosing visual aids and, 276
Responsibility(ies)
dividing group topic into areas of, 404
of ethical listener, 30–32
of ethical speaker, 25–29
group decision making as shared, 393
of group leaders, 399–402
of small group members, 397–99
Revision of group presentation, 405
Rhetoric, The (Aristotle), 320
Rhetorical questions, **179**
Richards, Ann, 347
Richards, I.A., 5
Roe v. *Wade*, 157
Rogers, Will, 225
Roosevelt, Eleanor, Stevenson's eulogy of, 315, 370–72
Ruggiero, Vincent Ryan, 229

S

Safety needs, 82, 83
Safire, William, 231
Sample speeches, 424–54
Sanford, Terry, 76
Satisfaction in motivated sequence, 355, 356
Schaefer, William, 336

Scheidel, Thomas, 5, 72
Schjeldahl, Peter, 231
Schnathorst, Shelley, 432
Schriver, Karen, 222
Schulz, Charles, 345
Schwartz, Tony, 306
Schwarzkopf, Norman, 362
Scope of content, testing, 196–97
Scott, Willard, 40
Segmentation, audience, **76**
Selection, audience, 76
Selective perception, 58–59
Self-actualization needs, 83, 84
Self-esteem, 3
Self-generated topics, **102**–5
Self-perception, theory of, 48
Selleck, Tom, 40
Semantic distractions, **61**
Senses, appealing to one's listeners', 226–28
Setting, physical, 14
Sexism, 77–78, 233–34
Sexist language, **233**–34
Shalit, Gene, 65
Shared meaning, 5
Signposts, **174**, 175, 176
Silas, C.J., 229
Silences, 246
Similarities in argument by analogy, relevance of, 336–37
Simile, **230**
Singer, Isaac Bashevis, 414
Slang, 216
Slides, **273**
Slippery slope fallacy, 343–**44**
Small groups, 389–407
defined, **391**
group discussion and decision making, 392–402
principles of, 393–94
process of, 394–97
responsibilities of leaders, 399–402
responsibilities of members, 397–99
group presentation, 402–5
importance of, 390
types of, 391–92

Smathers, George, 214
Smith, Donald, 23
Social bonds, language and strengthening of, 216–17
Social needs, 82–83, 84
Social-oriented group, **391**–92
Solutions in problem solving process, 396–97
Source citations, 35, 323, 373
Sources, tests of, 161–63
Spatial division (organization), **171**, 289, 290, 293
Speaker's Journal, 415–23
Speaking
  differences between writing and, 168–69
  to entertain, 114
  ethical, 25–29
  extemporaneously, **258**–59
  from manuscript, **257**–58
  from memory, **257**
  rate of, 65, 244–46, **245**
Speaking outline, 198, **208**–10
Special occasions, speaking on, 361–87
  acceptance speech, **367**–69
  impromptu speech, **257**, **377**–79
  oral report, **372**–74
  question-answer period, **379**–81
  speech of introduction, **362**–65
  speech of presentation, **365**–67
  speech of tribute, **369**–72, 442–44
  speech to entertain, **114**, **374**–77
  videotaped speech, 381–85, **382**, 421
Specificity
  of critique, 411
  of informative speeches, 298
  of language, clarity and, 221–22
Specific purpose statement, 114–**15**
Speech
  acceptance, **367**–69
  to actuate, **113**–14, **314**
  to convince, 113, **313**–14
  to entertain, **114**, **374**–77
  impromptu, **257**, **377**–79
  to inform. *See* Informative speech (speech to inform)

to inspire, **314**–15
of introduction, **362**–65
knowing one's, 46
to persuade, **113**–14. *See also* Persuasion
placement in program, 92
of presentation, **365**–67
of tribute, **369**–72, 442–44
videotaped, 381–85, **382**, 421
Speech file, **124**–25
Speech principles, knowledge of, 44
Speed of speaking, 65, 244–46
Spielberg, Steven, 368
Stage fright. *See* Nervousness
Standards. *See* Ethics
Statement of idea, 174, 176
Statement of purpose, 185
Statistics, **159**–60, 163
Steinbeck, John, 101
Stereotyping
  of audience, 76, 77–80
  sexist language and, 233
Stevenson, Adlai, 315, 370–72, 399
Still projections, 272, 273–74
Streep, Meryl, 40
Streisand, Barbra, 40
Strengths and weaknesses, knowing one's, 44
Stress
  chemical and physiological responses to, 41–42
  knowing one's reactions to, 43
Structure of persuasion. *See under* Persuasion
Structures of speech, using, 228–31. *See also* Organization
Study group, **392**
Style manuals, 141–43
Subject, knowing one's, 322–23
Subordinate ideas, **197**
Substitution, 249
Sufficiency, testing inductive argument for, 335
Summary, **187**, 188
  by group leaders, 401
  of key ideas, 175, 176
  to reinforce message, 66
Support among group members, 399

Supporting materials, 147–65, 174–75, 176
  appropriate, 300
  for informative speech, limiting, 299
  purposes of, 148–50, 265
  in speaking outlines, 208–9
  types of, 150–63
    comparison and contrast, **157**–58, 163
    definition, **153**–55, 163
    examples, **150**–53, 163
    narration, **155**–57, 163
    statistics, **159**–60, 163
    testimony, **160**–63
Swift, Al, 337
Syllogism, **339**
Symbols, **5**–6
Symposium, **402**
Synesthesia, **228**
Synonym, definition by, **153**
Synthesis of ideas in oral report, 373

T

Tact
  in critique, using, 411–12
  in speech to entertain, 376
Tactile images, **227**
Task-oriented group, **392**
Taste in speech to entertain, 376
Technical language, 104–5, 128
Television, information from, 140
Terminal credibility, **321**–22
Testimony, **160**–63
Thermal image, **227**
Thesis in speech to entertain, 374–75
Thesis statement, **115**, 347
  wording, 115–16
Third-person narrative, **156**–57
Timbre, **248**–49
Time magazine, 214
Time of delivery, 92
Title, developing, 115–17
Todd, Alden, 143
Tone, **232**
  of speech of introduction, 363–64

of speech to entertain, 376
Topic(s), 99–119
  clothing choice and, 253
  establishing importance of, 186
  ethical speaking and choice of, 27
  focusing, 112–13
  generating ideas for, 101–11
    audience-generated topics, **105**–6
    occasion-generated topics, **106**–8
    research-generated topics, **108**–11
    self-generated topics, **102**–5
  group leader's introduction of new, 401
  importance to audience, persuasion and, 317
  positive attitude toward, 46–47
  purpose of speech, 113–15
    determining general, 113–**14**
    formulating specific, 114–**15**
  selecting, 100–101, 111–12, 419–20
  stating, 185
  thesis statement, **115**–16
  title, developing, 115–17
  See also Informative speech (speech to inform); Research
Topical division (organization), **170**, 171, 288–89, 290, 293, 294, 295
Tradition, appeal to, **345**
Transitions, **176**–78
  causal, **177**
  chronological, **177**–78
  complementary, **176**–77
  contrasting, **177**
Transparencies, **273**
Transparent language, 218, 224
Transportation of visual aids, 277
Transposition, 249
Triangle of meaning, 5–6
Tribes (Morris and Marsh), 157–58
Tribute, 229
  speech of, **369**–72, 442–44
Trustworthiness, **323**
Truth, testing inductive argument for, 335

Turabian, Kate, 141
Twain, Mark, 332, 342

U

Undecided audience, 88
Understanding
audience, 59, 93
seeking knowledge for, 285
Unfavorable audience, 88–89
Uninformed audience, 88
Unintentional plagiarism, 34

V

Valenti, Jack, 48
Value(s), **85**–87
instilling, 309
intensification of, 309–10
proposition of, **350**
in pyramid of persuasion, 310–13
tapping audience, 326
Verbal cues, 14
Videotaped speech, 381–85, **382**, 421
Videotapes, **274**
research using, 140
Visual aids, 205, 263–81, 421
to enhance emotional appeals, 326
importance of using, 264–66
for oral report, 373
to show relationships among statistics, 160
in speeches about places, 290
strategies for using, 276–80
before speech, 276–78
during speech, 278–80
types of, 266–75
audio aids, **275**, 326
graphics, 266, **267**–72
handouts, **274**–75, 279
objects, **266**–67
projections, 272–74

Visual brainstorming, **109**, 110, 112, 201, 202
Visual examples, 155
Visual images, **227**
Visualization in motivated sequence, 355, 356
Vividness
of language, 223–31
supporting materials for, 149, 150
Vocal delivery, elements of, 244–51
articulation and pronunciation, **249**–51
pitch and inflection, **247**–**48**
rate and pause, 244–46, **245**, **246**
voice quality or timbre, **248**–49
volume, **246**–47
Voice, active, 226
Voice quality, **248**–49
Volume, **246**–47
Voluntary audience, **87**, 88

W

Wallace, Bill, 436
Waller, Bruce, 344
Wall Street Journal Index, The, 129
Walpole, Horace, 32
Wasserstein, Wendy, 40
Weaknesses and strengths, knowing one's, 44
White, Ryan, 362
Witnesses, selective perceptions of, 58
Wooden, John, 415
Woodward, Joanne, 40
Wording. *See* Language
Working groups, 392
Working outline, **201**–5
Writing, differences between speaking and, 168–69, 232–33
Wuthering Heights (Brontë), 189

Y

Yearbooks, 134